Targum Neofiti 1: Exodus

Targum Pseudo-Jonathan: Exodus

THE ARAMAIC BIBLE
• THE TARGUMS •

PROJECT DIRECTOR
Martin McNamara, M.S.C.

EDITORS
Kevin Cathcart • Michael Maher, M.S.C.
Martin McNamara, M.S.C.

EDITORIAL CONSULTANTS
Daniel J. Harrington, S.J. • Bernard Grossfeld

The Aramaic Bible

Volume 2

Targum Neofiti 1: Exodus

Translated, with Introduction and Apparatus

BY

Martin McNamara, M.S.C.

and Notes

BY

Robert Hayward

Targum Pseudo-Jonathan: Exodus

Translated, with Notes

BY

Michael Maher, M.S.C.

A Michael Glazier Book
THE LITURGICAL PRESS
Collegeville, Minnesota

About the Authors:

Martin McNamara, M.S.C., is Professor of Sacred Scripture at the Milltown Institute of Theology and Philosophy, Dublin. He has a licentiate in Theology from the Gregorian University, Rome, and a licentiate and doctorate in Sacred Scripture from the Biblical Institute, Rome. His doctoral dissertation was entitled *The New Testament and the Palestinian Targum to the Pentateuch* (1966; reprint 1978). His other publications on the Targums and Judaism include *Targum and Testament* (1972); *Palestinian Judaism and the New Testament* (1983); *Intertestamental Literature* (1983).

Robert Hayward received his doctorate from the University of Oxford. He is Lecturer in Old Testament at the University of Durham in England. His publications include *Divine Name and Presence: The Memra*.

Michael J. Maher, M.S.C., is Lecturer in Scripture at the Mater Dei Institute of Religious Education, Dublin. He studied at Hebrew Union College, Cincinnati, and earned his Ph.D. in Semitic Languages at University College Dublin. His publications include *Genesis* (Old Testament Message, 2).

First published in 1994 by The Liturgical Press, Collegeville, Minnesota 56321.
Copyright © 1994 by The Order of St. Benedict, Inc., Collegeville, Minnesota. All rights reserved.

Library of Congress Cataloging-in-Publication Data

Bible. O.T. Exodus. English. McNamara. 1994.
    Targum Neofiti 1, Exodus / translated with introduction and
apparatus by Martin McNamara ; and notes by Robert Hayward. Targum
Pseudo-Jonathan, Exodus / translated with notes by Michael Maher.
        p.   cm. — (The Aramaic Bible ; v. 2)
    Includes bibliographical references and index.
    ISBN 0-8146-5477-0
    1. Bible. O.T. Exodus. Aramaic. Targum Yerushalmi–
–Translations into English.   2. Bible. O.T. Exodus. Aramaic.
Targum Yerushalmi—Criticism, Textual.   3. Bible. O.T. Exodus.
Aramaic. Targum Pseudo-Jonathan—Translations into English.
4. Bible. O.T. Exodus. Aramaic. Targum Pseudo–Jonathan–
–Criticism, Textual.   I. Hayward, Robert, 1948– . II. Maher,
Michael, 1933– . III. Bible. O.T. Exodus. English. Maher.
1994.   IV. Title.   V. Series: Bible. O.T. English. Aramaic Bible.
1987 ; v. 2.
BS709.2.B5   1987 vol. 2
[BS1243]
221.4′2 s—dc20
[222′.12042]   94-2487
                                                                          CIP

Logo design by Florence Bern.
Typography by Graphic Sciences Corporation, Cedar Rapids, Iowa.
Printed and bound in the United States of America by Edwards Brothers, Inc., Ann Arbor, Michigan.

TABLE OF CONTENTS

EDITORS' FOREWORD

While any translation of the Scriptures may in Hebrew be called a Targum, the word is used especially for a translation of a book of the Hebrew Bible into Aramaic. Before the Christian era Aramaic had in good part replaced Hebrew in Palestine as the vernacular of the Jews. It continued as their vernacular for centuries later and remained in part as the language of the schools after Aramaic itself had been replaced as the vernacular.

Rabbinic Judaism has transmitted Targums of all books of the Hebrew canon, with the exception of Daniel and Ezra-Nehemiah, which are themselves partly in Aramaic. We also have a translation of the Samaritan Pentateuch into the dialect of Samaritan Aramaic. From the Qumran library we have sections of a Targum of Job and fragments of a Targum of Leviticus, chapter 16, facts which indicate that the Bible was being translated into Aramaic in pre-Christian times.

Translations of books of the Hebrew Bible into Aramaic for liturgical purposes must have begun before the Christian era, even though none of the Targums transmitted to us by rabbinic Judaism can be shown to be that old and though some of them are demonstrably compositions from later centuries.

In recent decades there has been increasing interest among scholars and a larger public in these Targums. A noticeable lacuna, however, has been the absence of a modern English translation of this body of writing. It is in marked contrast with most other bodies of Jewish literature, for which there are good modern English translations, for instance the Apocrypha and Pseudepigrapha of the Old Testament, Josephus, Philo, the Mishnah, the Babylonian Talmud and Midrashic literature, and more recently the Tosefta and Palestinian Talmud.

It is hoped that this present series will provide some remedy for this state of affairs.

The aim of the series is to translate all the traditionally-known Targums, that is those transmitted by rabbinic Judaism, into modern English idiom, while at the same time respecting the particular and peculiar nature of what these Aramaic translations were originally intended to be. A translator's task is never an easy one. It is rendered doubly difficult when the text to be rendered is itself a translation which is at times governed by an entire set of principles.

All the translations in this series have been specially commissioned. The translators have made use of what they reckon as the best printed editions of the Aramaic Targum in question or have themselves directly consulted the manuscripts.

The translation aims at giving a faithful rendering of the Aramaic. The introduction to each Targum contains the necessary background information on the particular work.

In general, each Targum translation is accompanied by an apparatus and notes. The former is concerned mainly with such items as the variant readings in the Aramaic texts, the relation of the English translation to the original, etc. The notes give what explanations the translator thinks necessary or useful for this series.

Not all the Targums here translated are of the same kind. Targums were translated at different times, and most probably for varying purposes, and have more than one interpretative approach to the Hebrew Bible. This diversity between the Targums themselves is reflected in the translation and in the manner in which the accompanying explanatory material is presented. However, a basic unity of presentation has been maintained. Targumic deviations from the Hebrew text, whether by interpretation or paraphrase, are indicated by italics.

A point that needs to be stressed with regard to this translation of the Targums is that by reason of the state of current Targumic research, to a certain extent it must be regarded as a provisional one. Despite the progress made, especially in recent decades, much work still remains to be done in the field of Targumic study. Not all the Targums are as yet available in critical editions. And with regard to those that have been critically edited from known manuscripts, in the case of the Targums of some books the variants between the manuscripts themselves are such as to give rise to the question whether they have all descended from a single common original.

Details regarding these points will be found in the various introductions and critical notes.

It is recognized that a series such as this will have a broad readership. The Targums constitute a valuable source of information for students of Jewish literature, particularly those concerned with the history of interpretation, and also for students of the New Testament, especially for those interested in its relationship to its Jewish origins. The Targums also concern members of the general public who have an interest in the Jewish interpretation of the Scriptures or in the Jewish background to the New Testament. For them the Targums should be both interesting and enlightening.

By their translations, introductions, and critical notes, the contributors to this series have rendered an immense service to the progress of Targumic studies. It is hoped that the series, provisional though it may be, will bring significantly nearer the day when the definitive translation of the Targums can be made.

Kevin Cathcart   Martin McNamara, M.S.C.   Michael Maher, M.S.C.

PREFACE

This present volume is numbered Volume 2 in the whole series, even though two volumes (Volumes 1A and 1B) were required for the Targums of Genesis, other than that of Onqelos.

The original plan was to publish the entire corpus of Palestinian Targums (Neofiti, Neofiti glosses, Fragment Targums, Pseudo-Jonathan) in the first five volumes of this series—one volume for each of the books of the Pentateuch. It was also planned to have Neofiti, with its Apparatus and notes, on pages facing the corresponding text and notes of Pseudo-Jonathan. Detailed examination of the midrashim common to both would be in the Pseudo-Jonathan section, with reference to this in the notes to Neofiti. Such a presentation of texts and notes proved too cumbersome from the publishing point of view, principally because the space required for each of the two blocks would not correspond. It was finally decided to present each of the two (Neofiti and Pseudo-Jonathan) separately, and further, to devote a volume to each for Genesis (Volume 1A and 1B of this series). It has been found possible to combine both in one volume for Exodus.

The introduction to Neofiti treats briefly of Exodus in Jewish tradition and of the Book of Exodus and rabbinic midrash. It then goes on to examine in some detail the translation techniques in Targum Neofiti Exodus.

The text of Neofiti had already been translated by Michael Maher and the present writer for the *editio princeps* under the editorship of Alejandro Díez Macho (1970). The editor has completely revised this translation for the present work.

In this translation, as in all volumes in this series, words in italics in the translation proper denote deviation in the Targum from the Hebrew Text.

This first part of the volume contains all the material of the Palestinian Targums of Exodus, with the exception of Pseudo-Jonathan. The Apparatus contains all the marginal variants in the manuscript of Codex Neofiti 1, apart from merely orthographical and grammatical ones. The significant variants of the other Palestinian Targum texts are also given. When it is perceived (as, for instance, Exod 12:42; 20:1-17) that other texts contain a recension worthy of reproduction in full, this is done. In such cases the reproduction of the simple variants would fail to do justice to the texts.

As in the case of Neofiti Genesis, notes to Neofiti Exodus (by Robert Hayward) concentrate on the features and peculiarities of Neofiti's text, with the minimum of reference required for an understanding of the midrash common to Neofiti and Pseudo-Jonathan. For fuller treatment the reader is constantly referred to the notes on this latter. This concentration on the peculiarities of Neofiti is a feature of all the books of the Pentateuch. From this it becomes clear that in good part, at least, Neofiti represents a unified approach to the understanding and translation of the Torah.

The second part of this volume has a translation of Targum Pseudo-Jonathan, with accompanying notes. Much of what is said in Volume 1B (pp. 2–11) about the Halakah and Haggadah in Pseudo-Jonathan, and about the language of this Targum, remains true for Pseudo-Jonathan's version of Exodus. The reader of the footnotes will notice how frequently Pseudo-Jonathan's interpretations in Exodus 1–11 are paralleled in *Exodus Rabbah*. Similarly, the notes on Pseudo-Jonathan Exodus 12–23 show that in these chapters the Targum has many parallels to the *Mekilta*. It seems that Pseudo-Jonathan must have known a version of both *Exodus Rabbah* and the *Mekilta*.

Acknowledging once again our debt to Michael Glazier for the initiation of this series, we must also express gratitude to The Liturgical Press for having agreed so generously to continue it; to Mark Twomey, managing editor, for general supervision; and particularly to John Schneider, who took over the task of editing the volumes in this series and overseeing their publication. The quality of these volumes owes much to his exceptional editorial skills. Finally, we once again thank Mrs. Chrissie Moore, who painstakingly and carefully keyed into the computer the entire text of this work.

Michael Maher, M.S.C.   Martin McNamara, M.S.C.
Dublin, Ireland

ABBREVIATIONS

Abod. Zar.	Abodah Zarah
Ant.	Josephus, *Jewish Antiquities*
Arakh.	Arakhin
ARN A	Aboth de-Rabbi Nathan, a
ARN B	Aboth de-Rabbi Nathan, b
b.	Babylonian Talmud
B	First *Biblia Rabbinica* (1517–18)
B. Bat.	Baba Bathra
B. Mez.	Baba Mezia
B. Qam.	Baba Qamma
Bek.	Bekhoroth
Ber.	Berakhoth
Bikk.	Bikkurim
Cant. R.	Canticles Rabba (Midrash)
Chronicles of Moses	(Page references are to Gaster's translation.)
CTg (A, B, C, etc.)	Cairo Genizah (Pal.) Tg. Manuscript
De conf. ling.	Philo, *De confusione linguarum*
De Dec.	Philo, *De Decalogo*
De spec. leg.	Philo, *De specialibus legibus*
Deut. R.	Deuteronomy Rabbah
Eccl. R.	Ecclesiastes Rabbah
ed. pr.	*Editio princeps*
Erub.	Erubin

Exod. R.	Exodus Rabbah
Frg. Tg(s).	Fragment Targum(s)
Gen. R.	Genesis Rabbah
Hag.	Hagigah
Hor.	Horayoth
HT	Hebrew Text
Ḥul.	Ḥullin
j.	Jerusalem (or Palestinian) Talmud
J	MS Jewish Theological Seminary (Lutzki) 605, folios 6, 7
Jub.	Book of Jubilees
Ker.	Keritot
Ketub.	Ketuboth
L	Frg. Tg. Leipzig MS
LAB	Pseudo-Philo's *Liber Antiquitatum Biblicarum*
Lam. R.	Lamentations Rabbah
Leq. Tob	Leqah Tob
Lev. R.	Leviticus Rabbah
Lond.	British Library MS 27031 of Pseudo-Jonathan
LXX	The Septuagint
m.	Mishnah
Makk.	Makkoth
Meg.	Megillah
Mek. RI	Mekilta de R. Ishmael (see Bibliography: Lauterbach and Horovitz-Rabin).
Mek. RSbY	Mekilta de R. Simeon b. Yohai (see Bibliography: Epstein-Melamed).
Men.	Menahoth
M. Qat.	Mo'ed Qatan
MT	Masoretic Text
Mus.	Benjamin Musafia, *Sefer Musaf ha-'Aruk* (in ed. Amsterdam of the *Aruk*)
N	Nürnberg Frg. Tg. Manuscript
Ned.	Nedarim

Nf	Neofiti
Nfi	Neofiti interlinear gloss
Nfmg	Neofiti marginal gloss
Nid.	Niddah
Num. R.	Numbers Rabbah
Onq.	Onqelos
P	Paris BN Frg. Tg. Manuscript
Pal. Tg(s).	Palestinian Targum(s)
Pesah.	Pesahim
Pesh.	Peshitta
Pes. R.	Pesiqta Rabbati (see Bibliography: Braude).
PG	Patrologia Graeca (Migne)
PRE	Pirqe de R. Eliezer (see Bibliography: Friedlander).
PRK	Pesiqta de Rab Kahana (see Bibliography: Braude-Kapstein).
Ps.-J.	Targum Pseudo-Jonathan
Qidd.	Qiddushin
Rosh Hash.	Rosh Ha-Shanah
RSV	Revised Standard Version
Sam. Tg.	Samaritan Targum
Sanh.	Sanhedrin
Sefer ha-Yashar.	(See Bibliography: Noah.)
Shabb.	Shabbath
Shebu.	Shebu'oth
Shek.	Shekalim
Sifra	Sifra on Leviticus
Sifre Deut.	Sifre on Deuteronomy
Sifre Num.	Sifre Numbers
Sukk.	Sukkah
Symm.	Symmachus
Syr	Syriac translation of the Bible
t.	Tosefta
Ta'an.	Ta'anith

Tanḥ. A	Midrash Tanhuma. Warsaw, 1871
Tanḥ. B	Midrash Tanhuma, ed. S. Buber. Vilna, 1885. Reprint Jerusalem, 1964.
Tg.	Targum
V	Vatican Library Frg. Tg. MS
Vulg.	Vulgate
Yeb.	Yebamoth
Zeb.	Zebahim

JOURNALS AND SERIES

CBQ	Catholic Biblical Quarterly
EJ	Encyclopaedia Judaica
Est. Bib.	Estudios Bíblicos
HTR	Harvard Theological Review
HUCA	Hebrew Union College Annual
JBL	Journal of Biblical Literature
JFPT	Jahrbuch für protestantische Theologie
JJS	Journal of Jewish Studies
JPS	Jewish Publication Society
JQR	Jewish Quarterly Review
JSJ	Journal for the Study of Judaism
JSS	Journal of Semitic Studies
MGWJ	Monatsschrift für Geschichte und Wissenschaft des Judentums
NT	Novum Testamentum
NTS	New Testament Studies
PG	Patrologia Graeca (Migne)
RB	Revue Biblique
REJ	Revue des Études Juives
TDNT	Theological Dictionary of the New Testament
VT	Vetus Testamentum
ZAW	Zeitschrift für die Alttestamentliche Wissenschaft
ZDMG	Zeitschrift der deutschen morgenländischen Gesellschaft
ZNW	Zeitschrift für die Neutestamentliche Wissenschaft

BRIEF INTRODUCTION
TO
THE PALESTINIAN TARGUMS OF EXODUS
Martin McNamara, M.S.C.

I. THE BOOK OF EXODUS IN JEWISH TRADITION

The Book of Exodus treats of central events in Jewish self-understanding, i.e., the Exodus from Egypt, the covenant with Moses, and the giving of the Law. The presentation of these great events in the biblical narrative itself represents a lengthy development and an elaborate redaction.

Fewer non-canonical writings on the Exodus events have been preserved than is the case for the Book of Genesis. The events themselves, and the Book of Exodus itself, have, however, been the basis for reflection and written composition among the Jews. Rather naturally they were of particular interest for Jewish scholars, writing in Egypt and in Greek. Ezekiel, the Jewish tragedian (2nd century B.C.E.), in his work *Exagôgê*, retells the story of the Exodus. He seems to make use of the Greek Septuagint version. Occasionally he introduces material extraneous to the biblical narrative, but this may possibly be explained through the canons and demands of Greek drama rather than derive from older Jewish haggadic tradition. The Jewish philosopher Aristobulus (2nd cent. B.C.E.) treats of questions connected with the Book of Exodus (e.g., the Passover; anthropomorphisms). The book is also used by the Jewish chronographer Demetrius (3rd cent. B.C.E.), in whose writing we also find some apocryphal lore. Moses and the Exodus events also figure in the writing *Peri Iudaiôn* ("About the Jews") of the Jewish writer Artapanus (3rd–2nd cent. B.C.E.). This work has certain non-biblical developments, which can probably be explained by early Jewish apologetics depicting Moses as the father and inventor of culture. According to the Jewish Hellenistic writer Eupolemus (ca. 150 B.C.E.), Moses was the inventor of the alphabet, which came into possession of the Phoenicians and, through them, passed to the Greeks.

A rich legendary tradition concerning Moses grew up and has been preserved in the writings of Philo (*Vita Mosis*), Josephus (*Ant.*, Bks. 2–4), and rabbinic sources.[1] Legends developed also concerning the magicians who opposed Moses according to Exod

---

[1] See B. Beer, *Leben Moses nach Auffassung der jüdischen Sage*, 1883; W. X. Lauterbach, "Moses," *Jewish Encyclopedia* 9:46–54; J. Jeremias, *TDNT* 4:852–73; H. Schoeps, *Theologie und Geschichte des Judenchristums*, 1949, 87ff.; B. Botte, G. Vermes, and R. Bloch, *Moïse l'homme de l'Alliance*, 1955, 55–167; D. Daube, *The New Testament and Rabbinic Judaism*, 1956, 5–12.

1

7:8-11. In the biblical text these are anonymous; they receive names in later legend: Jahneh (*Yhnh*) and his brother, Jannes and Johanan, Jannes and Jambres (Mambres in Latin sources). This particular legend has been transmitted in Hebrew and Greek, in Palestinian and Greek sources. It is found in written form in the composition entitled *The Book of Jannes and Jambres* (see Ps.-J. Exod 7:11f.; 1:15).[2]

The story of Moses, the Exodus, and the giving of the Law is briefly retold at the end of the Book of Jubilees (Jub. 47–50). We have a detailed rewriting of Exod 1, 14, 19, 20, 32, and 34 in the *Liber Antiquitatum Biblicarum* (9:1–13:2) of Pseudo-Philo, a work generally taken as a witness of the manner in which the Bible was understood in Palestinian synagogues prior to 70 C.E., and as a link to the material gathered in the midrashic collections.[3]

II. THE BOOK OF EXODUS AND RABBINIC MIDRASH

The biblical Book of Exodus is part narrative, part religious law (halakah). The legal section begins with the ordinances on the Passover in chapter 12. The legal material which this book, and the other books of the Pentateuch contain, represents many centuries of development and codification. The many earlier developments are enshrined in the book, which attained its final state some time after the Exile. Even when the work became canonical, the development in the halakah it enshrined went on, partly as necessary interpretation but also in an effort to make relevant for later generations the biblical prescriptions, regarded as manifestations of God's will for his people. These later developments could no longer be written into the sacred text. They were either transmitted orally or consigned to writing in non-canonical compositions. We can presume that this development and interpretation of the biblical laws went on from the promulgation of the Book of the Law by Ezra about 400 B.C.E., and this in different ways, in keeping with the different traditions within Judaism, e.g., Sadducees, Pharisees, scribes, Essenes, the rabbis. The task of assigning precise cultural origins and dates to any given form of Jewish halakah is no easy matter, but one not without importance for situating the halakah we meet in the different recensions of the Palestinian Targums. I here note some of the rabbinic writings which are relevant for an understanding of the midrash (both haggadic and halakic) of the Palestinian Targums of Exodus.

1. *The Mekilta of Rabbi Ishmael*

This is our oldest rabbinic midrash on the Book of Exodus. It contains an exposition of twelve of the forty chapters of Exodus, beginning with Exod 12 (Exod 12:1–23:19),

---

[2] See G. Vermes and M. Goodman, in E. Schürer, *The History of the Jewish People in the Age of Jesus Christ* 3/2, rev. and ed. G. Vermes, F. Millar, and M. Goodman, 1987, 781–83; A. Pietersma and R. Lutz, in J. Charlesworth, ed., *The Old Testament Pseudepigrapha*, 1985, 2:427–42.

[3] See D. Harrington, in J. Charlesworth, ed., *The Old Testament Pseudepigrapha*, 1985, 2:362.

together with comments on two other passages (31:12-17; 35:1-3). The midrash concentrates on the legal material (which really begins with chapter 12), without, however, neglecting the narrative sections. The work has been regarded as our oldest extant halakic midrash, going back to the teaching of R. Ishmael (ca. 130 C.E.) or his school. It is now recognized that the work is not a single unit, but has a rather long history of redaction, stretching probably from the time of R. Ishmael into the Middle Ages (8th century or so). [4]

2. *The Mekilta of Rabbi Simeon ben Yohai*

This work, cited by medieval Jewish writers, was believed lost until rediscovered in the nineteenth and twentieth centuries. The extant portions contain a midrashic exposition of Exod 3:2, 7-8; 6:2; 12:1–24:10; 30:20–31:15; 34:12, 14, 18-26; 35:2. Its medieval name, "Mekilta of the Bush" (cf. Exod 3:2), shows that it was known to begin, as today, with Exod 3. It gets its name from the repeated occurrence in its exposition of R. Simeon ben Yohai, the disciple of R. Aqiba. Its exegetical approach is also that of Aqiba and his school. [5]

3. *Exodus Rabba*

This is a haggadic exposition of the Book of Exodus. Two distinct traditions are found in the work. Part I, on Exod 1–10, is in the style of Genesis Rabba, of which it may be a continuation. Part II, on chapters 12–40 is in the style of the Tanhumah-Yelamadenu midrashim. Part II is the older section and of Palestinian origin. Part I has Babylonian Aramaic and uses the Babylonian Talmud. [6]

III. TRANSLATION TECHNIQUES IN TARGUM NEOFITI EXODUS

In the introduction and notes to Genesis (Vol. 1A in this series), I have examined some of the translation techniques of the Palestinian Targum as found in Codex Neofiti. The partial examination there carried out indicates that the translator or translators tend to be consistent in the rendering of words and phrases of the Hebrew Text. I here list the information on this matter for Nf's rendering of the Book of Exodus.

(*Note*: Throughout this volume, the designation "Vol. 1A" refers to the first volume in this series: M. McNamara, *Targum Neofiti 1: Genesis*.)

---

[4]See H. Strack-G. Stemberger, *Einleitung in Talmud und Midrasch*, 7th ed., 1987, 236–41; English trans. by M. Bockmuehl, *Introduction to the Talmud and Midrash*, 1991, 274–80.

[5]Ibid., 241–44, English trans., 280–83; M. D. Herr, "The Mekhilta of R. Simeon ben Yohai," *Encyclopedia Judaica* 11 (1971), cols. 1269–70.

[6]See H. Strack-G. Stemberger, op. cit., 284f.; M. D. Herr, "Exodus Rabbah," *Encyclopedia Judaica* 6 (1971), cols. 1067–69.

1. "increase" (HT *prh*) of the HT is rendered by "be strong." See note to Nf Gen 1:22. So also in Exod (Exod 1:7). Nf Exod 23:30 is an exception.

2. HT *šbt*, verb and noun ("rest"), is rendered as "rest and repose (before him/your God. . .)." Thus Nf Exod 20:10; 20:11; 31:17. See note to Nf Gen 2:23.

3. HT *twldwt*. Nf Gen generally renders by double *yḥws twldwt* ("pedigree of the genealogy"; "genealogical pedigree"). See note to Nf Gen 2:4. The only occurrences in HT Exod are Exod 6:16, 19; 18:10, where Nf renders by single *yḥws* ("pedigree").

4. HT *śdh*, rendered in three different ways in Nf Gen, one of which is *(b)'py br'*, "in the open field." See note to Gen 2:5. The term occurs in Exod 1:14; 9:19; 27:22, 25, and is always rendered in Nf Exod by *(b)'py br'*.

5. HT *nṭh*, "stretch out," is generally rendered in Nf by *'rkn*, "incline." Thus Exod 6:6; 7:5, 19; 8:1, 2, 12, 13; 9:22, 23; 10:12, 13, 21, 22; 14:16, 21, 26, 27; 15:2; 23:2; 33:7 (all in Qal); in Hifil Nf Exod 23:2, 6. See also Nf Gen 12:8; 26:25; 33:19; 38:1, 16; 39:21; 49:15 (all in Qal); in Hifil Nf Gen 24:14.

6. HT *mhr*, "hurried." Nf Gen renders by Afel of *yḥy*; Nfmg generally with verb *zrz* (see Vol. 1A, p. 27). The verb occurs five times in HT Exod: 2:18; 10:16; 12:33; 22:8; 34:8. In 2:18; 10:16; 34:8 Nf renders by root *yḥy*; in 12:33 by *zrz*; in 32:8 as adverb (*bpry'*).

7. As in Nf Gen, generally (see note to Gen 1:7, Vol. 1A, p. 53), "made" (*'śh*) of HT, with God as subject, is rendered by "create." Thus Nf Exod 20:11; 31:17.

8. The HT term *qṭr*, in the Hifil, "burn (incense)" occurs in Exod 29:13, 25 (+ "on the altar"); 29:18; 30:7, 8, 20; 40:27 (and frequently in Leviticus). In Nf Exod it is invariably rendered by the verb *sdr*, "set in order," "arrange" (on top of the altar).

9. The Hebrew word *mšpṭ* (found but rarely in Genesis: Gen 18:19, 25; 40:13) occurs frequently in Exod-Deut: Exod 15:25; 21:1, 9, 34; 23:6; 24:3; 26:30; 28:15, 29, 30, in Exodus in the singular with the exception of 21:1 and 24:3. The proper rendering of the term, in the singular or plural, presents a problem for translators of any age. Nf Exod renders both the singular and plural by the double *sdr dyn*, lit. "order of judgment," without any apparent rule governing the choice. Thus HT sing. (*mšpṭ*) is rendered by *sdr dyn* ("order of judgment") at Nf Exod 21:9; 26:30; by *sdry dyn* ("orders of judgment") at Nf Exod 23:6; 28:29, 30. The HT plur. (*mšpṭym*) is rendered by the simple *dynyy'* ("judgments") at Nf Exod 21:1; by *sdry dyn'* ("orders of the judgment") at 24:3; cf. *sdry dynyhwn* ("orders of their judgments"), Nf Exod 28:30 (sing. in HT).

10. The HT *tm*, "perfect," when referring to sacrificial animals, is rendered "perfect, without blemish" (Nf Exod 26:24; 36:29). See note to Nf Gen 6:9 (Vol. 1A in this series, p. 73).

11. The HT term *zr'*, "seed," when referring to humans is in Nf rendered as "sons" (see Vol. 1A, p. 26). The term in this sense occurs but rarely in Exodus (Exod 28:43; 30:21; 32:13; 33:1). In Nf Exod it is rendered by "sons" in 28:43; 32:13 (twice); by the singular "(your) son" in 33:1, and by "seed of sons" (more proper to Nfmg) in 30:21.

12. HT "elder(s)" (*zkn[ym]*) is in Nf rendered by "wise men" (as already in Nfmg Gen 50:7). Thus Nf Exod 3:16, 18; 4:29; 10:9; 12:21; 17:5, 6; 18:12; 19:7; 24:1, 9, 14. This is in keeping with a rabbinic principle set out in *b. Qidd.* 32b.

13. When "servants" of the HT refers to those of Pharaoh, Nf renders as "rulers"

(*šlyṭyn*). Thus Nf Exod 5:21; 7:20, 28, 29; 8:5, 7, 17, 20, 25; 9:14, 20 (twice), 30, 34; 10:1, 6; 12:30; 14:5. Not so in Nf Exod 7:10; 10:7. In other cases, Nf renders with the cognate Aramaic word ("servants").

14. The HT "priest (*khn*) of Midian" is in Nf rendered as "lord of Midian." Thus Nf Exod 2:16; 3:1; 18:1.

15. The HT "land flowing with milk and honey" (Exod 3:8, 17; 13:5; 33:3) is in Nf rendered generally as "(a land) producing good fruits, pure as milk and sweet as honey" (a minor variant, omitting "good" in Nf Exod 3:17).

16. On Nf rendering of HT *yštḥw* see note to Nf Gen 18:2 (Vol. 1A, p. 103). When this HT verb is used in the sense of "worship," "praise" (God), Nf renders accordingly. Thus *w'qdw w'wdw wšbḥw* (or similar verbal forms) in Nf Exod 4:31; 12:27; 34:8. In Exod 11:8; 18:7, Nf renders as *š'l bšlm*, "inquire about the welfare of . . . ," in keeping with the absence of *'rṣh* in the HT (see note to Nf Gen 18:2). When the HT term refers to false gods, Nf renders by *sgd*, "bow down to." Thus Nf Exod 20:5; 23:24; 34:14.

17. As in Nf Gen (see note Nf Gen 7:13, Vol. 1A of this series, p. 76) and generally, Nf Exod renders the HT *b'ṣm hywm hzh* ("the selfsame day") as "at the time of this day" (or similar words). Thus Nf Exod 12:17 (*bzmn ywm' hdyn*), 12:5 (*hyk zmn ywm' hdyn*). The same Aramaic expression in Nf Exod 19:1, where the HT has *bywm hzh*, "this day."

18. As in Nf Gen (see note to Nf Gen 8:1, Vol. 1A, p. 77), Nf Exod adds "in his good mercies" to the verb "remembered" when the subject is God. Thus Nf Exod 2:24; 32:13.

19. In keeping with the translation practice in Nf Gen, Nf Exod renders HT *pqd* ("visit") as "remembered," adding "in his good mercies" when the subject is God and when the action is in his people's favor. See note to Nf Gen 21:1 (Vol. 1A, p. 112). Thus Nf Exod 3:13; 4:31; 13:19; 32:34; 34:7—otherwise when the contexts indicate a different meaning. Thus Nf Exod 20:5 (visit to punish; Nf, "be avenged"); 30:12 (twice), 13, 14; 38:25, 26 (make a census).

20. In keeping with another translational principle already noted in Genesis (see note to Nf Gen 15:2; 18:3, Vol. 1A, pp. 94, 104), Nf inserts "I beseech by the mercies that are before you (O Lord)," when in the HT God is addressed directly in petition. Thus Nf Exod 4:13.

21. As elsewhere in its text, Nf Exod uses the double *šry wšbq*, "forgive and pardon," where the HT has but a single verb, and occasionally in free paraphrase. Thus Nf Exod 23:2 (HT, "pardon," "lift transgressions"); 32:32 (HT, "pardon," "lift iniquity"); 34:9 (HT, "pardon," *slḥ*). See also Nf Exod 34:7; in Nf Exod 10:17 *šry* alone.

22. As already noted for Nf Gen (see note to Nf Gen 6:8, Vol. 1A, p. 73), where the HT has the simple term *ḥn* ("grace"), Nf adds *wḥsd* ("and favor") to give the better-known formula. Thus Nf Exod 32:5; 33:12, 16, 17; 34:9. Apparent exceptions are Nf Exod 3:21; 11:3; 12:36, where, however, *ḥn* ("favor") is a property of the people, not a position in the sight of God, e.g., *ḥn* ("favor") in the sight of the Egyptians.

23. Nf Exod inserts many references to "redemption" (from Egypt) into the HT, e.g., "I redeemed you and brought you out redeemed from the land of Egypt." Thus Nf Exod 2:25; 3:10, 11; 6:6, 7 (twice in both cases); 7:5; 12:17, 41, 42, 51; 13:3, 4, 8, 9, 13, 14,

15, 16, 18; 14:8, 30; 15:2, 16; 16:6, 32; 18:1; 19:1; 20:2; 23:15; 29:45; 32:7, 11; 33:1; 34:18, 20. See note to Nf Exod 3:10.

24. In keeping with its general practice, Nf Exod tends to specify persons where HT uses personal or tribe names, e.g., "the men of," "the sons of," etc., e.g., Exod 1:1, 5.

25. Nf Exod (as Nf elsewhere) has a predilection for the use of certain words and phrases, e.g., *šlyṭ*, "ruler," 5:21; 7:20; 8:5, 17, 20, 25, 27, 28, 29; 9:14, 20, 30, 34; 10:1, 6; 11:3; 12:30; 14:5; 17:16. Also, *rb wšlyṭ* ("lord and ruler"), Nf Exod 2:14; 7:1; *mlk(yn) wšlyṭ(yn)*, "king(s) and ruler(s)," 17:16; 34:24.

26. Nf Exod likes to insert a reference to "instruction," "the instruction of the Law," "to seek instruction from (before) the Lord." Thus Nf Exod 4:16; 18:15, 19; 19:2, 4; 23:17; 24:1; 34:28. The expression "stiff-necked people," *'m qšh 'rp* of the HT is rendered "a people difficult (*qšyyn*) to receive instruction." Thus Nf Exod 32:9; 33:3; 34:9.

27. Another expression worthy of note is "plagues of my punishment," Nf Exod 3:20; 7:4, 5; 9:3, 5.

28. Nf Exod has no regular, single rendering for the term *gr* (RSV: "sojourner") of the HT. The term occurs alone in HT Exod 2:22; 18:3; 20:10; 23:9; 23:12. Nf Exod renders *gr* alone of 2:22 as *dyyr wtwtb* (see note to Nf Gen 15:13; 23:4, Vol. 1A, pp. 96, 120); of 18:3 as *gywr wtwtb*; simple form *gr* with suffixes, etc., as *gywrykwn*, etc. (Nf Exod 20:10; 23:12). Both the sing. and plur. forms, *gr, grym*, occur in HT 22:20 and 23:9. Nf renders respectively as *gywr'; dyyryn; gywr', gwwryn*. The HT *gr w'zrḥ* is rendered in Nf Exod 12:19 as *gywr' wyṣyb* and in Nf Exod 12:49 and 12:48 as *dyyr yṣyb'*.

29. At Exod 3:4, Nf retains the Hebrew word *hnny*, "Behold, here I am," of the HT in Moses' reply and identifies it as Hebrew: "Moses said in the language of the sanctuary." See note to Nf Gen 2:19, Vol. 1A, p. 58.

30. Coins, weights, and measures: see Vol. 1A, pp. 32f. HT term *sheqel* is rendered universally in Nf as *sl'* (sela). See Introduction and note to Nf Gen 23:15, Vol. 1A, pp. 32, 121. Thus Nf Exod 21:32; 30:13, 15, 24; 38:24, 25, 27, 29. HT *kkr* (*kikkar*) is rendered as *centenarium* (a weight being intended) in Nf Exod 25:39; 37:24, while the HT *kikkar* is retained in Nf Exod 38:24, 25, 27, 29.

INDEX OF VERSES PRESERVED IN THE
FRAGMENT-TARGUMS OF EXODUS

The following list is taken from M. L. Klein, *The Fragment-Targums of the Pentateuch According to Their Extant Sources* (Rome: Biblical Institute Press, 1980), vol. I, pp. 244–246, and is reproduced by the kind permission of the publisher.

EXODUS

1:8		V B
1:10-11		V B
1:15	P	V B
1:19	P	V B
1:21	P	V B
2:1	P	V B
2:3	P	V B
2:10	P	V B
2:12	P	V B
3:2-3		V B
3:5		V B
3:14	P	V B
3:22		V B
4:3-4		V B
4:6	P	V B
4:10	P	V B
4:13		V B
4:16		V B
4:25-26	P	V B
4:31		V B
6:3	P	V B
6:9	P	V B
6:20	P	
7:9		V B
7:15	P	V B
7:19	P	V B
8:1	P	V B
8:5	P	V B
8:10	P	V B
8:17		V B
9:9		V B
9:17		V B
9:20	P	
9:31		V B
10:4		V
10:21		V B
10:28-29	P	V B
12:2	P	
12:9		V B
12:11	P	V B
12:33	P	V B
12:34		V B

12:38		V B
12:42		V B/N
12:45	P	V N
13:10		V N
13:13		V N
13:17	P	
13:18-22	P	V N
14:1	P	J
14:2-3	P	V N
14:4	P	
14:5	P	V N
14:6	P	
14:7	P	V
14:8-9	P	V N
14:10-12	P	
14:13-14	P	V N J
14:15-16	P	V N
14:17-18	P	
14:19	P	V
14:20-21	P	V N
14:22	P	
14:23	P	V
14:24-27	P	V N
14:28	P	V
14:29-31	P	J
15:1	P	V N J
15:2-4	P	V N
15:5	P	V
15:6	P	V N
15:7-8	P	
15:9	P	V N
15:10-11	P	
15:12	P	V N
15:13-15	P	
15:16-18	P	V N
15:19	P	
15:20	P	V N
15:21	P	
15:22	P	V N
15:23	P	V
15:24-26	P	V N
15:27		V N

CATALOGUE OF CAIRO GENIZAH FRAGMENTS OF
PALESTINIAN TARGUMS OF EXODUS

The following list is taken from M. L. Klein, *Genizah Manuscripts of Palestinian Targum to the Pentateuch* (Cincinnati: Hebrew Union College Press, 1986), vol. I, pp. xlvi–xlviii, and is reproduced by the kind permission of the publisher.

Exod 4:7-26	MS A
Exod 4:25, 26 (tosefta)	MS FF
Exod 5:20–6:10	MS D
Exod 7:10-22; 9:21-33	MS D
2 acrostic poems to Exod 12:1-2	MS GG
Acrostic poem to Exod 12:2	MS MM
Acrostic poem to Exod 12:2	MS JJ
4 poems to Exod 12:2	MS KK
Acrostic poems (omens) to Exod 12:2	MS HH
Exod 12:1-3	MS HH
Exod 12:1-42	MS AA
Exod 12:42; 12:21-34	MS AA
Exod 12:42 (tosefta)	MS FF
Exod 13:17 (tosefta)	MS X
Exod 14:13, 14 (tosefta)	MS FF
Exod 14:1, 13-14, 29-31; 15:1	MS J
Poems to Exod 14:29-31	MS PP
Acrostic poem to Exod 14:30(?)	MS MM
Acrostic poem to Exod 14:30	MS X
Acrostic poem to Exod 14:30	MS T
Exod 15:1, 3, 12, 18 (toseftot)	MS FF
Exod 15:3-8	MS U
Exod 15:7-21	MS W
Exod 15:6-10 (Targumic acrostic poem)	MS G
Exod 15:10-16 (continuation of preceding item)	MS G
Exod 17:8-16	MS AA
Exod 17:12, 16 (tosefta)	MS FF
Exod 17:15-16; 19:1-8	MS J
Exod 19:1-7	MS NN
Exod 19:7-14	MS U
Exod 19:1–20:23(26)	MS F
Exod 20:26	MS FF
Exod 19:1-10	MS Y
Exod 19:25–20:13 (expansive)	MS S
Exod 19:25–20:2	MS BB
Exod 20:13-14/17 (expansive)	MS CC
Exod 20:2-3, 7-8 (expansive)	MS Q
2 acrostic poems to Exod 20:1, 2	MS G
2 poems to Exod 20:2, 3 (the first is a continuation of preceding item)	MS G
Exod 20:24/25–23:14	MS A
Exod 39:23-37	MS D
Exod 40:9-27	MS D

Targum Neofiti 1: Exodus

Translation

CHAPTER 1

1. These are the names of the children of Israel that entered Egypt with Jacob: every man and *the men of* his house entered: 2. Reuben, Simeon, Levi and Judah; 3. Issachar, Zebulun and Benjamin; 4. Dan and Naphtali, Gad and Asher. 5. And all the persons who came forth from the *loins* of Jacob were seventy persons, and Joseph *who* was[1] in Egypt.[a] 6. And Joseph died and all his brothers and all that generation. 7. And the children of Israel *grew strong* and *begot children* and multiplied.[2] 8. And a new[b] king arose over Egypt who did not know Joseph *and did not walk in his customs.*[c3] 9. And he said to his people: "Behold, the people,[d] the children of Israel, have multiplied and have become stronger than us. 10. Come, *let us take*[e] *evil counsels against them;*[4] *let us pass laws (by which) we will reduce them* before they multiply, and should it come to pass that battle lines[f] are drawn they also join our enemies and wage war against us and *set over themselves a king* and go up from the land." 11. And they set taskmasters over them so

---

Apparatus, Chapter 1

[a] Nfmg: "(who) was still (in Egypt)."
[b] In v. 8 Nf = VB, except "in the beginning" for "new."
[c] Greek loan word, *nomos.*
[d] Nfmg: "the peoples of."
[e] Nfmg: "now let us advise one another (regarding) the secrets of war."

[f] Nfmg: "battle lines against us and they drive us away (reading: *ytrk[w]*) and we have to go up (= depart) from the land"; VN: "and they kill us and they go up in peace (= safely) from the land."

Notes, Chapter 1

[1] Tg. Nf seems to be aware of a debate about the exact identity of the seventy persons. This arose from the fact that in Gen 46:26–27 only sixty-nine descendants of Jacob are named; various suggestions, therefore, were made about the identity of the seventieth person to make the information of Genesis coincide with this verse. See *Gen. R.* 94,9; *Exod. R.* 1,7; *Lev. R.* 4,6; *Num. R.* 3,8; 13,10; *b. B. Bat.* 123ab; *Jub.* 44:12–33; Rashi on this verse; Tg. Ps.-J. of this verse; later midrashim cited by M. Kasher, *Torah Shelemah*, vol. 7 (Genesis); in Hebrew, pp. 1690–91; Jerome, *Hebraicae quaestiones in libro Geneseos* on Gen 46:26–27; 48:1; 48:5–6; and M. Rahmer, 1861, 51–52.

[2] Verse 7 in Hebrew has: "And the Israelites were fruitful and swarmed and multiplied and became very strong; and all the land was filled with them." Tg. Nf lacks a translation of all the words following "and multiplied." B. B. Levy, *Targum Neophyti 1. A Textual Study*, vol. 1 (New York, 1986) 339, offers a conjectural reconstruction of the missing words. For its rendering of the first part of the verse, cf. Tg. Nf Gen 1:28, Tg. Onq., and Tg. Ps.-J. The Hebrew verb "swarm" was considered inappropriate with human beings as subjects; thus the Targum bowdlerizes. See B. Grossfeld, 1988B, 2, and cf. Pesh. and *Exod. R.* 1,8. Vulg. also tones the word down with "quasi germinantes."

[3] For Nf's addition to the end of the verse, which is otherwise rendered literally, see Tg. Ps.-J.; Tg. Onq.; Frg. Tg. V; *b. Erub.* 53a; *b. Sotah* 11a; *Exod. R.* 1,8; and *Tanḥ. Shemot* 7. According to Josephus, *Ant.* II.ix.1, the Egyptians forgot Joseph's good deeds. See also Philo, *De confusione linguarum*, XVI §§71–72, and Grossfeld, 1988B, 2.

[4] Hebrew has: "Come, let us act shrewdly with them lest they increase; and when war happens they also be joined with our enemies and go up from the land." Cf. Tg. Ps.-J.; *Exod. R.* 1,9; *b. Sotah* 11ab; Tg. Ezek 16:5, cited by Le Déaut, 1979 (*Exode*) 14. See also *Jub.* 46,13. The mention of a king may refer to a tradition of Egyptian scribes recorded by Josephus, *Ant.* II.ix.2, that an Israelite child would be born who would shatter Egyptian sovereignty and give power to the Israelites.

that they might oppress them with their (forced) labor.[g] And they built fortified cities[5] for Pharaoh: *Tanis and Pelusium.*[h] 12. But the more they oppressed them, the more did they multiply, and the more did they grow strong. And *the Egyptians*[6] (were) *afflicted* before the *people*, the children of Israel. 13. And the Egyptians enslaved the children of Israel with rigor. 14. And they made bitter their lives by harsh work in clay and in bricks and in every work in the open field—every work in which one works with rigor. 15. And the king of Egypt[i] said to the Hebrew midwives—the name of one *of them*[7] was Shiphrah and the name of the second was Puah— 16. and he said: "When you serve as midwife to the Hebrew women, you shall see (them) upon *the birthstools*; if it is a *male* son you shall kill him, and if it is a *female* daughter she shall live." 17. But the midwives feared *before*[j] the Lord,[8] and they did not do as the king of Egypt had spoken with them but let the children live. 18. And the king of Egypt called the midwives and said to them: "For what reason have you done this thing, that you have let the children live?" 19. And the midwives said to Pharaoh:[k] "Because the Hebrew women are not like the Egyptian women, for they are vigorous. Before the midwife comes to them, *they pray before their Father in the heavens,*[m] *and he answers them and*[9] they give birth."[k]

Apparatus, Chapter 1

[g] Nfmg: "in servitude."

[h] "Tanis and Pelusium"; also in VN.

[i] In v. 15 Nf = VN (except that both have different Aramaic terms for "midwives") and P: Nfmg: "(Shiphrah), she was Jochabed and the name of the second was Puah, who was Miriam"= VN.

[j] Lit.: "from before"; Nfmg same with different Aramaic word for "midwife."

[k-k] In v. 19, "because . . . in giving birth"; Nf = VN, with variants (usual different term for "midwives");

P: "And the midwives said to Pharaoh: Now the ways of the Egyptian women are unlike (those of) the Hebrew women, for these are vigorous. Before the midwife comes in to them, they raise their eyes in prayer to their heavenly Father (lit.: Father in heaven) and he hears the voice of their prayer, and he answers them and they give birth."

[m] Nfi: "Before the Lord (MS: he) and he answers them and (they bear)"; (correcting final word).

Notes, Chapter 1

[5] Hebrew has: "store-cities"; with Tg. Nf, which seems to convey the notion of fortified cities, cf. Tg. Ps.-J.; LXX; *Jub.* 46,14; Ezekiel the Tragedian, *Exagôgê*, lines 9–11; and the general drift of Josephus, *Ant.* II.ix.1. Hebrew has Pithom and Raamses for Tanis and Pelusium; see also Tg. Ps.-J. and Frg. Tg. V. Raamses is further identified with Pelusium in Tg. Nf Exod 12:37; Num 33:3, 5 (so also Tg. Ps.-J.); Frg. Tg. P and V of Num 33:3. Also see note to Nf Gen 47:11.

[6] For the addition of "the Egyptians," see LXX, Vulg.

[7] For the addition "of them," see LXX, Vulg.

[8] Hebrew has: "But the midwives feared God." The identification of the deity with the God of Israel is particularly important in the light of what the Targum has to say later about the midwives.

[9] Tg. Nf's material is an addition to the Hebrew text, otherwise literally translated; similar material is found in Nfmg, Tg. Ps.-J., and Frg. Tg. P, V, *b. Sotah* 11b, and *Exod. R.* 1,16; it may owe its origin to an interpretation of the Hebrew *ḥyyt*, "vigorous," as meaning "righteous": see Kasher, *Torah Shelemah*, vol. 6 (Exodus) 43. For the formula "their Father in heaven," see Nfmg, Frg. Tg. P Gen 21:33; Frg. Tg. P Exod 15:12; 17:11; Frg. Tg. V Num 20:21; Tg. Ps.-J. Deut 28:32; Tg. Nf Deut 33:24; Frg. Tg. P, V Deut 32:6; Le Déaut, 1979 (*Exode*) 19, and the literature cited there; M. McNamara, 1972, 115–19; and A. N. Chester, 1986, 354.

20. And *the Lord*[10] dealt favorably with the midwives, and the people multiplied and grew strong. 21. And it came to pass[n] that because the midwives feared *before the Lord, they acquired a good name for themselves in the midst of the house of Israel,*[o] and he made houses for them,[p][11] *the house of kingship*[q] *and the house of the high priesthood. Miriam took the crown of kingship, and Jochabed took the crown of the high priesthood.*[r] 22. And Pharaoh commanded all his people, saying: "Every *male* son that is born *to the Jews,*[12] throw him into the river but keep alive every *female* daughter."

Apparatus, Chapter 1

[n] Paraphrase of v. 21 also in VNP; as Nf with variants noted below.

[o] P: "before their father who is in heaven"; VN: "among (lit.: "in the midst of") the generations"; Nfmg: "the generations and they made for themselves houses" = VN.

[p] Nfmg: "houses of the high priesthood, and houses of prophecy and houses (text: from the houses) of kingship."

[q] Nfmg: "of the kingdoms."

[r] P: "Jochabed took the crown of kingship, and Miriam took the crown of the high priesthood" (absent from VN).

Notes, Chapter 1

[10]Hebrew has "God" for "the Lord"; see on v. 17.

[11]Hebrew has: "And because the midwives feared God, he made houses for them." The exegesis depends on the notion that fear of God has its reward in the present; hence the midwives' good name in Israel, and in the future, hence Tg.'s understanding of the vague "houses" as royal and priestly dynasties. For the "good name" associated with pious deeds, see Tg. Nf and Tg. Ps.-J. Exod 31:2; Nfmg and Tg. Ps.-J. Exod 33:12, 17; 35:30. The phrase "high priesthood" is very common in Tg. Nf: see, e.g., Gen 14:18; Exod 28:1, 3, 4; Lev 7:35; Num 3:3; Deut 10:6; A.O.H. Okamoto, "A Geonic Phrase in Ms. Targum Yerushalmi, Codex Neofiti 1," *JQR* 66 (1976) 160–67. The general statement that the women were granted royal and priestly offspring is found also in Tg. Ps.-J. and Frg. Tg. V; the latter part of the aggadah is, however, dependent on the identification of the midwives with Miriam and Jochebed, respectively the sister and mother of Moses. This identification is explicit in Tg. Ps.-J. and Frg. Tg. P, V of Exod 1:15; *b. Sotah* 11b; *Exod. R.* 1,17; *Sifre Num.* 78; *Tanḥ. Wayyaqhel* 4; Rashi on this verse. See further J. Heinemann, 1974A, 85–89; R. Le Déaut, 1964A; L. Díez Merino, 1984. *m. Aboth* 4:13 lists three crowns of the Torah, the priesthood, and the kingship, but ranks the crown of a good name above them all (R. Simon); cf. *ARN* A 41; *ARN* B 48.

[12]Tg. Nf has added "to the Jews"; so also Tg. Ps.-J., Tg. Onq., and Sam. Tg.; cf. *b. Sanh.* 101a; *Exod. R.* 1,18; *Tanḥ. Wayyaqhel* 4, 5. LXX have added "to the Hebrews"; Josephus, *Ant.* II.ix.2, "to the Israelites"; cf. Ps.-Philo, *LAB* 9,1; *Jub.* 41,1–2. Le Déaut, 1979 (*Exode*) 20, notes that *b. Sotah* 12ab considers that Pharaoh ordered the death of all male infants irrespective of nationality; cf. Grossfeld, 1988B, 4–5.

CHAPTER 2

1. And a man*ᵃ* from the house of Levi went and took as wife the daughter of Levi. 2. And the woman conceived and bore a son and saw that he was handsome, and she hid him three months. 3. And, being able to hide him no longer, she took for him a basket (made) of bullrushes and daubed it with bitumen and pitch; and she placed the boy in it and placed it in the *meadow*¹ beside the river.*ᵇ* 4. And his sister stood in readiness at a distance to know what would be done to him.*ᶜ* 5. And the daughter of Pharaoh came down *to refresh herself*² by the river, and her maidens walked by the edge of the river;*ᵈ* and saw the basket within the *meadow*ᵉ¹ and sent her maidservant to fetch it. 6. And she opened (it) and saw the boy, and, behold, the boy (was) crying, and she had pity on it and said: "This one is from the children of the Hebrews." 7. And his sister said to the daughter of Pharaoh: "Shall I go and call a nurse from the Hebrew women for you so that she may suckle the boy for you?" 8. And the daughter of Pharaoh said to her: "Go." And the maiden*ᶠ* went and called the mother of the boy. 9. And the daughter of Pharaoh said to her: "*Rear*³ this boy and suckle it for me, and I will give you your wages." And the woman took the boy and suckled it. 10. And the boy grew, and she took him to the daughter of Pharaoh and he became a son for her, and she called his name Moses and she said: "I have *rescued* him from the waters."⁴ 11. And it came to pass that in those days when Moses had grown up, he went out to his brethren and saw their

---

Apparatus, Chapter 2

ᵃ In text and P determinate state, with indeterminate sense. In V, N and Nfmg: indeterminate state. Nfmg: "a Levite man from the tribe of Levi" = V; P: "and a man from the house of Levi went and took himself his aunt Jochabed as wife"; ending ("aunt . . . wife") = Nfmg.

ᵇ "and placed . . . river"; also in V.
ᶜ Nfmg: "(what would be) the end of the boy (*ṭly'*).
ᵈ In text: "her maiden" (*rbyth*): Nfmg: "by the bank of the river and the girls (*ṭlyyt'*)."
ᵉ Nfmg: "the bullrushes."
ᶠ Text: "his maiden"; or "maidens."

Notes, Chapter 2

¹Hebrew has: "the reeds" for Tg. Nf's "meadow"; so also Frg. Tg. P, V. Cf. *Jub.* 47,4.

²Hebrew has "to wash" for Tg. Nf's "to refresh herself": so also Tg. Ps.-J., which explains that the Lord had sent burning ulcers on the Egyptians, so that they needed cooling waters for refreshment. Perhaps Tg. Nf refers obliquely to that aggadah, which is found, e.g., in *b. Sotah* 12b; *Exod. R.* 1,23. *PRE* 48,3 and has Pharaoh's daughter as a leper: cf. *Lev. R.* 1,3 and *Tanḥ. Shemot* 7. The Hebrew word *'mth* may be rendered as "hand" or "maidservant": see *b. Sotah* 12b; *Exod. R.* 1,23; Grossfeld, 1988B, 5.

³The translation "rear," found also in Tg. Ps.-J. and some witnesses to Tg. Onq., represents the problematic and uncertain Hebrew word *hylyky*, which both Targums seem to have understood as *hwlyky*, "carry, bring up." The ancient commentators were puzzled by the word. LXX has "take this child (away). . ." (so Grossfeld, 1988B, 5); Vulg.: "receive, take"; Pesh. has "behold, it is yours," which is similar to *b. Sotah* 12b and *Exod. R.* 1,25.

⁴Hebrew has: "because I drew him out of the water." The tradition that Moses had been so named because he had been rescued or saved from the water is found in Josephus, *Ant.* II.ix.6, with the claim that the name's etymology is Egyptian: see also *Contra Apionem* I.31 and Philo, *De Vita Mosis* I. IV §17.

toils.[g] And he saw an Egyptian man striking a Hebrew man from (among) his brethren. 12. And he looked hither and thither[5] and saw that no one was there, and he *killed* the Egyptian and hid him in the sand.[h] 13. And he went out the second day and, behold, two[i] Hebrew men were fighting, and he said to the guilty one: "Why, *I pray*, do you strike your fellow?" 14. <And he said>:[j] "Who has set you a lord and ruler over us? Do you mean to kill me as you killed the Egyptian?" And Moses was afraid and said: "Behold, now, the thing is known."[k] 15. And Pharaoh heard this thing and he sought to kill Moses. And Moses fled from before Pharaoh and dwelt in the land of Midian; and he sat down beside a well. 16. And the *lord*[6] of Midian had seven daughters; and they came and drew water and filled the watering troughs to water their father's flock. 17. And shepherds came and drove them away; and Moses stood up and delivered them, and he watered their flock. 18. And they came to their father Reuel, and he said: "For what reason have you come so quickly[m] this day?" 19. And they said: "An Egyptian man delivered us from the hands of the shepherds, and he has also drawn water for us and has watered *our* flock."[n][7] 20. And he said to his daughters: "And where is he? Why, I pray, have you forsaken the man? Call him and let him eat[o] *food*." 21. And Moses began to dwell by the man, and he gave Moses his daughter Zipporah *in marriage*.[p] 22. And she bore a son, and *she* called his name Gershom because he said: "*A dweller and inhabitant*[8]

Apparatus, Chapter 2

[g] Nfmg: "in their enslavements" (bondage).

[h] Nfmg 1°: "in a spirit of prophecy in this world and in the world to come and saw, and behold, no just man was coming forth from him and he struck the Egyptian and buried him in the sand": Nfmg 2°: "Moses (looked) on the holy spirit in the two worlds and saw and, behold, there was no proselyte destined to": Nfmg 2° = V, N, P, which continue: "(destined) to arise from that Egyptian, and he killed the Egyptian and buried him in the sand."

[i] Nfmg: "Dathan and Abiron Hebrew men fighting."

[j] Missing in text.

[k] Nfmg: "of a truth it is known."

[m] Lit.: "have you hastened to come"; Nfmg: "have you hurried."

[n] Nfmg: "the flock."

[o] Nfmg: + "a little" (written erroneously as *klyl*: ("a crown").

[p] Nfi: "and he gave" = Ps.-J.

Notes, Chapter 2

[5]The opening of this verse in the Hebrew may be translated literally as: "And he turned hither and thither." Tg. Nf may, Nfmg does, have knowledge of the aggadah that Moses looked into the future through the Holy Spirit to see that no proselyte or righteous person would descend from the Egyptian: cf. Tg. Ps.-J.; Frg. Tg. P, V; *b. Ned.* 64b; *Exod. R.* 1,29. Philo, *Leg. Alleg.* I. XIII §38, heavily stresses the fact that Moses looked. Hebrew has "and he smote" for "and he killed."

[6]Hebrew has: "And the priest of Midian," as in Exod 3:1; 18:1. "Priest" is a designation which Tg. reserves for priests of the God of Israel. See Le Déaut, 1979 (*Exode*) 24; Tg. Onq. of this verse and Gen 41:45; Exod 3:1; 18:1; *Exod. R.* 2,16; *Mek. RI Amalek* 3:60–61.

[7]Hebrew has: "the sheep." Tg. Nf stresses that Moses' help was directed to Reuel's daughters only: so LXX and Josephus, *Ant.* II.xi.2. Against this interpretation, see Nfmg and Le Déaut, 1979 (*Exode*) 24, who notes how *Exod. R.* 1,32 insists that Moses drew water even for the wicked shepherds: see also *Lev. R.* 34,8.

[8]Hebrew has *gêr*, "sojourner," in the sense of "resident alien" for "a dweller and inhabitant"; cf. our Tg. of Gen 23:4. See M. Ohana, 1974, 317–32, who suggests that Tg. Nf is reluctant to render the word as "proselyte" in the manner of the other Targums.

am I in a foreign land." 23. And it came to pass that in those many days the king of Egypt died, and the children of Israel groaned because of their toil, and they cried out, and their plaint because of their toil *q* went up *before the Lord.* [9] 24. And their plaint *was heard before the Lord*: And *the Lord,*[r] *in his good mercies*, recalled the covenant *he had sworn* with Abraham, with Isaac and with Jacob. [10] 25. And the *servitude*[s] of the sons of Israel *was manifest before the Lord*, and he *determined in his Memra to redeem them.*[11]

CHAPTER 3

1. And Moses was pasturing the flock <of his father-in-law Jethro, the *lord* of Midian, and he led the flock>[a] behind[b] the wilderness, and he reached Mount Horeb, *above which the Glory of the Shekinah of the Lord was revealed.*[1] 2. And the angel of the Lord was *revealed* to him in flames of fire[c] from the midst of the thorn

Apparatus, Chapter 2

[q] Nfmg: "their labor."
[r] Nfmg: "the Memra of the Lord."

[s] Nfmg: "the plaint."

Notes, Chapter 2

[9]Hebrew has: "went up to God."
[10]Hebrew has: "And God heard their groanings; and God remembered his covenant with Abraham, with Isaac, and with Jacob." On the covenant as a sworn oath and God's good mercies in this Targum, see C.T.R. Hayward, 1981A, 39–98. See also Tg. Nf of Exod 6:5; 13:19; 32:13. Targum also removes ambiguity in the Hebrew by insisting that God remembered the covenant with the patriarchs, rather than the patriarchs themselves; see Levy, 1986, 342.
[11]Hebrew has: "And God saw the Israelites, and God knew." The enslavement of Israel is a recurrent theme of Tg. Nf and Nfmg in these early chapters, and contrasts with the redemption which will follow at the Exodus. The terse and somewhat obscure Hebrew might raise the question, What was it that God saw, and what was the significance of his knowledge? Targum answers both queries. See also Tg. Onq., *Exod. R.* 1,36, and, for the Memra and its place in redemption, Hayward, 1981A, 42–43; D. Muñoz León, 1974, 292–93.

Apparatus, Chapter 3

[a] Omitted in text by homoioteleuton.
[b] Nfi: "in the way of."

[c] Nfmg: "the Glory of the Shekinah of the Lord (lit.: "of the Name") (came: original text uncertain) above it in flames of fire."

Notes, Chapter 3

[1]Hebrew has: "Now Moses was pasturing the sheep of Jethro, his father-in-law, the priest of Midian; and he led the sheep to the back of the wilderness and came to the mountain of God, to Horeb." On the lord of Midian, see 2:16; and on the Glory of the Shekinah (cf. Exod 18:5), and the similar rendering of Tg. Nf and Tg. Onq., see D. Muñoz León, 1977, and the critical discussion of this verse by Chester, 1986, 159–60, and Levy, 1986, 342–43.

bush;[d] and he saw, and, behold, the thorn bush was aflame in the fire, but the thorn bush was not *burned.*[2] 3. And Moses said: "I will turn aside now and I will see this great vision: why the thorn bush is not burned."[e] 4. And *it was manifest before* the Lord that *Moses* had turned aside to see, and *the Memra[f] of the Lord* called to him from the midst of the thorn bush and said to him: "Moses, Moses." *Moses answered in the language of the sanctuary* and said: "HERE I AM."[g][3] 5. And he said: "Do not draw nigh hither. Put off your shoes[h] from off your feet because the place upon which you stand is holy *place.*"[4] 6. And he said: "I *am* the God of your father, the God of Abraham, the God of Isaac and the God of Jacob." And Moses hid his face because he was afraid to look on *the Glory of the Shekinah of the Lord.*[5] 7. And the Lord said: "I have truly seen[i] the affliction of my people who are in Egypt, and I have heard their plaint on account of their oppressors because their *servitude[j] is manifest before me.*[6] 8. And I have *been revealed in my Memra* to deliver them from the hands of the Egyptians, to bring them[k] up from this land, to a land good and broad, to a land *producing good fruits, pure as* milk and *sweet[m] as* honey, to the *land* of the Canaanites[7] and the Hittites[n] and the Amorites and the Perizzites[o] and

Apparatus, Chapter 3

[d] Nfmg: "in the thorn bush" (*'sny'* with *sin*) = *sny* (with *samech*) of Nf.

[e] Nfmg: "and the thorn bush was green and not burned"; VB.

[f] Nfmg: "the angels."

[g] Hebrew left untranslated.

[h] Nfmg: "to come; draw off your sandals" = VB.

[i] Nfmg: "the Memra of the Lord (said: The affliction . . .); manifest before me."

[j] Nfmg: "their tribulations."

[k] Thus Nfmg; text: "you."

[m] Nfmg: "(sweet) and tasty."

[n] Nfmg gives a different gentilic ending -*'y* for *yy*- (that found in Ps.-J.) for the last five names.

[o] In text "and the Amorites" repeated after "Perizzites."

Notes, Chapter 3

[2] For the reading in Nfmg, see the literature on 3:1. Hebrew has "eaten, consumed" for "burned." With Tg. Nf, cf. Tg. Ps.-J. and Frg. Tg. V.

[3] Hebrew has: "And the Lord saw that he had turned aside to see; and God called to him from the midst of the bush and said: Moses! Moses! And he said: Here I am." On the Memra, see Hayward, 1981A, and, most recently, Chester, 1986, 293–313, and the bibliographies they cite. For the phrase "language of the sanctuary" (= Hebrew), see, e.g., Tg. Nf of Gen 2:19, and 22:1, where the response "Here I am" is retained, as here, in Hebrew; Gen 11:1; 35:18 (both also Tg. Ps.-J.); Tg. Nf of Lev 8:9; 16:32; Num 28:7; 35:25; J.P. Schäfer, 1972, 137–39; Le Déaut, 1978 (*Genèse*) 142–43.

[4] "Holy place" is read by Tg. Onq. and Tg. Ps.-J.; Hebrew has "holy ground." Josephus, *Ant.* II.xii.1, relates a belief that God dwelt in the area, and cf. the exegesis of the verse in *Exod. R.* 11,2.

[5] Hebrew has: "he was afraid to look upon God." For the Glory of the Shekinah, see 3:4. Tg. Ps.-J. introduces the same expression here; cf. D. Muñoz León, 1977, 71–72.

[6] Hebrew has: "for I know their sorrows." With Targum, cf. Symm., *tas kataponêseis,* and above, 2:25.

[7] Hebrew has: "And I have come down to deliver them . . . to a land flowing with milk and honey, to the place of the Canaanites." Tg. Ps.-J. has God manifesting himself to save by means of his Memra; see Hayward, 1981A, 16, and the important matter of God's revelation, found also in Tg. Onq. and discussed by Chester, 1986, 109–10. The rendering of "a land flowing with milk and honey" as "producing good fruits, pure as milk and sweet as honey" is standard and consistent in Tg. Nf: see Exod 3:17; 13:5; 33:3; Lev 20:24; Num 13:27; 14:8; 16:13, 14; Deut 6:3 (also Frg. Tg. V); 11:9; 26:9, 15; 27:3; 31:20, following the view of R. Eliezer as quoted in *Mek. RSbY,* p. 38, as opposed to the literalism of R. Akiba.

Amorites and the Hivites and the Jebusites. 9. And now, behold, the plaint of the children of Israel has *come up* to me, and the oppressions with which the Egyptians oppress them *are* also *manifest before me.*[8] 10. And now, come and I will send you to Pharaoh, and you shall bring my people, the children of Israel, *as redeemed ones*[p][9] out of Egypt." 11. And Moses said *before the Lord*: "Who am I that I should go to Pharaoh and that I should bring up[q] the children of Israel *redeemed* from Egypt?"[10] 12. And he said: "But I, *[in] my Memra,*[r] will be with you,[s] and this *will be* a sign that *my Memra*[t] has sent you: when you have brought out the people from Egypt, you will worship *before the Lord* upon the mountain."[11] 13. And (Moses)[u] said *before the Lord*:[12] "Behold, I go to the children of Israel and say to them: 'The God of your fathers has sent me to you.' And they say: 'What is his name?' What will I say to them?" 14. And[w] *the Lord* said to Moses: "I AM WHO I AM." And he said: "Thus shall you say to the children of Israel: *'The one who said and the world came into existence from the beginning; and is to say to it again: Be, and it will be,*

Apparatus, Chapter 3

[p] Nfmg: "redeemed" (without "as"; as in v. 11).

[q] Nfmg: "bring (you) out."

[r] Lit.: "I, my Memra will be" (HT: "I will be"); Nfmg: "(my Memra) will be" (3rd pers.).

[s] Nf = HT; Nfmg: "(will be) at your aid and this to you" = Ps.-J.

[t] Nfmg: "I have sent you, when you have brought out."

[u] In lemma; missing in text of Tg.

[w] Nfmg 1°: "the Memra of the Lord (said) to Moses: He who said to the world: 'Be,' and it came into being, and who will again say to it: 'Be,' and it (will be) (correcting text, which has imperat. or past tense, as in VB). And he said: Thus shall you say to the children

of Israel: ("WHO I AM (*'hyh*) has sent (me)" = V; Nfmg 2°: "I have existed before the world was created and have existed after the world has been created. I am he who has been at your aid in the Egyptian exile, and I am he who will (again) be at your aid in every generation. And he said: Thus shall you say to the children of Israel. I AM (*'HYH*) sent me to you"; P: "And the Memra of the Lord said to Moses: The one who said to the world from the beginning: Be and it was and will again say to it: 'Be' and (it will) be (text: imperat. or past tense). And he said: Thus should you say to the children: He (*hw'*; corrected to: *'HYH*: I AM) that sent me to you."

Notes, Chapter 3

[8]Hebrew has: "has come to me, and I have also seen the affliction. . . ."

[9]On the addition of "as redeemed ones," which is very frequent, see, e.g., Tg. Nf of Exod 3:11; 6:7; 7:5; 12:17, 41, 42; 13:3, 4, 8, 9, 14; Lev 25:38; 22:33; 26:45; and Hayward, 1981A, 23. God is thus described as a redeemer God or as One who redeems by means of his Memra—Gen 17:8; 28:21; Exod 6:7.

[10]Hebrew has: "And Moses said to God . . . and that I should bring out the Israelites from Egypt?" On the addition of "redeemed," see 3:10.

[11]Hebrew has: "and he said: Because I shall be with you. And this shall be for you the sign that I have sent you . . . you shall serve God upon this mountain." Here Tg. Nf appears to present the Memra of the Lord as subject of the verb "to be" in the first person. For an explanation of this, see Hayward, 1981A, 16–17, and the criticisms of Chester, 1986, 307–8.

[12]Hebrew has: "And Moses said to God. . . ."

has sent me to you.'"[13] 15. And he[14] said again to Moses: "Thus[x] shall you say to the children of Israel: 'The Lord, the God of your fathers, the God of Abraham, the God of Isaac and the God of Jacob, has sent me to you.' This is my name for ever and this is my memorial for all generations. 16. Go and gather the *wise men* of Israel and say to them: 'The Lord, the God of your fathers, has been revealed to me, the God of Abraham, Isaac and Jacob,[y] saying: "*The Lord has surely remembered you*[z] and what *the Egyptians* have done to you.[aa][15] 17. And I have determined—*in his Memra*—to bring you up from the *servitude*[bb] of *the Egyptians* to the land of the Canaanites and the Hittites and the Amorites and the Perizzites and the Hivites and the Jebusites, to a land *bearing fruits,*[cc] *pure as* milk and *sweet*[dd] *as* honey.'"[16] 18. And they will listen to your voice,[ee] and you and the *wise men*[17] of Israel shall

---

Apparatus, Chapter 3

[x] Nfmg: "the Memra of the Lord (said) to Moses a second time. Thus."

[y] Nfmg: "the God of Isaac, the God of Jacob."

[z] Nfmg: "I remembered you in my (text: "his") good mercies."

[aa] Nfi: "from your servitude"; Nfmg: "from the tribe (a time of)."

[bb] Nfmg: "which they have done, enslaving you in Egypt."

[cc] Nfmg: "good"; probably should go with "fruit" ("good fruits"); cf. 3:8, etc.

[dd] Nfmg: "tasty"; see *m* in Apparatus to Exod 3:8.

[ee] Nfmg: "to the voice of your words and you shall go in."

Notes, Chapter 3

[13]Hebrew has: "And God said to Moses: I AM WHO I AM. And he said: "Thus you shall say to the Israelites, I AM has sent me to you." Tg. Nf retains in Hebrew I AM WHO I AM, as do Tg. Onq., Pesh., and Sam. Tg. The third I AM is left untranslated by Tg. Onq., Pesh., and Sam. Tg. but provides the occasion for Tg. Nf's exegesis of God's self-revelation. For full discussion of this verse, Nfmg, and its interpretation in the other Targums, see M. McNamara, 1966, 97–112; Hayward, 1981A, 16–20; Muñoz León, 1974, 300–304; Chester, 1986, 301–2. Tg. Nf's exposition of the Name is similar to Frg. Tg. P, V. "He who said, and the world came into existence" is an Aramaic rendering of the common Hebrew title *my š'mr whyh h'wlm*: see E. E. Urbach, 1969, 161–89 (Hebrew). It has possibly entered the Targum's text through rabbinic revision. Nfmg expounds the Name on the principle that no word of Scripture being redundant, the three I AM's must all have different references.

[14]Hebrew has: "And God again said. . . ."

[15]Hebrew has: "Go and assemble the elders of Israel . . . saying, I have surely visited you, and (I have seen) what is done to you in Egypt." The rendering of "elders" as "wise men" is almost entirely consistent throughout Tg. Nf: see Exod 4:29; 12:21; 17:5, 6; 18:12; 19:7; 24:1, 9, 14; Lev 4:15; 9:1; Num 11:16, 24, 25, 30; 22:4 (but not Num 22:7, where "princes" is the translation); Deut 5:23; 19:12; 21:2, 3, 4, 6, 19, 20; 22:15, 16, 17, 18; 25:7, 8, 9; 27:1; 29:9; 31:9, 28; 32:7. This rendering is not found in Genesis. Such consistency of translation is not shared by the other Targums, although they can render "elders" as "wise men": so Tg. Ps.-J. of Deut 21:2, 3, 4, 6, 19, 20; 31:9, 28. In this verse, LXX have *tēn gerousian* for "elders"; the word used by King Antiochus III in his letter to Ptolemy (so Josephus, *Ant.* XII.iii.1) to describe the "senate" of the Jews, a formally constituted body which was probably the forerunner of the Sanhedrin and its Sages; and "wise men" are indicated also in *b. Qidd.* 32b. For God's visiting understood as "remembering," see Tg. Nf, Tg. Onq., Tg. Ps.-J. of Gen 50:24; Exod 4:31; Tg. Nf of Exod 32:34; and *t. Rosh Hash.* 4:6; *b. Rosh Hash.* 32b; *Mek. RSbY* Jethro 106.

[16]Hebrew has: "And I said: I will bring you up from the affliction of Egypt . . . to a land flowing with milk and honey." For the Memra here, see Le Déaut, 1979 (*Exode*) 32–33; the Targum's specification of servitude is discussed under 2:25, and further by Grossfeld, 1988B, 7. For the understanding of "a land flowing with milk and honey," see 3:8.

[17]Hebrew has "elders" for "wise men"; cf. LXX *gerousia*, and see above, 3:16. Hebrew has: "the God of the Hebrews has met with us"; cf. 5:3, and see the detailed discussion of Tg. Nf and the other Targums in Chester, 1986, 140–41.

go to the king of Egypt, and you shall say to him: 'The Lord, the God of the Hebrews, *has been revealed* to us; and now, let us go, we pray, *a journey distance* of three days in the wilderness that we may sacrifice *before* the Lord our God.' 19. And I know that the king of Egypt will not *permit* you to go, not even by a hand *that is* strong.*[ff]* 20. And I will send*[gg]* *the plague of my punishment*, and *I will kill*[hh] the Egyptians[18] by all my wonders which I will do amongst them. 21. And I will give this people favor in the sight of the Egyptians, and it shall come to pass that when you go*[ii]* <you shall not go>*[ii]* empty. 22. And a woman shall ask of her fellow inhabitant*[jj]* and of the neighbor *sojourning*[19] in her house objects of silver and objects of gold clothing; and you shall put them on your sons and on your daughters, and you shall despoil the Egyptians."

CHAPTER 4

1. And Moses answered and said: "And if they do not believe me and do not listen to my voice because they will say: 'The Lord was not revealed to you?'"*[a]* 2. And the Lord*[b]* said to him: "What is that in your hand?" And he said: "A staff." 3. And he said: "Cast*[c]* it on the ground." And he cast*[c]* it on the ground, and it became a serpent. And Moses fled from before it. 4. And the Lord said to Moses: "Stretch out your hand and take hold of it by its tail"—*[d]* and he stretched out *his*

Apparatus, Chapter 3

[ff] Tg. follows HT; "even" inserted for sense; LXX, Vg and M: "except by a mighty hand."
[gg] Nfmg: "and I will unleash."

[hh] Nfmg: "and I will smite."
[ii] Omitted in text through homoioteleuton.
[jj] mgyrth (also in VB and Nfi); HT: mšknth (only here in fem. sing.).

Notes, Chapter 3

[18]Hebrew has: "And I shall stretch out my hand and smite Egypt." Biblical writers often use the Lord's hand as a symbol of his power to smite Israel's enemies. The Targum makes this symbol into a prosaic statement of fact, as do Tg. Onq. and Tg. Ps.-J. "The plague of my punishment" is found also at 7:4, 5; 9:3, 15; Tg. Nf and Tg. Ps.-J. of Deut 32:23; and the Lord's hand regularly becomes, in Targum, his power or might: see Hayward, 1987, 31. The final words "amongst them" represent Hebrew "in his midst." Targum gives the natural meaning, as do LXX.

[19]The Targum indicates that Israelites were lodging in Egyptian houses, a tradition represented also by LXX, Tg. Onq., and *Mek. RSbY*, p. 31: see Grossfeld, 1988B, 9.

Apparatus, Chapter 4

[a] Nfmg: "to you the Memra of the Lord."
[b] Nfmg: "the Memra of the Lord."
[c] Nfmg: "throw"; = VB.

[d] VB: "and take hold of the place of its tail" (lit.: "tails"); Nfmg (with slight correction): "the place of its tail."

hand and took hold of it, and it became a staff in the palm *of* his *hand*[e1] 5. —"so that they may believe[f] that the Lord, the God of their fathers, the God of Abraham, the God of Isaac and the God of Jacob, was revealed to you." 6. And *he*[g] said[2] to him again: "Put, I pray, your hand into your bosom."[h] And he put his hand into his bosom;[h] and he took it out and, behold, his hand was leprous, like snow. 7. And he said: "Put, *I pray*, your hand back into your bosom."[3] And he put his hand back into his bosom; and he took it out from his bosom, and, behold, it was restored, to be like his flesh. 8. "And it shall be that if they do not believe you and do not listen to the voice of the first signs, they will believe the voice of the last[i] sign. 9. And it shall be that if they do not believe even these two signs and do not listen to your voice, you shall take from the water of the river and pour (it) out on[j] the dry ground; and the water you will take from the river will become blood on the dry ground." 10. And Moses said *before* the Lord: "I beseech, *by the mercy before you, O Lord*, I am not one who is *master* of speech, neither from yesterday nor from *before it* nor even from *the time*[k] that you have spoken with your servant, because *halting*[m] of mouth, *halting*[n] *of speech* am I."[4] 11. And the Lord[o] said to *Moses:*[5] "Who has made <a mouth for> *the son of* man, or who has made the dumb or the deaf or those with sight or the blind[p] but I the Lord?[q] 12. And now go, and I, *with my Memra,*[r] will be with *the speech of* your mouth,[6] and I will teach you[s] what to

Apparatus, Chapter 4

[e] Nfmg: "a staff in the palm of his hands."
[f] Nfi: "that he may believe."
[g] Nfmg: "the Memra of the Lord."
[h] "put in his bosom"; also in P.
[i] Nfmg: "the latest."
[j] Nfmg: "upon."
[k] Nfmg: "from the hour."
[m] VB: "for I am halting of tongue (lit.: mouth) and dif-

ficult of speech"; P: "halting of tongue" (lit.: "mouth").
[n] Nfmg: "difficult."
[o] Nfmg: "the Memra of the Lord."
[p] Nfmg: "him who sees, or him who is blind."
[q] Nfmg: "is it not I the Lord?"
[r] Nfmg: "in my Memra."
[s] Nfmg: "and I will show."

Notes, Chapter 4

[1] Hebrew has, literally: "and it became a rod in his palm."

[2] Hebrew has: "and the Lord said to him. . . ."

[3] Hebrew has: "And he said: Return your hand. . . ." With Tg. Nf, cf. the Targum fragment of this verse in M. L. Klein, 1, 1986, 172.

[4] Hebrew has: "And Moses said to the Lord: O Lord, I am not an eloquent man, neither beforehand nor since you have spoken to your servant, because I am slow of speech and slow of tongue." Targum's exposition of Moses' exclamation to the Lord, in Hebrew *by 'dny*, as a call to his mercy, is found also in Gen 15:2, 8; 19:18; 20:4; Exod 4:13; 5:22; Deut 3:24; 9:26; and see Hayward, 1981A, 39–40; Chester, 1986, 326–30. The Hebrew expression *gm mtmwl gm mšlšm* is an idiom meaning "formerly, heretofore"; but it is joined to what follows by another *gm*, "also," which encourages Targum to give the three expressions joined by *gm* specific reference, "yesterday," "before it," "from the time": cf. LXX, Tg. Ps.-J., *Seder Olam Rabbah* 5, and the complex interpretation in *Exod. R.* 3,14. Vulg. is very close to Tg. Nf with its description of Moses' tongue as halting and tardy.

[5] Hebrew has: "And the Lord said to him . . .": for the addition of Moses, cf. LXX.

[6] Hebrew has: "And now go: and I shall be with your mouth." Cf. Tg. Onq., Tg. Ps.-J. with Tg. Nf.

say." 13. And he said: "I beseech,[t] *by the mercy before you, O Lord*, send, I pray, by the hand of *the one who is suited to be sent*."[u][7] 14. And the anger of the Lord was enkindled against Moses, and he said: "Is (there) not Aaron, your brother, the Levite? I know that he will surely speak. And, behold, he even *comes*[w] to meet you.[8] He will see you or be glad in his heart. 15. And you will speak with him and place the words in his mouth; and I, *in my Memra*, will be with *the speech*[x] of your mouth and with *the speech* of his mouth,[9] and I will teach you what you shall do. 16. And he shall speak beside you[y] to[z] the people, and he will be an *interpreter*[aa] for you, and you shall be for him *as one seeking instruction from before the Lord*.[10] 17. And this staff, by which you will do signs of *wonders*, take in your hand." 18. And Moses went and returned[bb] to *Jethro*,[11] his father-in-law, and he said to him: "I will go now and return to my brethren who are in Egypt, and I will see whether they are still[cc] alive." And Jethro said to Moses: "Go in peace." 19. And the Lord said to Moses in Midian: "Go, return to Egypt because all the men who sought[dd] *the evil of* your life[12] are dead."[ee] 20. And Moses took his wife and his

Apparatus, Chapter 4

[t] Nfmg: "(I beseech) of you, my master, send"; VB: "send, I pray . . . " = Nf.

[u] Nfmg 1° = N, with variant form of infinitive; Nfmg 2°: "by the hand of the angel (corrected to: "King") Messiah who is to be sent."

[w] Nfmg: "who comes out."

[x] Nfmg: "will be with the speech (variant form from Nf) of your mouth and with the speech (same variant) of his mouth (variant form) and I will instruct you."

[y] Nfmg: "with you."

[z] Nfmg: "for the people."

[aa] Nf: *l-twrgmn*; VB: *l-mtwrgmn*; otherwise VB in v. 16b verbatim as Nf.

[bb] Nfmg: "went back."

[cc] Nfmg has a slightly different phrase.

[dd] Nfmg: "who sought your life to kill you."

[ee] Nfmg: "they have come down from their possessions, and behold, they are reckoned as dead persons" = Ps.-J.

Notes, Chapter 4

[7]Hebrew has: "And he said: O my Lord! Send now by the hand of the one whom you shall send." For the rendering of "O my Lord!" see 4:10. "The one who is suited to be sent" (cf. Tg. Onq., Frg. Tg. V) is somewhat vague. This may be intentional, to allow the Targum maximum latitude of interpretation. Thus we may have here an oblique reference to the Messiah (so, explicitly, Nfmg) as King or angel (or even an angel *tout court*: see *Exod. R.* 3,16); or to Phinehas-Elijah, the messenger (angel) of the end of days, as in Tg. Ps.-J.

[8]Hebrew has: "he is going out to meet you."

[9]Hebrew has: "and I shall be with your mouth and with his mouth." See notes on 4:12.

[10]Hebrew has: "and he shall be a mouth for you, and you shall be to him as God." Tg. Nf puts Aaron in place of a *twrgmn*, a Targumist, in relation to Moses, who is to search out divine instruction: the same idea occurs in Frg. Tg. V. Tg. Onq., Tg. Ps.-J., Pesh., *Exod. R.* 3,17 make Aaron a *mtwrgmn* in respect to Moses, who is *rab*, "master": see Le Déaut, 1979 (*Exode*) 37. But the biblical text, which makes Moses almost a Godlike figure, would catch the attention of the Targumist, as noted by Chester, 1986, 337. The Targum may reflect contemporary synagogue practice in its description of the seeker of divine instruction (the reader of the Hebrew Bible) and the translator (the Targumist). See further on 7:1; Philo, *De mig. Abr.* XV §§81, 84, and, on *mtwrgmn*, W. Bacher, 1899, 28. Vulg. has a rendering not far removed from Tg. Nf: "and you shall be to him in those things which pertain to God."

[11]Hebrew has: "And Moses went and returned to Jether." The reading "Jethro" is found in one Hebrew MS, the Samaritan, Vulg., Pesh., and Tg. Ps.-J. Seven names are accorded to Jethro, of which Jether is one: see *Mek. RI* Amalek 3:31–40, which comments on the change from "Jether" to "Jethro" by the addition of an extra letter; *Sifre Num.* 78; *Exod. R.* 27,8; *Tanḥ.* Jethro 13.

[12]Hebrew has: "all the men who were seeking your life"; the Targum makes precise what they were seeking to do to Moses. See also 35:23 and Levy, 1986, 347.

sons and mounted them on an ass and went back to the land of Egypt. And Moses took in his hand the staff *by which signs were done before the Lord.* [13] 21. And the Lord[ff] said to Moses: "As you go to return to Egypt, see all the signs that I have placed in your hand. [gg] And you shall do them before Pharaoh, and I will harden his heart and he shall not let the people go. 22. And you shall say to Pharaoh: 'Thus says the Lord: Israel is my first-born son. [hh] 23. And I have said to you: Let my son go that he may worship *before* me; and you have refused to let him go. [ii] Behold, I kill your first-born son.'" 24. And it happened on the way, in the resting-house, that *an angel from before* the Lord overtook him and sought to kill him. [14] 25. And Zipporah took a flint[jj] and circumcised the foreskin of the[kk] son and brought it near[mm] the feet of the *destroyer* and said: "In truth the bridegroom *sought to circumcise, but his father-in-law did not permit him. And now may* the blood *of this circumcision atone*[nn] *for the sins of this bridegroom.*"[15] 26. And *the angel*[oo] let him go

Apparatus, Chapter 4

[ff] Nfmg: "the Memra of the Lord to Moses; when you shall go to go."

[gg] Nfmg: "before you; and you shall do them before."

[hh] Nfmg: "the Memra of the Lord; my sons, my first-born are Israel."

[ii] Nfmg: "my sons (*bryy*) that they may worship before me, and you have refused to let them go."

[jj] PVB: "and Zipporah took a flint and circumcised the foreskin of her son and brought it near before the feet of the angel (P: of the Destroyer) and said: 'The bridegroom wanted to circumcise, but the father-in-law would not permit him. And now may the blood

of this circumcision atone, which has rescued the father-in-law from the hands of the angel of death'"; cf. v. 26b.

[kk] Probably scribal error for "her son."

[mm] Nfmg: "and cast it under the feet of."

[nn] "may it . . . atone," with PVB; Nf text: "and atoned."

[oo] PVB: "and when the Destroyer let him go free from him, then Zipporah gave praise and said: 'How beloved (P: How powerful) is the blood of the circumcision which has saved the (P: this) father-in-law from the hands of this angel of death.'"

Notes, Chapter 4

[13]Hebrew has: "and Moses took the staff of God in his hand." Targum had to modify this theologically naive expression and state the exact significance of the staff in almost the same language as Tg. Onq.: cf. *Tanḥ.* Shemot 23, and see Grossfeld, 1988B, 11. The most recent study of the staff is found in G. Bienaimé, 1984, 71–75; but the aggadah found in Tg. Ps.-J. of Exod 2:21; 4:40; Deut 34:12 is entirely lacking in Tg. Nf.

[14]Hebrew has: "and the Lord met him, and sought to slay him." Targum had of necessity to modify this shocking statement: hence the introduction of the angel, as in LXX, Tg. Onq., Tg. Ps.-J., and *Exod. R.* 5,8. According to *Jub.* 48,2–3, it was Mastema who tried to kill Moses. For the interpretation of this verse and the two following verses in other rabbinic sources, see G. Vermes, 1973A, 178–92; the review of this article by J. Heinemann, *Tarbiz* 35 (1965–66) 86–88; and Le Déaut, 1979 (*Exode*) 38–39. Philo, Josephus, and *LAB* entirely omit this episode.

[15]Hebrew has: "And Zipporah took a flint and cut off her son's foreskin, and made it touch his feet. And she said: Surely you are a bridegroom of blood to me." Targum's interpretation is very close to those of Frg. Tg. V, P; Tg. Ps.-J.; and the fragments in Klein, 1, 1986, 172. See also *j. Ned.* 3:9.

from him. Then *pp* *Zipporah gave praise and* said: "*How beloved is* the blood *qq* *that has delivered this* bridegroom *rr* *from the hand ss* *of the angel of death.*" *tt* 16 27. And the Lord *uu* said to Aaron: "Go to meet Moses to the wilderness." And he went and met him on the mountain *ww* *of the sanctuary of the Lord,* 17 and he kissed him. 28. And Moses related *xx* to Aaron all the words of the Lord who had sent him <and all the signs that he had planned to do>. *yy* 29. And Moses and Aaron went and gathered all the *wise men* 18 of the children of Israel. 30. And Aaron spoke all the words which the Lord *zz* had spoken with Moses and did the signs before the eyes of the people. *a* 31. And these people believed *in the name of the Memra of the Lord* and heard that the Lord, *in his good mercies, had remembered* the children of Israel *b* and that *c* their tribulations *were manifest before him.* And they bowed down *and gave thanks and praised.* 19

Apparatus, Chapter 4

pp Nfmg: "the angel, the Destroyer; behold, then he (read: she?) gave praise."

qq Nfi: "(blood of) circumcision."

rr Nfmg: "which has delivered the bridegroom."

ss Nfi: "from the hands of"; cf. PVB.

tt Nfmg: "the Destroyer."

uu Nfmg: "the Memra of the Lord."

ww Nfmg: "on the mountain on which the glory of the Shekinah of the Lord was revealed."

xx Lit.: "showed"; Nfmg: "told."

yy Missing in text.

zz Nfmg: "the Memra of the Lord."

a Nfmg: "before Pharaoh."

b Nfmg: "the Memra of the Lord (had remembered) the children of Israel."

c "and heard that he had remembered" repeated in text.

Notes, Chapter 4

16 Hebrew has: "And he left off from him. Then she said: A bridegroom of blood in regard to the circumcision." Closest to Tg. Nf here are the fragments in Klein, 1986, 172, and Frg. Tg. P, V. *Exod. R.* 5,8 and Tg. Ps.-J. have a similar aggadah. The verb *šbḥ*, "give praise," is common in Tg. Nf as introducing addresses to God: it is frequently conjoined with the verb "give thanks." See below, 4:31; 15:1; and Grossfeld, 1988B, 40–41.

17 Hebrew has: "and he met him at the mountain of God." This expression might be open to crude misconstruction, and is therefore defined either as the Temple Mount or (so Nfmg) as a place where God was revealed (possibly the Temple Mount, more probably Mount Sinai). See Chester, 1986, 160, and Levy, 1986, 347.

18 On "wise men" for MT's "elders," see 3:16. LXX have *gerousia* here.

19 Hebrew has: "And the people believed, and heard that the Lord had visited the Israelites, and that he had seen their affliction; so they bowed their heads and worshiped." For the "Name of the Memra of the Lord," see Gen 4:26; 8:20; 12:7, 8; 13:4, 18; 15:5; 16:13; 21:33; 22:14; 24:3; 26:25; 35:1; Exod 5:23; 14:31; 17:15; 32:13; 34:5; Lev 16:8, 9; Num 14:11; 18:9; 20:12; Deut 1:32; 9:23; 10:8; 18:5, 7, 19, 20, 22; 21:5; 32:51. It occurs most often in cultic settings and probably refers to the Tetragrammaton pronounced with its proper vowels: so Hayward, 1981A, 100–111; but see Chester, 1986, 343–47. It is introduced here to avoid the suggestion that the people believed in Moses; cf. 14:31 and Levy, 1986, 348. On Targum's use of "remember" for Hebrew "visit," see 3:16; the aspect of mercy is implied here by Philo, *De Vita Mosis* I. XV §86, and discussed by Hayward, 1981A, 42–43. For "gave thanks and praised," which is a biblical phrase (Dan 2:23), see Exod 12:27; 15:1, 21; and above, 4:26.

CHAPTER 5

1. After this, Moses and Aaron went in and said to Pharaoh: "Thus said the Lord,[a] the God of Israel: 'Let go the people that they may *celebrate* a feast before me in the wilderness.'" 2. And Pharaoh said: "Who is the Lord that I should listen to his voice to let Israel go? *Pharaoh* does not know who the Lord *is*;[1] and I will not let Israel go." 3. And they said: "The God of the Hebrews *was revealed* to us.[2] Let us go, we pray, a *journey distance* of three days, and we will sacrifice *before* the Lord our God, lest[b] he meet us[b] with the plague or with the sword." 4. And the king of Egypt said to them: "Why, *now*, should you Moses and Aaron make the people rest from their work? Return to your labors." 5. And Pharaoh said: "Behold, the people <of the land>[c] *are* now many, and you make them rest from their labors!"[d] 6. And Pharaoh commanded the officers of the people and their oppressors that day, saying: 7. "You shall no longer give the people straw to make bricks, not like yesterday *and earlier*;[3] they shall go and gather straw for themselves. 8. But the number of bricks they made yesterday and *earlier*[3] you shall lay upon them. You shall not diminish them, because they are idle; because of this they cry out, saying: 'Let us go and let us sacrifice *before* our God.' 9. You shall impose harsher work on the men, and they shall work at it, and they shall not busy themselves[e] with words of lying men." 10. And the oppressors of the people and their officers went out to the people, saying: "Thus said Pharaoh: 'I will not give you straw. 11. Go, gather straw for yourselves from where you will find it, but nothing shall be diminished[f] of your labors.'" 12. And the people were scattered[g] in all the land of Egypt to gather stubble for straw. 13. And the oppressors oppressed (them), saying: "Complete your work, the *amount* for each day (is to be) as when the straw *was given* to you."[h][4] 14. And the officers of the children of Israel, whom oppressors of Pharaoh's had set over them, were beaten, being asked: "Why, neither yesterday nor today, have you not completed as *previously*[3] the amount allotted to you[i] for brickmaking?" 15. And the officers of the children of Israel came and cried out[j] before

Apparatus, Chapter 5

[a] Nfmg: "the Memra of the Lord."
[b] Nfmg: "the God of the Hebrews lest."
[c] Added interlinearly.
[d] Nfmg: "their bondage."
[e] Nfmg: "rely on."

[f] Nfmg: "I will not diminish."
[g] Nfi: "were dispersed."
[h] Nfmg: "as there was straw."
[i] Nfmg: "the amount of bricks."
[j] Nfmg (with corr.): "and they sighed"(?).

Notes, Chapter 5

[1] Hebrew has: "I do not know the Lord." For the change, see Levy, 1986, 348.
[2] Hebrew has: "the God of the Hebrews has met with us." See 3:18 and Chester, 1986, 141–42. The "plague" in the language of Tg. Nf is literally "death"; so Sam. Tg., Tg. Ps.-J., Tg. Onq., LXX; cf. 9:15.
[3] For the translation here and in vv. 8 and 14, see 4:10 and cf. Tg. Onq. and Tg. Ps.-J.
[4] Hebrew has: "Complete your works, each task on its day, as when there was straw." Cf. Tg. Onq. and Tg. Ps.-J., and LXX, Vulg.

Pharaoh, saying: "Why, *we pray*, do you act thus[k] with your servants? 16. Straw is not given to your servants, and you say to us,[m] your servants: 'Make bricks.' Behold your servants are punished, but *Pharaoh* and *the* people are at fault."[n5] 17. And he said: "You are idle, you are idle; wherefore do you say, 'We will go and will make an offering[o] *before* the Lord'? 18. And now, go, work; and straw will not be given but the number of bricks you must deliver." 19. And the officers of the children of Israel saw that they were in an evil plight when they said: "You shall not diminish the daily *amount* of your bricks."[6] 20. And they met Moses and Aaron standing[p] before them when they came out from *before* Pharaoh.[q] 21. And they said to them: "May the Lord[r] *be revealed against you* and judge that you have made our *name evil*[s] in the sight of Pharaoh and in the sight of his *rulers*,[7] giving[t] a sword into their hands to kill us." 22. And Moses returned before the Lord[u] and said: "*I beseech by the mercy before you, O Lord*: why, *I pray*, have you done evil to this people, and why, I pray, have you sent me?[8] 23. And from the time that I came[w] to Pharaoh to speak in the name of your *Memra*,[9] he has done evil to this people, and you certainly have not redeemed[x] your people."

Apparatus, Chapter 5

[k] Nfi: "(is it) done thus?"

[m] Nfmg: "they say to us."

[n] Nfmg: "are guilty" (Hebrew ending).

[o] Nfmg: "we will sacrifice."

[p] Nfmg: "standing in readiness."

[q] CTg D (which resumes in Exod 5:20): "they went out from the presence of Pharaoh."

[r] Nfmg: "the Memra of the Lord"; = CTg D.

[s] CTg D: "that you have spread abroad an evil remembrance"; Nfmg: "(and judge) you that you have made our breath offensive before Pharaoh and before his servants, putting."

[t] CTg D: "setting."

[u] Nfmg = "in prayer."

[w] CTg D: "from the hour I went in."

[x] CTg D: "you certainly have not rescued."

Notes, Chapter 5

[5]Hebrew has: "and behold, your servants are beaten, but the fault is in your own people."

[6]See notes on v. 13.

[7]Hebrew has: "May the Lord see you and judge, because you have made our smell to stink rankly in Pharaoh's sight and in his servants' sight." The consonantal text might be vocalized otherwise so as to yield: "May the Lord be revealed over you and judge. . . ." See Chester, 1986, 79–80, 175. Note how Targum, like the Tg. fragment in Klein, 1, 1986, 175, changes colorful metaphor for fact and replaces the "bad stink" with a "bad name," while Nfmg keeps something of the power of the original Hebrew expression.

[8]Hebrew has: "And Moses returned to the Lord and said: O my Lord! Why have you treated this people badly? Why have you sent me?" For Targum's additions, see notes on 4:10. Moses makes petition before the Lord: the notion is ancient, being represented by LXXb; so also the Tg. fragment in Klein, 1, 1986, 174.

[9]"In the Name of your Memra" stands for Hebrew "in your Name"; cf. Tg. fragment in Klein, 1, 1986, 175, and notes to 4:31.

CHAPTER 6

1. And the Lord^a said to Moses: "Now you shall see what I will do to Pharaoh, because with a strong hand^b he shall let them go, and with a strong hand^b he shall drive them out from the land."[1] 2. And *the Lord*^a spoke *with* Moses[2] and said to him: "I *am* the Lord. 3. And I was revealed^c in *my Memra* to Abraham, to Isaac and to Jacob as the God *of the heavens but*^d my *mighty* name, the Lord, I did not make known to them.[3] 4. And I also established my covenant with them to give them the land of Canaan, the land of their sojournings in which they sojourned. 5. And I also have heard the plaint of the children of Israel whom the Egyptians enslave, and *in mercy*[4] I have remembered my covenant. 6. *By an oath*; say to the children of Israel: 'I am the Lord, and I will bring you out *redeemed* from^e beneath the *yoke of the servitude* of the Egyptians, and I will deliver you from your toils and redeem you with *a strong hand*^f and with numerous judgments.[5] 7. And I will *set* you *aside to my Name* as a people of *holy ones,*^g and *my Memra* will be to you *a redeemer* God, and you shall know that I *am* the Lord your God *who redeemed*^h and

Apparatus, Chapter 6

^a Nfmg, CTg D: "the Memra of the Lord."
^b In Nf, determinate form (*yd'*) used; in CTg D and Nfmg indeterminate.
^c In v. 6 VB = Nf, with variants as below.
^d PVB; Nfmg: "and the name of the Memra of the Lord"; CTg D: "and my holy Name, the Lord."

^e CTg D: "(bring) you out from under the bondage of the Egyptians"; Nfmg: "from the bondage."
^f Nfi: "with an uplifted arm" = CTg D.
^g Nfmg: "as a holy nation."
^h CTg D: "who brought you out redeemed": Nfmg: "brought you out redeemed from."

Notes, Chapter 6

[1] Hebrew has: "from his land." There is possibly an error here in the Targum's text, which elsewhere reads "his land"; so 6:11; 7:2.

[2] Hebrew has: "And God spoke to Moses. . . ." With Tg. Nf, cf. Tg. Onq. and Tg. Ps.-J., Vulg.

[3] Hebrew has: "And I appeared to Abraham . . . as El Shaddai; but my Name YHWH I did not make known to them." For revelation in the Memra and God of the heavens, cf. Frg. Tg. V, and Klein, 1, 1986, 175. Hayward, 1981A, 22, discusses the significance of this Targum and Nfmg with respect to Memra and the different qualifications of God's Name set out in this verse.

[4] Hebrew has: "and I have remembered my covenant." On mercy, see 2:24.

[5] Hebrew has: "Therefore say to the children of Israel: . . . and I shall bring you out from beneath the burdens of the Egyptians; and I shall deliver you with an arm stretched out and with great judgments." For this promise as a divine oath, see *Mek. RSbY*, p. 4; *Exod. R.* 6,4; *Lev. R.* 23,2; and later midrashim cited by Kasher, *Torah Shelemah*, vol. 6 (Exodus) 8–9. Field, 1875, quotes as a reading of *Allos* the curious *eis to bebaion*, which has overtones of firmness, perhaps implying a sworn oath. On the addition of "redeemed," see 3:10 and the Tg. fragment in Klein, 1, 1986, 177. The "yoke of servitude" allies this verse to earlier references such as 2:25; 3:7, and points forward to 6:7 and 18:10, where the expression occurs again; cf. Grossfeld, 1988B, 15. The "strong hand" (see also 32:11) suggests that Tg. Nf is not, as is often supposed, overconcerned with the removal of anthropomorphisms; see 3:20, and Chester, 1986, 265–92, for the most recent discussion of this matter.

brought you out from beneath the *yoke of the servitude* of the Egyptians.[6] 8. And I will bring you into the land which I raised[i] my hand *in oath*[7] to give to Abraham, to Isaac and to Jacob, and I will give it to you as <an inheritance>[j] and a *possession*, I[k] the Lord.'" 9. And Moses spoke thus with the children of Israel, but they did not listen to *the words of*[8] Moses because of *broken* spirits[m8] and harsh bondage. 10. And the Lord[n] spoke to Moses, saying: 11. "Go in; speak with Pharaoh, the king of Egypt, that he let the children of Israel go from his land."[o] 12. And Moses spoke before the Lord, saying: "Behold, the children of Israel have not listened to <my>[p] *words* and how will Pharaoh listen to me,[q] I who am *halting*[r] *of speech*?"[9] 13. And the Lord[s] spoke *with* Moses and *with* Aaron and commanded them *concerning* the children of Israel and *concerning* Pharaoh, the king of Egypt, to lead out[t] the children of[u] Israel from the land.[10] 14. These are the heads of the house of their fathers: the sons of Reuben, the first-born of Israel: Hanok and Pallu, and Hezron and Carmi; these are the descendants *of the sons* of Reuben. 15. And the sons of Simeon: Jemuel and Jamin and Ohad and Jachin and Zohar and Shaul, the sons of the Canaanite woman; these are the descendants *of the sons*[11] of

Apparatus, Chapter 6

[i] Nfmg: "that I lifted up my hand."

[j] Correcting text.

[k] Nfi:"said (the Lord)." CTg D: "I will give it to you as an inheritance, said the Lord."

[m] Lit.: "shortness of breath"; Nfmg: "to Moses because of the shortness (of breath)"; PVB: "shortness of breath."

[n] Nfmg = CTg D: "the Memra of the Lord"; in Nf at the beginning of this verse, the opening words of preceding verse are repeated.

[o] Nfi: "from the land."

[p] In text: "his."

[q] Text lit.: "listen from me"; Nfmg: "they did (not) listen to me (lit.: "receive from me"), and how will (Pharaoh) listen to me" (lit.: "receive from me").

[r] Nfmg: "hard."

[s] Nfmg: "the Memra of the Lord."

[t] Nfmg + "redeemed."

[u] Text repeats: "the children of."

Notes, Chapter 6

[6]Hebrew has: "And I shall take you to myself as a people, and I shall be your God; and you shall know that I am the Lord your God who brought you out from under the burdens of the Egyptians." The Tg. fragment published by Klein, 1, 1986, 177, is very close to Tg. Nf. The expression "set aside to my Name" is much favored in cultic contexts, as in 13:2 (with reference to first-born sons); 13:12 (also Tg. Ps.-J.); 25:2; 29:18; 30:37; and Chester, 1986, 324–27. The people "of holy ones" anticipates 19:6. For the Memra as a redeemer God, see 3:10; note again the stress on the "yoke of servitude" (as in v. 6) and the corresponding portrayal of the Exodus as a redemption from slavery.

[7]"In oath" is an addition to the Hebrew, found also in the Tg. fragment edited by Klein, 1, 1986, 177. Tg. Onq. and Tg. Ps.-J. present the Lord as swearing by his Memra: on this, see Hayward, 1981A, 71–98. The somewhat tautological reference to the oath is probably intended to recall the divine oath of redemption in v. 6 and to reflect the nature of the land of Israel as a promised "possession," also clearly stated. Tg. Nf's omission of the word "inheritance " and the emphasis on "possession " suggest knowledge of a rabbinic debate about how the land of Israel could be a gift of God and yet a promised inheritance at the same time: see *j. B. Bat.* 8:2; *b. B. Bat.* 117a; *Exod. R.* 6,4; *Mek. RI Pisḥa* 18:12–13; *Tanḥ. Bo'* 12.

[8]Addition of "the words" of Moses is found also in Tg. fragment in Klein, 1, 1986, 177. For Targum's expression "broken spirits," cf. Tg. Ps.-J.; Frg. Tg. P, V; Klein, 1, 1986, 177.

[9]Hebrew has: "have not listened to me. Then how would Pharaoh hear me, when I am uncircumcised of lips?" See notes on 4:10.

[10]On Nfmg's addition of "redeemed," see 3:10. Hebrew has: ". . . from the land of Egypt."

[11]See LXX for addition of "of the sons."

Simeon. 16. And these are the names[w] of the sons of Levi according to their pedigrees:[x] *Gershom*[12] and Kohath and Merari; and the years of the life of Levi were one hundred and thirty-seven years. 17. The sons of Gershon:[y] Libni and Shimei, according to their descendants. 18. And the sons of Kohath: Amram and Izhar and Hebron and Uzziel; and the years of the life of Kohath were one hundred and thirty-three years. 19. And the sons of Merari: Mahli and Mushi. These *are* the descendants *of the sons* of Levi according to their pedigrees. 20. And Amram took as wife Jochabed, *the daughter*[z] *of the brother of his father,*[13] who bore him Aaron and Moses; and the years of the life of Amram were one hundred and thirty-seven years. 21. And the sons of Izhar: Korah and Nepheh and Zichri. 22. And the sons of Uzziel: Mishael and Elzaphan and Sithri. 23. And Aaron took as wife Elisheba, the daughter of Amminadab, the sister of Nahshon, and she bore him Nadab and Abihu and Eleazar and Ithamar. 24. And the sons of Korah: Assir and Elkanah and Abiasaph; these *are* the descendants *of the sons* of *Korah.*[14] 25. And Eleazar, Aaron's son, took as wife from the daughters of Putiel, and she bore him Phinehas. These are the heads of the Levite fathers according to their descendants. 26. These are Aaron and Moses to whom the Lord[aa] <said>:[bb] "Bring out the children of Israel[cc] from the land of Egypt according to their hosts." 27. These are they who spoke with Pharaoh, king of Egypt, about bringing out the children of Israel from Egypt, this Moses and Aaron. 28. And it happened on the day that the Lord[dd] spoke with Moses in the land of Egypt 29. that the Lord[ee] spoke *with* Moses, saying: "I am the Lord; speak with Pharaoh, king of Egypt, all that I[ff] speak *with* you." 30. And Moses said before the Lord; "I am *halting*[gg] *of speech;*[15] and how will Pharaoh listen to me?"

Apparatus, Chapter 6

[w] Nfi: "(these are) they."

[x] Nfi: "according to their genealogies."

[y] With HT, for "Gershom."

[z] Nfmg: "(took as wife) the beloved (or: aunt, father's brother's wife) to himself"; P: "his beloved" (or: aunt, father's brother's wife").

[aa] Nfmg: "the Memra of the Lord."

[bb] Missing in text.

[cc] Nfmg + "redeemed."

[dd] Nfmg: "the Memra of the Lord."

[ee] "Lord" missing in text; Nfmg: "the Memra of the Lord."

[ff] Nfmg + "now."

[gg] Nfmg: "hard."

Notes, Chapter 6

[12]On Gershom for Hebrew Gershon, see Le Déaut, 1979 (*Exode*) 49. Gershon appears in v. 17 in accordance with MT.

[13]Hebrew has: "And Amram took Jochebed, his father's sister, *ddtw*, as wife." In view of the law of Lev 20:20 that a man should not marry his uncle's wife, *ddtw*, Targum has expounded the verse to bring the pious Amram's conduct into agreement with the commandments of the Torah. Cf. LXX; *b. Sanh.* 58b; Rashi on this verse; Le Déaut, 1979 (*Exode*) 50–51; *j. Yeb.* 11:2; *Gen. R.* 18,5. Philo, *De Vita Mosis* I. II §7, sidesteps the issue.

[14]Hebrew has: "these are the families of the Korahites." Cf. Tg. Ps.-J., Tg. Onq., and LXX.

[15]Hebrew has: "I am uncircumcised of lips. . . ." See notes on 4:10 and 6:12.

CHAPTER 7

1. And the Lord[a] said to Moses: "See, I have made[b] you *lord and ruler* to Pharaoh; and Aaron, your brother, will be your *interpreter.*[c1] 2. And you shall speak all that I have commanded[d] you; and Aaron your brother will speak with Pharaoh, that he let the children of Israel go from his land. 3. And I will make stubborn[e] the heart of Pharaoh, and I will multiply <my>[f] signs and wonders[g] in the land of the Egyptians, 4. but Pharaoh will not listen to you. And I will set *the plagues of my punishment* in Egypt,[2] and I will bring out the hosts of the people of the children of Israel from Egypt in plentiful judgments. 5. And the Egyptians will know that I am the Lord when I set *the plagues of my punishment* upon Egypt and bring out the children of Israel *redeemed* from among them."[3] 6. And Moses and Aaron did as the Lord[h] commanded them; thus they did. 7. And Moses *was*[4] eighty years old and Aaron eighty-three years old when they spoke with Pharaoh. 8. And the Lord[h] said to Moses and Aaron, saying: 9. "When Pharaoh speaks with you, saying: 'Give a sign for yourselves,' you shall say to Aaron: 'Take your staff and cast[i] *it* before Pharaoh'; *and*[5] it will become a serpent." 10. And Moses and Aaron went in to Pharaoh and did thus, as the Lord[h] had commanded them. And Aaron cast down his staff before Pharaoh and before his servants,[j6] and it became a serpent. 11. And Pharaoh also called his wise men and his sorcerers, and they also[k]—the sorcerers of the Egyptians—did likewise by their sorceries. 12. And each one cast

Apparatus, Chapter 7

[a] Nfmg: "the Memra of the Lord."

[b] Nfmg: "behold, I have set you as a lord to Pharaoh."

[c] Lit.: "Targeman (*trgmn*); M: "Tur(geman)"; cf. 4:16.

[d] Nfmg: "which I command," or: "I shall command."

[e] Nfmg: "harden."

[f] Text: "his"; Nfmg: "my signals and my (text: "his") signs."

[g] Nfi: "the miracle (lit.: "astonishment"; cf. Ps.-J.) of the Lord."

[h] Nfmg: "the Memra of the Lord" = CTg D in vv. 13, 14.

[i] VB: "and throw it before Pharaoh"; Nfmg: "throw" = VB.

[j] Nfmg, and CTg D (which resumes here): "and his rulers."

[k] CTg D: "likewise"; Nfmg: "they too."

Notes, Chapter 7

[1] Hebrew has: "And the Lord said to Moses: See, I have set you as God to Pharaoh; and Aaron your brother shall be your prophet." For "God," Hebrew *'lhym,* as "lord and ruler," see Tg. Onq., which has "lord"; Tg. Ps.-J.; Tg. Nf Exod 22:27; Philo, *De mutatione nominum* XII §128–29; *b. Sanh.* 56b; *Exod. R.* 2,6; and P. Alexander, 1972, 60–71. On the *mtrgmn* as "prophet," cf. *t. Meg.* 4:3, and see notes on 4:16. Possibly Targumists sometimes saw themselves in the role of prophets: so B.D. Chilton, 1983, 52–56.

[2] Hebrew has: "and I will set my hand against Egypt": see notes on 3:20.

[3] Hebrew has: "I am the Lord, when I stretch out my hand against Egypt and bring out the Israelites from their midst." See above, v. 4, notes on 3:20, and, for the addition of "redeemed," notes on 3:10.

[4] For the addition of "was," see also LXX, Vulg.

[5] For "*and* it will become a serpent," see LXX, Vulg.

[6] Nfmg's addition "and his rulers" anticipates the common rendering in these chapters of "servants" as "rulers": see notes on 7:20.

down[m] his staff, and they became serpents. But Aaron's staff swallowed up their staffs. 13. And the heart of Pharaoh was hardened, and he did not listen to them, as the Lord[h] had spoken. 14. And the Lord[h] said to Moses: "The heart of Pharaoh is hardened; he refuses to let the people[n] go. 15. <Go to>[o] Pharaoh in the morning; behold, he goes out *to refresh himself by the river*;[p][7] and you shall place yourself before him on the bank of the river, and the staff that was turned into a serpent take in your hand. 16. And you shall say to him: 'The Lord, the God of the Hebrews, has sent me to you to say: "Let my people go, that they may worship *before me*[q] in the wilderness; for behold, thus far you have not listened."[r] 17. Thus said the Lord:[h] "in this shall you know[s] that I am the Lord: behold, I strike the water which is in the river with the staff that is in my hand, and it shall be turned into blood. 18. And the fish that are in the river shall die, and the river shall become foul,[t] and the Egyptians will weary themselves[u] (in vain) to drink the waters of the river."''" 19. And the Lord[h] said to Moses: "Say to Aaron: 'Take your staff and *incline* your hand over the waters of the Egyptians, over the rivers, and over their *springs*,[w][8] and over their canals,[x] and over every gathering of their waters; and they will become blood in all the land of Egypt, in (vessels of) wood[y] and (of) stone.'" 20. And Moses and Aaron did thus, as the Lord had commanded; and he raised his staff[z] and struck the waters that were in the river *before* Pharaoh and *before his rulers*;[9] and all the waters of the river were turned into blood. 21. And the fish that were in the river died, and the river turned foul,[aa] and the Egyptians were not able to drink the water from the river; and there was blood in all the land of Egypt. 22. And the sorcerers of the Egyptians did likewise with their sorceries; and the heart of Pharaoh was hardened, and he did not hearken[bb] to them, as the Lord[cc] had spoken. 23. And Pharaoh turned[dd][9a] and entered within his house and did not

Apparatus, Chapter 7

[m] Nfmg: "threw."
[n] Nfmg: "his people."
[o] Missing in text.
[p] PVB: "to refresh himself by the waters"; Nfmg: "by the waters."
[q] Nfmg: "before him."
[r] Nfmg: "you have (not) heeded" (lit.: "received").
[s] CTg D: "this time you shall know"; Nfmg: "the Memra of the Lord, this time you shall know."
[t] Nfmg: "shall stench" = CTg D.
[u] Nfmg: "and they shall labor."

[w] Nfmg: "their pools" (?) = *sgyyhwn*— (? dialectical variant of *sqyyhwn*: cf Ps.-J.).
[x] CTg D = "marshlands"(?).
[y] Nfmg: "and in their irrigation canals" (?).
[z] Nfmg: "the Memra of the Lord (had commanded) and brandished his staff."
[aa] Nfmg: "and stank" (Afel, but in sense of Qal).
[bb] Nfmg: "and did not heed them"(lit.: "did not receive from them").
[cc] Nfmg, CTg D: "the Memra of the Lord."
[dd] Nfmg: "reflected."

Notes, Chapter 7

[7]Hebrew has: "Go to Pharaoh . . . behold, he will go out to the waters, and you shall stand to meet him. . . ." Cf. Frg. Tg. P, V, and that edited by Klein, 1, 1986, 179; for the exegesis here, see notes on 2:5.

[8]"Springs" renders Hebrew *y'ryhm*, "their streams, canals"; so also Frg. Tg. in Klein, 1, 1986, 181.

[9]For "before," see also LXX, Vulg. The "rulers" represent Hebrew "servants," as in 7:20; 8:5, 7, 17, 20, 25, 26, 27; 9:14, 20, 30, 34; 10:1, 6; 14:5, and other places throughout. Targum specifies that these are Pharaoh's high officials of state, his ministers, as does *Exod. R.* 18,1.

[9a]"Turned" is Aramaic *wkwyn* (or: "directed himself"), for Hebrew root *pnh*. Nf renders this Hebrew verb in the same manner in Gen 18:22; Exod 16:10; 32:15; Num 17:7; 21:33; Deut 1:40.

pay attention even to this *plague.*[ee][10] 24. And all the Egyptians dug round about the river <for water to drink, for they could not>[ff] drink from the water of the river. 25. And seven days passed after the Lord[gg] had struck *the waters of the river and he healed it.*[11] 26. And the Lord[hh] said to Moses: "Enter to Pharaoh and say to him: 'Thus said the Lord:[hh] Let the people go that they may worship *before* me.[ii] 27. If you decline to let them go, behold, *I will blot out*[jj][12] all your territory by frogs. 28. And the river will swarm with frogs, and they shall come up and go into your house and into the bed-chambers of your sleeping quarter, upon your bed and in the houses of your *rulers,*[kk][13] and in your people <*and in all your rulers*>,[mm] and in your ovens and in your kneading troughs. 29. And the frogs shall come up on you and your people and all your *rulers.*'"[nn]

CHAPTER 8

1. And the Lord[a] said to Moses: "Say to Aaron: '*Incline* your hand with your staff over the rivers and over the pools and over the swamps, and make frogs come up upon the land of Egypt.'"[b] 2. And Aaron *inclined* his hand over the waters of the Egyptians, and frog*s*[1] came up and covered[c] the land of Egypt. 3. And the sor-

Apparatus, Chapter 7

[ee] Nfmg: "bitterness" (*mrrwt'*; read?: *mrdwt'*, "chastisements, punishments").
[ff] Missing in text.
[gg] Nfmg: "the Memra of the Lord and (text apparently corrupt: read: healed?) the river."
[hh] Nfmg: "the Memra of the Lord."

[ii] Nfi: "before him."
[jj] Nfmg: "I will destroy."
[kk] Nfmg: "your servants and your peoples."
[mm] Probably wrongly introduced from following verse.
[nn] Nfi: "your servants."

Notes, Chapter 7

[10]Hebrew has: "did not pay attention even to this matter."
[11]Hebrew has: "after the Lord had smitten the river." For the healing of the water, see Tg. Ps.-J.; *Exod. R.* 9,12.
[12]Hebrew has: "I shall smite all your border with frogs." Cf. *Exod. R.* 10,2.
[13]In this and the following verse, "rulers" translates Hebrew "servants"; see notes on 7:20.

Apparatus, Chapter 8

[a] Nfmg: "the Memra of the Lord."
[b] Nfi: "(of the Egypt)ians."

[c] Nfmg: "frogs and they overspread."

Notes, Chapter 8

[1]Targum, like Vulg., has plural "frogs" for MT's singular. For the aggadah of the single, huge amphibian which appeared, see *Exod. R.* 10,4 and discussion in Grossfeld, 1988B, 20.

cerers did likewise by the sorceries, and they made frogs come upon the land of Egypt. 4. And Pharaoh called Moses and Aaron and said: "*Pray before* the Lord that the frogs may cease[d2] from me and from my people; and I will let the people go that they may sacrifice *before* the Lord." 5. And Moses said to Pharaoh: "*Give me a sign[e] and trust me[f]* until when I shall pray for you and for your *rulers[g]* and for your people, to blot out the frogs from you and from *the men of* your house;[3] only those which are in the river[h] shall be left." 6. And he said: "Tomorrow." And he said: "(Be it done) according to your words,[i] so that you may know that there is none like the Lord our God. 7. And the frogs shall go[j] from you and from *the men of* your house and from your *rulers[k4]* and from your people; only those which are in the river[m] shall be left." 8. And Moses and Aaron went out from the presence of Pharaoh; and Moses *prayed before* the Lord[5] concerning the frogs which he had sent to Pharaoh. 9. And the Lord[n] did according to the words of Moses, and the frogs died out of the houses and out of the courtyards and out of the fields. 10. And they gathered them into heaps and heaps,[o] and the land stank.[p] 11. And Pharaoh saw that there was an *hour* of respite,[6] and he hardened his heart and he did not hearken to them,[q] as the Lord[r] had spoken. 12. And the Lord said to Moses: "Say to Aaron: '<*Incline*>[s] your staff and strike the dust of the earth, and it shall become vermin in all the land of Egypt.'" 13. And they did thus; and Aaron *inclined* his hand with the staff and struck the dust of the earth, and there was vermin on all the *sons of* man and on beast. All the dust of the land became vermin in all the land of Egypt. 14. And the sorcerers did likewise by their sorceries, (trying)

Apparatus, Chapter 8

[d] Nfmg: "that they may pass away."
[e] PVB: "give a sign and I will trust you (P+) until when I shall pray for you."
[f] Nfmg: "you"; cf. PVB.
[g] Nfmg: "and for your servants."
[h] Nfi: "in the river shall they be left."
[i] Nfmg: "according to your words" (a different term).
[j] Nfmg: "and (all the frogs) shall pass."
[k] Nfmg: "and from your servants."

[m] Nfi: "(those) in the river."
[n] Nfmg: "the Memra of the Lord."
[o] VB: "heaps and heaps" (= Nf); P: "heaps."
[p] Nfmg: "and (the land) grew foul."
[q] Nfmg and Nfi: "and he did not hear them" (lit.: "receive from them").
[r] Nfmg: "the Memra of the Lord."
[s] Missing in text.

Notes, Chapter 8

[2]Hebrew has: "And Pharaoh called Moses and Aaron, and said: Entreat the Lord, that he may remove the frogs." For "pray before the Lord," see Tg. Onq., Tg. Ps.-J., LXX, Vulg., and Tg. Nf Exod 8:5, 24, 25; 9:28.

[3]Hebrew has: "And Moses said to Pharaoh: Assume honor over me (to decide) when I should entreat for you and for your servants . . . to cut off the frogs from you and from your house." For "give me a sign and trust me," see also Frg. Tg. V; on "pray," see notes on v. 4 and cf. LXX; and on "rulers" for "servants," see notes on 7:20.

[4]Hebrew has: "And the frogs shall depart from you and from your house and from your servants. . . ." See notes on 7:20.

[5]Hebrew has: "and Moses cried out to the Lord." For "crying out" as prayer, see Tg. Ps.-J., Tg. Onq., Pesh., and Grossfeld, 1988B, 21.

[6]Hebrew has: "And Pharaoh saw that there was respite." Cf. *Exod. R.* 10,6.

to make vermin come out, but they could not. And there was vermin in man and in beast. 15. And the sorcerers said to Pharaoh: "This is the finger[t] of *might from before the Lord*."[7] And the heart of Pharaoh was hardened, and he did not hearken to them,[u] as the Lord had spoken. 16. And the Lord[w] said to Moses: "Arise early in the morning and be in readiness before Pharaoh; behold, he comes out *to refresh himself by*[x] *the river*; and you shall say to him: 'Thus says the Lord:[w] "Let my people go so that they may worship *before* me.'[y8] 17. If you do not let my people go, behold, I *unleash*[z] against you and your *rulers*[aa] and your people and *the men of* your house a mixed swarm[bb] (of gnats); and the houses of the Egyptians shall be filled with the swarm (of gnats), and (also) the land in which they *dwell.*[cc9] 18. And *I will do signs and wonderful things* on that day with the land of Goshen, upon which my people *dwell*, so that no swarm (of gnats) shall be there, so that you may know that I *am* the Lord *whose Memra dwells*[dd] within the land.[10] 19. And I will set redemption[ee] between my people and your people. Tomorrow shall this sign be."'" 20. And the Lord did so. And there came a great swarm (of gnats) into the *palace*[11] of Pharaoh and into the houses of his *rulers*,[ff] and in all the land of Egypt. And the land was destroyed before the swarm (of gnats). 21. And Pharaoh called Moses and

Apparatus, Chapter 8

[t] Nfmg: "(this is) the might."

[u] Nfmg: "and he did not hear them" (lit.: "receive from them").

[w] Nfmg: "the Memra of the Lord."

[x] Nfmg: + "the brink of."

[y] Nfi: "before him."

[z] Nfmg: "I will send."

[aa] Nfmg: "on your servants."

[bb] In Aramaic '*rbrwb*'; VB (sole word to verse): '*rwbrwbh*, rendering '*rb* of HT. This Aramaic term, also occurring in Samaritan Aramaic, is found in the sense of "vermin" in Nf Exod 8:17, 18, 20, 25, 27,

and of "mixed multitude" in Pal. Tg. texts Exod 12:38; Num 11:4. See Sokoloff, 1990, 419. It is related to obscure '*rwb*' of Onq., = "mixed swarm"? (of wild beasts?); Nfmg: "a swarm" ('*rwb*') (of gnats?; wild animals?). Ps.-J.: '*yrbwt*.

[cc] Nfmg 1°: "in which they dwell" (orthographical variants); Nfmg 2°: "in which they reside."

[dd] Nfmg: "the glory of whose Shekinah dwells."

[ee] A literal translation of a probably corrupt word of the HT.

[ff] Nfmg: "into the house of Pharaoh and into the houses of his servants."

Notes, Chapter 8

[7]Hebrew has: "it is the finger of God." See notes on 3:20; 7:4, 5; and cf. *Exod. R.* 10,7; *Tanḥ Wa'era* 14; *b. Sanh.* 95ab.

[8]Hebrew has: "he will go out to the water. . . . Let my people go, that they may serve me." See notes on 2:5.

[9]Hebrew has: "behold, I shall send on you and on your servants and on your people and on your house the flies . . . and also the ground which they are on." See notes in Apparatus and on 7:20. *Leqaḥ Ṭob*, quoted by Kasher, *Torah Shelemah*, vol. 6 (Exodus) 70, understands the "servants" as those who see the king's face, i.e., the high state officials.

[10]Hebrew has: "And I shall make separate on that day the land of Goshen on which my people stand . . . so that you may know that I am the Lord in the midst of the land." Targum has interpreted "I shall make separate," which derives from the root *plh*, as if it were derived from root *pl'*, "to be wonderful, extraordinary": cf. Tg. Ps.-J. and Vulg. Tg. Onq. has "on which my people dwell." Instead of the Memra dwelling in the land, Nfmg has the Glory of the Shekinah: see Muñoz León, 1974, 309–10.

[11]For "palace," Hebrew has "house." The Hebrew has "the house of his servants" for Targum's "the houses of his rulers": for plural houses, see LXX and Vulg.; and on "rulers," see notes to 7:20.

Aaron and said: "Go, sacrifice *before the Lord* your God in the land*[gg] of Egypt.*"[12] 22. And Moses said: "It is not right to do so, because *the idols of the* Egyptians are an abomination, *from which we must take* to sacrifice before*[hh]* the Lord, our God. Behold, if we sacrifice *the idols[ii] of* the Egyptians in their presence, *it is impossible* that they should not stone us.[13] 23. We will go a *journey distance* of three days in the wilderness and sacrifice *before* the Lord, our God, as he has spoken to us." 24. And <Pharaoh>*[jj]* said: "Behold, I let you go, and you shall sacrifice *before* the Lord, your God, in the wilderness. *Only* that you shall not go very far distant. *Pray*[14] *also* for me."*[kk]* 25. And Moses said: "Behold, I go out from your presence, and *we will pray[mm]*[15] *before* the Lord, and he will make the mixed swarm*[nn]* (of gnats) pass from Pharaoh and from his *rulers* and from the people tomorrow. Only let Pharaoh not lie again by not letting the people go that they may sacrifice *before* the Lord." 26. And Moses went out from the presence of Pharaoh and *prayed before* the Lord.[16] 27. And the Lord*[oo]* did according to the words of Moses and made the swarm (of gnats) pass from Pharaoh and from his *rulers[pp]*[17] and from the people, and not *even* one remained. 28. And Pharaoh hardened his heart also this time and did not let the people go.

Apparatus, Chapter 8

[gg] Nfmg: "worship God in the land."

[hh] Nfmg: "the lambs, they are the abomination of the Egyptians; we must take from them and sacrifice before."

[ii] Nfmg: "the abomination of the Egyptians."

[jj] Missing in text.

[kk] Nfmg: "you shall pray also for me."

[mm] Probably = "I will pray."

[nn] 'rbrwb'; see note *bb* above.

[oo] Nfmg: "the Memra of the Lord did according to the words."

[pp] Nfmg: "his servants."

Notes, Chapter 8

[12]Hebrew has: "Go, sacrifice to your God in the land." Cf. Tg. Ps.-J.; they are not to sacrifice in the land of Israel but in Egypt. For God specified as the Lord, see LXXa.

[13]Hebrew has: "for we shall be sacrificing to the Lord our God the abomination of the Egyptians. If we sacrifice the abomination of the Egyptians in front of them, will they not stone us?" Both the Targum and Nfmg are quite clear that the Egyptians worshiped animals as divine beings, a point endorsed by Tg. Onq., Tg. Ps.-J., *Exod. R.* 11,3, and *Cant. R.* 2,16; see further Grossfeld, 1988B, 21. That the Hebrews might sacrifice Egyptian sacred animals is highlighted by Vulg., "quod si mactaverimus ea quae colunt Aegyptii coram eis," and by Philo, *Quaestiones in Exodum* 1 §8.

[14]"Pray" represents Hebrew "make entreaty": see v. 4, Tg. Onq., Tg. Ps.-J., LXX, Pesh., and *Exod. R.* 11,3.

[15]For "pray," cf. LXX, Vulg., and see notes on v. 4. Hebrew has: "I shall entreat," discussed by Le Déaut, 1979 (*Exode*) 62–63. On "rulers" for "servants," see note on 7:20.

[16]Cf. LXX, Vulg., and see notes on v. 4.

[17]See notes on 7:20.

CHAPTER 9

1. And the Lord[a] said to Moses: "Go in to Pharaoh and say to him:[b] 'Thus says the Lord, the God of the *Jews*:[c][1] "Let my people go so that they may worship before me.[d] 2. Because (if) you refuse to let (them) go and still detain (them), 3. behold, the *plagues of my punishment*[2] shall be[e] upon the cattle of the field, the horses and the donkeys, the camels, the oxen and the sheep—a very strong plague. 4. And the Lord will make a distinction between the cattle of the Egyptians and the cattle of Israel,[3] and nothing whatsoever shall die[f] from all that belongs to the children of Israel."'" 5. And the Lord[a] set a time, saying: "Tomorrow the Lord[g] will do this thing in the land."[h] 6. And the Lord[a] did this thing on the following *day*,[4] and all the cattle[i] of the Egyptians died, and not *even* one died from the cattle[j] of the children of Israel. 7. And Pharaoh sent and, behold, not as much as one had died from the cattle[k] of Israel; but the heart of Pharaoh was hardened, and he did not let the people go. 8. And the Lord said to Moses and Aaron: "Take handfuls[m] of ashes of the oven and throw them towards the heavens[n] before Pharaoh. 9. And it shall become dust upon all the land of Egypt, and upon the *sons of* man and upon beast it shall become an inflammation (that) breaks through, *producing blisters*,[o] in all the land of Egypt." 10. And they took the ashes of the oven and stood before Pharaoh, and Moses threw them towards the heavens, and they became an inflammation that broke out, producing *blisters*,[p] in *the sons* of man and in beast. 11. And

Apparatus, Chapter 9

[a] Nfmg: "the Memra of the Lord."

[b] Nfmg: "and you shall speak with him: Thus said the Memra of the Lord."

[c] Nfmg: "of the Hebrews."

[d] Nfi: "before him."

[e] Nfmg: "comes on your flocks that are in the open field and on the mares and on the asses. And it shall distinguish." These last four words belong to v. 4.

[f] Nfmg: "and the Memra of the Lord shall set a distinguishing mark between the flocks of Israel and the flocks of the Egyptians and there shall not die of their cattle."

[g] Nfmg: "the Memra of the Lord (will perform) this sign."

[h] Nfmg: "word (i.e., thing) to the land."

[i] Nfmg: "the flocks of."

[j] Nfi: "and from the flocks of."

[k] Nfmg: "from the flocks of."

[m] Lit.: "full of your palms"; Nfmg: "full of the hollow of your hands."

[n] Nfmg: "heavenwards."

[o] "blisters": in Nf.: *slpwqyn* (in vv. 9, 10); VB *slbwqyyn* (v. 9); a rare word, found only in these texts and in Christian Palestinian Aramaic; see Sokoloff, 1990, 551, s.v. *slbwqy*. In VB misplaced after 17.

[p] Nfmg: "inflammation (producing) blisters."

Notes, Chapter 9

[1] Hebrew has: "the God of the Hebrews," which Tg. Nf has allowed to stand unchanged at 3:18; 5:3; 7:16; 10:3. Tg. Onq. and Tg. Ps.-J. of this verse have "the God of the Jews"; perhaps Tg. Nf has been influenced by them, since they have "the God of the Jews" at 3:18; 5:3; 7:16; and 9:13, and in this last verse Tg. Nf agrees with them.

[2] "The plagues of my punishment" renders Hebrew "my hand." See notes on 3:20.

[3] Targum here renders literally the Hebrew "and the Lord will make a separation," as also in 11:7. See notes to 8:18, and contrast the exegesis there, which is actually shared in this verse by Tg. Ps.-J. Hebrew has "the cattle of Israel and the cattle of Egypt."

[4] Hebrew has "the morrow" for "the following day"; cf. Tg. Onq.

the sorcerers were not able to stand before Moses because of the inflammation, because there was inflammation on the sorcerers and on all the Egyptians. 12. And the Lord*ᵃ* hardened the heart of Pharaoh, and he did not listen to them, as the Lord*ᵃ* had spoken with Moses. 13. And the Lord*ᵃ* said to Moses: "Arise early in the morning and be in readiness before Pharaoh and say to him: 'Thus said the Lord,*ᵃ* the God of the *Jews:*ᵃ⁵ "Let the people go that they may worship *before* me.'*ʳ* 14. Because this time, behold, I will send all my plagues upon your heart,*ˢ* on your *rulers*ᵗ⁶ and your people so that you may know that there is not like to me*ᵘ* in all the land. 15. Because (even) now I had (almost) sent the *plagues of my punishment* and blotted out*ʷ* you and your people by the pestilence; and you shall be blotted out, *O Pharaoh*, from the earth.⁷ 16. *But, not that it go well with you have I kept you alive until now; but* for this reason have I kept you alive *until now:* to show*ˣ* you the *might* of my strength and so that you may recount my *Holy* Name in all the land.⁸ 17. *Behold*, until now you lord it*ʸ* over my people, not letting them go. 18. Behold, at (this) hour*ᶻ* tomorrow I will make very strong hail *descend*,⁹ the like of which was not in Egypt from the day it was founded*ᵃᵃ* until now. 19. And now, send, *gather*¹⁰ your cattle*ᵇᵇ* and all that belongs to you on the face of the field, all men and beasts that are left in the field. If they are not gathered*ᶜᶜ* within the house,

Apparatus, Chapter 9

ᵃ Nfmg 1° and 2°: "of the Hebrews."
ʳ Nfi: "before him."
ˢ Nfmg: "I shall unleash my plagues on all of them, and they shall reach to your heart."
ᵗ Nfmg: "the plague of my punishment upon the heart of Pharaoh and upon your servants."
ᵘ Nfmg: "like to the Memra of the Lord."
ʷ Nfi: "and I would have blotted out."
ˣ Nfmg: "in order to show you what is the might of my strength and in order to recount my name" (with Hebrew form for the sign of accusative).

ʸ VB: "(you) have grown strong" (sole word in VB for verse).
ᶻ Nfmg 1°: "at this time"; Nfmg 2°: "this day and tomorrow (I will make) hail."
ᵃᵃ Lit.: "appointed"; Nfmg: "that it was established."
ᵇᵇ Nfmg: "your flock."
ᶜᶜ Nfmg: "shall (not) be gathered within the houses, shall come down."

Notes, Chapter 9

⁵On "the God of the Jews," see note to v. 2.
⁶On "rulers" for "servants," see note on 7:20.
⁷Hebrew has: "For now I might have stretched my hand and smitten you and your people with plague, so that you were cut off from the earth." Cf. Tg. Onq. and see notes on 3:20. The pestilence denotes "death," as in Tg. Onq., Tg. Ps.-J., and LXX, and midrashim cited by Grossfeld, 1988B, 23.
⁸Hebrew has: "But for this reason I have caused you to stand, that I may show you my power, and that my Name may be recounted in all the earth." It is possible that the Targum knew the tradition that Pharaoh was himself a first-born son who alone was spared the twelfth plague and preserved alive; so R. Nehemiah in *Mek. RI Beshallah* 7:44–49; *Pisha* 13: 17:25; *Tanh. Bo' 7*; *Mek. RSbY*, pp. 67–68. For God's *Holy* Name, see Tg. Ps.-J.; Tg. Nf Exod. 23:1; and Chester, 1986, 67–68.
⁹For "descend," Hebrew has "rain down"; cf. Tg. Onq. and Tg. Ps.-J.
¹⁰Hebrew has *h'z*, "hasten in," or, according to Grossfeld, 1988B, 25, "bring in to safety." For "gather," see Tg. Onq., Tg. Ps.-J., LXX, Vulg., Pesh., and Kasher, *Torah Shelemah*, vol. 6 (Exodus) 90.

the hail will come down upon them and they will die.""" 20. Anyone of Pharaoh's *rulers*[dd] who feared[ee] before the Lord[11] chased his servants and his cattle within the house.[ff] 21. And whosoever paid no attention to the words of the Lord[gg] left his servants and his cattle[hh] in the open field.[12] 22. And the Lord[ii] said to Moses: "*Incline* <your hand>[jj] to the heavens[kk] that there may be hail, in all the land of Egypt, upon the *sons of man*, upon the beast, and upon every plant in the open field in the land of Egypt." 23. And Moses *inclined*[mm] his staff to the heavens, and the Lord[ii] gave[nn] thunder and hail, and fire walked[oo] within the land, and the Lord[ii] made hail *come down*[13] upon the land of Egypt. 24. And there was *strong* hail, and the fire *was leaping* in the midst of the hail:[14] very strong, the like of which there was not in the land of Egypt from the time[pp] it became a nation *and a kingdom.*[qq] 25. And in all the land of Egypt the hail blotted out all *that was* in the open field, from *the sons of man* to[rr] beast; and every plant that was in the open field the hail blotted out,[ss] and all the trees that were in the open field it broke. 26. Only in the land of Goshen, where the children of Israel *dwelt*, there was no hail.[tt] 27. And Pharaoh sent and called Moses and Aaron and said to them: "I have

Apparatus, Chapter 9

[dd] Nfmg: "servants."

[ee] P: "and Job, although he was from among Pharaoh's counselors, was fearing the decree of eternal life (or: of him who gives life to the world) chased his rulers and his cattle in (corr. to: "from"?) the open field"; Nfmg: "Job who feared the word of the Lord" = Ps.-J.

[ff] Nfmg: "his flocks within the house."

[gg] Nfmg: "and Balaam who did not pay attention to the wo(rd) of the Lord"; = Ps.-J.; CTg D resumes at v. 21, with text identical with Nf apart from variants noted below.

[hh] Nfmg: "his flocks."

[ii] CTg D: "the Memra of the Lord."

[jj] Missing in text; in CTg D.

[kk] Nfmg: "raise your hand toward the heavens."

[mm] Nfmg: "and (Moses) raised."

[nn] Nfmg: "appointed."

[oo] CTg D: "and fire was withheld (?; thundered?) in the land, and the Memra of the Lord rained down hail"; Nfmg: "and the fire danced within the hail, and the Memra of the Lord rained down hail upon."

[pp] Nfmg: "the hour"; CTg D: "from the day that it became a nation."

[qq] Nfmg: "a nation"; = CTg D.

[rr] Nfmg: "and every (beast)."

[ss] Nfmg: "was destroyed."

[tt] Nfmg: "(there was no) hail there."

Notes, Chapter 9

[11] Hebrew has: "Those of the servants of Pharaoh who feared the word of the Lord." On "rulers" for "servants," see note on 7:20. Nfmg introduces here the aggadah of Job as Pharaoh's counselor, found also in *j. Soṭah* 5:6; *b. Soṭah* 11a; *Tanḥ. Wa'era* 16; see also J.R. Baskin, 1983, 11.

[12] Nfmg's aggadah about Balaam is found also in the sources listed for v. 20, and *Exod. R.* 1,9.

[13] "Come down" stands for MT's "rained": see note on v. 18 and Tg. Ps.-J.

[14] The Hebrew lacks "strong," which is Tg. Nf's addition. "Was leaping" represents Hebrew *mtlqḥt*, a word of uncertain meaning, possibly "taking hold of itself, enfolding itself"; Tg. Nf's interpretation is shared by Tg. Ps.-J., as is the additional phrase "and a kingdom." LXX has: "so there was hail, and flaming fire in the hail." See also *Exod. R.* 12,4; *Num. R.* 12,8.

sinned[uu] this time; the Lord is just, and *Pharaoh* and his people are *guilty.*[ww][15] 28. *Pray*[xx] *before* the Lord that he *withhold*[yy] the thunder *from before the Lord* and the hail,[16] and I shall let you go and you shall stay no longer." 29. And Moses said to him: "As I go out of the city I will stretch out the palms[zz] *of my hands before* the Lord; the thunders will be withheld,[a] and there will be no more hail so that you may know that the earth *is of* the Lord. 30. But (as for) you and your *rulers,*[b][17] I know[c] that formerly[d] you feared before the Lord[e] our God." 31. And the flax and the barley were beaten down, because the barley *was* early[f] and the flax *was* in bud *and had shed*[g] *its blossom.*[18] 32. But the wheat and the spelt[h] were not beaten down, because they were late. 33. And Moses went out of the city[i] from the presence of Pharaoh and spread out the palm[j] of his hands *before* the Lord; and the thunder and the hail were withheld,[k] and rain did not come down[m] on the earth. 34. And when Pharaoh saw that the thunder and the rain and the hail had ceased,[n] he sinned yet again and his heart was hardened, he and his *rulers.*[o][19] 35. And the heart of Pharaoh was hardened, and he did not let the children of Israel go, as the Lord[p] had spoken with Moses.

Apparatus, Chapter 9

[uu] Nfmg: "I have sinned because I have rebelled against the Memra of the Lord this time. It is manifest."

[ww] CTg D: "the Lord is guiltless and (I and my people) are guilty."

[xx] Nfmg + "now."

[yy] Nfmg: "that it cease before him, for the Lord is guiltless."

[zz] Nfmg: "the palm."

[a] Correcting *wtmn'wn* of text to *ytmn'wn* with CTg D; Nfmg: "will cease."

[b] CTg D: "your servants"; Nfmg: "and (as for) you, Pharaoh, and your servants (I) know."

[c] Nfmg: "that until the plagues reached you, you did not humble yourselves before (the Lord)."

[d] Nfmg: "that still you do not fear"; CTg D: "that formerly you did (not) fear before the Lord."

[e] Nfmg: "the Memra of the Lord."

[f] Nfmg: "was late."

[g] VB: "the flax was in bud and had shed its blossom" = Nf: "shed" in Nf, VB *'trt*, Nfmg: *'tr't* (root *tr'*); "shed its blossom" not in CTg D.

[h] In Nf: *kwntyh*; CTg D: *kwppyyt'*, vocalized in the MS as: *kûppîyata'*.

[i] Nf, which = CTg D, reproduces the HT construction of use of the sign of the accusative for indication of *terminus a quo* (also HT Exod 9:29; Deut 14:22; cf. Gen 44:4; Jer 10:20b); Nfmg: "outside of the city."

[j] CTg D, Nfmg: "the palms of his (hands)."

[k] Nfmg: "ceased."

[m] CTg D: "did not come down in wrath (?) upon the earth."

[n] Nfmg 1° + 2°: "the rain, hail and thunder had ceased."

[o] Nfmg: "and his servants."

[p] Nfmg: "the Memra of the Lord through the hands of (= through) Moses."

Notes, Chapter 9

[15]Hebrew has: "and I and my people are guilty."

[16]On "pray" for Hebrew "make entreaty," see note on 8:4, and LXX, Vulg., Tg. Ps.-J., Tg. Onq., fragment in Klein, 1986, 185. "Withhold" stands for Hebrew *wrb*, "there has been enough."

[17]"Rulers" for MT's "servants"; see note on 7:20.

[18]". . . and had shed its blossom" is an addition to MT; cf. Frg. Tg. V and *Exod. R.* 12,6.

[19]"Rulers" for MT's "servants"; see note on 7:20.

CHAPTER 10

1. And the Lord*ᵃ* said to Moses: "Go in to Pharaoh, because I have hardened his heart and the heart of his rulers*ᵇ* so as to set these signs*ᶜ* among them,¹ 2. so that you may relate in the hearing of your *sonsᵈ* and *your son's sons* how *I have confounded* the Egyptians*ᵉ*² and the signs that I have set among them,*ᶠ* that you may know*ᵍ* that I am the Lord." 3. And Moses and Aaron came*ʰ* to*ⁱ* Pharaoh and said to him: "Thus said the Lord, the God of the Hebrews: 'How long will you decline to humble yourself before *the Lord*?³ Let my people go*ʲ* that they may worship before me. 4. Because if you decline to let my people go, behold, tomorrow I will bring the locusts into your territory. 5. And they will cover the *view* of the land,⁴ and you will not be able*ᵏ* to see the land; and they shall eat the remnant that has been spared, that has been left*ᵐ* to you from the hail, and they shall eat all the trees that grow for you from the open field. 6. And your houses and the houses of all your *rulers*, and the houses of all the Egyptians,*ⁿ* shall be filled by them, which your fathers or your fathers' fathers have not seen from the day they were*ᵒ* upon the earth until this day.'" And he *hurriedᵖ* and went out from before Pharaoh.⁵ 7. And Pharaoh's servants said to him: "How long will this one be a snare for us? Let *the people*⁶ go*ᑫ* that they may worship *before* the Lord their God before you (come to)

Apparatus, Chapter 10

ᵃ Nfmg: "the Memra of the Lord."
ᵇ Nfi: "of his servants."
ᶜ Nfmg: "and my wonders."
ᵈ Nfmg: "to recount in the hearing of your sons."
ᵉ "how I confounded the Egyptians"; Nf almost verbatim as citation in *Aruk*; Nfi: "that I have confounded" (mere orthographical variant).
ᶠ Nfmg: "I was avenged of the Egyptians and the signs of my wonders I set among you."
ᵍ Nfmg: "and they shall know."
ʰ Nfi: "and he went in."

ⁱ Nfmg: "before."
ʲ Nfmg: "before him: let my people go."
ᵏ Nfmg: "Pharaoh will not be able."
ᵐ Nfmg: "and it shall eat the remainder that has been spared, that has been left to you."
ⁿ Nfmg: "(of all) your servants and the houses of (text: sons) all the Egyptians."
ᵒ Nfmg: "they dwelt."
ᵖ Nfmg: "and directed himself."
ᑫ Nfmg: "the men."

Notes, Chapter 10

¹"Rulers" for MT's "servants"; see note on 7:20. Nfmg "signs and wonders" (cf. also v. 2) reproduces a standard phrase which occurs in biblical descriptions of the Exodus: e.g., Deut 29:3; 34:11.

²Hebrew has: "So that you may recount in the ear of your son and your son's son what I did ruthlessly to (or: how I mocked) the Egyptians." The word *ht'llty* may be rendered in two ways, as above. On its translation in Targum generally, see Grossfeld, 1988B, 26–27, and Le Déaut, 1979 (*Exode*) 73. The plural forms of the Targum occur also in LXX and Vulg.

³Hebrew has: "How long will you refuse to humble yourselves before me?"

⁴Hebrew has: "And they shall cover the face (lit.: eye) of the earth." So also Tg. Ps.-J., LXX, and v. 15, possibly suggesting that men could not see the earth because the sun was obscured as related in Tg. Onq., on which see Grossfeld, 1988B, 27.

⁵Hebrew has: "servants" for "rulers" (see note on 7:20), and "he turned and went out" for "he hurried and went out," perhaps agreeing with *Exod. R.* 13,5 that Pharaoh had believed Moses, so that the latter left immediately before Pharaoh should change his mind!

⁶Hebrew has: "the men" for "the people."

know[r] that Egypt is blotted out."[s] 8. And he brought back[6a] Moses and Aaron to Pharaoh, and they said to them: "Go, sacrifice *before* the Lord your God. But who are those that go?" 9. And Moses said: "With our young men[t] and our old men we shall go, with our sons and our daughters, with our sheep and our oxen we shall go, because we have a feast *before* the Lord." 10. And he said: "Let, *now*, the *Memra*[u] *of* the Lord be with you[w7] when I let you and your little ones go. See! There is evil before your faces. 11. Not thus! Go now, men (among you), and worship before the Lord, because you have desired it." And they were driven out from before the presence of Pharaoh. 12. And the Lord[a] said to Moses: "*Incline* your hand over the land of Egypt for the locusts, and let them come down upon the land of Egypt and eat every plant, and[x] the land,[8] and all that the hail has left." 13. And Moses *inclined* his staff over the land of Egypt, and the Lord[y] brought a wind from the east[z] upon the land all that day and all the night. Morning came and the eastern wind had borne the locusts. 14. And the locusts came up upon all the land of Egypt and dwelt in all the territories of Egypt in great numbers. Before them there were not such locusts like them, and after them there will not be such.[aa] 15. And they covered *all* the *view* of all the land,[9] and the land darkened,[bb] and they ate every plant of the land and all the fruits of the tree that the hail had left, and a green thing was not left on a tree or on a plant[cc] of the open field in all the land of the Egyptians. 16. And Pharaoh hastened[dd] to call Moses and Aaron and said: "I have sinned *before* the Lord[10] your God and against you. 17. And now, forgive, I pray, my *debts*[ee] only this time, and *pray before* the Lord your God that he may make this *plague*[ff] also pass from me."[11] 18. And he went out from before Pharaoh and *prayed before*

Apparatus, Chapter 10

[r] Nfmg: "is it that you did not have consideration to (come to) know?"

[s] Nfmg: "has been blotted out."

[t] Nfmg: "our youths."

[u] Nfmg: "thus let the Memra."

[w] Nfmg: "at your aid."

[x] This text probably an error for "of the land."

[y] Nfmg: "and his Memra"; or "this (his) Memra of (the Lord)."

[z] Nfmg: "an easterly (wind)."

[aa] Nfmg: "and after him there will not be such" (lit.: "there will not add to be such").

[bb] Nfmg: "and (the land) grew black" (a different word for "was darkened").

[cc] Nfmg: "green in tree and herb."

[dd] Nfmg: "and (Pharaoh) hurried."

[ee] Nfmg: "(forgive) and remit the debts," i.e., sins.

[ff] Nfmg: "the anger."

Notes, Chapter 10

[6a]"He brought back" is *whzr*, followed by the sign of the accusative *yt* before "Moses and Aaron." Nf understood Hebrew *wywšb*, MT *wayyûšab*, lit. "and there was brought back Moses and Aaron," as active, not passive.

[7]Hebrew has: "And he said to them: So may the Lord be with you." Cf. Tg. Onq., Tg. Ps.-J., and Nfmg; and see Hayward, 1981, 21, and Le Déaut, 1979 (*Exode*) 74.

[8]Hebrew has: "the plant of the land."

[9]See notes to v. 5, and cf. Tg. Ps.-J. and LXX.

[10]For "before the Lord," cf. LXX.

[11]Hebrew has: "and entreat the Lord your God that he remove only this death from me." See notes to 8:4; 9:15; Tg. Onq., Tg. Ps.-J., and LXX, Vulg.

the Lord.[12] 19. And the Lord turned a very strong west[gg] wind, and it bore the locusts and cast[hh] them into the Reed Sea; a single locust was not left in all the territory of the Egyptians. 20. And the Lord hardened the heart of Pharaoh, and he did not let the children of Israel go. 21. And the Lord said: "*Incline* your hand to the heavens,[ii] and let there be darkness upon the land of Egypt, and let the darkness be *palpable*."[jj][13] 22. And Moses *inclined*[kk] (his) hand to the heavens, and there was thick darkness in all the land of Egypt three days. 23. No one saw his brothers, and no one rose from his *place*[14] for three days. But there was light[mm] in their dwelling places[nn] for all the children of Israel. 24. And Pharaoh called Moses *and Aaron*[15] and said: "Go and worship *before* the Lord; only your sheep and your oxen shall remain[oo] here; your little ones shall go with you." 25. And Moses said: "You shall also give into our hand[pp] sacrifices and holocausts, and *we will sacrifice before* the Lord[16] our God. 26. And our cattle[qq] shall also go with us; the hoof *of a foot*[17] shall not be left behind them, for it is from among them we shall take *to sacrifice before* the Lord, our God; and as for us, we do not know *how* we shall *worship before* the Lord, our God, until the time we enter there."[rr] 27. And the Lord[ss] hardened *his*

Apparatus, Chapter 10

[gg] Lit.: "in the sea" as HT; Nfmg: "the Memra of the Lord (turned) a very strong westerly wind."

[hh] '*ql'* a rare word (Sokoloff, 1990, 495); also in Pal. Tg.citations of this verse in *Meturg.*, MS Angelica, Rome ("he cast it"), and ed. Isny; Nfmg: "and threw (*ṭlq*) them into the sea."

[ii] Nfmg: "and the Memra of the Lord said: Lift up your hand toward the heavens."

[jj] Lit.: "and let there be feeling (palpability or "substance") in the darkness"; VB: "and let there be feelings (!: or: "let them be persons feeling") in the darkness"; Nfmg: "and let them be like people feeling (or: groping) in the darkness."

[kk] Nfmg: "and (Moses) lifted up."

[mm] Nfmg: "they had light because they busied themselves with the words of the Law in their dwellings."

[nn] Nfmg: "in their tents."

[oo] Nfmg: "leave; take only your little ones."

[pp] Nfi: "into our hands."

[qq] Nfmg: "our flocks we shall take with us."

[rr] Nfmg: "what we must offer before the Lord until we enter there."

[ss] Nfmg: "the Memra of the Lord."

Notes, Chapter 10

[12]Hebrew has: "and he entreated the Lord." See note on 8:4; Tg. Onq., Tg. Ps.-J., and LXX. Vulg. has "ask."

[13]Hebrew describes the darkness as *wymš ḥšk,*, "that one may feel the darkness"; another possible rendering would be "darkness in which people grope around." Both these possibilities are exploited by the different Targums, as indicated in the Apparatus. LXX has darkness that may be felt; cf. Vulg. In *Exod. R.* 14,1 it is said to be as thick as a *dinar* coin. For its palpability, see also *Mek. RSbY* on this verse, and *Exod. R.* 14,3.

[14]"From his place" represents Hebrew *mtḥtyw*, "from beneath, instead of, him"; cf. Vulg. Nfmg, like Tg. Ps.-J. and *Exod. R.* 14,3, explains the light as arising from their Torah-study, which is a source of enlightenment; indeed, Targum regularly translates Torah as "illumination" or "enlightenment."

[15]Targum has added Aaron's name: so also two Hebrew MSS, Sam, LXX, and Vulg.

[16]For "we will sacrifice" Hebrew has, literally, "we will make, do," and Targum gives what is clearly the meaning of the expression: see *Exod. R.* 14,4 and MS sources cited by Kasher, *Torah Shelemah*, vols. 10–11 (Exodus) 22–23; Vulg. and below, 12:48; 29:36.

[17]Targum adds "of a foot" to MT's "there shall not be left a hoof." "To sacrifice" translates Hebrew *l'bd*, "to serve, worship."

heart,"[tt][18] and he did not desire to let them go. 28. And Pharaoh said to him:[uu] "Go away from me[ww] and never again *speak before me one of those harsh words*;[xx] *I would surely rather die than hear any of your words*. Take heed[yy] *that my anger be not kindled against you* and *I deliver you into the hands of the people who sought your life and they kill you*."[zz][19] 29. And Moses said[a] to him:[b] *"Fittingly and the truth[c] have you spoken. I was being notified[d] while yet residing in Midian to the effect[e] that: 'All the men who were seeking your life are dead.' And not only after I was making petition for you from before the Lord was I praying for you, and the plague was withheld from you. And this plague is the tenth one for Pharaoh. With the first-born of Pharaoh it will begin."[f] And Moses said *to Pharaoh*: "Fittingly and with truth have you spoken; I shall never again[g] see your *countenance*." [20]

Apparatus, Chapter 10

[tt] Nfmg, Nfi: "(the heart) of Pharaoh."

[uu] P: "And Pharaoh said to him: Go away from me. Take heed for yourself, never again to speak to him (read: me?) any of these evil words. Pharaoh wishes to die rather than hear your speech, and beware lest my anger grow strong against you and I hand you over into the hands of the people who were seeking you to kill you"; VB: "And Pharaoh said to him: Go away from me and take heed of yourself lest my anger grow strong against you, saying: Are not these harsh words that you say to me? Pharaoh, however, would prefer to die rather than to hear your words. Take heed lest my anger grow strong against you and I hand you over into the hands of those people who sought you to kill you."

[ww] Nfmg +: "take heed of yourself"; = P.

[xx] Nfi: "he"; = VB.

[yy] Nfmg: "these words; wherefore he said to him, take heed."

[zz] Nfmg: "saying: Are not these harsh words that you say to me? However, I would wish to die rather than listen to your words. Take heed lest my anger grow strong against you and I hand you between the hands of these people who sought you to kill you"; cf. VB.

[a] P: "And Moses said: You have spoken fittingly. I was notified while I was residing in Midian that the men who were seeking my life to kill me had died. It was not because mercy had come upon you that I used to pray for you, and the plague was withheld from you. But this plague is the tenth one for Pharaoh, and with your first-born son I begin. And Moses said: Fittingly have you spoken: I shall never again see your countenance"; VB: "And Moses said: You have spoken the truth. I was notified from the first time while I was still residing in Midian that all the men who were seeking my life to kill (me) had died. It was not that (?; lit.: at the end) mercy had come to you that I used to pray for you and the plague was withheld from you. But this plague is the tenth one for Pharaoh; with the first-born son of Pharaoh I begin. And Moses said to him: You have spoken the truth. I shall never more see your countenance."

[b] Nfi: "to Pharaoh."

[c] Nfi: "of truth" ("truly").

[d] Nfmg: "I was notified from the first time that I was residing (correcting *yhyb* to *ytyb*) in Midian. It was not that (? lit.: not at the end) mercy had come to you that I used to pray for you and the plague"; cf. VB.

[e] Lit.: "saying."

[f] Nfi: "From your first-born son (Hebrew form of word) I begin"; cf. P.

[g] Nfmg: "(never) more" = VB.

Notes, Chapter 10

[18]Hebrew has: "And the Lord hardened Pharaoh's heart."

[19]Hebrew has: "And Pharaoh said to him: Go from me; take care for yourself; do not see my face again, for on the day you see my face you shall die." Cf. Frg. Tg. P, V; Tg. Ps.-J., Nfmg. Pharaoh's anger is related by Josephus, *Ant.* II.xiv.5.

[20]Hebrew has: "And Moses said: thus have you spoken. I shall not see your face again." Cf. Frg. Tg. P, V; Tg. Ps.-J., Nfmg. The exegesis is built up from Exod 4:19; for an analysis of its structure, see Levy, 1986, 355–56.

CHAPTER 11

1. And the Lord said to Moses: "One more plague will I bring*ᵃ* upon Pharaoh and upon the Egyptians; and after that he will let you go from here; when he lets you go, he will drive you out*ᵇ* from here *in all haste.*ᶜ¹ 2. Speak, I pray, in the hearing of the people, that each man ask of his neighbor, and every woman of her neighbor, objects of silver and objects of gold." 3. And the Lord*ᵈ* gave favor to the people in the sight of the Egyptians. Moreover, Moses was a very powerful man in the land of Egypt in the sight of the *rulers*ᵉ² of Pharaoh and in the sight of the people. 4. And Moses said: "Thus said the Lord:*ᶠ* 'In the middle of the night *my Memra will be revealed* in the midst of Egypt.³ 5. And all the first-born in the land of Egypt *shall be killed,*ᵍ from the first-born of Pharaoh *who was* to sit*ʰ* upon the throne *of his kingdom* to the first-born of the maidservant who *grinds* behind the mill,⁴ and every first-born of the cattle. 6. And there shall be*ⁱ* a great cry in all the land of Egypt such as there has never been and such as will not be *seen*ʲ again. 7. But against any of the children of Israel—either against man or beast—no dog shall *bark* with its tongue,⁵ that you may know that the Lord makes a distinction between the Egyptians and Israel.' 8. And all these your servants will come down to me, and they will *salute* me saying: "Go out, you and all the people who are with you"'";*ᵏ⁶* and after that I will go out."'" And he went out *from before*ᵐ Pharaoh in hot anger. 9. And the Lord*ᵈ* said to Moses: "Pharaoh will not listen to you, so as to multiply *the signs*ⁿ *of* my wonders in the land of Egypt."⁷ 10. And Moses and Aaron did all these wonders before Pharaoh, but the Lord*ᵈ* hardened Pharaoh's heart, and he did not let the children of Israel go out of his land.

Apparatus, Chapter 11

ᵃ Nfmg: "I will unleash."
ᵇ "drive (you) out," also in *Meturg.*, MS Ang. and ed. Isny and in *Aruk* ("drive you out from here").
ᶜ Nfmg: "completely."
ᵈ Nfmg: "the Memra of the Lord."
ᵉ Nfmg: "the servants."
ᶠ Nfmg: "the Memra of the Lord: At midnight my Memra."
ᵍ Nfi: "and I will kill."

ʰ Nfmg: "(who was to) loathe all the thrones": or, by emending *lmt'b*: "to desire"; or "to seek" (*lmtb'*); or "to sit upon" (*lmtb b-*).
ⁱ Lit.: "and there was"; cf. HT construction.
ʲ Nfmg: "(not) be (again)."
ᵏ Nfmg: "that are in your hand."
ᵐ Nfi: "from beside."
ⁿ Nfmg: "these (signs)."

Notes, Chapter 11

¹"In all haste" is an interpretation of Hebrew *klh*, "completely"; cf. 12:11, and *Mek. RI Pisha* 7:5–20.
²"Rulers" stands for MT's "servants"; see note on 7:20.
³Hebrew has: "at midnight I shall go out in the midst of Egypt." See Chester, 1986, 148–49.
⁴Hebrew has: "And all the first-born in the land of Egypt shall die, from the first-born of Pharaoh who sits upon his throne, to the first-born of the slave-woman who is behind the mill-wheels." For the description of Pharaoh's son, see Tg. Onq. and Tg. Ps.-J.
⁵Hebrew has: "a dog shall not whet its tongue." For "bark," see LXX; Philo, *De somniis* II. XL §267; Tg. Onq.; Tg. Ps.-J.; Pesh.; *Mek. RI Pisha* 7:7–8; *Exod. R.* 31,9; *PRK* 11:12.
⁶Hebrew has: "And all these your servants shall go down and worship me, saying, . . . all the people who are at your feet. . . ." Worship, of course, is reserved for God; hence the Targum's changes. A similar procedure operates at 18:7.
⁷Hebrew has: "so that (I may be able) to increase my wonders in the land of Egypt." For Targum, see note on 10:1.

CHAPTER 12

1. And the Lord[a] spoke to Moses and Aaron in the land of Egypt saying:
2. "This month[b] *of Nisan* will be for you[c] the beginning of the months; it shall be the first for you *and for all the beginnings* of the months of the year.[1] 3. Speak with

Apparatus, Chapter 12

[a] Nfmg: "the Memra of the Lord."

[b] P: "This month, Nisan, shall be for you the beginning of months. *And it came to pass when the Lord was revealed to redeem the people of Israel with seraphim and clouds and Shekinahs, he was revealed and stood between all the heads (or: beginnings) of the months in order to come to know the praises of each one the dignity of each single one and <to ascertain> in which of them the Israelites should be redeemed and which of them had taken the crown. Iyyar (it was) that answered and said: In me they should be redeemed, and I am the one to take the crown of kingship, since in me Noah the survivor (of the flood) went into the Ark in safety. Sivan answered and said: In me they should be redeemed, and I am the one to take the crown of kingship, since in me the Mount of Sinai arose, perfect (or: adorned) as a bridegroom, and all Israel arose listening to (or: obedient to) the hearing of the Two Laws (? dynwmys = Greek di-nomos; or "power," Greek dynamis) of life (? corr. Aramaic hywn) (from the mouth of the living One) (M. Klein, correcting Aramaic text; hywn mm pshy'). Tammuz answered and said: In me should they be redeemed, and I am the one to take the crown, since in me the spies entered the land of Canaan, and brought some of the fruit of the land (as) a gift to the people. Ab answered and said: In me should they be redeemed and I am the one to take took the crown, since in me all the months are (come) together seeking to stone him (read: me): (saying): Go away from us, master of shops (? pltrwt'; Greek loan word: poleterion; (or "palaces"; Greek praitorion), since in you all debts are collected, and in you the king burned his bridal chamber. Elul answered and said: In me they should be redeemed, and I am the one to take the crown, since my shofar is the shofar of life and my breath is the breath of life. Tishri answered and said: In me should they be redeemed and I am the one to take the crown, since in me all souls stand in affliction in the Fast Day of Kippurim, and when I see the merits of Israel flying and ascending before their God who is in heaven, I myself will tip the scales (lit.: "weigh in the pan of the scales") recalling many merits in Israel's favor. Marheshvan answered and said: In me should they be redeemed and I am the one to take the crown, since in me the four quarters begin to be divided in quarters (Klein: the winter rains begin to fall) and the four gates (Greek loan word: pyle) are shaken to the ground. Kislew answered and said: In me should they be redeemed and I am the one to take the crown, since in me Moses erected the Tent of Meeting and brought it and consecrated it and all its utensils and plated it with refined gold. Tebeth answered and said: In me should they be redeemed and I am the one to take the crown, since I am good and in me all good is a gift (Greek loan word: doron). Shebat answered and said: In me should they be redeemed and I am the one to take the crown of kingship, since in me all the trees from of old have arisen. When they see me they open their mouths and praise the Living God with their leaves. Adar answered and said: I do not reply (lit.: turn) to you at this hour, since this is the hour of great tribulation. The writs of the enemy are spread out upon the columns of the synagogues (or: the assemblies) to wipe out and destroy the enemies of Israel. And now, I shall neither rest nor be at ease until the time that I (or: we) break the writs and he mixes (the cup of punishment?) for his own; the cup that he mixed he shall drink, and the pit that he dug he shall fill. While they were gathered together, one to the other, Moses the prophet and the scribe of Israel came and said to them: Arise, go out to Pontus. The month of Nisan is the beginning of all the months, since in it the Lord redeemed his people, the children of Israel, and in it he is again to redeem them. For which reason the Scripture explains and says: <This> month, Nisan shall be for you the beginning of months. It is appointed the first of all the beginning of months (i.e.: new moons) of the year."*

[c] Nfmg: "for all."

Notes, Chapter 12

[1] Hebrew has: "This month shall be for you the first (lit.: head) of months: it shall be for you the first of the months of the year." For Nisan as the first of all months, see Tg. fragment in Klein, 1, 1986, 209; Philo, *Quaestiones in Exodum* I. §1; Tg. Ps.-J.; *Mek. RI Pisḥa* 2:13–15, 21ff.; *t. Rosh Hash.* 1:3; 3; *j. Rosh Hash.* 1:1–2; *Shek.* 1:1; *b. Rosh Hash.* 7a. The poem on the dispute of the months found at this point in Frg. Tg. P is of a quite distinct genre, which differs in character from Targum of the usual kind: see Klein, 1, 1986, xxxviii; 2, 1986, [56]. For brief comments on this poem, which has not been systematically studied, see Klein, 1, 1986, 186, 188; *idem*, 2, 1980, 37–39; and S.P. Brock, 1985, 181–211.

all the congregation *of the children* of*ᵈ* Israel: On the tenth *day*ᵉ of this month they shall take*ᶠ* every man a lamb according to their father's house—a lamb for *every* house.[2] 4. And if the *people of the household* are too few *to be reckoned sufficient* for the *paschal* lamb, they and the neighbor who is near to it shall take according to the number of persons;*ᵍ* according to what each can eat, you shall make count for the *paschal* lamb.[3] 5. Your lamb shall be perfect, *without blemish*, male, a year old; from among the lambs or from among the kids *the young of* goats you shall take it *for yourselves*.[4] 6. And you shall keep it until the fourteenth day*ʰ* of this month, and all the assembly of the congregation *of the sons* of Israel[5] shall slaughter it at twilight.*ⁱ* 7. And they shall take some of the blood and put it on the two doorposts and on the lintel of the houses in which they shall eat *the passover*.*ʲ*[6] 8. And they shall eat the flesh on the night *of Passover*,[7] roasted on fire; unleavened bread with bitter herbs they shall eat. 9. Do not eat any of it lightly roasted*ᵏ* or even *overcooked*, cooked in water,[8] but only roasted on fire—the head with its legs*ᵐ* and the inner parts. 10. And you shall leave none of it over until morning; and anything that does remain of it until morning you shall burn in the fire. 11. And according to *this order* you shall eat it: your loins girded,*ⁿ* your shoes on your feet, and your staffs in your hands. And you shall eat*ᵒ* it in a hurry. It is the paschal *sacrifice before* the Lord.[9] 12. And I will pass in my *Memra*ᵖ through the land of Egypt this

Apparatus, Chapter 12

ᵈ Nfmg; "(the congregation) of Israel."

ᵉ Lit.: "in the ten days."

ᶠ Lit.: "take for yourselves"; Nfmg: "for them."

ᵍ Nfmg: "according to the total of persons."

ʰ Lit.: "on the fourteen days."

ⁱ Lit.: "between the suns," or "services."

ʲ Nfmg: "in which they eat it."

ᵏ "lightly roasted" (*mhbhb*); same word in VB: also in

Aruk; in some MSS of *Aruk* a fuller text: "you shall not eat any of it lightly roasted."

ᵐ Text: *rglwy*; same word in Aruk; Nfmg: "his legs" (*krʿwy*); cf. Onq.

ⁿ PVB: "your loins girded with the precepts of the Law"; Nfmg + "with the precepts of the Law."

ᵒ Nfmg: "they shall be eaten"; possibly error for: "and you shall eat" (a mere orthographic variation).

ᵖ Nfmg: "and I will be revealed in my Memra."

Notes, Chapter 12

[2] Hebrew has: "Speak to all the congregation of Israel . . . a lamb for the house." For the addition of "children of," cf. LXX, Vulg. For the addition of "day" and "each," see Tg. fragment in Klein, 1, 1986, 209; *Mek. RI Pisḥa* 3:50–54. Tg. probably has in mind the legislation of v. 36: see also Philo, *Quaestiones in Exodum* I. §3.

[3] Hebrew has: "And if the house be too small for a lamb, then he and his neighbor next to his house . . . you shall make your count for each lamb." Very similar is the Tg. fragment in Klein, 1, 1986, 209; for the notion of the men being too few to be sufficient, see Tg. Onq. and Vulg.

[4] Hebrew has: "It shall be for you a perfect lamb, a male, one year old; you shall take it from the sheep or from the goats." For "without blemish," see Tg. fragment in Klein, 1, 1986, 209; *Mek. RI Pisḥa* 4:3; *j. Pes.* 9:5; *alia exempla* quoted by Field, 1875, on this verse. For "the young of goats," see Klein, *ibid.*: according to *Mek. RI Pisḥa* 4:1–2, the word *śh*, "lamb," includes the young of goats as well as lambs.

[5] Hebrew has: "the assembly of the congregation of Israel." For the addition of "sons of," cf. Vulg.

[6] Hebrew has: "where they are eating it."

[7] Hebrew has: "And they shall eat the flesh on this night." See Tg. fragment in Klein, 1, 1986, 209; Tg. Ps.-J. specifies the fourteenth of Nisan up to midnight; cf. *Mek. RI Pisḥa* 6:29–43; *Jub.* 49:12-13; *Mek. RSbY*, p. 13 (R. Eleazar b. Azariah); *b. Ber.* 9a; *b. Meg.* 21a; *b. Zeb.* 57b; Philo, *Quaestiones in Exodum* I. §13.

[8] Hebrew has: "You shall not eat of it raw, nor boiled at all in water"; cf. the Tg. fragment in Klein, 1, 1986, 211, and Grossfeld, 1988B, 31. The prohibition is against eating it raw *or* boiled: see *Mek. RI Pisḥa* 6:66-70; *b. Pes.* 41ab; *j. Pes.* 2:7. On the language used here, see Levy, 1986, 359–60.

[9] Hebrew has: "And thus you shall eat it . . . it is the Lord's Passover." The *order* of the ritual is emphasized by Tg. Nf in several passages dealing with sacrificial law: see, e.g., 29:35 and the constant rendering of "and you shall burn" as "and you shall set in order," e.g., Exod 29:13, 18. See also for this verse Klein, 1, 1986, 211.

night *of the Passover*, and I will kill all the first-born in the land of Egypt from the *sons of* man to beast. And I will execute *different* judgments on all the idols of Egyptians," says the Lord. [q10] 13. "And the blood will be for you as a sign over the houses where[r] they *dwell*; and I will see the blood and I will pass by,[s] and *I in my Memra will defend* you,[t] and there will be no destroying *death* among you when I kill *all the first-born* in the land[u] of Egypt. [11] 14. And this day shall be for you a good memorial; and you shall celebrate[w] it as a feast *before* the Lord:[x12] you shall celebrate it for your generations as an eternal statute. 15. Seven days you shall eat[y] unleavened bread. Even on the first day you shall put away leaven out of your houses, because whoever eats leavened bread from the first day to the seventh day, that *man*[z] will be blotted out from Israel. 16. On the first day you shall have *a feast day*[aa] and a holy convocation, <and on the seventh day *a feast day* and a holy convocation>.[bb] No work shall be done on them. But whatever *is done*[cc] *for any* vital *need*, that alone may be done by you. [13] 17. And you shall observe the unleav-

Apparatus, Chapter 12

[q] Nfmg: "I am he."

[r] Nfmg: "in which."

[s] Nfmg: "and he will spare."

[t] Nfmg: "and I in my Memra will defend."

[u] Nfmg: "and the destroying angel who is appointed over death will not have power to injure (you) when I am revealed to slay the first-born in the land."

[w] Text: "they shall be celebrated," writing initial *waw* as *yod*.

[x] Nfmg + "your God."

[y] Nfmg: "they shall eat."

[z] Nfi: "that soul" (= "that person").

[aa] Nfmg: "a feast day and a convocation and on the seventh day."

[bb] Omitted in text.

[cc] Nfmg: "all by which (things) are eaten."

Notes, Chapter 12

[10]Hebrew has: "And I shall pass through the land of Egypt on this night, and I shall smite . . . both of man and beast; and I shall perform judgments on all the gods of Egypt. I am the Lord." For the Memra, its revelation (Nfmg) and its passing through the land, see Chester, 1986, 144–49; the fragment in Klein, 1 1986, 211, is almost identical with Tg. Nf. The "different" judgments probably refer to the four divine punishments inflicted on idols made of metal, stone, clay, and wood listed in Tg. Ps.-J.; cf. *Mek. RI Pisha* 7:51-58; *Mek. RSbY*, p. 15; *Exod. R.* 15,15.

[11]Hebrew has: "on the houses where you are; and I shall see the blood and pass over you, and there shall be no plague upon you as a destroyer when I smite the land of Egypt." For "they dwell," see Tg. Ps.-J.; and cf. the discussion in *Mek. RI Pisha* 7:66-69; *Mek. RSbY*, p. 16. For the Memra, see the fragment in Klein, 1, 1986, 211. "Defend" is *'gn*: for this interpretation, cf. LXX, "protect," and see *Mek. RI Pisha* 11:90-92; 7:86-93; *Exod. R.* 15,12; S.P. Brock, 1982A, 27–34; *idem*, 1982B, 222–33.

[12]Hebrew has: "And this day shall be for a memorial to you, and you shall keep it as a feast to the Lord." For the *good* memorial, see fragment in Klein, 1, 1986, 211, and *Jub.* 49:15 (acceptable memorial). Tg. Nf uses this qualification at Exod 13:9; 17:14; 28:12, 29; 30:16; Lev 23:24; Num 10:10; 17:5; 31:54 to contrast with the memorial of sin referred to in (e.g.) in Num 5:15, 18. Tg. Ps.-J. has the expression at Exod 30:16; Num 10:10; 31:54.

[13]Hebrew has: "And on the first day there shall be a holy assembly, and on the seventh day there shall be a holy assembly for you. No work shall be done on them, except what each person shall eat: that alone may be done for you." Tg. Nf adds to the expression "holy assembly" the term "feast day," *ywm tb*; so also fragment in Klein, 1, 1986, 211–13. This is very common: see Tg. Nf and fragment in Klein, 1986, 311–17 of Lev 23:2, 3, 4, 7, 21, 24, 27, 36, 37; Tg. Nf of Num 28:18, 25, 26; 29:1, 7, 12; Tg. Ps.-J. of Lev 23:14. *Mek. RI Pisha* 7:105-120 and *Mek. RSbY*, p. 18, use *ywm tb* throughout this discussion. For "whatever is done for any vital need," see *Mek. RI Pisha* 9:53-68; *j. Shabb.* 3:3; *Bezah* 2:5; *b. Pesah.* 83b-84a; *b. Shabb.* 25a, 133a.

ened bread,*dd* because on this very day*ee* I brought your hosts *redeemed*[14] out*ff* of the land of Egypt, and you shall observe this day throughout your generations *as* an eternal statute. 18. In the first *month*, on the fourteenth day*gg* of the month in the evening *at twilight,*hh* you shall eat unleavened bread,[15] (and so) until the twenty-first day of the month, in the evening. 19. For seven days no leaven shall be found*ii* within your houses, because whoever eats leavened bread, that person will be blotted out from the congregation of Israel, whether he is a stranger or a native of the land. 20. You shall eat nothing leavened. In all your dwelling places[16] you shall eat unleavened bread." 21. And Moses called all the *wise men* of Israel and he said to them: "Appoint (the participants) and take[17] one of the flock*jj* according to your families and sacrifice the Passover. 22. And take a bunch of hyssop and dip it in the blood which is in the vessel*kk*[18] and come,*mm* and you shall put upon the lintel and on the two doorposts *some of the blood that is in the vessel*; and let no one of you go out of the door of his house until morning. 23. And *the Glory of the Shekinah* of the Lord*nn* will pass through to blot out*oo* the Egyptians; and he will see the blood upon the lintel and upon the two doorposts, and he will pass by,*pp* and the *Memra of* the Lord will *defend* the door of *the fathers of the children of Israel*, and he will not give *permission* to the Destroyer*qq* to enter within your houses

Apparatus, Chapter 12

dd I.e., the feast of Unleavened bread; Nfmg: "the precepts of unleavened bread."

ee Lit.: "at the time of this day"; Nfmg: "as the time."

ff Nfmg: "he brought you out."

gg Lit.: "from (= on) the fourteen days."

hh Lit.: "between the suns," or "services."

ii Nfmg: "shall not be seen."

jj Nfmg: "withdraw your hand from foreign worship and afterwards sacrifice a lamb."

kk Nfmg: "which is in the cup."

mm "and come" or "and you"; probably a dittography from the occurrence of the same word later in this verse.

nn Nfmg: "the Memra of the Lord."

oo Nfmg: "to destroy."

pp Nfmg: "and he will spare."

qq Nfmg 1°: "when the destroying angel is empowered"; Nfmg 2°: "to the destroyer" (a variant writing).

Notes, Chapter 12

[14]Hebrew has: "I brought out your armies." On "redeemed," see note on 3:10 and cf. Tg. Ps.-J.

[15]Hebrew has, lit.: "In the first, on the fourteenth day of the month, at evening, you shall eat unleavened bread." Tg. qualifies evening with "twilight," lit. "between the suns," its rendering of Hebrew *byn h'rbym* used at 12:6 to designate the time for the slaughter of the Pesaḥ victim. The same interpretation of this verse is found in the fragment edited by Klein, 1, 1986, 213; *Jub.* 49:12-13.

[16]Hebrew has: "in any of your dwellings." With Tg., cf. Tg. Ps.-J. and Klein, 1, 1986, 213.

[17]Hebrew has: "And Moses called to all the elders of Israel and said to them: Draw out and take. . . ." On "elders" as "wise men," see note on 3:16; LXX has *gerousia; Mek. RI Pisḥa* 11:1-2 says that Moses constituted the elders as a Beth Din.

[18]Hebrew has: "which is in the basin." Tg. Nf uses *bmnh* to render Hebrew *bsp*, which might equally mean "on the threshold." Tg. Nf uses the same word as Tg. Onq. and *Mek. RI Pisḥa* 11:38-39 (R. Akiba).

to destroy."[rr][19] 24. You shall observe this word as a statute for yourselves and for your sons for ever.[20] 25. And when you come into the land which the Lord[nn] will give you as he said, you will observe this service. 26. <And when your children say to you: 'What does this service mean for you?'>,[ss][21] 27. you shall say: 'It is the sacrifice of the Passover *before* the Lord, who passed by and *defended*[tt] the houses of the children of Israel in Egypt when he *killed* the Egyptians[uu] and delivered our houses.'" And the people bowed down and *gave thanks and praised*.[22] 28. And the children of Israel went and did so: as the Lord[nn] had commanded Moses and Aaron, so they did. 29. And in the middle of the night the Lord *slew*[ww] all the first-born in the land of Egypt, from the first-born of Pharaoh who *was to* sit upon the throne *of the kingdom*[23] to the first-born of the captive who was in prison, and every first-born of the cattle. 30. And Pharaoh rose up at night, he and all his *rulers*[xx] and all the Egyptians, and there was a great cry in Egypt, because there was not a house *there* in which there were no dead.[yy][24] 31. And he called Moses and Aaron at night, and he said: "Rise up, go out from the midst of my people, both you and the children of Israel, and go, worship *before* the Lord as you have spoken. 32. <Take also your flocks and your herds as you said>,[zz] and go and *pray* also *for me*."[25] 33. The Egyptians urged the people, to hurry (them), to send them forth

Apparatus, Chapter 12

[rr] Nfmg + : "you."

[ss] Omitted in the text.

[tt] Nfmg: "the Memra of the Lord spared and defended the."

[uu] Nfmg: "when he destroyed the Egyptians."

[ww] Nfmg: "at midnight the Memra of the Lord slew."

[xx] Nfmg: "his servants."

[yy] Nfmg: "a house in which there was no dead one of the Egyptians."

[zz] Omitted in the text; as in CTg AA.

Notes, Chapter 12

[19] Hebrew has: "And the Lord will pass through . . . and the Lord will pass over the door, and he will not let the destroyer come into your houses to smite." For the Glory of the Shekinah and the Memra (Nfmg), see Chester, 1986, 146–48. According to *Exod. R.* 17, 5: *Cant. R.* 3:15; Philo, *Quaestiones in Exodum* 1. §22; and the Passover Aggadah, it was God himself who smote the Egyptians. On "defend," see note on 12:13; and on "the door of the Fathers" see Le Déaut, 1979 (*Exode*) 90, and *t. Soṭa* 3:1: "We find in Abraham's case that with the measure he meted out it was measured to him: of Abraham it says, 'And he stood over them.' So God protected *hgyn* his sons in Egypt, as it is said, And the Lord will pass over the door."

[20] Tg. Nf and the fragment in Klein, 1, 1986, 215, have second person plural verbs for Hebrew second person singular.

[21] Hebrew has: "And when your sons say to you: What does this service mean to you?"

[22] Hebrew has: "And you shall say, it is the sacrifice of the Lord's Passover, who passed over the houses of the Israelites . . . then he smote the Egyptians. . . . And the people bowed down and worshiped." For "defended," see note on 12:13, and cf. LXX and Klein, 1, 1986, 215; 15:1, 21; and note on 4:31. "Praise" features also in *Mek. RI Pisha* 12:75-79.

[23] Hebrew has: "the Lord smote all the first-born . . . the first-born of Pharaoh who sits on his throne." "Slew" is found in Tg. Onq., Tg. Ps.-J.; Klein, 1, 1986, 215. "Who was to sit upon the throne of the kingdom" features in Tg. Onq.; Tg. Ps.-J.; Klein, 1986, 215; see note on 9:16; *Mek. RSbY*, p. 28.

[24] For "rulers," Hebrew has "servants"; see note on 7:10. Hebrew has: "for there was not a house where there was not one dead." The nuanced translation of the Targum may hint at the question whether all houses had first-born in them, and the possible answers; see *Mek. RI Pisha* 13:51-54 (R. Nathan); *Mek. RSbY*, p. 29.

[25] Hebrew has: "Take both your sheep and your cattle as you have said, and go; and bless me also." For "pray," see Tg. Onq.; *Mek. RI Pisha* 13:95-96.

from the land, for^a they said:^b *"If the Israelites^c delay here but one hour,* behold, all *the Egyptians* are dead." [26] 34. And the people loaded their cakes of dough [27] before it was leavened,^d their kneading bowls^e wrapped up in their mantles^f on their shoulders. 35. And the children of Israel did according to the words of Moses, and they asked of the Egyptians objects of silver and objects of gold and clothes. 36. And the Lord^g gave favor to the people in the sight of the Egyptians,^h and they lent to them; and *the children of Israelⁱ* despoiled the Egyptians *of their property.* [28] 37. And the children of Israel <journeyed>^j from *Pelusium^k* to Succoth, about six hundred thousand *men* on foot, besides the little ones. [29] 38. And many *strangers^m* also went with them, [30] and sheep and oxen, very many cattle.ⁿ 39. And they baked *their own* leaven which they had brought out of Egypt, unleavened cakes,^o *before* it was leavened; for they had been driven out of Egypt^p and could not wait, [31] and they had not even made provisions^q for themselves. 40. And the sojourn of the children of Israel which they sojourned in Egypt was four hundred and thirty years. 41. And it happened that at the end of four hundred and thirty years, on that very day,^r all the hosts of the Lord went out *redeemed* [32] from the land of the Egyptians. 42. It is a night reserved *and set aside^s* for *redemption to the name of the Lord at the time the children of Israel* were brought out^t *redeemed* from the land of Egypt. *Truly, four nights are those that are written^u* in the Book of Memorials.

Apparatus, Chapter 12

^a PVB: "For the Egyptians said: If the children of Israel delay here one hour, behold, all the Egyptians are dead."

^b Nfmg +: "the Egyptians (said)" = PVB.

^c Nfmg: "if the children of Israel delay here (one) hour"; cf. PVB.

^d Nfmg: "their dough before it was leavened."

^e VB: "the remainder of the paschal sacrifices bound up in their mantles upon their shoulders"; Nfmg: "What remained of the unleavened bread and the bitter herbs wrapped up in their clothes, laden upon their shoulders."

^f Nfi:+ "placed upon."

^g Nfmg: "the Memra of the Lord."

^h Nfmg: "(of) the Egyptians and they asked."

ⁱ Nfmg: "Israel (despoiled) the Egyptians by (= of?) their beasts."

^j Missing in text.

^k HT: Rameses.

^m VB + Nfmg 1°, 2°: "and likewise; mixed multitudes."

ⁿ Nfmg: "very numerous flocks."

^o Nfmg: "unleavened pancakes"; *Aruk* almost = Nf text: *ḥwrrn dpṭyryn; Aruk: ḥrrn pṭyrn.*

^p Nfmg: "the Egyptians had driven them out."

^q Nfmg: "delay, and neither had they made provisions for the journey."

^r Lit.: "as the time of this day."

^s Full midrash of four nights in VBN; identical with Nf, apart from variants noted below; in P at Exod 15:18.

^t Nfmg: "it is for redemption before the Lord at the coming out" = VBN.

^u Nfmg: "because four nights are those that are written"; VBN: "because four nights are written."

Notes, Chapter 12

[26]Hebrew has: "for they said: We are all dead men." Cf. Tg. Ps.-J., Frg. Tg. P, V.

[27]Targum has *their* dough, plural for singular: all the people are involved, as in Tg. Ps.-J., Pesh., LXX.

[28]Hebrew has: "so they lent (things) to them. And they despoiled the Egyptians." For "property," see Tg. Ps.-J., Ezekiel the Tragedian, *Exagôgê,* 162–66; *b. Sanh.* 91a.

[29]For Pelusium as a rendering of Raamses, see note on 1:11; Tg. Ps.-J., fragment in Klein, 1, 1986, 217.

[30]Hebrew has: "And also a great mixed company went up with them." For Targum's "many strangers," *gywryn sgyn,* cf. Tg. Onq., Tg. Ps.-J., and Le Déaut, 1979 (*Exode*) 94.

[31]Hebrew has: "the dough . . . for it was not leavened . . . and they could not wait."

[32]For "redeemed," see Tg. Ps.-J., fragment in Klein, 1, 1986, 217, *Tanḥuma Bo',* and note on 3:10.

The first night: when the Lord[w] was revealed over the world to create it.[x] The world was without form and void, and darkness was spread over the face of the abyss, and the Memra of the Lord was the Light,[y] and it shone;[z] and he called it the First Night.

The second night: when the Lord[aa] was revealed to Abram,[bb] a man of a hundred years, and Sarah his wife, who was a woman of ninety years, to fulfill what the Scripture says: Will Abram, a man of a hundred years, beget,[cc] and will his wife Sarah, a woman of ninety years, bear?[dd] And Isaac was thirty-seven years when he was offered[ee] upon the altar. The heavens were bowed down[ee] and descended, and Isaac saw their perfections, and his eyes were dimmed because of their perfections,[ff] and he called it the Second Night.[gg]

The third night: when the Lord[hh] was revealed against the Egyptians at midnight; his hand[ii] slew the first-born of the Egyptians, and his right hand protected[jj] the first-born of Israel to fulfill what the Scripture says: Israel is my first-born son.[kk] And he called it the Third Night.

The fourth night: when the world reaches its appointed time to be redeemed:[mm] the iron yokes shall be broken and the generations of wickedness[nn] shall be blotted out,[oo] and Moses will go up[pp] from the midst of the desert <and the king Messiah from the midst of Rome.>[qq] One will lead at the head of the flock,[rr] and the other will lead at

Apparatus, Chapter 12

[w] VBN: "the Memra of the Lord."

[x] Nfi: "(to create) the World."

[y] Aramaic: "(and the Memra of the Lord) *whwh nhwr'* (lit.: "and it was the light") is probably a scribal error; Nfi: "(was) light (*nhwr*); VBN: "and the Memra of the Lord was bright and illuminating (*hwh nhyr wmnhr*, "was light and illumination," M. Klein); P (from Exod 15:18): "and in his Memra he was bright and illuminating" (*hwh nhyr wmnhyr*).

[z] Nfi: "and illuminating"; Nfmg: "and illuminating and he called"; cf. VBN, P.

[aa] VBN: "when the Memra of the Lord."

[bb] VBN: "to Abram between the pieces. Abram was a son of a hundred years, and Sarah was a daughter of ninety years."

[cc] VBN: "Behold Abram (is) a son of a hundred years; is it possible for him to beget?"

[dd] VBN: "and Sarah a daughter of ninety years; is it possible for her to bear?"

[ee] Nfmg, VBN: "was not (VBN + "our father) Isaac a son of thirty-seven years at the time he was offered?"

[ff] Nfi: "from (their perfections)"; VBN: "from (=because of) the heights."

[gg] Nfmg: "his first-born son is Israel and he called it the Second Night. The Third Night," apparently a misplaced and partly corrupt text, to be placed at end of the Third Night as in VBN and Nf.

[hh] VBN: "the Memra of the Lord."

[ii] VBN: "his left hand"; Nfmg: "his right hand."

[jj] VBN: "rescued."

[kk] In Nf the gloss given above (*gg*) wrongly placed here.

[mm] Or, in this context less probably: "to be dissolved" (R. Le Déaut, R. Bloch, B. Walton).

[nn] Nfi: "and the wicked."

[oo] VBN: ". . . to be redeemed. The workers of evil will be blotted out and the iron yokes shall be broken." Nfmg: "the members of the wicked (error for: "the workers of evil"?) and the iron yokes shall be blotted out from Israel."

[pp] VBN: "shall come out."

[qq] Missing in text of Nf, probably by error; omission denoted (it would seem) by omission signs to text, but not supplied in margins. VBN: "and King Messiah from the midst of Rome" (*mn gw rwm'*); P: (Exod 15:18): "Moses will come forth from the desert (*mmdbr'*), and King Messiah will come forth from Rome" (? *mrwmh, Meturgeman* in ed. lsny *mn rwmy*; or: "from on high"). VBN (*mn gw rwm'*) seems best translated: "from the midst of Rome" (rather than "from on high"), since "from the midst of the height" (*mn gw rwm'*) seems an unnatural expression. Since Nf has preserved "from the midst of the desert," the missing section must have been "from the midst of *roma'*." The original text may have been as P: "from the desert . . . from *roma'*" = "from on high."

[rr] "flock," '*n'*; thus Nf and all independent MSS of Frg. Tg. The first Rabbinic Bible (1517–1518) has "at the head of the cloud" ('*nn'*), and so also editions dependent on this; so also, the Sassoon MS 264 of Frg. Tg. This, however, is a MS copy of the Rabbinic Bible.

the head of the flock,*rr* and his Memra*ss* will lead between the two of them, and I and they will proceed together. This is the night *of the Passover to the name of* the Lord: it is a night reserved *and set aside* for the *redemption of* all Israel, throughout their generations.[33] 43. And the Lord said to Moses and to Aaron: "This is *the decree* of the Law of the Passover:[34] no gentile shall eat of it. 44. And every slave of anyone bought*tt* for money *you* shall circumcise, then he *will be fit* to eat it.[35] 45. *My people, children of Israel,* no *gentile* sojourner for wages shall eat of it.*uu* [36] 46. *In groups* it shall be eaten; *you* shall not bring outside any of the flesh from the house *for a group, and not even from one group for another,* [37] and a bone you shall not break in it.*ww* 47. And all the congregation of Israel shall keep *the Passover.*

Apparatus, Chapter 12

ss VBN: "and the Memra of the Lord will be between them both, and I and they will walk together"; P: "and the Memra of the Lord will lead between both of them, and they shall walk together."

tt Nfmg: "(slave) of purchase, when you have circumcised (him)."

uu Nfmg, PVBN: "a man's resident (worker) and the hired person, when he is a Gentile (lit.: "a son of the peoples") cannot eat of it"; Nfi: "a resident and the hired person a son of the nations."

ww Nfmg: "(of) the houses, any of the flesh from outside. And a bone you shall not annul from it"; possibly, however, we should read "precept" instead of what in Neofiti MS appears to be *wgwrm'*: "and a bone," e.g., thus: "Do not take any flesh outside of the houses, and do not neglect in its regard the precept not to (break a bone)" (Le Déaut).

Notes, Chapter 12

[33]Hebrew has: "It is a night of watching for the Lord, to bring them out from the land of Egypt; it is this night which is to be observed to the Lord, for all the Israelites for their generations." Various forms of this famous paraphrase are found in Nfmg; Tg. Ps.-J.; Frg. Tg. V, P (at Exod 15:18); Klein, 1, 1986, 217–21. Chester, 1986, 192–94, gives a convenient summary of the relationships of the various Targums of this verse, and the whole tradition is subject of an exhaustive study by R. Le Déaut. *La Nuit Pascale* (Pontifical Institute: Rome, 1963), to which reference should be made. Specific items in the aggadah are treated as follows: (1) The book of Memorials: see Le Déaut, *Nuit Pascale,* 66–71. (2) Revelation of the Lord and surrogates for the divine Name: see Chester, 1986, 194–99. (3) Memra, creation, and light: N. Séd, 1964, 532; M. McNamara, 1967, 115–17; Hayward, 1981A, 51–53. (4) On the announcement of Isaac's birth, Targum refers to Gen 17:17 but not to its own version of that text. (5) The sacrifice of Isaac is placed at Passover by *Jub.* 17:18; on the whole matter see G. Vermes, 1973B, 193–227. P. R. Davies and B. D. Chilton, 1978, 514–46, regard the reference to Isaac's sacrifice here as a secondary development; see also Davies, 1979, 59–67. Their thesis is questioned by C.T.R. Hayward, 1981B, 127–50. (6) The notion that Messiah shall come from Rome is discussed by Le Déaut, 1963, 359–69. For full discussion of the textual problems and the structure of this verse, see Levy, 1986, 362–68.

[34]Hebrew has: "this is the ordinance of the Passover." On the whole section 12:43-51, see M. Ohana, 1973, 385–99.

[35]Hebrew has: "you (sing.) shall circumcise him: then he shall eat of it."

[36]Hebrew has: "The resident (alien) and the hired men shall not eat of it." For the expression "My people, sons of Israel," see note on Exod 20:2. The "resident," Hebrew *twšb*, is designated a gentile by Frg. Tg. P, V. R. Eliezer in *Mek. RI Pisha* 15:46-47 declares that *twšb* is a resident alien, and the "hired man" a gentile; Targum's interpretation, however, differs from this and seems determined by v. 48, which it deems to deal with resident aliens; since their concerns are covered by that verse, Targum holds that this present verse must deal with a different category of persons, namely, gentiles.

[37]Hebrew has: "In one house it shall be eaten; you (sing.) shall not bring any of the flesh out of the house outside." Targum orders that the lamb be eaten *ḥbwrn ḥbwrn,* "in groups"; see Josephus, *Ant.* II.xiv.6; III.x.5; *War* VI.ix.4. Tg. Onq. and Tg. Ps.-J. lay down that it be eaten *bhbwrh ḥd',* "in one group": this terminology differs from Tg. Nf's and seems to correlate with the explicit requirement of *Mek. RI Pisha* 15:64-75; *Mek. RSbY,* p. 36; *Tanḥ. Bo'* 10; *b. Pes.* 85b that it should not be eaten in two *ḥbwrwt.* However, the Mekhiltas are concerned to prevent individuals changing from one group to another; as long as the *ḥbwrh's* membership remains intact, it may move as a *ḥbwrh* from one house to another. This restriction seems adequately represented by Tg. Nf's exposition of the latter part of the verse. "You shall not bring out" is plural for MT's singular; so also LXX.

48. And if a resident who resides with you wishes to keep the Passover *before* the Lord, when he circumcises every male, then he *will be fit* to keep it, and he will be as the natives of the land; but no *gentile* shall eat of it. [38] 49. There shall be one *decree* of law[xx] for the nations and for the sojourners who sojourn among you." [39] 50. And all the children of Israel <did it>:[yy] as the Lord commanded Moses and Aaron, thus they did. 51. And it came to pass that on that very day[zz] the Lord brought the children of Israel *redeemed*[40] from the land of Egypt, according to their hosts.

CHAPTER 13

1. And the Lord[a] spoke *with* Moses, saying: 2. "Sanctify *to my name*[b] every first-born that opens every womb, in the children of Israel, in the *sons of* man and in cattle; they are to *my name*."[c] [1] 3. And Moses said to the people: "Remember this day in which you have come out *redeemed*[2] from Egypt, from the house of bondage, because by a strong hand the Lord[a] has led you out hence, and you shall not eat leaven. 4. This day you shall go out *redeemed*, at the *time* of the month of

Apparatus, Chapter 12

[xx] Nfmg: "there shall one law."
[yy] Missing in text.

[zz] Lit.: "as the time of this day."

Notes, Chapter 12

[38]Hebrew has: "and then he shall draw near to offer (lit.: make) it. . . . But anyone who is uncircumcised shall not eat of it." Targum here differs from *Mek. RI Pisha* 15:131-134 and *b. Shabb.* 87a, which understand the uncircumcised here referred to as uncircumcised Israelites. See further Levy, 1986, 369–70.

[39]Hebrew has: "There shall be one law. . . ." For the formula "decree of law," see 12:43; 13:10; and Hayward, 1981A, 67–68. "The sojourners who sojourn" is *gywryyh dmtgyyryn*, which may in this instance mean "the proselytes who have converted": see Le Déaut, 1979 (*Exode*) 101, 427, and note on 2:22. *Mek. RI Pisha* 15:135-141, however, takes this apparently redundant verse to counter the view that the proselyte is like a Jew only in respect of the law of Pesah; rather, he is like a Jew in all respects.

[40]On "redeemed," see note on 3:10. Nfmg seems to stress the fact that all this happened on this very same day; so Tg. Ps.-J., *Sifre Deut.* 337.

Apparatus, Chapter 13

[a] Nfmg: "the Memra of the Lord."
[b] Nfmg: "all the first-born before him (corr. to: before me), those who open the womb in the sons."

[c] Nfmg: "they are: Thus says the Lord."

Notes, Chapter 13

[1]"To my Name" represents Hebrew "to me"; see 6:7. Before Aaron's election as priest, the first-born performed the functions of the priesthood and were thus peculiarly dedicated to the Lord's Name: see Philo, *De spec. leg.* I. XXVII §138; *Cant. R.* 7, 2; and note on 19:22.
[2]For "redeemed," see note on 3:10.

*Abiba.*³ 5. And when the Lord has brought *you* in to the land of the Canaanites and the Hittites and the Amorites and the Hivites and the Jebusites, which *the Lord* swore to your fathers to give *you*, a land that *produces good fruits, pure as* milk *and sweet as* honey^d—you shall offer this service on this month:⁴ 6. seven days *you* shall eat unleavened bread, and on the seventh day (there shall be) a feast *before* the Lord. 7. Unleavened bread shall be eaten for seven days, and leaven shall not be seen with you, and nothing leavened shall be seen with you in all *your* borders. 8. And *you* shall tell your sons on that day saying: 'It is because *of the precept of un-leavened bread* (that) the Lord worked for *us our battle victories* when *we* came out *redeemed* from Egypt.'^{e5} 9. And they shall be for you as *signs* upon *your arms* and as a good memorial upon *your faces*, so that the Law of the Lord may be *constantly* on your mouths; because by a strong hand he has brought you redeemed out of Egypt.⁶ 10. And *you* shall observe the *statutes of this* Law in its time, from *year* to *year.^{f7}* 11. And when the Lord^a brings you in to the land of the Canaanites, as he swore to you^g and to your fathers, and gives it to *you*, 12. *you shall set aside* to *the name of* the Lord every *firstling* that opens the womb;^h and everything that opens

---

Apparatus, Chapter 13

^d Nfmg: "(as) milk and tasty as honey."

^e Nfmg 1°: "because of this precept of the unleavened breads and the bitter herb and this passover flesh, the Lord has worked signs for me when I come out of Egypt"; Nfmg 2°: "the Memra of the Lord (has worked signs) for us when they came out."

^f Lit.: "from time of days to time of days"; VN: "from those days to those months"; Nfmg: "this statute at

the (appointed) time to be performing it from those days to those months" (end: "from those days . . . months" = VN).

^g Nfmg: "to you" (plur.; in text sing.).

^h Nfmg: "the first: (everything) that opens the womb" (lit.: "breaks through the womb"): same Aramaic phrase as in VN Exod 34:19.

Notes, Chapter 13

³See note on 3:10 for "redeemed." Hebrew has: "in the month Abib." With Tg. Nf, cf. Tg. Ps.-J.

⁴All Israel is affected by this law, so Targum changes Hebrew second person singular to plural throughout the section vv. 5-16. On "and land that produces good fruits," see note on 3:8. With Nfmg's "as tasty as honey," cf. *j. Ber.* 1:3; *b. Meg. 6a.*

⁵Hebrew has: "And you shall declare to your son on that day, saying, it is because of what the Lord did for me when I came out of Egypt." On the precept of unleavened bread as constituting the reason for what the Lord did, see Tg. Ps.-J. and *Mek. RI Pisḥa* 9:86-89; both "commandments" and "unleavened bread" have the same consonants *mṣwt* in Hebrew, and Targum has punned on this word: see Le Déaut, 1979 (*Exode*) 102. "The victories of our battle" provides the object of what the Lord did; closely related is the object "signs and wonders" provided by Tg. Ps.-J.; cf. Nfmg and *m. Pesaḥ.* 10:5; *b. Pesaḥ.* 116b. These, of course, include Israel's victories, but also much more.

⁶Hebrew has: "And it shall be a sign for you upon your hand, and a memorial between your eyes, so that the law of the Lord may be in your mouth; for with a strong hand the Lord brought you forth from Egypt." See further v. 16. Hebrew "hand" is understood as "arms" by R. Eliezer, *Mek. RI Pisḥa* 17:118-129; cf. *Mek. RSbY*, p. 40; *b. Men.* 37b; *Tanḥ. Bo'* 14: *Sifre Deut.* 35. On the "good" memorial, see note on 12:14 and the ruling in *Mek. RI Pisḥa* 17:115-117; *Mek. RSbY*, p. 40, that the *tefillin* are made up of four sections in one single container. Hence they may be described as plural "frontlets," v. 16, and signs, as here, and also as singular, a "good memorial," as here and also v. 16, where this phrase ren-ders Hebrew "frontlets." "Your faces" for "your eyes" represents the ruling of *b. Men.* 37b; *Sifre Deut.* 35; *Ber.* 13a; *b. Arak* 1b; *Mek. RI Pisḥa* 17:145-153; *Mek. RSbY*, p. 40. For the addition of "continually," see Vulg. On "redeemed," see 3:10.

⁷Hebrew has: "And you shall keep this ordinance in its season from year to year." For "the statutes of this Law," see 12:49. The notices of time, set out in the Apparatus to this verse, may obliquely allude to rules governing times and sea-sons when *tefillin* are to be used: see *Mek. RI Pisḥa* 17:181-187, 188-209, and the sources cited in note on v. 9.

the womb of a beast which you have, the males shall be for *the name of* the Lord.[8] 13. Everything that opens the *womb* of a donkey *you* shall redeem with a lamb, and if *you* do not redeem *it you shall kill* it;[i] and all males of the *sons of* man among *your* sons *you* shall redeem.[9] 14. And when tomorrow *your* sons ask,[j] saying: 'What is this?' you shall say to (them): 'By a strong hand has the Lord[k] brought us out *redeemed*[10] from the house of bondage.[m] 15. And it came to pass that Pharaoh hardened against letting us go, and the Lord killed all the first-born in the land of Egypt, from the first-born of the *sons of* man to the first-born of beasts; because of this *we* offer *before* the Lord all males that open the womb,[n] and every male of *our* sons[o] *we* redeem.'[p] 16. And it shall be[q] a sign[r] upon *your arms* and as *a good memorial* upon *your faces*, that by a strong hand the Lord led us out *redeemed* from[s] Egypt."[11] 17. And it came to pass[t] when Pharaoh let the people go,[u] the Lord[w] did

Apparatus, Chapter 13

[i] VN: "and you shall kill it" = Nf. Nfmg: "you shall kill them with the head of an axe."

[j] Nfmg +: "you" (plur.).

[k] Nfmg: "the Memra of the Lord from."

[m] Nfmg: "(from) Egypt, from the house of bondage"; however, we should probably read: "from the house of the bondage of Egypt."

[n] Nfmg: "to the name of the Lord everything that first opens the womb."

[o] Nfmg: "my sons I will redeem."

[p] Nfmg + "them."

[q] Nfmg: "they shall be as signs (a different word) upon."

[r] Nfmg has: "phylacteries" (*tephillim*).

[s] Nfmg: "redeemed and brought us out from."

[t] P: "and it came to pass that when Pharaoh let the people go he did not lead them by the way of the land of the Philistines although (M. Klein: "because") it was near. Two hundred thousand (was the number of those) who went out of Egypt thirty years before the Lord's predetermined time—two hundred thousand warrior infantrymen; they were all from the tribe of Ephraim, holding shields and implements of war

and spears. They, they are the dry bones that the Lord revived through the hands of the prophet Ezekiel in the valley of Dura. And from those bones were (made) the drinking vessels from which the wicked Nebuchadnezzar drank. And at the time the Lord had revived them by the hands of the prophet Ezekiel, they slapped that wicked one on his mouth. And the bones drew near one to the other and they came to life and stood upon their feet, very, very many camps. All of them arose except one man who did not arise. The prophet said before the Lord: What were the deeds of this one man that he did not arise? And therefore the Lord said to him [i.e., Moses]: He gave (loans) against pledges and collected with interest. So he shall not come to life. And thus the Lord showed the prophet Ezekiel this sign that [Hebrew particle!] he is to revive the dead. And therefore the Lord said to him: Lest the people tremble when they see their dead brothers and fear and go back to Egypt."

[u] Nfmg: "at the time he let (the people) go."

[w] Nfmg: "the Memra of the Lord by the road."

Notes, Chapter 13

[8]Hebrew has: "Then you shall set apart to the Lord every first offspring of the womb, and every first offspring of a beast (*ptr šgr*, lit.: what opens the womb of newly born beasts) which belongs to you: the males shall belong to the Lord." Targum's "you shall set aside" is *wtpršwn*, "and you shall separate," a technical term for the separation of priestly and Temple dues. The same word is used by Tg. Ps.-J.; cf. *Mek. RI Pisha* 10:20-21; 18:20-21; *Tanḥ. Bo'* 14; b. Zeb. 100a; LXX; Vulg.; Syr.-Hex. Grossfeld, 1988B, 36, suggests that Tg. Nf, like Tg. Onq. and Pesh., omits *šgr*. The expression "womb of a beast" occurs in LXX here. On the Name of the Lord and separation of dues, see note on 6:7. Vulg.'s "you shall consecrate" at the end of the verse stresses the cultic element.

[9]Hebrew has: "And every firstling of an ass you shall redeem with a lamb; but if you will not redeem it, then you shall break its neck. And every first-born of man among your sons you shall redeem." LXX have "everything that opens the womb of a donkey . . ."; and the command to *kill* the beast is found in Symm., Vulg. and Frg. Tg. V. Nfmg states that an axe-head shall be used for this purpose: so Rashi and *b. Bekh.* 10b.

[10]On "redeemed," see 3:10.

[11]Hebrew has: "And it shall be as a sign on your hand and as frontlets between your eyes; because with strength of hand

not lead them by the way of the land of the Philistines, although that was near, because *the Lord*[x] said: "Lest the *heart of* the people *be broken* when they see battle *array* and they return to Egypt."[12] 18. And *the Lord* led[y] the people about[z] by the way of the wilderness (towards) the Reed Sea. And *armed in good work*, the children of Israel went up *redeemed* from the land of Egypt.[13] 19. And Moses took[aa] the bones of Joseph with him because he[bb] had made the children of Israel swear, saying: "*The Lord shall* surely *remember* you *in his good mercies*,[cc][14] and you shall take my bones with you from here." 20. And they journeyed from Succoth and encamped in Etham, on the edge[dd] of the wilderness. 21. And *the Word* of the Lord led on before them[15] during the daytime in a pillar of cloud to lead them on the way,[ee] and by night[ff] in a pillar of fiery cloud to give them light, that they might journey[gg] by day and night. 22. The pillar of cloud[hh] did not cease during the daytime, nor the pillar of fire[ii] at night, *leading and standing in* readiness *and shining* before the people.[jj][16]

Apparatus, Chapter 13

[x] Nfmg: "the Memra of the Lord in the thought of them" (read: "of his heart"?).

[y] Vv. 18-20 fully in P; partially in VN.

[z] Nfmg: "the Memra of the Lord led the people" = VN; P: "the Lord led the people."

[aa] P: "brought up."

[bb] P: "because Joseph while alive had made. . . ."

[cc] Nfmg: "the Memra of the Lord (will remember) you in his (good) mercies."

[dd] Nfi: "the end of"; Nfmg: "which is on the edges of" = VN; cf. P.

[ee] P: "to prepare for them a resting place on the way"; Nfmg: "to show them the way."

[ff] P: "and also by night."

[gg] Nfmg: "(that) they might go and ha<ve light?>."

[hh] P: "the light of the pillar of cloud. . . ."

[ii] P: "nor the illumination of the pillar of fire."

[jj] Nfmg: "(of) the house of Israel."

Notes, Chapter 13

the Lord brought us out from Egypt." Verse 9 is very similar: see the notes to it for the rendering of "hand" as "arms"; the *good* memorial; "your faces" for "between your eyes"; and the addition of "redeemed." Hebrew "sign" is here rendered by Targum with the Greek loan word *sēmeion*. Vulg. is very close to Tg. Nf here in regarding the *tefillin* as a memorial. It translates "frontlets" as *et quasi adpensum quid ob recordationem*.

[12]Hebrew has: "that God did not lead them by the way of the land of the Philistines . . . for God said: Lest the people change their mind when they see war." Targum's slight divergencies from the Hebrew may indicate some acquaintance with the aggadah set out in the Apparatus, which is found also in Tg. Ps.-J.; *Exod. R.* 20, 11; *Mek. RI Beshallah* 1:45-51; Tg. Cant. 2:7; Tg. 1 Chr. 7:21; Tg. Jerushalmi of Ezek 37:1-14, published by A. Díez Macho, "Un segundo Fragmento del Targum palestinense a los Profetas," *Biblica* 39 (1958) 198–205; *PRE* 48:2; J. Heinemann, 1975, 1–15.

[13]Hebrew has: "And God led the people round . . . and the Israelites went up armed [*ḥmšym*] from the land of Egypt." For *ḥmšym* as "armed in good work," see Frg. Tg. P, V; for "armed," cf. Tg. Onq., Aq., Symm., *Mek. RI Beshallah* 1:71-74 interprets the word as "zealous," which certainly implies good deeds; see also *Mek. RSbY*, p. 45; *Num. R.* 11, 3; *PRE* 42:1. On "redeemed," see 3:10 and Frg. Tg. P, V. See also 33:4-6.

[14]Hebrew has: "God will certainly visit you." See notes on 2:24; 3:16; 4:31; and Frg. Tg. P, V; Tg. Nf of Gen 21:1; 50:24.

[15]Hebrew has: "and the Lord went before them." For the Word, see Frg. Tg. P and Muñoz León, 1974, 332–33.

[16]"Leading" is included also by Tg. Ps.-J., and Frg. Tg. P refers to the light of the cloud and fire; cf. Neh 9:19; *Mek. RI Beshallah* 1:234-38; *b. Shabb.* 23b.

CHAPTER 14

1. And[a] the Lord[b] spoke with Moses, saying: 2. "Speak with the children of Israel and let them return and encamp before the *Taverns*[c] *of Hirata*[d1] between Migdol and the sea, before the *idol* Zephon;[e] facing[f] (it) you shall encamp by the sea.[g] 3. And Pharaoh <will say>[h] *concerning the people* of the children of Israel: 'They are gone astray *on the way*;[i] *my idol*[j] Baal Zephon has barred against them the *passes* of the wilderness.'[k2] 4. And I will harden the heart of Pharaoh, and he will pursue after them, and I will be glorified[m] <in> Pharaoh and in all his hosts; and the Egyptians will know that I am the Lord." And they did thus.[n] 5. When it was reported[o] to the king of Egypt that the people had fled, the heart of Pharaoh and of his *rulers* was changed towards[p] the people, and they said: "What is this which we have done that we have let Israel go from serving *before* us?"[3] 6. And he harnessed his chariots and took people, *men of war*,[q4] with him. 7. And he took six hundred chariots[r] and all the chariots[s] of the Egyptians, and *lords*[t] *were appointed*

Apparatus, Chapter 14

[a] Chapter 14 in its entirety in P; all verses in whole or in part in VN, except 1, 4, 6, 10-12, 18, 22, 29-31; verses 1, 13-14, 29-31 in CTg J (=MS 605 of the Jewish Theological Seminary).

[b] Nfmg: "the Memra of the Lord"; CTg J: "The Memra of Adonai"; P: "the Dibbera of the Lord" (*dybryh dyyy*).

[c] Greek loan word: *pandokeion*: in all Pal. Tgs. texts of Exod 14:2.

[d] "*Ḥirata*"; MT: "Pi-Hahiroth." Nfmg: "and encamp the Taverns of Licentiousness" (*ḥyrwt'*) (omitting "before").

[e] MT: "Baal Zephon"; P: "before Baal Zephon the idol."

[f] VN: "before it you shall encamp."

[g] P: "by the shore of the sea."

[h] Missing in text of Nf: in P; VN: "and Pharaoh said."

[i] PVN: "in the wilderness."

[j] P: "the idol Baal Zephon"; VN: "the idol Peor."

[k] Nfmg: "Pharaoh is to say to Dathan and Abiron, who remained in Egypt, concerning the children of Israel:

My idol Peor, etc., they are seized (?) in the land; they are gone astray on the way; the idol Zephon has barred against them the passes (correcting text) of the wilderness"; cf. Ps.-J.

[m] Nfmg: "and he will pursue aft(er them) and I will glorify my (text: hi[s]) Memra in Ph(araoh)"; P: "and my Memra will be glorified in Pharaoh."

[n] P + : "according to his Memra" (or: "command").

[o] Nfmg: "and the slave drivers (Latin loan word: *actores*) who journeyed with the camps of Israel and had acted against the people reported"; cf. Ps.-J.

[p] P: "against."

[q] P: "men who wage war."

[r] Nfmg: "(six) hundreds of war chariots"; P: "select chariots."

[s] Nfmg: "war chariots of Egypt and men (read: "warriors") appointed."

[t] Nfmg: "generals" (Greek loan word *polemarchos*); P: "and warriors divided into three divisions, with weapons."

Notes, Chapter 14

[1] For the Taverns of Hirata, see Frg. Tg. P, V; the reading of Nfmg, "Taverns of Licentiousness," is reflected in Tg. Ps.-J. of Num 33:8; *Mek. RI Beshallaḥ* 2:15-17; *Num. R.* 20, 23; *Tanḥ. Balak* 17.

[2] Hebrew has: "And Pharaoh will say of the Israelites: They are entangled in the land: the desert has shut them up." Frg. Tg. P, V, are very similar to Tg. Nf. For Nfmg's reference to Dathan and Abiram, see also Tg. Ps.-J.: this is apparently a tradition peculiar to the Targum: Le Déaut, 1979 (*Exode*) 109.

[3] For Nfmg's reference to the "slave drivers," see *Mek. RI Beshallaḥ* 2:94-96; *Mek. RSbY*, p. 49; Tg. Ps.-J. On "rulers" for "servants," see note on 7:20.

[4] For the addition of "men of war," cf. Frg. Tg. P and *Tanḥ. Shofetim* 13.

over all of them.[5] 8. And the Lord[u] hardened the heart of Pharaoh, king of Egypt, and he pursued after the children of Israel,[w] and the children of Israel went out *redeemed, with head uncovered.*[x][6] 9. And the Egyptians pursued after them, and they reached them (as they were) encamped by the sea[y]—all the horses, the chariots of Pharaoh, and his horsemen and his hosts—*near the Taverns*[z] *of Hirata,* before *the idol* Zephon.[7] 10. And Pharaoh drew near,[aa] and the children of Israel lifted up their eyes and, behold, the Egyptians marched after them and they feared greatly. And the children of Israel *prayed*[bb] *before* the Lord.[8] 11. And they said to Moses: "Is it because there are no tombs[cc] in Egypt that you have led[dd] us *to kill us* in the wilderness?[ee] What is this that you have done to us in bringing us[ff] out of Egypt? 12. Is not this the word that we spoke with you in Egypt, saying: 'Let us alone[gg] that we may serve *before* the[hh] Egyptians'? For it would be better[ii] for us to serve *before* the[hh] Egyptians[jj] than *to kill us* in the wilderness."[kk] 13. *The children of Israel were formed into four groups at the time they were standing beside the Reed Sea.*[mm] *One said: "Let us fall into the sea";*[nn] *and one said: "Let us return to Egypt";*

Apparatus, Chapter 14

[u] P: "and the Memra of the Lord hardened."

[w] P: "after the people of the children of Israel."

[x] P: ". . . went out redeemed with head uncovered"; VN: "went out redeemed."

[y] P: "by the shore of the sea."

[z] Greek loan word: *pandokeion.*

[aa] P: "drew near to come and the children of Israel raised their eyes"; Nfmg: "and Pharaoh offered sacrifices to Baal Zephon."

[bb] Nfmg: "and they cried."

[cc] P, Nfmg: "there were no tombs for us."

[dd] Nfmg: "to bring (us)."

[ee] Nfmg +: "of Zephon."

[ff] Nfmg: "them."

[gg] Nfmg: "leave (us)."

[hh] P: "serve the."

[ii] P: "it is better."

[jj] Nfmg: "that we should serve with the Egyptians."

[kk] Nfmg: "in tents" (?; *bskt*).

[mm] CTg J = Nf, with minor variants P. v. 13: "And Moses said to the people, the children of Israel: Do not fear, stand prepared and see the redemption of the Lord, that he will work for you this day, because as you have seen the Egyptians this day you shall not see them again for ever"; VN: vv. 13-14: "The children of Israel were formed into four groups when they were standing by the Reed Sea. One said: Let us fall into the sea. Another said: Let us set battle array against them. And another said: Let us shout out against them and confound them. And another said: Let us return to Egypt. To the group that said: Let us fall into the sea, Moses said: Do not fear; stand prepared and see the redemption of the Lord which he will work for you this day. To the group that said: Let us return to the Egyptians, Moses said: Do not fear, because as you have seen the Egyptians this day, you shall never see them again in bondage for ever. To the group who said: Let us set battle array against them, Moses said: Do not fear, the Lord in the Glory of his Shekinah is he who works your battle victories for you. To the group who said: Let us shout against them and confound them Moses said: Do not fear; stand; be silent and give glory and praise and exaltation to our God."

[nn] Nfmg: "into the Sea and one said: Let us set battle array against (them)." (This puts group three, second place, as in VN).

Notes, Chapter 14

[5]Hebrew has: "and captains over all of them." The military aspects of the operation are likewise stressed by Nfmg, Tg. Onq., Tg. Ps.-J. Frg. Tg. P, V, *Mek. RI Beshallaḥ* 2:200-201; *Mek. RSbY,* p. 52.

[6]Hebrew has: "went out with a high hand." On "redeemed," see 3:10; Frg. Tg. P, V. "With head uncovered" is used also by Tg. Onq., Frg. Tg. P; *Mek. RI Beshallaḥ* 2:231-32; *Mek. RSbY,* p. 52; and it also renders "with a high hand" in Tg. Nf, Tg. Onq., and Tg. Ps.-J. of Num 15:30; 33:3; Nfmg of Lev 26:13. See also Tg. Nf, Frg. Tg. P, V of Gen 40:18, and M. McNamara, 1966, 176–77.

[7]See notes to v. 2.

[8]Nfmg has Pharaoh sacrificing to Baal-Zephon: so Tg. Ps.-J.; *Mek. RI Beshallaḥ* 3:10-15; *Tanḥ. Beshallaḥ* 8. "Prayed before the Lord" renders Hebrew "cried out to the Lord"; so Frg. Tg. P; Tg. Ps.-J.; prayer is assumed by *Mek. RI Beshallaḥ* 3:26-65; *Mek. RSbY,* p. 53.

and one said: "Let us set battle array against them"; and one said: "Let us shout out against them and confound them." To the group that said: "Let us fall into the sea," Moses said: "Fear not, stand prepared and see the redemptions of the Lord which he does for you this day." *And to the group that said: "Let us return to Egypt," Moses said: "Fear not, because* as you have seen the Egyptians this day, you shall never see them again, *in bondage,*[oo] forever." 14. *And to the group that said:*[pp] *"Let us set battle array against them," Moses said: "Fear not,* the Lord[qq] *himself works your battle victories for you." And to the group that said: "Let us shout against them and confound them," Moses said: "Fear not; stand;* be silent *and give glory and praise and exaltation to our God."*[9] 15. And the Lord[rr] said to Moses: *"How long will you stand praying before* me? *Your prayer has been heard before me. Besides, the prayer of the children of Israel has anticipated*[ss] *yours.* Speak to the children of Israel and let them go forward.[10] 16. And as for you, raise[tt] your staff and *incline* your hand over the sea and divide it, that the children of Israel may enter the midst of[uu] the sea on dry land. 17. And as for me, behold, I harden the heart of the Egyptians, and they shall enter after them,[ww] and I shall be glorified in Pharaoh and in all his hosts, in his chariots and in his horsemen. 18. And the Egyptians shall know that I am the Lord when I am glorified in Pharaoh, in his chariots and his horsemen." 19. And the angel of the Lord who *was ready* to walk[xx] before the camps of Israel, *in front of them,* moved and *stood* behind them.[11] And the pillar of cloud moved from before them and stood behind them, 20. and it went in between the camps of

Apparatus, Chapter 14

[oo] Omitted in CTg J.
[pp] CTg J v. 14 = Nf, with variants noted below. P: v. 14: "the Memra of the Lord will wage battle for you; stand; be silent and give glory and praise to your God."
[qq] Nfmg: "in the Glory of his Shekinah is the one who works"; misplaced gloss; = VNV 13.
[rr] Nfmg: "the Memra of the Lord" = PVN.

[ss] Nfmg: "of my people has been anticipated" = PVN.
[tt] P: "and (as for) you Moses lift up."
[uu] P: "in the middle of."
[ww] Nfmg: "after you and I will glorify (my? his?) Memra"; cf. P: "after them and my Memra will be glorified."
[xx] P: "who was leading before the camps of Israel and came behind them.

Notes, Chapter 14

[9] Hebrew has: "And Moses said to the people: Do not be afraid. Stand and see the salvation of the Lord, which he will perform for you today. For just as you have seen the Egyptians today, you shall not ever see them again. The Lord will fight for you, and you shall be quiet." The tradition that Israel divided into groups, to whom Moses addressed different exhortations, is found in Tg. Ps.-J.; Frg. Tg. V; Tg. fragment in Klein, 1, 1986, 225; Tosefta Tg. in Klein, 1, 1986, 223. The tradition is possibly of pre-Christian origin, being found in embryonic form in Philo, *De Vita Mosis* I. XXXI §§170-75; in the first century C.E., *LAB* 10:3 knows of a division of Israel into three groups: see P.-M. Bogaert and C. Perrot, 1, 1976, 108–9, and the literature cited there. See also *Mek. RI Beshallaḥ* 3:128-35; *Mek. RSbY*, p. 56; *j. Ta'an.* 2:5; *b. Sotah* 36b; and later sources quoted by Kasher, *Torah Shelemah*, vol. 14, 1951, 47–48. Discussion of the aggadah is found in J. Heinemann, 1974A, 78–84; W.S. Towner, 1973, 101–18, esp. 113–17; A. Shinan, 1, 1979, 77–78 (in Hebrew).

[10] Hebrew has: "And the Lord said to Moses: Why are you crying out to me? Speak to the Israelites, that they may journey forward." Cf. Tg. Ps.-J.; Frg. Tg. P, V; *Mek. RI Beshallaḥ* 4:1-7 (R. Eliezer), 92–94; *Mek. RSbY*, p. 57; *Exod. R.* 21, 4, 8; *Lev. R.* 28, 7; *PRK* 8:2. Particularly important is the declaration of R. Abtalos (Absalom?), in *Mek. RI Beshallaḥ* 4:29-41, that God is already reconciled to his children: in this source the merits of the Fathers are to the fore. See also *Mek. RSbY*, p. 57, and *Exod. R.* 21, 8.

[11] Hebrew has: "And the angel of God who went in front of the camps of Israel journeyed and went behind them."

the Egyptians and the camps of Israel; and the cloud became *yy* darkness *and in part light: obscuring darkness for the Egyptians and light for Israel* all the night. And one group did not draw nigh to the other *for battle array* all the night. *zz*[12] 21. And Moses *inclined* his hand over the sea, and the Lord drove the sea by a strong east wind all the night and made the sea dry land, and the waters were divided. 22. And the children of Israel entered into the midst of *a* the sea on dry land, and the waters were walls *of water* for them *b* to their right and to their left.[13] 23. And the Egyptians followed on and entered after them—all the horses of Pharaoh, his chariots and his horsemen—into the midst of *a* the waters. 24. And it came to pass at morning *time* *c* that the Lord scrutinized *d* *in anger* the camps of the Egyptians, *and he hurled upon them asphalt* *e* *and* fire *and hailstones;* *f* and he confounded the hosts of the Egyptians.[14] 25. And he *g* *untied* the chariot wheels, and *they* carried *them* away, *dragged* *h* *backwards, the way of the she-mules, being dragged by the wheels*

Apparatus, Chapter 14

yy Nfmg 1° and 2° PVN: "and the cloud was part light and part darkness; the light shone upon Israel, and the darkness cast darkness upon the Egyptians. And one group did not draw near to the other to wage war on them the whole night."

zz Nfmg: "Israel shone(?) during the night; one camp did not draw near to the other. However the angels of the service did not say the service all the night."

a P: "into the middle of."

b P: "were for them high walls" (corr. to: "walls of water"?).

c Nf and P: lit.: "morning times"; VN: "morning times."

d Nfmg, VN: "and the Memra of the Lord scrutinized."

e Greek loan word: *naphta* (also in VN).

f Nfi: "and hail" (omitting "stores").

g Or: "it," i.e., thunder; cf. Mekilta, *Beshallah 6 in loc.* (in Hebrew).

h PVN: "and he (or "it" = "thunder") broke off the wheels of their chariots (*rdwwthwn*; Latin loan word: *rhaeda*, also used in Greek: *raida*; cf. Rev 13:14) which led them, dragged from behind. It is the way of the mules (Latin loan word: *mula*; also used in Greek: *moulē*) to pull the wheels (P +: and the shafts). The wheels and the chariots (*rhaeda, raida*), (however,) turned round to pull the mules and cast (them) into (VN: upon) the sea. The Egyptians answered and said to each other, (P +: rather, let us turn round and) let us flee from before the people of the sons of Israel, because this is the Lord who wrought the order of their battle victories for them while they were still dwelling (VN: found) with (lit.: beside) us in Egypt, (P +: and also here)"; Nfmg: "their chariots which led (them) were dragged from behind, the way of mules." In Nf and Nfmg "chariot" = *rhaeda*; "mule": *mula, moulē*.

Notes, Chapter 14

[12]Hebrew has: "and there was the cloud and the darkness, and it gave light in the night: and the one did not draw near to the other all night." On darkness for the Egyptians and light for Israel, see Tg. Ps.-J.; Frg. Tg. P, V; Nfmg; Tg. Ps.-J. of Exod. 13:21; *Mek. RI Beshallah* 5:37-46; *Mek. RSbY* p. 60; *Tanh. Tesawweh* 4; *Exod. R.* 14, 3; *Lev. R.* 21, 1. The one group did not approach the other for war all night: see *Mek. RI Beshallah* 5:55-57; *Mek. RSbY*, p. 61; Grossfeld, 1988B, 39. Nfmg records a tradition found also in *b. Meg.* 10b and *Sanh.* 39b that the angels did not offer the heavenly liturgy on the night of the Exodus from Egypt.

[13]Hebrew has: "and the water was a wall for them on their right hand and on their left." A later, well-known tradition in *PRE* 42, 2 tells of the walls of water forming twelve paths for the twelve tribes. The path through the sea and the wall of water evokes comment also in *b. Yoma* 4b; *Tanh. Beshallah* 10; *Wa'ethannan* 6.

[14]Hebrew has: "And at the morning watch, the Lord looked out at the camp of the Egyptians through the pillar of fire and cloud, and brought confusion to the camp of Egypt." For "at morning time," cf. Frg. Tg. P, V; *Mek. RI Beshallah* 6:75-93; Vulg. For "scrutinized in anger," cf. Frg. Tg. P; Tg. Ps.-J. *Mek. RI Beshallah* 6:116-17; *Exod. R.* 23, 23, 24; *Lev. R.* 18, 5. For "asphalt, fire and hailstones," cf. Frg. Tg. P, V; Pss. 18:14-15; 77:16-20; Josephus, *Ant.* II.xvi.3.

and the shafts. The <wheels and the chariots> turned round, dragging the she-mules,[i] and cast them into the sea. When the Egyptians *saw this praiseworthy thing,* they said *one to the other: "Let us flee from the people,[j] the children of* Israel, be-cause *it is* the Lord *who worked* their *battle victories for them when they were yet* in Egypt, *and he is about to work their battle victories for them again at the Reed Sea."* [15] 26. And the Lord[k] said to Moses: *"Incline* your hand over the sea and let the waters return upon the Egyptians, upon their chariots and horsemen." 27. And Moses *inclined* his hand over the sea and caused the sea to turn back, at morning time[m] *to its strength.[n]* And the Egyptians fled against it, and the Lord *left[o]* the Egyptians in the midst of the sea. [16] 28. And the waters returned[p] and covered their chariots and the horsemen[q] and all the hosts of Pharaoh who had entered after them into the sea. Not *even* one among them was left. [17] 29. And the children of Is-rael walked on dry land in the midst of the sea, and the waters *were* walls[r] of water

Apparatus, Chapter 14

[i] Lit.: "dragging (or: being dragged) like she-mules."

[j] Nfmg: "dragging the wheels. The wheels of the chari-ots (*rhaeda*) turned round to drag the mules (*moula, moulē*) casting them upon the sea. The Egyptians an-swered and said to each other: Rather, let us flee from before the people."

[k] Nfmg, P: "the Memra of the Lord."

[m] Nf, P, V literally: "at the morning times."

[n] Nfmg: "to its places"; VN: "to its place."

[o] Nfmg, P: "and the Egyptians fled against it and the Memra of the Lord suffocated (*snq*) the Egyptians in the midst of (P: in the middle of) the sea"; VN: "and the Lord suffocated (correcting text with Nfmg, P) the Egyptians." Nf *sbq* may = *snq* or be an error for it.

[p] Nfmg +: "these to these."

[q] Nfmg: "their horsemen."

[r] Nfmg, P, CTg J: "like walls of water"; P: alphabetic (acrostic) poem after v. 29: "(*Aleph*) Go, Moses, and stand by the sea and say to the sea, Move from before me; (*Beth*) in my name you shall go and say to the sea (that): I am the messenger of Him who Created in the Beginning (lit.: formed). (*Gimel*) Uncover your way

for a brief while (lit.: "a little hour") so that within you the redeemed of the Lord (Greek loan word: *Kyrios*) may pass. (*Daleth*) Since the tribes of Jacob dwell in distress and those who hate them pursue after them, (*He*) Behold, you have closed (the way) before them and the Wicked Pharaoh is coming after them. (*Waw*) And Moses went and stood beside the sea and said to the sea: Move from before God. (*Zain*) And the sea moved from before Moses when it saw the rod of the miracles in his hand. (*Heth*) Anger and wrath entered the sea, and it made a big deal about turning backward. (*Teth*) Behold, it is an error for you, son of Amram. I shall not be subdued before one born of woman. (*Yod*) I am three days older (lit.: greater) than you, since I was created on the third day and you on the sixth. How can you seek to subdue me? (*Caph*) When Moses saw the sea agitated, and its waves growing greater against him, (*Lamed*) (he said): This time (lit.: hour) is no time (lit.: hour) for disputations since Israel dwells in distress. You are not against me, nor am I against you. (*Mem*) Moses replied and said to the Sea: I am the messenger of Him who created (lit.: formed) in the Beginning (*in*

Notes, Chapter 14

[15]Hebrew has: "And he clogged their chariot wheels, so that they drove heavily; and the Egyptians said: Let me flee from before Israel, for the Lord is fighting for them against the Egyptians." See Apparatus for Frg. Tgs. and Nfmg, which are very close to Tg. Nf here. See the elaborate description of the rout of Egypt in *Mek. RI Beshallah* 6:127-36; *Mek. RSbY*, p. 65, which ends in the comment that formerly the mules had pulled the chariots, but when God acted, the chari-ots dragged the mules! "Let us flee": see LXX and Tg. Onq. For victories in Egypt and at the Red Sea, see *Mek. RI Beshallah* 6:143-46.

[16]Hebrew has: "and the Lord shook off the Egyptians in the midst of the sea." See Apparatus, and the textual problem discussed by Le Déaut, 1979 (*Exode*) 118–19.

[17]For addition of "even," cf. LXX, Vulg.

for them on their right and on their left. [18] 30. And on that day *the Memra* of the Lord *redeemed*[s] and delivered Israel from the hands of the Egyptians; and the Israelites saw the Egyptians dead, *cast* upon the shore of the sea. [19] 31. And Israel saw the strong hand[t] (with) which the Lord worked in Egypt, and the people feared *before* the Lord and they believed[u] *in the name of the Memra of* the Lord and in *the prophecy of* Moses, his servant. [20]

CHAPTER 15

1. Then Moses and the children of Israel sang[a] this song *of praise*[b] *before* the Lord and said thus: *"We will give thanks and praise before* the Lord,[c] who *by his Memra takes revenge of every one who exalts himself before him*: horse[d] and riders, *because they had exalted themselves and had pursued after the people, the children of*

Apparatus, Chapter 14

Hebrew). (*Nun*) The Sea turned itself around (*Hebrew verb form*) when it heard his words and arose to perform the will of the Master of the Heavens. (*Samek*) The end of the affair was (that) the sea said to Moses: I am not being *subdued* before one born of woman. (*Ain*) Moses answered and said to the sea: One who is greater than me and you will subdue you. (*Pe*) Moses opened his mouth in a song (an)d praised thus in song and in praise. (*Sade*) The prayer of Moses entered in petition, and in supplication: he said his words. (*Qof*) He called out: He said (= it was said) to me in the book of the Law: Now you shall see what I shall do to Pharaoh. (*Resh*) O Master of the World, do not hand over your people into the hands of the wicked Pharaoh. (*Resh*) The Exalted One has given him the staff of miracles to destroy all rebels. (*Shin*) The Sea heard the voice of the holy Spirit that spoke with Moses from the midst of the fire. (*Tav*) The Sea turned back from its waves and the children of Israel passed over through its midst."

[s] P: "the Lord redeemed Israel."

[t] P: "the might of the strong hand (with) which the Lord avenged them of the Egyptians"; CTg J: "the might of the strong hand (by) which the Memra of the Lord was avenged.

[u] Nfmg: "the strength of the arm of might with which the Memra of the Lord had worked signs in Egypt and they believed."

Notes, Chapter 14

[18] See note to v. 22. Frg. Tg. P here adds an alphabetic acrostic poem, which consists of a debate between Moses and the Red Sea. See J. Heinemann, 1973, 362–75 (in Hebrew).

[19] Hebrew has: "And the Lord saved Israel on that day . . . dead on the seashore." Cf. Tg. fragment in Klein, 1, 1986, 227; and Muñoz León, 1974, 340–42. The addition of "cast" is found also in Frg. Tg. P and Tg. Ps.-J. Possibly it is connected with the tradition that Israel had of necessity to see the dead bodies of the Egyptians; so *Mek. RI Beshallah* 7:94-108, which gives four reasons for the public display of the corpses, and Philo, *De conf. ling.* X §36.

[20] Hebrew has: "and they believed in the Lord and in his servant Moses." See Tg. Ps.-J., Tg. Onq., Frg. Tg. P, and Tg. fragment in Klein, 1, 1986, 227. Belief in God is not to be considered on a par with belief in Moses; hence the introduction of prophecy, for which see Grossfeld, 1988B, 40.

Apparatus, Chapter 15

[a] Lit.: "praised"; likewise PVN, CTg J.

[b] CTg J as Nf: Nfmg, PVN: "the praise of this song."

[c] Nfmg, PVN, CTg J: "who is high above the high(est), and exalted above the exalted and every one (Nfmg: every thing) who exalts himself."

[d] VN: "the horses of Pharaoh and their riders"; P: "the Egyptians and their horses and their chariots"; CTg J: "he casts (down) according to (?) their spirits (?) the exalted of spirit; the horses and their riders."

Israel, he cast them down *and drowned^e* in the Sea *of Reeds.*[1] 2. *Our* strength and the *magnitude^f of our* praise is the one *Feared^g of all ages, the Lord.* He *decreed in his Memra* and became for us *a Redeemer." The children of Israel said:^h "He* is *our God and we will praise* him, the God of *our* fathers and *we will extol* him.[2] 3. The Lord is a man making wars, the Lord is his name; *according to his name, so in his might; may his name be blessed for all ages.^{i3}* 4. The chariots of Pharaoh and his hosts,*^j* he shot *against them arrows of fire*, in the sea; and *the best of his young men,*

Apparatus, Chapter 15

^e CTg J, Nfmg, PVN: "he buried."

^f "Magnitude," reading *rwb* with Nf, P, VN; Ps.-J. and Parma, *Bibl.* MS 3089 Palatina (978): "master" (*rab*).

^g "fear," with VN; P: "behold, the Lord of all ages."

^h Nfmg, VN: "from the breasts of their mothers the sucklings signaled with their fingers to their fathers and said to them: This is our father who nourished us with honey from the rock and anointed us with oil from the flint of stone. The children of Israel answered and said one to the other: He is our God, let us praise him; the God of our (Nf: their) fathers, let us exalt him."

^i VN: "the Lord, in the glory of his Shekinah, he it is who works your battle victories for you, in every generation he makes known his mighty deeds for his people, those of the house of Israel, the Lord is his name. As his name so also is his might. Let his name be praised for ever and ever"; P: "The children of Israel were formed into four groups when they were standing by the Red Sea, one of which was saying: Let us fall into the sea. And one said: Let us return to Egypt. And one said: Let us set battle array against them. And one said: Let us shout (*nmny*: thus M.

Klein: with reference to PVN, Num 21:34) against them and confound them. To the group which said: Let us fall into the sea, Moses said: Do not fear, <but stand firm and you shall see the redemption which the Lord will work for you this day. To the group that said: Let us return to Egypt, Moses said: Do not fear>, because as you have beheld the Egyptians this day you shall never see them again for ever. To the group that said: Let us set battle array against them, Moses said: Do not fear, but give glory and the praise to your God. To the group that said, Let us shout (?) against them and confound them, Moses said: The Lord, the warrior, who performs for you battle array, your battle victories—the Lord is his name. As his name, so also is his might, so also is his power, so his kingdom. May his great name be blessed for ever and for ever and ever."

^j P: "the chariots of Pharaoh the wicked and his host, he cast into the sea, and the pick of his young warriors he cast them down and drowned them in the Red Sea"; VN: "the chariots of Pharaoh and his hosts, he shot arrows against them in the sea; the pick of his young warriors he drowned in the Red Sea."

Notes, Chapter 15

For an analysis and examination of this chapter, see E. Levine, "Neofiti I. A Study of Exodus 15," *Biblica* 54 (1973) 301–30; P. Grelot, "Un poème acrostiche araméen sur Exode 12," *Semitica* 38 (1990) 159–65; and Levy, 1986, 376–85.

[1] Hebrew has: "Then Moses and the Israelites sang this song to the Lord, and uttered, saying: I will sing to the Lord, for he is very highly exalted. The horse and his rider he has thrown into the sea." See also Tg. Ps.-J.; Frg. Tg. P, V; and the fragment in Klein, 1, 1986, 241. On the song of *praise*, see Frg. Tg. P, V; Tg. Onq.; Tg. Ps.-J.; Klein, 1, 1986, 241. For the first person plural, cf. Pesh., Vulg., and Sam.: it may reflect the view of R. Akiba in *b. Sotah* 30b about the manner in which this song was sung, on which see Grossfeld, 1988B, 40–41. For "we will give thanks . . . everyone who exalts himself before him," see Tg. Ps.-J.; Frg. Tg. P, V; and Klein, 1, 1986, 241; *Mek. RI Shirta* 2:12ff.; *Exod. R.* 23, 13. For the verse as a whole, see also McNamara, 1966, 200–204; Bienaimé, 1984, 156.

[2] Hebrew has: "The Lord is my strength and my song, and has become my salvation: this is my God, and I will praise him; my father's God, and I will exalt him." For "our strength . . . is the Lord," see Tg. Ps.-J., Frg. Tg. P, V; M. Klein, 1975, 61–67. For "he decreed . . . Redeemer," see Tg. Onq.; Tg. Ps.-J.; Frg. Tg. P, V. For "the children of Israel . . . will extol him," see Frg. Tg. P; *Exod. R.* 23, 15. For the aggadah about the sucklings, found in Nfmg, Tg. Ps.-J., and Frg. Tg. V, see *Mek. RI Shirta* 1:148-51; *Exod. R.* 23, 8; *t. Sotah* 6:4; *j. Sotah* 5:6; *b. Sotah* 30b; and P. Grelot, 1961, 49–60.

[3] Hebrew has: "The Lord is a man of war: the Lord is his Name." The Targumic exegesis in the latter part of the verse is reflected in Tg. Ps.-J. and Frg. Tg. V. It is here that Frg. Tg. P and the Targum in Klein, 1, 1986, 241, 243, have the midrash of the Four Divisions, discussed above at 14:13-14. See *Mek. RI Shirta* 4:40ff.; *Mek. RSbY*, p. 82.

the warriors of Pharaoh, he *cast them down* and drowned [k] in the Sea of Reeds. [4]
5. The abyss covered over [m] them, they went down *and sank* into the depths *of the
waters, they were likened* to a stone. [5] 6. Your right hand, O Lord, *how* beautiful [n] it
is in power; your right hand, O Lord, broke *Pharaoh,* the hater, and *the adversary.* [o6]
7. And in the greatness of your exaltedness you destroy [p] *the adversaries of your people*; you send *on them the might of* your anger, *you consume them* [q] as *the fire burns*
in straw. [7] 8. And *by a decree from before you, Lord,* the waters *were made to be
piles upon piles*; bundles rose up like water bags of running waters; the depths congealed in the midst of the Great Sea. [8] 9. *Pharaoh, the wicked,* the hater, *and the adversary, said:* 'I will pursue *after the people, the children of Israel, and* I will reach
*them encamped by the shore of the Sea; I will take many of them captive, and I will
plunder great booty from them.* [r] I will divide *the booty* [s] *among my people*, who fight
the battle, *and when* my soul is sated with them, *then* shall I unsheath my sword
and my *right* hand will blot them out.'" [r9] 10. You blew with a breath [u] from *before*

Apparatus, Chapter 15

[k] Nfmg: "drowned" (without cast down; missing also
in V).

[m] P: "the abyss covered over them: the waters of the
sea; they sank into the depths of the Great Sea like a
stone"; VN: "the abyss covered over them; they went
down into the depth; they were likened to stones."

[n] Nfmg, VN: "(how) praiseworthy it is in might, your
right hand, O Lord, which has crushed and crushes
the wall (VN: walls) of the enemies of your people."

[o] Nfmg: "and in the vastness of your strength you
broke the walls of the enemies (of)" (from v. 7; see
VN).

[p] Nfmg: "You have broken the walls of the enemies";
= P: "and in the greatness of your excellence you
have broken the walls of the enemies of your people.
You have sent the angel of your anger, who was en-
raged and set them alight, as fire sets straw alight."

[q] Nfmg: "and you will destroy them."

[r] VN, v. 9 as in Nf, with variants as below. P: "Pharaoh
the wicked, the hater, the adversary, said: I will pursue after the people of the children of Israel. I will
confound them as they are encamped beside the
coast of the sea. I will take from them great booty,
and I will take captive from them many captives. I
will divide them up among my people, who fight the
battle, until my soul is sated with them, and after that
I will unsheath my sword from the scabbard (Greek
loan word: *thēkē*) and I will blot them out with my
right hand."

[s] Nfmg: "all the possessions of"; VN: "I will make division of their possessions."

[t] Nfmg, PVN: "and I will blot them out (PVN: + with
my right hand)."

[u] Nfmg: "your breath blew"; or: "you blew your
breath."

Notes, Chapter 15

[4] Hebrew has: "The chariots of Pharaoh and his army he has thrown into the sea; and the pick of his captains are sub-
merged in the Sea of Reeds." For the Lord's shooting arrows, cf. Frg. Tg. V; "the best of his young men, the warriors of
Pharaoh," cf. Frg. Tg. P, V; Tg. Ps.-J.

[5] Hebrew has: "The deeps covered them; they went down into the depths like a stone." The Targum closest to Nf is
Ps.-J.; see also Klein, 1, 1986, 243.

[6] Hebrew has: "Your right hand, O Lord, is exalted in strength; your right hand, O Lord, has broken the enemy." With
Tg. Nf and Nfmg, cf. *Mek. RI Shirta* 6:2-9, 41-45; *Exod. R.* 23, 9.

[7] Hebrew has: "You have destroyed those who rise up against you. You sent forth your anger: it devoured them like
chaff." For "the adversaries of your people," cf. Tg. Ps.-J.; Tg. Onq.; and for the verse as a whole and for Nfmg, see *Mek.
RI Shirta* 6:1-9, 73-76; Bienaimé, 1984, 25-29; and W. Baars, 1961, 340-42.

[8] Hebrew has: "And at the breath of your nostrils the waters stood in heaps: the streams stood up like a heap, the deeps
were congealed in the heart of the sea." Cf. Tg. Ps.-J.; Frg. Tg. P; Klein, 1, 1986, 243, 245; *Mek. RI Shirta* 6:110-11; and
the detailed discussion in Bienaimé, 1984, 28–29.

[9] Hebrew has: "The enemy said: I will pursue, I will overtake, I will divide the spoil; my soul shall be filled with them. I
will empty my sword, my hand shall destroy them." See also Tg. Ps.-J.; Frg. Tg. P, V; Klein, 1, 1986, 245. The enemy is
identified as Pharaoh in *Mek. RI Shirta* 7:17, 27.

you, O Lord; the waters of the sea covered them over; *they went down and* sank like lead in the powerful waters. *[w]* [10] 11. Who is like you among the gods *on high*, O Lord? Who is like you, glorious in holiness to be feared in praises *during all ages, performing signs[x] and wonders for your people, the house of Israel?*[11] 12. *The sea and the land disputed, both of them together,[y] and said: 'The sea said to the land: "Receive your sons." And the land said to the sea: "Receive your slain."' The sea did not want to receive them and the land did not want to swallow them up. The land feared the judgment of the great day, lest it require them of her in the world to come. Immediately you inclined your right hand in an oath over the earth, O Lord, that you would not require them of it in the world to come. And[z] the earth opened its mouth and* swallowed them up. [12] 13. In your mercy *[aa]* you have led this people which you have redeemed; you lead *them[bb]* in your might to the *dwelling place of the house of the Shekinah* of your holiness. [13] 14. The peoples*[cc]* have heard; they have quivered; trembling has grasped the inhabitants*[dd] of the land* of Philistia. [14] 15. Then were the lords of the Edomites confounded; trembling grasped the mighty ones of the

---

Apparatus, Chapter 15

[w] P: "they were immersed like lead in the majestic waters."

[x] P: "feared in praises, performing for them signs, and mighty deeds for your people, the house of Israel."

[y] P: "The sea and the land disputed together. The sea said to the land: Receive your sons; and the land said to the sea: Receive your slain. The sea did not want to receive them nor did the Lord want to receive her (text: his) slain ones. A fear grasped the earth from her Father in heaven that he would not want them (back) (for) the world to come, <and with a command (*memar*) from before you, you inclined your right hand in an oath, and you swore to the earth that you would not seek them from it in the world to come>. Immediately the earth opened its mouth and swallowed them up"; VN: "The land and the sea were disputing, one opposite the other. The sea said to the earth: Receive your sons. And the earth said to the Sea: Receive your slain. The earth did not want to

swallow them up, nor did the sea want to cause them to sink (reading: *ṭm'*, as *ṭm'*). But by a command (*memar*) from before you, you inclined your right hand in an oath and swore to the earth that you would not demand them from it in the world to come. Behold, then, the earth opened its mouth and swallowed them up"; Nfmg, VN: "One disputed against the other: The sea < . . . > receive your slain < . . . > the sea did not want to cause them to sink (*ṭm'*) and by a command (*memar*) from before you, you inclined your hand in an oath and it was sworn (or: "you swore," or as VN) to the earth that (they/you would) not."

[z] Nfmg: "Behold, then (the earth opened)" = VN.

[aa] P: "in your goodness."

[bb] P: "you carried them with (lit.: by) your might."

[cc] P: "the nations."

[dd] P: "has grasped them, all the inhabitants of."

Notes, Chapter 15

[10]Hebrew has: "You blew with your wind: the sea covered them; they sank like lead in the mighty waters." Cf. Tg. Ps.-J.; Frg. Tg. P; Klein, 1, 1986, 245.

[11]Hebrew has: "Who is like you among the gods, O Lord? Who is like you, glorious in holiness, fearful in praises, performing wonders?" See Tg. Ps.-J.; Frg. Tg. P; Klein, 1, 1986, 245; *Mek. RI Shirta* 8:27-41; *b. Rosh Hash.* 31b.

[12]Hebrew has: "You stretched forth your right hand: the earth swallowed them up." The question naturally arises why the earth, not the sea, swallowed them, which Tg. proceeds to answer. On the dispute of the sea and the land, which features also in Tg. Ps.-J.; Frg. Tg. P, V; Klein, 1, 1986, 241, 245, see *Mek. RI Shirta* 9:7-15; *Mek. RSbY*, p. 95; *b. Pesah.* 118b; *PRE* 42:5; *Lam. R.* 1, 9; *Mid. Pss.* 22:17.

[13]Hebrew has: "to the place of your holiness." Cf. Frg. Tg. P; Klein, 1, 1986, 247; *Mek. RI Shirta* 9:49-52.

[14]Hebrew has: "the inhabitants of Philistia." Cf. Tg. Ps.-J.; Frg. Tg. P; Klein, 1, 1986, 247.

Moabites;*ee* *their hearts* melted*ff* *within* all inhabitants *of the land* of Canaan.[15] 16. The fear *of you* and dread *of you* fall upon them.*gg* By *the* strength of the arm *of your strong might they stand silent* like stones until the time your people, O Lord, have passed over *the torrents of the Arnon*, until this people which you *redeemed* passed over *the ford of the Jordan.*[hh][16] 17. You shall bring them in[ii] and *give* them *possession* on the mountain of the house of your possession; *the place*[jj] *set aside; the house of the Shekinah* which you have acquired[kk] *for yourself*, O Lord; *your sanctuary, O Lord*; your *two* hands have perfected it.[17] 18. *The children of Israel said: 'How the crown of* kingship *becomes you, O Lord! When your sons saw the signs of your wonders in the sea, and the might between the waves, at that hour they opened their mouths together and said: "Of the Lord is the kingship* before the world and *for all ages."'"*[mm][18] 19. For the horses of Pharaoh with his chariots and horsemen went

Apparatus, Chapter 15

ee Nfmg: "Moab. Trembling took hold of them; they melted in their hearts, of the inhabitants of the land."

ff P: "were broken."

gg Translating, with Hebrew, Aramaic imperfects as present tense: "fall" or "you cause to fall." P: "There fall (or: you made fall), upon them fear and fright; in the greatness of your might, they remain silent like a stone until your people, O Lord, crossed the Arnon, until this your people which you redeemed crossed over the fords of the Jabbok"; VN: "There falls upon them the fear of death and destruction; in the strength of the arm of your might, they are struck dumb like stones until these people which you redeemed pass over the fords of the Jabbok and the fords of the Jordan, until the time these people which you acquired for your name have passed over." Nfmg: "the fear of death and destruction, in the strength"; = VN.

hh Nfmg: "the fords of the Jordan until the time these people which you acquired for your name have passed over" = VN.

ii In v. 17 Nf = P, with minor variants; VN: "you shall bring them in and plant them on the mountain of the place of your inheritance, the dwelling place of the Shekinah of your holiness. You appointed (read with Nf: "prepared") for yourself, O Lord, a sanctuary; O Lord, your two hands have perfected it."

jj Nfmg: "in the dwelling place of the Shekinah of your holiness, O Lord, which you prepared for yourself, O Lord, your sanctuary, O Lord, your two hands perfected it" = VN.

kk Nfmg: "prepared."

mm VN: "when the children of Israel saw the signs and wonders that the Holy One, Blessed be he had worked for them beside the shore of the Sea—may his name be blessed for ever and ever—they gave

Notes, Chapter 15

[15]Hebrew has: "all the inhabitants of Canaan were melted." Cf. Tg. Ps.-J.; Klein, 1, 1986, 247.

[16]Hebrew has: "Terror and fear fell upon them: by the greatness of your arm they are as still as a stone, until your people, O Lord, should cross over, until the people whom you have acquired should cross over." Cf. Tg. Ps.-J.; Tg. Onq.; Frg. Tg. P, V; Klein, 1, 1986, 247; *Mek. RI Shirta* 9:115-117; *Sifre Num.* 34; *b. Ber.* 4a; *PRE* 42:5 in MS. Casanatensia 10. IV. 1: see M. Pérez Fernández. 1984, 300. Hebrew "acquired" is rendered as "redeemed" by Theod. and *alia exempla* in Field, 1875, 108; Pesh.; Frg. Tg. P, N; Klein, 1, 1986, 247.

[17]Hebrew has: "You shall bring them in and plant them on the mountain of your inheritance, the place which you have made for your dwelling, O Lord; the sanctuary, O Lord, which your hands have established." Cf. Frg. Tg. P, V; Klein, 1, 1986, 247. The house of the Shekinah features in Tg. Onq. and Tg. Ps.-J.; God's *two* hands in Tg. Ps.-J.; *Mek. RI Shirta* 10:38-42; *b. Ketub.* 5a. Vulg. has the sanctuary as "most firm." Nfmg and the Frg. Tgs. are aware that the earthly sanctuary corresponds to the heavenly: this is clearly stated in *Mek. RI Shirta* 10:24-28; *Exod. R.* 33, 3; *j. Ber.* 4:5; *b. Ber.* 33b; *Num. R.* 4, 13.

[18]Hebrew has: "The Lord shall reign for ever and ever." Close to Tg. Nf is the fragment in Klein, 1, 1986, 241; Frg. Tg. V is not far removed, and the exegesis finds clear echoes in the more extended paraphrase in Tg. Ps.-J. For extended discussion of this verse and its relationship with Rev 4:2-11, see McNamara, 1966, 204–8. Frg. Tg. inserts here the poem on the four Nights, discussed in notes on 12:42.

into the sea, and the Lord made return upon them the waters of the sea; and the children of Israel walked on dry land in the midst of the sea.[nn] 20. And Miriam, the prophetess, Aaron's sister, took timbrels in her hand, and all the women went out after her; *they danced* to the timbrels.[oo][19] 21. And Miriam answered them:[pp] *"Let us praise and glorify* before the Lord, the exalted, *who is majestic above the exalted and lofty above the lofty.* Horses and their riders *because they were exalted and pursued after the people, the children of Israel,* he cast them down *and buried* in the Sea *of Reeds."*[20] 22. And Moses made Israel journey from the Reed Sea, and they went out[qq] to the wilderness[rr] *of Haluza;*[ss] and they marched a *journey-distance* of three days[tt] in the wilderness and did not find water.[21] 23. And they came to

Apparatus, Chapter 15

glory and praise and exaltation to their God. The children of Israel answered and said to one another: Come, let us put the crown on the head of the Redeemer, who causes to pass but is not himself made to pass (away)(cf. Ps.-J), who causes change but is not himself changed, who is king of kings in this world and to whom also belongs the crown of kingship in the world to come. And his it is for ever and ever" (cf. Ps.-J); P: "Four nights are written in the Book of the Memorials. The first Night when the Lord was revealed upon the world to create it. The world was void and empty, and darkness was spread upon the face of the abyss, and in his Memra he was bright and illuminating (*wmnhr*; cf. VN, Exod 12:42) and he called it the First Night. The Second Night, when the Lord was revealed above Abraham, between the pieces, Abraham was a hundred years old and Sarah his wife was ninety years, to fulfill what the Scripture had said: Abraham, a hundred years old will beget, and Sarah his wife ninety years old will give birth. Was not Isaac thirty-seven years old the time he was offered on top of the altar? The heavens inclined and descended, and Isaac saw their perfections and his eyes flowed (with tears) to the height, and he called it the Second Night. The Third Night when the Lord was revealed against Egypt at the middle of the night. His left hand slew the first-born of the Egyptians and his right hand rescued the first-born of Israel, to fulfill what the Scripture says: My first-born is Israel. And he called it the Third Night. The Fourth Night when the world will have completed its (determined) end to be redeemed. The iron bonds will be broken and the workers of evil will be blotted out. Moses will come forth from the desert and King Messiah will come forth from Rome. The one will lead at the head of the flock and the other will lead at the head of the flock, and the Memra of the Lord will lead between them both. And they shall walk together. And the children of Israel shall say: To the Lord belongs the kingship in this world, and in the world to come his it is." This in other Pal. Tg. texts at Exod 12:42.

[nn] "And the Lord made return . . . the middle of the Sea" of v. 20 repeated through homoioteleuton.

[oo] P as Nf, but ends: . . . "all the women went out after her with the timbrel and in dance chorus; and they were dancing."

[pp] P: "And Miriam sang to them: Let us praise and glorify before the Lord, since he is exalted above the exalted and made himself majestic above the majestic and who in his Memra revenges himself of everyone who extols himself before him. Their horses and their riders, since they come against his people, the house of Israel, he cast them down and buried them in the Reed Sea." Nfmg: "And Miriam answered them: Let us praise and glorify before the Lord (lit.: Name) because he is exalted above the exalted."

[qq] P: "and they went."

[rr] Nfmg: "the land of."

[ss] MT: "Shur." P: "the wilderness of Haluza"; VN: "the way of Haluza."

[tt] P: "and they went three days."

Notes, Chapter 15

[19]Hebrew has: "after her, with drums and dances." Cf. Frg. Tg. P, V.

[20]Hebrew has: "And Miriam answered them, saying: Sing to the Lord, for he is very highly exalted; the horse and his rider he has thrown into the sea." Cf. Tg. Ps.-J.; Frg. Tg. P; fragment in Klein, 1, 1986, 247; and notes to v. 1. Vulg. issues Miriam's command in the first person plural.

[21]Hebrew has: "in the desert of Shur; and they journeyed for three days in the desert." For Haluzah, see Tg. Ps.-J.; Frg. Tg. P, V; Bienaimé, 1984, 10; for "a journey distance of three days," see Tg. Onq.

Marah, *ᵘᵘ* and they could not drink the waters from Marah because they were bitter; for this reason they called its name Marah. 24. And the people murmured *ʷʷ* against Moses, saying: "What are we to drink?" 25. And he *ˣˣ* *prayed before* the Lord, and the Lord *ʸʸ* showed him a tree, *ᶻᶻ* *and the Memra of the Lord took from it a word* of *the Law*, and he cast it into the midst of the water and the waters were made sweet. There he gave *ᵃ* statutes and the orders of judgments, and there he tested him. *ᵇ²²* 26. And he said: "If *you* listen to the voice of the *Memra* of the Lord, *your* God, and do *ᶜ* what is proper in his sight, and obey the precepts *ᵈ* and observe all his statutes, I will not set upon you all the *evil* plagues that I *have brought* *ᵉ* on the Egyptians, because I am the Lord *who* heals *you*."*ᶠ²³* 27. And they came to Elimah, where there were twelve springs *ᵍ* of water *corresponding to the twelve tribes of Israel*, and seventy *date* palms, *ʰ* *corresponding to the seventy* <ancients> *ⁱ* *of the Sanhedrin* of Israel. And they encamped there by the waters. *²⁴*

Apparatus, Chapter 15

ᵘᵘ In Nf and P lit.: "Marta," "the Lady."

ʷʷ PVN: "and the people quarreled. . . ."

ˣˣ Thus Nf, with HT; P: "And Moses prayed before the Lord and the Memra of the Lord taught him a word of the Law which is comparable to the Tree of Life, and he cast it into the waters and the Waters were made sweet. There he read to him statutes and legal ordinances, and there he tested him and he stood (firm) in his test"; VN: "and Moses prayed before the Lord and the Memra of the Lord showed him an oleander tree, and he threw it into the waters and the waters were made sweet. There the Memra of the Lord showed him statutes and legal ordinances, and there he tested him with the tenth test."

ʸʸ Nfmg: "the Memra of the Lord" = VN.

ᶻᶻ Nfmg 1°: "an oleander (tree) and he threw (it) into the waters and (the waters) were made sweet" = VN;

Nfmg 2°: "an oleander tree and he wrote on it the Distinguished Name (= the Tetragrammaton; Yahweh) and he cast it to the waters."

ᵃ Nfmg: "the Memra of the Lord showed him" = VN.

ᵇ Nfmg: "he tested him with the tenth test"; cf. VN.

ᶜ Nfmg: "and you do what is proper before him"; cf. P.

ᵈ Nfmg: "commandments."

ᵉ Nfmg: "that I have placed"; P: "that I have sent."

ᶠ Nfmg 1°: "who by my Memra heal you" = PVN; Nfmg 2°: "who heals by the Memra of the Lord."

ᵍ In Nf. Greek loan word *pēgē*; in Nfmg (which = VN) the regular Aramaic term is used.

ʰ N: "palm trees" (*dyqlyn*); Nf has composite *dqlyn dtmryn*).

ⁱ Missing in text; in VN. Orthographical variants in Nfmg, also found in VN.

Notes, Chapter 15

*²²*Hebrew has: "And he cried to the Lord, and the Lord showed him a tree; and he cast it into the water, and the water was made sweet. There he appointed for him an ordinance and a statute; and there he tested him." For Hebrew "cry" interpreted as "pray," see 8:8; it is assumed by *Mek. RI Vayassa'* 1:95-105; Josephus, *Ant.* IV.i.1. Tg. Nf does not give the species of the tree but understands it as a teaching of the Torah: so R. Simeon b. Yohai in *Mek. RI Vayassa'* 1:109-12 and the *dōreshē reshūmōt* in *Vayassa'* 1:113-15; cf. *Mek. RSbY*, p. 104. Le Déaut, 1979 (*Exode*) 129, notes how Tg. Nf of Gen 3:24 equates Torah with the Tree of Life; cf. Frg. Tg. P to that verse. The wood referred to here in Exod 15:25 is taken from the Tree of Life according to Philo, *De mig. Abr.* VIII §§36-37, and *LAB* 11:15. On the whole verse, see Bienaimé, 1984, 11–16; 42–44, and Levy, 1986, 384. Nfmg 1° and other Tgs. noted in the Apparatus identify the tree as an oleander, *'rdpny*: this is the view of R. Joshua b. Karha in *Mek. RI Vayassa'* 1:108-109. But there is debate about it, as in *Exod. R.* 23, 3. Nfmg 2° has Moses inscribe the Holy Name on this tree; so also Tg. Ps.-J. For the tenth test, see also Tg. Ps.-J. Plural "statutes and ordinances" is read by Vulg.

*²³*Hebrew has: "And he said: If you (sing.) will indeed listen to the voice of the Lord your God, and do what is upright in his sight and attend to his commandments and keep all his statutes, I shall not put upon you any of the diseases which I put upon the Egyptians: for I am the Lord your healer." For Nfmg's reference to healing by means of the Memra, see Hayward, 1981A, 119.

*²⁴*Hebrew has: "And they came to Elim, and there were there twelve springs of water and seventy palm trees; and they camped there by the water." See also Tg. Ps.-J. and Frg. Tg. V; *Mek. RI Vayassa'* 2:8-12 (R. Eleazar of Modi'im); *Mek. RSbY*, p. 105; Philo, *De Vita Mosis* I. XXXIV §188-89; Bienaimé, 1984, 47–53.

CHAPTER 16

1. And they journeyed from Elim, and all the congregation of the children of Israel[1] came to the wilderness of Sin which is between Elim and Sinai, on the fifteenth day of the second month, after they had come out from the land of Egypt. 2. And all the community *of the congregation* of the children of Israel murmured against Moses and Aaron in the wilderness, 3. and the children of Israel said to them: *"Would[a]—who will give—*that we had died[a2] *before* the Lord in the land of Egypt when we sat beside the fleshpots eating bread[b] to the full; for you have brought us out to this desert to kill all this assembly with hunger." 4. And the Lord[c] said to Moses: "Behold, I will make bread[d] *come down* from heaven for you, and the people shall go out and collect the daily *amount* so as to test them, whether they[e] *observe the precepts of the Law* or not.[3] 5. And on the sixth day they shall *set aside[f]* what they have brought,[g] and it shall be the double of the daily *amount* they collect."[4] 6. And Moses and Aaron said to all the children of Israel: "In the evening you shall know that the Lord[c] had led you out *redeemed[5]* from the land of Egypt. 7. And in the morning you shall see the Glory of *the Shekinah of* the Lord, and your murmuring has been heard *before* the Lord. And as for us, what *are we reckoned as,[h]* that you murmur against us?"[6] 8. And Moses said: "When[i] the Lord shall give you flesh to eat in the evening, and in the morning bread to the full, when[j] your murmuring which you murmured[k] against me is heard *before* the Lord. And as for us, what *are we reckoned as?[h]* Your murmuring is not against us but *before* the Lord."[7] 9. And Moses said to Aaron: "Say to all the congregation of the

Apparatus, Chapter 16

[a] This phrase "would . . . died" is in the Hebrew of the MT without translation (unlike, e.g., Num 11:29; Deut 28:67).

[b] Nfmg: "and we ate food."

[c] Nfmg: "the Memra of the Lord."

[d] Nfmg: "food."

[e] Nfmg: "(to test) you, whether you."

[f] Nfmg: "and they shall prepare."

[g] Nfi: "what they have gathered."

[h] Or: "of what importance are we?"; also in VN.

[i] "You shall know it," presupposed before "when"; cf. Ps.-J.

[j] Nfmg: "as food and provision for the morning to satiate you, for your murmurings with which you have murmured are manifest before the Lord. Not against us."

[k] Nfmg: (apparently to this word): + "in prayer."

Notes, Chapter 16

For particular studies of this chapter, see B. Malina, "The Manna Tradition in the Palestinian Targum," in *The Palestinian Manna Tradition* (Leiden: Brill, 1968); and G. Vermes, "He Is the Bread," in *Neotestamentica et Semitica,* Studies in Honour of M. Black, ed. E. E. Ellis and M. Wilcox (Edinburgh: Clark, 1969) 256-63.

[1] Hebrew has: "And all the congregation of the Israelites." Cf. Tg. Onq., and see J. Potin, 1, 1971, 204–7.

[2] Hebrew has: "Would that we had died. . . ."

[3] Hebrew has: "Behold, I will rain down for you bread from heaven . . . and gather a day's portion each day, so that I may test them, whether they will walk in my Law or not." On "come down" for "rain down," cf. notes on 9:18, 13. For the daily amount, *skwm ywm bywmyh,* cf. R. Eleazar of Modi'im, *Mek. RI Vayassaʿ* 3:23-25 (not so R. Joshua!); *b. Men.* 103b; *Mek. RSbY,* p. 106; *Tanḥ. Shemot* 20, and, very clearly, Vulg. For the "precepts of the Law," cf. Tg. Ps.-J.

[4] Hebrew has: "they shall prepare what they bring . . . what they gather day by day." See note to v. 4.

[5] For the addition of "redeemed," see 3:10.

[6] Hebrew has: "the glory of the Lord . . . against the Lord: and what are we, that you murmur against us?" On the glory of the Shekinah, see Chester, 1986, 80–81, and cf. Tg. Ps.-J. For "what are we reckoned as?," cf. Tg. Ps.-J.; Frg. Tg. V; *Mek. RI Vayassaʿ* 3:56-58.

[7] See note to preceding verse.

children of Israel: 'Offer sacrifice before the Lord because your murmuring *has been heard before the Lord.'*"[8] 10. And it came to pass that when Aaron spoke with all the congregation *m* of the children of Israel and they directed themselves[8a] to the wilderness, that the Glory of *the Shekinah*[9] of the Lord was revealed in the cloud. 11. And the Lord *n* spoke with Moses, saying: 12. "The murmurings *o* of the children of Israel *have been heard* before me:[10] speak with them, saying: 'At twilight you shall eat flesh, and in the morning you shall be filled with bread, *p* and you shall know that I *am* the Lord your God.'" 13. And it came to pass in the evening that quails *q* came up and covered the camps, and in the morning there was a *little cloud* *r* of dew round about the camp. 14. And the *little cloud* *r* of dew went up and, behold, (there was) on the face of the wilderness a thin substance, *s* in particles, thin like white frost, *t* upon the earth. 15. And the children of Israel saw and said one to the other: "What is it?" because they did not know (what it was). And Moses said to them: "It is bread, which the Lord has given to you to eat."[11] 16. This is the thing which the Lord has commanded: 'Gather from it, each man according as he can eat, an omer a head, according to the number of your persons, each one shall take according to the number that is in his tent.'" 17. And the children of Israel did thus, and they gathered, some more, some less. *w* 18. And when they measured with an omer, he who *x* took much had nothing over, and he who took little had no lack; each gathered according to what he could eat. 19. And Moses said to them: "Let no one leave any of it until morning." 20. And they did not listen to Moses, and some people *y* left some of it until morning, and it *bred* *z* worms[12] and became foul; *aa* and

Apparatus, Chapter 16

m Nfmg: "before all the people of the congregation."

n Nfmg: "the Memra of the Lord."

o Nfmg: "your murmurings are manifest before him" (corr. to ?: "before me").

p Nfi: "food."

q Nfmg: "and at evening pheasants (Greek loan word: *phasianos*: also in Ps.-J.) came up."

r Or: "layer"; Nf in both cases has *'nnyt*, a form otherwise unattested. The *Aruk*, MSS and editions, has *'nwt* (= *'anuta'* or *'anwata'*; also otherwise unattested), which Levy renders (*Wörterbuch*) as "layer" ("die Lage, Schichte"), derived probably from *'ny*, "to lie low" ("niedrig liegen"); Sokoloff, 1990, 413, *'nny* = "covering."

s "a thin substance," *dqyq mpsps*; also in P; M. Klein, "fine and flaky"; Sokoloff, 1990, 154, 441, "crushed," "spread out."

t Nfmg: "white, thin like hoarfrost"; VN: "like hoarfrost"; *Meturgeman* MS: "hoarfrost on the ground."

u Nfmg: "by the Memra of the Lord for you as food."

w Nfmg 1°: "one tribe more, another tribe less"; Nfmg 2°: "some and others; (this one more) and the other less."

x Nfmg: "the tribe (that)."

y Lit.: "and men"; Nfmg: "men; Dathan (Dathan repeated) and Abiram guilty men."

z Nfmg: *wrm rm* or *whm rm*. Read probably *wrmrm* (as V corrected; MS *wdmdm*) = "and it elevated" = reared, produced?: M. Klein, "it gave forth." If we read as *whm rm, rm* = "it lifted"; *hm* could be a variant to "it bred" (Aram.: *'bd*) and *whm* = "and grew hot," a variant to "rose upon it" of v. 21, where the *Meturgeman* has: "and when the sun grew hot it melted."

aa Nfi: "and it decayed."

Notes, Chapter 16

[8]Hebrew has: "because he has heard your murmurings." Cf. Tg. Onq.; Tg. Ps.-J.

[8a]For "directed themselves" or "turned," see note on 7:23.

[9]Hebrew has: "the glory of the Lord." Cf. Tg. Ps.-J.; Chester, 1986, 57–58.

[10]Hebrew has: "I have heard the murmurings of the Israelites." Cf. Tg. Onq.; Tg. Ps.-J.

[11]See Muñoz León, 1974, 357–58; Vermes, 1969, 256–58.

[12]Targum reads lit.: "it made worms": see the Apparatus for Nfmg and possible solutions of the somewhat confused text. Nfmg also names Dathan and Abiram as the guilty parties: so Tg. Ps.-J. and *Exod. R.* 25, 10; *Lev. R.* 13, 1; and cf. *Tanḥ. Teṣawweh* 11.

Moses became angry against them. 21. And they gathered it *every* morning, each according as he could eat; and *when* the sun *rose*[bb] *upon* it, it melted.[cc][13] 22. And on the sixth day they gathered bread in double quantity: two omers for each *head;*[dd][14] and all the lords of the congregation[ee] came and told Moses. 23. And *Moses* said: "This is the *word* which the Lord[ff] has spoken.[15] 'Tomorrow is a rest, a holy sabbath *before* the Lord. Bake what you will bake and boil what you will boil, and what is left over, set it aside for yourselves to keep until the morning.'" 24. And they set it aside until the morning as the Lord had commanded[gg] Moses, and it did not get foul and there was no worm within it.[hh] 25. And Moses said: "Eat it this day, because this day is a sabbath *before* the Lord; you shall not find it this day in the open field. 26. Six days you shall gather it, and the seventh day is the sabbath; on it there shall be none of it." 27. And it came to pass on the seventh day that some of the people went out[ii] to gather but did not find (any).[16] 28. And the Lord said to Moses: "How long do you refuse to observe my precepts *and my judgments?*[jj][17] 29. See that the Lord has given you the sabbath; therefore he gives you bread *(in) double portion* on the sixth day; let every one[kk] dwell *in his place;*[18] let no one go out from his place on the seventh day." 30. And the people rested on the seventh day. 31. And *the children* of Israel[19] called its name manna, and it is like the coriander seed, white and its taste is like pancakes[mm] with honey. 32. And Moses said: "This is the thing the Lord[nn] has commanded: 'Fill an omer of manna[oo] to keep for your generations so that they may see[pp] the bread with which I fed you[qq] in the wilderness when I brought you out *redeemed*[20] from the land of

Apparatus, Chapter 16

[bb] Nfmg: "set."
[cc] *Meturgeman*: "and when the sun grew hot on it, it melted"; cf. note *z* above; VN: "it melted."
[dd] Nfmg: "for a man" (or: "for each").
[ee] Nfmg: "of the people of the congregation."
[ff] Nfmg: "the Memra of the Lord."
[gg] Nfmg: "had spoken."
[hh] Nfmg: "had (not) become foul and neither had the worms gained control of it."
[ii] Nfmg: "wicked persons went out from the people."

[jj] Nfmg: "my commandments and the instruction of my Law."
[kk] Nfmg: "two days food: let every one reside."
[mm] *sisin*: pancakes made of cooked lentils and honey; VN v. 31b = Nf.
[nn] Nfmg: "the Memra of the Lord."
[oo] Reading *mnh* of Nf as "manna"; LXX: "of it," with HT and Ps.-J.
[pp] Nfmg: "my food that they might see."
[qq] Nfmg: "my food that I gave to eat."

Notes, Chapter 16

[13]Hebrew has: "but the sun became hot, and it melted." The readings in the Apparatus to this and the preceding verse reflect debates about when precisely the sun melted the manna. The fourth hour of the day was a widely agreed time: so *Mek. RI Vayassa'* 5:24-27; *Mek. RSbY*, p. 112; Tg. Ps.-J.; *b. Ber.* 27a.; *Tanḥ. B.* II. 66-67.

[14]Hebrew has: "two omers for one person."

[15]Hebrew has: "And he said to them: It is what the Lord spoke. . . ." LXX introduces both *Moses* and *word* here.

[16]For Nfmg, see note on v. 20.

[17]Hebrew has: "my commandments and my laws?"

[18]Hebrew has: "bread of two days. Let each man stay in his place." For the double portion, cf. R. Joshua in *Mek. RI Vayassa'* 6:17-19; *Mek. RSbY*, p. 114, Vulg. *cibos duplices*. For the command to each Israelite to dwell "in his place," cf. Tg. Ps.-J., which expands the ruling to include explicit reference to Sabbath halakhah, like *Mek. RI Vayassa'* 6:20-23; *b. Erub.* 51a.

[19]Hebrew has: "And the house of Israel. . . ." For "children of Israel," cf. LXX.

[20]On "redeemed," see 3:10.

Egypt.'" 33. And Moses said to Aaron: "Take a *flask* and put within it an omerful of manna, and put it aside before the Lord *as a testimony* to keep for your generations."[21] 34. As the Lord commanded Moses, so did Aaron set it aside before the Testimony to keep it. 35. And the children[rr] of Israel ate the[ss] manna forty years until they entered the land of *their* residences;[tt] they ate the manna until they entered the borders of the land of Canaan. 36. And one omer is the tenth part of *three seahs.*[uu][22]

CHAPTER 17

1. And all the congregation of the children of Israel journeyed from the wilderness of Sin, and their journeyings (were) according to *the decree of the Memra of the Lord.* And they encamped at Rephidim, and they had no water which the people could drink.[a][1] 2. And the people quarreled with Moses and said: *"Give*[2] us water that we may drink." And Moses said to them: "Why do you quarrel with me? Why do you tempt *before* the Lord?"[b] 3. And the people[3] thirsted for water there, and the people murmured[c] against Moses and said *to him:* "Why, we pray, have you brought us out of Egypt to kill *us* and *our* sons and *our* cattle with thirst?" 4. And Moses *prayed before* the Lord, saying:[4] "What shall I do to this people? Yet a little[d]

Apparatus, Chapter 16

[rr] Nfmg: "the people of."
[ss] Nfmg: "manna."

[tt] Nfmg: "of their encampments."
[uu] MT: "of an epha."

Notes, Chapter 16

[21]Hebrew has: "a pot . . . as something to be kept for your generations." For "flask," cf. Tg. Onq.; Tg. Ps.-J. Possibly Tg. Nf implies that it is of earthenware: so *Mek. RI Vayassa'* 6:65-70; *Mek. RSbY*, p. 116.
[22]Hebrew has: "the tenth part of an ephah." See Tg. Onq.; Tg. Ps.-J.; LXX; *Mek. RSbY*, p. 117; Grossfeld, 1988B, 47, who also cites *b. Men.* 77a.

Apparatus, Chapter 17

[a] Nfmg: "water to drink."
[b] Nfmg: "the glory of my Shekinah"; or more probably: "the Shekinah of (of the Lord)."

[c] Nfmg: "and (the people) disputed."
[d] Nfmg: "to these people? Behold, a little while and they will stone him" (corr. to: "me").

Notes, Chapter 17

[1]Hebrew has: "at the command of the Lord . . . and there was no water for the people to drink." For the "decree of the Memra of the Lord," see Tg. Onq.; Tg. Ps.-J.
[2]"Give" is a singular imperative, as in LXX; Pesh.; Vulg.; Sam.; Tg. Ps.-J. For the Targums of vv. 2-6, see Bienaimé, 1984, 61–67.
[3]"People" is singular in the Hebrew, as are the pronouns and suffixes. Targum reads plural; so also LXX.
[4]Hebrew has: "Moses said to the Lord. . . ." For Moses' prayer, see Tg. Onq.; Tg. Ps.-J.; and Josephus, *Ant.* III.i.7.

and they will stone me." [e] 5. And the Lord [f] said to Moses: "Pass before the people and take with you from among the *wise men* [5] of Israel, and the staff with which you struck the river you shall take in your hand and go. 6. Behold, *my Memra* shall stand *in readiness* [g] on the rock at Horeb, and you shall strike the rock and water shall come out from it, and the people shall drink." And Moses did so before the eyes of the *wise men* [5] of Israel. 7. And he called the name of the place *"His Temptation"* [h] and *"His Contentions,"* [i] because the children of Israel had contended and tempted *before* the Lord, [j] saying: "Does the *Glory of the Shekinah of* the Lord *truly dwell* among us [k] or not"? [6] 8. And *the lords* of [m] Amalek came and set *battle array* with [n] Israel in Rephidim. [7] 9. And Moses said to Joshua: "Choose for us *warrior* men, and go out and set *battle array* with [n] *those of the house of* Amalek tomorrow. Behold, I *will stand* [o] ready on the top of the height and in my hand the staff *by which signs were done before the Lord."* [8] 10. And Joshua did as Moses, *his master,* had said to him, setting *battle array* with [n] *those of the house of* Amalek, [9] and Moses and Aaron and Hur went up to the top of the height. 11. And it happened that when Moses raised his hands *in prayer,* [p] *those of the house of* Israel would prevail *and were victorious;* [q] and when he would withhold his hands *from praying, those of the house of* Amalek would prevail, *and they would fall by the sword.* [r][10] 12. And the

Apparatus, Chapter 17

[e] Nfmg 2°: a word of uncertain reading: *skyn'* or *sbyn'* = "(and) my life is in danger" (?); or: "our elders"; or: "the elders" (corr. to *sbyy'*, and as variant with HT to "wise men" of v. 5).

[f] Nfmg: "the Memra of the Lord."

[g] Correct? *mt'dt* of text to *mt'td*; Nfmg: "in readiness (*m'td*) before you."

[h] HT: *Massah.*

[i] HT: *Meribah.*

[j] Nfmg: "the place of the Temptation and of the wran-

gling, because the children of Israel had wrangled and because the Lord had tempted them."

[k] Nf text has "among them among us."

[m] Nfmg +: "of the house of."

[n] Nfmg: "opposite."

[o] Nfmg: "tomorrow I will stand."

[p] P +: "toward his Father who is in heaven."

[q] P +: "in battle"; otherwise P = Nf in v. 11.

[r] VN: "and they fell in the battle array." Otherwise VN= Nf in v. 11.

Notes, Chapter 17

[5] Hebrew has "elders" for "wise men": see note to 3:16. For the rendering of v. 6, cf. Muñoz León, 1974, 359; Bienaimé, 1984, 285.

[6] Hebrew has: "And he called the name of the place Massah and Meribah. . . . Is the Lord in our midst or not?"

[7] Hebrew has: "Then came Amalek and fought with Israel in Rephidim." See Tg. fragment in Klein, 1, 1986, 263, which, however, lacks "lords."

[8] Hebrew has: "Choose for us men, and go out, fight against Amalek: tomorrow I shall stand on the top of the hill, and the rod of God shall be in my hand." See also fragment in Klein, 1, 1986, 253 (almost *verbatim*). Tg. Ps.-J. has the main elements of Nf's exegesis but adds material, some of which is found in Nf of v. 12. Tg. Onq. has the addition relating to the rod, on which see note to 4:20. The military aspect of the preparations is stressed in Josephus, *Ant.* III.ii.3; *Exod. R.* 26, 3; "men" are understood as "warriors" by R. Eleazar of Modi'im in *Mek. RI Amalek* 1:88; cf. *Mek. RSbY*, p. 120; *Tanḥ. Beshallaḥ* 26; *PRE* 44,1-2.

[9] Hebrew has: "And Joshua did as Moses had said to him, so as to fight with Amalek." Cf. Klein, 1, 1986, 253; for Moses *and* Aaron, see LXX.

[10] Hebrew has: "And it was, that when Moses held up his hand, Israel prevailed; but when he let his hand rest, then Amalek prevailed." Cf. very closely related Tg. fragment in Klein, 1, 1986, 253; Frg. Tg. P, V, Tg. Ps.-J. For "prayer," see *PRE* 44:2; *b. Rosh Hash.* 29a; and *Mek. RI Amalek* 1:119-123, which tells of Moses raising his hand "to heaven," which is similar to Frg. Tg. P. See further Bienaimé, 1984, 65, and H. Maneschg, 1981, 215–48.

hands of Moses were *raised in prayer*; and they took a stone and placed it under him and he sat on it, and Aaron and Hur *took hold of* his hands,[s] one at one *side* and one at the other[t] *side*. And the hands *of Moses* were *raised in prayer, recalling the faith of the pious fathers Abraham, Isaac and Jacob, and recalling the faith of the pious mothers Sarah, Rebekah, Rachel and Leah* until the setting of the sun."[11] 13. And Joshua *blotted out* Amalek and his people[12] at the edge[w] of the sword. 14. And the Lord[x] said to Moses: "Write this as a *good* memorial[13] in a book and place it in the hearing (of)[y] Joshua, that I will surely blot out[z] the memory of Amalek from beneath the heavens." 15. And Moses built an altar and prayed[aa] there in the name of *the Memra of* the Lord *who had worked signs for him.*[14]

Apparatus, Chapter 17

[s] Nfmg: "of his two hands."
[t] Lit.: (as P): "one at this side and one at this side"; P continues "recalling the faith of the three pious fathers who are comparable to the mountains, Abraham, Isaac and Jacob, and the faith of the four pious mothers who are comparable to the hills, Sarah, Rebekah, Rachel and Leah. And his hands were raised in prayer until the setting (lit.: sinkings) of the sun."
[u] Lit.: "until the sinkings of the sun"; Nfmg: "raised in prayer until the sinkings of the sun" = P.

[w] Nfmg: "the curse of the Lord is the death penalty, and he smote (Amalek . . .) with the edge (of the sword)."
[x] Nfmg: "the Memra of the Lord."
[y] Text: "and (Joshua)."
[z] Nfmg: "You shall blot out the memory of."
[aa] CTg J: "An altar, and worshiped and prayed"; otherwise CTg J v. 15 = Nf. Nfmg: "the altar (= an altar) and worshiped."

Notes, Chapter 17

[11]Hebrew has: "Now Moses' hands were heavy . . . then Aaron and Hur supported his hands, one on the one side, and the other on the other side: so his hands were firm (*'mwnh*) until the sun went down." Very similar is Frg. Tg. P; Klein, 1, 1986, 253, has a shorter form of the paraphrase; and Tg. Onq. refers to Moses' prayer. It is the word *'mwnh* which triggers the reference to the patriarchs and matriarchs, as in *Mek. RI Amalek* 1:148-152 (R. Eleazar of Modi'im as opposed to R. Joshua); *Mek. RSbY*, pp. 121, 122; *Exod. R.* 26, 3; cf. also *PRE* 44, 2. The comments of Nf and of those rabbinic texts which refer to the merits of the patriarchs and matriarchs are based on the traditional notion that the words "mountains" and "hills" may properly represent in similitude the pious ancestors of Israel; see especially *Sifre Deut.* 414. Earlier in this chapter (17:9), Ps.-J. had already interpreted Moses' standing "on top of the hill" as a reference to the patriarchs, matriarchs, and their merits: the same kind of exegesis is found also in Ps.-J., Nf, and Frg. Tg. P, V of Gen 49:26; Num 23:9; and Deut 33:15. But Nf of this verse has made a further exegetical "jump" by referring Hebrew *'mwnh*, "firmness" or "faith," to the ancestors, something which is stated just as clearly in Frg. Tg. P of this verse. Nf's interpretation seems to proceed from this Hebrew word's association with the words "justice" and "*mountains* of God" in Ps 36:6-7, to forge a link with the "mountains" who, by traditional exegesis, symbolize Israel's forefathers. On the merits of the matriarchs, see further S. Schechter, 1961, 172–73; and for discussion of the Targumic verses listed here, see R. Syrén, 1986, 58–60; 125–26.

[12]Hebrew has: "So Joshua laid Amalek and his people low." Cf. Klein, 1, 1986, 253; Kasher, *Torah Shelemah*, vol. 14, 266; *PRK* 3, 1.

[13]On the *good* memorial, see note to 12:14; Klein, 1, 1986, 253, and discussion in *Pes. R.* 12:1; *Tanḥ. Noaḥ* 9.

[14]Hebrew has: "and he called its name YHWH-Nissi." See fragment in Klein, 1, 1986, 253, for "worshiped and prayed"; Tg. Onq., Klein, 1, 1986, 255, have "the Lord who worked signs for him." Tg. Nf and Tg. Ps.-J. seem to exclude the naming of the altar by Moses, which would possibly be in line with the view of R. Eleazar of Modi'im, as against that of R. Joshua, that God called its name Nissi, since God performed the miracle for his own sake: so *Mek. RI Amalek* 2:163-70; cf. *Mek. RSbY*, p. 126; *Tanḥ. Beshallaḥ* 28. This tradition seems to be an old one: according to Josephus, *Ant.* III.ii.5, Moses named God, not the altar. See further Le Déaut, 1979 (*Exode*) 145. On the Name of the Memra, see note to 4:31.

16. And he said: [bb] *"An oath has gone out from beneath the throne of the Glory of the Lord of all the world: The first (king)* [cc] *who is to arise* [dd] *from the tribe of Benjamin shall be Saul, the son of Kish. He shall wage war on* [ee] *the house of Amalek and shall kill kings with rulers; and Mardocai and Esther shall blot out what remains of* [ff] *them."* And the Lord decreed in his Word to blot out the memory of Amalek for all generations. [15]

CHAPTER 18

1. And Jethro, the *lord* of Midian, Moses' father-in-law, heard all that *the Lord* had done [1] for Moses and for Israel his people, that the Lord [a] had led out Israel *re-*

Apparatus, Chapter 17

[bb] P: "And he said: An oath has gone forth from beneath the throne of the glory of the Lord of all the worlds, the Lord: the first king who is to arise to sit upon the throne of the kingdom of Israel is Saul the son of Kish and he will set battle array against those of the house of Amalek, and what is left of them Mardocai and Esther will blot out. And the Lord in his Memra decreed to blot out the memory of Amalek for generation and generation." VN: "and he said: An oath went forth from beneath the throne of the glory of the Lord of all the worlds. The first king that is to arise is from those of the house of Israel is Saul the son of Kish. He will set battle array with those of the house of Amalek and will slay some of them, kings with rulers, and what remains of them, Mardocai and Esther will slay in Shushan the fortress. And the Lord decreed in his Memra to blot out the memory of

Amalek for generation to generation"; CTg J: "And he said: An oath < . . . . > the first king that is to sit upon the throne of the kingdom of Israel will be from the tribe of the sons of Benjamin. He is Saul, the son of Kish. He will set battle array with those of the house of Amalek and from among them he will slay kings with rulers. And what remains of them still, Mardocai and Esther will slay them. And the Lord (in text: Adonai) said in his Memra to blot out the memory of Amalek for generation and generation."

[cc] Correcting text of Nf, "hundred" (*m'h*) to *mlkh*.

[dd] Nfmg: "to sit upon the throne of the kingdom of the children of Israel, he is Saul the son of Kish and he"; cf. VN.

[ee] Nfmg: "against those of the house of Amalek" = VN.

[ff] Lit.: "in them"; Nfmg + MT: "of them."

Notes, Chapter 17

[15]Hebrew has: "And he said: For a hand is upon the throne of the Lord: the Lord will have war against Amalek from generation to generation." See Frg. Tg. P, V, and the various fragments in Klein, 1, 1986, 253, 255. The oath also features in Tg. Onq., and is suggested by the Lord's *hand* which he raises in oath-swearing, Deut 32:40; cf. Gen 14:22-23. R. Eleazar of Modi'im relates the oath at this point: see *Mek. RI Amalek* 2:174-75. For "Lord of all the world," see Chester, 1986, 365. The utter destruction of Amalek is predicted in Josephus, *Ant.* III.ii.5; cf. *Mek. RSbY*, p. 127. The repetition of the word "generation" gives rise to the exegesis that Amalek will be destroyed at various points in the future. There are references not dissimilar to the Targum in *Mek. RI Amalek* 2:12-14; *Mek. RSbY*, p. 127; but the tradition is found more clearly in *b. Sanh.* 99a; *PRE* 44:2, 5; *Tanḥ. Ki Teṣe'* 11.

Apparatus, Chapter 18

[a] Nfmg: "the Memra of the Lord (had led out) the children of Israel."

Notes, Chapter 18

[1]Hebrew has: "the priest of Midian . . . all that God had done." For the "lord" of Midian, see *Mek. RI Amalek* 3:60-61 (R. Eleazar of Modi'im, as opposed to R. Joshua); *Tanḥ. Jethro* 5. LXX and Tg. Onq., Tg. Ps.-J. have "the Lord" for "God." On "redeemed," see note to 3:10.

deemed from Egypt. 2. And Jethro, Moses' father-in-law, took Zipporah, Moses' wife, after he had left her. 3. And his two sons, the name of one of whom was Gershom, because he said: "I am a stranger[b] and *a sojourner* in a foreign land"; 4. and the name of *the other* was Eleazar because: *"The Memra of* the God of my father[2] was at my aid[c] and delivered me from the sword of Pharaoh." 5. And Jethro, Moses' father-in-law, and his sons and his wife came to Moses to the wilderness where he was dwelling, *where the Glory of the Shekinah of the Lord dwelt.*[3] 6. And he said to Moses: "I Jethro, your father-in-law, am come to you and your wife and her two sons with h(er)."[d] 7. And Moses went out to meet his father-in-law and *saluted* him and kissed him;[4] and they exchanged words of salutation, one with the other, and they went into the tent. 8. And Moses recounted to his father-in-law all that the Lord,[e] had done to Pharaoh and to the Egyptians on account of Israel, all the distress that overtook them on the way and (how) the Lord[f] had delivered them. 9. And Jethro rejoiced over all the good that the Lord[e] had done for Israel, who had delivered them from the hands of the Egyptians. 10. And Jethro said: "Blessed be the Lord who delivered you from the hands of the Egyptians and from the hands of Pharaoh, who saved the people from beneath the yoke of bondage of the Egyptians.[5] 11. *Behold, now* I know and *it is manifest to me* that the Lord *is* mightier than the gods, *and Lord above all lords,* because by the thing *which the Egyptians devised* concerning *Israel—to cast their children into the river—by that* (same) *thing has the Lord revenged himself of them. The Lord* determined in his *Memra and buried their chariots in the Sea of Reeds."*[g][6] 12. And Jethro, Moses' father-in-law, took holocausts and sacrifices *of consecrated objects* for *the name of the Lord;*[h] and Aaron and all the *wise men* of Israel came to eat bread[i] with the fa-

---

Apparatus, Chapter 18

[b] HT: *ger.*
[c] HT: *'ezri.*
[d] Nf text: "with him."
[e] Nfmg: "the Memra of the Lord."
[f] Nfmg: "the Memra of."

[g] Nfmg: "with that (same) plan Pharaoh (corr. to: the Lord) avenged himself of them, and buried their chariots in the Sea of Reeds."
[h] Nfmg: "from before the Lord."
[i] Nfmg: "to eat food."

Notes, Chapter 18

[2]Hebrew has: "because the God of my father. . . ."

[3]Hebrew has: "where he was camping at the mountain of God." Tg. Onq. and Tg. Ps.-J. refer to the Glory of God: see Chester, 1986, 161; *b. Ta'an.* 21b.

[4]Hebrew has: "and bowed down and kissed him." See note on 11:8: the rendering is similar to Tg. Onq., and cf. *Mek. RI Amalek* 3:165-69.

[5]On the yoke of bondage, see notes to 6:6, 7, and cf. *Mek. RI Amalek* 3:201-2.

[6]For Jethro's confession, see J.R. Baskin, 1983, 47–61. Unlike Tg. Ps.-J., which made of Jethro a convert to Judaism (Exod 18:6-7, 27), Tg. Nf is somewhat lukewarm, even though Jethro confesses the God of Israel as "Lord above all lords": he does not unambiguously espouse monotheism as he does in Tg. Onq. On the "measure for measure" principle in punishment, see Tg. Ps.-J. *Mek. RI Amalek* 3:215-17; *Mek. RSbY*, p. 131; *Exod. R.* 22, 1; *Tanḥ. Jethro* 7, and Levy, 1986, 390.

ther-in-law of Moses before *the Lord.*[7] 13. And it came to pass that on the follow-ing *day* Moses sat to judge the people, and the people stood *before* Moses from morning until evening.[8] 14. And the father-in-law of Moses saw all that he was doing for the people, and he said: "What is this thing that you are doing for the people? Why do you sit alone and all the people stand about you from morning until evening?" 15. And Moses said to his father-in-law: "Because the people come to me to seek *instruction from before the Lord.*[9] 16. When they have an affair of *judgment of words*, they come to me and I judge between man and his neighbor, and I make *them* know the statutes of *the Lord and the decrees of the Law.*"[10] 17. And Moses' father-in-law said to him: "This thing which you are doing is not good. 18. Both you and these people who are with you are tired because the thing is too hard for you; you cannot do it alone. 19. Now, listen to my voice: I will give you advice and *the Lord*[e] will be with you; be, you, for the people *as one seeking in-struction from before the Lord*, and you shall bring the words *before the Lord.*[11] 20. And you shall explain to them the statute and *the decree*[j] *of the Law*,[12] and you shall make known to them the way in which they must walk and the thing[k] they must do. 21. And you shall look out for men from all the people, men of valor, who fear *before* the Lord, trustworthy[m] men, who hate *wealth (unjustly gained)*,[n][13] and you shall appoint them lords of thousands and lords of hundreds and lords of fifty and lords of ten. 22. And they shall judge the people at all times;[o] and every major affair they shall bring to you, and every minor affair they themselves shall judge; and (the burden) shall be made light[p] for you, and they shall bear (it) with you.

Apparatus, Chapter 18

[j] Nfmg: "the instructions of."
[k] Or: "words"; Nfmg: "the deed."
[m] Nfmg: "true."
[n] Erased by censor.

[o] Lit.: "at every hour."
[p] Nfmg 1°: "minor affairs." Nfmg 2°: "a minor affair, they themselves shall judge, and it shall be made light for you and they will bear."

Notes, Chapter 18

[7]Hebrew has: "whole burnt offerings and sacrifices for God: and Aaron came, and all the elders of Israel . . . before God." Tg. Nf often renders Hebrew *zbḥ*, "sacrifice," as "sacrifice of holy things"; see, e.g., Exod 23:18; 24:5; 34:25; the same phrase may be used to render *šlmym*, the so-called "peace offerings," as, e.g., at Exod 20:24; 29:28; Lev 3:1. See fur-ther Grossfeld, 1988B, 29, citing *b. Zeb.* 116b. For "wise men" rendering "elders," see note on 3:16.

[8]Cf. Tg. Onq. for the opening of the verse.

[9]Hebrew has: "the people come to me to seek God." The exegesis occurs again in v. 19; 19:3, 4; and in Tg. Onq., Tg. Ps.-J. The "instruction" is, of course, instruction in the Law. Moses is depicted as a Torah scholar or rabbi giving legal ad-vice and rulings on the halakhah. Cf. here Vulg.: "seeking the decision of God."

[10]Hebrew has: "For when they have a matter, they come . . . then I make known the statutes of God and his laws." For "judgment of words," cf. Tg. Onq., Tg. Ps.-J., LXX.

[11]Hebrew has: "and may God be with you. Do you be for the people towards God; and do you bring the words to God." For "instruction from before the Lord," see Tg. Onq., Tg. Ps.-J., and above, v. 15.

[12]Hebrew has: "And you shall teach them the statutes and the laws."

[13]Hebrew has: "from among the people men of ability, fearers of God . . . who hate unjust gain." Cf. Tg. Onq., Tg. Ps.-J., *Mek. RI Amalek* 4:66-70 (R. Joshua), Vulg.

23. If you do this thing, and *the Lord*[14] (so) commands you, you shall be able to endure;[q] and this people likewise will go into their places in peace." 24. And Moses listened to the voice[r] of his father-in-law and did all that he had said. 25. And Moses chose *men*, men of valor, from all Israel and appointed them as heads over the people, lords of thousands and lords of hundreds and lords of fifty and lords of ten. 26. And they judged the people at all times;[o] the major affair they brought to Moses, and the minor affair they themselves judged. 27. And Moses let his father-in-law depart, and he went his way to his (own) land.

CHAPTER 19

1. In the third month,[a] at the time the children of Israel went out[b] *redeemed* from the land of Egypt,[c] on that *very* day,[d] they entered the wilderness of Sinai.[1] 2. And they departed from Rephidim and came to the wilderness of Sinai and encamped in the wilderness, and *Israel*[d bis] faced[e] there[2] towards the mountain. 3. And Moses went up *to seek instruction from before*[f] *the Lord*, and the *Dibbera*[g]

Apparatus, Chapter 18

[q] Nfmg: "the Memra of the Lord (commands) you and you will be able to endure."

[r] Nfmg: "to the voice of the words of."

Notes, Chapter 18

[14]Hebrew has "God" for "the Lord"; see Tg. Onq. and Tg. Ps.-J.

Apparatus, Chapter 19

[a] Ch. 19 in entirety in PV; vv. 1-8 in CTg J; in all cases only minor variants from Nf.
[b] V: "at the going out of."
[c] V: "from Egypt."
[d] Lit.: (as in CTg F, P, V, J): "according to the time of this day."
[d bis] CTg E: "all (Israel)."

[e] *kwwnw* (same verb in CTg J, rendering HT *ḥnh*, generally rendered "dwell" in Nf); Nfmg: "and they encamped" (= CTg F); cf. "encamp," Onq. and Ps.-J.
[f] P: "before the Lord."
[g] *Dibbera* = "divine voice revealing God's will to man"; same term in PVNL; CTg J: *dybyry*; in CTg F: *dbry dyy* ("the Dibbera of the Lord").

Notes, Chapter 19

For special studies on this chapter as a whole, see J. Potin, *La Fête juive de la Pentecôte*, 2 vols. (Paris: Cerf, 1971), and J. Luzarraga, *Los Tradiciones de la Nube en la Biblia y en Judaismo primitivo* (Rome: Pontifical Biblical Institute, 1973).

[1]On "redeemed," see note to 3:10. Hebrew has "on this day" for "on that very day": although Tg. Nf, Frg. Tg. P, V, and fragments in Klein, 1, 1986, 257, 261, stress this point, they do not specify the day, as do, e.g., *Mek. RI Baḥodesh* 1:42-44; b. *Shabb.* 86b; *Tanḥ. Jethro* 7.

[2]Hebrew has: "and Israel encamped there"; cf. Frg. Tg. P, and Klein, 1, 1986, 257.

of the Lord called to him from the mountain, saying: "Thus shall you say to *those of* [h] the house of Jacob and shall you relate to the *tribe(s)* [i] *of* the children of Israel: [3] 4. 'You have seen (all) [j] that I have done to the Egyptians [k] and (that) I have borne you *on the clouds of the Glory of my Shekinah* upon the wings [m] of *swift* eagles, and *brought you nigh to the instruction of the Law.* [n] [4] 5. And now, if you hearken to the voice of *my Memra* and observe my covenant, you shall be to my name a *beloved* people, [o] *as* a special possession from all the nations, because all the earth *is mine.* [p] [5] 6. And you shall be to *my name kings and* priests and a holy nation. [6] These are the words [q] you shall speak [q] with the children of Israel.'" 7. And Moses came and called the *wise men* of the people [r] and set in order before them all these words [s] which the Lord [s] had commanded him. [7] 8. And all the people answered to-

Apparatus, Chapter 19

[h] PVN: "to the men of," CTg J= Nf. Nfmg: "to the men of the house of Israel"= CTg F PVN.

[i] Nf: "tribe"; P, CTg J: "tribes"; CTg E, VN: "and you shall narrate teaching to the congregation of the children of Israel"; Nfmg: "to the women of the house of Jacob and you shall narrate to the men of the house of Israel."

[j] Nf: "the voice," *ql'*, probably error for *kl'* ("all"), as Nfi; CTg F, VN: "you have seen how I was avenged of the Egyptians and carried you upon swift clouds as upon eagles' wings and brought you near to the instruction of the Law"; P: almost as CTg F, VN, with variants "bore you up upon the clouds of glory of my Shekinah as upon swift eagles' wings. . . ."

[k] Nfmg: "that I was avenged of the Egyptians and carried you on swift clouds as upon eagles' wings"= VN. P, CTg J: "avenged of the Egyptians."

[m] Expressed by different words in P (*gdpy*) and CTg J (*gppy*).

[n] CTg F, PJ: "my law."

[o] Nfmg +: "another" (=distinct) (people); cf. VN: "as a people, another (= distinct) and beloved, as a special possession . . . ."

[p] Nfmg: "of the Name of the Lord is all"; = CTg F VN; P, CTg J: "of the Lord is all."

[q] "words" (*ptgmy'*); Nfmg: "holy (nation). These are the utterances (*dbyr[y]* or: commandments) which": = CTg F, VN, CTg J; P: "these are the praiseworthy utterances" (lit.: "praise of the utterances," *dbyry'*).

[q bis] CTg F = : "O Moses."

[r] Nfmg: "the wise men of Israel" = VN.

[s] Nf: *ptgmy'*; P: "all the praise of these utterances" (*dybry'*) = CTg F (but reading uncertain); VN, CTg J: "all these utterances" (*dbyry'*).

[s bis] CTg F +: "O Moses."

Notes, Chapter 19

[3] Hebrew has: "And Moses went up to God. . . . Thus you shall say to the house of Jacob, and declare to the sons of Israel." The exegesis is very close to the fragment in Klein, 1, 1986, 257, and Frg. Tg. P. For "seek instruction," see note on 18:15. For the *Dibberah*, see M. Ginsburger, 1891, 265–67; V. Hamp, 1938, 93–97; Muñoz León, 1974, 668–79; Chester, 1986, 115. Nfmg interprets the house of Jacob to refer to the women, the house of Israel to the men: so *Mek. RI Bahodesh* 2:6-7; *PRE* 41, 3; *Exod. R.* 28, 2.

[4] Hebrew has: "You yourselves have seen what I did to the Egyptians, and how I carried you on eagles' wings and brought you to myself." Cf. Frg. Tg. P, V; fragments in Klein, 1, 1986, 257, 261. For the instruction of the Law, see note to 18:15 and *Mek. RI Bahodesh* 2:20-21 (R. Akiba).

[5] Hebrew has: "And now, if you will truly listen to my voice and keep my covenant, then you shall be for me a peculiar treasure out of all the peoples: for all the earth is mine." Very close to Tg. Nf is material in Klein, 1, 1986, 257, 261; Frg. Tg. P, V. See *Jub.* 16:18; 2 Macc 2:18; Philo, *De sobr.* XIII §66; *De Abr.* XII §56. Tg. Onq. renders "peculiar treasure" as "beloved"; so do Tg. Ps.-J.; *Mek. RSbY*, p. 139; *Mek. RI Bahodesh* 2:48-49.

[6] Hebrew has: "And you shall be for me a kingdom of priests and a holy nation." See Frg. Tg. P, V; fragments in Klein, 1, 1986, 257, 261; and Tg. Ps.-J.; Tg. Onq. also has "kings, priests, and a holy people." Cf. Symm.; Theod.; Philo, *De sobr.* XIII §66; *De Abr.* XII §56; 1 Pet 2:5, 9; Rev 1:6; 5:10; and the extended discussion in Potin, 2, 1971, 218–30; McNamara, 1966, 227–30; *idem*, 1972, 148–59.

[7] Hebrew has "elders" for "wise men": cf. Frg. Tg. P, V; Klein, 1, 1986, 257–61; "set in order" stands for Hebrew "placed": so also Frg. Tg. P, V; Tg. Ps.-J.; Klein, 1, 1986, 257, 261, probably reflecting *Mek. RI Bahodesh* 2:82-83; *Mek. RSbY*, p. 140.

gether *in a perfect heart*[8] and said[*t*]: "All that the Lord[*u*] has spoken we shall do." And Moses brought back the words[*w*] of the people *in prayer before* the Lord. 9. And the Lord[*x*] said to Moses: "Behold, *my Memra will be revealed* to you in the might[*y*] of the cloud so that the people may hear when I speak with you and also[*z*] that they may always believe in *your prophecy, Moses, my servant.*"[9] And Moses related the words of the people[*aa*] before the Lord. 10. And the Lord[*bb*] said to Moses: "Go to the people and sanctify them this day and tomorrow and let them wash their garments, 11. and they shall be in readiness for the third day, because on the third day *the Glory of the Shekinah* of the Lord *will be revealed* to the eyes of all[*cc*] the people[10] upon Mount Sinai. 12. And you shall set bounds for the people round about, saying: 'Take care that you do not go up into the mountain or draw near to the *lower parts*[*dd*] of it; anyone who draws near to the mountain *shall surely be slain.*[11] 13. Let not the hand *of man*[*ee*] approach it, because he shall surely be stoned, or *arrows of fire* shall be hurled,[*ff*] shall *be thrust,*[*gg*] at him; whether it be beast or man,[*hh*] it shall not live.' When the trumpet[*ii*] is sounded,[*jj*] Moses and Aaron they *are authorized to* come up into the mountain."[12] 14. And Moses went down from the mountain to the people, and he sanctified the people; and they washed their garments. 15. And he said to the people: "Be in readiness for three days; let

---

Apparatus, Chapter 19

[*t*] P, CTg J: "answered together and said."

[*u*] Nfmg: "the Memra of the Lord" = CTg F, PVNJ.

[*w*] *mlyhwn*; Nfmg: "the words (*ptgmy*) of the people"= VN, CTg J.

[*x*] Nfmg: "the Memra of the Lord" = CTg F, PVN.

[*y*] CTg F, VN; "in the thick of"; cf. Onq., and Ps.-J.; word glossed in CTg F as "might" (Nf's term).

[*z*] CTg F, P: "likewise."

[*aa*] CTg F, PVN +: "in prayer."

[*bb*] Nfmg: "the Memra of the Lord" = PVN.

[*cc*] Nfmg: "the Memra of the Lord will be revealed, all (the people) seeing"; = VN; CTg F, P: "the Memra of the Lord will be revealed opposite all the people."

[*dd*] Nfmg: "the edges"; = CTg F; VN, P = Nf. CTg F has: "its edges, its lower parts"; the first term deleted through dots.

[*ee*] CTg F: "of a son of man"; P: "of death" (= of the executioner).

[*ff*] Reading uncertain (correcting *ygrr* [last *r* deleted in text] to *ygrw*); absent from CTg F, PVN.

[*gg*] Nfmg: "will be shot at him"; = VN; CTg F: "shall be thrust and shall be shot at him"; P = Nf.

[*hh*] CTg F, P: "son of man."

[*ii*] Nfmg: "the horn."

[*jj*] Nfmg: "at the sound of the trumpet they shall ascend the mountain."

Notes, Chapter 19

[8] "In a perfect heart" is an addition: see Frg. Tg. V; Klein, 1, 1986, 261. The expression is used in exegesis of v. 2 by Tg. Ps.-J.; *Mek. RI Baḥodesh* 1:110-11; 2:85-86; *Mek. RSbY*, p. 140; *Lev. R.* 9, 9.

[9] Hebrew has: "Behold, I am coming to you in a thick cloud . . . and also that they may believe in you for ever." For the revelation of the Memra, see Frg. Tg. P, V; Klein, 1, 1986, 259, 261; and Chester, 1986, 131–32. The same Targums also refer to the prophecy of Moses the servant. It is proper for Israel to believe in God *alone*; hence Targum specifies that, as regards Moses, it is his prophetic words that are to be accepted.

[10] Hebrew has: "for on the third day the Lord will come down in the sight of all the people." Tg. Nf alone has reference to the Glory of the Shekinah. For the other Targums, see Chester, 1986, 110–11.

[11] Hebrew has: "touch its border: whoever touches the mountain shall surely be put to death." Cf. Tg. Onq.; Tg. Ps.-J.; Frg. Tg. V; Klein, 1, 1986, 259–61.

[12] Hebrew has: "Let no hand touch it: he shall surely be stoned or entirely shot through; whether beast or man, he shall not live. When the horn sounds, they shall come up to the mountain." The exegesis of Tg. Ps.-J. is similar: see also Frg. Tg. V; Klein, 1, 1986, 261.

no man of you have marital intercourse." kk 13 16. And on the third day, *at* the morning *time*, 14 there were thunders and lightnings and a thick cloud upon the mountain, and the trumpet, mm which was very strong, and all the people that were in the camp trembled. 17. And Moses led out the people from the camp to meet *the Glory of the Shekinah of the Lord,* nn and they stood in readiness *at the foot* of the mountain. 15 18. And Mount Sinai, all of it, smoked, oo because *the Glory of the Shekinah of* the Lord *was revealed* upon it in fire; 16 and the smoke went up like the smoke of a furnace, pp and all the mountain trembled greatly. qq 19. And the voice of the trumpet went on growing very strong; Moses spoke *in a pleasant voice, and from before the Lord* answer was made to him in thunder. rr 17 20. And *the Glory of the Shekinah of* the Lord *was revealed* ss upon Mount Sinai, upon the top of the mountain; and *the Memra* tt *of* the Lord called to Moses *from* the mountain, uu 18 and Moses went up. 21. And the Lord ww said to Moses: "Go down, warn the people lest

Apparatus, Chapter 19

kk Lit.: "draw near for the use of the bed."

mm CTg F VN: "and the voice of the trumpet (was) very strong"; P: "and the voice of the trumpet was going and growing very strong."

nn CTg F: "to meet the Shekinah of the Lord"; P: "to meet the Memra of the Lord"; VN = Nf.

oo CTg F, P: "and Mount Sinai, all of it, smoked and was covered (?; *'ty*; corr. to *'tr*: "smoking"; cf. VN) because (lit.: "from before"; cf. HT) the glory of the Shekinah of the Lord was revealed upon it in flames of fire, and its smoke rose up like the incense (of) the smoke of a furnace and all the mountain was greatly shaken " = P; VN: "and Mount Sinai, all of it, smoked [. . . as in CTg F] . . . and its smoke went up as the smoke of a furnace, and all the people who were in the camp trembled."

pp Nfmg: "trembled and it was filled with the splendor of the glory of the Shekinah of the Lord, and the

smoke (or: incense) went up like the smoke (or: incense) of a furnace."

qq Nfmg: "in the flame of fire and the smoke went up like the incense (of) the smoke of a furnace and all the people who were in the camp trembled"; cf. VN.

rr CTg F; PV: "Moses used to speak, and from before the Lord answer was made (PVN: to him) by a sweet and pleasant voice"; P: "in a sweet voice and on a light chant" (to be corrected according to CTg F?): V: "in a pleasant voice."

ss Nfmg: "and the Memra of the Lord was revealed" = PV; CTg F = Nf.

tt PV: "The Debira (V: *dbyrh*; P: *dbr'*) of the Lord"; CTg F = Nf.

uu PV: "from the top of the mountain"; CTg F: "upon the top of the mountain."

ww Nfmg: "the Memra of the Lord" = CTg F, PVN.

Notes, Chapter 19

13 Hebrew has: "do not draw near to a woman." Cf. Frg. Tg. P, V; Klein, 1, 1986, 263; Tg. Ps.-J.; Vulg. "to your wives." See also *b. Shabb.* 87a; *Sifre Num.* 103; *b. Yeb.* 62a.

14 Hebrew has: "when it was morning"; cf. Frg. Tg. P, V; Tg. Ps.-J.; Klein, 1, 1986, 263. *Mek. RSbY*, p. 142, stresses that it was morning, not night: so also Josephus, *Ant.* III.v.2; Vulg.

15 Hebrew has: "to meet God . . . and they stood at the lower part of the mountain." For the Glory of the Shekinah, see Frg. Tg. V; Klein, 1, 1986, 263; and Chester, 1986, 66–67.

16 Hebrew has: "because the Lord came down upon it in fire"; cf. Frg. Tg. P, V; Klein, 1, 1986, 263; Chester, 1986, 112–14. For the smoke and furnace, see *Mek. RI Baḥodesh* 4:7-15.

17 Hebrew has: "Moses spoke, and God answered him with a voice." Tg. Nf is peculiar, asserting that Moses spoke in a pleasant voice, whereas other sources ascribe the pleasant sound to God's answer: so sources in Apparatus of this verse, and Tg. Ps.-J.; *LAB* 11:3.

18 Hebrew has: "And the Lord came down on Mount Sinai . . . and the Lord called Moses to the top of the mountain." See Chester, 1, 1986, 114–16. *Mek. RI Baḥodesh* 4:45-55 has references to the glory.

they press forward *before* the Lord to see, and numerous *multitudes*[xx] of them fall.[19] 22. And let the priests also, who *stand*[yy] *and serve before* the Lord, sanctify themselves lest there *be*[zz] *wrath from before* the Lord on them."[20] 23. <And Moses said to the Lord>:[a] "The people cannot go up into Mount Sinai because you have warned us saying: 'Set bounds to the mountain and sanctify it.'" 24. And the Lord[b] said to him: "Go, descend and take up Aaron with you; and the priests and the people shall not press forward to come up *before* the Lord, lest *wrath be*[c] on them."[21] 25. And Moses went down from *the mountain* to the people, and he said to them: "*Draw near; receive the ten words.*"[d][22]

CHAPTER 20

1. And *the Lord*[a] spoke all *the praise of* these words,[b] saying:[1] 2. *The first word*[c]

Apparatus, Chapter 19

[xx] Greek loan word *ochlos* (also in CTg F, PVN), (possibly = a large multitude?).
[yy] Nfmg: "who draw near."
[zz] Nfmg: "be enkindled" (lit.: "grow strong") = CTg F, P, VN.
[a] Missing in Nf; in CTg F, PVN.

[b] CTg F, PVN: "the Memra of the Lord."
[c] CTg F, PVN: "be enkindled" (lit.: "grow strong"); see zz above. P has : "lest a great wrath."
[d] *dbyryy'*, i.e., the (ten) commandments; same term in CTg F: PVN.

Notes, Chapter 19

[19] Hebrew has: "to the Lord to see, and a great number of them fall." Cf. Frg. Tg. P, V; Klein, 1, 1986, 263; *Mek. RSbY*, p. 145.

[20] Hebrew has: "And also let the priests, who draw near to the Lord, sanctify themselves, lest the Lord break out upon them." For "stand and serve before," see Frg. Tg. P, V; Klein, 1, 1986, 265; and, to some degree, Tg. Onq. and Tg. Ps.-J. There was debate about the identity of these priests. They were regarded either as the first-born, or Nadab and Abihu: see b. Zeb. 115b; *Mek. RI Baḥodesh* 4:71-74; *Mek. RSbY*, p. 145; *Num. R.* 12, 7. The language of Tg. Nf suggests that it identifies the priests as Nadab and Abihu: see Exod 28:1.

[21] Hebrew has: "to the Lord, lest he break out upon them." See Klein, 1, 1986, 265; Frg. Tg. P, V.

[22] Hebrew has: "So Moses went down to the people and said to them." Cf. Frg. Tg. P, V; Tg. Ps.-J.; *Mek. RI Baḥodesh* 4:92-93.

Apparatus, Chapter 20

[a] VN: CTg F: "And the Memra of the Lord spoke all the praise of these words (*dbyry'*) saying"; P: "and the Dibberah of (*dybryh*) the Lord spoke all the praise of these words (*dybry'*) saying"; Nfmg: "the Memra of the Lord."

[b] *dybyryy'*, i.e., the Ten Words or commandments.
[c] Text: *dbwryy'*, "words."

Notes, Chapter 20

For a special study, see G. J. Kuiper, "Targum Pseudo-Jonathan in Relation to the Remaining Targumim at Exodus 20:1-18, 25-26," *Augustinianum* 11 (1971) 105–54; and cf. Y. Komlosh, *The Bible in the Light of the Aramaic Translations* (Tel-Aviv: Bar Ilan University-Dvir, 1973) 259–67 (in Hebrew); Y. Maori and S. Kaufman, "Aspects and Implications of the Targumim to Ex. 20," *Textus* 16 (1991) 13–78.

[1] Hebrew has: "And God spoke all these words and said." For the *Dibberah*, see note on 19:3.

that[d] went out from the mouth of the Holy One, may his name be blessed, (was) like shooting stars and lightnings and like torches of (fire),[e] a torch of fire to the right and a torch of fire to the left. It flew and winged swiftly in the air of the heavens and came back,[f] and all Israel saw it and feared; and returning, it became engraved on the two tables of the covenant and said: "My people, children of (. . .)."[g] And it came back and hovered over the camps of Israel and, returning, it became engraved on the tables of the covenant and all Israel beheld it. Then it cried out[h] and said: "My people, children of[g] Israel, I am the Lord, your God, who redeemed you and led you out redeemed from the land of Egypt, from the house of slavery."[2] 3. The second word,[i] when it went out from the mouth of the Holy One, may his Name be blessed, (was) like shooting stars and like lightnings and like torches of fire, a torch of fire on

Apparatus, Chapter 20

[d] CTg F, v. 2: "The first word (*dbyrh*) when it went forth (from) the mouth of the Holy One, may his name be praised, (was) like shooting stars, like lightnings, like torches (*lpdyn*, Greek loan word), a torch (*lpd*) of fire to the right and a torch of fire (*'š'*) to the left. It flew and winged swiftly in the air of the heavens, and all Israel saw (*ḥmyyn*) it and feared it. And it came back and was engraved on the two tables of the covenant and said: People of the children of Israel, I am the Lord your God who redeemed and brought you out of the land of Eg(ypt) from the house of the bondage of slaves"; Nfmg: "when it (went forth)." Cf. P: "the first word (*dbr'*) when it went forth from the mouth of the Holy One, Blessed be, may his great name be blessed and praised for ever, (was) like shooting stars and lightnings and like torches (*lpdyn* = Greek loan word, *lampas*) of fire, a torch of fire (*nwr*) to its right and a torch of fire (*'š'*) to its left. It flew and winged swiftly in the air (Greek loan word *aēr*) of the firmament of heaven. It went and encircled the camp of Israel. It returned and was inscribed upon the tables of the covenant and was turned about (?*mthpk*) in them from side to side. And it cried out thus and said: My

people, my people (of the) house of Israel, I am the Lord your God who brought you out and redeemed you from the bondage of the Egyptians, when you labored under the hands of the Egyptians in the house of bondage."

[e] Correcting *nzr* ("crown, vow") to *nwr*.

[f] Nfmg: "and all Israel saw it and feared, and it came back and was inscribed on the two tables of the covenant and said: My people, children of Israel."

[g] Text of Nf apparently disturbed by insertion of the section ("And it come . . . . children of") from another source, possibly Oriental (*ḥz'*, rare in Nf for regular *ḥm'*, for "beheld").

[h] Nfmg 1°: "And thus it cried out and said, and all Israel beheld it when it cried out and said: My people, children of Israel"; Nfmg 2°: "and thus it cried out and said and all Israel beheld it."

[i-i] This section, ("when . . . . said") a repetition of that of preceding verse and absent from other texts, may be an insertion into Nf. CTg F, v. 3: "My people, children of Israel, you shall not have another God outside of me," but with the marginal gloss: "The second word (*dbyr'*), as it emerges from the mouth of the Holy One, may his name be praised."

Notes, Chapter 20

[2] Hebrew has: "I am the Lord your God, who brought you out of the land of Egypt, from the house of slaves." See Tg. Ps.-J.; Frg. Tg. P; fragment in Klein, 1, 1986, 265; Tg. Nf of Deut 5:6; Tg. preserved in Maḥzor Vitry; Philo, *De Dec.* XI §§46–47; Potin, 1, 1971, 280–98. The "first word" is specifically singled out by Josephus, *Ant.* III.v.5. The divine title "Holy One blessed be he" is discussed by S. Esh, 1957. For the fire imagery, see *LAB* 11:5, 14; *Mek. RI Baḥodesh* 9:26–28; *b. Shabb.* 104a; *PRE* 41:5. For the word's flight in the air and return, see 4 Esdras 3:19. That Israel saw it is the view of R. Akiba, *Mek. RI Baḥodesh* 9:3–5. It was engraved on two tablets: this is the view of "the sages," *Mek. RI Baḥodesh* 8:98–102, as opposed to the view that five commandments were engraved on one tablet and five on the other; cf. *Exod. R.* 47, 6. On the expression "my people, children of Israel," which is liturgical in character, see I. Elbogen, 1931, 188, 192; McNamara, 1966, 137–38. For "redeemed," see note on 3:10. On the nature and content of the doublet formed by this and the following verse, see R. Kasher, "Targumic Conflations in the Ms. Neofiti 1," *HUCA* 57 (1986) 10–11 [in Hebrew].

the right and a torch of flame to the left. It flew and winged swiftly in the air of the heavens and came back, and all Israel saw it and feared; and, returning, it became engraved on the two tables of the covenant and all Israel beheld it, and thus it cried out and said:[i] *"My people, children of*[j] *Israel*, you shall have no other God *beside me.*[3] 4. *You shall*[k] not make *for yourselves*[k4] (an image or a figure)[m] or any likeness (of anything) that is in heaven above or in the earth beneath or in the sea under the earth *beneath.*[n] 5. *You* shall not[o] bow down[k] to them or worship[k] *before* them,[p] because I am the Lord, *your* God, a jealous and *revenging* God who *takes*[q] *revenge with zeal on the wicked*, upon the *rebellious* sons, until the third and fourth generation on those who hate me; *when the so(n)s continue in sin after their fathers, I call them those who hate me.*[5] 6. *'But I observe* grace *and goodness*[s] to thousands *of generations* for the *just* who love him[t] and for those who observe my command-

---

Apparatus, Chapter 20

[j] P for v. 3: "My people, my people (of the) house of Israel, you shall not have another God outside of me, since I all alone created the whole world, and there was no other God together with me; thus also you shall not kneel down to another God but only to the one to whom the power belongs."

[k] In Nf and CTg F in plural; in P as in MT, in singular.

[m] Erased by censor; in CTg F; P: "an image."

[n] In v. 4 CTg F as Nf, with minor differences; P adds at end "below the earth, because all of them have I created in six days and they tremble before me when they go forth and bow down before me in great fear; so also shall you bow down before me in great fear."

[o] P: "You shall not bow down to them nor shall you worship them because I am the Lord your God, a God jealous and revenging, who takes revenge with zeal; for I will eventually collect my due from all who bow down to them provoking anger (correcting

text from: "bowing down") before me. And I will also execute judgment on (lit.: "of") them because they bowed down to them, created beings, for I am the God who visits the sins of wicked fathers on rebellious children until the third and the fourth generation, on those who hate me, when the children continue to sin after their fathers, because they rebelled before me and because they transgressed my words." CTg F = Nf, with variants as indicated.

[p] CTg F: "to their idols."

[q] CTg F: "and takes revenge, remembering the sins of the wicked fathers . . . on those who hate me"; Nf's ending absent.

[r] In Nf no separation between this and preceding verse. In v. 6 CTg F, P = Nf, with variants as indicated.

[s] P: "I observe goodness."

[t] "who love them," as in P; "love me," Nfmg, CTg F.

Notes, Chapter 20

[3]Hebrew has: "You shall not have other gods before my face." See comment on v. 2, and Tg. Nf of Deut 5:7; Tg. Ps.-J.; and fragment in Klein, 1, 1986, 267. Note that Hebrew "gods" is changed to singular "God," as in Tg. Onq.; Tg. Ps.-J.; Frg. Tg. P; and Klein, 1, 1986, 267: for the significance of this change, see Grossfeld, 1988B, 54. For "beside me," cf. LXX. Vulg., like Tg., issues the command in the plural.

[4]Hebrew has: "You shall not make for yourself. . . ."

[5]Hebrew has: "You (sing.) shall not bow down to them or worship them; for I am the Lord your (sing.) God, a jealous God, visiting the iniquity of the fathers upon the sons to the third and fourth (generation) of those who hate me." Cf. very closely Frg. Tg. P; Tg. Ps.-J.; and Klein, 1, 1986, 267. For God's revenge and punishment of the wicked, see *Mek. RI Baḥodesh* 6:100-103; *Mek. RSbY*, p. 147. On the matter of the rebellious sons who continue their fathers' sins, see *Mek. RI Baḥodesh* 6:125-128; *b. Ber.* 7a; *b. Sanh.* 27b; *LAB* 11:6. On "I call them those who hate me," found in no other Targum, see Le Déaut, 1979 (*Exode*) 165, who cites Komlosh to the effect that the clause is a late gloss. The word "generation" is implied by the Hebrew, although not actually written; Tg. Onq., Tg. Ps.-J., Frg. Tg. P, and Pesh. all supply it.

ments.*[u]*[6] 7. *My people,*[w] *children of Israel,* let *no one of you* take the Name of the Lord his God in vain, because *on the day of the great judgment* the Lord will not acquit the one who shall take the Name of *the Lord his God in vain.*[x][7] 8. *My people,*[y] *children of Israel,* remember[z] the sabbath day to sancti(f)y it.*[aa][8]* 9. *[bb]* Six*[cc]* days shall *you* labor (and) do all *your* work,*[dd][9]* 10. *[bb]* and the seventh day is a rest *and repose* before the Lord *your* God. *You* shall do no work, neither *you* nor *your* sons, *your* daughters, *your* manservants, *your* maidservants, *your* beasts, nor *your* proselytes who are in *your cities.*[10] 11. *[bb]* Because during six*[ee]* days the Lord created*[ff]* the heavens, the earth, the seas and all that are in them, and *there was rest*

Apparatus, Chapter 20

[u] Nfmg: "the precepts of (my?; the?) law"; CTg F: "the precepts of my law"; P: "my commandments and my law."

[w] CTg F: "my people, children of Israel, no one of you shall swear in the name of the Memra of the Lord his God a false oath, because the Lord will not acquit the guilty in the day of great judgment, anyone who swears in his name and lies." This almost as Nfmg: "(no) one of you shall swear in the name of the Memra of the Lord your God falsely because the Lord will not acquit your guilt (corr. to: "the guilty" or "the guilt of") in the day of judgment, <anyone> who swears in his name falsely"; P: "my people, house of Israel, you (sing.) shall not take an oath in the name of the Lord your (sing.) God, and you shall not swear in my name and speak falsely, since I am the Lord your (pl.) great (and) avenging God, who is to take revenge of anyone who swears falsely in my name, because in my great name was the world created and anyone who swears in my name lying, it is manifest before me that on account of his sins I will devastate it for him. And anyone who guards himself and does not swear lyingly, it is

manifest before me that by his righteousness the world is sustained. And anyone for whose sake the world is sustained, it is profit for him (or: "happy is he") in this world and for the world to come."

[x] Nfmg: "who swears by my name lyingly"; cf. CTg F.

[y] Nfmg prefixes: "the fourth word" (*dbyr'*, i.e., Commandment); P: "my people, my people, house of Israel."

[z] CTg F: "be attentive to."

[aa] Emending a slight scribal error in text.

[bb] No separation in text between this and preceding verse.

[cc] Similar orthographical variant in Nfi and CTg F; CTg F: "in (during) six."

[dd] Nfi: "(all) work"; in v. 9, CTg F as Nf.

[ee] Identical orthographical variant in Nfmg and CTg F; Nfmg: "the Memra of the Lord (created) and perfected."

[ff] CTg F, v. 11: "For (in) six days the Lord created and perfected the heavens and the earth and the seas and everything that is in them, and he was rested himself on the seventh day. For this reason the Memra of the Lord blessed the sabbath day and

Notes, Chapter 20

[6]Hebrew has: "And performing steadfast love for thousands of those who love me and keep my commandments." See Tg. Ps.-J., Frg. Tg. P, and Klein, 1, 1986, 267. The "thousands of generations of the just" are suggested by *Mek. RI Baḥodesh* 6:134-143.

[7]Hebrew has: "You (sing.) shall not take the Name of the Lord your God in vain: for the Lord will not regard as innocent one who takes his Name in vain." For "my people, children of Israel," see note on v. 2. For "in vain," Tg. Nf, like Tg. Ps.-J., uses the phrase *'l mgn*. On this matter, see Grossfeld, 1988B, 55–57, who points to sources which distinguish between general taking of the Lord's Name in vain and its use in false oaths, e.g., *Pes. R.* 22:112b; *b. Shebu.* 20b-21a. Nfmg clearly relates the second occurrence of "in vain" to false swearing. Vulg. repeats "the Name of the Lord his God" at the end of the verse, like Tg.

[8]Hebrew has: "Remember the sabbath day, to sanctify it." Cf. Tg. Ps.-J.; Frg. Tg. P; Klein, 1, 1986, 267. For "my people," see note on v. 2.

[9]Hebrew has: "Six days you (sing.) shall work, and do all your labor." Cf. Tg. Ps.-J.; Klein, 1, 1986, 267.

[10]Hebrew has: "For the seventh day is Sabbath to the Lord your God." Hebrew has singular verbs and suffixes throughout, while the Targum has plural. Cf. Tg. Ps.-J.; Klein, 1, 1986, 267. Proselytes are presumably meant here rather than "resident aliens": so Tg. Ps.-J., Tg. Onq., and discussion in *Mek. RI Baḥodesh* 7:97-99.

and repose before him[gg] on the seventh day.[11] Because of this the Lord[hh] blessed the sabbath day and sanctified it. 12. *My people,*[ii] *children of Israel, each one shall pay attention to the honor of his* father and *to the honor of his* mother, so that *your* days may be many upon the land which the Lord *your* God gives to *you.*[12] 13. *My people,*[jj] *children of Israel, you shall not be murderers or companions or partners with the murderers,*[kk] *and murderous people shall not be seen in the congregations of Israel,*[mm] *lest your sons arise after you*[nn] *and they also*[oo] *learn to be a murderous people, because by the sins of murderers the sword goes out upon the world.*[pp] [13] 14. *My people,*[qq] *children of Israel,*[rr] *you shall not be adulterers or companions or partners with adulterers,*[ss] *and adulterous people shall not be seen in the congregation of Israel,*[tt] *lest your children arise after you*[uu] *and they also*[ww] *learn to be an adulterous people, because by the sins of the adulterer pestilence comes upon the*

Apparatus, Chapter 20

sanctified it"; P: "for (in) six days the Lord made the heavens and the earth and the sea and all that is in them and he rested on the seventh day. Wherefore, the Lord blessed the sabbath day and sanctified it. It is first among all the feasts and the most important (or: "stringent") of all the (fixed) times and the most desirable of the precious gifts (or: "stringent regulations") for the children of Israel is its Law. And everyone who honors the sabbath is the equivalent before me as anyone who honors me upon my throne of glory. For the reason of the honor of the sabbath, the children of Israel will inherit the world to come, the whole of which is sabbath."

[gg] Nfmg: "and he rested himself on the (seventh?) day"; cf. CTg F.

[hh] Nfmg: "because of this the Memra of the Lord"; cf. CTg F.

[ii] Nfmg prefixes: "the fifth word (or: commandment *dbyr[']*)." P: "my people, my people, house of Israel, pay attention to the glory of your (pl.) father and the glory of your (pl.) mother, since anyone who honors his father and his mother, I will give him length of days and plentifulness of years, because for the sake of the honor of father and mother I (will) make him possess the world to come." CTg F: "My people, children of Israel, be attentive each one of you to

the glory of (his) father and mother, so that (your days may be multiplied upon) the land which the Lord your God is giving to you."

[jj] Nfmg: "the sixth word (or: commandment, *dbyr(')* (my people)"; P: "my people, my people, house of Israel." In v. 13 P and CTg F = Nf, apart from variants noted below.

[kk] P, CTg F: "with murderers."

[mm] Nfmg: "murderers (in the congregations) of the children of Israel lest."

[nn] Nfmg: "their sons after them."

[oo] "also" not in P; Nfmg: "they likewise (learn to be) murderers."

[pp] Nfmg: "comes up on the world"; CTg F: "death comes upon the world."

[qq] P, CTg F = Nf, with variants noted below.

[rr] P: "my people house of Israel"; Levita, *Meturgeman*: MS Angelica: "my people, children of Israel, you shall not be adulterers"; Levita, *Meturgeman*, ed. Isny: "my people, house of Israel, you shall not be adulterers."

[ss] Nfmg: "to adulterers."

[tt] Nfmg: "adulterers (shall not be seen in the congregation) of the children of Israel."

[uu] Nfmg: "their children after them."

[ww] "also" not in P; P: "and they learn your ways."

Notes, Chapter 20

[11]Hebrew has: "the Lord made the heavens . . . and he rested on the seventh day."

[12]Hebrew has: "Honor your father and your mother, so that your days may be long upon the land which the Lord your God gives you." For "my people," see note on v. 2. Cf. Frg. Tg. P; Tg. Ps.-J.; and Klein, 1, 1986, 269.

[13]Hebrew has: "You shall not commit murder." Cf. Tg. Ps.-J.; Frg. Tg. P; Klein, 1, 1986, 269. The final five commandments have a formulaic type of exegesis in Targum, exhorting the congregations not to commit the transgressions or to associate with those who do, and warning of the consequences for future generations and the appropriate punishment for each sin. It is not paralleled exactly elsewhere and probably derives from a homiletic-liturgical milieu; *m. Aboth* 5:7-8, however, lists particular consequences for particular breaches of individual laws. For "my people," see note on v. 2.

world.[xx][14] 15. My people, children of Israel,[yy] *you shall not be thieves or companions or partners with thieves,*[zz] *and people who steal*[a] *shall not be seen in the congregation of Israel, lest your children arise after you*[b] *and they also learn to be people who steal,*[c] *because by the sins of thieves famine comes to the world.*[15] 16. *My people, children of Israel,*[d] you shall not be false witnesses *or companions or partners with false witnesses,*[e] *and people who give false witness shall not be seen in the congregation of Israel, lest your children arise after you*[f] *and they also learn to be people who give false witness,*[g] *because by the sins of false witnesses wild beasts cause childlessness*[h] *among the sons of man.*[16] 17. *My people, children of Israel,*[i] *you shall not be covetous or companions or partners with those who covet,*[j] *and covetous people shall not be seen in the congregation of Israel,*[k] *lest your children arise after you*[m] *and they also learn to be a covetous people.* No *man of you* shall covet the house of *his* neighbor, or *his* companion's wife, or *his* manservant or *his* maidservant, or *his* ox, or *his* ass or anything that belongs to your neighbor, *because by the sins of the covetous the ruling powers are incited against the sons of man.*"[n][17] 18. And all the

---

Apparatus, Chapter 20

[xx] Nfmg, CTg F: "death comes to (CTg F: "upon") the world."

[yy] In v.15, P, CTg F = Nf, with variants as noted below. P: "my people, my people, house of Israel."

[zz] Nfmg: "to thieves."

[a] Section: "and people . . . of Israel" absent from P; Nfmg: "thieves (shall not be seen in the congregation) of the children of Israel lest."

[b] Nfmg: "their children after them."

[c] Nfmg: "they likewise (learn to be) thieves"; CTg F: "they also to be thieves."

[d] In v. 16, P, CTg F = Nf, with variants as noted below. P: "my people, my people, house of Israel."

[e] Nfmg: "to false witnesses."

[f] Nfmg: "their children after them."

[g] Nfmg: "they likewise (to be) false witnesses."

[h] Nfmg: "the clouds go up and the rain does not come down"; CTg F: "the clouds go up" (remainder of

wording of verse lost); P: "the kingdom (or: kingship) is excited against the children of men, and exile comes upon the world."

[i] P as Nf except: "my people, my people, house of Israel . . . arise after you to be a people who covet and no one of you will covet his neighbor's wife nor his male servant, nor his female servant, not his ox, nor his donkey, nor anything belonging to his neighbor, because for the sins of the covetous the clouds go up and the rain does not come down and drought comes upon the world." CTg F (where preserved) = Nf, with variants as noted below.

[j] Nfmg: "to those who covet."

[k] Nfmg: "covetous (shall not be seen in the congregation of) the children of Israel."

[m] Nfmg: "their children after them."

[n] Nfmg and CTg F +: "and exile comes upon the world."

Notes, Chapter 20

[14]Hebrew has: "You shall not commit adultery." See note on v. 13. Cf. Tg. Ps.-J.; Frg. Tg. P; Klein, 1, 1986, 269. Philo, *De Dec.* XXIV §127, urges readers not to associate with adulterers.

[15]Hebrew has: "You shall not steal." See note on v. 13. Cf. Tg. Ps.-J.; Frg. Tg. P; and Klein, 1, 1986, 269.

[16]Hebrew has: "You shall not bear false witness against your neighbor." The penalty of wild beasts for this crime does not appear in the other Targums.

[17]Hebrew has: "You shall not covet your neighbor's house; you shall not covet your neighbor's wife, nor his servant, nor his handmaid, nor his ox, nor his ass, nor anything that is your neighbor's." Tg. Ps.-J. has affinities with Nf but the penalty here involves the stirring up of the ruling powers against mankind. See S. Lyonnet, "Tu ne convoiteras pas," in *Neo-Testamentica et Patristica* (Leiden: Brill, 1962) 157–65.

people saw the thunders and the torches *o* and the sound *p* of the trumpet and the mountain smoking, and the people *q* saw and trembled [18] and stood *r* afar off. 19. And they said to Moses: "Speak you with us and we will hear, and let it not *be spoken* with us *from before the Lord,* *s* [19] lest we die." 20. And Moses said to the people: *t* "Fear not, because it was to test you that *the glory of the Shekinah of the Lord has been revealed to you,* and so that the fear *of the Lord* *u* [20] may be upon your faces and that you may not sin." *w* 21. And the people stood afar off and Moses drew near to the cloud where *the Glory of the Shekinah of the Lord dwelt.* [21] 22. And the Lord *x* said to Moses: "Thus shall you say to the children of Israel: *y* 'You have seen that I have spoken with you from the heavens. 23. You shall not make *before* *z* me *idols* of silver, and *idols* of gold [22] you shall not make for yourselves. 24. An altar *you shall build fixed upon* the earth *aa* to *my Name*, and you shall offer upon it *your* holocausts and *your sacrifices of holy things* and *your* sheep and *your* oxen; in every place that *you* remember my Name *in prayer* *bb* I *will be revealed* to you in (my) *Memra* and I will bless you. [23] 25. And if *you build* an altar of stones to *my Name,* *cc* *you* shall not build them of hewn stones, because if you pass

Apparatus, Chapter 20

o Greek loan word *lampas*; also in CTg F.

p Nfmg: "sounds"; CTg F: "sounds," or "the sound," i.e., "sound of."

q CTg F: "all the people."

r CTg F, P: "stood praying."

s CTg F, VN, Nfmg 1° + 2°: "and let (not) the Memra of the Lord speak."

t In v. 20 CTg F = Nf, with variants, most of which are in Nfmg.

u CTg F: "the law of the Lord."

w Nfmg: "constantly on your mouth so that you may not incur guilt"; = CTg F, VN.

x Nfmg, VN: "the Memra of the Lord."

y Nfi: "in the people (of Israel)."

z VN: "before him"; CTg F: ". . . to act provokingly before me."

aa Nfmg, VN: "You shall make in (on) the earth."

bb Nfmg: "(in every) place to pray in my holy name, his (read: my?) Memra will be revealed to you and bless you"; VN and CTg F (insofar as legible): "in every place in which you recall my holy Name, my Memra will be revealed to you and bless you."

cc CTg F: "you built before me."

Notes, Chapter 20

[18]Targum renders "trembled," Hebrew root *nw'*, with *w'zd'z'w*: cf. *Mek. RI Baḥodesh* 9:42-43.

[19]Hebrew has: "but let not God speak with us": cf. Tg. Ps.-J. and Tg. Onq.

[20]Hebrew has: "God has come to test you . . . the fear of him." Cf. Frg. Tg. V; Klein, 1, 1986, 271. On the Glory of the Shekinah, see Chester, 1986, 133.

[21]Hebrew has: "where God was." Cf. Frg. Tg. V; Klein, 1, 1986, 271; Tg. Ps.-J.

[22]Hebrew has: "You shall not make me gods of silver . . . and gods of gold." For "before me," cf. Tg. Onq., and see Grossfeld, 1988B, 57.

[23]Hebrew has: "An altar of earth you shall make for me, and on it you shall sacrifice your whole burnt offerings, and your peace offerings, your sheep and your oxen. In every place where I make my Name to be remembered, I shall come to you and bless you." Cf. Frg. Tg. V and Klein, 1, 1986, 271. The altar is fixed on the earth, like the ladder in Jacob's dream, Tg. Nf of Gen 28:12; and see *Mek. RI Baḥodesh* 11:2-4; *Gen. R.* 82, 2. For the expression "to my Name," see note on 6:7. For "sacrifices of holy things," see note on 18:12. This verse is the proof that the Shekinah is present even with one person in a synagogue: so *Mek. RI Baḥodesh* 11:51-52; *m. Aboth* 3:6; *Tanḥ. Naso'* 26, *Wayyeḥe'* 10. Such use corresponds with the Targumic alteration: men call on God, and God blesses them; so also Vulg. But see also *b. Sotah* 38a, which seeks to safeguard God's unique Presence in the Temple.

iron, *(of which)* the sword *is made, over them,* you defile *them.*[dd][24] 26. *And you, priests, sons*[ee] *of Aaron, who stand and serve upon my altar,*[ff] *you* shall not go up by steps upon my altar[gg] lest your nakedness by revealed upon it.'[hh][25]

CHAPTER 21

1. "And these are the judgments which you shall place before them:[a] 2. When you buy a Hebrew slave, he shall serve six years *before you,*[b] and in the seventh *year you shall send him away* to freedom for nothing.[1] 3. If he came in alone, he shall go out alone; if he is married, his wife shall go with him. 4. If his master should give him[c] a wife and she bears him sons or daughters, the wife and her sons shall belong to her master and he shall go out alone. 5. But if the slave clearly says: 'I love my

[dd] Nfmg 1°: "of hewn stone because iron—the sword is made from it—if you pass iron over it you profane it"; = PVN; CTg F: "if (. . . text illegible) iron over them you profane them"; Nfmg 2°: "from it wars (read?: swords) of death have been made for all (?): take care that you do not unbare (lit.: "empty") your sword upon it lest you (lit.: "and you shall not") profane it." The scribe hesitates between "empty," *tryq,* and "lift up," *trym*; cf. Ps.-J.

[ee] CTg F, P: "and sons of."
[ff] P: "serve before me upon the altar."
[gg] Nfmg: "make a connection to the altar and do not go up by steps."
[hh] Nfmg and CTg F leave the ending in Hebrew ("lest . . . revealed upon it") untranslated; P omits.

Notes, Chapter 20

[24]Hebrew has: "And if you make an altar of stones for me, you shall not build them as hewn stones. For if you wield your sword upon it, you profane it." See Tg. Ps.-J.; Frg. Tg. P, V; Klein, 1, 1986, 271; *Mek. RI Baḥodesh* 11:85-89.
[25]Hebrew has: "And you shall not go up by steps upon my altar, so that your nakedness be not revealed upon it." Cf. Frg. Tg. P, V; Klein, 1, 1986, 271; Tg. Ps.-J. Nfmg appears to have in mind the ramp or bridges of Tg. Ps.-J.

Apparatus, Chapter 21

[a] CTg A (very early; 8th–9th cent. or earlier) extant for most of ch. 21; almost verbatim as Nf. Variants noted below.

[b] Nfmg: "(six years) of days he shall serve with you."
[c] CTg A: "to him."

Notes, Chapter 21

[1]Cf. Deut 15:13. Hebrew *ḥpšy,* "free," becomes *lḥyrwth,* "to freedom"; cf. Tg. Onq., Tg. Ps.-J., where he becomes *lbr ḥwryn.*

master, my wife and my children; I will not go out to freedom,' 6. his master will bring *d* him to *the judges*,[2] and he will bring him to the door or to the doorposts; *e* and his master will pierce his ear with an awl, and he will be a slave to him, *enslaved* forever.*f* 7. And when a man sells his daughter as a slave, she shall not go out according to *the laws*[g] of the male slaves.[3] 8. If she is displeasing in the sight*h* of her master, who does not designate her, then he shall let her be redeemed; but he will not have the power*i* to sell her to a *gentile man*, because he has *given up his power* over her.[4] 9. And if he designates her for his son, he will deal with her according to the order of judgment for daughters.*j*[5] 10. If he takes another*k* (wife) to himself, he shall not withhold her food, her clothing*m* or *cohabitation*[n] (from her).*o*[6] 11. And if he does not do those three *things* for her, he will send her away to *freedom*, for nothing, without money.*p* 12. *Whoever* strikes a man and he should die shall surely *be put to death.*[7] 13. And for him who does not intend it,*q* and *whose sin happened from before the Lord*, (God) bringing (him) to his hands, I will

Apparatus, Chapter 21

d Correcting error in text; CTg A: "and his master will bring him near to the door of the house of judgment or to the doorposts; and his master will perforate his ear . . . with an awl, and he will be for him a laboring slave."

e Nfmg: "to the door of the house of judgment or to one of the doorposts"; cf. CTg A.

f Nfmg: "and his master shall bore his right ear with a punch, and he shall serve with him until the Jubilee Year."

g Greek loan word *nomos*.

h Nfi: "in the eyes of"; cf. CTg A.

i Nfmg: "he is not empowered."

j Nfmg: "of the daughters of Israel."

k Nfmg: "and if (another) woman"; = VN.

m Text *tksyth* (= HT *kswth?*); PVN, Levita, *Meturgeman*: *tksyth*: "her ornaments"; Nfmg: "besides (?) her, her ornaments, her articles of"; also in Nf 22:26; Sokoloff, 1990, 581:*tksy* = "garment".

n Lit.: "his going and coming out to her."

o Added explicitly in PVN.

p Nfmg: "he shall have (her) redeemed, free, without (money)."

q Nfmg: "he did (not) intend to strike him."

Notes, Chapter 21

[2]"Judges" represents Hebrew *'lhym*, "God": so Tg. Onq.; Tg. Ps.-J.; Pesh.; *Mek. RI Nezikin* 2:51-52; *j. Qidd.* 1:2. LXX have "the judgment seat of God"; cf. Nfmg. There was discussion whether the slave were to serve his master in perpetuity or only until the Jubilee year. Tg. Nf, Tg. Onq. indicate the former position, Nfmg and Tg. Ps.-J. the latter: see *Mek. RI Nezikin* 2:91-98, *b. Qidd.* 17b; *j. Qidd.* 1:2; *Sifra 'Emor* 4.

[3]Hebrew has, lit.: "according to the going out of (male) slaves." See *Mek. RI Nezikin* 3:56-57; *b. Qidd.* 18a; *j. Qidd.* 1:2.

[4]Hebrew has: "to sell her to a foreign people, *l'm nkry*, because he has acted deceitfully, *bbgdw*, with her." *Mek. RI Nezikin* 3:86-87 interprets *l'm nkry* as "Gentile." Targum understands *bbgdw* as though it were connected with *bgd*, "garment": the spreading of a garment over a woman constitutes a man's authority over her, according to Ruth 3:9. For the exegesis, see *b. Qidd.* 18ab (R. Akiba); *Mek. RI Nezikin* 3:94-95; and comments of Le Déaut, 1979 (*Exode*) 165; Grossfeld, 1988B, 59-60.

[5]Nfmg specifies that daughters of Israel are meant: so Tg. Ps.-J., a position adopted by R. Josiah and challenged by R. Jonathan in *Mek. RI Nezikin* 3:103-111.

[6]See Frg. Tg. P, V; Tg. Ps.-J.; *Mek. RI Nezikin* 3:118-19 (R. Josiah); *b. Ketub.* 47b-48a.

[7]"Whoever" is added, to yield the sense: Hebrew has: "and one smiting. . . ." "He shall surely be put to death," *mtqtl' ytqtl*, lit.: "he shall surely be killed" is the constant rendering of the words *mwt ywmt* in this Targum; cf. here Tg. Onq. and Tg. Ps.-J.

appoint for *you* a place, *a city of refuge*, to where you can flee.[r]8 14. <And if>[s] a man <willfully attacks>[s] another to kill him treacherously,[t] *even if he is the high priest who stands and serves at* my altar, *you* shall take him *from there and you shall kill him.*[9] 15. And *whoever* strikes[u] his father or his mother *shall be surely put to death.*[10] 16. And *whoever* steals a man, whether he sells him or (whether) he is found in his hand, he *shall* surely *be put to death.*[10] 17. <Whoever curses his father or his mother *shall* surely *be put to death*>.[w] 18. And when men quarrel,[x] and one strikes another with a stone or with the fist and he does not die, but is cast[y] on a *sick* bed,[11] 19. if he gets up and goes about the marketplace upon his crutch,[z] he who struck him[aa] shall be acquitted; only he shall pay *the wage of* his *enforced idleness* and *the wage of the doctor who* heals *him.*[bb][12] 20. When a man strikes his slave or his maidservant with a rod and he dies under his hand,[cc] revenge shall be taken *of him;*[dd][13] 21. but if he survives a day or two,[ee] revenge shall not be taken of him[ff] because he is a money-*purchase.*[gg][14] 22. When men struggle together and trample upon[hh] a woman with child, and there is a miscarriage[ii] but there is no accident, he

Apparatus, Chapter 21

[r] Nfmg: "where you can flee."

[s] Missing in text; supplied from PVN, all with the root *ḥšb* (lit.: "plan"); CTg A has same root as HT(*zyd*), also used in Onq.

[t] Lit.: "in ambush"; P: "with premeditation," "intentionally."

[u] Nfmg: "who hits" (or: "who hit").

[w] Omitted in text.

[x] Nfmg: "wrangle."

[y] CTg A: "but falls (cf. HT) into shame" (?) (or: "condition requiring indemnity").

[z] In text (as in *Aruk*) *mrdnyth*; Nfi: *mrdkytyh*; other texts: *mrdtykh*; CTg A: "his staff" (*ḥwṭrh*).

[aa] Nfmg: "his support; the one who struck him shall be acquitted."

[bb] Nfmg: "who healed"; cf. CTg A.

[cc] CTg A: "his hands."

[dd] CTg A, PVN: "he shall certainly be punished" (or: "fined"); Nfmg: "by punishment (or: "fine") he shall be punished" (or: "fined").

[ee] Nfmg: "but after a day or after two days."

[ff] CTg A: "punishment shall not be exacted of him."

[gg] Nfmg: "because he is enslaved to him, and to his son and to his son's son."

[hh] CTg A: "knock down."

[ii] Nfmg: "a pregnant Canaanite woman and she has a miscarriage."

Notes, Chapter 21

[8]Hebrew has: "But if a man lie not in wait, but God let him fall into his hand, then I will appoint for you a place for him to flee to." For "intend," *'tkwwn*, see also fragment in Klein, 1, 1986, 283, and cf. LXX. Tg. Onq. has: "and from before the Lord he has been surrendered into his hand." For the city of refuge, see Philo, *De spec. leg.* III. XXI §123 in the context of this law; *Mek. RI Nezikin* 4:47-51; *b. Makk.* 10b; 12b.

[9]Hebrew has: "And if a man come intentionally against his colleague to kill him with guile, you shall take him from my altar to die." For "treacherously" the Targum has *bkmn'*, lit.: "in an ambush": so Philo, *De spec. leg.* III. XV §86; Vulg. The second half of the verse is found in very similar words in Frg. Tg. P, V; cf. Klein, 1, 1986, 283, and Tg. Ps.-J.; see *b. Yeb.* 7a; *b. Sanh.* 95b; *b. Yoma* 85a; *b. Makk.* 12a; *j. Makk.* 2:7; *Mek. RI Nezikin* 4:72-73.

[10]See note on v. 12.

[11]Hebrew legislates for what happens if a man "falls to the bed"; Targum specifies that he is *sick*, as do Frg. Tg. P, V, and Tg. Ps.-J.; Philo, *De spec. leg.* III. XIX §106; Josephus, *Ant.* IV.viii.33.

[12]Hebrew has: "only he shall pay for his idleness (i.e., loss of time), and the wage of the doctor who healed him." Very close is fragment in Klein, 1, 1986, 285; cf. also Tg. Onq., Tg. Ps.-J.; *Mek. RI Nezikin* 6:1-5, 53-65; *b. B. Qam.* 85b; Philo, *De spec. leg.* III. §106; Josephus, *Ant.* IV.viii.33.

[13]Nfmg's penalty of a fine stands opposed to the death penalty required by Tg. Ps.-J. and *Mek. RI Nezikin* 7:58-64.

[14]"Money-purchase" is a spelling-out of the clear sense of the Hebrew; so fragment in Klein, 1, 1986, 285.

shall surely be fined according as her husband*jj* imposes on him *according to the judges.*[kk][15] 23. But if there is an accident, he will give life *as indemnity*[16] *for life,* 24. eye *as indemnity* for eye, tooth *as indemnity* for tooth, hand *as indemnity* for hand, foot *as indemnity* for foot, 25. burn *as indemnity* for burn, wound *as indemnity* for wound, scar*mm* *as indemnity* for scar.*mm* 26. And when a man strikes the eye of his slave or the eye of his maidservant and destroys it, he shall send him away to freedom for his eye's sake.*nn* 27. And if he knocks out*oo* the tooth of a manservant or of a maidservant, he shall send him to freedom for his tooth's sake. 28. And when an ox gores*pp* a man or a woman and he dies, the ox shall surely be stoned and its flesh shall not be eaten, but the owner of the ox shall be acquitted. 29. But if the ox has been goring for some time, and it has been made known to its owners, and they would not watch it, and a man or woman *was killed,*[qq] the ox shall be stoned and its owner also shall *be put to death.*[rr][17] 30. If a fine *of money*[18] is imposed on him, he will pay as redemption of his life whatever is imposed on him. 31. If it gores a male son*ss* *of the children of Israel* or*tt* a female daughter *of the children of Israel*, it shall be done to him according to this order of judgment.[19] 32. If the bull gores*pp* a slave or*uu* a maidservant, thirty *selas*[20] of silver shall be given to its owner and the ox will be stoned. 33. And when a man opens a pit, or when a man digs a pit and does not cover it and an ox falls in there or an ass, 34. the

Apparatus, Chapter 21

[jj] CTg A: "the husband of the woman."

[kk] Nfmg: "the decree of the judges."

[mm] Aramaic *rwšm*, as in *Aruk*; HT: *ḥbwrh* (RSV: "stripe"); retained in CTg A; P: "*glwpss* (=wound?), a word of uncertain meaning, otherwise unattested; Ps.-J.: *hlksws*, "swelling, bruise, sore" (Jastrow); Onq.: *msqwpy*, "knock, bruise."

[nn] Nfmg: "in exchange for his eye."

[oo] From root *ntr*, in CTg A ("knock out") from verb *npl*, as HT.

[pp] Verb *ngš* (as in VN, *Aruk* in v. 27); CTg A verb *ngḥ*, as HT.

[qq] Nfi, CTg A: "and it should kill."

[rr] Nfi: "shall die."

[ss] Aramaic *bar*; Nfmg: "if a son" (*bîr*); CTg A: "or if it gores (verb *ngḥ*) a male son or gores (verb *ngḥ*) a female daughter, it shall be done to him according to this procedure."

[tt] Nfmg: "and if."

[uu] Lit.: "if"; CTg A: "or."

Notes, Chapter 21

[15]Hebrew has: "and he shall pay as the judges determine." With Tg. Nf cf. fragment in Klein, 1, 1986, 285; *Mek. RI Nezikin* 8:53-56.

[16]The phrase "as indemnity for" is *tšlwmy*, representing Hebrew *tḥt*, "instead of": see R. Ishmael's repeated use of Hebrew *btšlwmyn* in respect of these laws in *Mek. RI Nezikin* 8:68-72; Le Déaut, 1979 (*Exode*) 179 and the literature there cited; B. S. Jackson, 1973, 273–304; and Tg. Nf of Lev 24:20; Deut 19:21; and the extended discussion in *b. B. Qam.* 83b-84a.

[17]For the forms "was killed," "be put to death," cf. Tg. Onq.; Tg. Ps.-J.; fragment in Klein, 1, 1986, 285–87; and note on v. 12.

[18]For the fine *of money*, see fragment in Klein, 1, 1986, 287, and Tg. Ps.-J.; Tg. Onq. has "money" only. See also Pesh. and *b. B. Qam.* 40a, cited by Grossfeld, 1988B, 61, and Vulg. ("pretium")

[19]For this ruling, see Tg. Onq., Tg. Ps.-J. (without reference to male and female); *Mek. RI Nezikin* 11:1-8 (includes proselytes); *b. B. Qam.* 44a.

[20]The word *sela* stands for Hebrew *šeqel*, as usual in this Targum. *Sela* was the major silver coin of the Talmudic period: see also Exod 30:13, 15, 24; 38:24, 29; B. Grossfeld, 1988A, 83, citing *b. Bek.* 50a.

owner of the pit shall make it good; he shall give back money to its owners, and (the profit of) [ww][21] the dead beast shall be his. [xx] 35. And when the ox of one man gores the ox of another and it dies, they shall sell the live ox and they shall divide the price of it; and even *the profit of* [22] that which is dead they shall divide. [yy] 36. But if it was known that the ox has been goring for some time and its owner would not watch it, he shall make it good, ox instead of [zz] ox, and *the profit of* that which is dead shall be his. [a][23] 37. And when anyone steals an ox or a lamb and slaughters or sells it, he shall repay five oxen for the ox and four sheep for the lamb. [b]

CHAPTER 22

1. "If a thief is found breaking in [a] and is struck [b] and dies, there shall be no *sin of shedding innocent* blood for him. [c][1] 2. If the sun has risen upon him, there is for him the *sin of shedding innocent* blood. [d] He shall surely make restitution. If he has nothing, he shall be sold for his theft. [2] 3. If the stolen (thing) is found alive in his hand, [e] whether it is an ox or an ass or a lamb, he shall pay double. [f] 4. If a man *sets*

Apparatus, Chapter 21

[ww] Word written wrongly by copyist.

[xx] Nfmg: "and the hide of the dead beast shall be his"; CTg A: "and the slain (beast) will be his"; cf. HT.

[yy] VN as Nf; CTg AS: "and even the killed (beast) they shall divide"; cf. HT.

[zz] CTg A: "in place of"; Nfmg: "in repayment for."

[a] CTg A: "and what is killed shall be his"; cf. HT.

[b] Nfmg: "in repayment for oxen; four lambs in repayment for the lamb"; CTg A: ". . . four sheep in place of the lamb."

Notes, Chapter 21

[21]Restoration of "the profit" involves reading *whnyyth* for *whd'* in the light of the following verses: so also Le Déaut, 1979 (*Exode*) 80. Nfmg's view that the *hide* belongs to the sufferer is at variance with *Mek. RI Nezikin* 11:76-79, that the whole carcass is his. See also *b. B. Qam.* 10b-11a.

[22]For the profit of the beast, see Frg. Tg. P, V; Tg. Onq. and Tg. Ps.-J. refer to its value. See Grossfeld, 1988B, 62, who refers to Tg. Nf and Frg. Tg., and *Mek. RI Nezikin* 12:13-31.

[23]See note on v. 35.

Apparatus, Chapter 22

[a] CTg A extant for Exod 22:1-27; as Nf, with variants noted below.

[b] In Nf verb *lqy*; in Ps.-J. verb *mhy*. CTg A here damaged. P. Kahle restores from root *mhy*; M. Klein from root *lqy*.

[c] CTg A: "there is no seeker of blood for him" ("blood avenger").

[d] CTg A: "there is for him a seeker of blood."

[e] Nfmg: "should surely be found with him."

[f] CTg A: "a double price" (Greek or Latin loan word: *diplos*).

Notes, Chapter 22

[1]Hebrew has: "there shall be no blood for him." With Tg. Nf, cf. Tg. Ps.-J. In this and the following verse there is an ambiguity in the Hebrew which the Targum does not resolve: does the matter of shedding innocent blood refer to the householder or to the thief? Rashi and *b. Sanh.* 72a clearly refer the matter to the thief, ibn Ezra to the householder.

[2]See also Tg. Ps.-J.

fire[g] to a field[h] or a vineyard and leaves *the fire to spread,* and (thus) *causes fire* in the field of another,[i] he shall give in restitution the best of his field and the best of (his)[j] vineyard.[3] 5. When fire breaks out and catches thorns[k] and consumes the stacked grain or the standing grain on the field, whoever caused the fire shall make full restitution. 6. If a man gives to his neighbor money or utensils to keep and they are stolen from the man's house, if the thief[m] is found he shall pay double.[n] 7. If the thief is not found, the master of the house shall come to the *judges* (to swear) that he has not put out[o] his hand on the acquisitions of his neighbor.[4] 8. In every sinful affair,[p] whether for an ox, an ass, a lamb, clothes,[q] or any lost thing of which one says: 'This is it,' the words of both parties shall come to *the judges: he* whom *the judges* declare guilty shall pay double[n] to his neighbor.[5] 9. And when a man gives his neighbor an ass or an ox or a lamb or any beast to take care of, and it dies or is hurt or driven away without anyone seeing it, 10. let there be an oath[r] of the Lord between them both (to the effect) that he has not put out his hand on the acquisitions[s] of his neighbor, and his master shall accept[t] (the oath), and he shall not make recompense. 11. But if it be truly stolen from him, he shall pay its owner.[u] 12. If it is torn to pieces, they shall bring *witnesses;*[w] he shall not make

Apparatus, Chapter 22

[g] Root *yqd*, rendering root *b'r* of the HT as elsewhere in Nf (Exod 3:3; 22:4; Lev 6:5). Nfmg 1°: *ypqr* (from *pqr*): "breaks into," "trespasses on"; CTg A: *ybqr* "visits" or "clears" (?), but possibly *bqr = pqr*, through confusion of *b/p* common in Galilean Aramaic. Nfmg 2°: *ylpy*, probably = *ylby* (from *lby; lhb*), "burns"; *ylpy* with same meaning "to burn" in Ps.-J. Lev 6:12. But possibly metathesis for *yply*, "searching"; as this renders same Hebrew word *b'r* in Onq. 26:13; cf. Exod 23:16.

[h] Aramaic *ḥql*; Nfmg: "a portion" (*ḥlq*).

[i] Nfmg: "in the field of another, the best of another."

[j] Thus CTg A; Nf text: "the vineyard."

[k] Nfmg: "(cut) timbers" (*qwṣṣyn*); CTg A; *qwṣnyn*; cf. *qwṣ*, "a thorn."

[m] Lit.: "the robber man"; CTg E: "thief."

[n] Nfmg, CTg E: "in the double" (Greek or Latin loan word, *diplos*; see *f* above).

[o] CTg A: "stretch out," *pst* (but reading uncertain);

Nfmg: "that she will (or might) not stretch out (*twšyṭ*; read *'wšyṭ*, that he has not stretched out) (his/her hand) on the work."

[p] Nfmg: "affair of guilt concerning."

[q] CTg A: "garments" (Greek or Latin loan word *stolê*, *stola*).

[r] Expressed by a different word in Nf (*šbw't'*); CTg A (*qymh*); Nfmg: *mwmt'*; Nfmg: "let there be an oath of the Lord upon them both."

[s] Nfmg: "on the work of" (correcting text, *'tydtyh*), slightly).

[t] Nfmg: "his masters (will accept) from him"; CTg A: "and his neighbor shall take (accept) it."

[u] Nfmg, CTg A: "from his presence he shall repay its owners."

[w] VNP, Nfmg (VN, Nfmg only): "and if he was really killed) he shall bring him some of its limbs as a witness; (PVN continue) he shall not make recompense for the dead one"; CTg A: "if it was really killed, then he shall bring its limbs."

Notes, Chapter 22

[3]Hebrew has: "If a man lay waste a field or vineyard, and shall send in his beast and devastate another's field, he shall pay the best of his field and the best of his vineyard." With Tg. Nf, cf. the fragment in Klein, 1, 1986, 289. Much has been written on this famous halakhah, which is clearly opposed to the ruling in *m. B. Qam.* 1:1; 6:2-5; *b. B. Qam.* 3ab. See P. Kahle, 1927, 15*; *idem*, 1959, 205-8; J. L. Teicher, 1951, 125-29; G. Schelberg, 1958, 253-63; J. Heinemann, 1969, 294-96; *idem*, 1974B, 117; B. S. Jackson, 1974, 127-29; A. Díez Macho, 2, (*Exodo*) 41*-43*.

[4]For "judges," Hebrew has "God." With Targum, cf. Tg. Onq., Tg. Ps.-J.; fragment in Klein, 1, 1986, 291; Pesh.; *Mek. RI Nezikin* 15:38-40; *b. Sanh.* 3b; Philo, *De spec. leg.* IV. VII §34; see also above, 21:6.

[5]See note on v. 7; cf. Tg. Onq., Tg. Ps.-J.; *Mek. RI Nezikin* 15:73-88; *b. Sanh.* 3b.

recompense for that *which was killed.*[x6] 13. If a man borrows (a beast) from his neighbor and it is hurt or dies, its owner not being with it, he shall surely make recompense. 14. If its owner was with it, he shall not make recompense; if it was hired it is received for hire.[y] 15. And when a man seduces[z7] a virgin who is not betrothed and lies with her, he shall surely take her as wife by payment of the bridal pre[s]ent[aa] for her. 16. If her father resolutely refuses to give[bb] her to him (for wife), he must (still) weigh out money for her according to the law[cc8] of the bridal present of a virgin.[dd] 17. *My people, children of Israel,*[9] you shall not allow *a sorcerer or* a sorceress to live. 18. Whoever lies with a beast[ee] *shall be put to death.*[10] 19. Whoever sacrifices *before other idols*—except before the Lord alone—shall be blotted out.[ff11] 20. You shall not ill-treat the sojourner, and *you shall* not oppress them,[gg] because you were dwellers[hh12] in the land of Egypt. 21. *My people, children*

Apparatus, Chapter 22

[x] Nfmg: "he shall take him the body of the mangled animal and he shall not make recompense."

[y] PVN: "if he was hired his hire shall cover (lit.: go for) the loss" (*psyd'*); CTg A: "(text damaged) . . . the loss" (*'psdh*); Nfmg 1°: "he receives the hire"; Nfmg 2°: "he brings in all the losses of the hire"; Nfmg3°: "its hire shall cover the loss" = PVN.

[z] VN, CTg A: "leads astray" (= seduces).

[aa] Slight scribal error in word.

[bb] CTg A: "not giving (different word from Nf) her to him, he shall weigh out money according to the marriage present of the virgin"; Nfmg: "not giving" (= CTg A).

[cc] Greek loan word *nomos*.

[dd] Nfmg: "the money to (the amount of) two hundred (*zuzim*) shall be paid as the dowry of the virgin."

[ee] CTg A: "My people house of Israel . . . a beast. . . ."

[ff] Nfmg: "all idols shall be blotted out except."

[gg] CTg A: "you shall not afflict the sojourners and do not ill-treat them"; Nfmg: "you shall not oppress them and you shall not afflict them."

[hh] Nfmg, CTg A: "sojourners."

Notes, Chapter 22

[6]Hebrew has *yb'hw 'd*, "let him bring it for witness"; Targum renders as *yytwn shdyn*, which may mean "they shall bring witnesses," "witnesses shall come," or even "witnesses shall bring (it)," thus increasing ambiguity rather than defining the law more closely. See Le Déaut, 1979 (*Exode*) 185 for bibliography. For the bringing of witnesses, see *Mek. RI Nezikin* 16:66-68; *b. B. Qam.* 75a. For "that which was killed," see Frg. Tg. P, V.

[7]Tg. Nf alone of the Aramaic versions uses the form *ytps* for "seduces." See Nf of Deut 22:28, and Levy, 1986, 402.

[8]The words "according to the Law" are added by Tg. Nf; no other Tg. does this. The amount of money is set at fifty sheqels of silver according to *Mek. RI Nezikin* 17:47-63; *b. Ketub.* 10a, 38b; Tg. Ps.-J. Nfmg has two hundred *zuzim*, which equals one hundred sheqels of the sanctuary.

[9]For the addition of "My people," see note on 20:2; cf. Tg. Ps.-J. and Klein, 1, 1986, 293. The law applies to male and female witches: so fragment in Klein; Philo, *De spec. leg.* III. XVII §94; *Mek. RI Nezikin* 17:54; *Mek. RSbY*, p. 209; *b. Sanh.* 67a. Cf. also Tg. Ps.-J.

[10]For the Targumic alteration, see note to 21:12. Death by stoning is the penalty: see *Mek. RI Nezikin* 17:71-84; *Mek. RSbY*, p. 210; *b. Sanh.* 54a.

[11]Hebrew has: "He who sacrifices to gods, except to the LORD alone, shall be put to the ban." The interpretation "before other idols" is shared with the fragment in Klein, 1, 1986, 293; Tg. Ps.-J. and Tg. Onq. have "idols of the nations." The word "other" is introduced by assimilation of this verse to the same law in Deut 11:16; 13:7, and it is found also in LXX and the Sam. Tg.

[12]"Dwellers" represents Hebrew *grym*: so Tg. Onq., Tg. Ps.-J., which like Tg. Nf and the fragment in Klein, 1, 1986, 293, have plural verbs for Hebrew singular.

of Israel,[ii][13] do not afflict any widow[jj] or orphans. 22. If *you* afflict them and he cry out *before* me *against you,*[kk] I shall hear *the voice of his prayer, for I am gracious*[mm] *and merciful;*[14] 23. *lest* my anger grow strong and I kill you[nn] with the sword, *lest* your wives become widows, and your sons orphans. 24. If you lend money to my people, to a poor man *who is* among you, you shall not be for him an *exacting* creditor, and you shall not impose on him interest *or usury.*[oo][15] 25. If you take your neighbor's garment in pledge,[pp] you shall return it to him before the sun goes down, 26. for it is his only covering, *the mantle*[qq] of the skin *of his flesh.* In what shall he sleep?[rr] And if he cries out *before* me against you, I will hear *the voice of his prayer,* for I am gracious[ss] *and merciful.*[16] 27. *My people, children of Israel*: do not despise *your judges*[17] and do not curse the lord who is in *your* people. 28. Do not delay *in collecting your tithes and your priestly share.*[tt] You shall consecrate[uu] *to my name* the first-born of your *male* sons.[18] 29. You shall *do* like-

Apparatus, Chapter 22

[ii] Opening words not in CTg A.

[jj] CTg A: "widows."

[kk] "against you" (sing.); CTg A: "if he cries out against you (pl.) before YHWH. I will hear. . . ."

[mm] Nfmg: "because if he cries out before him I will surely hear the voice of the prayer because (I am) a gracious God."

[nn] Nfmg: "and I blot (you) out."

[oo] Nfmg, VN: "you lend to my people, the poor which are among your people, you shall not be pressing creditors for them. You shall impose on them neither

interest nor usury."

[pp] CTg A adds: "beside you."

[qq] CTg A: "the robe" (*'styl'*, from Greek or Latin loan word *stola*).

[rr] Nfmg: "in what shall he stand?"

[ss] Nfmg: "if he cries before him I will certainly hear the voice of his prayer because (I am) a gracious God"; CTg A + at end: "says the Memra of YHWH."

[tt] Text: *dema'*.

[uu] Nfmg: "You shall set aside."

Notes, Chapter 22

[13]For "My people," see note on 20:2.

[14]Hebrew has: "If you do indeed afflict them, so that they cry out at all to me, I shall surely hear their cry." Hebrew has singular verbs and suffixes, Tg. plural. With Nf, cf. closely the fragment in Klein, 1, 1986, 295; Tg. Ps.-J. has "the voice of their prayer."

[15]For the addition "who is," see Tg. Onq., Tg. Ps.-J., Frg. Tg. P, V; Klein, 1, 1986, 295. For the *exacting* creditor (Hebrew has: "like a creditor"), see Frg. Tg. V and Klein, 1, 1986, 295. The addition of "or usury" is shared with Tg. Ps.-J., Frg. Tg. V, and Klein, 1, 1986, 295.

[16]Hebrew has: "it is his garment for his skin . . . when he cries out to me, then I shall hear, for I am gracious." The fragment in Klein, 1, 1986, 295, is very similar. Nf points out that the garment covers his flesh, i.e., his private parts: see also Philo, *De somniis* I. XVI §97. The reference to God as gracious and merciful is found also in v. 22; see also *Mek. RI Kaspa* 1:58-59.

[17]For "My people," see note on 20:2, Tg. Ps.-J., and Klein, 1, 1986, 295. "Your judges" represents Hebrew *'lhym*, "God"; so Tg. Onq., Tg. Ps.-J., Klein, 1, 1986, 295; *Mek. RI Kaspa* 1:63-64; b. *Sanh.* 66a; *Exod. R.* 31, 8, 16.

[18]Hebrew has: "You shall not delay your fullness (i.e., produce) and your 'tear' (*wdm'k*, i.e., fruit juice, wine): the first-born of your sons you shall give to me." The Targum needed to elucidate this somewhat obscure verse and makes "fullness" refer to tithe (so Vulg.) and *dm'k* to priestly dues (Vulg. has first-fruits). Tg. Nf agrees with other Targums in its general reference to Temple offerings and priestly dues; in details, however, it seems quite different. Tg. Onq. and Tg. Ps.-J. understand "fullness" as first-fruits of the produce, not tithe; Tg. Ps.-J. then speaks of "wine," and Tg. Onq. uses a word which resembles the Hebrew original, *dm'kwn*, the close similarity of which to *demai*, "uncertainly tithed produce," suggests priestly dues, *Terumah*. In this they reflect faithfully the language of *Mek. RI Kaspa* 1:80-81; *Mek. RSbY*, p. 213. Both these sources, however, continue to speak of the order in which the various dues, including tithes, should be presented: by putting tithes first in the list, the Targum may be making a point in connection with the debate set out in the *Mekhiltas*. For "you shall consecrate," lit.: "you shall separate," see also Tg. Onq. and Tg. Ps.-J.

wise with *your* oxen and with *your* sheep. Seven days [ww] it shall be reared behind its mother, and on the eighth day [xx] they shall *separate* it to *my name.* [19] 30. And you shall be a *people of consecrated ones* to *my name.* You shall not eat flesh torn from a *wild beast, killed* in the field; you shall throw it to the dog, *or you shall throw it to the gentile stranger, who is comparable to the dog.* [yy] [20]

CHAPTER 23

1. "You shall not accept *false witness.* Do not *join* your hand with the sinner [a] to be for *him a false* witness. [1] 2. *My people, children of Israel,* [b] *you* shall not *go* after

Apparatus, Chapter 22

[ww] Nfmg: "and from the (seventh) day."
[xx] Nfmg: "and from the eighth day."
[yy] PVN: "(VN) and flesh torn from a wild beast thrown

on the open field you shall not eat (PVN). You shall give it to the gentile who is comparable to the dog."

Notes, Chapter 22

[19] Hebrew has: "So you (sing.) shall do for your ox, for your sheep: seven days it shall be with its mother. On the eighth day you shall give it to me." Targum has had an eye to the same law in Lev 22:27, which specifies that the young beast shall be after, *tht*, rather than *with*, its mother. R. Nathan in *Mek. RI Kaspa* 1:113-117 understands *tht* as "behind," implying time for the *rearing* of the animal, as in our Targum; so also Tg. Ps.-J., which envisages the mother suckling her young; see *b. Bek.* 26b. Targum uses the verb "separate" as in the preceding verse, to indicate the formal setting apart of priestly dues: so also Tg. Onq. and Tg. Ps.-J.: see Grossfeld, 1988B, 65. For the expression "to my name," see note on 6:7.

[20] Hebrew has: "And men of holiness you shall be to me: and you shall not eat flesh in the field torn by beasts. You shall cast it to the dogs." "A people of consecrated ones" is an expression found often in Tg. Ps.-J., e.g., at Lev 26:12; Deut 7:6; 26:19; 32:9. This law deals with *trēfāh*, flesh torn from a living animal. In ruling that it may be given to a Gentile, Targum is following the rules laid down for carrion, *nebēlāh*, in Deut 14:21. This corresponds to the way in which the verse is treated in *Mek. RI Kaspa* 2:23-39, *Exod. R.* 31, 9, and the arguments adduced for dealing with *trēfāh* in this fashion. But as Levy (1986, 404) makes clear, the Hebrew is ambiguous and may refer to two forbidden things, dead flesh in the field and flesh from a living animal. The words of Nf can be translated such that they also include this ambiguity. Tg. Ps.-J. also rules that *trēfāh* should be given to dogs: see *b. Hul.* 68a; *j. Orlah* 3:1. The comparison of the Gentile with a dog is found in Frg. Tg. P, V, Nfmg, *Mek. RI Kaspa* 2:23-25. See also *b. Pesah.* 21b-22a.

Apparatus, Chapter 23

[a] Nfmg: "my people, children of Israel, none of you shall swear falsely in the name of the Memra of the Lord your God, and you shall not put your hands with the sinner."

[b] Nf seems to have double paraphrase for verse 2; the first ("my people . . . in judgment") repeated verbatim in Nfmg; also in P and V, with few variants noted below.

Notes, Chapter 23

[1] Hebrew has: "You shall not bear a false report . . . to be a witness for violence." Targum here understands Hebrew's "violence," *hms*, as "unrighteousness," as does Tg. Onq. Similarly Tg. Ps.-J. interprets the verse of a witness who testifies falsely; so *Mek. RI Kaspa* 2:52-56; *b. Shebu.* 31a; Philo, *De spec. leg.* IV. VIII §44; Vulg.; and LXX, *martus adikos.* For Nfmg's "My people," see note on 20:2.

the many to do evil, but rather *to do good*; and let *none of you refrain from pleading in favor^c* of his neighbor in judgment. And (you shall not)^d *say in your hearts*: '*Justice^e* is with the many.'^f Do not *go* after the many to do evil. Do *not* hold back *from asking what is in your heart about your neighbor* in judgment, *lest you go astray and say: 'Perfect justice* is with the majority.'² 3. *My people, children of Israel*, you shall not *favor* in judgment the poor man *who has become guilty, because there is to be no accepting of persons in judgment.*³ 4. When you meet the ox or the ass of him who hates you going astray, you shall bring it back to him. 5. If you see the ass of one who hates you lying under its load and *you would refrain* from *removing (it) with him, you shall surely abandon whatever is in your heart against your neighbor,^g and you shall remove (it) with him, and you shall surely load* (it) with him.⁴ 6. You shall not pervert the judgment of the needy^h man in the judgment.ⁱ 7. You shall keep far removed from lying words and put *no one* to death who is innocent *in judgment,^j* because the guilty will not be acquitted *before me.*^{k5} 8. And

Apparatus, Chapter 23

^c Aramaic *lmlph zkwwn* (in Nf: *zmn*) = Hebrew *lmd zkwt*, (lit.: "teach justice"), "making known the merits of," "plead in favor of the defendant." Nf MS has false reading *zmn* as also Nfmg and V; N(ur), *zkw*; P: *zkwwn*.
^d Missing in text of Nf.
^e Or: "judgment, legal decision"; Nfmg: "good (judgment)."
^f Lit.: "Justice (or judgment, legal decision) is after (= according to) the majority"; note Nf second para-

phrase: "Perfect justice is after (= according to) the majority."
^g Nfmg: "which is in your heart against him."
^h Emending text slightly.
ⁱ Nfmg: "My people, children of Israel, you shall not pervert the poor person's judicial procedure (lit.: order of judgment) in the hour of his judgment."
^j Nfmg: "and the innocent and upright in judgment."
^k Nfmg: "because, the Lord will not acquit the guilty in the hour of judgment."

Notes, Chapter 23

²Hebrew has: "You shall not follow the majority for evil; and you shall not bear witness in a case to turn aside after the majority to pervert (justice)." For "My people," see Tg. Ps.-J., Frg. Tg. P, V, and note on 20:2. For "you shall not go," see Frg. Tg. P, V. Our Targum differs greatly from Tg. Onq., which states that the Law follows the majority: see Grossfeld, 1988B, 66–67. Tg. Ps.-J. is similar to Tg. Nf in exhorting the hearer to follow the many not to do evil but to do good (cf. *Mek. RI Kaspa* 2:64-74; *Mek. RSbY*, p. 214; *b. Sanh.* 2a), and not to refrain from testifying in a trial to his colleague's innocence. On the doublet in this verse of Nf, see Kasher, 1986, 11–12.

³Hebrew has: "You shall not favor a poor man in his case." For "My people," see note on 20:2. Targum has interpreted this verse in the light of its fellow, Lev 19:15, and the exegesis is very close to that of Tg. Ps.-J. For "there is to be no accepting of persons in judgment," see *Mek. RI Kaspa* 2:75-79, where the law of Leviticus is stated; *Mek. RSbY*, pp. 214–15; *Sifra Qedoshim* 8; *Sifre Deut.* 17.

⁴Hebrew has: "If you see your enemy's ass lying under his load, and you would forbear to release (*m'zwb*) it for him—you shall certainly release ('*zb t'zb*) it for him." There are here three occurrences of the verb '*zb*, which means ordinarily "to leave, forsake" and may also, more uncommonly, mean "to help." Tg. Nf has taken the first occurrence of the word in the sense of "remove," i.e., unloose the ass's burden, using Aramaic root *prq*: cf. *Mek. RI Kaspa* 2:132-45. The second occurrence is in the form of a Hebrew Infinitive Absolute, '*āzōb*, which is understood as "leave, forsake," to give "you shall surely abandon whatever is in your heart. . . ."; cf. Tg. Onq.; Tg. Ps.-J. The third occurrence is the Imperfect *t'zb*, which is taken to mean "you shall remove it with him," as before: so also *Mek.* as quoted, *b. Baba Metsia* 32b; *Sifre Deut.* 222. For a comparison of this rendering with that of Tg. Onq., see Grossfeld, 1988B, 67.

⁵Hebrew has: "You (sing.) shall keep far from a false matter; and do not slay the innocent and the righteous, for I shall not justify the wicked." Targum's interpretation is not entirely clear. It may refer to the case envisaged by Tg. Ps.-J. of one acquitted by the court but later found to have been guilty; or of one convicted of crime, but later found to be innocent: there is discussion of this in *b. Sanh.* 33b; *Sifre Deut.* 144; *Mek. RI Kaspa* 3:42-52.

do not accept a bribe,*[m]* because a bribe blinds *the eyes of those who take it and removes*[n] the words *of* just *judgment*[o] *in judgment.*[p6] 9. *You* shall not oppress a sojourner, *because* you know the soul of the sojourner,*[q]* for you were sojourners in the land of Egypt.*[7]* 10. For six years*[r]* you shall sow *your* land and gather its produce,*[8]* 11. and in the seventh *year* you shall leave it fallow, and *leave it free*[s] that the poor of your people may eat;*[t]* and what is left the beasts of the field*[u]* will eat. You shall do likewise with your vineyards and with your olive orchards.*[9]* 12. Six days you shall do*[w]* your work, and on the seventh day *you shall rest; so that your ox*[x] and your ass may rest, and that the son of your *Jewish* bondmaid*[y]* and the sojourner may rest.*[10]* 13. And pay attention*[z]* to everything I have said to you, and you shall not remember the name of other *idols*,*[11]* and let it not be heard in your mouths. 14. Three*[aa]* *times* in the year *you* shall keep a feast *before* me.*[bb12]* 15. *You* shall observe the feast of Unleavened Bread: seven days *you* will eat unleavened

Apparatus, Chapter 23

[m] Nfmg: "and a bribe of wealth (Aramaic: *mamon*). You shall not take."

[n] Or: "makes waver."

[o] Or: "of the righteous judge."

[p] Nfmg: "(of) the wise in judgments and confounds and corrupts the words of the innocent in the hour of the judgments."

[q] Nfi: "and you understand the souls of the sojourners"; Nfmg: "you understand the bitterness of soul of the sojourner."

[r] Nfmg +: "of days."

[s] Reading *tbqrwn* (Nf MS: *tbqdwn*) with P (text) *Aruk*, ed. Kohut; *Aruk*, ed. Breslau, "declare free and

ownerless" (? *tbqrwn wtpqrwn*); P: marg. gloss: *tbqr kmw hpqr*—"*tbqr* is the same as *hpqr*": "You shall declare free is the same as you shall declare ownerless."

[t] Nfmg: "and you shall give it to eat to the poor who are among your people and what."

[u] Nfmg: "the beasts that are on the face of the field."

[w] Verb in pl.; pronom. suffix in sing.; both sing. in HT.

[x] Nfmg: "so that your (pl.; in text sing.) oxen may eat."

[y] Nfi: "of your (pl.; text sing.) handmaids."

[z] Nfmg: "you shall observe."

[aa] Nfmg prefixes: "children of Israel."

[bb] Nfmg: "each year you shall celebrate a feast before me."

Notes, Chapter 23

[6]Hebrew has: "And you shall not take a bribe: for a bribe blinds those who have sight and perverts the words of the righteous." For "you shall not accept," cf. Tg. Onq., although it has a singular verb, and Deut 16:19. LXX, Sam., Pesh., twelve Hebrew MSS and Deut 16:19 include the eyes being blinded. The last phrase of the Hebrew, very literally rendered as "the words of the righteous," is *dbry ẓdyqym*. Its meaning is ambiguous, since it may refer to the judges themselves, (b. *Ketub.* 105ab), to the Law (so *Mek. RI Kaspa* 3:67-68), or to the plea of the innocent parties who did not bribe the judge. Rather than attempt to resolve the ambiguities, the Targum and Nfmg seem to exploit the various possibilities of meaning in the phrase.

[7]LXX, Tg. Ps.-J., Tg. Onq. have plural verbs and *because* (LXX; cf. Vulg.), like Tg. Nf. Nfmg's reference to the bitterness of the sojourner's soul is found also in Tg. Ps.-J.

[8]Targum has plural verbs and suffixes for Hebrew singular; so also fragment in Klein, 1, 1986, 297.

[9]Targum has plurals, as in preceding verse; so Klein, *ibid.*, which also adds *year*.

[10]Targum has plurals, as in preceding verse; so Klein, *ibid.* The son is here specified as Jewish: not so Tg. Ps.-J., b. *Yeb.* 48b, *Mek. RI Kaspa* 3:135-138, where he is said to be an uncircumcised slave, a possibility entertained by Nfi.

[11]"Other idols" represents Hebrew "other gods"; see note on 22:19.

[12]Hebrew has: "Three times you shall keep a feast to me in the year." *Times* is added in the light of the wording of the same law in 23:17; so also Tg. Onq., Tg. Ps.-J., fragment in Klein, 1, 1986, 297. *Mek. RI Kaspa* 4:32-37 emphasizes that the law requires a man to keep festival at three specified times *per annum*, not at any random time nor more than once on any given festival. So also Vulg., "per singulos annos."

bread as I have commanded you, at the (appointed) time of the month of Abiba, for in it *you* came *redeemed* out of Egypt. And *you* shall not be seen before me empty(-handed).[cc13] 16. And (you shall observe) the feast of harvest, of the first fruits of the work *of your hands*, of what *you bring out* and sow[dd] in the field, and the feast of ingathering at the end of the year, when *you* gather in from the field the work *of your hands*.[ee14] 17. Three times *every year all your males shall appear*[ff] *seeking instruction* before the Master *of all ages*, the Lord.[15] 18. You shall not[gg] sacrifice the blood of my *holy* sacrifice[hh] with leavened bread, and the fat of my feast shall not remain till morning.[ii16] 19. The beginning of the first *fruits of your produce*[jj] you shall bring to the *sanctuary* of the Lord, *your God. My people, children of Israel,*[kk] you shall not boil *and you shall not eat flesh* with milk, *mixed together, lest my anger be enkindled against you and we boil*[mm] *your bundled wheat, the wheat and the straw* mixed together.[17] 20. Behold, I[nn] send an angel *of mercy* before *you* to guard *you* in the land,[oo18] to bring *you* into the place which I have prepared.

Apparatus, Chapter 23

[cc] Nfmg: "out of Egypt. My people, children of Israel, you are not permitted to be seen before your God void of every precept."

[dd] Nfmg: "Your produce which you shall sow against" (or "toward": correcting *ylpy* to *klpy*).

[ee] Nfmg: "your produce which you will sow."

[ff] Nfmg: "shall be seen."

[gg] Nfmg prefixes: "my people, children of Israel."

[hh] Nfmg: "the sacrifices of holy things."

[ii] Nfmg: "the flesh which you sacrifice on the first night of the feast day of passover from evening until morning."

[jj] *Aruk*: "the beginning of the first fruits of your (sing.) land"; P: "the beginning of the first fruits of your (pl.) land you shall bring to the sanctuary of the Lord your God. My people, my people, house of Israel, you are not permitted either to boil or to eat flesh and milk, the two of them mixed together, lest my anger be enkindled against you and I boil your wheat, piled up in your threshing floors; the wheat and the straw both of them mixed together"; Nfmg: "you are not permitted to boil and eat flesh and milk mixed together"; cf. P.

[kk] See also Nf Exod 34:26.

[mm] Or rather: "I boil," (= P), with use of 1st per. pl. form.

[nn] Nfmg: "his Memra."

[oo] Read probably: "on the way."

Notes, Chapter 23

[13] Targum has plural verbs for Hebrew singular; so LXX. On "redeemed," see note to 3:10. Nfmg's understanding of "empty" as "void of every precept" is shared by Tg. Ps.-J. See also 34:20.

[14] Hebrew has: "And the festival of harvest, the first-fruits of your labors which you have sown in the field, and the festival of ingathering at the going out of the year, when you gather in your labors from the field."

[15] For *every* year, see 23:14. Hebrew has: " all your males shall appear to the face of the Lord God." On "seeking instruction," see note on 18:15. "Lord God" is *h'dwn YHWH*; for its interpretation as Master of all ages, see Chester, 1986, 326–30.

[16] See note on 18:12. Nfmg refers the latter part of this verse to the Passover, no doubt linking it with its parallel in 34:25: see *j. Pesah.* 5:4, and *Mek. RI Kaspa* 4:74-75, *b. Men.* 78b.

[17] Hebrew has: "The first-fruits of the firstlings of your ground you shall bring to the house of the Lord your God. You shall not boil a kid in its mother's milk." The first-fruits are to be brought to the Temple: so Tg. Onq., Frg. Tg. P; see Grossfeld, 1988B, 68–69, who cites *m. Bikk.* 1:9; *t. Shek.* 3:24; *m. Shek.* 8:8; *j. Peah* 5:5. On "My people," see note on 20:2. Note that Targum prohibits both the cooking and the eating of milk and meat, two out of the three prohibitions (the other is a prohibition of deriving benefit from it) derived from this verse by R. Simeon b. Yohai in *Mek. RI Kaspa* 5:28-31. The same two prohibitions are listed in Tg. Ps.-J.; Frg. Tg. P; and cf. *b. Hul.* 115b; *t. Makk.* 4:7; *Mek. RSbY*, p. 219; Grossfeld, 1988B, 69. The threat of God's anger and the fate of the wheat and straw are found also in Tg. Ps.-J. and Frg. Tg. P, but not elsewhere: see Le Déaut, 1979 (*Exode*) 195, who cites B. J. Bamberger, 1975, 29, and S. Gronemann, 1879, 92, and Levy, 1986, 410–11.

[18] Hebrew has: "an angel before you . . . in the way."

21. Pay attention[pp] before him and listen to (his)[qq] voice, and do not rebel against *his words, for my holy name is invoked upon him*, for he will not *forgive or* pardon your sins, for my *holy* name *is invoked upon him.*[rr][19] 22. But if you listen to the voice *of my Memra* and do all that *it* says, I will hate whoever hates *you*, and I will oppress whoever oppresses *you*.[20] 23. Because my angel[ss] will go before *you* and will bring *you* into the *land* of the Amorites, of the Hittites and the Perizzites and the Canaanites and the Hivites and the Jebusites, and I will blot them out. 24. *You* shall not bow down to their *idols*,[21] and *you* shall not worship *before* them,[tt] and *you* shall utterly overthrow[uu] them and shatter their pillars. 25. But you shall worship *before* the Lord, your God, and he will bless *your* bread[ww] and *your* waters, and *he* will remove the *evil* plagues[xx] from among *you*.[22] 26. There shall be neither a childless nor a barren woman in your[yy] land. *You* shall *fulfill* the number of your days[zz] *in peace*.[23] 27. I will send my terror[a] before *you*, and I will confound all the peoples among whom *you* enter, and I shall place[b] all *your* enemies before you, their necks *broken*.[24] 28. And I will send hornets before *you*, and they will drive out the Hivites and the Canaanites and the Hittites before *you*.[24] 29. I will not drive them out before you in one year lest the land become deserted, lest the wild beasts multiply[c] against you.[24] 30. Little by little I will drive them out from before you until *you* multiply and possess the land.[24] 31. And I will set *your* boundaries from the Reed Sea to the Sea of the Philistines, and from the desert to the *Great River*;[d] for I will deliver into your hands *all* the inhabitants of the land, and *I* will

Apparatus, Chapter 23

[pp] Nfmg: "pay attention to yourselves."

[qq] Text: "my voice"; Nfmg: "to the voice of his Memra. Do not rebel."

[rr] Nfmg: "the name of my Memra (will be invoked; corr. text) upon him."

[ss] Nfmg: "angel of mercy."

[tt] Nfmg: "(worship) them."

[uu] Nfmg: "(you shall) demolish" (*mpkr'*) = V; P: "but split (or: smash, *mmpk'*)"; V: "but you shall surely demolish (*pkr*) them and shatter their pillars."

[ww] Nfmg: "your provisions."

[xx] Nfmg: "your waters and I will remove the plagues."

[yy] Text sing.: Nfmg: "in your (pl.) land."

[zz] Nfmg: "I will fill your days with good."

[a] Nfmg: "the plague of my punishment."

[b] Nfmg: "I will blot out the entire people to whom you are entering and shall place."

[c] Lit.: "that they would not multiply"; Nfmg: "and (the wild beasts) would multiply."

[d] Nfmg: "to the river Euphrates."

Notes, Chapter 23

[19] Hebrew has: "Take heed from before him and listen to his voice: do not rebel against him, for he will not forgive your rebellion: for my name is in him." Targum is similar to Tg. Ps.-J. "Forgive" is read by Tg. Onq., without "pardon." On the holy Name, see Chester, 1986, 343.

[20] Hebrew has: "For if you will certainly listen to his voice and do all that I speak, then I shall be hostile to your enemies, and an adversary to your adversaries."

[21] Targum has "idols" for Hebrew *'lhym*, as at 22:19; 23:13.

[22] Hebrew has: "and he will bless your (sing.) bread and your water; and I shall remove sickness from the midst of you." Targum has plural suffixes. For the *evil* plagues, cf. Tg. Onq.

[23] Hebrew has: "I shall fulfill the number of your days." Targum's second person plural is echoed by the second person singular which Philo uses to express this verse, *De praemiis* XIX §111.

[24] The Targum has second person plural verbs and suffixes for Hebrew singular.

drive them out from before you.[25] 32. *You* shall not make a covenant with them or with their *idols.*[26] 33. They shall not dwell in *your* land, lest they make *you* sin before me, because *you* would worship before[e] their idols, and they would be a snare for *you.*"

CHAPTER 24

1. And he said to Moses: "Go up, *seek instruction from before*[a] the Lord, you and Aaron, Nadab, and Abihu, and seventy *wise men* of Israel. And you shall *pray* from afar off.[1] 2. And Moses alone shall approach *before* the Lord, and they shall not approach, and the people shall not go up with him." 3. And Moses came and related to the people all the words of the Lord and all the orders of judgment.[b] And the people replied with one voice and said:[c] "All the words which the Lord[d] has spoken, we will do."[2] 4. And Moses wrote down all the words of the Lord. And he got up early in the morning and built an altar at the foot of the mountain, and twelve pillars for the twelve tribes *of the children* of Israel.[3] 5. And he sent the

Apparatus, Chapter 23

[e] In Nfmg the sign of accusative for "before"; i.e., "you worship their idols."

Notes, Chapter 23

[25] Again, second person plurals are used for Hebrew singulars. The Great River is the Euphrates: so also Tg. Onq., Nfmg, Tg. Ps.-J., and LXX. The addition of "all" is shared with Tg. Ps.-J., and the first person "I will drive" out with LXX, Sam., Vulg. in place of Hebrew "you will drive out."

[26] Second person plural for Hebrew singular continues. "Idols" represents Hebrew *'lhym*: see v. 24 and notes on 22:19; 23:13.

Apparatus, Chapter 24

[a] Nfmg: "and seek instruction before."
[b] Nfmg: "his judgments."

[c] Nfmg: "together with a perfect heart and soul."
[d] Nfmg: "the Memra of the Lord."

Notes, Chapter 24

For the chapter as a whole, see the special studies referred to at the beginning of comment on Chapter 19.

[1] Hebrew has: "And to Moses he said: Go up to the Lord, you and Aaron . . . and seventy of the elders of Israel, and you shall prostrate yourselves from afar off." On the phrase "seek instruction from before the Lord," see note on 18:15. On "wise men" for elders, see note on 3:16; Philo, *De mig. Abr.* XXXI §168 has *gerousia.*

[2] For Nfmg's use of the phrase "a perfect heart," see note on 19:8.

[3] Hebrew has: "twelve tribes of Israel."

young men of the children of Israel, and they *arranged*[e] holocausts, and they *offered* oxen as sacrifices *of holy things before* the Lord.[4] 6. And Moses took half the blood and put it in a bowl, and half the blood he sprinkled[f] on top of the altar. 7. Then he took the Book of the Covenant and read (it) in the hearing[g] of the people; and they said: "All that the Lord has spoken we will do and we will obey." 8. And Moses took the blood and sprinkled (it) on the people and said: "Behold the blood of the covenant which the Lord *established*[h] with you, all these words."[5] 9. And Moses and Aaron, Nadab, and Abihu and seventy of the *wise men*[6] of Israel went up. 10. And they saw the *Glory of the Shekinah of the Lord;*[i] and under the *footstool*[j] *of* his feet there (was) like brick-work of sapphire,[k] as *a vision of the* heavens, *when they are* pure *from cloud.*[m][7] 11. And he did not stretch out his hand to the *young men*[n] of the children of Israel; and they saw the *Glory of the Shekinah*

Apparatus, Chapter 24

[e] Nfmg: "and he sent the first-born of the children of Israel, because until that time (lit.: hour) the worship was with the first-born, since as yet the tent of meeting had not been made and as yet the priesthood had not been given to Aaron and they offered"; cf. Ps.-J.

[f] Nfmg: "in the bowls and the other half of the blood he sprinkled."

[g] Nfmg: "which the Memra of the Lord had spoken."

[h] Nfmg: "which the Memra of the Lord has established."

[i] Nfmg: "the God of Israel"; P: "and they saw the Glory of the Shekinah of the God of Israel . . . ," etc., as in Nf, with variants noted below. VN, v. 10b as Nf, with variants as noted below.

[j] Text: *'pwpwdn*; Greek loan word *hypopodion*. Nfmg:

'pypwdwn; Aruk: "the footstool (*'pypwdyn*) of his feet"; also in Pal. Tg. citations in the *Meturgeman* (*'pwpryn*) and of Rashi: "under his footstool" (*'pypwryn*).

[k] Greek loan word *sanpheironon*; also in *Aruk: spyrynwn*.

[m] Nfmg: "they were pure from the clouds" = VN; P ". . . from clouds"; cited in j. *Sukka* 54c; *Lev R.* c. 23, 167a; cf. McNamara, 1966A, p. 53.

[n] Nfmg 1°: "to the lords"; Nfmg 2°: "to Nadab and Abihu, the handsome young men who had been appointed over the children of Israel"; Levita, *Meturgeman* and *Aruk (Mus.)* "the youths" (*z'ṭwty*); PV in v. 11a = Nf except ". . . he did not stretch out his hand to destroy."

Notes, Chapter 24

[4]Hebrew has: "and they offered up whole burnt offerings and sacrificed peace offerings to the Lord." Nfmg shares with Tg. Ps.-J. the identification of the "young men" as the first-born, who functioned as priests before Aaron's appointment and the setting up of the Tabernacle: see j. *Meg.* 1:11; b. *Zeb.* 112b; 115b; *Num. R.* 4:8; *Mek. RSbY*, p. 220; *Tanḥ B. Toledoth* 67; *Aggadath Bereshith* 42–43; Tg. Nf of Gen 49:3; Jerome, *Hebraicae Quaestiones* on Gen 27:15; Epistle lxxiii *Ad Evagrium (Evangelum)*. The beginnings of the tradition may be discerned in Philo, *De agric.* XII §51; *De conf. ling.* XXVIII §146; *De congressu* XVIII §98; *De somniis* I. XXXVII §§213–15. Targum's "arranged" renders Hebrew "offered up," as very frequently in this text: see further on 29:13. On the rendering of "peace offerings," cf. Tg. Onq., Tg. Ps.-J., and see note on 18:10.

[5]On the language of the Targum here, see Hayward, 1981A, 59–63.

[6]On "wise men" for elders, see 3:16; LXX have *gerousia*.

[7]Hebrew has: "And they saw the God of Israel: and under his feet as it were a work of pavement of sapphire, and as it were the body of heaven for purity." As noted in the Apparatus, a Pal. Tg. of this verse is quoted in j. *Sukk.* 4:3 (54c); *Lev. R.* 23, 3. This verse was a *locus classicus* for the rabbis in the matter of appropriate translation of the clause "and they saw the God of Israel": so, famously, R. Judah b. Ilai in t. *Meg.* 4:41; b. *Qidd.* 49a. Tg. Onq. and Tg. Ps.-J. follow the rabbinic rule and state: "and they saw the Glory of the God of Israel." For further discussion of the rabbinic rule, see Le Déaut, 1966, 43. For analysis of Tg. Nf's exegesis, see Muñoz León, 1977, 95–99. Hebrew "body" of the heaven becomes "vision": so Tg. Onq. Absence of cloud is a feature of Tg. Ps.-J., Frg. Tg. P, V, and Vulg.

of the Lord,[o] *and they rejoiced*[p] *over their sacrifices, which were received, as if* they ate and drank.[8] 12. And the Lord said to Moses: "Come up to me to the mountain and be there; and I will give you the tables of stone and the Law and the Covenant which I have written to instruct them."[q] 13. And Moses arose, and Joshua, his servants,[r] and Moses went up to the mountain, *on which the Glory of the Shekinah of the Lord had been revealed.*[9] 14. And to the *wise men* he said: "Stay, wait for me here,[s] until we return to you. And behold Aaron and Hur are with you; whoever *has a judicial affair of* words, let him approach them."[10] 15. And Moses went up to the mountain, and the cloud covered the mountain. 16. And the Glory *of the Shekinah* of the Lord rested on Mount Sinai, and the cloud covered it six days; and on the seventh day he called[t] to Moses[u] from the midst of the cloud.[11] 17. And the appearance of the Glory *of the Shekinah* of the Lord (was) like a devouring fire, *a devouring fire* on the top of the mountain, in the eyes[w] of the children of Israel.[12] 18. And Moses came into the midst of the cloud and went up the mountain. And Moses was on the mountain forty days and forty nights.

Apparatus, Chapter 24

[o] Nfmg: "the God of Israel"; see note *i* above.

[p] P: ". . . and they saw the glory of the Shekinah of the Lord and they appeared as if they ate and drank"; Nfmg: "they appeared as if they ate."

[q] Nfmg: "and the commandments I have written to show them."

[r] Nfmg: "his servant."

[s] Nfmg: "(wait) for yourselves here."

[t] Nfmg: "the Dibbera (*dbyr'*) of the Lord (called)."

[u] Nfmg: "to Moses on the seventh day upon the mountain."

[w] Nfmg: "(the children of Israel) seeing."

Notes, Chapter 24

[8]Hebrew has: "And to the nobles of the sons of Israel he did not stretch out his hand; and they saw God and ate and drank." The "nobles" are rendered as "young men" by Frg. Tg. P and Tg. Ps.-J.; the latter Targum shares with Nfmg 2° their identification as Nadab and Abihu, who, in some sources, had already been identified as priests designated to go up to Mount Sinai: see note on 19:22. On the Glory of the Shekinah, see above, v. 10. They appeared to eat and drink: so Tg. Ps.-J., Tg. Onq., Nfmg, and Frg. Tg. P. In this respect they were like the angels, who only appear to eat and drink: see Tob 12:19; Tg. Ps.-J., Tg. Nf of Gen 18:8; Tg. Ps.-J. of Gen 19:3; *Gen. R.* 48, 11, 14; Philo, *Quaest. in Exod.* II. §39.

[9]Hebrew has: "to the mountain of God." See Tg. Ps.-J., note on 4:27, and Chester, 1986, 161–62.

[10]Hebrew has: "And to the elders he said: Wait for us here. . . . whoever has a case, let him go to them." Tg. Ps.-J. also has "wise men" for "elders": see note on 3:16. For "a judicial affair of words," cf. Tg. Ps.-J. and LXX. Philo, *Quaest. in Exod.* II. §44, regards them as judges.

[11]Tg. Ps.-J. has Shekinah here. For Nfmg's reference to the *Dibbera*, see note on 19:3.

[12]The description of the theophany is not unlike that in Tg. Ps.-J., although the latter is slightly more elaborate. Cf. Tg. Ps.-J. of Gen 38:25; Deut 4:24; *Num. R.* 11, 3.

CHAPTER 25

1. And the Lord[a] spoke to Moses, saying: 2. "Speak with the children of Israel that they may *set separated* offerings *aside* for *my name*; you shall receive *separated* offerings from everyone whose heart prompts them.[1] 3. And this is the *offering of separation* which you shall receive[b] from them: gold and silver and bronze, 4. blue and purple and *precious* crimson[2] material and byssus and goats' hair, 5. reddened[bbis] rams' skins, and *sasgona*[c3] skins, and acacia wood; 6. oil for the illumination, spices for the anointing oil and for the fragrant incense, 7. *precious* stones[d] and stones for setting, *for inserting*[e] in the ephod and in the breastpiece.[4] 8. And they *shall build* a sanctuary *to my name* that I *may make the Glory of my Shekinah* dwell among them.[5] 9. (According to)[f6] whatever I will show you concerning the design of the tabernacle and concerning the design of all its utensils, thus you shall do. 10. And they shall make the ark[g] of acacia wood; its length shall be two cubits and a half, and its breadth shall be a cubit and a half, and a cubit and a half shall be *the measure of* its height,[7] 11. and you shall overlay it with pure gold; inside and outside you shall overlay it, and you shall make it a molding *round about.*[8] 12. And you shall cast four rings of gold for it, and you shall place them on the four corners: two rings on one side and two rings on the second side. 13. And

Apparatus, Chapter 25

[a] Nfmg: "the Memra of the Lord."
[b] Nfmg: "you shall take."
[b bis] I.e., "tanned."
[c] Cf. 26:14; 35:7; rendering *tahaš*, an unidentified animal, of the MT; Nfmg: "of *shsgwnyn*," otherwise unattested.
[d] *Aruk, Mus.* here and 28:9: "pearls of beryl" (*mrglyyn*

dpyrwlyn, read *dbyrwlyn*; Greek loan word: *beryllion*); MT: "of *šoham*," RSV: "onyx."
[e] Nfmg: "with which to insert the ephod and the breastplate."
[f] Missing in text; in Nfmg.
[g] Nfmg: "an ark."

Notes, Chapter 25

[1] Hebrew has: "that they may take offerings for me." Targum's "set aside" is "separate," root *prš*, used by Tg. Onq. See note to 22:29, and Grossfeld, 1988B, 75, who also points to the technical use of this term to indicate the setting aside of priestly dues. On "to my Name," see note on 6:7.

[2] Targum will, throughout the following chapters, qualify the crimson material as "precious"; so, e.g., 26:1, 31; 27:16; 28:5, 33; 35:6, 23, 25, 35; 36:8, 35, 37.

[3] On the Sasgona, see *b. Shabb.* 28ab, which explains it as a special animal living only at the time of the building of the Tabernacle. Its name is expounded as meaning that it took delight (*sas*) in its color (*gōna'*).

[4] Hebrew has: "*šoham* (beryl? onyx?) stones and stones for setting for the ephod and for the breastplate." The identity of the precious stones named in this and the following chapters is not always clear, and the ancient commentators often had as much difficulty as the moderns: see below, on 28:17-20. Tg. Nf sometimes qualifies the stones as "precious"; so here and 35:9, 27; 39:6. "For inserting" is the reading of Tg. Onq., Tg. Ps.-J.

[5] Hebrew has: "And make for me a sanctuary, so that I may tabernacle in their midst." See note on 6:7 on "to my Name." Both Tg. Onq. and Tg. Ps.-J. have Shekinah: see further Muñoz León, 1977, 100–101.

[6] There is a similar omission of "according to" at 29:35.

[7] Hebrew has: "and a cubit and a half its height." Targum almost invariably adds "the measure of" to phrases of this kind throughout the following chapters.

[8] "Round about" represents *hzr wmqp*, which is Tg. Nf's almost invariable translation of Hebrew "around" in these chapters. Similar here is Frg. Tg. V.

you shall make poles of acacia wood, and you shall overlay them with gold, 14. and you shall introduce the poles into the rings on the sides of[h] the ark to carry the ark by them. 15. The poles shall be in the rings of the ark: they shall not move from it. 16. And you shall place within the ark the testimony which I shall give you. 17. And you shall make a mercy seat of pure gold: two cubits and a half its length, and a cubit and a half its breadth. 18. And you shall make two cherubin[i9] of gold; hammered you shall make them, at the two sides of the mercy seat, 19. and you shall make one cherub at this side—one here—and another cherub at the other side—there; you shall make the cherubin of one piece with[j] the mercy seat, at its sides, its two sides. 20. And the cherubin shall spread their wings upward, over-shadowing the mercy seat with their wings, and their faces *turned*[10] one toward another; toward the mercy seat shall the faces of the cherubin be. 21. And you shall place the mercy seat upon the ark <above; and in the ark>[k] you shall place the testimony which I shall give you. 22. I shall appoint *my Memra* to *meet* you there, and I shall speak with you from above the mercy seat which is upon the ark of the testimony,[m] from between the two cherubin, all whatsoever I shall command[n] you concerning the children of Israel. 23. And you shall make a table of acacia wood: two cubits its length, a cubit its breadth, and a cubit and a half *the measure*[11] of its height. 24. And you shall overlay it with pure gold, and you shall make for it a molding of gold round about.[8] 25. And you shall make a border[o] of a hand's-breadth[p] round about,[8] and you shall make a molding of gold for its border round about.[8] 26. And you shall make for it four rings of gold, and you shall place the rings on the four corners of its four legs. 27. The rings will be opposite its border as *places*[12] for the poles to carry the table. 28. And you shall make the poles of acacia wood, <and you shall overlay>[q] them with gold, to carry[r] the table with them. 29. And you shall make its bowls,[s] and its dishes[t] and its flagons and its libation

Apparatus, Chapter 25

[h] Nfmg: "on the side of."

[i] Nfmg: "figures" (i.e., images); cf. 26:1.

[j] Lit.: "you shall make the cherubin from the mercy seat."

[k] Omitted in text through homoioteleuton.

[m] Nfmg: "from between the two cherubin which are above the ark of the testimony."

[n] Nfi: "I shall speak."

[o] P: "a border"; = Nf *Aruk*: "a border of a hand-breadth" = Nf; Levita, *Meturgeman*: "a border (of) a span," cf. Nfmg; VN: "a border of a span all round about."

[p] Nfmg: "a span"; cf Levita, *Meturgeman*, VN.

[q] Missing in text.

[r] Nfi: "to bear."

[s] Greek loan word *phialē*; also in P and *Aruk*.

[t] Nfi, *Aruk*: "its distributors" (or: "dishes").

Notes, Chapter 25

[9]Nfmg's rendering of Cherubim as "figures" occurs also in Tg. Nf itself, e.g., 26:1, 31.

[10]The addition of "turned" suggests the rendering of Tg. Ps.-J., which explicitly states that the Cherubim are to be op-posite one another: so *b. Sukk.* 5ab; Vulg.; Philo, *Quaest. in Exod.* II. §66. See also *b. B. Bat.* 99a.

[11]For the addition of "measure," see note on v. 10.

[12]Hebrew has "houses" for Tg.'s "places". The Hebrew is a little poetic, and Tg. gives it its "real," prosaic meaning: so Tg. Onq.; Tg. Ps.-J.; Pesh.; and Sam. Tg. See further Grossfeld, 1988B, 75, and other occurrences of the rendering in 30:4; 36:34; 37:14; 38:5.

jars, with which *service* shall *be made;* [u][13] of pure gold you shall make them.
30. And you shall place the *arrangement* [14] of the bread [w] of the Presence upon the
table before *him* [x] always. 31. And you shall make a lampstand of pure gold; the
lampstand shall be made of hammered work, and its *base* [y] and its shaft; its cups, its
apples [z] and its lilies [aa] shall be of one piece with it. 32. And there shall be six
branches going out of its side: three branches of the lampstand from one side [bb] and
three branches of the lampstand from the second side; 33. three *decorated* [15] cups [cc]
on one branch, apple and lily; [dd] thus on the six branches which come out of the
lampstand; 34. and on the lampstand four *decorated* [15] cups, its apples and its lilies,
35. and an apple of one piece with it under two branches, and an apple of one
piece with it under the (other) two branches, [ee] for the six branches that come out of
the lampstand. 36. Their apples and their branches shall be one piece with it, all of
it one hammered piece of pure gold. 37. And you shall make the seven lamps; and
you shall arrange [16] the lamps to give light over against it. 38. And its snuffers and
its trays you *shall make* [17] of pure gold. 39. Of a *centenarium* [ff][18] of pure gold you
shall make it, with all these utensils. 40. And see that you make (them) according
to their designs which you see on the mountain.

Apparatus, Chapter 25

[u] Nfi: "(with which) the anointing shall be done."

[w] Nfi: "the bread of arrangement."

[x] Nfi: "before me."

[y] *bsys* (loan word) also in *Aruk*, Nfmg.

[z] I.e., its bulbs.

[aa] Or: "flowers."

[bb] In text: "three branches in one side" written twice in
text.

[cc] Nfi: "with figures."

[dd] Text: "three decorated . . . and lily," here and in par.
37:19, only once in text, as in LXX; in MT, Onq., Ps.-
J. twice; cf. v. 35.

[ee] Phrase "and an apple . . . two branches" here, in par.
37:21 and in LXX only twice; three times in MT,
Onq., Ps.-J.

[ff] A Latin loan word, *centenarium*; cf. 37:24; also in P.
Aruk, and Levita, *Meturgeman*.

Notes, Chapter 25

[13]Hebrew has: "jars, with which to pour out. . . ." It is not made clear what is to be poured out: is it libations of wine or
oil? Targum specifies only that they are for use in Temple service, as does Tg. Ps.-J.; but Nfi has them as vials for anointing oil.

[14]Targum adds "arrangement" when the Bread of the Presence is discussed, since the word features in the laws concerning that bread: see Lev 24:5-9.

[15]Hebrew has *mšqdyn*, "made like almond blossoms," which Tg. has rendered with the similar-sounding word *mšq'yn*,
"decorated." Nfi's rendering recalls the Cherubim: see note on v. 18. Perhaps Tg. Nf's vagueness here is intentional, al-
lowing for the detailed description given in *b. Men.* 25ab.

[16]"And you shall arrange" renders Hebrew "and bring up," giving the proper sense.

[17]Targum has added "you shall make."

[18]Tg. Ps.-J. also has *centenarium*.

CHAPTER 26

1. "And you shall make the tabernacle with ten curtains of twined byssus and blue and purple, and *precious* crimson material; with *figures*[a] you shall make them, the work of an artist.[1] 2. The length of one curtain: twenty-eight cubits *for each curtain*; and the breadth: four *cubits according to the (ordinary)* cubit for each curtain, the same measure for each curtain. 3. Five curtains shall be joined one against the other, <and the other five curtains shall be joined one against the other>.[b] 4. You shall make loops of blue upon the side of the *outer* curtain in the place of joining; and thus you shall do on the side of the *outer* curtain in the second[c] place of joining. 5. You shall make fifty loops on one curtain, and you shall make fifty loops on the side of the curtain which is in the second place of joining; the loops *shall be* directed one toward the other. 6. And you shall make fifty hooks of gold, and you shall join the curtains one against the other with the hooks, and the tent shall be one *whole*.[2] 7. And you shall make curtains of goats' hair *to spread over*[3] the tabernacle: eleven curtains you shall make. 8. The length of one curtain shall be thirty *cubits according to the (ordinary)* cubit and the breadth four *cubits according to the ordinary* cubit: the same measure for the eleven curtains. 9. And you shall join five curtains by themselves, and you shall double the sixth curtain against the front of the tabernacle. 10. And *you shall make*[4] fifty loops on the side of an *outer* curtain at the place of joining, and *you shall make* fifty loops on the side of the curtain at the second place of joining. 11. And you shall make fifty hooks of bronze, and you shall introduce the hooks into the loops, and you shall join the tent together, and it shall be all one whole. 12. And the remaining part that hangs down from the curtains of the tabernacle, the half of the curtain that remains, you shall let hang over its extremities of the tabernacle toward the sea. 13. And the cubit that remains in the length of the curtains[d] of the tabernacle, on one side and on the other, shall hang down upon the side of the tabernacle, on one side and on the other,[e] to cover it. 14. And you shall make a covering[f] for the tabernacle of reddened[g] rams' skins, and above it a covering of *sasgona*[h] skins.

Apparatus, Chapter 26

[a] MT: "cherubim"; cf. 25:18.
[b] Missing in text; but in MT, Onq., and Ps.-J.
[c] Nfmg: "the other."
[d] Nfmg: "of one curtain shall hang."

[e] Thus Nfmg; Nf literally: "from here and from there."
[f] Nfmg: "the covering."
[g] I.e., tanned.
[h] See to 25:5.

Notes, Chapter 26

[1] For the addition of "precious," see note on 25:4; and for "figures" rendering MT's Cherubim (*added* by Tg. Ps.-J. at this point), see note on 25:18.
[2] Targum's rendering "one whole" occurs again at 36:13, 18.
[3] Hebrew has "for the tent," which Tg. regularly explains as "to spread over"; cf. 36:14; 40:19.
[4] For "and you shall make," cf. LXX.

15. And you shall make upright planks of acacia wood for the tabernacle. 16. Ten cubits shall be the length of a plank, and a cubit and a half shall be the breadth of each plank, 17. two tenons for each plank which fit in[i] one against the other;[j] thus shall you do for all the planks of the tabernacle. 18. And you shall make the planks for the tabernacle: twenty planks for the south side, to the south. 19. And you shall make forty sockets of silver under the twenty planks, two sockets under the twenty planks,[k] two sockets under one plank for its two tenons, and two sockets under another plank for its two tenons. 20. And for the second side of the tabernacle, for the north side, twenty planks. 21. And their forty sockets of silver: two sockets under one plank and two sockets under another plank. 22. And for the extremity[m] of the tabernacle, *to the west,*[5] you shall make six planks, 23. and you shall make two planks for the *corners*[n] of the tabernacle in the rear. 24. And they *shall correspond*[o] below and they *shall correspond*[6] on top within one ring: thus shall it be with two of them, they shall form two *sides.* 25. And there will be eight planks and their sockets of silver, sixteen sockets; two sockets under one plank, and two sockets under another plank. 26. And you shall make bars of acacia wood: five for the planks of one side of the tabernacle, 27. and five bars for the planks[p] of the second side of the tabernacle, and five bars for the planks of the sides of the tabernacle in the extremity *to the west.*[7] 28. And the *second*[q] bar, in the middle of the planks, shall reach[r] from one side to the other. 29. And the planks you shall overlay with gold, and their rings you shall make of gold, *places*[8] for the bars;[s] you shall overlay the bars[s] with gold. 30. You shall erect the tabernacle according to the order of judgment which you saw on the mountain. 31. And you shall make a veil[t] of blue and purple and *precious* crimson material and twined byssus; the work of an artist he shall make it,[u] *with figures.*[9] 32. And you shall place it over four pillars of

Apparatus, Chapter 26

[i] *Aruk,* Mus.: "directed" (same word as in 26:5).
[j] Lit.: " . . . this against this"; Nfmg: "each (lit.: "one") (plank) which fit in one against the other."
[k] The phrase "two pockets under the twenty planks" seems superfluous.
[m] Levita, *Meturgeman* : "and in the extremity of"; *Aruk* has Nf reading.
[n] P: "at its overlapping"; VN "to the west."
[o] Nfmg: "they shall join"; or "they shall bound, form boundaries," "form borders " (correcting *mthmmyy'* to *mthmy[n]*); see Apparatus 36:29.

[p] Nfmg: "cross-bars"; VN: "and the five bars of the planks, the sides (= corners) of the tabernacle"; Levita, *Meturgeman*: "and the five bars, the planks."
[q] The text is probably corrupt, *tnyynh,* "the second," a false reading for *tykwnh* or *msy'yh*; cf. Exod 36:33.
[r] Correcting text with Nfmg.
[s] Nfmg: "the cross-bars."
[t] Nfmg: "a screen."
[u] Nfmg: "you shall make it."

Notes, Chapter 26

[5]The addition of "to the west" is intended to direct the reader's attention back to v. 12, and forward to the rule of v. 27. Cf. *b. Shabb.* 98b: the entrance is toward the east, so the extremity will be toward the west.
[6]Hebrew has: "And they shall be double . . . and they shall be entire. . . ." Cf. Tg. Onq.
[7]See above, v. 22.
[8]On "places," see note on 25:27.
[9]On "precious," see note on 25:4. The "figures" render MT's Cherubim: see note on 25:18.

acacia overlaid with gold, with their clasps[w] of gold on four sockets of silver. 33. And you shall hang the veil under the hooks, and you shall introduce there within the veil the ark of the testimony, and the veil will separate for you the holy *from* the holy of holies. 34. And you shall place (the mercy seat)[x] upon the ark of the testimony within the most holy place. 35. And you shall place the table outside the veil[y] and the lampstand opposite the table, at the side of the tabernacle to the south;[z] and you shall place the table *at the north*, to the north side. 36. And you shall make a screen for the door of the tent, of blue and purple and fine crimson material[10] and twined byssus, a work of *embroidery*. 37. And you shall make for the screen five pillars of acacia, and you shall overlay them with gold, and their clasps shall be of gold, and you shall cast for them five sockets of bronze.

CHAPTER 27

1. "And you shall make the altar of acacia wood, five cubits wide; the altar shall be square, and the measure of its height[1] shall be three cubits. 2. And you shall make horns for it on the four corners *from the measure of the height*.[2] Its horns shall be of one piece with it. And you shall overlay it with bronze. 3. And you shall make pots to clean it of ashes,[a] shovels,[b] its sprinkling basins, forks and trays. All its utensils you shall make of bronze. 4. And you shall make for it a grating,[c] a net-

Apparatus, Chapter 26

[w] *qlwwthwn*; in Nfmg, Levita, *Meturgeman*, VN, a different form: *'nqlwwtyhwn*; presumably a Greek loan word, *agkolê (ankolê)*.
[x] Following the correction by a second hand; in text: "the veil"; a variant Nfmg to v. 35: "the mercy seat" probably belongs to this verse.

[y] Nfmg: "the mercy seat"; probably belongs to v. 34; see note *x*.
[z] Nfi: "to the west."

Notes, Chapter 26

[10] For the addition of "fine," see note on 25:4.

Apparatus, Chapter 27

[a] Aramaic *lmdsn'*; cf. *diššûn (dśśwn)*, "removal of ashes, cleaning"; HT: *le͏daššenô* (root *dśn*). Great variety in terms used to render Hebrew: V: *lmydwdh*, "to clean" (Klein); N(ur), Ps.-J., *ed. pr.* 1590 *lmydrdh*.

[b] VN, Levita, *Meturgeman*; "scrapers" or "sweepers."
[c] Greek (*kinklis*) or Latin (*cancellus*) loan word; also in VN, *Aruk*; cf. 35:16; 38:4, 30; 39:39.

Notes, Chapter 27

[1] For "the measure of its height," see 25:10, 23; 30:2.
[2] Hebrew has "of it" for "from the measure of the height"; see above, v. 1, and notes to 25:10.

work of bronze, and on the net you shall make four rings of bronze at the four corners. 5. And you shall place it under the circuit [d] of the altar underneath, and the net shall reach to the middle of the altar. 6. And you shall make poles of acacia wood [e] for the altar, and you shall overlay them with bronze. 7. And you shall put the poles [f] in the rings, and the poles will be on the two sides of the altar to carry it. [g] 8. You shall make it hollow with boards; as <I have shown> [h] you on the mountain, this shall they do. 9. And you shall make the court of the tabernacle on the south side, to the *south*, [3] and the court will have hangings [i] of twined byssus, a hundred *cubits wide, according to the (ordinary)* cubit, on one side. 10. And the pillars shall be twenty, and their sockets twenty, of bronze; the clasps [j] of the pillars and their fastenings shall be of silver. 11. And likewise for the north side, for (its) length, there shall be hangings a hundred *cubits* long; [4] and its columns shall be twenty, and the bases shall be twenty, of bronze, and the clasps of the pillars, and their fastenings [k] shall be of silver. 12. And (for) the breadth of the court on the *west* side there shall be fifty cubits of hangings; their pillars [m] shall be ten, and their sockets shall be ten. 13. And the breadth of the court on the east side, to the east, shall be fifty cubits. 14. And the hangings on one *side* [5] shall be fifteen cubits; their pillars shall be three, and their sockets three. 15. On the second *side* [5] there shall be fifteen hangings; their pillars shall be three and their sockets three. 16. And the door of the court shall have a screen of twenty cubits of blue and purple and *precious* crimson material [6] and twined byssus, the work of an embroiderer; [n] their pillars four cubits and their sockets four. 17. And the pillars of the court round about shall be fastened together with silver, and their clasps [j] of silver and their sockets of bronze. 18. The length of the court shall be a hundred *cubits, according to the (ordinary)* cubit, and its breadth will be fifty by fifty, and the *measure of* its height [7] five cubits, (with curtain) of twined byssus and their sockets of bronze. 19. All the utensils of the tabernacle for every service, and all its pegs and all the pegs of the court,

Apparatus, Chapter 27

[d] Nfmg: "the grating"; = P.

[e] Nfmg: "poles for the altar, poles of (acacia) wood."

[f] Nfmg: "its poles."

[g] Nfmg: "to bear it."

[h] Missing in text; cf. 26:30; Nfmg: "the vision(s)."

[i] Greek (*bēlon*) or Latin (*velum*) loan word; also in VN.

[j] *qlwwt*; Nfmg: *'wnqlwwt*, Greek loan word *ankylē*; (cf. Exod 26:32; 38:10) "clasps."

[k] Nfmg: *sqy'wwyyhwn*; "their staples"(?), "their clasps"(?); cf. Nfmg Exod 36:38; 38, 10, 17. Sokoloff, 1990, 548, understands as "cavity."

[m] Nfmg: "and their pillars"; probably a variant of "its columns" of preceding verse.

[n] Cf. 26:36, where same HT word is rendered as "of embroidery."

Notes, Chapter 27

[3] Targum is quite concerned to give proper orientation as in 26:18. Cf. Vulg.

[4] For "cubits," see LXX, Sam., and Vulg.

[5] "Side" renders Hebrew "shoulder": so LXX, Vulg.

[6] For "precious," see 25:4.

[7] Hebrew has: "and its height"; for Tg., see note on 25:10.

shall be of bronze. 20. And you shall command the children of Israel, and they shall take *and bring to you* pure olive oil, crushed, for lighting, for *the arranging* of lamps° continually.⁸ 21. In the tent of meeting, outside the veil which is beside the testimony, Aaron and his sons shall keep it in order from evening to morning, before the Lord. It shall be an eternal statue for their generations from the children of Israel.

CHAPTER 28

1. "And you, bring near to you Aaron your brother, and his sons with him from among the children of Israel, to *serve before him*ᵃ *in the high priesthood*:¹ Aaron, Nadab and Abihu, Eleazar and Ithamar, sons of Aaron. 2. And you shall make holy garments for your brother Aaron for glory and praise. 3. And you shall speak to all who are wise of heart, whom I have perfected with a spirit of wisdom, and they shall make the garments of Aaron to consecrate him to *serve before him*ᵃ *in the high priesthood*.² 4. And these are the garments which they shall make: a breastpiece, an ephod, a robe, a knitted coat, turbans, and girdles.ᵇ And they shall make holy garments for Aaron your brother and for his sons to *serve before him in the high priesthood*.³ 5. And they will receiveᶜ gold and blue and purple and *precious* crim-

Apparatus, Chapter 27

° Nfi: "a lamp."

Notes, Chapter 27

⁸Targum adds "and bring to you" to make the ruling absolutely precise. Hebrew has: "to set up a lamp continually" in place of "for the arranging of lamps": cf. Tg. Onq., Tg. Ps.-J., and Pesh. for plural "lamps."

Apparatus, Chapter 28

ᵃ Nfmg: "before me."
ᵇ Nfmg: "and the coat of byssus, and the turban and the girdle."

ᶜ Nfmg: "and they shall take."

Notes, Chapter 28

¹Hebrew has: "to appoint him as priest to me"; Targum's rendering of the Hebrew terminology in this way is very common: see (e.g.) 28:3, 4, 41; 29:1, 44; 30:30; 40:13, 15. Tg. Onq. and Tg. Ps.-J. have "to serve before me"; for the high priesthood, see *Exod. R.* 37, 2, and note on 1:21. Both Philo, *De vita Mosis* II. XXIII §109; *Quaest. in Exod.* II §107 and Josephus, *Ant.* III.vii.1, refer this chapter to the high priest.
²See above, v. 1.
³See note on v. 1. "Girdle" is *hmyyn*, a Persian loan word, translating Hebrew *'bnt*: so Tg. Onq. and Josephus, *Ant.* III.vii.2. See Le Déaut, 1979 (*Exode*) 220–21.

son material [4] and byssus. 6. And they shall make the ephod of gold, of blue and purple and *precious* crimson material [d4] and twined byssus, the work of an artist. 7. Two shoulder pieces shall be joined to it from its two sides. And it shall be joined. 8. And the girdles of the ephod which is upon it shall be of the same workmanship of one piece with it: [e] gold and blue and purple and *precious* crimson material [4] and twined byssus. 9. And you shall take two *precious* stones, [5] and you shall inscribe on them the names of the children of Israel, 10. six of their names on the one stone, and the names of the *six that remain* [f] over on the second stone according to their pedigrees. [g] 11. The stone *shall be* the work *of an artist,* [6] inscribed, engraved; [h] you shall inscribe the two stones according to the names of the children of Israel: set [i] in gold settings [j] you shall make them. 12. And you shall place the two stones on the shoulder pieces of the ephod as stones of *good* remembrance [7] for the children of Israel, and Aaron shall *receive* [k] their names before the Lord on his two shoulder pieces for a good remembrance. 13. And you shall make settings [j] of gold 14. and two chains of pure gold. (Like) cords [m] you shall make them, plaited [n] work. And you shall place the chains of plaited work in the settings. [o] 15. And you shall make the breastpiece of judgment, the work of an artist; like the work of the ephod you shall make it. Of gold, blue and purple and *precious* crimson material [8] and twined byssus you shall make it. 16. It should be square, double, a hand's-breadth its length and a hand's-breadth (its) breadth. 17. And you shall fill [p] in it [q] a filling of stone: four rows of *precious* [r] stones. The *first* row: a carnelian, topaz [s] and carbuncle: [t] one row. [u] *And written and clearly expressed upon them shall be the*

Apparatus, Chapter 28

[d] Nfi: "crimson-colored," (*gwwn' zyhwry*; text *ṣb' zhwry*).

[e] Lit.: "from it"; Nfmg: "(from it) and in it they shall be."

[f] Nfmg: "the six (names) remaining over."

[g] Nfmg: "according to their genealogies."

[h] Nfmg: "stone: engraved by an engraver; you shall engrave."

[i] *mqpn*; lit.: "encircled"; Nfmg: "inserted" (*msq'n*, the term used by Onq.).

[j] Or: "mountings, brooches."

[k] Thus text which is probably corrupt and to be corrected with Nfmg: "shall bear."

[m] Lit.: "forming borders"; cf. Exod 28:22; 39:15, and see HT.

[n] Nfmg: "twisted."

[o] Nfmg: "(the chains) in the form of a cord upon the settings" (a different word for "settings").

[p] Verse 17 in VN, almost identical with Nf; variants noted below.

[q] VN: "with it."

[r] Also in VN; not in MT nor (apparently) Nfmg.

[s] *yrqth*; also in N; identification uncertain.

[t] *brqth*; identification uncertain.

[u] "one row," not in VN.

Notes, Chapter 28

[4] For "precious," see 25:4.

[5] Hebrew has: ". . . two *šōham* stones": see 25:7.

[6] Hebrew has: "the work of an engraver." For "artist," cf. Tg. Onq., Tg. Ps.-J.

[7] For the "good" memorial, see note on 12:14.

[8] For "precious," see 25:4.

name of three tribes: Rueben, Simeon, Levi.[9] 18. And the second row: a chalcedony, [w] a sapphire[x] and a calf's eye. [y] *And written and clearly expressed upon them shall be the name of three tribes: Judah, Issachar, Zebulun.* [10] 19. And the third row: a jacinth and a beryl[z] and an emerald. *And written and clearly expressed upon them the name of three tribes: Dan and Naphtali and Gad.* [11] 20. And the fourth row: beryl[aa] of *the Great Sea* and a bdellium, [bb] and a pearl. [cc] *And written and clearly expressed upon them shall be the name of three tribes: Asher, Joseph and Benjamin.* [12] They shall be set[dd] in gold <in their settings> [ee] 21. <The stones shall be>[ff] according to the names of the children of Israel, twelve, according to their names. They shall be inscribed, *engraved,*[gg][13] <each one> according to its name, for the twelve tribes. [hh] 22. And you shall make on the breastpiece chains like a cord, plaited work, of pure gold. 23. And you shall make on the breastpiece two rings of gold. 24. And you shall put the two plaits of gold upon the two rings within[ii] the sides of the breastpiece. 25. And the two sides of the two plaits you shall put in the two settings,[jj] and you shall put (them) on the shoulder pieces of the ephod, in

Apparatus, Chapter 28

[w] Greek loan word: *chalkēdōn.*

[x] *sprynh*; VN: *smpwryn'*; Greek or Latin loan word (?): *sappheirinon.*

[y] *'yn 'gl*—an unidentified precious stone; = "diamond"?

[z] Greek loan word: *beryllion.*

[aa] Greek loan word: *chrōma*; lit.: "color (of the Great Sea)"; VN: "color (*chrōma*) of the Sea (= Sea Green," "aquamarine," a species of bdellium).

[bb] A Semitic loan word, also in Greek and Latin (*bdellium*).

[cc] Greek or Latin loan word: *margaritēs/margarita.*

[dd] Nfmg, VN: "inserted."

[ee] Missing in Nf; in VN.

[ff] Missing in text.

[gg] Nfmg: "engraved (by) a seal-maker upon"; cf. v. 11; 39:14.

[hh] Nfmg: "they shall be the twelve (uncertain reading) tribes of Israel."

[ii] Nfmg: "in the sides."

[jj] Nfmg: "inserted"; cf. v. 20; 39:15.

Notes, Chapter 28

[9]For "precious," see 25:4. Tg. Onq., Tg. Ps.-J., and Frg. Tg. V specify the *first* row and name the same stones (with minor orthographical variations) as Tg. Nf. Tg. Ps.-J. also points out that they make one row. For the formula "and written . . . three tribes," see Frg. Tg. V; Tg. Ps.-J. notes that the names are "clearly expressed." The names Reuben, Simeon, and Levi make up the first row also in Frg. Tg. V; Tg. Ps.-J., *Exod. R.* 38, 8–9; *Num. R.* 2, 7; and Philo, *Leg. alleg.* I. XXVI §81.

[10]The names of the stones do not correspond with the list in Tg. Onq. Frg. Tg. V is closest to our Targum; Tg. Ps.-J. also has sapphire in second place. For the formula "and written and clearly expressed," see note to v. 17. The names Judah, Issachar, Zebulun, found in that order also in *Exod. R.* 38, 8–9; *Num. R.* 2, 7 for the second row, are only partly represented in other sources. Thus Philo, *Leg. alleg.* I. XXVI §81, lists Judah and Issachar, and then stops enumerating the tribes; Tg. Ps.-J. has Judah in first place; and *LAB* 25:6 juxtaposes Issachar and Zebulun before continuing in the same basic order as that found here in Tg. Nf, although not with reference to the tribes listed on the breastplate.

[11]Frg. Tg. P, V here places our Targum's last two stones and proceeds to add another of its own. Neither Tg. Onq. nor Tg. Ps.-J. have much in common with this list of stones. For the formula "and written . . . ," see note on v. 17. The names Dan, Naphtali, and Gad are found in Frg. Tg. V and *Exod. R.* 38,8–9; *LAB* 25:6. *Num. R.* 2,7 has the order Dan, Gad, Naphtali.

[12]The names of the stones are almost identical with those in Frg. Tg. V. The first two stones have similar names in Tg. Ps.-J. For the formula "and written," see note on v. 17. The names Asher, Joseph, Benjamin are found in Frg. Tg. V; *Exod. R.* 38, 8–9; *Num. R.* 2, 7. *LAB* 25:6 has Asher, Manasseh, Ephraim (the two sons of Joseph), and Benjamin.

[13]For "engraved," see Tg. Ps.-J.

front. 26. And you shall make two rings of gold, and you shall put them on the two sides of the breastpiece, on the *inside*[kk] border of the ephod. 27. And you shall make the two rings of gold, and you shall place them on the two shoulder pieces of the ephod, underneath and in front, opposite its joining above the girdle of the ephod. 28. And they shall spread out[mm] the breastpiece by its rings to the ring of the ephod[nn] by a thread of blue, so that it shall be over the girdle of the ephod, and so that the breastpiece shall not move from over the ephod. 29. And Aaron will carry[oo] the names of the children of Israel in the breastpiece of judgment upon[pp] his heart, when he enters within[qq] the sanctuary, for a *good*[14] remembrance[rr] before the Lord continually. 30. And you shall put the Urim and the Thummin in[ss] the breastpiece of judgment, and they shall be upon the heart <of Aaron when he enters before the Lord>,[tt] and Aaron will bear the *order of* the judgments of the sons of Israel upon his heart before the Lord continually. 31. And you shall make the robe of the ephod entirely[uu] of blue. 32. And it will have an opening for the head in the middle;[ww] its opening shall have a border all around, the work of weavers; it shall be like the opening of a coat of mail. It shall <not>[xx] be torn. 33. And on its lowest edge *all around* you shall make pomegranates of blue, purple and *precious* crimson material[15]—on its lowest edge all around—and bells of gold between them round about, 34. bells of gold and a pomegranate; bells of gold and a pomegranate on the lowest edge of the robe round about. 35. And it shall be upon Aaron when he ministers, and its sound shall be heard when he goes into the sanctuary before the Lord and when he comes out, lest he die. 36. And you shall make a plate of pure gold and you shall inscribe on it, inscribed, engraved:[yy] 'Holy to[zz] *the name* of the Lord.'[16] 37. And you shall put it on a thread of blue, and it shall be on the tur-

---

Apparatus, Chapter 28

[kk] Nfmg: "upon the inner border which is in the front of the ephod"; cf. 39:19.

[mm] Nfmg: "and they shall fasten"; or: "press upon"; cf. Nfmg Exod 39:21.

[nn] Lit.: "from its rings (to) within the ring of the ephod"; Nfmg: "its rings to the rings of the ephod.

[oo] Nfmg: "he shall bear."

[pp] Nfmg: "on the girdle on the ephod upon."

[qq] Nfmg: "to the sanctuary."

[rr] Nfmg: "to the sanctuary a remembrance."

[ss] Nfmg: "within the breastplate."

[tt] Missing in text; supplied from Ps.-J.

[uu] Nfmg: "of a thread of blue."

[ww] VN, v. 32a: "and it shall have an opening for the (lit.: his) head in the middle; there shall be a border (a different form of the word from Nf) surrounding its opening round about, the work of weavers. It shall be like the opening of a coat of mail. It shall not be torn."

[xx] Missing in text; in VN.

[yy] Nfi: "inscribed"; N and M: "of an engraver."

[zz] Nfmg: "before the Lord."

Notes, Chapter 28

[14]For "good" remembrance, see note on 12:14.

[15]Targum has added "all around" to MT. On "precious," see 25:4.

[16]Hebrew has: "Holy (or: Holiness) to the Lord."

ban; on the front of the turban it shall be, 38. and it shall be upon the forehead of Aaron, and Aaron shall carry the sins [17] of the holy[a] (offering) which the children of Israel will sanctify as their holy gifts. And it shall be upon his forehead continually that there may be favor upon them before the Lord. 39. And you shall knit[b] a cloak of byssus, and you shall make turbans of byssus, and you shall make a girdle,[c] the work of an embroiderer.[d] 40. And for the sons of Aaron you shall make cloaks, and you shall make girdles for them, and you shall make caps for them for glory and praise. 41. And you shall put them on Aaron your brother, and on his sons with him, and you shall anoint them, and you shall complete *the offering of* their hands,[e] and you shall sanctify them, and they *will minister before him*[f] *in the high priesthood.*[18] 42. And you shall make for them undergarments[g] of byssus to cover the flesh of *their* nakedness; from *the belt of* their loins[19] to their thighs they shall reach. 43. And they shall be on Aaron and on his sons when they enter[h] the tent of meeting or when they draw near the top of the altar to minister within the sanctuary, lest they contract guilt, lest they die. (This shall be) an eternal statute for them and for their sons after them.[i][20]

Apparatus, Chapter 28

[a] Or: "the faults they may commit in the holy offerings."

[b] Nfmg: "and you shall engrave (root *šq'* rendering, HT *šbṣ*; see to Exod 28:11, Nfmg) cloaks of byssus."

[c] Nfmg: "and girdles."

[d] Nfmg: "of embroidery."

[e] MT: "you shall fill their hands," i.e., with the instruments of their office; i.e., you shall ordain them.

[f] Nfi: "before me."

[g] Nfmg: "breeches" ('*brqsyn*; from Greek *brakai*; Latin *brac(c)ae*); cf. 39:28 VN: "breeches" ('*bryn*; corr. with Nfmg).

[h] Nfmg: "when he enters."

[i] Nfmg: "the sanctuary lest they contract guilt (lit.: debts) and die: an eternal statute for him and for the descendants of his sons after him."

Notes, Chapter 28

[17]Targum has plural "sins" for Hebrew singular; so also LXX, Vulg.

[18]Hebrew has: "and you shall fill their hands . . . that they may minister to me as priests." Targum's usual rendering of "fill the hands" is "complete the offering of the hands": so 29:9, 29, 33, 35; 32:29; Lev 8:33; 16:32; 21:10; Num 3:3; see further Grossfeld, 1988B, 81. On "minister in the high priesthood," see notes on 1:21; 28:1.

[19]See also Tg. Ps.-J. for "from the belt of their loins."

[20]"For them and for their sons after them" renders Hebrew "for him and for his seed."

CHAPTER 29

1. "And this is what you shall do to them to sanctify them *to minister before him[a] in the high priesthood*: Take[b] one young ox and two rams, perfect *without blemish*,[1] 2. and unleavened bread and unleavened cakes saturated with oil. With fine wheaten flour you shall make them. 3. And you shall put them <in a basket and you shall bring them>[c] in the basket, and (you shall bring) the ox and the[d] two rams. 4. And you shall bring Aaron and his two sons near to the door of the tent of meeting, and you shall *sanctify*[2] them with water. 5. And you shall take the garments and you shall put the cloak on Aaron, and the robe of the ephod, and the ephod, and the breastpiece, and you shall gird him with the girdle of the ephod. 6. And you shall put the turban[e] on his head, and you shall put the crown *of the sanctuary*[3] on the turban. 7. And you shall take the anointing oil, and you shall pour it on his head, and you shall anoint him. 8. And you shall make his sons draw near, and you shall clothe them with cloaks. 9. And you shall gird[f] them with girdles, Aaron and his sons, and you shall put[g] <the turbans>[h] on them, and the priesthood <will be theirs>[h] for an eternal statute.[i] And you shall complete *the offering* of the hands of Aaron and *the offering* of the hands of his sons.[4] 10. And you shall bring the ox before the tent of meeting, and Aaron and his sons will lay their hands upon the head of the ox. 11. And you shall slaughter the ox before the Lord at the door of the tent of meeting. 12. And you shall take some of the blood, and you shall put it on the horn of the altar with your finger, and you shall pour all the (remaining) blood at the base of the altar. 13. And you shall take all the fat that covers the entrails, and whatever remains of the *lobes of the* liver and the two kidneys, and the fat that is on them, and you shall *arrange* (it) *upon* the altar.[5]

Apparatus, Chapter 29

[a] Nfi: "before me."
[b] Nfmg 1° and 2°: "to take (= taking) an ox."
[c] Omitted in text through homoioteleuton.
[d] With slight correction of text (*dkryh* for *dkryhw*); or: "their (two) rams" (*dkryhwn*).

[e] Nfi: "a turban."
[f] Nfmg: "gird" (imper. sing.).
[g] Nfmg: "and you shall fasten" (or "press").
[h] Missing in text, through homoioteleuton.
[i] Nfmg: "ministry for an eternal statute."

Notes, Chapter 29

[1] Hebrew has: "to act as priest to me" : see notes on 1:21; 28:1. Tg. Onq. and Tg. Ps.-J. have "to serve before me." See note on 12:5 for addition of "without blemish."

[2] Hebrew has: "and you shall wash them." This is the ritual ablution technically known as "sanctification," and Targum renders accordingly here and elsewhere, e.g., 30:18, 19, 20, 21.

[3] Hebrew has: "the crown of holiness."

[4] "Girdle" is singular in Hebrew, plural in Targum, LXX, Symm. Hebrew has: "and you shall fill Aaron's hands and his sons' hands"; see note on 28:41; Tg. Ps.-J.; and cf. Tg. Onq.

[5] Targum usually puts "the lobes of the liver" for Hebrew "the liver"; a similar rendering occurs in LXX, who have *lobos*, and Tg. Ps.-J. Hebrew has: "and you shall burn them upon the altar," which Targum normally renders as "you shall set them in order": see, e.g., 24:5; 29:18, 25; 30:1, 7, 8, 9; 40:27, and cf. LXX *epithéseis*.

14. And the flesh of the ox, the skin and its dung you shall burn with fire outside the camp; it is a sin offering. 15. And you shall take one of the rams, and Aaron and his sons shall lay their hands upon the head of the ram. 16. And you shall slaughter the ram and take its blood and sprinkle *it* upon the altar round about. 17. And you shall divide the ram into pieces and wash its entrails and its legs[j] and put them upon its pieces and upon its head. 18. And you shall *arrange* the whole ram upon the altar; it is a holocaust to *the name of* the Lord for a pleasing odor; it is *an offering before* the Lord.[k6] 19. And you shall take the second ram, and Aaron and his sons shall lay their hands upon the head (of the ram).[m] 20. And you shall slaughter the ram, and you shall take some of its blood, and you shall put it on *the tip*[n] of Aaron's ear and upon *the tip* of the ears of his sons[7]—of the right one[o]— and upon the thumb of their hands—of the right one[p]—and upon the great toe of their feet—of the right one[q]—and you shall sprinkle the blood upon the altar round about. 21. And you shall take some of the blood that is[r] upon the altar and some of the anointing oil and asperse Aaron and his garments, and his sons and his son's garments with him; and he shall be sanctified, he and his garments, and his sons, and his sons' garments with him. 22. And from the ram you shall take the fat, and the fat tail, and the fat that covers the entrails, and what remains of the lobes of the liver[s8] and the two kidneys and the fat which is on them, and the right thigh; for it is a ram of initiation.[t] 23. And one loaf[u] of bread and one cake of bread *saturated*[9] with oil, and one roll from the basket of unleavened bread which is before the Lord. 24. And you shall put all these on the palms[w] <*of the hands* of Aaron and on the palms>[x] *of the hands* of his sons, and you shall wave them for *a wave* offering[y] before the Lord. 25. And you shall receive[z] them from their hands, and you shall *ar-*

Apparatus, Chapter 29

[j] PVN= Nf for v. 17, except that P has different word for "its legs" (*kr'wy*; cf. HT; Nf *rglwy*).

[k] Nfmg: "it is an acceptable offering to the name of the Lord."

[m] Text, erroneously: "of the ox."

[n] *Aruk*, Mus.: "you shall put on the cartillage (*ḥshws*) (of the ear)"; = Ps.-J.

[o] Nfi: "the right (ear)."

[p] Nfi: "the right"; Nfmg: "of his right."

[q] Nfmg: "of her right."

[r] Nfmg: "which there is."

[s] Levita, *Meturgeman*: "what remains of the liver."

[t] Nfmg: "of the initiations."

[u] Nfmg + P: "a roll (*'iggul*); Pal. Tg. citation in Rashi: "one roll (*'ygwl*) of bread."

[w] Nfmg: "the palm."

[x] Omitted from text by homoioteleuton; added in margin.

[y] Text: *'npw*; HT: *tenupah*; Nf renders as *'npw(th)* in Exod 29:24; 35:22; 38:24, 29.

[z] Nfmg: "and you shall take."

Notes, Chapter 29

[6]Hebrew has: "And you shall burn, offer, the whole ram"; see note on v. 13. "To the Name of the Lord" represents Hebrew "to the Lord"; see note on 6:7. Hebrew has: "a fire-offering to the Lord": so Tg. Ps.-J., Tg. Onq., Pesh., Vulg.: *victimae Dei*, and below, 29:25, 41; 30:20; Lev. 2:3. The rendering is discussed by Grossfeld, 1988B, 83.

[7]Targum has, literally, "upon the upper part, *rwm*, of Aaron's ear and . . . of his sons"; so Tg. Onq. Cf. Symm. and Hebraios in Field, 1875, *ad. loc.*

[8]On the lobes of the liver, see v. 13 and LXX.

[9]The addition of "saturated" compares with that of "kneaded" in Tg. Ps.-J.

range them *upon* the altar, upon the holocaust, as a pleasing odor before the Lord; it is *an offering before* the Lord.*aa*[10] 26. And you shall take the breast (from) the ram of initiation of Aaron, and you shall wave (it)*bb* for a wave offering before the Lord; and it shall be your portion. 27. And you shall sanctify the breast of the wave offering,*cc* and the thigh of the *separated* offering*dd*—which had been waved*ee* or which has been *separated*[11] from the ram of initiation from*ff* that of Aaron and from that of his sons. 28. And it shall be*gg* for Aaron and for his sons as an eternal statute from the sons of Israel, for it is a *separated* offering (for the priests); and there will be a *separated* offering from the sons of Israel from *your*hh sacrifices of *holy things.*ii It shall be *your*jj *separated* offering to *the name of* the Lord.*kk*[12] 29. And the holy garments*mm* which are Aaron's shall be for his sons after him, to be anointed in them*nn* and to be ordained*oo* in them.[13] 30. The priest who*pp* *shall arise* after him[14] shall wear them seven days, when he goes *into* the tent of meeting to minister within the sanctuary.*qq* 31. And you shall take the ram of initiation,*rr* and you shall boil the flesh in a holy place. 32. And Aaron and his sons shall eat*ss* the flesh*tt* of the ram and the bread that is in the basket at the door of the tent of meeting. 33. And they shall eat those things with which atonement has been made to ordain them,*uu* to sanctify*ww* them; but a profane person shall not eat them be-

Apparatus, Chapter 29

aa Nfmg: "acceptable to the name of the Lord."
bb Text: "them," by dittography from v. 24.
cc "the breast of the wave offering"; also in VN ("the breast," only) P, *Aruk*; Levita, *Meturgeman.*
dd Aramaic; *'pršwt'*; HT: *terumah* (from *rûm*, "rise"); offering, contribution (for sacred uses), RSV: "wave offering."
ee Nfmg: "which he had waved"; probably error for "which has been raised."
ff Nfmg: "of the initiations, from that which belongs to Aaron and from that which belongs to his sons."
gg Nfmg: "and they shall be."
hh Nfmg: "their."
ii HT: "from the peace offerings."
jj Nfmg: "his"; see *hh* above.

kk Nfmg: "before the Lord."
mm Nfmg +: "of the house (of holiness)" = the sanctuary, temple.
nn Nfmg: "of Aaron shall be for his sons after him to be anointed in it" (i.e., in the garment).
oo Lit.: "to complete by them the offering of his hands."
pp Nfmg: "(the priest) from his sons (who comes) after him."
qq Nfmg: "in the sanctuary."
rr Nfmg: "of the initiations."
ss Nfmg: "and (Aaron) shall eat."
tt Nfmg: "(the flesh) of the initiations and the flesh that is in the basket."
uu Lit.: "to complete the offering of their hands."
ww Nfmg: "and to sanctify."

Notes, Chapter 29

[10]On "arrange" and "an offering before the Lord," see note on v. 18 and Tg. Ps.-J. Vulg. simply has "offering."

[11]Hebrew has: "which has been waved and which has been lifted up, *hwrm*." The last word recalls for the Targumist the *Terumah*, the priestly due, which is rendered by Targum with the root *prš*, "separate": hence "has been separated"; cf. Tg. Onq., Tg. Ps.-J., and LXX, Vulg., *b. Sukk.* 37a.

[12]For the rendering of peace offerings as "sacrifices of holy things," see note on 18:10 and Tg. Onq.; Tg. Ps.-J. Targum has changed Hebrew third person suffixes into second person suffixes. On "the Name of the Lord," see note on 6:7. "Separation" renders Hebrew *Terumah*: see note on v. 27.

[13]Apparatus gives a literal rendering of the Aramaic, for which see note on 28:41.

[14]Hebrew has: "The priest after him from his sons"; with Targum, cf. Tg. Ps.-J.

cause they are a holy thing.[15] 34. But if any of the flesh of initiation or any of the bread[xx] is left over until the morning, you shall burn whatever is left over in fire; it shall not be eaten, because it is[yy] a holy thing. 35. And thus you shall do to Aaron, to his sons, according to all[zz] that I have commanded you; for seven days you shall ordain[a] them.[16] 36. And *you shall offer* an ox every day as a sin offering[b] for atonement; and you *shall anoint* the altar when you make atonement upon it; and you shall anoint it to sanctify it.[17] 37. Seven days you shall make atonement upon the altar, and you shall sanctify it, and the altar shall be most holy.[c] Whatever touches the altar shall become holy. 38. *According* to this *order you shall make offerings* upon[d] the altar: two lambs a year old every day continually.[e][18] 39. One of the lambs *you shall offer*[f] in the morning, and the second lamb *you shall offer* at twilight.[g][19] 40. *According to this order you shall offer:*[h] with one lamb *a measure of* fine flour saturated with a fourth of a hin of beaten oil, and a libation of a fourth of him of wine.[20] 41. And *you shall offer* the second lamb at twilight; *you shall offer* it as the cereal offering of the morning *lamb* and as its libation.[i] *It shall be received*[j] as a pleasing odor, *an offering before* the Lord.[k][21] 42. It shall be a continual holocaust throughout your generations,[m] at the door of the tent of meeting, *before the* Lord, where I will meet you,[n] to speak with you there. 43. And I—*my Memra*—

Apparatus, Chapter 29

[xx] Nfmg: "of the initiations and of the food."

[yy] Nfmg: "they are."

[zz] Nfmg: "according to this order; according to all that."

[a] Nfmg: "you (sing.) shall ordain"; cf. vv. 29, 31; pl. in text.

[b] Nfmg: "as the sin offering."

[c] Nfmg: "all who offer upon the altar shall be made holy."

[d] Nfmg: "and according to this order which you shall offer upon."

[e] Nfmg: "of one year, perfect (cf. LXX), without blemish, two each day, a perpetual holocaust."

[f] Nfmg: "and one lamb you shall offer"; Nfi: "a lamb you shall offer."

[g] Lit.: "between the suns," or "services."

[h] Nfmg: "you shall offer," i.e., suppresses "according to this order" with HT.

[i] Nfmg: "and as its libations, thus shall you offer it."

[j] Nfi: "it is received."

[k] Nfmg: "received to the name of the Lord."

[m] Nfmg: "a perpetual holocaust throughout your generations."

[n] Nfi: "that I will meet"; Nfmg: "where my Memra will meet you"; cf. 30:6,36.

Notes, Chapter 29

[15]See note to v. 29.

[16]With "according to this order," Nfmg anticipates a cliché of Tg. Nf found already at 12:11 and below, vv. 38, 40. On "ordain," see note to verse 29.

[17]Hebrew has, lit.: "And you shall make, do an ox"; the verb '*sh*, "make, do," may have the sense of "sacrifice," as in 10:25; 12:49; and Vulg., so that the Targum interprets accordingly, and so also in vv. 38, 39, 41. Hebrew has: "and you shall purify the altar when you make atonement upon it."

[18]Hebrew has: "And this is what you shall do upon the altar." For Targum, see notes on vv. 35 and 36, and Tg. Ps.-J. Nfmg's addition incorporates the version of the law of Tamid found in Num 28:3-4.

[19]See note to v. 36.

[20]See notes to 12:11; 29:35.

[21]For "offer," see note to v. 36 and Vulg. Targum makes precise the law that the evening sacrifice is to proceed exactly like the morning one, a matter stressed also by Vulg. "It shall be received . . . an offering before the Lord" is Targum's standard rendering of "an agreeable odor, a fire-offering to the Lord."

will meet the children[o] *of* Israel there, and it will be sanctified[p] *within* my Glory.[q][22] 44. And I will sanctify the tent of meeting and the altar; and Aaron and his sons I will sanctify *to minister before* me[r] *in the high priesthood.*[23] 45. And I will *make my Shekinah[s] dwell* in the midst of the children[t] of Israel, and *my Memra* will be for them a *redeeming* God.[24] 46. And they shall know *that I* am the Lord their God, who brought them forth out of the land[u] of Egypt so that *the Glory of my Shekinah* might dwell among them.[25] I the Lord, their God.

CHAPTER 30

1. "And you shall make an altar for *arranging* the incense;[a] of acacia wood you shall make it.[1] 2. A cubit (shall be) its length and a cubit its breadth; it shall be square, and two cubits shall be *the measure of* its height; its horns (coming) from it[b] shall be its height.[2] 3. And you shall overlay it with pure gold, its upper parts and its sides round about, and its horns; and you shall make a molding of gold round about for it.[3] 4. And two rings of gold you shall make for it; under its molding on the two corners, upon its two sides, you shall make (them), and they shall

Apparatus, Chapter 29

[o] Lit.: "join myself to the children of"; Nfmg: "upon the children of."

[p] "it"; i.e., the tent; Nfi, (and LXX, Syr, Onq.): "and I shall be sanctified."

[q] Nfmg: "in my glory."

[r] Nfmg: "before him."

[s] Nfi: "the glory (of my Shekinah)."

[t] Nfmg: "the glory of my Shekinah among the children."

[u] Nfmg: "(I . . .) who have redeemed and brought them out redeemed from."

Notes, Chapter 29

[22] On the Memra here, cf. Tg. Onq. and Tg. Ps.-J.; and see Hayward, 1981A, 104–6.

[23] See notes on 1:21; 28:1.

[24] Hebrew has: "And I shall dwell (*wšknty*) in the midst of the Israelites, and I shall be God for them." On the Shekinah, see Tg. Onq. and Tg. Ps.-J., and cf. Muñoz León, 1977, 100–101. For the Memra as a redeemer God, see note on 6:7, and cf. Hayward, 1981A, 23–24.

[25] Hebrew has: "so that I should dwell (*lškny*) in their midst." See Tg. Onq., Tg. Ps.-J.

Apparatus, Chapter 30

[a] Nfmg: "altar of incenses; of acacia wood."

[b] Nfmg: "(from it) and in it shall its horns be."

Notes, Chapter 30

[1] See note on 29:13.

[2] See note on 25:10.

[3] See note on 25:11.

serve as *places* for poles whereby to carry it.[c4] 5. And you shall make the poles of acacia wood, and you shall overlay them with gold. 6. And you shall place it before the veil which is by the ark of the testimony, where *my Memra* will meet you.[d5] 7. And Aaron *shall arrange*[e] incense[f] of *good* aromas upon it; every morning when he arranges the lamps *Aaron shall arrange* it.[6] 8. And when Aaron *arranges* the lamps at twilight, he shall *arrange* it, a perpetual incense[g7] before the Lord throughout your generations. 9. You shall not arrange[8] strange incense, nor holocausts, nor cereal offerings, nor shall you pour libations[h] upon it. 10. And Aaron shall make atonement *on it once* a year,[i9] upon its horns. With the blood of the sin offering of atonement he shall make atonement on it once a year, *on its horns*, throughout your generations. It shall be most holy to *the name of* the Lord." 11. And the Lord[j] spoke to Moses saying: 12. "When you take the sum *total*[k] of the children of Israel, to make a census of them, each man will give a ransom for himself to *the name of* the Lord when you count them,[m] so that there will not be[n] among them any *destroying* plague at the time you count them.[10] 13. Whoever passes[o] the census will give *according* to this *order:*[p] *from*[q] half a *sela* according to the *sela* of the sanctuary—the *sela* is twenty *ma'in*[r]—a half *sela* as a *separated* of-

Apparatus, Chapter 30

[c] Nfmg: "to bear it."
[d] Cf. 29:42; 30:36.
[e] Nfmg: "and you shall arrange."
[f] Nfmg: "incenses."
[g] Nfmg: "incenses always."
[h] Nfmg: "strange incenses, holocausts and cereal offering; and you shall not pour a libation."
[i] Nfmg: "shall meet (probably an error for "once") each year, with the blood of the sin offering of atonement he shall meet (?), each year he shall make atonement."
[j] Nfmg: "the Memra of the Lord."
[k] VN: "the sum total reckoning"; otherwise VN, v. 12 = Nf.

[m] Nfmg: "at the time in which you are (counting them)."
[n] Nfmg: "and (there will) not (be)."
[o] Nfmg: "this is the proportion of the *sela* that appeared to Moses on Mount Sinai: about one denarius (*Latin loan word*) of fire, and thus it said to him: Like this shall all who pass give."
[p] Nfmg: "the enumerations."
[q] "from" probably due to taking *mem* of HT *maḥaṣit* (= half), a mistake not made in other renderings of the Hebrew term in Nf.
[r] MT: *gerah.*

Notes, Chapter 30

[4] See note on 25:27.
[5] For the Memra, cf. Tg. Onq., Tg. Ps.-J., and see Hayward, 1981A, 104–6.
[6] See note on 29:13. The addition of "good" is commonplace when this Targum speaks of the incense.
[7] Hebrew has: "and when Aaron sets up the lamps . . . he shall offer it as incense." Targum uses "arrange" for both verbs. See note on 29:13, and below, v. 9.
[8] Hebrew has: "You shall not bring up," for which the Targum has used "arrange"; Hebrew root *'lh* is used here and in v. 8. The listed sacrifices appear in the singular in the Hebrew text.
[9] For the addition of "upon it," see LXX. Targum makes explicit that this be done once a year: so also Tg. Ps.-J. See note on 6:7 for "to the Name of the Lord."
[10] For "sum total," cf. Frg. Tg. V. See note on 6:7 for "to the Name of the Lord." The "destroying" plague refers to the events of 12:13.

fering *to the name of* the Lord. [11] 14. Everyone who passes the census from twenty years old and upward will give the *separated* offering[s] to *the name of* the Lord. [t][12] 15. He who is rich shall not give more, and he who is poor shall not give less than half a *sela* when giving the *separated* offering[s] of the Lord to make atonement for yourselves. [12] 16. And you shall take the redemption money from the sons of Israel, and you shall give it for the service of the tent of meeting; and it will be for the sons of Israel for a *good* remembrance [13] before the Lord, as atonement for yourselves." 17. And the Lord[u] spoke with Moses saying: 18. "You shall make a basin of bronze, with the base thereof of bronze, for washing. [14] And you shall place it[w] between the tent of meeting and the altar, and you shall put water within it. 19. Aaron and his sons shall wash their hands and their feet from it.[x][15] 20. When they enter the tent of meeting or when they draw near to the top of the altar to minister, to arrange offerings before the Lord, they shall wash in water so that[y] *they may not die.* [16] 21. And they shall wash their hands and their feet lest they die; and it shall be[z] for them an eternal statute:[aa] for *them* and for the descendants *of their sons and* throughout their generations." [17] 22. And the Lord[bb] spoke to Moses, saying: 23. "And you, take the finest[cc] incense, *precious spices, choicest* myrrh, as weighed out[dd] five hundred *selas*, aromatic cinnamon half *as much,*[ee] (that is) two hundred and fifty (*selas*); and aromatic cane, *a weight of* two hundred and fifty (*selas*), [18] 24. and of cassia, *a weight of* five hundred *selas*, according to the *sela* of

---

Apparatus, Chapter 30

[s] Aramaic *'prśw*; HT's *terumah*; see note *dd* to Exod 29:27.

[t] Nfmg: "the Lord's separated offering."

[u] Nfmg: "the Memra of the Lord."

[w] Nfmg: "and he will place" (corr. to: "and place"); Nfmg: "and you shall put (it)."

[x] *Aruk*, (Mus.): "and they shall take from it in a pure ladle."

[y] Nfmg: "and (they) shall not (die)."

[z] Nfmg: "and they shall be."

[aa] Nfmg: "an eternal statute for them for ever."

[bb] Nfmg: "the Memra of the Lord."

[cc] Lit.: "the heads of incense"; Nfi: "the head of."

[dd] Aramaic: *mtql*; Nfmg: "a weight of" or "weighty" (*tql*) = VN; VN: "and you take the heads of precious spices, choicest myrrh weighing (*tql*) five hundred *sela'in*."

[ee] Lit.: "half in weight."

Notes, Chapter 30

[11] Hebrew has: "This they shall give" for "according to this order," on which see note to 12:11. Twenty *ma'in* are also required by Tg. Ps.-J. and Tg. Onq. See note on 6:7 for "to the Name of the Lord." For the offering of separation, see notes on 29:27, 28. Nfmg relates the tradition that this was shown to Moses on Sinai: so also Tg. Ps.-J., *Tanḥuma Ki Tissa'* 4, and *PRK* 2:10; *Pes. R.* 16:7.

[12] See note on v. 13.

[13] On the good remembrance, see note to 12:14.

[14] Targum has, literally, "for sanctification" instead of "for washing," like Tg. Onq. and Tg. Ps.-J. See note on 29:4; Le Déaut, 1979 (*Exode*) 242; and Grossfeld, 1988B, 85.

[15] See note on v. 18.

[16] "To arrange offerings before the Lord" renders Hebrew "to offer up fire offerings to the Lord": see note on 29:13, 18, and cf. Tg. Onq. and Tg. Ps.-J. On the washing in water, see note on v. 18.

[17] On washing, see note on v. 18. Hebrew has: "for him and for his seed for their generations"; cf. Tg. Onq., Tg. Ps.-J.

[18] Tg. has added "precious spices": see v. 7, and Frg. Tg. V. "Choicest" represents "liquid" of MT: see also Tg. Ps.-J., Frg. Tg. V, LXX, Vulg., and Josephus, *Ant.* III.viii.3. "Weight" is an addition here and in the following verses; so Tg. Onq. and Tg. Ps.-J.; cf. Grossfeld, 1988B, 86.

the sanctuary, and olive oil a hin-full.[19] 25. And you shall make of it a holy anointing[ff] oil, a blend of a spice-blender, work of a perfumer. It shall be holy anointing oil. 26. And with it you shall anoint the tent of meeting and the ark of the testimony, 27. and table and all its utensils, and the lampstand and all its utensils,[gg] and the altar of incense, 28. and the altar of holocausts and all its utensils, and the basin and the base thereof. 29. And you shall consecrate them, and they shall be most holy; everything that draws near them shall be holy.[hh] 30. And you shall anoint Aaron and his sons, and you shall consecrate them to *serve before* me[ii] *in the high priesthood.*[20] 31. And you shall speak[jj] with[kk] the children of Israel, saying: 'This shall be for me a holy anointing oil throughout your generations. 32. It shall not be rubbed upon the flesh of an *ordinary*[mm] son of man[nn] and according to its likeness, similar to it, you shall not make *for yourselves.*[21] It is holy, and it shall be holy for you. 33. Anyone who blends its like and who puts any of it upon an outsider[oo] shall be blotted out from the midst of his people.'" 34. And the Lord said to Moses: "Take the *finest*[pp] *incenses, precious spices,* balsam, *an ear (of) myrrh*[qq] and galbanum[rr] and clear[ss] frankincense:[22] of each there shall be equal weight. 35. And you shall make with it an incense[tt] *blended,*[23] the work of a

Apparatus, Chapter 30

[ff] Nfmg: "a work of holiness"; probably through some error.

[gg] Nfmg: "the utensils and the basins and the base thereof; *and the altar* (in Hebrew; = lemma cf. v. 28). And the altar of incense and the altar of the holocausts and (correcting text) all its utensils. *And you shall consecrate*" (in Hebrew; = lemma v. 29).

[hh] Nfmg: "all that draw near to them (or: that touch them) shall be made holy."

[ii] Nfmg: "before me."

[jj] Aramaic, *tmll*; Nfmg: "you shall speak" (*tdbr*, Hebrew).

[kk] Nfmg: "to the children of."

[mm] Greek loan word *idiôtês*; here one without a priestly or royal office; cf. M. Kasher, *Torah Shelemah*, 21 (Jerusalem 1954), 35; cf. also 30:37.

[nn] Nfmg: "(flesh of) a man."

[oo] or: "a profane person."

[pp] Lit.: "heads of incenses"; Nfmg: "(take) spices," indicating its text lacked "incenses."

[qq] VN: "balsam, and an ear (of) myrrh (*swbl' mwryy'*) and galbanum"; Levita, *Meturgeman*, "balsam and an ear"; "myrrh and galbanum"; *Aruk* 1°: "an ear myrrh," *Aruk* 2°: "ears"; cf. "spikenard" (*spica nardea*); "myrrh nard," Mark 14:3.

[rr] Nfmg: "and galbanums" (pl.).

[ss] Nfmg: "bitter (frankincense)."

[tt] Nfmg: "incenses."

Notes, Chapter 30

[19]For "a weight of," see note on v. 23. On the full hin, Grossfeld, 1988B, 87 recalls the information given in *b. Men.* 87b that the hin-measuring vessel had several gradated marks upon it indicating fixed portions of the measure.

[20]Hebrew has: "to be priests to me." See notes on 1:21; 28:1.

[21]See Le Déaut, 1979 (*Exode*) 244. The addition of "for yourselves" is found also in LXX.

[22]Hebrew has: "Take for yourselves sweet spices, stacte, and onycha and galbanum; sweet spices with pure frankincense." See note on v. 23, and cf. Tg. Onq. and Tg. Ps.-J. They should be of equal weight: Grossfeld, 1988B, 87, notes the same requirement in Tg. Onq., Tg. Ps.-J., Pesh., Vulg., and *b. Ker.* 5a, which notes that the measures were interpreted generously.

[23]For "blended," cf. Tg. Ps.-J. and Frg. Tg. P, V: Hebrew has "tempered."

perfumer, mixed, *uu* pure, holy. *ww* 36. And you shall pound some of it and grind it to powder and put some of it before the testimony in the tent of meeting, where *my Memra* will meet you; *xx* it shall be *yy* most holy for you. [24] 37. And the incense which you shall make, in its likeness, you shall not make (it) for yourselves; it shall be holy *for you* to the name of the Lord. [25] 38. Anyone who should make like to it *to enjoy* it shall be blotted out from the midst of his people." [26]

CHAPTER 31

1. And the Lord *a* spoke with Moses, saying: 2. "See, *Moses*, that I have *designated and* called *b* by the *good* name of *master*, *c* Bezalel, son of Uri, son of Hur, of the tribe of the sons of Judah. [1] 3. And I have perfected him with a spirit of holiness *d from before the Lord*, in wisdom, [2] in skill *e* and in knowledge and all

Apparatus, Chapter 30

uu Or: "seasoned" (with salt); Aramaic *mmzg*; attested also in PVN, *Aruk*, Elias, *Meturgeman*. HT: *mmlḥ* ("salted").

ww Lit.: "pure of holiness"; cf. Org: "pure for holiness."

xx Better than: "I will make my Memra meet you": *'zmn* of text = *yzmn*; or: "I, my Memra, will meet you."

yy Nfmg: "they shall be."

Notes, Chapter 30

[24] See Tg. Onq. and Tg. Ps.-J., and note to v. 6.

[25] Hebrew has: "it shall be holy for you (sing.) to the Lord." For second person plural, cf. LXX, Vulg., and Tg. Ps.-J.; and see note on 6:7.

[26] Hebrew has: "to smell" for "to enjoy"; with Tg., cf. Vulg.

Apparatus, Chapter 31

a Nfmg: "the Memra of the Lord."

b VN: "See, Moses, behold I have anointed and called by a good name Bezalel." Nfmg 1°: "behold, I have anointed and called" = VN; Nfmg 2°: "that I have remembered and called by a good name from the days of eternity."

c Nfi: "(I have appointed) Bezalel" (omitting intervening section).

d The text of Nf reads: "(with) a spirit of a prophet draw near (*qrb*; to be corrected to: *qry* = "read") of holiness." The explanation seems to be that the scribe wrote "of a prophet" and, recognizing his mistake, continued: "Read" (= correct to) "of holiness." This reading confirmed by Nf's almost identical rendering of the same HT in 35:31.

e Nfmg: "(spirit) of skill from (before)."

Notes, Chapter 31

[1] Hebrew has: "See, I have called by name Bezalel the son of Uri . . . of the tribe of Judah." Frg. Tg. V is similar to our Targum, having "I have anointed and called": the verb *rby*, "anoint," which is used here also by Tg. Onq., carries with it also the lesser significance of "appoint." Tg. Ps.-J. adds "Moses" and the "good" name. "Master" is Rabban: see further 33:12, 17; 35:30; and Le Déaut, 1979 (*Exode*) 246–47.

[2] Hebrew has: "And I have filled him with the spirit of God, with wisdom." There is confusion in the text: see discussion in Levy, 1986, 420, and Apparatus, which notes the reading "spirit of prophecy," for which cf. witnesses G, v, 1 of Tg. Onq. in Sperber's edition. LXX has *pneuma theion sophias*.

work, 4. and *for teaching*[f] *craftsmanship* and for working in *the art*[g] *of* gold and in the art of silver[h] and in the art of bronze,[3] 5. and in *the art* of setting *precious stones*[i4] and in woodcarving, to work in every (kind of) work.[j] 6. And behold, I have placed Oholiab, the son of Ahisamach, of the tribe of *the men* of Dan,[k] with him, and in the hearts of all the able of heart[m] I have placed ability that they may make all that I have commanded[n] you: 7. the tent of meeting and the ark for the testimony and the mercy seat which is thereon and all the utensils of the tent,[o] 8. and the table and its utensils,[p] and the pure lampstand and all its utensils, 9. and the altar of holocaust and all its utensils, and the basin and the base thereof, 10. and the garments of the service and the holy[q] garments of Aaron the priest,[r] and the garments of his sons for the *service;*[s5] 11. and the anointing oil and the fragrant incense for *sanctification.*[t6] *You* shall make everything[u] that I have commanded you." 12. And the Lord[w] said to Moses, saying: 13. "And you, speak with the children of Israel, saying: 'You shall surely keep my *holy* sabbaths because they are a sign[x] between me and you for your generations, that (you) may know that it is I the Lord who sanctified you.'[y] 14. And you shall keep the sabbath day[z] because it is holy for you. Whoever profanes it *shall surely be put to death;*[7] whoever does any work on it,[aa] that person[bb] shall be blotted out[cc] from the midst of his people. 15. Six days shall work be done,[dd] and on the seventh day (there shall be) a sabbath of rest holy *before* the Lord:[ee] whoever does work <on the sabbath day>[ff] *shall*

Apparatus, Chapter 31

[f] Nfmg: "to instruct."
[g] Nfmg: "and for working the art."
[h] Nfmg: "and silver and the art of."
[i] Levita, *Meturgeman:* "in the shaping of (precious) stone."
[j] Nfmg: "and of cutting precious stones for setting and in woodcarving to work all work."
[k] Nfi: "(of the tribe) of Dan."
[m] I.e., men of ability.
[n] Nfmg: "I shall command."
[o] Lit.: "of his tent"; HT: "of the tent."
[p] Nfmg: "(and) all its utensils."
[q] Nfi: "(the garments of) the sanctuary."
[r] in the text "the priest" is also written in Hebrew.
[s] Nfmg: "(to minister) before him in the high priesthood."

[t] The text has *qidduš,* washing of hands and feet before officiating.
[u] Nfi: "according to all."
[w] Nfmg: "the Memra of the Lord."
[x] Nfmg: "hope between my Memra and between." We should probably read "sabbaths" instead of "hope."
[y] Nfmg: "that my Memra sanctifies you."
[z] Nfi: "the sabbath."
[aa] Nfmg: "who does work on it."
[bb] Nfi: "(that) man."
[cc] Nfi: "he shall be blotted out": i.e., that man; text has feminine—"that person," lit.: "soul."
[dd] Nfi: "you shall do" (with LXX).
[ee] Nfmg: "to the name of the Lord."
[ff] Added interlinearly in note by copyist.

Notes, Chapter 31

[3]Hebrew has: "To devise cunning works, to work in gold, and in silver, and in bronze." Tg. Onq. renders "for teaching craftsmanship" and "working in the art."

[4]Hebrew has: "And in the cutting of stone"; cf. Tg. Onq. for "and in the art."

[5]For the rendering, cf. Tg. Onq., Tg. Ps.-J., LXX, Pesh.

[6]Hebrew has: "and sweet-smelling incense for holiness (or: for the sanctuary)." Targum's "for sanctification" may be a mistake for "for the sanctuary": see Le Déaut, 1979 (*Exode*) 249. Hebrew has: "they shall make everything."

[7]Hebrew has: "the Sabbath"; "day" is added to bring the wording of the commandment into line with Exod 20:8. For the formula "shall surely be put to death" for Hebrew *mwt ymwt*, see Tg. Onq., Tg. Ps.-J., and above, 21:12.

surely be put to death.[8] 16. And the children of Israel shall keep the sabbath *day,*[9] observing[gg] the sabbath *day*[hh] throughout their generations as a perpetual covenant. 17. *The sabbath* is a sign forever between *his Memra* and the children of Israel that in six days the Lord *created*[ii] the heavens and that on the seventh day *there was* rest and repose *before the Lord.*"[jj][10] 18. And he gave to Moses, when he had completed speaking with him on Mount[kk] Sinai, (the) two tables (of) the testimony, tables of stone, written by the finger of *the Might from before the Lord.*[11]

CHAPTER 32

1. When the people saw that Moses delayed to come down from the mountain, the people gathered themselves together to Aaron *AND THEY SAID TO HIM*: *"ARISE; MAKE US GODS WHO SHALL GO BEFORE US,*[a] because this man Moses who *brought us out* of the land of Egypt, we do not know what has happened to him *in the end.*"[1] 2. And Aaron said to them: "Break open[b] the gold rings which

Apparatus, Chapter 31

[gg] Lit.: "doing."
[hh] Nfmg: "doing (lit.: "to be doing") the sabbath day."
[ii] Nfmg: "and the Memra of the Lord perfected."

[jj] Nfmg: "before him."
[kk] Nfmg: "from the mountain."

Notes, Chapter 31

[8]For "shall surely be put to death," see note on v. 14. The words "that soul shall be destroyed from the midst of his people" have been written in the MS and erased: see Levy, 1986, 421.

[9]On the addition of "day," see note on v. 14.

[10]Hebrew has: "It is a sign between me and between the Israelites for ever; for in six days the Lord made heaven . . . , and on the seventh day he rested and was refreshed." For the sabbath as a sign between God's Memra and Israel, see Tg. Onq. and Tg. Ps.-J. For the formula "created and perfected" in Nfmg, see Tg. Ps.-J. The notion of "rest and repose" before the Lord is clearly designed to avoid any suspicion that God may have "slept" on the sabbath. Vulg. has it that God ceased from work.

[11]On the exegesis here, see 32:16 and Nfmg.

Apparatus, Chapter 32

[a] The words in capitals are in Hebrew without an Aramaic translation because, as is said in Nfmg: "it is read but not translated."

[b] Nfmg: "take off."

Notes, Chapter 32

For studies of Targum of this chapter, see L. Smolar and M. Aberbach, "The Golden Calf Episode in Postbiblical Literature," *HUCA* 39 (1968) 91–116; M. Ginsburger, "Verbotene Thargumim," *MGWJ* 44 (1900) 1–7; P. S. Alexander, "The Rabbinic Lists of Forbidden Targumim," *JJS* 27 (1976) 177–91; M. McNamara, *New Testament and Palestinian Targum* 48–49; A. Díez Macho, *Neophyti* I, vol. 1, 62*; I. J. Mandelbaum, "Tannaitic Exegesis of the Golden Calf Episode," in *A Tribute to Geza Vermes*, ed. P. R. Davies and R. T. White (Sheffield: Sheffield Academic Press, 1990) 207–23. Words and phrases set in capital letters are not translated, but retained in the original Hebrew.

[1]The words not translated do not agree with the ruling of *m. Meg.* 4:10; *t. Meg.* 4:31; *b. Meg.* 25ab, which allow the "first story of the calf," but not the "second story of the calf," to be put into the Targum. The "second story," according to *b. Meg.* 25b, is Exod 32:21–25, which may be read (in Hebrew) but not translated (into Aramaic). It is possible that Tg. Nf's treatment of this chapter derives from a time before the mishnaic ruling was adopted, when more stringent rules applied and even the first story of the calf was left in Hebrew: see Alexander, *art. cit.*, 181–82, 184, 188. But see M. Klein, 1988, 89. Vulg., like Tg., has "brought out" for Hebrew "brought up."

are on the ears of your wives,^c on your sons and on your daughters, and bring (them)^d to me." 3. And all the people took off the gold rings <which were>^e on their ears and brought (them) to Aaron.^f 4. And he received them from their hands and cast (them) into a mold² *AND THEY MADE A MOLTEN CALF; AND THEY SAID: "THESE ARE YOUR GODS, O ISRAEL, WHO BROUGHT YOU OUT OF THE LAND OF EGYPT."*^g 5. And Aaron saw *Hur the prophet before it*^h *and was afraid*; and he built an altar before it; and Aaron made announcementⁱ and said: "A feast *before* the Lord tomorrow!"^{j 3} 6. And they arose early the following day and *set* holocausts^k in order beside them ^m and brought sacrifices of holy things, and the people sat down to eat and drink and rose up to sport obscenelyⁿ *in foreign worship.*⁴ 7. And the Lord^o spoke with Moses: "Go, descend, because the people whom you have *brought redeemed* out⁵ of the land of Egypt have corrupted themselves;^p 8. they have turned aside quickly from the way which I have commanded them; *THEY HAVE MADE FOR THEMSELVES A MOLTEN CALF AND HAVE BOWED DOWN TO IT AND SACRIFICED TO IT AND SAID: 'THESE ARE YOUR GODS, O ISRAEL, WHO BROUGHT YOU OUT OF THE LAND OF EGYPT.'"*^q 9. And the Lord^o said to Moses: "This people *is manifest before me,*^r and, behold, they are a difficult *people to receive*^s *instruction.*⁶ 10. And now, re-

Apparatus, Chapter 32

^c Nfmg: "which there are on the ears of your wives."

^d Nfmg: "(bring) them (to me)."

^e Absent from text; supplied in Nfi.

^f Nfmg: "which there were on their ears and brought them to Aaron."

^g Words in capitals are only in Hebrew; cf. to v. 1.

^h Nfmg: "and Aaron saw Hur sacrificing before it"; PVN: "And Aaron saw Hur (P +: "his sister's son) sacrificing before it and he was afraid, and built an altar before it (VN adds: "and Aaron called and said: a feast")."

ⁱ Nfmg: "and he shouted."

^j Nfmg: "and Aaron made announcement and said: Would that the sacrifice be against him (correcting text *by*) as the feast of the wicked before the Lord tomorrow."

^k Nfmg: "and they brought holocausts near " (or: "they offered holocausts").

^m The word is probably due to dittography and should be deleted.

ⁿ Or: "to act licentiously"; M: "playing (licentiously)," = PVN.

^o Nfmg: "the Memra of the Lord."

^p Nfmg 1°: "have corrupted their good works"; Nfmg 2°: "have corrupted their works."

^q Text in capitals in Hebrew only, without Aramaic translation.

^r HT: "I have seen this people."

^s Nfmg: "stiff-necked to receive."

Notes, Chapter 32

²The casting of the rings into a mold is found also in Tg. Ps.-J.

³Hebrew has: "And Aaron saw, and built an altar in front of him; and Aaron called and said: A feast to the Lord tomorrow!" The Targum needed to indicate what Aaron saw, for the verb in Hebrew has no object. Tg. Nf may have preserved a small relic of a tradition according to which Hur the prophet had objected to the calf, and had been killed for his pains by the mob: see *b. Sanh.* 7a; *Exod. R.* 41, 7; 48, 3; 51, 8; *Lev. R.* 10, 3; *PRE* 45, 2, 5; *Num. R.* 15, 21,*Tanhuma Tesawweh* 10; *Tanhuma B.* II. 113; and Le Déaut, 1979 (*Exode*) 251, who notes that this tradition was known also to Ephraim Syrus. By this means, Targum attempts to exonerate Aaron of blame for making the calf: had he not agreed to make it, the people would have killed him as surely as they had killed Hur.

⁴Hebrew has: "So they rose up the next day, and offered whole burnt offerings, and brought near peace offerings; and the people sat down to eat and drink, and rose up to sport." For "set holocausts in order," see note on 29:13; for "sacrifices of holy things," see note on 18:12; and for "foreign worship," the literal Aramaic rendering of Hebrew *'abodah zarah,* "idolatry," see *Exod. R.* 41, 7; Frg. Tg. P, V; and Tg. Ps.-J.

⁵Targum has "brought out" for Hebrew "brought up"; cf. LXX, Vulg. On "redeemed," see note on 3:10.

⁶Hebrew has: "I have seen this people, and, behold, it is a stiff-necked people." For "is manifest before me," cf. Tg. Onq. and Tg. Ps.-J. Tg. Nf regularly renders "stiff-necked people" as "a people difficult to receive instruction," referring to their unwillingness to accept the commandments of the Law; this is what the biblical phrase actually means. See also 33:3; 34:9.

frain yourself[t] *from beseeching mercy for them before me* that my anger may be enkindled against them and that I may *blot* them *out*, and *it is possible before me to constitute* <you a people>[u] *greater and stronger than they.*"[7] 11. And Moses *prayed before* the Lord[w] his God and said: "Why, O Lord,[x] is your anger kindled against your people which you brought out *redeemed* from the land of Egypt by *your* great power[y] and with *your outstretched arm?*[z8] 12. Why, *I pray*, should the Egyptians say:[aa] 'For their evil has been their coming out; for having them slain on the mountains and for blotting them out[bb] from off the face of the earth'?[cc] Turn, *I pray*, from the might of your anger and let there be regret *before* you[dd] concerning the evil *which you have planned to bring*[ee] upon your people.[9] 13. Remember, in your good mercies, Abraham,[ff] Isaac and Israel, your servants, to whom you swore by *the name of your Memra* and spoke: 'I will multiply your *sons*[gg] like the stars of the heavens, and I will give to your *sons*[hh] all this land which I have said and they shall possess *it* forever.'"[10] 14. And *there was regret before* the Lord concerning all

---

Apparatus, Chapter 32

[t] Nfmg: "and now restrain yourself (from beseeching) and my anger will be enkindled."

[u] Missing in text and added interlinearly as a note; Nfmg: "and I will constitute you, Moses, nations."

[w] Nfmg: "and Moses began to beseech mercy from before the Lord."

[x] Nfmg: "(why) I pray, O Memra of the Lord?"

[y] Nfmg: "from Egypt by your power."

[z] Nfmg: "and with outstretched arm."

[aa] Lit.: "say, saying."

[bb] Nfmg: "the Egyptians saying: For their evil has he

brought them out, to slay them on the mountains and blot them out."

[cc] Nfi: "(from above) the earth."

[dd] Nfmg: "and have compassion upon (all)."

[ee] Nfmg: "to bring (it)"; or: "to bring" (a different writing).

[ff] Nfmg: "in your mercies (or: "your friends") Abraham."

[gg] Nfmg: "I shall surely multiply the descendants of your sons."

[hh] Nfmg: "the descendants of your sons."

Notes, Chapter 32

[7]Hebrew has: "And now, leave me alone, and my anger shall be kindled against them, and I shall devour them; but you I shall make into a great nation." For Moses beseeching mercy, see Tg. Onq. and Tg. Ps.-J. The point is that Moses should not pray for the people; and the Hebrew "leave me alone" is thus understood by *b. Ber. 32a; Tanḥuma Ki Tissa'* 22; and Targums of Deut 9:14, sources cited also by Grossfeld, 1988B, 89. The rendering "blot out" for Hebrew "devour," which is, of course, a metaphorical expression "decoded" by the Targum, is shared with Tg. Onq. and Tg. Ps.-J., Vulg. The final sentence is not found in the other Targumim: its precise implications are uncertain, and it would possibly provide a pretext for anti-Jewish polemic in the hands of the unscrupulous. Are passages like Tg. Jer 31:36 a kind of antidote to this Targum?

[8]Hebrew has: "And Moses besought the face of the Lord his God . . . whom you brought out from the land of Egypt, with great power and a strong hand?" For Moses' prayer, see Tg. Onq.; LXX; Pesh.; *b. Ber.* 30b, 32a; *Exod. R.* 43, 1; *Sifre Deut.* 26; Vulg. On "redeemed," see note on 3:10. The "outstretched arm" features in the Hebrew text of Exod 6:6, where Tg. Nf (see note to the verse) renders it as "strong hand," the very expression used in the Hebrew of this verse! Clearly, the Targum regarded the expressions as interchangeable, no doubt noting Deut 4:34; 5:15; 7:19; Ps. 136:12; Jer 32:21. But Targum retains "strong hand" at Exod 6:1; 13:9.

[9]On both occasions, "I pray" is an addition peculiar to this Targum, emphasizing the intercession of Moses. Hebrew has: "of your wrath, and repent of the evil to your people." The Targum must dispel any notion that God would do evil to his people, both for the sake of his own honor, and for the sake of Israel. Both Tg. Onq. and Tg. Ps.-J. expound in accordance with Tg. Nf.

[10]Targum adds "in your good mercies": see note to 2:24. Hebrew has: " to whom you swore by yourself." For the Name of the Memra, cf. Tg. Onq. and Tg. Ps.-J., and see Hayward, 1981A, 42, 71–94. Targum's "sons" stands for Hebrew "seed," as in Tg. Onq. and Tg. Ps.-J.

the evil which he had planned *to bring* upon the people.[11] 15. And Moses turned[11a] and went down from the mountain and the two tables in his hand(s),[ii] tables written on both sides; on the one side and on the other *side* they were written. 16. And the tables were the work *of the Power[jj] from before the Lord,* and the writing was written and *clearly expressed[kk] from before the Lord,*[12] engraved upon the tables. 17. And Joshua heard the voice of the people as they *ran to and fro[mm]* and said to Moses: "The voice of battle *array[nn]* (is) in the camp."[13] 18. And he said: "It is not the voice *of men victorious in battle[oo] I hear*; nor is it the voice of the feeble, defeated in battle[pp] I hear; the voice *of those who sing praise[qq] in a foreign worship* I hear; *the voice of those who sing praise."[qq][14]* 19. And it happened that when he drew near the camp *AND SAW THE CALF AND THE DANCING,[rr]* Moses' anger was kindled, and he threw the tables from his hands and broke them at the foot of the mountain.[ss] 20. *AND HE TOOK THE CALF WHICH THEY HAD MADE AND BURNED IT WITH FIRE, AND GROUND IT UNTIL IT WAS POWDER, AND SCATTERED IT UPON THE WATER AND MADE THE CHILDREN OF IS-RAEL DRINK IT.[rr]* 21. And Moses said to Aaron: "What has this people done[tt] to you that you have brought great sins[uu][15] upon them?" 22. And Aaron said *to*

Apparatus, Chapter 32

[ii] Text: "his hand."
[jj] Nfmg: "(work) of the finger of the power."
[kk] "the writing was *ktb mprš*" i.e., "a writing clearly expressed." See note for meaning of *mprš*.
[mm] P, Nfmg: "acting unpleasantly" (or: "doing evil") = PVN.
[nn] Nfmg: "I hear."
[oo] Nfmg: "of warriors, men who go forth victorious (or: "singing"?) to battle array."

[pp] Nfmg: "in battle array."
[qq] Or: "who tramp," "stamp."
[rr] Text in capitals in Hebrew without Aramaic translation; see note *a* above.
[ss] Nfmg: "below the mountain."
[tt] Nfmg: "have they done."
[uu] Lit.: "debts"; Nfmg: "a great debt" (i.e., "sin").

Notes, Chapter 32

[11]Hebrew has: "And the Lord repented about the evil which he had spoken (thought) to do to his people." Cf. Tg. Ps.-J. and Frg. Tg. P, and note to v. 12.

[11a]For "turned," see note on 7:23.

[12]Hebrew has: "And the tablets were a work of God, and the writing was writing of God." See 32:18. Both Tg. Onq. and Tg. Ps.-J. also insist that the writing was *mprš*. The word *mprš* refers to items which are distinctly and plainly set out; often it is used with a word meaning "inscribed, engraved," as at 28:17, 18, 19, 20; 39:12, 13, and very frequently in Tg. Ps.-J., to refer to the Divine Name when it is expressed and set forth in its authentic characters: see Tg. Ps.-J. of Exod 2:21; 4:20; 14:21; 28:30; and 33:6, which it shares with Tg. Nf and Frg. Tg. P. The word indicates the Divine Name itself in these verses: no substitute or surrogate is meant, but the clear reality. Traditionally, the occurrence of the form *mprš* in Hebrew at Neh 8:8, where Ezra and the Levites expound the Law to the people, is held to refer to the Aramaic Targum, which, of course, lays bare with absolute clarity the meaning of the sacred text.

[13]Hebrew has: "And Joshua heard the sound of the people as they shouted, *br'h* . . ." Nfmg has understood the last word as if it derived from Hebrew *ra'*, "evil"; the Targum itself has paraphrased.

[14]Hebrew has: "And he said: It is not the sound of the cry *'nwt* of mastery, and it is not the sound of the cry *'nwt* of defeat: I hear the voice of songs, *'nwt*." The thrice-repeated *'nwt* is naturally given three different explanations. The first refers to men victorious in battle: Tg. Onq. and Tg. Ps.-J. are very close to Tg. Nf here, as are LXX (*phônê exarchontôn kat' ischun*) and Theod. (*phônê polemou exarchontôn kat' ischun*). The second refers to the sound of defeat; so also Tg. Onq. and Tg. Ps.-J.; cf. LXX and Theod. The third refers to those praising in "foreign worship" (see note on v. 6): see also Frg. Tg. P, V; Tg. Ps.-J.; *Exod. R.* 41, 1; *j. Ta'an* 4:5; *Eccles. R.* 9:11.1; and Levy, 1986, 423.

[15]"Debts" represents Hebrew "sin," in the singular.

Moses: "Let not the anger of my master be enkindled; you know the people, that [ww] they are *evil*,[xx][16] 23. *AND THEY SAID TO ME: MAKE US GODS WHO SHALL GO BEFORE US*,[rr] because (as for) this Moses who *brought us out* from the land of Egypt, we do not know what has happened to him *in the end*.[17] 24. And *he*[yy] said to them: 'Any one of you who has gold, take *it* off and give it to me.' *AND I PUT IT INTO THE FIRE AND THIS CALF CAME OUT*."[zz] 25. And Moses saw that the people were stripped, because *they* had stripped off *the crown of gold that had been on their heads, upon which the Distinguished Name was engraved;*[a] *because*[b] they did not listen to the words of Aaron[c] they acquired[d] an evil name for themselves for all generations;[e][18] 26. and Moses stood at the door of the camp and said: "*Let* every one who *fears before* the Lord *come* to me." And there was gathered to him all *the tribe*[f] *of* Levi.[19] 27. And he said to them: "Thus said the Lord,[g] the God of Israel: 'Place every man his sword upon his thigh; go to and fro from door to door in the camp and kill every man his brother, and every man his companion, and every man his neighbor.'" 28. And the sons of Levi[h] did according to the words of Moses. And there fell of the people on that day about three thousands of men. 29. And Moses said: "*Complete the offering*[i] *of your hands* this day *before* the Lord, because everyone of you *has smitten* his son and his brother,[20] that he may bestow blessings[j] upon you this day." 30. And on the following *day* Moses said to the peo-

Apparatus, Chapter 32

[ww] Nfmg: "that the evil inclination has taken dominion of it and has led it do."

[xx] Nfmg: "that it acts unpleasantly" (or: "does evil"); see note *mm* above.

[yy] Thus text: perhaps from respect for Aaron; MT: "and I said."

[zz] Text in Hebrew without Aramaic translation. Nfmg: "and I said to them: Whoever has gold strip it off and bring it. And they brought it to me and I threw it into the fire and Satan (or: "the tempter") entered within it and the likeness of this calf came forth from it."

[a] VN +: "(engraved) from Mount Horeb"; Pal. Tg.

text: "were stripped . . . engraved," *Meturgeman* of Elias Levita.

[b] Nfmg: "and because."

[c] P: "of Moses."

[d] Or: "they created"; Nfmg: "they acquire" (="acquired") or "they create" (= "created") = VN.

[e] Nfmg: " among the generations."

[f] Nfmg: "(all) the sons of."

[g] Nfmg: "the Memra of the Lord."

[h] Nfmg: "the sons of the tribe of Levi."

[i] Reading "offering" (*qrbn*), not "offer" (*qrbw*) as text.

[j] Nfi+: "many" (blessings).

Notes, Chapter 32

[16]LXX also has "to Moses." Nfmg blames the evil *inclination* for their behavior: so also Tg. Ps.-J.; *b. Shabb.* 89a; *Tanḥuma Ki Tissa'* 26; *b. Ber.* 32a. For Nfmg's note that they act unpleasantly, see note to v. 17.

[17]Hebrew has "this man Moses"; Targum omits "man," and has "brought out," like LXX, Vulg., for Hebrew "brought up." The addition "in the end" parallels the interpretation of v. 1.

[18]Hebrew has: "And Moses saw the people, that they were stripped; for Aaron had let them break loose to their shame among their enemies." For the crown of gold on their heads, see exactly Frg. Tg. P, V. Tg. Ps.-J. has "the holy crown," and adds that Aaron had stripped them of it. The Divine Name was engraved on these crowns: so also *b. Shabb.* 88a, 119b, whose relationship to Nf of this verse is discussed by Levy, 1986, 424–25. For their acquisition of an evil name, see Tg. Onq.; Tg. Ps.-J. and Frg. Tg. Le Déaut, 1963, 230, links this tradition to the expulsion of Adam and Eve from Eden.

[19]For the details, see also Tg. Onq. and Tg. Ps.-J.

[20]Hebrew has: "Fill your hands today for the Lord: for each man (has been) against his son and against his brother." For "complete the offering," see note on 28:41. The words "has smitten" supply the missing verb; so also Tg. Ps.-J.

ple: "You have committed great sins. And now I shall go up to *beseech[k] mercy from before* the Lord; <perhaps I can make atonement for your sins>."[21] 31. <And Moses returned *before* the Lord>[m] and said: "I beseech (you); this people have sinned[n] great sins[o] AND HAVE MADE FOR THEMSELVES GODS OF GOLD.[p] 32. And now, if you will forgive *and remit* their debts! And if not strike me out[q] from the book *of your Law[r]* which you have written."[22] 33. And the Lord[s] said to Moses: "Whoever has sinned before me, I will strike him out from the book *of my Law.*[23] 34. And now, go; lead the people to the *place* which[t] I have spoken to you. Behold, my angel will lead on before you. And on the day *I remember[u]* them, I shall *remember* their sins against them."[24] 35. And the Lord smote[w] the people *BE-CAUSE THEY MADE THE CALF WHICH AARON MADE.[x]*

CHAPTER 33

1. And the Lord[a] spoke with Moses: "Go, ascend from here, you and the people which you have brought up *redeemed* from[b] the land of Egypt, to the land which I swore to Abraham, to Isaac, and to Jacob, saying: 'To your *son* I will give it.'[c][1]

Apparatus, Chapter 32

[k] Nfmg: "and we (= Nfi) will beseech"; an Aramaism, 1st per. pl. for 1st per. sing.
[m] Omitted from text by homoioteleuton; supplied in Nfmg.
[n] Nfmg: "by the mercy before you, O Lord, this people has sinned."
[o] Lit.: "debts"; Nfmg: "a great debt" (= "sin").
[p] Text in Hebrew without Aramaic translation; Targum added in Nfi.

[q] Nfmg+: "now," or "I pray."
[r] Nfi: "of the Law."
[s] Nfmg: "the Memra of the Lord."
[t] Nfmg: "that (which)."
[u] Nfmg: "an angel of mercy shall go (Nfmg 2°: "shall lead," "shall accompany") before you and in the day of my remembrance I shall remember."
[w] Nfmg: "and the Memra of the Lord destroyed."
[x] Text in Hebrew only, without Aramaic translation.

Notes, Chapter 32

[21]See note on 4:10 for the beseeching of mercy, and see above, vv. 10, 11. Tg. Ps.-J. has Moses go up to pray.
[22]Hebrew has: "And now, if you will forgive their sin [do so]; but if not, blot me out of your book which you have written." Targum's "forgive and remit" is a cliché: see McNamara, 1972, 129–30. God's book is the book of the Law according to *Exod. R.* 47, 9.
[23]For "before me," cf. Tg. Ps.-J. and Tg. Onq.; Hebrew has "to me." On the book of the Law, see note on v. 32.
[24]Hebrew has: "and on the day that I visit, I shall visit their sin upon them." See note on 3:16.

Apparatus, Chapter 33

[a] Nfmg: "the Memra of the Lord."
[b] Nfmg: "I brought out from"; the text is probably to be corrected to: "you brought out from."

[c] Nfi: "to your sons I shall give it"; Nfmg: "to the descendants of your sons I shall give."

Notes, Chapter 33

[1]For "redeemed," see note on 3:10. On the singular "your son" for Hebrew "your seed," see Le Déaut, 1979 (*Exode*) 260.

2. And I will send an angel before you,[d] and he will drive out the Canaanites, the Amorites, the Hittites, the Perizzites, the Hivites and the Jebusites, 3. to a land that *produces[e] good fruits, pure as* milk and *sweet[f] as* honey; but[g] I will not make *the Glory of my Shekinah* go up from among *you,*[h] because they are a difficult people *to receive[i] instruction*[2]—lest I blot you out on the way." 4. When the people heard this evil word, they mourned and no one put his *articles of weaponry.*[3] 5. And the Lord[a] said to Moses: "Say to the children of Israel: 'You are a difficult[j] people *to receive instruction*; if[k] I should make *the Glory[m] of my Shekinah* go up from among you for a little while, I would blot you out. And now, let everyone put off his *articles of weaponry* and I will know what to do with you.'"[n4] 6. And the children of Israel stripped[o] themselves of their *articles of weaponry, on which the Distinguished Name was engraved*—from Mount Horeb (onward).[5] 7. And Moses took[p] the tent and spread[q] it outside the camp, far away from the camp; and he called[r] it the tent of meeting. And everyone who sought *instruction[s] from before*[6] the Lord went out to the tent of meeting which was outside the camp. 8. And whenever Moses used to go out[t] to the tent, all the people used to rise up and stand,[u] each at the door of his tent, looking[w] after Moses until he went into his tent.[x] 9. And when Moses used to enter *the door of* the tent, the column of cloud descended[y] and stood[z] at the door of the tent and he spoke with Moses. 10. And

Apparatus, Chapter 33

[d] "You" (sing.); Nfmg: "before you" (pl.).

[e] Nfi: "to a land that produces."

[f] Nfmg: "that are tasty."

[g] Lit.: "because," translating, as usual, Hebrew *kî*.

[h] Or perhaps: "shall I not make . . . from among you"? Ps.-J. however, translates without seeing a question in it. Hebrew text has: "I will not go up among you." Possibly we should understand the word (*'rwm*) rendered "because" as "even though (they are . . .)."

[i] Nfmg: "My Memra will not go up before you because you are a stiff-necked people to receive."

[j] Nfmg: "stiff-necked."

[k] Nfmg: "behold (if)."

[m] Nfmg: "I should take the Glory."

[n] Nfmg: "your articles of ornament(s) from off you and I will know what."

[o] Nfmg 1°: "and they emptied"; Nfmg 2°: "and they were emptied."

[p] Nfmg: "would take"; or "will take."

[q] Nfmg: "and would spread"; or "will spread."

[r] Nfi: "and would call it" or "will call it."

[s] Nfmg: "and it was for him a tent of meeting and it came to pass that all who sought instruction."

[t] Nfmg: "would go out" (*yppwq*).

[u] Nfmg: "and it came to pass that when Moses went out to the tent all the people arose and stood.

[w] Nfmg: "and they used to look."

[x] Nfmg: "till his entry into his tent."

[y] Nfmg: "And it came to pass that when Moses entered the tent there descended" (or "they lowered").

[z] Nfmg: "and it stood" (*wq'm*; text: *qyym*).

Notes, Chapter 33

[2] Hebrew has: "to a land flowing with milk and honey": see note on 3:8. Hebrew continues: "for I shall not go up among you," a difficult text (see Grossfeld, 1988B, 92–93) which Tg. Nf appears to have understood in the same way as Tg. Onq. and Tg. Ps.-J. The difficult people to receive instruction are, in the Hebrew, "stiff-necked"; see note on 32:9.

[3] Hebrew has "ornaments"; our Targum uses the same word as Tg. Onq. and Tg. Ps.-J., which is used at 13:18 to render Hebrew *ḥmšym*, "armed," a point noted by Le Déaut, 1979 (*Exode*) 261.

[4] See notes to vv. 3–4, and cf. Tg. Onq. and Tg. Ps.-J.

[5] Hebrew has: "So the Israelites stripped themselves of their ornaments from Mount Horeb." Cf. Tg. Onq., Tg. Ps.-J., Frg. Tg. P; notes to vv. 3–5 and 32–35; *Exod. R.* 45, 2, 3; 51, 8; *b. Shabb.* 88a.

[6] Hebrew has: "everyone who sought the Lord"; see Tg. Onq.; note to 18:15; 19:3–4; and Vulg.: "all the people who had any kind of question."

all the people saw the column of cloud that stood^{aa} at the door of the tent; and all the people *used to* stand^{bb} and pray,^{cc} each at the door of his tent.^{7} 11. And the Lord^{dd} spoke with Moses, *speech to speech,*^{ee} as one speaks to his companion. And he returned to the camp, but his minister, Joshua, the son of Nun, a youth, did not move from within^{ff} the camp.$^{gg\,8}$ 12. And Moses said *before* the Lord: "See, you say to me: 'Bring up this people'; and you^{hh} have not made known to me whom you will send with me, and (yet) you have said: '*See that I have designated* you with the name of *master*, and you have also^{ii} found grace *and favor before* me.'^{9} 13. And now, if, I pray, I have found^{jj} grace and *favor before* you, make known, I pray, your ways to me and I shall fear before you, because I have found grace *and favor* in your sight; and see^{kk} that this *great*^{10} nation is your people." 14. And he said: "*The Glory*^{mm} *of my Shekinah* will *accompany among* you, and *I will prepare*^{nn} *a resting place for you.*"^{11} 15. And he said *before* him: "If *the Glory*^{oo} *of your Shekinah* is not *among us*, do not make us go up from here.^{12} 16. And in what will it be known, now, that I have found grace *and favor* before you, I and your people, if not by *the Glory of your Shekinah* accompanying^{pp} with us, and signs *and wonders shall be performed with us*, I and your people, (a nation distinct)^{qq} from all peoples that are

Apparatus, Chapter 33

^{aa} Nfmg: "standing" (*q'm*).

^{bb} Nfmg: "and they arose" (*qmw*); (text: *w-qyymyn*).

^{cc} Nfmg: "and they bowed down."

^{dd} Nfmg: "the Memra of the Lord."

^{ee} Or: "orally"; lit.: "speech against (opposite corresponding to) speech"; HT: "face to face."

^{ff} Nfmg: "a tender youth, he did not cease (= depart) from within the"; = PVN.

^{gg} For "camp" read "tent" with Nfmg (= MT); Nfmg: "an adolescent, did not withdraw from within the tent of the house of instruction."

^{hh} Nfmg: "in your Memra."

^{ii} Nfmg: "you said in your Memra: I know you by a good name, and also."

^{jj} Nfmg: "and now, if, I pray, I have found," i.e., "I shall show you reverence."

^{kk} Nfmg: "(your) good (ways) and may I know you to find favor and mercy before you, and see."

^{mm} Nfi: "behold (the Glory)."

^{nn} Nfmg: "the face of my good-pleasure will lead you and give you rest."

^{oo} Nfmg: "(he said) to him: 'If the Glory (. . .) not.'"

^{pp} Nfmg: "by the glory (of your Shekinah) speaking."

^{qq} Another rendering: "and there shall be performed with us (with) me and your people—signs and wonders, above all the people that are upon the face of the earth." HT (cf. RSV), v. 16: "For how shall it be known that I have found favor in your sight. I and your people? Is it not in your going with us, so that we are distinct, I and your people, from all other people that are upon the face of the earth?"

Notes, Chapter 33

^{7}Hebrew has: "and each man bowed down at the door of his tent." For the rendering of "bow down" by "pray," see 24:1. The Hebrew verb is normally used to describe full prostration of the worshipers in the Temple service. This is obviously inappropriate here, and the Targumist renders accordingly.

^{8}Cf. Tg. Onq., and see Le Déaut, 1979 (*Exode*) 262. The "house of instruction" (see Nfmg) was, of course, a fundamental institution in post-biblical times, and is frequently introduced by the Targumists: see Tg. Nf and Tg. Ps.-J. of Gen 24:62; 25:22, 27; Tg. Ps.-J. of Exod 39:33; Num 24:2, 6.

^{9}Hebrew has: "and you have said, I know you by name, and you have also found favor in my sight." Moses is here described in the same terms as was Bezalel b. Uri in 31:2. On the addition of "favor," see vv. 13, 16 and 17.

^{10}LXX here describe Israel as "great."

^{11}Hebrew has: "And he said: My Presence (lit.: Face) will go and I will give you rest." For the Glory of the Shekinah, see Muñoz León, 1977, 105–7. Tg. Onq. has Shekinah alone.

^{12}Hebrew has: "And he said to him: If your Presence (lit.: Face) does not go (with us), do not bring us up from here." See note on v. 14; Tg. Onq. again has Shekinah alone.

upon ^{rr} the face of the earth." ^{13} 17. And the Lord said to Moses: "This word also ^{ss} which you speak ^{tt} I shall do because you have found grace *and favor* in my sight, and I have *designated* you by the name of *master*." $^{uu\,14}$ 18. And he said: "Show, me, I pray, your Glory." $^{ww\,15}$ 19. And he said: "Behold, I made the entire measure of my goodness ^{xx} pass before you, ^{yy} and I will have pity on whoever ^{zz} *is worthy* ^{a} of pity, and I will have mercy on whoever *is worthy of* mercy." ^{16} 20. And he said: "You will not be able to see my face, because it *is* not *possible* that a son of man see my face and live." $^{b\,17}$ 21. And the Lord ^{c} said: "Behold, (there is) a place set aside ^{18} beside me, and you shall stand in readiness upon the rock. 22. And it shall come to pass that when the Glory *of my Shekinah* passes by, I shall place you in a cleft of the rock. And I shall spread my palm ^{d} over you until *the troops of angels, which you*

Apparatus, Chapter 33

^{rr} Nfmg: "(with us) and we will remain hidden. I and your people, from every people there is upon."

^{ss} Nfmg: "the Memra of the Lord to Moses: Also."

^{tt} *mmllt*: participle *pael* with termination of finite verb.

^{uu} Nfmg: "before him and I have made you known (cf. "I know you," v. 12) by a good name."

^{ww} Nfmg: "Moses (said) before the Lord: Show me, I pray, the splendor of your Glory."

^{xx} Nfmg: "(behold) I shall make all the troops of angels that minister before me pass by your face" (text: my face).

^{yy} VN adds: "and I will proclaim the good name of the Lord before you."

^{zz} Nfi: "on what" = VN; *Meturgeman* citation as Nf ("whomsoever").

^{a} Nfmg: "to him (who is fitting) to have mercy shown to him" = VN.

^{b} Nfmg: "a son of man (= "a human being") does not see me and live" (lit.: "(be) alive").

^{c} Nfmg: "the Memra of the Lord."

^{d} Nfmg: "and I, cause the palm of my hand to pass"; VN: "and I will cause my hand to pass."

Notes, Chapter 33

^{13}See Apparatus for Hebrew text. On the Glory of the Shekinah, for which Tg. Onq. has Shekinah alone, see note on v. 14. In Nfmg, the Shekinah speaks with Israel: so Tg. Ps.-J. On the distinctness of Israel and the signs and wonders, see Tg. Onq., which is very close to Tg. Nf, and the discussion of Grossfeld, 1988B, 95. The Targum is actually taking up points made earlier about Israel's distinctness, which the Lord makes clear (Hebrew verb *plh*), and the signs and wonders which God performed for them (Hebrew root *pl'*): see note on 8:18; 9:4; 11:7. Cf. also *b. B. Bat.* 15b; *b. Ber.* 7a; *Seder Olam R.* 21.

^{14}See note on verse 12.

^{15}The post-biblical exegesis of this and the following verses is analyzed by P. Vermes, "Buber's Understanding of the Divine Name related to Bible, Targum, and Midrash," *JJS* 24 (1973) 147–66; she pays particular attention to Targum on pp. 155–60. Useful commentary will also be found in Chester, 1986, 78, 148, 361, and Muñoz León, 1977, 108–10; 213–17; 442–43. It should be noted that throughout this section the Targums approximate closely to the traditions preserved in *b. Ber.* 7a.

^{16}Hebrew has: "And he said: I will make all my goodness pass before your face, and I shall call on the Name of the LORD before you; and I will be gracious to whom I will be gracious, and merciful to whom I will be merciful." For the "measure of my goodness," see Tg. Ps.-J.; Frg. Tg. V; *Exod. R.* 45, 6; and Le Déaut, 1979 (*Exode*) 266–67, citing M. Kadushin, 1965, 99, 202; and W. Bacher, 1, 1899, 965, 102; 2, 106. Tg. Nf apparently omits "and I shall call on the Name of the LORD before you." For the rest of the verse, cf. Tg. Ps.-J. and Frg. Tg. V.

^{17}Hebrew has: "for man shall not see Me and live." Cf. Tg. Ps.-J. for the addition of "it is not possible."

^{18}Targum adds "set aside," *mzmn*, cf. Tg. Onq. and Tg. Ps.-J., which have *mtqn*. These additions perhaps indicate that the Targums agree with the view that God is the place of the Universe and not vice-versa: see R. Jose b. R. Hanina in *Exod. R.* 45, 6.

will see, pass by.[e][19] 23. *And I will make the troops of angels pass by, and they will stand and minister before me*, and you will see *the Dibbera[f] of the Glory[g] of Shekinah*, but *it is* not *possible that* you see[h] the face *of the Glory of my Shekinah*."[20]

CHAPTER 34

1. And the Lord said to Moses: "Cut[a] two tables of stones like the first ones; and I will write[b] upon the tables the words[c] that were upon the first tables which you broke. 2. And you shall be[d] prepared[e] for the morning, and in the morning you shall come up to Mount Sinai, and you shall stand in readiness there beside me on top of the mountain.[f] 3. And no one shall go up with you; neither shall anyone be seen in all the mountain, nor shall sheep or oxen[g] graze opposite that mountain." 4. And Moses cut two tables of stones like the first ones; and Moses rose early in the morning and went up to Mount Sinai as <the Lord>[h] had commanded him, and took two tables of stones in his hand. 5. And *the Glory of the Shekinah of the Lord[i] was revealed* in the cloud, and it stood beside him[j] there, and he *prayed* there in the name of *the Memra of* the Lord.[1] 6. And *the Glory of the Shekinah of* the

Apparatus, Chapter 33

[e] Nfmg: "(until) we (= "I"?) pass," lit.: "until the time we pass."

[f] Nf: *dbr'*; P: *dybwr'*; VN: *dbyr'*.

[g] Nfmg: "and I make (you) see the *Dibburah* (*dbwr'*) of (my) Glory."

[h] Nfmg: "(it is not possible) for you to see" = VNP.

Notes, Chapter 33

[19] Hebrew has: "And when my glory passes by, I shall put you in a cleft of the rock, and cover you with my palm until I have passed by." The troops of angels are to feature in the following verse. With the Targum, cf. *Exod. R.* 14:19; *Pes. R.* 10. For the relationship of this and the following verse to other Targums, and for a possible history of Nf's textual development, see Levy, 1986, 427–28.

[20] Hebrew has: "And I shall remove My hand, and you shall see My back; but My Face shall not be seen." For the angels who stand and minister, see Tg. Ps.-J., Frg. Tg. P, V. The *Dibbera* features in Frg. Tg. P, V; see note on 19:3. "The face of the Glory of the Shekinah" occurs in Tg. Ps.-J.; cf. Frg. Tg. V. Frg. Tg. P has "the Glory of the Shekinah." See also Vulg. and *b. Men.* 35b.

Apparatus, Chapter 34

[a] Nfmg: "the Memra of the Lord to Moses: Cut."

[b] Nfmg: "like the first ones and you shall write."

[c] I.e., "the commandments."

[d] Nfmg: "and be."

[e] Nfi: "prepared" (*zmyn*; text: *mzmn*).

[f] Nfmg: "and you will be carried over there beside me upon the top of the mountain."

[g] Nfmg: "sheep nor oxen."

[h] Omitted in text; added in Nfi; Nfmg: "the Memra of the Lord."

[i] Nfmg: "and the Memra of the Lord was revealed."

[j] Nfmg: "with him."

Notes, Chapter 34

[1] Hebrew has: "And the Lord came down in the cloud and stood with him there; and he called on the name of the Lord." Cf. Tg. Ps.-J., and see Chester, 1986, 110–11; 117–18. On the Name of the Memra, see note on 4:31.

Lord passed[k] by, and *Moses prayed and said*: "O Lord, O Lord, gracious and merciful[m] God, patient,[n] *far removed from anger and nigh of mercy* and bounteous *to do* grace and truth,[2] 7. keeping grace *and goodness*[o] for thousands *of generations*, forgiving *and pardoning* sins,[p] *and passing by rebellions and procuring forgiveness* for sins, but by no means leaving (sins) go unpunished;[q] *on the day of the great judgment* he *will remember* the sins of the *wicked* fathers on the sons and on the sons of *rebellious* sons, to the third generation and to the fourth *generation.*"[3] 8. And Moses hurried[r] and bowed down to[s] the ground and *gave thanks and praised,*[4] 9. and he said: "If, now,[t] I have found grace *and favor before* you, O Lord,[u] let *your Glory, O Lord,* lead on among us, although they are difficult[w] people *to receive instruction*, and forgive *and remit* our *debts*[x] and our sins and take us as your possession."[5] 10. And he said: "Behold, I make a covenant; opposite[y] your

Apparatus, Chapter 34

[k] Nfmg +: "before him" (*qwdmwy*); = VN (*qdmwy*), P (*qwmwy*).

[m] Nfmg: "merciful and gracious"; = VN.

[n] Lit.: "long of spirit"; absent in VN. The continuation in Nf ("far removed from . . . mercy") might also be rendered: "the One who makes anger distant and brings near compassion."

[o] VN: "keeping goodness for thousands of generations, forgiving and pardoning debts (= sins) and offenses, but by no means will the Lord acquit (= leave unpunished) sins (lit.: debts) on the day of the great judgment (text: judgments); and remembering the sins (lit.: debts) of the wicked father upon the rebellious sons to the third generation and to the fourth generation"; Nfmg: "the offenses and debts"; cf. VN.

[p] Nfmg: "the offenses and debts"; cf. VN.

[q] Nfmg: "the Lord (will not acquit = leave unpunished) sins (lit.: = VN debts) on the day of"; = VN.

[r] Nfmg: "and he hurried"; = VN.

[s] Nfmg: "upon the (ground)"; = VN, Levita, *Meturgeman.*

[t] Nfmg: "I pray."

[u] Nfmg: "let, now, the Glory of the Shekinah of the Lord pass."

[w] Nfmg: "stiff-necked."

[x] I.e., sins; Nfmg: "their debts."

[y] Nfmg: "before."

Notes, Chapter 34

[2]Hebrew has: "And the Lord passed by before his face, and cried: The Lord, the Lord, a God merciful and gracious, patient and abounding in steadfast love and truth." For the Glory of the Shekinah, see Frg. Tg. P, V; Tg. Onq. and Tg. Ps.-J. have the Shekinah alone: see Chester, 1986, 148. For Moses' prayer, see above, v. 5, and cf. Frg. Tg. P, V, which make it clear that Moses is the subject of the verb.

[3]Hebrew has: "Keeping steadfast love for thousands; forgiving iniquity, rebellion, and sin; and acquitting he does not acquit; visiting the iniquity of fathers upon sons and on sons' children to the third and fourth generations." For the addition of "goodness," see Tg. Ps.-J.; Tg. Onq. and Frg. Tg. V so translate "steadfast love." For the addition of "generations," see Frg. Tg. V, Tg. Ps.-J., and Tg. Onq. On the phrase "forgiving and pardoning," see note to 32:32; it is used here by Tg. Ps.-J. and Frg. Tg. V. For the rest, cf. Tg. Ps.-J. and Frg. Tg. V. The rendering of the difficult Hebrew, literally translated as "acquitting he does not acquit," is by no means as clear and straightforward as the exegesis provided by Tg. Onq. and Tg. Ps.-J.; it seems likely, however, that the fundamental approach to the Hebrew text is similar in all three Targums. See also Tg. Mic. 7:18. Like Tg. Onq., Tg. Nf has its own exegesis of 20:5 in mind here, but it does not make clear that God forgives those who return to the Torah, clears the guilt of those who repent, and punishes the impenitent, as do the other two Targums, and *b. Yoma* 86ab; *b. Shebu.* 39a; *b. Sanh.* 27b.

[4]Hebrew has: "and worshiped, prostrated" for "gave thanks and praised": see note on 33:10, 12:27, and Frg. Tg. V, and Le Déaut, 1963, 138.

[5]Hebrew has: "And he said: If I have now found favor in your sight, O Adonai, let now Adonai go in our midst; for this is a stiff-necked people; and forgive our iniquities and our sins, and take us as your inheritance." Tg. Onq., Tg. Ps.-J., and LXX have "before you" for "in your sight." Adonai, the Lord, is specified as YHWH by our Targum, Tg. Onq., and Tg. Ps.-J. For the rendering of "stiff-necked" as "difficult to receive instruction," i.e., in the Law, see note on 32:9; and on the phrase "forgive and remit," see 32:32 and Tg. Nf of Gen 4:13.

entire people I will do signs *and wonders*[6] which have not been wrought in all the earth nor in any nation; and all the people among whom *you dwell* shall see[z] the works of the Lord; awesome[aa] are (the things) which I shall do with you. 11. Pay attention to what I shall command you[bb] this day. Behold, I drive out before you the Amorite and the Canaanite and the Hittite and the Perizzite and the Jebusite.[cc][7] 12. Pay attention lest you make a covenant[dd] with the inhabitants of the land within which *you* go,[ee] lest they become[ff] a stumbling block[gg] among you.[8] 13. For you shall destroy their *objects of divination*,[gg][9] and you shall break their pillars, and you shall cut their Asherin,[hh] 14. because *you* shall not bow down to another god, because the Lord,[ii] whose name is "Jealous," is a jealous God and *surely takes revenge*[jj] *in (his) jealousy*— 15. lest[kk] *you* make a covenant with the inhabitants of the land and when they go astray[mm] after their *idols*[10] and sacrifice to their *idols* and call you, and *you* eat from their sacrifices, 16. and you take (wives) from their daughters for *your* sons, and their daughters go astray[nn] after their *idols*, and they lead *your* sons astray[oo] after their *idols*. 17. *My people, children of Israel, you shall not make yourselves deities*,[pp] idols of cast metal.[qq][11] 18. The feast of unleavened bread you shall observe. Seven days *you* shall eat unleavened bread as I have commanded *you*, at the time of the month of Abiba <because in the month of Abiba>[rr] *you* came out *redeemed* from Egypt.[12] 19. All that opens[ss]—the first fruits of—the womb[tt] *are* for *my name*, and all *your* male cattle[uu] that open *the*

Apparatus, Chapter 34

[z] Nfmg: "they shall see."
[aa] Nfmg: "mighty."
[bb] Nfmg: "(I command) you" (pl.; in text sing.).
[cc] Nfmg: "(from) before you the Amorites, the Canaanites, the Hittites, the Perizzites, and the Jebusites."
[dd] Nfmg: "take care for yourselves lest you make a covenant."
[ee] Nfi: "you enter" (*'lyln*).
[ff] Nfmg: "may be."
[gg] Nfmg: "you shall knock down their altars and."
[hh] I.e., sacred pillars of Canaanite worship. Nfmg: "you shall destroy their idols."
[ii] Nfmg: "the Memra of the Lord."
[jj] Nfi: "(lest) he take revenge" (*mppr'*; text: *mtpr'*).
[kk] Lit.: "you shall not make"; Nfmg: "lest."

[mm] Nfmg: "with (? lit.: "to," "for") the inhabitants of the land and you go astray after."
[nn] Nfmg: "and they will turn aside."
[oo] Nfmg: "and they will cause to turn aside"; = VN.
[pp] Nfmg: "my people (you shall not make) idols."
[qq] *mtkh*; Nfmg: "molten" (*mtkwwh*).
[rr] Omitted in text by homoioteleuton.
[ss] VN: "every first-born (lit.: "every first breakthrough of the womb") you shall set aside for my name, all your first-born males, every first-born (lit.: "every first breakthrough of the womb") of cattle (lit.: "of cow") and sheep (lit.: "lamb")."
[tt] I.e., "all the first-born"; "the first fruits of" possibly a gloss; Nfmg: "the first that opens the womb"; Levita, *Meturgeman*, Exod 34:19; 13:12, 15; Num 3:12; 18:15; "breakthrough of the womb"; cf. VN.
[uu] Nfmg: "you shall set aside (the males)."

Notes, Chapter 34

[6]"Signs and wonders" stands for MT's "wonders." For the covenant terminology here, see Hayward, 1981A, 57–70. Tg. Ps.-J. also adds "you dwell."
[7]Targum has omitted the Hivites from the list of nations.
[8]Targum has plural verbs and suffixes for MT's singular until v. 26. LXX has plural forms in vv. 12–14.
[9]Hebrew has "their altars" for "objects of divination."
[10]Targum's "idols" renders Hebrew *'lhym*, "gods"; so Tg. Onq. and Tg. Ps.-J.
[11]Hebrew has: "Molten gods you shall not make for yourself." For "My people . . . ," see note on 20:2. Hebrew "gods" is translated as *dḥln*, "objects of fear, idols"; so also Tg. Onq. and Tg. Ps.-J.
[12]On "redeemed," see 3:10.

womb^{ww} of cow or of sheep.^{xx13} 20. Those which open the womb^{yy} of a donkey *you shall* redeem with a lamb, and if *you* do not redeem it, *you shall slay* it. And all the first-born of *your* sons *you* shall redeem. And they shall not be seen before me void^{zz} *of every precept.*¹⁴ 21. Six days you shall work, and on the seventh day *you shall rest*; and on *the feast of ingathering*^a and on *the feast of* harvesting *you shall rest.*¹⁵ 22. And you shall perform the feast of weeks, *that is 'Asarta,*^b the first fruits of the wheat harvest,^c and the feast of ingathering at the end^d of the year. 23. Three times in the year all *your* males shall be seen *before* the Lord *of all ages,* the Lord, the God of Israel.^{e16} 24. For I *shall blot* out the nations^f before *you,* and I will enlarge *your* borders, and no one, *prince or ruler,* shall covet^g *your* land when *you* go up to *be seen before the Lord* your God three times in the year.^{h17} 25. *You* shall not offer the blood of my sacrifices *of holy things* with leaven, nor shall the sacrifice of the feast of Passoverⁱ remain overnight until the morning.¹⁸ 26. The beginning of the first fruits of your land^j *you* shall bring to the sanctuary of the

Apparatus, Chapter 34

^{ww} I.e., the first-born; Nfmg: "the first that opens the womb."

^{xx} Lit.: "lamb."

^{yy} Nfmg: "and all the first-born that opens the womb."

^{zz} Nfmg: "my people, children of Israel, you are not permitted to be seen before the Lord, your God empty"; = PVN (with minor variants).

^a Nfmg: "at the ploughing and at the harvesting you shall rest." Nf omits rendering of v. 21b. HT: "in ploughing time and in harvest you shall rest"; Nfmg: "at the ploughing time (rare word: *rdy'*) and at the harvest time you shall rest"; VN: "at the ploughing time" (*rdy'*); Levita, *Meturgeman*: "at the ploughing time (*rdy'*) and harvest time"; *rdy'* also in P, Deut 25:4.

^b I.e., a festive gathering for the conclusion of a festive season, or a concluding feast. It was applied especially to the concluding feast of the Passover cycle, i.e., the feast of Weeks, or Pentecost; cf. Josephus, *Ant.*, 3, 10, 6, p. 252; Nfi: omits "that is *'asarta.*"

^c Nfmg: "of the harvests of."

^d M +: "when you gather your produce from the earth"; cf. 23:16.

^e Nfmg: "my people, children of Israel, three times in every year all your males shall be seen seeking instruction before the Lord, their (?) God."

^f Nfmg: "I shall cast out nations."

^g Nfmg: "and no one shall covet."

^h Nfmg: "each year."

ⁱ VN: "You shall not offer (lit.: "slaughter"; "sacrifice") the blood of the Passover sacrifice together with (lit.: "upon," "beside") anything leavened; there shall not remain overnight from evening until morning any part of the meat (lit.: "flesh") that you offer (lit.: "sacrifice") on the night of the first festival day of Passover"; Nfmg: "(you shall not keep) any part of the flesh which you sacrifice on the night of the feast of Passover from night until morning"; cf. VN.

^j VN: "your produce."

Notes, Chapter 34

¹³See notes to 13:12, which this verse, in some degree, repeats. But here we encounter a difficulty in the Hebrew not found in 13:12, since the text refers to *wkl mqnk tzkr*, "and all your cattle that give birth to a male." The verb *tzkr* is feminine (so Rashi), and implies as subject the female animal giving birth. But female beasts are not given as firstlings to the Lord; hence it was necessary for Targum to specify the male firstlings by exegesis.

¹⁴See notes to 13:13. The end of the verse reads, in Hebrew: "and no one shall appear before me empty." For "void of every precept," see Frg. Tg. P, V, and Tg. Ps.-J., and Nfmg of 23:15. This may differ from *b. Ḥag.* 7a, which regards this verse as a ruling that the proper offering be brought for the appropriate festival, which has general affinity with Philo, *Quaest. in Exod.* II. 7, that men should come to God with full hands bearing fruits of the firstlings unblemished. But Philo goes on to say that it is impossible for anyone coming to God to be "empty," since he will be illuminated with God's light of good, knowledge, and wisdom.

¹⁵Hebrew has: "Six days you shall work, and on the seventh day you shall rest; in ploughing time and harvest you shall rest."

¹⁶See note on 23:17.

¹⁷"Blot out" renders Hebrew "dispossess." For no one coveting Israel's land, see *Mek. RI Pisḥa* 12:11–14; *b. Pesh.* 8b.

¹⁸See note on 23:18, and cf. *b. Pes.* 63a, 89a. For "sacrifices of holy things," see note on 18:10.

Lord your God. *My people, children of Israel, you* shall not boil, *and you shall not eat flesh*, with milk, *mixed together,[k] lest my anger be kindled against you and we boil[m] your bundled wheat, the wheat and the straw mixed together."* [19] 27. And the Lord[n] said to Moses: "Write these words, because according to *the decree* of these words have I made a covenant with you[o] and with Israel." [20] 28. And he was there *seeking instruction from before[p]* the Lord [21] forty days and forty nights; he neither ate bread[q] nor drank water. And he wrote upon the tables the words of the covenant, the ten words.[r] 29. And it came to pass that when Moses came down from[s] Mount Sinai, and the two tables of the covenant in the hands of Moses, as he came down from the mountain, Moses did not know that *the splendor of the glory of* his face[t] *shone* because his having spoken with him. [22] 30. And Aaron and all the children of Israel saw Moses, and, behold, *the splendor of the glory of Moses'* face[u] *shone*, [22] and they were afraid to draw near to him. 31. And Moses called to them; and Aaron and all the leaders in the congregation[w] returned to him, and Moses spoke with them.[x] 32. And after this all the children of Israel drew near, and Moses commanded them all that the Lord *had commanded them* [23] on Mount[y] Sinai. 33. And when Moses had finished speaking with them, he put a veil[z] on his face. 34. And when Moses used to go in before[aa] the Lord to speak with him, he used to remove the veil until[bb] he came out;[cc] and he used to come out and speak with the children of Israel what he had been commanded. 35. And the children of Israel saw the countenance of Moses, that *the splendor of the glory of* the face of Moses *shone*;[dd] and Moses used to put[ee] the veil over his face again until he went in to speak with him. [24]

Apparatus, Chapter 34

[k] Nfmg: "you are not permitted either to boil or to eat together"; = VN.

[m] I.e., 1st per. pl. for 1st sing. (= I boil); cf. Exod 23:19.

[n] Nfmg: "the Memra of the Lord."

[o] "with you" (Nfmg has pl.; sing. in text).

[p] Nfmg: "before."

[q] Nfmg: "food."

[r] I.e., commandments.

[s] Nfmg: "at the time he came down from."

[t] Nfmg: "(he did not know that) they praised the glory of his face"; = PVN.

[u] Nfmg: "that they praised the glory of his face."

[w] Nfmg: "of (lit.: "in") the people of the congregation."

[x] Nfmg: "to them," as in HT.

[y] Nfmg: "the Memra of the Lord had spoken with him on the mountain."

[z] Greek or Latin loan word (*soudarion; sudarium*); also in PVN, *Aruk*, Levita, *Meturgeman*.

[aa] Nfmg: "and when Moses went in before."

[bb] Correcting the text which says: "of his coming out."

[cc] Nfmg: "until he came out; and he came out and spoke."

[dd] Nfmg: "they praised the splendor on (of?) the face of."

[ee] Nfmg: "and Moses replaced (*'ḥzr*; text: *mḥzr*) the."

Notes, Chapter 34

[19] Hebrew has: "The chief of the first-fruits of your land you shall bring to the House of the Lord your God. You shall not boil a kid in its mother's milk." See notes to 23:19. For the sanctuary, see Tg. Onq., Tg. Ps.-J., and Frg. Tg. V. On "My people," see Frg. Tg. V and note on 20:2.

[20] For the covenant terminology, see note on v. 10.

[21] Hebrew has: "And he was there with the Lord." On "seeking instruction," see notes on 33:11 and 18:15.

[22] Hebrew has: "Moses did not know that the skin of his face beamed when he spoke with him." For the "splendor of the glory," cf. Frg. Tg. P, V, and Tg. Onq.; and see Grossfeld, 1988B, 99, who notes that the radiance of Moses' face derives from that of God's glory, as in *Tanḥuma B. Ki Tissa'* 20, 27; *Exod. R.* 47, 6; *Deut. R.* 3, 12. See also *b. Shabb.* 10b.

[23] Hebrew has: "all that the Lord had spoken"; for "commanded," see LXX[b].

[24] See note on vv. 29–30. An excellent discussion of the terms used in vv. 29–35 can be found in McNamara, 1966, 168–81.

CHAPTER 35

1. And Moses gathered all the congregation[a] of the children of Israel and said to them: "Those are the words which the Lord[b] commanded to do. 2. Six days you shall do[c] work; the seventh shall be for you holy, a sabbath of rest *before the Lord*; whoever shall do work on it shall be put to death. 3. You shall not light a fire in any *place of*[1] your dwellings on the sabbath day."[d] 4. And Moses said to all the congregation of the children of Israel, saying: "This is the thing that the Lord[b] has commanded saying: 5. Receive[e] from among you a *separated* offering for *the Name*[f] *of* the Lord;[2] everyone whose heart shall prompt him shall bring the Lord's *separated* offering: gold, silver and bronze; 6. blue and purple, and *precious* crimson material[3] and byssus; and goats' hair, 7. reddened[g] rams' skins, *sasgona*[h] skins; and acacia wood, 8. and oil[i] for the illumination, and spices[j] for the anointing oil[k] and for the fragrant incense, 9. and *precious* stones, and stones for setting[m] *to insert them*[4] in the ephod and in the breastpiece. 10. And let everyone wise of heart *who is* among you come[n] and let them make all that the Lord[o] has commanded: 11. the tent and its *screen*[p][5] and the coverings and its hooks and its planks and its bars and its pillars and its sockets; 12. the ark and its poles and the mercy seat and the veil of the screen; 13. the table and its poles and all its utensils and the *arrangement*[6] of the bread of the Presence; 14. and the lampstand of the illumination, <its utensils, its lamps and the oil for the light; 15. the altar of incense and its poles and the oil of anointing, and the incense of perfumes and the screen of the door for the door of the tabernacle>;[q] 16. and the altar of holocaust and the grating of bronze thereof and its poles and all its utensils and the basin and

Apparatus, Chapter 35

[a] Nfmg: "the people of the congregation."

[b] Nfmg: "the Memra of the Lord."

[c] Nfmg: "there shall be done." This variant is erroneously given as a variant to "whoever shall do work"; cf. v. 2b.

[d] Nfmg: "on the day of the sabbath"; = VN.

[e] Nfmg: "take."

[f] Nfmg: "before (the Lord)."

[g] I.e., "tanned."

[h] See 25:5, note c.

[i] Nfi: "an oil."

[j] Nfi: "perfumes."

[k] Nfmg: "spices of the anointing oil."

[m] Nfmg: "by which to set the ephod and the breastpiece."

[n] Nfmg: "enter."

[o] "the Memra of the Lord."

[p] Nfmg: "its tent"; VN: "and its tent and the coverings and its hooks and its planks and its bars and its pillars and its sockets."

[q] Missing in the text; added in the margins.

Notes, Chapter 35

[1] For the addition of "place of," see Frg. Tg. V, and cf. Tg. Ps.-J.

[2] On Targum's "offering of separation," *'prshw* for Hebrew Terumah, see Tg. Onq., Tg. Ps.-J., and note to 13:12. For the Name of the Lord, see note on 6:7. Vulg. has: "separate first-fruits for yourselves."

[3] On "precious," see 25:4.

[4] "Precious stones" renders Hebrew *šoham*. See note on 25:7; as also for "to insert"; cf. Tg. Onq. and Tg. Ps.-J.

[5] Hebrew has: "The Tabernacle and its tent." For "the screen," see Tg. Onq. and Tg. Ps.-J., Vulg.

[6] For "arrangement," see note on 25:30.

the base thereof; 17. and the curtains of the court, its pillars and its bases *r* and the screen of the door of the court; 18. the pegs of the tabernacle and the pegs of the court and their cords; *s* 19. and the garments of ministry, for ministering [7] within the *t* sanctuary: the garments of holiness for Aaron the priest and the garments of his sons for *the ministry.*" *u* 20. And all *w* the congregation of the children of Israel went out before Moses. 21. And every man whose heart prompted him *x* and everyone whose spirit prompted him brought the Lord's *separated* offering *y*[8] for the making of the tent of meeting and for all the worship and for the garments of holiness. *z* 22. And the men came, *beside* *aa* the women; everyone whose heart prompted him brought necklaces *bb* and rings and signet rings and *emeralds* *cc*[9] and all objects of gold; and likewise every man who waved his wave-offerings of gold to the *Name of* the Lord. 23. And every man with whom was found blue or purple or *precious* crimson material [10] or *twined* byssus or goats' hair or reddened *dd* rams' skins or *sasgona* skins brought them. 24. Everyone who *had set aside* a *separated* offering [11] of silver or bronze brought the Lord's *separated* offering, and everyone with whom was found acacia wood for any use fin the work, *ee* brought them. 25. And every woman, skillful *ff* of hand, *gg* spun the blue and purple and the *precious* crimson material and the byssus. [12] 26. And all the women whose hearts prompted *hh* them with skillfulness spun the goats' hair. 27. And the lords brought *precious* stones and stones for setting, for the ephod and for the breastpiece, *ii*[13] 28. and the perfume and the oil for the illumination and for the oil of anointing and for the fragrant incense. *jj* 29. Every man and woman whose heart prompted

Apparatus, Chapter 35

r Nfmg: "its poles" (this variant is probably misplaced).

s Nfmg: "its bolts."

t Nfi: "in the (sanctuary)."

u Nfmg +: "before him in the high priesthood."

w Nfmg +: "the people (of)."

x Nfmg: "(whose spirit) was great."

y Nfmg: "whose spirit will prompt them, shall bring the (text: "of," probably by error) offering of separation."

z Nfmg: "and for the garments of the sanctuary."

aa Nfmg: "with the women."

bb Nfmg: "chains" (*šryyn* = *šyryn* = Onq.).

cc Nfmg: "broaches" (carried on their persons by the women).

dd I.e., tanned; cf. note *g* above.

ee Nfmg: "work of service."

ff Lit.: "wise of heart by her hand."

gg Nfmg: "wisdom (of heart by her hand)"; cf. below 35:35.

hh Nfmg 1°: "(whose heart) was big (spun)"; Nfmg 2°: "upon them."

ii Nfmg: "for setting, to set the ephod and breastpiece by them."

jj Lit.: "incense of the spices"; same (in different writing) in Nfi.

Notes, Chapter 35

[7] "For ministering" represents Hebrew "to act as priest"; cf. Tg. Onq., Tg. Ps.-J., and cf. note on 28:1; Nfmg has the full expression found most often in Tg. Nf.

[8] See note on 13:12 for "offering of separation."

[9] For "emeralds," Hebrew has "rings."

[10] On "precious," see 25:4.

[11] Hebrew has: "Everyone who lifted up a heave offering, *terumah* . . .": see notes on "offering of separation," 13:12; 29:27.

[12] See note on 25:4.

[13] See note on 25:7.

them to[kk] bring (anything) for the work which the Lord[mm] by Moses had commanded to do, brought it—all the children of Israel—as a free-will offering[nn] to *the name of* the Lord. 30. And Moses said to the children of Israel: "See, the Lord has *designated* by the name of *master*[oo] Bezalel, the son of Ur(i), the son of Hur, from the tribe *of the sons* of Judah.[14] 31. And a spirit of *holiness*[pp] *from before the Lord* has filled (him)[15] with wisdom and with understanding and with knowledge and with all work(manship), 32. to instruct artsmen[qq] to work in the art[rr] of gold and in the art of silver and in the art of bronze;[ss][16] 33. and in the art of (cutting) *precious* stones for setting[tt] and in woodcarving, to work in every work artistically.[17] 34. And he has also inspired him to teach, both him and Oholiab, son of Ahisamach, from the tribe *of the children* of Dan. 35. He filled (them)[uu] with skill[ww] in their hearts to do every work,[xx] of the woodcarver and artist, and of the embroiderer in blue and purple and *precious* crimson material and byssus and of the weavers, who do every work and teach crafts."[18]

CHAPTER 36

1. And Bezalel and Oholiab and every man skillful[a] in his heart, in whom the Lord has put skill[b] and understanding to know and to do all[c] the work of the (service)[d] of the sanctuary, worked according to all the Lord[e] had commanded.

Apparatus, Chapter 35

[kk] Nfmg: "whose heart was big (*ytrbrb*), to (bring)."
[mm] Nfmg: "the Memra of the Lord."
[nn] Nfmg: "a free-will offering" (*nsybh*; Nf text: *ndbh*, here rendered "offering."
[oo] Nfmg: "look: behold the Memra of the Lord has anointed and called Bezalel by a good name."
[pp] Nfmg: "of wisdom."
[qq] Or: "to each art (to work)." The text appears to be erroneous; cf. MT and 31:4.

[rr] Nfmg: "the art of gold and silver and the art of bronze."
[ss] Nfi: "of silver and bronze."
[tt] Nfmg: "and the cutting of precious stones for setting them"; almost verbatim as VN.
[uu] Text: "with them," reading *'tm* as *'ittam*.
[ww] Lit.: "wisdom"; Nfmg: "wisdom (= skill) of heart."
[xx] Nfi: "(to work) in all the works" (= "all kinds of work").

Notes, Chapter 35

[14]See note on 31:1 and cf. Tg. Ps.-J.
[15]Hebrew has: "And he has filled him with the Spirit of God." See note on 31:3 and LXX as there quoted.
[16]See note on 31:4 and cf. Tg. Onq. and Tg. Ps.-J.
[17]See note on 31:5. Hebrew has: "And in the cutting of stone"; cf. Tg. Onq., Tg. Ps.-J., and Frg. Tg. V for the idea of precious stones.
[18]See note on 25:4.

Apparatus, Chapter 36

[a] Lit.: "wise in his heart"; Nfmg: "wise of heart."
[b] Nfmg: "wise of heart in which the Memra of the Lord has put wisdom."

[c] Nfi: "(to know to work) in all."
[d] In the text: "of the workers."
[e] Nfmg: "the Memra of the Lord."

2. And Moses called Bezalel and Oholiab and all who were wise*f* of heart, in whose heart the Lord had put skill, everyone whose heart prompted him to approach the work to do it.*g* 3. And they took from before Moses every *separated* offering which the children of Israel had *set aside*[h1] for doing the work of the service of the sanctuary; and they brought free-will offerings to him again every morning.*i* 4. And all the skillful men,*j* who were doing*k* all the work*m* of the sanctuary, came, each from the work which they were doing. 5. And they said*n* to Moses, saying: "The people bring more than the service requires, for doing the work which the Lord*o* had commanded to do." 6. And Moses gave command, and they made a *public crier*[2] pass*p* through the camp saying: "Neither man nor woman shall do any more work for the *separated* offering of the sanctuary." And the people refrained*q* from bringing. 7. And the work*r* was sufficient for all the work to be done; and *(after) they had made* (it),[3] there remained over. 8. And all the skillful of heart among the doers of the work made the tabernacle (with) ten curtains; of twined byssus, blue and purple, and *precious* crimson material, with *figures,s* a work of art, they made them.[4] 9. The length of each curtain: twenty-eight *cubits, according to the (ordinary) cubit,t* and the breadth four cubits for each curtain;*u* all the curtains had the same measure. 10. And he joined five curtains one against the other. 11. And he made loops of blue on the side of the outmost curtain at the place of the joining;*w* and he did likewise on the side of the outmost curtain at the place of the second joining. 12. And he made fifty loops on the first curtain, and he made fifty loops on the side of the curtain that is in the place of the second joining; the loops were directed*x* one against the other. 13. And he made fifty hooks of gold and joined one curtain against the other by the hooks. And the tabernacle was one *whole.*[5]

Apparatus, Chapter 36

f I.e., "skillful."

g Nfmg: "and to every skilled (lit.: "wise of heart") man in whose heart the Memra of the Lord had put skill (lit.: "wisdom"), everyone whose heart was big (*rbrb*;cf. 35:29, Nfmg) to approach the work to do it."

h Nfmg: "had brought."

i Nfmg: "and those brought it again as free-will offerings every."

j Nfmg: "those (who)."

k Nfmg: "(who) would do."

m Nfmg: "of the service."

n Lit.: "they say."

o Nfmg: "the Memra of the Lord."

p Nfmg: "they sent" (lit.: "they made go out").

q Nfmg: "completed" i.e., "ended, stopped bringing."

r I.e., the material. Nf renders HT literally.

s Or: "embroidered."

t "According to ordinary cubit" not in Nfi or HT; see to 26:2.

u Nfmg: "cubits (according to ordinary cubit) of each curtain."

w VN: "(at) the joining."

x Nfmg: "the loops appearing"; VN: "appearing."

Notes, Chapter 36

[1] Cf. Tg. Onq. and Tg. Ps.-J., and see notes on "separation."

[2] "Public crier" stands for Hebrew "voice," and is in Aramaic *krwz* (cf. Tg. Onq. and Tg. Ps.-J.), possibly a loan word from Greek *kêrux*, a herald. Cf. Vulg., "praeco." On "separation," see notes on 13:12.

[3] "After they had made it" is a Targumic addition shared with Tg. Ps.-J.

[4] For "precious," see note on 25:4; and for "figures," note on 25:18.

[5] See also v. 18 for the Tabernacle being "one whole," a point made earlier in 26:6.

14. And he made curtains of goats' *hair as coverings* to *spread* over the tabernacle; [6] eleven[y] curtains he made them. 15. The length of each curtain was thirty *cubits according to the (ordinary)* cubit, and the breadth was four cubits for each curtain; all the eleven curtains had the same measure. 16. And he joined five curtains by themselves <and six curtains by themselves>[z7] 17. And he made fifty loops on the sides of the outmost curtain at the place of joining, and he made fifty loops on the side of the curtain at the place of the second joining. 18. And he made fifty hooks of bronze to join the tent together that it might be one *whole*.[8] 19. And he made for the tent a covering of reddened[aa] rams' skins and a covering of *sasgona* skins, above it. 20. And he made upright planks of acacia wood for the tabernacle.[bb] 21. The length of the planks was ten cubits, and the breadth of each plank was a cubit and a half. 22. Each plank had two tenons for fitting one against the other. Thus he did for all the planks for the tabernacle. 23. And he made for the tabernacle: twenty planks for the south side, southward; 24. and for the forty sockets of silver he made under the twenty planks, two sockets under each plank, for its two (tenons);[cc] 25. And for the second side of the tabernacle, for its north side, he made twenty planks, 26. and their forty sockets of silver, two sockets under one plank and two sockets under the other plank. 27. And for the extremity of the tabernacle *westward* he made six planks.[9] 28. And for the sides of the tabernacle at the *extremities*[dd] he made two planks. 29. And they were joined[ee] below, and together they were joined at the top within the first ring; he made the two of them thus, for its two *sides*.[ff] 30. And there were eight planks with their sockets of silver—sixteen sockets: two sockets under each plank. 31. And he made bars[gg] of acacia wood, five for the planks of one side of[hh] the tabernacle, 32. and five bars for the planks of the second side[ii] of the tabernacle, and five bars for the planks of

Apparatus, Chapter 36

[y] The text has "twenty-one" but, it appears, erroneously.

[z] Missing in text; added in margin; Nfmg: "he joined five curtains by themselves, corresponding to the five books of the Law, and six curtains by themselves corresponding to the six orders of the Mishnah"; cf. Ps.-J.

[aa] I.e., "tanned."

[bb] Lit.: "the tents" or "his tent." "The tent" of text is probably to be corrected; Nf throughout uses same word for "tabernacle" and "tent."

[cc] Thus in Nfi and in 26:19; in the text "for its two sides."

[dd] Nfmg: "at the hangings to the west"; VN: "at the hangings."

[ee] Nfmg 1° and 2° *mthmyn*, apparently from root *thm*, "forming borders" (with); VN: "and they were (= will be) forming borders with" (*whwwn mthmyn*). So also apparently at Nfmg 26:24 (*mthmmyy'*; correct accordingly); also Nfmg Exod 39:15 (where text of Nf has *mt'myn* as here).

[ff] I.e., "at the two corners."

[gg] Nfmg: "poles."

[hh] Nfmg: "for the planks of the sides of."

[ii] Nfmg: "of the sides of."

Notes, Chapter 36

[6] Hebrew has: "for the tent over the Tabernacle"; see note on 26:7 and cf. 40:19, Vulg.

[7] For Nfmg's symbolic understanding of the five curtains as the five Books of the Law, and the six curtains as the six Orders of the Mishnah, see Tg. Ps.-J. of this verse and of 26:9.

[8] See above, note to v. 13.

[9] Cf. Targum at 26:12, 22.

the tabernacle at the *extremity*[jj] westward.[10] 33. And he made the central bar to (pass)[kk] within the planks[mm] from one side to the other. 34. And he overlaid the planks with gold, and made their rings of gold (as) *places*[nn] for the poles, and overlaid the bars[oo] with gold.[11] 35. And he made the veil of blue and purple and *precious* crimson material and twined byssus; he made it[pp] a work of art *with figures*.[12] 36. And he made four acacia columns for it and overlaid them with gold; their clasps[qq] were of gold, and he cast for them four sockets of silver. 37. And he made a screen[rr] of blue and purple and *precious* crimson material[13] and twined byssus for the door of the tent, the work of an embroiderer, 38. and their five columns and their clasps.[ss] And he overlaid the tops of them and their fastenings[tt] with gold, and their five sockets (were) of bronze.

CHAPTER 37

1. And Bezalel made the ark of acacia wood; two cubits and a half (was) its length, and a cubit and a half its breadth, and a cubit and a half *the measure* of its height.[1] 2. And he overlaid it with pure gold within and without, and he made for it a molding of gold round about.[2] 3. And he cast for it four rings of gold for its four corners: two rings for one side and two rings for the second side. 4. And he made poles of acacia wood and overlaid them with gold. 5. And he put the poles into the rings upon the sides of the ark, to carry[a] the ark. 6. And he made the mercy seat of pure gold; two cubits and a half (was) its height and a cubit and a half its breadth. 7. And he made two cherubin[b] of gold—(of) hammered (gold) he made

Apparatus, Chapter 36

[jj] Nfi: "in its extremity"; Nfmg: "in the hangings."
[kk] In the text, probably corrupt, here, as in 26:28, "serving"; "feeling" or "reaching"; VN: "and he made the central bars to go through between the planks."
[mm] Nfmg: "to go through between the planks"; = VN.
[nn] I.e., "holders."

[oo] Nfmg: "poles."
[pp] Nfi: "them."
[qq] Nfmg: "their clasps" (written differently from Nf).
[rr] Nfmg: "a covering."
[ss] Nfmg: "clasps" (written differently).
[tt] Nfmg: "their fillets (?); coverings(?)."

Notes, Chapter 36

[10]For the addition of "extremity," cf. Tg. Ps.-J.
[11]See note on 25:27.
[12]On "precious," see note on 25:4; and for "figures," note on 25:18.
[13]On "precious," see note on 25:4.

Apparatus, Chapter 37

[a] Nfmg: "to bear."

[b] Nfmg: "images."

Notes, Chapter 37

[1]On the addition of "measure," see note on 25:10.
[2]On "round about," see note on 25:11.

them—at the two sides of the mercy seat, 8. one cherub at *this* side here and one cherub at *that* side yonder; from the mercy seat[c] he made the cherubin, from its two sides.[3] 9. And the cherubin spread their wings above, overshadowing the mercy seat with their wings, and their faces were *turned* one toward the other; toward the mercy seat were the faces of the cherubin.[4] 10. And he made the table of acacia wood; two cubits (was) its length, and a cubit its breadth, and a cubit and a half *the measure of* its height.[5] 11. And he overlaid it with pure gold, within and without, and he made for it a molding of gold round about. 12. And[d] he made a border of a hand's-breadth round about,[6] and he made a molding of gold for the border round about.[6] 13. And he cast for it four rings of gold and put the rings on the four corners of its four legs. 14. Opposite the border were the rings (as) *places*[7] for the poles, to carry[a] the table. 15. And he made the poles to carry[e] the table of acacia wood and overlaid them with gold. 16. And he made the utensils of pure gold which (were to be) upon the table, their bowls and the dishes[f] and the libation jars and flagons *to be used.*[g][8] 17. And he made the lampstand of pure gold; (of) hammered (gold) he made the lampstand; the base thereof and its shaft, its cups, its apples, and its lilies (were)[h] from it. 18. And six shafts went out from its side, three shafts of the lampstand from one side and three shafts of the lampstand from the second side, 19. three cups *engraved*[9] on the shaft; an apple and a lily; thus for the six shafts going out from the lampstand. 20. And on the lampstand[i] there were four *engraved*[9] cups, their apples and their lilies, 21. and an apple of one piece with it under the two shafts, and an apple of one piece with it under the two pairs of shafts, for each of the six shafts that went out from it. 22. Their apples and their shafts were of one piece with[j] it: all of it was one hammered piece of pure gold. 23. And he made seven lamps and its snuffers and its trays of pure gold. 24. He made it and all its utensils of a *centenarium*[k] of pure gold.[10] 25. And he made the altar of incense of acacia wood, its length (was) one cubit and its breadth was one

Notes, Chapter 37

[3] Cf. Tg. Onq. and Tg. Ps.-J.
[4] See note on 25:20.
[5] See note on 25:10.
[6] On "round about," see note on 25:11.
[7] Hebrew has: "houses" for "places"; see note to 25:27.
[8] See note on 25:29.
[9] For "engraved," see note on 25:33.
[10] Hebrew has: "a talent of gold" for "centenarius"; so Tg. Ps.-J.: see note on 25:39.

cubit; it was square, and two cubits was *the measure of* its height; [11] the horns were
<of one piece with it>. [m] 26. And he overlaid it with pure gold, the tops of it and
its sides round about, and he made a molding of gold for it round and about. [12]
27. And he made for it two rings of gold under the molding at the two corners
upon its two sides, as *places* [13] for the poles with which to carry it. [n] 28. And he
made the poles of acacia wood, and he overlaid them with pure gold. 29. And he
made holy anointing oil and the pure fragrant incense, the work of a perfumer. [o]

CHAPTER 38

1. And he made the table of holocaust of acacia wood; its length (was) five cubits, and its breadth was five cubits; (it was) square, and *the measure of* its height
(was) three cubits. [1] 2. And he made its horns upon its four corners; its horns were
from a measure [a] *of its height*, and he overlaid th(em) with bronze. [2] 3. And he
made all the utensils of the altar, the pots [b] and shovels [c] and the sprinkling bowls
and the forks and the trays; all its utensils he made of bronze. 4. And he made for
the altar a grating of network of bronze under the circuit, [d] half its way up from
below. 5. And he cast four clasps in the four corners of the grating of bronze (as)
places [3] for the poles. 6. And he made the poles of acacia wood and overlaid them

Apparatus, Chapter 37

[m] Omitted in text; Nfmg: "from it and in it were (its horns)."

[n] Nfmg: "by which to bear them."
[o] Nfmg: "of a blender (or perfumer)."

Notes, Chapter 37

[11] On the addition of "measure," see note on 25:10.
[12] After "and its sides round about," Targum omits MT's "and its horns." For the final "round and about," see note on 25:11.
[13] Targum has "places" for "houses"; see note on 25:27.

Apparatus, Chapter 38

[a] Nfmg: "from it and in it shall (its horns) be."
[b] Nfmg: "and its pots" (written differently from Nf).
[c] Nfmg: "and its pans (?) and its shovels and its sprin-

kling bowls and its forks and its trays and all its utensils."
[d] Nfmg: "the grating."

Notes, Chapter 38

[1] See note on 25:10.
[2] Hebrew has: "And he made its horns on its four corners: its horns were from it (i.e., they were of one piece with it)." See note on 25:10.
[3] Targum has "places" for Hebrew "houses"; see note on 25:27.

with bronze. 7. And he put the poles into the rings upon the sides[e] of the altar to carry it by them; he made it hollow,[f] of planks. 8. And he made the bronze basin and the base thereof of bronze, from the mirrors of the *just* women who *prayed* at the door[g] of the tent of meeting.[4] 9. And he made the court. For the *south* side, southward, the hangings for the court (were) of twined byssus, a hundred cubits according to the ordinary cubit.[5] 10. And their columns were twenty, and their sockets were twenty, of bronze; and the clasps[h] of the pillars and their fastenings[i] were of silver. 11. And for the north side, a hundred cubits, according to the ordinary cubit, and their pillars twenty, and their sockets twenty, of bronze, and the clasps[h] of the columns and their fastenings (were) of silver. 12. And for the *west*[6] side (there were) hangings of fifty cubits according to the ordinary cubit, their pillars ten and their sockets ten, and the clasps[h] of the pillars and their (fastenings)[j] (were) of silver. 13. And for the *east* side, eastward, fifty cubits.[7] 14. And the hangings for one side (of the gate) (were) fifteen cubits, their pillars three and their sockets three. 15. And for the second side: on this hand and on that hand by the gate[k] of the court (were) hangings of fifteen cubits, their pillars three and their sockets three. 16. All the curtains of the court round about were of twined byssus, 17. clasps of the pillars and their fastenings[m] of silver, and the overlaying[n] of their capitals[o] of silver; and all the pillars of the court were fastened with silver.[p] 18. And the screen[q] of the gate of the court was of embroidered work[r] of blue and purple and *precious* crimson material[8] and twined byssus, and it was twenty cubits long, five cubits in height and in breadth,[s] corresponding to the hangings of the court.

Apparatus, Chapter 38

[e] Nfmg: "(upon) the side of."

[f] Nfmg: "to bear them (read ?: "it"); hollow."

[g] Nfmg: "with mirrors of the chaste (or: "retired") women who lived in retirement at the door of"; PVN: (VN) "And he made the bronze basin and the base thereof of bronze (PVN) with the mirrors of retiring (= chaste women who lived in retirement at the door of the tent of meeting)."

[h] Nfmg: *wqlwwt*, "and the clasps (of)" (written differently: *w'nqlwwt*, but as Nfmg 27:11).

[i] Nfmg: "their fillets (?)"; cf. 36:38.

[j] The text mistakenly has "sockets."

[k] Nfmg: "to this and to the other side of the door."

[m] Nfmg: "and the sockets of the pillars were of bronze and the clasps of the pillars and their fillets (?)."

[n] Nfmg: "and their fillets (?)."

[o] Lit.: "the tops of them."

[p] Nfmg: "and all the pillars of the court had fillets (?) of silver."

[q] Nfmg: "and the covering of."

[r] Nfmg: "of an embroiderer."

[s] Nfmg: "(twenty) cubits long and the measure of the height to the breadth of five. . . ."

Notes, Chapter 38

[4]Hebrew has: "with the mirrors of the women who served, who served at the door of the tent of meeting." Cf. Tg. Onq., Tg. Ps.-J., Nfmg, and Frg. Tg. P, V, which record the same tradition in different words: see also Philo, *De vita Mosis* II. XXVII §§136–37; *De mig. Abr.* XVII. §97; *Num. R.* 9:14; *Tanḥuma Piqqude* 9; *Mek. RI Pisḥa* 16. LXX have "the women who fasted," presumably indicating their piety.

[5]See Targum of 26:9.

[6]"West" correctly interprets Hebrew "sea"; cf. Tg. Ps.-J.; Tg. Onq.; and LXX (37:10); Vulg.

[7]Cf. Tg. Onq.; Tg. Ps.-J.; and LXX (37:11).

[8]For "precious," see note on 25:4. For Nfmg's "measure," see note on 25:10.

19. And their pillars (were) four and their sockets four, of bronze; their clasps[t] of silver and the overlaying of their capitals and their fastenings[u] of silver. 20. And all the pegs for the tent and for the court round about[w] (were) of bronze. 21. This is the sum of (the things for) the tabernacle, the tabernacle of testimony, which were counted by *decree* of the mouth of Moses,[9] the service of the Levites[x] by the hands of Ithamar, son of Aaron, the priest.[y] 22. And Bezalel, the son or Ur(i), the son of Hur, of the tribe[z] *of the sons* of Judah made all which the Lord[aa] had commanded Moses. 23. And with him was Oholiab, the son of Ahisamach, from the tribe *of the sons,*[bb] of Dan, a (wood)carver, an artist, and an embroiderer in blue and purple and *precious* crimson material[cc][10] and in byssus. 24. All the gold that was used for the work,[dd] in all the work of the sanctuary—and it was the gold of the wave-offering[ee]—(was) twenty-nine *kikkars*[ff] and seven hundred and thirty *selas*, according to the *sela* of the sanctuary. 25. <And the silver of those numbered of the *people* of the congregation (was) a hundred *kikkars*[ff][11] and a thousand and seven hundred and seventy-five *selas*, according to the *selas* of the sanctuary>[gg] 26. <a *teba*[hh] per[ii] head, a half *sela*[jj] of the sanctuary>[kk] for [mm] everyone who passed over to them that were numbered from twenty years and upward, for six hundred thousand, three thousand and five hundred and fifty[nn] (men). 27. And the hundred *kikkars*[11] of si(l)ver were for casting[oo] the sockets of the sanctuary and the sockets of the veil: a hundred sockets for a hundred *kikkars*,[pp][11] a talent for *each* socket. 28. And of the thousand seven hundred and seventy-five *selas*[qq] he made clasps[rr]

Apparatus, Chapter 38

[t] Nfmg: "four, of bronze and their clasps" ("clasps" written differently, as for Nfmg v. 10; note *h* above).
[u] Nfmg: "and their fillets (?)."
[w] Nfmg: "for all the pegs of the tabernacle and of the court roundabout."
[x] Nfmg: "of the tabernacle of the testimony, which was commanded by decree of the mouth of Moses, the service of the Levites."
[y] Nfi: "the high (priest)."
[z] Nfi: "of the tribe of Judah."
[aa] Nfmg: "the Memra of the Lord."
[bb] Nfi: "of the tribe of Dan."
[cc] Nfmg: "and of color."
[dd] Nfmg: "used in the work."
[ee] MT: *tenuphah*; Nf renders by *'npu(th)*; see above to 29:26.

[ff] talents; Nfmg: "centenaria."
[gg] Forgotten in text; added in Nfmg.
[hh] Or: a half-sela; MT: *beqa'*.
[ii] Nfmg: "for" (= corresponding to) (a head).
[jj] Nfi: "a sela of the selas of."
[kk] Forgotten in text; added in Nfmg.
[mm] Nfmg: "for all who passed."
[nn] Nfmg: "for sixty times ten thousand and three (thousand . . .)."
[oo] Nfmg: "a hundred centenaria of silver were for casting."
[pp] Nfmg: "centenaria."
[qq] Introduced to make sense clearer.
[rr] Nf: *'wnqlwwn*; a Greek loan word, *ankylê*; cf. above 27:10, 11; Nfmg: "clasps," (*wwylwn*, to be read probably as *qlwwn*; see note *h* to v. 10 above).

Notes, Chapter 38

[9] Hebrew has, lit.: "by the mouth of Moses." For Nfmg's reference to the high priest, see note on 28:1.
[10] On "precious," see note on 25:4.
[11] Nfmg has "centenaria"; see note on 25:39. Targum Nf retains Hebrew *kikkar*, "talent".

for the columns and overlaid[ss] their capitals and fastened[tt] them. 29. And the gold of the wave-offering was seventy *kikkars*[uu][11] and a thousand four hundred *selas, according to the selas of the sanctuary*; 30. <and he made> the sockets of the door of the tent of meeting with it, and the bronze altar and the bronze grating for it[ww] and all the utensils of the altar, 31. and the sockets of the court round about and the sockets of the door of the court <and all the pegs of the tabernacle and all the pegs of the court>[xx] round about.

CHAPTER 39

1. And of the blue and of the purple and of the *precious* crimson material[1] they made the service garments <for ministering in the sanctuary; and they made the service garment>[a] of Aaron, as the Lord[b] had commanded Moses. 2. And he made the ephod of gold, blue and purple and *precious* crimson material[1] and twined byssus. 3. And they beat the gold foil and cut[c] it into threads to work (it) within the blue and within the purple and within the *precious* crimson material[1] and within the byssus: a work of art. 4. And they made for it shoulder pieces joined together; it was joined at its two ends. 5. And the girdle of the ephod which is upon it was of one piece with it,[d] of like workmanship (with it), gold and blue and purple and *precious* crimson material[1] and twined byssus, as the Lord[a] had commanded Moses. 6. And they made the *precious* stones[2] set in gold setting;[e] inscribed in engraved inscribing,[f] according to the names of the children of Israel. 7. And he set them upon the shoulder piece of the ephod as stones of remembrance[g] for the children of Israel, as the Lord[h] had commanded Moses.[3] 8. And he made the

Apparatus, Chapter 38

[ss] Nfmg: "and overlaid" (?), written differently.
[tt] Nfmg: "and filleted" (?) or "inserted" (?) or "covered" (?) (*wšq'*).
[uu] Nfmg: "centenaria."

[ww] Nfmg: "(the bronze grating) which it has" (lit.: "which there is to it").
[xx] Missing in text; omitted by homoioteleuton. Supplied in Nfmg.

Apparatus, Chapter 39

[a] Missing in text; supplied in Nfmg.
[b] Nfmg: "the Memra of the Lord."
[c] Nfmg: "and they cut (it) up."
[d] I.e., with the ephod.
[e] Nfmg: "inserted" (cf. Ps.-J.; Onq.).

[f] Nfmg: "(inscribing of) a seal (maker) (i.e., as cutters inscribe on seals) according to the names of."
[g] Nfmg: "of good remembrance."
[h] Nfmg: "the Memra of the Lord."

Notes, Chapter 39

[1] For "precious," see note on 25:4.
[2] Hebrew has "onyx/beryl stones." For Targum and Nfmg, see note on 25:7.
[3] For Nfmg's "good remembrance," see note on 12:14.

breastpiece, a work of art; like the work of the ephod, of gold, blue and purple and *precious* crimson material[1] and twined byssus. 9. It was square; they made the breastpiece double, a hand's-breadth[i] its length and a hand's-breadth its breadth, double. 10. And they filled in it four rows of *precious* stone. *The first* row: carnelian, topaz and carbuncle, one row. *And written and clearly expressed upon them (was) the name of the three tribes, Reuben, Simeon, Levi.*[4] 11. And the second row: a chalcedony and a sapphire and a "calf's eye." *And written and clearly expressed upon them was the name of the three tribes: Judah, Issachar, Zebulun.*[5] 12. And the third row: a jacinth and a beryl and an emerald. *And written and clearly expressed upon them was the name of the three tribes: Dan and Nephtali and Gad.*[6] 13. And the fourth row: a beryl of *the Great Sea,* and a bdellium and a pearl. *And written and clearly expressed upon them (was) the name of the three tribes: Asher, Joseph, and Benjamin.* (They were) set in gold setting,[j] in their settings.[7] 14. And the stones, according to the names of the children of Israel, were twelve according to their names; (they were) inscribed, engraved,[k] each according to its name, according to the twelve tribes.[m] 15. And they made upon the breastpiece chains of pure gold like a cord,[n] a plaited work. 16. And they made two (settings)[o] of gold and two rings[p] of gold, and they put two rings upon the two sides of the breastpiece. 17. And they put the two plaits of gold on the two rings upon the sides of the breastpiece. 18. And they put[q] the two sides of the two plaits upon the two settings.[r] And they set them upon the shoulder pieces of the ephod, in front. 19. And they made two rings of gold and put them upon[s] the two sides[t] of the breastpiece on the *inside* border of the ephod.[u] 20. And they made two rings of gold and placed them upon the two shoulder pieces of the ephod, underneath, in front, opposite its joining point, above the girdle of the ephod. 21. And they looped[w] the breastpiece from the ring to the rings[x] of the ephod <with a lace of blue so that it should lie upon the blue girdle>[xbis] *and so that the breastpiece should*

Apparatus, Chapter 39

[i] Nfmg: "a hand's-breadth (badly written, probably by contamination of *pšk* and *ptyh*) in its length, double."

[j] Nfmg: "inserted"; cf. v 6, note *e.*

[k] Nfmg: "of a seal-maker"; cf. v. 6, note *f.*

[m] Nfmg: "according to the number of the twelve tribes of Israel."

[n] Lit.: "twin-like," "joined"; Nfmg: "chains" making borders or bounding, *mthmyn*; see Apparatus, 28:22.

[o] The text is corrupt. This is the word to be substituted; Nfmg: "insertings of gold."

[p] Nfmg: "the (two) rings."

[q] Nfmg: "and they put the two insertings."

[r] Nfmg: "the (two) insertings."

[s] Nfmg: "the (two) rings of gold and they put (them) upon."

[t] I.e., "ends."

[u] Nfmg: "(on) the inside border which is in front of the ephod."

[w] Nfmg: "and they fastened."

[x] Lit.: "with the rings"; Nfmg: "to the rings."

[x bis] Missing in text.

Notes, Chapter 39

[4]See notes on 28:17. For "precious," see also Tg. Onq.; for "first row," see Tg. Onq. and Tg. Ps.-J.
[5]See note on 28:18.
[6]See note on 28:19.
[7]See note on 28:20.

not move[y] from upon the ephod, as the Lord[z] had commanded Moses. 22. And *they* made[8] the *robe* of the ephod, the work of weavers, completely[aa] of blue; 23. and the opening of the robe was its center like the opening of a coat of mail, with a border[bb] for the opening round about so that it was not torn. 24. And they made the skirts of pomegranates, of blue and purple and *precious* crimson material[9] and twined *byssus*. 25. And they made bells[cc] of pure gold and put the bells within[dd] the pomegranates upon the skirts, round about, within the pomegranates, 26. a bell[ee] and a pomegranate, a bell[ee] and a pomegranate upon the skirts round about for ministering, as the Lord[ff] had commanded Moses. 27. And they made the *robe*[gg] of byssus, weavers' work,[hh] for Aaron and for his sons. 28. And the turban of byssus, and the crowns, the caps, of byssus, and the byssus breeches of twined byssus.[ii] 29. And the girdle of twined byssus and blue[jj] and purple and precious crimson material,[9] work of an embroiderer, as the Lord[kk] had commanded Moses. 30. And they made the plate (of) the crown of the *sanctuary* of pure gold, and they wrote upon it an inscription, inscribed, engraved;[mm] "Holy to *the Name of the Lord.*"[nn][10] 31. And they *placed upon it a thread of blue to put it upon the turban, above, as the Lord*[kk] commanded Moses.[11] 32. And all the work of the tabernacle[oo] of the tent of meeting was completed. And the children of Israel had done all that the Lord[kk] had commanded[pp] Moses; thus they did. 33. And they brought[qq] <to Moses the tabernacle>,[rr] the tent and all its utensils; its hooks, its boards, its bars, its pillars and its sockets, 34. and the covering[ss] of goats' reddened skin, and the *sasgona*[tt] covering, and the veil of the screen; 35. and the ark of the testimony and its poles and the mercy seat; 36. and the table and all its utensils,

---

Apparatus, Chapter 39

[y] Nfmg: "(so that it should not) move" (same word written differently).
[z] Nfmg: "the Memra of the Lord."
[aa] Nfmg: "the thread of (blue)."
[bb] Or: "hem"; Nfmg: "the fringe."
[cc] Nf: *zwgyn*; Nfmg: "bells" (written differently, *zgwnyn*).
[dd] Nfmg: "the bells between."
[ee] Nf: *zwg*; Nfmg: "a bell" (*zgwn*); cf. *cc* above.
[ff] Nfmg: "the Memra of the Lord."
[gg] Nfi: "the robes."
[hh] Nfmg: "the robe of byssus, work of."
[ii] Nfmg: "of byssus; and the excellence—the work of the turbans—of byssus; and the trousers of byssus; byssus."

[jj] Nfi: "and of blue."
[kk] "the Memra of the Lord."
[mm] Nfmg: "of a seal-maker."
[nn] Nfmg: "holy before the Lord."
[oo] Nfmg: "and all the labor of the tabernacle was completed."
[pp] Nfi: "as he had commanded."
[qq] Nfi: "and they came" (should be corrected to "and they brought").
[rr] Missing in text; supplied in Nfi.
[ss] Nfmg: "the covering" (written differently).
[tt] Nfmg: "(the covering) of skins, reddened (= tanned) and the covering of the skins of *sasgonin*."

Notes, Chapter 39

[8]For "they made," see some Hebrew MSS.
[9]On "precious," see note on 25:4 and fragment cited by Klein, 1, 1986, 299.
[10]Hebrew has: "And they made of pure gold the flower of the holy crown . . . holy to the Lord." See fragment in Klein, 1, 1986, 299, and note on 28:33.
[11]See 28:37 and cf. Tg. Onq., and *b. Arakh.* 10a; *b. Zeb.* 19a.

and the arrangement of the bread of the Presence;^{uu} 37. and the pure lampstand^{ww} *and* its lamps of *illumination,*^{xx} and all its utensils and the oil of illumination;¹² 38. and the golden altar, and the anointing oil, and the fragrant incense, and the screen of the door of the tent; 39. the bronze altar and the bronze grating thereof,^{yy} and its poles and all its utensils and the basin,^{zz} and the base *of the basin*; 40. the hangings of the court, its pillar(s)^a and its socket(s),^b and the screen for the door of the court and their cords and their pegs, and the utensils^c of the service of the tabernacle, for the tent of meeting; 41. the garments of service for serving within^d the *sanctuary*, and all the garments of the sanctuary for Aaron the priest, and the garments of his sons for *serving.*^{e 13} 42. According to^f all that the Lord^g had commanded Moses, thus the children of Israel did all the work. 43. And Moses saw all *his* work^h and, behold, they had done it; as the Lord^g had commanded Moses, thus they had done. And Moses blessed them *and said to them: "May his Shekinahⁱ dwell in the work of your hands."*¹⁴

CHAPTER 40

1. And the Lord^a spoke to Moses, saying: 2. "On the first day of the first month^b you shall erect^c the tabernacle, the tent of meeting. 3. And you shall place there the ark of the testimony, and you shall cover the ark with the veil. 4. And you shall

Apparatus, Chapter 39

^{uu} Or simply "the bread of the Presence"; Nfmg inverts the order of Nf; cf. 40:23.
^{ww} I.e., "of pure gold."
^{xx} Nfmg: "of the altar."
^{yy} Nfmg: "which it has" (lit.: "which there is for it").
^{zz} Nfmg: "its basin."
^a Text: "its pillar."
^b Text: "and its socket."
^c Nfmg: "its bars and its pegs and all the utensils of."

^d Nfmg: "in the sanctuary."
^e Nfmg + : "before him in the high priesthood."
^f Nfi: "all (that)."
^g Nfmg: "the Memra of the Lord."
^h Nfmg: "the work."
ⁱ Nfmg: "may God grant (lit.: "may there be goodwill before the Lord") to make his Shekinah dwell in the work of your hands and that the nations may not rule in the work of your hands for all ages."

Notes, Chapter 39

¹²For the addition of "and," see fragment in Klein, 1, 1986, 301, and Tg. Ps.-J. Hebrew has "lamps of arrangement" for "lamps of illumination."

¹³For the rendering here, cf. Tg. Onq. and Tg. Ps.-J. For Nfmg's reference to the high priesthood, see note on 28:1; and see further *b. Yoma* 72ab. The point is that the high priest's forehead was visible in the gap between the priestly headdress and the golden band with the divine name. In this gap the priest would place the *tefillin shel ro'sh*: so Rashi on this verse.

¹⁴For the substance of Moses' blessing, which is not included in the Hebrew, see Tg. Ps.-J.; *Seder Olam Rabbah* 6; *Sifre Num.* 143; *Tanḥuma Berakhah* 1; *Naso'* 13; *Num. R.* 12, 9. The "blessing" is a quotation of Ps 90:17, whose authorship is traditionally ascribed to Moses himself.

Apparatus, Chapter 40

^a Nfmg: "the Memra of the Lord."
^b Nfmg: "on the first (lit.: "on one") day (of the first month)."

^c Nfmg: "Moses erected."

bring in the table and shall set its arrangements in order;[d] and you shall bring in the lampstand and *arrange* its lamps.[1] 5. And you shall put the golden altar for incense before the ark of the testimony, and you shall set up[e] the screen of the door for the tabernacle.[f] 6. And you shall put the altar of holocaust before the door of the tabernacle, the tent of meeting. 7. And you shall place the basin between the tent of meeting and the altar, and you shall put water within it.[g] 8. And you shall set up[h] the court round about, and you shall place a screen at the door of the court. 9. And you shall take the oil of anointing and shall anoint the tabernacle and all that is in it, and you shall consecrate all its utensils; and they shall be holy.[i] 10. And you shall anoint the altar of holocaust and all its utensils, and you shall consecrate the altar; and the altar shall be most holy; 11. <and you shall anoint the basin and its socket, and you shall consecrate it,[2] 12. and you shall bring Aaron and his sons near to the door of the tent of meeting, and you shall wash them with water. 13. And you shall clothe Aaron with the garments *of the sanctuary>,[j]* and you shall anoint them and consecrate him, and he shall[k] *minister before* me *in the high priesthood.* 14. And you shall bring his sons near and clothe them with cloaks, 15. and you, anoint them as you anointed their father, and they *shall minister before* me *in the high priesthood;*[3] and their anointing shall confer[m] on them an eternal priesthood[n] for their generations." 16. And Moses did (so); <according to>[o][4] all that the Lord[p] had commanded him, thus he did. 17. And on the first month, in the second year, on the first of the month,[q] *Moses* erected the tabernacle. 18. And Moses erected the tabernacle, and he laid its sockets and set up[r] its planks, and put in its poles,[s] and set up its pillars; 19. and he spread the *screen*[t][5] over the taberna-

---

Apparatus, Chapter 40

[d] I.e., "you shall place the bread of the Presence"; Nfmg: "its arrangement."

[e] Nfi: "and set up" (imper.).

[f] Nfmg: "a screen for the door, for the door of the tabernacle."

[g] Nfmg: "there, in it, water."

[h] Nfi: "and set."

[i] Nfi: "and it shall be."

[j] Omitted in the text by homoioteleuton.

[k] Nfmg: "and you shall anoint him and consecrate him and he shall serve me."

[m] Lit.: "and it shall be for them" (= to retain); Nfmg: "(before me) and (his anointing) shall be"; Nfi: "(in the high priesthood) and (his anointing) shall be."

[n] Nfmg: "an eternal ministry"; lit.: "(it shall be . . .) for an eternal ministry."

[o] Missing in Nf: present in Nfmg.

[p] Nfmg: "the Memra of the Lord."

[q] Nfmg: "(in the) second (year) on the first day (lit.: "on day one") of the month."

[r] Nfi: "and he put up."

[s] Nfmg: "its beams."

[t] Nfmg: "the tent of meeting."

Notes, Chapter 40

[1] Hebrew has: "and you shall bring up its lamps." For "set in order," rendering Hebrew *'lh,* see 25:37; 27:20; 30:8.

[2] Parts of vv. 11–13 are missing in the text, as noted in the Apparatus; they are found in Nfmg. For "garments of the sanctuary," see notes to 31:10; 35:19. For "minister before me in the high priesthood," see note on 28:1. "Minister" is the verb used by Tg. Onq. and Tg. Ps.-J.

[3] Hebrew has: "and they shall be priests to me." See note on 28:1.

[4] LXX also omits "according to."

[5] See note on 26:7 and cf. Tg. Onq., Tg. Ps.-J., and fragment in Klein, 1, 1986, 305. LXX have "curtains" for Hebrew's original "tent."

cle and put the covering of the tent over it, as the Lord*ᵖ* had commanded Moses. 20. And he took the testimony within the ark*ᵘ* and put the poles upon the ark *of the testimony* and placed the mercy seat above upon the ark. 21. And he brought in the ark within*ʷ* the tabernacle and set up the veil of the screen and (covered)*ˣ* the ark of the testimony, as the Lord*ᵖ* had commanded Moses. 22. And he placed the table in the tent of meeting at the extremity*ʸ* of the tabernacle, to the north, outside the veil. 23. And he arranged upon it the order of the bread *of the Presence*ᶻ before the Lord,⁶ as the Lord*ᵃᵃ* had commanded Moses. 24. And he set the lampstand*ᵇᵇ* in the tent of meeting, opposite the table at the extremity*ᶜᶜ* of the tent, to the south. 25. And he *brought in*ᵈᵈ⁷ the lamps before the Lord, as the Lord*ᵃᵃ* had commanded Moses. 26. And he put the table of gold in the tent of meeting before the veil; 27. and he *arranged*⁸ upon it the incense of *good* perfumes, as the Lord*ᵃᵃ* had commanded Moses. 28. And he put in place the screen of the door for the tabernacle. 29. And the altar of holocaust he put at the door of the tabernacle,*ᵉᵉ* the tent of meeting, and *arranged*⁹ upon it the holocaust <and the offering>,*ᶠᶠ* as the Lord*ᵃᵃ* had commanded Moses. 30. And he set the basin, with water*ᵍᵍ* for ablution in it,*ʰʰ* between the tent of meeting and the altar; 31. and Moses, Aaron and his sons washed their hands and their feet from it. 32. When they went in to the tent of meeting and when they drew near to the top of the altar, they washed themselves, as the Lord*ᵃᵃ* had commanded Moses. 33. And he erected the court round about the tabernacle and the altar, and set up the screen of the door of the court. And Moses completed the work. 34. And the cloud covered the tent of meeting, and the Glory*ⁱⁱ* of *the Shekinah of* the Lord filled*ʲʲ* the tabernacle.¹⁰ 35. And Moses could not enter the tent of meeting, because he had made *the Glory of the Shekinah of the*

Apparatus, Chapter 40

ᵘ Nfmg: "and Moses took the two tables of stone that were given at Horeb and they remained as a sign in the house of instruction, that is, the tables of the covenant, the tables of the testimony, in the ark."

ʷ Nfmg: "in the tabernacle."

ˣ In the text "and brought in" by error.

ʸ Nfmg: "at the side of."

ᶻ Or simply, "he arranged upon it the bread of the Presence"; Nfmg: "the order of the Presence" (= "of the bread of the Presence").

ᵃᵃ Nfmg: "the Memra of the Lord."

ᵇᵇ Nfmg: "the lampstands."

ᶜᶜ Nfmg: "the side of."

ᵈᵈ Nfmg: "and he arranged."

ᵉᵉ Nfmg: "at the opening (of: "entrance") of the tabernacle."

ᶠᶠ Missing in text; present in Nfi.

ᵍᵍ Nfmg: "and he put water there"; in Ps.-J.: "living water," i.e., running water.

ʰʰ Lit.: "there."

ⁱⁱ Nfmg: "and in the Glory."

ʲʲ Nfmg: "filled" (masc.; in text fem.).

Notes, Chapter 40

⁶Hebrew has: "the bread before the Lord," Targum "the bread of the presence"; Nfmg "the order of the Presence"; cf. Frg. Tg. V, and see note on 25:30.

⁷Hebrew has: "And he brought up," root *'lh*, rendered in Nfmg as "and he arranged"; see note on 25:27; 40:4.

⁸Hebrew has: "And he burned upon it sweet incense": see note on 29:13.

⁹Hebrew has: "And he brought up onto it the holocaust," rendering *'lh* as in v. 25: see note on 25:27.

¹⁰Hebrew has: "and the Glory of the Lord filled the Tabernacle." For the Shekinah, cf. Tg. Ps.-J.

Lord rest[kk] upon it, and the Glory *of the Shekinah* of the Lord filled[mm] the tabernacle.[11] 36. And when the cloud was taken up[nn] <from above the tabernacle>,[oo] the children of Israel used to journey in all their journeys. 37. And if the cloud was not taken up, they used not to journey until the day it was taken up. 38. Because the cloud of *the Glory of the Shekinah of* the Lord was[pp] upon the tabernacle[12] by daytime, and a fire was in it by night to the eyes of all the house[qq] of Israel in all their journeys.

Apparatus, Chapter 40

[kk] Nfmg: "(the Glory . . .) had rested."

[mm] Nfmg: "(on it) the cloud and filled it with the glory of the Shekinah of the Lord."

[nn] Nfmg: "and when it went up."

[oo] Missing in text, added in margin.

[pp] Nfmg: "was overshadowing"; = VN.

[qq] Nfmg: "(and fire) was shining upon it all the night, being seen by all the house (of Israel)"; = VN, which continues: "of Israel, in all their journeys."

Notes, Chapter 40

[11] Hebrew has: "because the cloud had tabernacled on it, and the glory of the Lord had filled the Tabernacle." Cf. Tg. Ps.-J.

[12] Hebrew has: "For the cloud of the Lord was upon the Tabernacle," Cf. Tg. Onq. and Tg. Ps.-J. for the Cloud of Glory.

Targum Pseudo-Jonathan: Exodus

Translation

CHAPTER 1

1. These are the names of the sons of Israel who entered Egypt with Jacob; they entered, each *with the members of*[1] his household. 2. Reuben, Simeon, Levi, and Judah; 3. Issachar, Zebulun, and Benjamin; 4. Dan and Naphtali, Gad and Asher. 5. The *sum total of* the persons[2] who were direct descendants of Jacob[3] was seventy persons, *with*[4] Joseph *and his sons who were*[5] in Egypt. 6. Joseph died, and *after him*[6] all[7] his brothers *died*, and all that generation. 7. But the Israelites multiplied and *begot children*;[8] they increased and became very[9] strong, so that the land was filled with them.[10] 8. Then a new king—as (if) *at the beginning*[11] (of his reign)

Notes, Chapter 1

[1]Or: "the men of"; = Onq. When Heb. *byt* means "household," as is the case in our present verse, the Targums very frequently make this meaning explicit by adding "the men of" before their translations of *byt*. See, e.g., the Targums of Gen 7:1; 12:17; 18:19; 34:30; 35:2; 45:11, 18.

[2]Lit.: "the sum of all the persons." The same idiom occurs in the same context in Ps.-J. in Gen 46:27 to translate the same Heb. idiom *kl (h)npš*, lit., "all the souls." It is worth noting that in Gen 46:15, 22, 25, 26 (twice) and in Num 31:35, which also deal with the numbering of persons, Ps.-J. translates the idiom *kl (h)npš* literally. Only in Gen 46:27 and Exod 1:5, both of which tell of the number of people who went down to Egypt with Jacob, does Ps.-J. use the phrase "the sum of all the persons." It would seem that Ps.-J. translated these two texts one in the light of the other, and this would seem to indicate that Ps.-J. as we know it is the result of conscious literary activity rather than the outcome of oral translation.

[3]"Who were direct descendants of Jacob"; lit.: "who came forth from the thigh (*yrk'*) of Jacob"; = Onq.; = HT: *yṣ'y yrk*. See also the Targums of Gen 46:26. This latter verse and our present verse (Exod 1:5) are the only texts in the Pentateuch where the Heb. idiom *yṣ'y yrk* occurs.

[4]Onq.: "with": = HT.

[5]Onq.: "and Joseph *who* was"; = Nf; Onq. and Nf include Joseph among the seventy who came to Egypt. See *Exod. R.* 1,7, which uses the phrase *'m ywsp,* "with Joseph," which we find in Ps.-J.'s version of our present verse; see Shinan, 1984, 43. Ps.-J. differs from Onq. and Nf in that he includes not only Joseph but also his sons among the seventy who came to Egypt. This is not in total agreement with Ps.-J. Gen 46:27, which, following *Gen. R.* 94,9, includes Joseph, his sons, and Jochebed among the seventy. See Ps.-J. Gen 46:27, and n. 25 to that verse (Maher, 1992, 151).

[6]One can deduce from Gen 50:24-25 that Joseph died before his brothers, and Ps.-J. took Exod 1:6 to mean that "Joseph died, and (then) all his brothers." Since Joseph was Jacob's eleventh son (see Gen 29:31–30:24), rabbinic tradition felt it necessary to explain why he should have died before his older brothers; see *ARN* B 22 (137); *Gen. R.* 100,3; *b. Ber.* 55a; *Sotah* 13b; see also *PRE* 39 (304–5).

[7]The word for "all" is omitted in Lond.

[8]= Onq. When Heb. *šrṣ,* "swarm, teem," which is normally used with reference to animals, is employed with reference to humans, as is the case in our present verse, it is usually translated in the Targums by *yld,* "beget." See Grossfeld, 1988B, 2, n. 3. See also Gen 8:17; 9:7, where Onq., Nf, and Ps.-J. render Heb. *šrṣ,* by *yld.* In these texts, however, Nfmg uses the verb *šrṣ,* as does CTg E Gen 9:7.

[9]*mnhwn* = Onq. The Targums make no effort to explain how the Israelites multiplied so speedily. They ignore the fanciful midrashic explanation which says that each woman gave birth to six (or twelve) children at once; cf. *Mek. RI* Exod 12:27 (1,95); *Exod. R.* 1,8; cf. *PRK* 11,11.

[10]*lhd'*; Onq.: *lḥd' lḥd',* = HT.

[11]In translating the biblical phrase "a new king," Ps.-J. translates "new" (*ḥdš*) by its Aramaic cognate (*ḥdt*; cf. Onq., Nf), and then as "as (if) at the beginning" (cf. V). This latter phrase seems to be an explanation of Heb. *ḥdš,* an explanation that is in line with the view which asserts that the king was "new" only in the sense that he issued new decrees. See *b. Erub.* 53a; *Sotah* 11a (52); *Tanḥ. A, Shemot* 5 (164–65); *Tanḥ. B, Shemot* 7 (2,4); *Exod. R.* 1,8. See also Isoʻdad of Merv, who said that the king was called "new" because "he was the first enemy of the Hebrews, and because of the new laws which he decreed against them"; see *Commentaire d'Išoʻdad de Merv sur L'Ancien Testament II.* Exode-Deutéronome, ed. C. van den Eynde; *Corpus Scriptorum Orientalium,* vol. 176; Scriptores Syri 80; Louvain: Secrétariat du Corpus *SCO,* 1958, Syriac text, p. 2; French translation, p. 2. See further Maher, 1988, 50–51.

arose over Egypt, who did not know Joseph, *and he did not walk according to his laws.*[12] 9. And he said to his people, "Behold, the people of the children[13] of Israel are *much* more numerous and stronger than we. 10. Come *now,* let us take counsel against *them; let us reduce*[14] *them with these laws*[15] *before* they increase, lest, should war come upon *us,* they too might join our enemies and *wipe us out*[16] *and not leave even one of us,* and *then* go up[17] out of the land. 11. So they set taskmasters[18] over *them* in order to afflict *them* in their slavery.[19] They built *fortified* cities as Pharaoh's *treasure houses,*[20] *Tanis and Pelusium.*[21] 12. But the more they afflicted *them,* the more they increased and the *stronger* they became, so that *the Egyptians*[22] *lived in dread* of[23] the Israelites. 13. The Egyptians harshly subjected the Israelites to slavery 14. and made their lives bitter with hard work in clay and bricks and in all (kinds of) work in the *open* country; with harshness they

Notes, Chapter 1

[12]*nymwswy* (Gr. *nomos*) = Nf, V. Onq. does not translate the biblical phrase "who did not know Joseph" literally, but interprets it as "who did not implement Joseph's decree." The Pal. Tgs., including Ps.-J., translate the phrase in question literally, but they add a phrase which has essentially the same meaning as the interpretation of Onq.

[13]*Ed. pr.:* "house."

[14]Or: "decimate." The verb *z'yr,* (Af.) "reduce, diminish," which both Ps.-J. and Nf use here, occurs also with humans as its object in Lev 26:22 (Ps.-J., Nf, Onq.) to translate Heb. *m't* (Hif.), which has the same meaning. In Num 22:6 (Ps.-J.) *z'r* translates Heb. *nkh* (Hif.), "smite," and Num 23:7 (Ps.-J., Nf, P, N; see also V), and 23:8 (Ps.-J., Nf, P, V, N), it renders Heb. *z'm,* "curse."

[15]Ps.-J. does not specify what "these laws" were. In *b. Sotah* 12a three decrees are mentioned. See also the Targumic Tosefta to Exod 15:2 published by Klein (1975, 62–63). *b. Sotah* 11a represents Pharaoh as considering different punishments (fire, the sword, water) that might be meted out to the Israelites. Cf. *Exod. R.* 1,9.

[16]*Sefer Ha-Yashar* 65 (205).

[17]*Ed. pr.:* "go out."

[18]Onq.: "*cruel* supervisors"; cf. Pesh.: "a cruel supervisor."

[19]*s'bwdhwn* = Nfmg; Nf: *pwlhnyhwn;* Onq.: *pwlhnhwn.* Heb. *sblwt,* "compulsory service, toil," which occurs only in the context of the slavery in Egypt (Exod 1:11; 2:11; 5:4, 5; 6:6, 7), is usually rendered by *pwlhn* in the Targums. Ps.-J. employs *s'bwd* only in our present verse. Nf has *s'bwd* in 6:6, 7, as does Nfmg in 1:11; 2:11, 5:5, and CTg D 6:6, 7.

[20]In translating Heb. *'ry msknwt,* "store cities," Ps.-J. first renders *msknwt* as *tlylyn,* "fortified" (= Nf: *tlyln;* cf. LXX: "strong cities"), and then adds "as (Pharaoh's) treasure houses"; cf. Onq., which also renders *msknwt* as "treasure house." *Exod. R.* 1,10 also takes Heb. *msknwt* to mean "treasure houses" (*bty 'wsrwt*), which corresponds to the Aramaic idiom used by Onq. and Ps.-J.; see Shinan, 1984, 51.

[21]Onq.: "Pithom and Raamses"; = HT. LXX: "Pitho and Raamses, and On, which is Heliopolis." The place-name Pithom occurs in the Bible only in our present verse (Exod 1:11). The name Tanis, which the Pal. Tgs. use to translate that word, occurs again in the Pal. Tgs. as a translation of the place-name On in Gen 41:45 (Ps.-J., Nf, P); 41:50 (Ps.-J., Nf); 46:20 (Ps.-J., Nfmg; in this verse Nf reads On). On the translation of the place-name Raamses in the Pal. Tgs., see n. 9 to Ps.-J. Gen 47:11 (Maher, 1992, 152).

[22]= Onq., LXX. Isenberg (1968, 92 and 123) claims that the addition of the words "the Egyptians," shared by Onq., Ps.-J., Nf, and LXX, may reflect an ancient Palestinian expansion of HT. However, he admits that since there is a change of subject in v. 12, the Targums and the LXX may have added the words "the Egyptians" independently.

[23]Lit.: "were distressed in their lives because of." The Heb. idiom *qws mpny,* "loathe, abhor," occurs in the Pentateuch only in our present verse and in Num 22:3. Ps.-J. renders that phrase in the same way in both texts. Nfmg translates in the same way as Ps.-J. in Num 22:3. See Gen 27:46, where Heb. *qsty bhyy mpny,* "I am weary of my life." The literal translation of the Targums' rendering (Onq., Nf, Ps.-J.) is "I am distressed in my life because of," which corresponds to Ps.-J.'s wording in our present verse and in Num 22:3.

made them do all their work. 15. *And Pharaoh said*[24] *(that while) he slept, he saw in his dream*[25] *that all the land of Egypt was placed on one balance of a weighing-scales, and a lamb, the young (of a ewe),*[26] *on the other balance of the weighing-scales; and the balance of the weighing-scales on which the lamb (was placed) weighed down. Immediately he sent and summoned all the magicians of Egypt and told them his dream.*[27] *Immediately Jannes and Jambres,*[28] *the chief magicians, opened their mouths* and said *to Pharaoh: "A son is to be born in the assembly of Is-rael, through whom all the land of Egypt is destined to be destroyed."*[29] *Therefore Pharaoh*, the king of Egypt, *took counsel* and said[30] *to the Jewish* midwives—one of whom was named Shiphrah, *she is Jochebed,*[31] and the other was named Puah, *she is Miriam, her daughter.*[32] 16. And he said: "When you act as midwives for the *Jewish* women, you shall look at the *birthstool:* if it is a *male* child,[33] you shall kill him; but if it is a *female* child,[34] she shall live."[35] 17. But the midwives feared *be-*

Notes, Chapter 1

[24]The verb "said" at the beginning of the verse is out of place from the point of view of syntax. Koch (1966, 80–81) claims that the repetition of the verb "said" (at the beginning of the verse and after the haggadic addition; the second "said" is omitted in *ed. pr.*) is a sign that the whole haggadic addition was taken from a literary source and inserted into the biblical verse. It is more likely that the repetition of the verb "said" is due to a copyist's error. The copyist began by writing "and Pharaoh said" as if he were copying a translation of the biblical verse, and then went on to copy the haggadah. Having completed this, he returned to the biblical verse and repeated the verb "said"; cf. Shinan, 1979, 1, 75, n. 124.

[25]See Ps.-J. Gen 9:24 (Maher, 1992, 46), which says that it was through a dream that Noah became aware of what had happened while he was drunk.

[26]*tly br ('ymrt')*. The word *'ymrt'* is omitted in Lond., but a blank space has been left for it. This is one of the few texts where *tly'* means "lamb." See Ps.-J. Gen 30:40 and n. 37 to that verse (Maher, 1992, 107). Vermes (1961, 93, n. 5) has noted that the fact that *tly'* can mean both "boy" and "lamb" explains why in the present haggadic addition the lamb can be taken to refer to a son who is to be born among the Israelites.

[27]Josephus, *Ant.* II.ix.2; *The Chronicles of Moses* (Gaster, 106); *Sefer Ha-Yashar* 67 (210). Cf. also *b. Sanh.* 101b; *PRE* 48 (377); *Exod. R.* 1,18. Compare Gen 41:8.

[28]Jannes and Jambres, who are also mentioned in Ps.-J. Exod 7:11; Num 22:22, are well known from Jewish, Christian, and pagan sources. Strack-Billerbeck (1961, 660–64) have collected many of the Jewish sources. See also H. Odeberg, "*'Iannēs, 'Iambrēs,*" *TDNT* 3, 192–93. R. Bloch (1955, 105, n. 21) and M. McNamara (1966, 82–96) have studied Jewish, Christian, and pagan sources. L. L. Grabbe (1979, 394–96) has briefly summarized them. J. G. Gager (1972, 137–40) has paid special attention to pagan writers who mention Jannes and Jambres, and A. M. Denis (1970, 146–49) has studied Christian sources that mention them. A. Pietersma and R. T. Lutz, (1985, 427–42) have published fragments from *The Book of Jannes and Jambres.* J. H. Charlesworth (1976, 1981, 133–34) lists several studies of the Jannes and Jambres theme. See also C. Burchard (1966).

[29]The closest parallels to Ps.-J.'s long haggadic addition to Exod 1:15 are found in *The Chronicles of Moses* (Gaster, 106) and in *Sefer Ha-Yashar* 67 (210). See further Maher, 1988, 79–88.

[30]Omitted in *ed. pr.*

[31]Omitted in Lond. Ps.-J. often identifies persons who are named in the Bible with better known biblical figures. On Ps.-J.'s tendency to name individuals who are not named in the Bible, see n. 10 to Ps.-J. Gen 6:4 (Maher, 1992, 38).

[32]On the identification of Shiphrah and Puah with Jochebed and Miriam, see *b. Sotah* 11b; *Sifre Num.* 78 (Horovitz, 74–75); *Tanḥ. A, Wa-Yakhel* 4 (335).

[33]*byr dkr.* Cf. Nf; Onq.: "a son (*br'*)." The Pal. Tgs. sometimes use *br (byr) dkr* to translate Heb. *bn,* "a son," or some equivalent. See, e.g., Gen 35:17; (Ps.-J., Nfmg); Exod 1:16 and 22 (Ps.-J., Nf); 2:22 and 12:24 (Ps.-J.).

[34]*brth nwqb'*; cf. Nf; Onq.: "a daughter (*brt'*)." The Pal. Tgs. sometimes employ the term *brth n(w)qbh,* lit., "a female daughter"; see, e.g., Exod 1:16 (Ps.-J., Nf); 1:22 (Nf); 21:31 (Nf); Lev 12:5 (Ps.-J., Nf, Nfmg).

[35]Onq.: "you shall let her live"; = Nfmg (with orthographical variations). See also Pesh. LXX: "save it." Onq., Ps.-J., and Nfmg translate HT *ḥyh,* "live," by *qwm.* Nf and Pesh. translate it by its Aramaic cognate.

fore the Lord, and they did not do as the king of Egypt told them but let the *sons*[36] live. 18. So the king of Egypt called the midwives and said to them, "Why *then* have you done this thing and let the *sons* live?" 19. The midwives said to Pharaoh, "Because the *Jewish* women are not like the Egyptian women, for they are *strong and skillful*.[37] Before the midwife comes to them, *they raise their eyes in prayer, praying and imploring mercy before their Father who is in heaven;*[38] *he hears the voice of their prayer, and they are answered immediately,*[39] and they give birth *and are delivered safely*."[40] 20. And *the Lord* dealt well with the midwives; and the people increased and became exceedingly strong. 21. And *when* the midwives feared *before the Lord, they acquired a good reputation for themselves for the generations, and the Memra of the Lord built* for them *the royal house and the house of the high priesthood*.[41] 22. *When* Pharaoh *saw this*, he commanded all his people saying, "Every *male* child that is born *to the Jews*[42] you shall throw into the river, but you shall let every daughter live."

CHAPTER 2

1. *Amram,*[1] a man *of* the *tribe* of Levi, went *and seated under*[2] the *bridal canopy and (in) the wedding chamber* Jochebed, *his wife, whom he had divorced because of*

Notes, Chapter 1

[36]In vv. 17-18 Ps.-J. and Onq. translate HT *hyldym,* "the male children," by *bny(y)',* "the sons." Nf remains closer to HT and uses the word *tly',* "(male) children, boys."

[37]Lit.: "strong (or: quick) and wise in their knowledge." These words translate HT *ḥywt* (RSV: "vigorous"), the meaning of which is not very clear. Cf. G. R. Driver, "Hebrew Mothers," *ZAW* 67 (1955) 246–48. The meaning of *ḥywt* was discussed in the Talmud; see *b. Sotah* 11b. Cf. also *Exod. R.* 1,16. See *The Chronicles of Moses* 3 (107). Nf, P, and V translate *ḥywt* by its Aramaic cognate. Ps.-J. offers a conflate rendering, first translating it as "strong," and then as "skillful" (*ḥkymn bd'tyhn*). This latter rendering conveys the same meaning as Onq., which reads *ḥkymn,* "wise, shrewd," and as Vulg.: *obstetricandi habent scientiam.* See further Grossfeld, 1988B, 5, n. 11.

[38]Besides our present text there are four other Targum texts that refer to prayer to the "Father in heaven"; see Gen 21:33 (Nfmg, P, V, N, L); Exod 17:11 (P); Num 21:9 (P, V, N); Deut 28:32 (Ps.-J.). McNamara (1972, 115–19) lists many texts where the title "Father in heaven" is used. To his list we may add Exod 1:21 (P); 15:12 (P); see also 15:2 (V, N), where the title "our Father" occurs.

[39]We know of no source for this haggadic addition to this verse; cf. Schmerler, 1933, 7.

[40]The Pal. Tgs., including Ps.-J., and Onq., translate HT *wyldw,* "they have given birth," by its Aramaic cognate. Ps.-J. alone adds *wprqn bšlm,* which we translate as "and are delivered safely." The Hebrew and Aramaic verb *prq* can mean "unload," and it seems to be used figuratively in our present verse. See also *Song of Songs R.* 1,5.3, where the corresponding Hebrew verb is used in a similar way.

[41]*b. Sotah* 11b; *Sifre Num.* 78 (Horovitz, 75); *Tanḥ. A. Wa-Yakhel* 4 (335); *Tanḥ. B, Wa-Yakhel* 5 (2, 122); *Exod. R.* 1,17; 48,4. See further V. Aptowitzer, 1927, 57–59 and 225–26, n. 23; Heinemann, 1974A, 85–89.

[42]= Onq. LXX: "to the Hebrews." Cf. *LAB* 9,1; Josephus, *Ant.* II.ix.2.

Notes, Chapter 2

[1]Moses' parents are named in Exod 6:20 and Num 26:59. Ps.-J. is the only Targum of our present verse to use the name Amram. On Ps.-J.'s tendency to name individuals who are unnamed in the Bible, see Maher, 1992, 38, n. 10.

[2]Lit.: "in."

Pharaoh's decree.[3] *Now, she was a hundred and thirty years old*[4] *when he took her back. But a miracle was performed for her, and her youth was restored just as she was when she was young (and) called*[5] a daughter of Levi. 2. The woman conceived and bore a son *at the end of six months.*[6] When she saw that he *was viable,*[7] she hid him for three months, *which gives a total of nine.* 3. It was no longer possible for her to hide him, *because the Egyptians had noticed her.*[8] So she took a basket of rushes for him and covered it with bitumen and pitch. She placed the child in it, and placed it among the reeds on the bank of the river. 4. And *Miriam,*[9] his sister, stationed herself at a distance to learn what would happen to him. 5. *The Memra of the Lord let loose inflamed scars*[10] *and blisters of the flesh against the land of Egypt.*[11] *Bithiah,*[12] Pharaoh's daughter, went down *to cool herself* at the river, and her maidens walked along *the bank of* the river. She saw the basket among the reeds *and stretched forth her arm*[13] and took it; *and immediately she was cured from the inflammation and from the blisters.*[14] 6. She opened (it) and saw the child; and behold, the boy was crying. She took pity on him and said, "This is one of the children of the *Jews.*" 7. Then his sister said to Pharaoh's daughter, "Shall I go and call you a nurse from

Notes, Chapter 2

[3]*b. Sotah* 12a; *Pes. R.* 43 (180a-b); *The Chronicles of Moses* (Gaster, 108–9); *Sefer Ha-Yashar* 68 (213). Ps.-J. (and Ps.-J. alone) mentions Amram's divorce in Num 11:26. On Ps.-J.'s tendency to repeat traditions, see Maher, 1992, 7.

[4]*b. Sotah* 12a; *B. Bat.* 119b–120a; *Exod. R.* 1,19; *PRE* 48 (375).

[5]*b. B. Bat.* 119b–120; *Sotah* 12a; *Exod. R.* 1,20. Ps.-J. is the only Targum to tell of Jochebed's marvelous transformation. This is in line with this Targum's fondness for the miraculous. See also Ps.-J. Gen 17:16 and n. 13 (cf. Maher, 1992, 65). Compare Gen 18:12 (Onq., Nf, V, N, L).

[6]Ps.-J. gives us to understand that Jochebed's pregnancy lasted only six months. See also *The Chronicles of Moses* (Gaster, 109). According to *Sefer Ha-Yashar* 68 (214), Jochebed gave birth after a pregnancy of seven months. According to rabbinic tradition, however, Jochebed was three months pregnant when Amram took her back (cf. Ps.-J., v. 1), and she gave birth six months later; cf. *b. Sotah* 12a; *Exod. R.* 1,20.

[7]*br qyywm'.* The same idiom, *bn qyym',* is used to refer to a viable infant in *b. Niddah* 26b. See also *m. Hul.,* where the same idiom (*bny qyym'*) is applied to viable nestlings. There is no need to change the text of Ps.-J. as suggested by Vermes (1961, 185, n. 1).

[8]Cf. *b. Sotah* 12a; *Exod. R.* 1,20; *Song of Songs R.* 2,15.2; *The Chronicles of Moses* (Gaster, 109); *Sefer Ha-Yashar* 48 (214).

[9]Ps.-J. is the only Targum of this verse to name the anonymous sister of HT. See above, n. 1 to v. 1. Since the Bible tells of a Miriam who was sister of Aaron and Moses (Num 26:59; 1 Chr 5:29 [6:3]) or Aaron's sister (Exod 15:20), it is not surprising that Jewish tradition identified the nameless sister of Exod 2:4-8 with Miriam. See, e.g., *m. Sotah* 1:9; *b. Meg.* 14a; *Sotah* 12b–13a. This is, of course, the Miriam whom Ps.-J. has earlier identified with Puah, one of the Hebrew midwives (Ps.-J. Exod 1:15).

[10]Lit.: "a scar of the inflammation (or boil)." The same idiom occurs in Ps.-J. Lev 13:23 to render a Heb. idiom which RSV translates as "the scar of the boil." In our present context (Ps.-J. Exod 2:5), such a translation of the Aramaic idiom, which describes a plague which the Lord sent, would scarcely be suitable.

[11]Ps.-J.'s statement that the Lord sent inflammation and blisters would explain why Pharaoh's daughter had to bathe in the river as any commoner might do. The closest parallel to Ps.-J.'s tradition occurs in *The Chronicles of Moses* (Gaster, 109–10). See also *Sefer Ha-Yashar* 68 (214); *PRE* 48 (378–79).

[12]Omitted in *ed. pr.* Once again Ps.-J., and only Ps.-J. among the Targums, names the daughter of Pharaoh. See above v. 1 and n. 1; v. 4 and n. 9. Bithiah, the daughter of Pharaoh, is mentioned in 1 Chr 4:18 (17).

[13]Ps.-J. uses the word *grmyd',* "arm, elbow," to translate HT *'mh,* "maid." Nf, Onq., and Pesh. translate that word by its Aramaic cognate and take it to mean "maiden." On the rabbinic debate about the meaning of HT *'mh* (does it mean "hand" or "handmaid"?), see *b. Sotah* 12b; *Exod. R.* 1,23.

[14]Several midrashic texts say that Pharaoh's daughter was cured of leprosy when she saved Moses from the Nile; cf. *Tanh. A, Shemot* 7 (166); *PRE* 48 (378–79); *Exod. R.* 1,23. Ps.-J., having spoken earlier in the verse of a plague of inflammation and blisters, now says that Bithiah was cured of these afflictions.

the *Jewish* women to nurse the child for you?" 8. And Pharaoh's daughter said to her, "Go!" So the girl went and called the child's mother. 9. And Pharaoh's daughter said to her, *"Bring* this child and nurse it for me, and I will give you your wages."[15] So the woman took the child and nursed him. 10. The child grew and she brought him to Pharaoh's daughter, and he was *as dear* to her *as* a son,[16] and she named him Moses, *for* she said, "I drew him out[17] of the water *of the river."* 11. One day, when Moses had grown up, he went out to his kinsfolk and saw *the anguish of their souls and the greatness of* their toil.[18] And he saw an Egyptian striking a *Jew*, one of his kinsmen. 12. *And Moses, in the wisdom of his mind, looked and considered every generation, and saw that no proselyte would arise from that Egyptian, and that no one from his children's children would ever repent.*[19] So he struck down the Egyptian and hid him in the sand. 13. When he went out next day, *he looked*, and he saw *Dathan and Abiram,*[20] *Jews,* quarreling. *And when he saw that Dathan raised his hand against Abiram to strike him,* he said *to him,* "Why do you strike your fellow?" 14. But *Dathan* answered *him:* "Who *is it that* appointed you prince and judge over us? Do you intend to kill me as you killed the Egyptian?" Moses was frightened and thought, *"In truth* the matter has *become public."* 15. When Pharaoh heard of this matter, he sought to kill Moses. But Moses fled from Pharaoh and settled[21] in the land of Midian; and he sat down beside a well. 16. Now the *ruler*[22] of Midian had seven daughters. They came and drew water, and filled the troughs to water their father's flock. 17. But the shepherds came and drove them away. Then Moses arose in *his mighty strength*[23] and saved them, and

Notes, Chapter 2

[15]The word *swṭr'*, "wages, reward," is used by Ps.-J., and only by Ps.-J., in our present verse and in 22:30; Lev 19:13; Deut 24:14, 15.

[16]Cf. *Exod. R.* 1,26: "she loved him as if he were her own son"; see also *Tanḥ. A, Shemot* 8 (166): "and she loved him."

[17]Ps.-J. agrees with Onq., against the Pal. Tgs., in using the verb *šḥl* to translate HT *mšh,* "draw out."

[18]Compare Exod 6:9. See Philo's description (Philo, *De vita Mosis* I.viii §40-41) of Moses' reaction to the cruel lot of the Israelites. Cf. also *Tanḥ. A, Shemot* 9 (167); *Exod. R.* 1,27.

[19]Ps.-J. takes *kh wkh,* "this way and that," of HT to mean "every generation," and he takes *wyr',* "and seeing" (RSV), to refer to a vision. By saying that no proselyte would ever arise from the Egyptian, Ps.-J. wishes to justify Moses' murderous deed. See *Exod. R.* 1,29; compare Tg. Gen. 4:10 (Nf, P, V, N, CTg B), which says that the blood of the righteous who would have arisen from Abel cried out against Cain. Many midrashic texts set out to justify Moses' killing of the Egyptian; cf., e.g., *Lev. R.* 32,4; *Tanḥ. A, Shemot* 9 (167); *Exod. R.* 1,28; *ARN* A 20 (96).

[20]On Ps.-J.'s tendency to give names to people who are anonymous in the Bible, see above, 2:1 and n. 1 to that verse. Dathan and Abiram are also named in this context in *PRE* 48 (380). The identification of the "two Hebrews" mentioned in Exod 2:13 with Dathan and Abiram is based on the use of the word *nṣym,* "struggling together," in that verse, and the use of the related word *hṣw,* "contended," in Num 26:9; see *b. Ned.* 64b; *Exod. R.* 1,29; *Mek. RI* Exod 18:4 (2,171). Because Dathan and Abiram are called "wicked men" in Num 16:25-26, all kinds of evil deeds can be attributed to them. Cf. *Tanḥ. A, Shemot* 10 (167-68).

[21]*wytyb* = Onq.; Nf: *šrh.*

[22]The word *'wnys* (= *ed. pr.;* Lond.: *'wnym*), which occurs here, and in the form *'wnws,* in Ps.-J. Exod 18:1. According to Jastrow (29) and Levy (1, 15), these are the only two occurrences of the word in the Targums. Jastrow derives it from the verb *'ns,* "take by force, oppress." Levy derives it from Gr. *eunoos/eunous,* "well-minded, benevolent," or *anax,* "lord, master." Levy rejects the interpretation of the *Aruk* according to which *'nws* corresponds to Gr. *onus,* "donkey." This *Aruk* interpretation is recorded in the margin of Lond. at Exod 18:1. The Targum deprives Jethro of the title priest which HT gives to him. On this latter point see Ps.-J. Gen 14:18, and n. 44 to that verse (Maher, 1992, 58).

[23]On the phrase "a mighty strength," see Ps.-J. Gen 44:13 and n. 7 to that verse (Maher, 1992, 145).

watered their flock. 18. When they came to Reuel, their *father's* father,[24] he said, "How is it that you have come so soon today?" 19. They said, "An Egyptian saved us from the shepherds, and drawing water *just once,*[25] he drew for us and watered the flock." 20. He said to his *son's* daughters, "And where is he? Why did you leave the man? Invite him to eat bread!" 21. *When Reuel learned that Moses fled from Pharaoh, he threw him into a pit. But Zipporah, his son's daughter, provided for him in secret for ten years. At the end of ten years he took him out of the pit.*[26] *Moses then went into Reuel's garden, and he gave thanks and prayed before the Lord who had performed miracles and mighty deeds for him. He noticed the rod that had been created at twilight,*[27] *on which was clearly engraved the great and glorious Name*[28] *with which he was to work wonders in Egypt, and with which he was to divide the Sea of Reeds, and bring water from the rock. It was fixed in the middle of the garden. And immediately he stretched forth his hand and took it.*[29] *Behold,* Moses *then* wished to stay with the man, and he gave Zipporah, his *son's* daughter,[30] to Moses. 22. She bore a *male* child whom he named Gershom, for he said, "I have been a resident in a foreign land *that is not mine.*" 23. After a long time the king of Egypt *was afflicted with leprosy, and he ordered the first-born of the Israelites to be killed so that he might bathe in their blood.*[31] The Israelites groaned because of the bondage *which lay heavily upon them,*[32] and they cried out. Their cry went up to *the high heavens of the Lord, and he decided in his Memra to deliver them from* the bondage. 24. Their cry *was heard before the Lord,* and his covenant *which he established* with Abraham, with Isaac, and with Jacob *was* remembered *before the Lord.* 25. *And the*

Notes, Chapter 2

[24]Ps.-J.'s addition brings Exod 2:16-21 (Reuel is Moses' father-in-law) into line with Num 10:29 (Reuel is the father of Moses' father-in-law). See *Sifre Num.* 78 (Horovitz, 72). See also Ps.-J.'s addition in v. 20 (*son's*) and his reference to Reuel's "son's daughter" in v. 21.

[25]Lit.: "he even drew one drawing." Cf. *Exod. R.* 1,32: "He only drew out one bucketful . . . for the water was blessed at his hands." *Exod. R.* and Ps.-J. give us to understand that a miracle was performed for Moses. On Ps.-J.'s love of the miraculous, see Maher, 1992, 6.

[26]The events mentioned here are told at greater length in *The Chronicles of Moses* (Gaster, 120) and in *Sefer Ha-Yashar* 76 (228); 77 (232).

[27]On the things that were created on the eve of the first sabbath, see Gen 2:2 and n. 4 to that verse (Maher, 1992, 21). *The Chronicles of Moses* (Gaster, 121) mentions that the staff was created when God finished creating all things.

[28]On Ps.-J.'s frequent use of the Ineffable Name, see Maher, 1992, 7. The tradition that the Name was written on the rod of Moses is recorded in *PRK* 19,6; *Deut. R.* 11,10; *The Chronicles of Moses* (Gaster, 121). See also *PRE* 40 (313). The idiom "clearly engraved" (*ḥqyq wmp[w]rš*) occurs frequently in Ps.-J. with reference to the divine Name; see, e.g., Exod 4:20; 14:21; 28:30; 32:16; 33:4. In our present verse both Lond. and *ed. pr.* read *ḥqyyn* rather than *ḥqyq*.

[29]Earlier in this verse Ps.-J. has said that the rod of Moses was created at twilight (on the eve of the first sabbath). He fails to tell us how it came to be in Reuel's garden. *PRE* 40 (312-13) fills in the missing details. Cf. *The Chronicles of Moses* (Gaster, 121); *Sefer Ha-Yashar* 77 (233).

[30]*Ed. pr.* mistakenly reads "his daughter's daughter."

[31]*Exod. R.* 1,34; *Sefer Ha-Yashar* 76 (228–29). These texts do not say, as does Ps.-J., that *first-born* children were to be killed. By referring to the *first-born* in our present verse, Ps.-J. may have intended to make the point that the slaughter of the Egyptian first-born (Exod 13:15) was a fitting punishment for the Pharaoh, who, according to Ps.-J.'s version of our present verse, killed the first-born of the Israelites.

[32]Or: "was hard on them"; = Onq.

affliction of the slavery of the Israelites *was revealed before the Lord*,[33] and *the repentance which they had undertaken in secret—so that one person did not know about the other—was revealed before him.*[34]

CHAPTER 3

1. Now Moses was tending the flock of his father-in-law Jethro, *chief*[1] of Midian, and he led the flock *to good grazing grounds*[2] *which are* beyond the desert, and he came to the mountain *on which the Glory of the Lord was revealed*,[3] to Horeb. 2. And *Zagnugel*,[4] the angel of the Lord, was revealed to him in flames of fire out of the midst of a bush. He looked, and behold, the bush was burning[5] in fire, but the bush was not *burned up or consumed*[6] *by the fire.* 3. And Moses said, "I must turn aside and see this great sight; why is the bush not burned?"[7] 4. And *it was revealed before* the Lord that he turned aside to see; and the Lord called to him out of the bush and said, "Moses! Moses!" And he said, "Here I am." 5. And he said, "Do not approach hither! Take off your shoes from your feet, for the place where you stand is a holy *place and on it you are to receive the Law to teach it to the children of Israel.*"[8] 6. Then he said, "I *am* the God of your father, the God of Abraham, the

Notes, Chapter 2

[33]*Ed. pr.:* "and the Lord saw."
[34]HT reads literally: "and God knew." The Targums expand on this laconic statement. Onq. reads: "and the Lord promised through his *Memra* to redeem them"; cf. Exod 3:8. Ps.-J.'s expansion is in line with rabbinic interpretation of Exod 2:25; cf. *Mek. RI* Exod 19:2 (2,196); *Mek. RSbY* Exod 19:1 (136–37); *Exod. R.* 1,36.

Notes, Chapter 3

[1]= Onq. See above, 2:16 and n. 22 to that verse.
[2]Lit.: "to a place of good pastures" = Onq. See Philo *De vita Mosis,* I.xii §65; Josephus, *Ant.* II.xii.1. The midrashim portray Moses as a good shepherd; cf. *Exod. R.* 2,2; *Tanh. B, Shemot* 10 (2, 6).
[3]= Onq. When translating biblical phrases which seemed difficult to harmonize with the spirituality of God (e.g., "the mountain of God" in our present verse and in 4:27; 18:5; 24:13; "the rod of God" in 4:20; "a fire of the Lord" in Num 11:3), the Targumists avoid a direct rendering of HT and choose some circumlocution.
[4]Perhaps we should read Zagzagel, as Levy (1, 211) proposes. This angel is mentioned in *Deut. R.* 11,10 (twice). Sasnigiel occurs in *3 Enoch* 18, 11–12 and 48D, 1–2 (Charlesworth, 1983, 1, 272 and 314) as the name of an angelic being. Zangaziel is the form of the name in *Midrash Petirat Moshe* (A. Jellinek, 1967, 1, 127). On other forms of the name, see H. Odeberg, 1973, 57. Ps.-J. is the only Targum of our present verse to name the angel who appeared to Moses. On Ps.-J.'s interest in angels, see Maher, 1992, 7.
[5]*mtryb* = Nfmg; *ed. pr.: mšryb.*
[6]In translating *'kl,* "consumed" (RSV), Ps.-J. combines the Pal. Tg. rendering (*yq[y]d*), "burned," with that of Onq. (*mt'kyl,* "consumed").
[7]*tryb;* cf. Nfmg: *mtrb; ed. pr.: šrb.* See v. 2 and n. 5.
[8]Ps.-J. locates the scene of the burning bush at Sinai. This identification is based on the similarity between the Hebrew words *snh,* "bush," and *syny,* "Sinai." See *PRE* 41 (321), where *snh* and *syny* are explicitly linked. See also *PRE* 40 (314); *Exod. R.* 3,4.

God of Isaac, and the God of Jacob." And Moses hid[9] his face, for he was afraid to look *towards*[10] *the Glory of the Shekinah of the Lord.*[11] 7. And <the Lord>[12] said, "The misery of my people who are in Egypt *has* indeed *been revealed before me*, and their cry because of those who enslave *them has been heard before me, because their sufferings have been revealed before me.* 8. *And I have revealed myself*[13] *to you today* in order to save *them*[14] by my Memra from the hand of the Egyptians and to bring *them* up from that *unclean*[15] land to a good land of spacious *borders*, to a land that *produces*[16] milk and honey, to a place *where* the Canaanites, the Hittites, the Amorites, the Perizzites, the Hivites, and the Jebusites *dwell.* 9. And now, behold the cry of the children of Israel *has come up before me*;[17] moreover, the oppression with which the Egyptians oppress them *has been revealed before me.* 10. Come, then, I will send you to Pharaoh, and you shall bring my people, the children of Israel, out of Egypt." 11. But Moses said *before the Lord*, "Who am I that I should go to Pharaoh and bring the children of Israel out of Egypt?" 12. And he said, "*My Memra will be at your assistance,*[18] and this (shall be) a sign for you that it was I who sent you: when you have brought the people out of Egypt you shall worship *before the Lord because you will receive the Law*[19] on this mountain." 13. And Moses said *before the Lord*, "If I *go*[20] to the children of Israel and say to them '*The Lord*, the God of your fathers sent me to you,' if they ask me, 'What is his name?' what shall I say to them?" 14. And *the Lord* said to Moses, "*He who said and the world was,*[21] *(who) said and everything was.*" Then he said, "Thus you shall say to the children of Israel 'I-am-*who-I-am-and-who-will-be*[22] has sent me to

Notes, Chapter 3

[9]Ps.-J. and Onq. use the verb *kbš*, while Nf employs *ṭmr.*

[10]= Onq.

[11]Onq.: "the Glory of the Lord."

[12]Omitted in Lond. and *ed. pr.*

[13]= Onq. The Targums avoid the anthropomorphic assertion that God "came down." See Ps.-J. Gen 11:5 and n. 11 to that verse (Maher, 1992, 50).

[14]Lond.: "to save you."

[15]Ps.-J. is the only one of the Targums to add the word "unclean." But the idea that Egypt was unclean and contaminated by idolatry and immorality is common; cf., e.g., Lev 18:3; Ezek 20:7; 23:3; *Mek. RSbY* Exod 6:2 (5); *PRE* 40 (316); 48 (382); *Exod. R.* 15,5.

[16]= Onq. The phrase "a land flowing with milk and honey" occurs fifteen times in the Pentateuch (Exod 3:8, 17; 13:5; 33:3; Lev 20:24; Num 13:27; 14:8; 16:13, 14, Deut 6:3; 11:9; 26:9, 15; 27:3; 31:20). Onq. regularly translates the phrase as it does in our present verse. Ps.-J. translates it in the same way as Onq. in all the texts from Exodus, Leviticus, and Numbers just listed, as well as in Deut 31:20. In four of the texts from Deuteronomy (6:3; 11:9; 26:9, 15), Ps.-J. translates the phrase in question as "a land whose fruit is as rich as milk and as sweet as honey," and in 27:3 Ps.-J. has a variation on this translation, reading, (by mistake, it would seem) "producing" instead of "sweet."

[17]= Onq.

[18]= Onq., Nfmg. See Ps.-J. Gen 26:3 and n. 2 to that verse (Maher, 1992, 91).

[19]*Ed. pr.:* "my law." Ps.-J. identifies the site of the burning bush with Sinai; see above v. 5 and n. 8 to that verse.

[20]Lit.: "behold I am going," = Nf; Onq.: "behold I am coming"; = HT.

[21]Or: "and came into being." The title "He who spoke and the world was" occurs in Tg. Gen. 11:2 (P, V, N); 21:33 (Nf, V, N, L). It is very common in rabbinic literature. Cf. A. Marmorstein, 1927, 89. In our present verse, Onq., like Nf, leaves HT "I am who I am" (RSV) untranslated. See Grossfeld, 1988B, 8, n. 16. See the comment on this verse in Nf.

[22]Onq. like V, Nfmg 1 and 2, leaves HT "I am" untranslated. See Grossfeld, 1988B, p. 8, n. 16.

you.'" 15. And *the Lord* said further to Moses, "Thus shall you say to the children of Israel: 'The God of your fathers, the God of Abraham, the God of Isaac, and the God of Jacob, has sent me to you': This *shall be* my name for ever, and thus I shall be remembered through *all* generations. 16. Go and assemble the elders[23] of Israel and say to them: 'The Lord, the God of your fathers, the God of Abraham, Isaac and Jacob, has been revealed to me and said, I have indeed *remembered*[24] you and the *humiliation* to which you have been subjected[25] in Egypt, 17. and I have decided *in my Memra*: I will bring you up out of the misery of *the Egyptians* to the land of the Canaanites, the Hittites, the Amorites, the Perizzites, the Hivites, and the Jebusites, to a land *that produces* milk and honey.' 18. They will listen to *you*;[26] then you and the elders of Israel, you shall go in to the king of Egypt, and you shall say to him, 'The Lord, the God of the *Jews*, has *been called*[27] upon us. And now, let us go, we pray, a three days' journey into the desert to offer sacrifice *before* the Lord our God.' 19. As for me, *it has been revealed before me* that the king of Egypt will not *let* you go, not *because of his* mighty *strength*,[28] but because (I have decided) by my Memra[29] to chastise him with evil plagues.[30] 20. *You shall be detained there until* I send *the blow of my strength* and smite the Egyptians with all the wonders which I will work among *them*; after that he will let you go. 21. And I will bring this people into favor in the eyes of the Egyptians; and when you go *thence redeemed*, you shall not go empty-handed. 22. Each woman shall ask of her neighbor,

Notes, Chapter 3

[23]When HT *zqn* has the meaning "elder" (as opposed to "old man"), the Pal. Tgs. (other than Ps.-J.) of the Pentateuch regularly translate it as *ḥkym*, "sage." See, e.g., Nf Exod 3:16, 18; 4:29; 12:21. Onq., on the other hand, regularly translates *zqn* as *sb'*, "old man elder," even when it has the meaning "elder." See, e.g., the texts from Exodus just referred to. Ps.-J. agrees with Onq. in the Books of Genesis (Gen 50:7 [twice]), Exodus (except 24:14, where Ps.-J. agrees with Nf), Leviticus, and Numbers. In the Book of Deuteronomy, Ps.-J. usually agrees with Nf in using *ḥkym*, rather than *sb'* of Onq.; see, e.g., Deut 5:20 (23); 19:12; 21:4, 6, 19, 20. Ps.-J. agrees with Onq. in Deut 27:1; 29:9, and in 21:3 Ps.-J. combines the reading of Nf with that of Onq.

[24]= Onq. The Targums of this verse translate HT "visit" by "remember." See also, e.g., Gen 21:1; 50:24, 25; Exod 4:31; 13:19. This is in line with the rabbinic interpretation, which declared that "visitation" is equivalent to "remembrance"; cf., e.g., *t. Rosh Hash.* 4 (2), 7 (Zuckermandel, 213); *b. Rosh Hash.* 32b; *Mek. RSbY* Exod 20:5 (148). See further B. Grossfeld, 1984, 83–101.

[25]Lit.: "the humiliation that has been done to you."

[26]= Onq. HT: "to your voice."

[27]= Onq. But some versions of Onq. read "has been revealed"; see Sperber, 1959, 1, 93. Onq. and Ps.-J. translate HT *nqrh*, "has met (with)" (RSV), as if it were *nqr'*, "has been called (upon)." See also LXX and Vulg.: "has called us." In Exod 5:3, where HT reads "the God of the Hebrews has met (*nqr'*) with us" (RSV), Ps.-J. and Onq. (Sperber) translate *nqr'* as "has been called." Nf, however, reads "was revealed," as in 3:18.

[28]Or: "not because (*l' mn d-*) his strength is mighty." Onq. is essentially the same: "not because (*l' mn qdm d-*) his strength is mighty." Etheridge (1862, 350) translates Onqelos as: "not even on account of him whose power is mighty." See also Grossfeld (1988B, 9): "not even on account of him whose strength is powerful."

[29]Lond.: "his Memra." A possible use of the 3rd person suffix in place of the 1st person.

[30]Ps.-J. explains why Pharaoh could refuse to let Israel go. It was not because of the Pharaoh's might, but because God intended to punish the king (for the suffering he had inflicted on Israel). See the comment on Exod 3:20 in *Exod. R.* 3,10. See also *Exod. R.* 5,7 and 11,6, which explains why God hardened Pharaoh's heart.

and of her who is *near the walls of* her house, [31] objects of silver and objects of gold, and clothing, and you shall *put* (them) *as ornaments* on your sons and on your daughters; (thus) you shall *empty out* [32] the Egyptians."

CHAPTER 4

1. But Moses replied and said, "But behold, they will not believe me or *listen to me*, for they will say, 'The Lord has not revealed himself to you.'" [1] 2. The Lord said to him, "What is that in your hand?" And he said, "A rod." 3. And he said, "Cast [2] it on the ground." So he cast it on the ground and it became a serpent and Moses fled from it. 4. But the Lord said to Moses, "Put out your hand and take hold of it by the tail"—so he put out his hand and seized it, and it became a rod in his *hand* [3]—5. "that they may believe that the Lord, the God of their [4] fathers, the God of Abraham, the God of Isaac, and the God of Jacob has revealed himself to you." 6. Again, the Lord said to him, "Put your hand into your bosom." [5] So he put his hand [6] into his bosom; and when he withdrew it, behold his hand was leprous; *it*

Notes, Chapter 3

[31] Onq.: "the one *near* to her house." Rieder (1965, 117) thinks that Ps.-J. took over the translation of Onq. but added "the walls of" to make it clear that "near to" does not refer to a blood relationship. But it is probable that Ps.-J. intended to say no more than that the Israelite woman was to take from the Egyptian who lived with her in the same house. Cf. LXX ("fellow lodger") and Nf. See further Grossfeld, 1988B, 9, n. 21.

[32] The Targums (Nf, Ps.-J., Onq.) translate HT *nṣl,* "plunder, strip," by *rwqn* in our present verse and again in 12:36, where it is said that the Israelites "stripped" the Egyptians. (See also Ps.-J. Gen 31:9 and n. 5 to that verse; cf. Maher, 1992, 108) The Targums avoid saying that the Israelites "plundered" the Egyptians. Jewish tradition explains that in taking the valuables of the Egyptians, the Hebrews were not unjustly despoiling them; see, e.g., Wis 10:17; *Jub.* 48, 18; Philo, *De vita Mosis,* I.xxv §§140-42; *Gen. R.* 61,7; *b. Sanh.* 91a.

Notes, Chapter 4

[1] = Onq. Lond. omits "to you."

[2] *ṭlwq;* Nf: *ṭlq;* Nfmg: *qlq;* Onq.: *rmy.* As in our present verse, Ps.-J. nearly always translates HT *šlḥ* (Hif.), "cast, throw," by *ṭlq.* See, e.g., Gen 21:15; 37:22, 24; Exod 1:22; 4:3ab; 7:9, 10, 12. Exceptions are Gen 37:20 and Exod 22:30, where Ps.-J. follows Onq. and uses the verb *rmy.* Like Ps.-J., Nf usually employs *ṭlq.* See, e.g., the texts just listed. Exceptions are Exod 32:24; Deut 9:21. In Num 19:6, Nf has a conflate reading. Onq. usually employs *rmy,* as in our present verse. See, e.g., all the texts mentioned in this note. Deut 29:27, where Onq. interprets the text, is an exception.

[3] = Onq. Compare Nf, Nfmg, HT: "in his palm."

[4] = *Ed. pr.;* Lond.: "your." Chester (1986, 47) suggests that the use of "your" in Lond. may reflect the meturgeman's wish to apply the text to his audience.

[5] In Exod 4:6ab and 7abc, where there are five references to Moses' putting his hand into his bosom, the Targums translate HT "bosom" literally. On other occasions when mention of the bosom might sound indelicate, the Targumists avoid a literal rendering of HT. See Ps.-J. Gen 16:5 and n. 7 to that verse (Maher, 1992, 62). In Exod 4:6ab and 7abc, Nf regularly translates HT "bosom" by *ḥwb.* Onq. regularly uses *'ṭp.* Ps.-J. agrees with Nf on four occasions and follows Onq. only once (v. 7a).

[6] *Ed. pr.:* "it"; *ed. pr.* read *ytyh* for *ydyh.*

was white as snow.[7] 7. And he said, "Put your hand back into your bosom." So he put his hand back into his bosom; and when he withdrew it from his bosom <behold>[8] it had become *healthy*[9] again like (the rest of) his flesh. 8. . . .[10] 9. "And if they do not believe even these two signs or listen to you,[11] you shall take some of the water *that is in*[11] the river and pour (it) on the dry ground, and the water that you take from the river will become blood on the dry ground." 10. And Moses said *before* the Lord, "O *Lord*, I beseech, I am not an eloquent[12] man, neither since yesterday nor since *before that*, nor since *the moment that* you spoke with your servant, for I am tongue-tied[13] and *I speak with difficulty*."[14] 11. But the Lord said to him, "Who *is it that* put *the speech of* the mouth *in the mouth of the first* man?[15] Or who made one who is dumb, or deaf, or seeing, or blind? Is it not I the Lord? 12. Now go, and I *in my Memra* will be with the *speech of* your mouth, and I will teach you what you are to say." 13. And he said, "I beseech *by the mercy from before you*, O *Lord*, send *your message* by the hand *of Phinehas, who is worthy to be sent at the end of days*."[16] 14. The anger of the Lord was enkindled against Moses, and he said, "Is there not your brother Aaron, the Levite? *It has been revealed before me* that he speaks fluently. And besides, behold, he is going out to meet you, and when he sees you he will rejoice in his heart. 15. You shall speak *with* him and put the words in his mouth. And my *Memra* will be with *the word of* your mouth and with *the word of* his mouth, and I will teach you what you are to do. 16. And he shall speak for you *with* the people, and he shall be your *interpreter*,[17] and you shall be his *teacher (who) seeks instruction from before the Lord*.[18] 17. And take in

Notes, Chapter 4

[7]Onq.: "and behold his hand was *white* as snow"; i.e., Onq. replaces HT "leprous" with "white." Nf, Pesh., and Vulg. translate "leprous" literally. Ps.-J. combines the rendering of Nf with that of Onq. LXX reads: "and his hand became as snow."

[8]Omitted in Lond. and *ed. pr.*

[9]Ps.-J. is the only Targum of this verse to use the word "healthy." *Exod. R.* 3,13 uses the word "healed" in the same context.

[10]V. 8 is omitted in Lond. and *ed. pr.*

[11]= Onq.

[12]The word *dbrn* which Ps.-J., and only Ps.-J., uses here is unusual. Levy (1, 161) and Jastrow (279) in their entries for this word refer only to our present verse (4:10).

[13]Or: "halting of speech"; (*ḥgr* [Lond. by mistake: *ḥgm*] *pwm*). The word *ḥgr* which Ps.-J. and the Pal. Tgs. use here can mean (1) "gird, tie," or (2) "halt, limp, hesitate." If we take *ḥgr* to mean "tie," the idiom *ḥgr pwm* means literally "mouth-tied," which would correspond to the English "tongue-tied." If we take *ḥgr* in its second meaning of "halt, limp," we can translate the Aramaic idiom as "halting of speech."

[14]Lit.: "and difficult of speech"; = Nfmg, V, N. See also Ps.-J. 6:12, 30.

[15]In *Otiyyot de R. Akiva* 80 (c. 700 C.E.) the words "who has made man's mouth?" (RSV) are taken to mean "who made the mouth of *the first* man?" See A. Jellinek, (1967, Dritter Theil) 43. See also *Exod. R.* 3,15.

[16]Cf. *LAB* 48, 1-2; *Tanḥ. A, Phinehas* 1 (592); *PRE* 29 (213); 40 (315); 47 (371). Ps.-J. gives great prominence to Phinehas; see Ps.-J. Exod 6:18; Num 21:32; 25:7-8, 12; 31:8; Deut 30:4; cf. also Ps.-J. Exod 40:10. On Phinehas in Jewish tradition see, e.g., Ginzberg, *Legends* 6, 316–17, n. 3; Schäfer, 1972, 78; Hayward, 1978, 22–34.

[17]The Targums (Onq., Nf, V, Ps.-J.) use the word *meturgeman* or *turgeman*. See also *Exod. R.* 3,17; *Song of Songs R.* 1,10.1. See Exod 7:1 (Nf, Nfmg).

[18]Onq.: "and you shall be his teacher." Compare the addition in Nf and Ps.-J. in our present verse with Tg. Exod 18:15, 19 (Nf, Ps.-J., Onq.); Num 15:32 (Ps.-J.).

your hand this rod with which you shall perform the signs." 18. Moses went back to *Jethro*, his father-in-law, and said to him, "Let me go back to my kinsmen who are in Egypt and see if they are still alive." And Jethro said to Moses, "Go in peace!" 19. And the Lord said to Moses in Midian, "Go back to Egypt; for all the men who sought *to take* your life have *been emptied out and have become impoverished, and behold, they are accounted as* dead." [19] 20. So Moses took his wife and his sons, mounted them on the ass, and went back to the land of Egypt. And Moses took in his hand the rod *which he had taken from the garden of his father-in-law. It was of sapphire from the throne of glory, its weight was forty seahs, and the great and glorious name was clearly engraved on it, and with it miracles were performed from before the Lord.* [20] 21. And the Lord said to Moses, "When you return to Egypt, see that you perform before Pharaoh all the wonders I have put in your power. I, however, will harden the *inclination of* his heart, and he will not let the people go. 22. And you shall say to Pharaoh, 'Thus says the Lord, Israel is my first-born son, 23. and I have said to you: Let my son go that he may worship *before* me! [21] Yet you refuse to let him go. Now I will kill your first-born son.'" 24. At a lodging place on the way *the angel of* [22] the Lord met him and sought to kill him *because of Gershom, his son, who had not been circumcised on account of Jethro, his father-in-law, who had not allowed him to circumcise him. But Eliezer had been circumcised according to an agreement which they had made between them.* [23] 25. Then Zipporah took a flint-stone and cut the foreskin of *Gershom*, her son, and brought *the circumcised foreskin* to the feet of *the Destroying Angel* [24] and said, "*The bridegroom wanted to circumcise, but his father-in-law prevented him. And now may* the blood *of this circumcision atone for* my husband." [25] 26. And the *Destroying Angel* left him alone.

Notes, Chapter 4

[19]Cf., e.g., *b. Abod. Zar.* 5a; *Ned.* 64b; *Gen. R.* 71,6; *Lam. R.* 3,2 to 3,6; *PRE* 40 (315).

[20]See above Ps.-J. 2:21. The fact that the rod was of sapphire and that it weighed forty *seahs* is mentioned in *Tanḥ. A, Wa-Era* 9 (195); *Tazriʻa* 8 (409); *Tanḥ. B, Tazriʻa* 10 (2,37); *Exod. R.* 8,3. A Targum Tosefta published by Kasher says that the rod of Moses was of sapphire stone from the throne of Glory; see R. Kasher, 1976–77, 9–17, especially p. 16. Ps.-J.'s addition about the rod in our present verse (see also Ps.-J. 34:12) supplements what we found in that Targum in 2:21. See also 14:21 (Ps.-J.). On Ps.-J.'s tendency to mention the same haggadic tradition in several places, see Maher, 1992, 5.

[21]Lond.: "before him."

[22]= Onq., LXX. Jewish tradition avoids attributing to God the attempt on Moses' life that is described in Exod 4:24 Cf. Vermes, 1961, 184.

[23]Ps.-J., alone among the Targums, explains that the attack on Moses was made because of his failure to circumcise one of his sons; cf. *Mek. RI* Exod 18:3 (2,168, 170); *j. Ned.* 3, 38b; *b. Ned.* 31b–32a. We find a similar tradition in the writings of Ephraem and Aphraat; cf. A. Guillaumont, 1977, 89–95. On Exod 4:24-26 in Jewish tradition, see Vermes, 1961, 178–92, and the review (in Hebrew) of this work by Heinemann, *Tarbiz* 35 (1965–66), 86–87; see also Heinemann, 1974A, 155.

[24]Apart from Exod 4:24-26, there are a few other texts where the Pal. Tgs. introduce supernatural beings in order to avoid attributing destructive action to God. See Exod 12:13 (Ps.-J., Nfmg); 12:23 (Ps.-J.; Nfmg 1); 15:7 (P). Ps.-J. refers to destroying angels in Exod 12:12; (cf. Nfmg 12:13); Deut 9:19. On other occasions Ps.-J. refers to demons; see, e.g., Num 6:24; 22:28. See further Shinan, 1983B, 191–96; idem, 1979, 2, 271–77.

[25]Onq.: "in virtue of this blood of circumcision let the bridegroom be given (back) to me." The Targums do not explain how Zipporah linked the attack on Moses' life with the fact that one of his sons was uncircumcised. *Exod. R.* 5,8 explains; cf. also *b. Ned.* 32a.

Then *Zipporah praised (God) and* said, "*How precious is* the blood of *this* circumcision *that saved* the bridegroom *from the hands of the Destroying Angel.*"[26] 27. The Lord said to Aaron, "Go to meet Moses in the desert." He went and met him at the mountain *on which the Glory of the Lord was revealed,*[27] and he kissed him. 28. Moses told Aaron <all>[28] *these* things which (the Lord) had entrusted to him, and all the signs which he had commanded him *to perform.* 29. Then Moses and Aaron went and gathered all the elders of the children of Israel. 30. Aaron spoke all the words that the Lord had spoken *with* Moses, and he performed the signs in the eyes of the people. 31. And the people believed. And when they heard that the Lord *remembered* the children of Israel, and that their *servitude* was *revealed before him,* they bowed down and worshiped.

CHAPTER 5

1. After that Moses and Aaron went in and said[1] to Pharaoh: "Thus said the Lord, the God of Israel, 'Let my people go that they may *make* a feast to me in the wilderness.'" 2. But Pharaoh said: "*The name of the Lord has not been revealed* to me[2] that I should listen to his *word* and let Israel go. I *have* not *found the name of* the Lord *written in the Book of the Angels.*[3] *I do not fear him,* and moreover I will not let Israel go." 3. They said, "*The name of* the God of the *Jews* has been called upon us.[4] Let us go a three days' journey in the wilderness that we may sacrifice a *festive offering before* the Lord our God, lest he fall upon us with *death*[5] or slaugh-

---

Notes, Chapter 4

[26]Onq.: "were it not for this blood of circumcision the bridegroom would have been condemned to death." Cf. *Mek. RI* Exod 18:3 (2, 169–70); *Exod. R.* 5,8.
[27]= Onq. See above, n. 3 to chap. 3.
[28]Omitted in *ed. pr.*

Notes, Chapter 5

[1]In Lond. the verb "said" is in the singular.
[2]"To me" is omitted in Lond. In reading "The name of the Lord . . . his word" Ps.-J. is following Onq.
[3]Onq. translates HT "I do not know the Lord" as "the name of the Lord has not been revealed to me." Ps.-J.'s rendering ("I have not found . . . Angels") reflects a rabbinic tradition according to which Pharaoh searched his records but could not find the name of the God of Israel among the gods recorded in his lists; cf. *Tanḥ. A, Wa-Era* 5 (189); *Exod. R.* 5,14. In the light of this tradition, Rieder (1984, Hebrew section, 108, n. 2) suggests that Ps.-J. should read the "Book of the Gods" rather than the "Book of the Angels."
[4]Ps.-J. and Onq. (Sperber) read HT *nqr'*, "has met" (RSV), as if it were derived from *qr'*, "call." See above 3:18, and n. 27 to that verse. For the idea that the name of God is called upon Israel, see, e.g., Deut 28:10; Jer 14:9; 2 Chr 7:14.
[5]= Onq., LXX. HT *dbr*, "pestilence," is rendered in Nf as *mwtn'* (with variations in orthography), which has the same meaning, in our present verse and in 9:15; Lev 26:25; Num 14:12; Deut 28:21. In Exod 9:3, however, Nf reads *mwt'*, "death." In all the texts just listed Ps.-J. and Onq. read *mwt'*, except in Lev 26:25, where both Ps.-J. and Onq. read *mwtn'*. See further Grossfeld, 1988B, 23, n. 4.

ter." 4. The king of Egypt said to them, "Why, Moses and Aaron, do you make the people cease from their work? Go to your work!" 5. And Pharaoh said, "Behold, the people of the land *whom* you cause to cease from their work are now many." 6. On that day Pharaoh commanded the rulers of the people and their officers, saying, 7. "You shall no longer give the people straw to *cast*[6] bricks as yesterday *and before that*. Let them go and gather straw for themselves! 8. But you shall *assign* to them the same amount of bricks as they made yesterday *and before that*. You shall not take from it, for they are idlers. That is why they cry out, saying, 'Let us go and sacrifice *a festive offering before* our God.' 9. Let heavier work be laid upon the men, and let them *occupy themselves*[7] with it, and let them not *trust*[8] in lying words." 10. Then the rulers of the people and their officers went out and said to the people:[9] "Thus says Pharaoh: 'I will not give you straw. 11. Go yourselves, (and) take straw for yourselves from whatever *place*[7] you find (it), because nothing will be taken from your work.'" 12. The people were scattered throughout all the land of Egypt to gather stubble for straw. 13. And the rulers pressed (them), saying, "Complete your work, each day's task, as *you did* when straw *was given* to you."[10] 14. And the officers of the children of Israel whom the rulers of Pharaoh had appointed over them were punished, saying, "Why *then* have you not completed, either today or yesterday, *what was decreed for you*, (namely), that you *cast*[6] bricks as yesterday *and before that*?" 15. Then the officers of the children of Israel came and cried out *before* Pharaoh, saying, "Why do you deal thus with your servants? 16. No straw has been given to your servants, and they say to us 'Make bricks!' And behold, your servants are punished; but the guilt of your people *is great and goes up*."[11] 17. But he said, "You are idlers! Idlers! Therefore you say, 'Let us go and sacrifice *a festive offering before our God*.'[12] 18. And now, go and work! But no straw will be given to you, and you shall deliver the (same) amount of bricks." 19. The officers of the people of Israel saw that they were in a bad (situation) when (Pharaoh) said,[13] "You shall not take anything from your daily number of bricks." 20. As they came forth from *before* Pharaoh, they came upon Moses and Aaron standing to meet them, 21. and they said to them, "May *our humiliation be re-*

Notes, Chapter 5

[6]See Ps.-J. Gen 11:3, and n. 5 to that verse (Maher, 1992, 49).

[7]= Onq.

[8]Compare Nfmg. For Ps.-J.'s idiom "trust in lying words," see Jer 7:4, 8. Tg. Jon. of these verses in Jeremiah uses the same verb (*rḥṣ*) as Ps.-J. in our present verse.

[9]*l'mr*, "saying," of HT is omitted in Lond. and *ed. pr.*

[10]Ps.-J.'s rendering ("as you did . . . given to you") follows that of Onq., apart from minor grammatical changes.

[11]HT is obscure. See Driver, 1911, 37; Durham, 1987, 66–67. Onq.: "and your people sin *against them*." Ps.-J. seems to mean that the sin of the Egyptians "is great and increases," or possibly that their sin "is great and goes up (to God)"; (compare Gen 4:10: "your brother's blood cries out to me").

[12]LXX: "to our God." See v. 8, where HT has "to our God." Perhaps Ps.-J. (and LXX) were influenced by v. 8 in their rendering of the final words of our present verse.

[13]Lit.: "saying"; = HT. One might also translate Ps.-J.'s phrase as "having to say," i.e., one might take "saying" to refer to the unpleasant message the officers had to bring to the people.

vealed before the Lord,[14] *and, moreover, may he take revenge*[15] *on you* for making us loathsome[16] before Pharaoh and his servants, *for you have been responsible for* putting a sword in their hands to kill us." 22. Then Moses returned to *before* the Lord and said, "*O Lord*, why have you done evil to this people, and why did you ever send me? 23. From the time that I came to Pharaoh to speak in your name, this people *has been badly treated*,[17] and you have not delivered your people."

CHAPTER 6

1. Then the Lord said to Moses, "Now you shall see what I will do to Pharaoh, for he will let them go because of[1] a strong hand; indeed, because of[1] a strong hand he will drive them from his land." 2. And *the Lord* spoke to Moses and said to him, "I am the Lord, *he who revealed myself to you in the midst of the bush and said to you, 'I am the Lord.'* 3. I revealed myself to Abraham, Isaac, and Jacob as El Shaddai, but (by) my name Yahweh—*except by the presence of my Shekinah*[2]—I did not make myself known to them. 4. I also established my covenant with them, to give them the land of Canaan, the land of their habitations in which they dwelt. 5. Moreover, the affliction of the children of Israel, whom the Egyptians are enslaving, *has come before me*,[3] and I remember my covenant. 6. Say therefore to the children of Israel, 'I *am* the Lord, I will bring you out from *the midst of the oppression of*[4] the servitude of the Egyptians, and I will release you from their servitude. And I will redeem you with an uplifted arm and with great judgments. 7. And I will *bring you near*[5] *before* me as (my) people: I will be your God, and you shall

Notes, Chapter 5

[14]Ps.-J. takes HT "The Lord look upon you" to mean "May the Lord look on our humiliation."

[15]= Onq. HT: "judge." See further Grossfeld, 1988B, 15, n. 12.

[16]Lit.: "making our odor offensive"; = Nfmg.

[17]= Onq. (Sperber); but, like Nf and CTg D, some versions of Onq. have a direct translation of HT "he has done evil to this people" (RSV).

Notes, Chapter 6

[1]Or: "with."

[2]This addition, which is found only in Ps.-J., is obscure. In this context one might expect Ps.-J. to read "but *not* by the presence of my Shekinah," since it is said of Moses that he saw the Glory of the Shekinah; cf. the Pal. Tgs. of Exod 24:11; *Exod. R.* 3,1. The name "Yahweh" was revealed to the patriarchs; cf. Gen 15:7; 28:13. The rabbis explained that the name was revealed to them, but not its meaning (*Tanḥ. B, Wa-Era* 5 [2, 21]). On the interpretation of Exod 6:3, see S. D. Fraade, 1984, 200–201.

[3]"Has come" is omitted in Lond. Onq.: "has been heard before me."

[4]= Onq.; cf. also v. 7.

[5]= Onq.; cf. Grossfeld, 1988B, 15, n. 7.

know that I am the Lord your God who brought you out from *the midst of the oppression of* the servitude of the Egyptians. 8. And I will bring you into the land which I *swore by my Memra*[6] to give to Abraham, Isaac, and Jacob, and I will give it to you as a possession, I the Lord.'" 9. Moses spoke thus to the children of Israel, but they did not listen to Moses, because their spirits were crushed,[7] and because of the terrible *idolatry they practiced.*[8] 10. And the Lord spoke to Moses saying, 11. "Go in (and) tell Pharaoh, the king of Egypt, to let the children of Israel go from his land." 12. But Moses spoke before the Lord, saying, "Behold, the children of Israel did not listen to me. How, then, will Pharaoh listen to me when *I speak with difficulty?*"[9] 13. So the Lord spoke to Moses and Aaron, *warning them concerning*[10] the children of Israel, and *he sent them* to Pharaoh, the king of Egypt, to bring the children of Israel out of the land of Egypt. 14. These are the heads of their ancestral houses: the sons of Reuben, Israel's first-born: Enoch and Pallu, Hezron and Carmi. These are the families of Reuben. 15. The sons of Simeon: Jemuel, Jamin, Ohad, Jachin, Zohar, and Saul, *he is Zimri who abandoned himself*[11] *to debauchery like the Canaanites.* These are the families of Simeon. 16. These are the names of the sons of Levi according to their lineage:[12] Gershon, Kohath, and Merari; and the years of Levi's life were one hundred and thirty-seven years. *He lived until he saw Moses and Aaron, the redeemers of Israel.*[13] 17. The sons of Gershom: Libni and Shimei according to their families. 18. The sons of Kohath: Amram, Izhar, Hebron, and Uzziel; and the life of Kohath *the pious* was one hundred and thirty-three years. *He lived until he saw Phinehas, he is Elijah the high priest who is to be sent to the exiles of Israel at the end of days.*[14] 19. The sons of Merari: Mahli and Mushi. These are the families of Levi according to their line-

Notes, Chapter 6

[6] = Onq. The Targums explain the Hebrew oath formula "I raised my hand." See Ps.-J. Gen 14:22 and n. 48 to that verse (Maher, 1992, 58). Cf. also Exod 15:12 (Pal. Tgs., Ps.-J.); Num 14:30 (Onq., Pal. Tgs., Ps.-J.); Deut 32:40 (Pal. Tgs., Ps.-J.).

[7] Lit.: "from shortness of spirit"; = HT. In Num 21:4, where HT has a similar idiom (lit.: "the soul of the people was short"), Ps.-J. does not translate the verb literally.

[8] Lit.: "because of the hard idolatry that was in their hands." Ps.-J. takes HT *'bdh,* "labor," in the sense of "worship," another meaning which that word has. Cf. *Mek. RI* Exod 12:6 (1,38): ". . . it was hard for them to part with their idols." The same tradition is recorded in *Exod. R.* 6,5.

[9] See above, 4:10, and n. 14 to that verse.

[10] According to *Sifre Num.* 91 (Horovitz, 91), God warned Moses and Aaron that the people would be stubborn, and that they would even curse Moses and Aaron and stone them. The same tradition is recorded in *Exod. R.* 7,3. See also *Lev. R.* 10,2; Matt 10:16.

[11] Lit.: "lent his soul." Ps.-J. plays on the name Saul (*š'wl*), which he links with the verb *š'l* (Af.), "lend." His source is *b. Sanh.* 82b. See Ps.-J. Gen 46:10 (Maher, 1992, 149).

[12] *yyḥwsyhwn* = Nf; Onq.: *twldthwn:* "their generations"; Onq. renders HT by its Aramaic cognate. The word *yyḥws,* which Ps.-J. uses in this verse to translate Heb. *twld(w)t,* is used by the same Targum to translate *mšpḥ,* "family," in vv. 14, 15, 17, 19, 24, 25. In v. 19 Ps.-J. uses *gnys',* "family," to translate Heb. *twld(w)t.*

[13] There is no known source for this addition which contradicts Exod 1:6, according to which Joseph and all his brothers died before the Israelites were subjected to slavery. Compare *b. B. Bat.* 121b, which tells of seven men the sum of whose life-spans corresponded with the whole period of human existence.

[14] Phinehas is identified with Elijah in *LAB* 48:1-2; *PRE* 29 (213). This tradition was known to Origen; cf. *PG* 14, 225. Elijah is called high priest in Ps.-J. Exod 40:10; Deut 30:4. See above 4:13 (Ps.-J.), and n. 16 to that verse.

age. 20. Amram took Jochebed, his aunt,[15] as wife, and she bore him Aaron and Moses; and the years of the life of Amram *the pious*[16] were one hundred and thirty-seven years. *He lived until he saw Rehabiah, son of Gershom, the son of Moses.*[17] 21. The sons of Izhar: Korah, Nepheg, and Zichri. 22. The sons of Uzziel: Mishael, Elzaphan, and Sithri. 23. Aaron took to wife Elisheba, daughter of Amminadab and sister of Nahshon, and she bore him Nadab and Abihu, Eleazar and Ithamar. 24. The sons of Korah: Assir, Elkanah, and Abiasaph. These are the families of Korah. 25. Aaron's son Eliezer took to wife one of the daughters of *Jethro—he is* Putiel[18]—and she bore him Phinehas. These are the heads of the ancestral houses of the Levites according to their families. 26. These are Aaron and Moses, to whom the Lord said, "Bring forth the children of Israel *redeemed* from the land of Egypt by their hosts." 27. It was they who spoke to Pharaoh, king of Egypt, to bring forth the children of Israel from Egypt; these are Moses *the prophet* and Aaron *the priest*. 28. On the day that the Lord spoke to Moses in the land of Egypt *Aaron was inclining his ear and heard what he said to him.*[19] 29. And the Lord spoke to Moses, saying, "I *am* the Lord; speak to Pharaoh, king of Egypt, all that I will tell you." 30. Moses said before the Lord, "Behold, <I>[20] *speak with difficulty.*[9] How[21] then will Pharaoh listen to me?"

CHAPTER 7

1. The Lord said to Moses, "*Why are you afraid*? See, I have *already* made you (an object of) *fear*[1] to Pharaoh *as if* (you were) his God,[2] and your brother Aaron will be your prophet.[3] 2. You shall speak *to Aaron* all that I command you, and

Notes, Chapter 6

[15]Onq.: "his father's sister." Onq., Ps.-J., Nfmg and P do not change HT, in spite of the fact that Lev 18:12 and 20:19 forbid marriage to one's aunt.

[16]According to *b. Shabb.* 55b and *b. B. Bat.* 17a, Amram died because of the sin of Adam and Eve, and not because of any sin he committed himself. The merit of Amram brought back the Shekinah; cf. *PRK* 1,1.

[17]We know of no source for Ps.-J.'s addition. Compare *b. B. Bat.* 121b, which says that Ahijah the Shilonite (cf. 1 Kgs 11:29) knew Amram. See Schmerler, 1933, 31. According to 1 Chr 23:17; 26:25, Rehabiah was the son of Eliezer.

[18]Cf., e.g., *Mek. RI* Exod 18:1 (2,164); *b. Sotah* 43a; *Sanh.* 82b; *B. Bat.* 109b; *Exod. R.* 7,5.

[19]See *Mek. RI* Exod 12:1 (1,1), which tries to harmonize Exod 12:1 ("The Lord said to Moses and Aaron . . .") and the words "when the Lord spoke to Moses" in our present verse (6:28). See also *Mek. RI* Exod 12:3 (1,22). In this latter text the wording ("Aaron inclined his ear to listen . . .") is very similar to Ps.-J.'s text.

[20]"I" is omitted in Lond.

[21]Lit.: "thus" (*kdyn*); we read *hkdyn* with Nf.

Notes, Chapter 7

[1]Onq.: "I have appointed you prince (or master, teacher; *rb*)."

[2]See *Tanḥ. A, Wa-Era* 9 (193): ". . . he will see you and say 'This is God,'" i.e., he will recognize your superior power. The same tradition occurs in *Exod. R.* 8,2. See also *Tanḥ. B, Wa-Era* 8 (2, 23 and 25).

[3]Onq.: "your interpreter."

your brother Aaron will speak to Pharaoh, and he will let the children of Israel go from his land. 3. But I will harden *the inclination of*[4] Pharaoh's heart, and I will multiply my signs and marvels in the land of Egypt. 4. But Pharaoh will not listen to you, and *I will let loose deadly arrows against them, and* I will lay *the blow of the strength of* my hand[5] upon Egypt, and I will bring out <my hosts>,[6] my people the children of Israel, *redeemed*, from the land of Egypt with great judgments. 5. And the Egyptians shall know that I *am* the Lord when I *raise up the blow of my strength* against Egypt and bring forth the children of Israel *redeemed* from among them." 6. Moses and Aaron did as the Lord commanded them: thus they did. 7. Moses was eighty years old and Aaron eighty-three years old when they spoke with Pharaoh. 8. The Lord spoke to Moses and Aaron, saying, 9. "When Pharaoh speaks to you, saying, 'Perform some marvel,' you shall say to Aaron, 'Take your staff and throw *it* before Pharaoh, (and) let it become a *venemous* serpent; *for all the inhabitants of the earth will hear the sound of the cry of the Egyptians when I shatter them, as all creatures heard the cry of the serpent when it was stripped at the beginning.*'"[7] 10. So Moses and Aaron went in to Pharaoh and did just as the Lord had commanded. Aaron threw his rod before *the sight of* Pharaoh and before *the sight of* his servants, and it became an adder. 11. Then Pharaoh summoned the wise men and the sorcerers; *and, Jannes and Jambres*, the sorcerers *who were in* Egypt, also did the same with the spells *of their divinations.*[8] 12. Each man threw down his rod, and they became adders; *but immediately they were transformed and were as at the beginning,*[9] and Aaron's rod swallowed their rods. 13. But *the inclination of* Pharaoh's heart was hardened, and he did not listen to them, as the Lord had said.[10] 14. And the Lord said to Moses, "*The inclination of* Pharaoh's heart has hardened; he refuses to let the people go. 15. Go to Pharaoh in the morning;

Notes, Chapter 7

[4]Ps.-J. makes this addition in the same context in Exod 7:3, 13, 14, 22; 8:15; 9:7, 12, 35; 10:1, 20, 27; 11:10; 14:4, 8, 17. See also Deut 5:26 (29).

[5]Ps.-J. gives a double interpretation of HT "I will lay my hand." The first interpretation ("I will let loose . . . against them") makes it clear that "hand" of HT refers to God's punishing hand. The second interpretation ("I will lay . . . my hand") is essentially that of Onq. ("I will lay the blow of my power"), although Onq. is more careful to avoid the anthropomorphic word "hand." See also v. 5, where Ps.-J.'s rendering of HT "when I stretch forth my hand" is the same as that of Onq.

[6]Omitted in Lond. and *ed. pr.*

[7]See Ps.-J. Gen 3:14, with notes 24 and 25 to that verse (Maher, 1992, 27). The cry of the serpent mentioned by Ps.-J. in our present verse must be the cry uttered by the serpent when its legs were cut off; cf. *Gen. R.* 20,5; *PRE* 34 (254). The mention of a serpent in Exod 7:9 prompted Ps.-J. to take up the tradition he had introduced into Gen 3:14. See also Ps.-J. Num 21:6. On Ps.-J.'s tendency to repeat haggadic traditions, see Maher, 1992, 6.

[8]Other sources (*b. Men.* 85a; *Exod. R.* 9,7), which say that Jannes and Jambres taunted Moses and Aaron, do not say that these two Egyptians actually performed a miracle. On Jannes and Jambres, see above Ps.-J. 1:15 and n. 28 to that verse.

[9]Ps.-J. records a double miracle, saying explicitly that the rods which had become adders were again turned into rods. See *b. Shabb.* 97a; *Tanh. A, Wa-Era* 3 (187); *Exod R.* 9,7; *The Chronicles of Moses* (Gaster, 124); *Sefer Ha-Yashar* 79 (236–37). The midrash is based on the fact that HT says that "Aaron's *rod* swallowed up their *rods*."

[10]"had said" is omitted in Lond.

behold, he is going out *to observe*[11] *omens on* the water *like a magus.*[12] Station yourself before him on the bank of the river. *But* take in your hand *Aaron's* rod that was turned into a snake. 16. And say to him, 'The Lord, the God of *the Jews* sent me to you to say, "Let my people go that they may worship *before* me in the wilderness." And behold, you have not yet listened. 17. Thus says the Lord, "By this *sign* you shall know that I am the Lord." Behold, I will strike the water that is in the river with the rod that is in my hand, and it will be turned into blood; 18. and the fishes that are in the river will die, and the river will stink, and the Egyptians will be loathe to drink water from the river.'" 19. And the Lord said to Moses, "Say to Aaron: 'Take your rod and *raise*[13] your hand over the waters of the Egyptians, over their rivers, their swamps,[14] their canals, and over all their reservoirs, and they will become blood. There will be blood in all the land of Egypt, both in *vessels of*[15] wood and in *vessels of*[15] stone.'" 20. And Moses and Aaron did so, just as the Lord commanded. He raised the rod and struck the water that was in the river *in the sight* of Pharaoh and *in the sight* of his servants, and all the water that was in the river was turned into blood. 21. And the fishes that were in the river died, and the river stank, so that the Egyptians were not able to drink the water from the river; and there was *a plague of* blood in all the land of Egypt. 22. But the magicians of Egypt did the same with their charms, *and they turned some of the water of Goshen into blood.*[16] But *the inclination of* Pharaoh's heart was hardened, and he did not listen to them as the Lord had spoken. 23. Pharaoh *satisfied his needs*[17] and went into his house, and he did not pay any attention even to this *plague.* 24. And the Egyptians[18] dug round about the river for drinking water—*but they did not find clear (water)*[19]—because they could not drink the water that was in the river. 25. Seven days passed after the Lord had struck the river, *and after that the Memra*

Notes, Chapter 7

[11]Reading *lmntwr* with *ed. pr.* (cf. 8:16, Lond., *ed. pr.*) rather than *lmptwr* of Lond.

[12]Gr. *magos*, a Magus, a Persian priest or wise man. The word is used again by Ps.-J. in 8:16. *b. M. Qat.* 18a, the source of Ps.-J.'s addition to our present verse, applies the same Greek term to Pharaoh.

[13]= Onq.

[14]Reading *bysyhwn* with Lond. (cf. also 8:1); HT: "canals" (RSV). *Ed. pr.* has *psydyhwn*, "trenches, rivulets"; cf. also 8:1. The word *bys'* used by Lond. in 7:19 and 8:1 to translate HT *y'r*, "canal" (RSV), is used to translate the following word of HT, *'gm*, (RSV 7:19 "pond"; 8:1[5] "pool") by Nf (7:19; 8:1) and P, V (8:1).

[15]= Onq.; *Tanḥ. B, Wa-Era* 14 (2, 29) and *Exod. R.* 9,10 specify that "all their pools of water" (RSV) in v. 19 includes "what was in the pitchers."

[16]There is no known source for Ps.-J.'s addition. The addition explains how the magicians could turn water into blood if all the water in Egypt had become blood already (cf. vv. 20-21). Ps.-J. takes it that there was still water in Goshen where the Israelites lived. Compare 8:18 (22); 9:26. See Schmerler, 1933, 34; Rieder, 1975, 429.

[17]I.e., he went aside to defecate. See *Exod. R.* 9,8 to Exod 7:15; *Tanḥ. A, Wa-Era* 14 (198) and *Tanḥ. B, Wa-Era* 16 (2, 31). Ps.-J.'s interpretation of our present verse is based on the fact that HT *pnh*, "turned" (RSV), can also mean "ease oneself" in Mishnaic Hebrew. Ps.-J., who does not refrain from referring to indelicate matters (see Maher, 1992, 7), is the only Targum of this verse to refer to Pharaoh's bodily needs.

[18]"All" of HT is omitted in Lond. and *ed. pr.*

[19]Compare *Exod. R.* 9,11: "The whole of Egypt's water supply was smitten with blood."

of the Lord purified[20] *the river.* 26. And the Lord said to Moses, "Go in to Pharaoh and say to him, 'Thus says the Lord: Let my people go that they may worship *before me.* 27. If you refuse to let (them) go, behold, I will smite all your territory with frogs. 28. And the river will *produce*[21] frogs, and they will come up and enter your house, and your bedchamber and your couch, and into the houses of your servants, and of your people, and into your ovens and your kneading-bowls. 29. And the frogs *will have control* over *your body* and over *the bodies of*[22] your people, and over all your servants.'"

CHAPTER 8

1. And the Lord said to Moses, "<Say to Aaron>,[1] '*Raise*[2] your hand with the rod over the rivers, over the swamps,[3] and over the canals, and bring up the frogs upon the land of Egypt.'" 2. And Aaron *raised* his hand over the waters of Egypt, and *a plague of* frogs came up and covered the land of Egypt. *But Moses did not strike the water either with the blood or with the frogs, for through them he had (found) deliverance when his mother threw him into the river.*[4] 3. But the magicians did the same with their charms, and they brought up frogs upon the land of Egypt. 4. Then Pharaoh summoned Moses and Aaron and said, "*Pray before*[5] the Lord that he may remove the frogs from me and from my people, and I will let the people go to sacrifice *festive offerings before* the Lord." 5. And Moses said to Pharaoh, "Glorify yourself in my regard! Whenever *you wish, I will pray* for you, for your servants and for your people, that the frogs be wiped out from you and your house; only those that are in the river shall remain." 6. And he said, "For tomorrow." And (Moses) said, "As you say, that you may know that there is none like the Lord our God. 7. The frogs shall depart from you and from your house, from your servants

Notes, Chapter 7

[20]Lit.: "healed." One rabbinic opinion claimed that the plague lasted seven days; see *Tanḥ. A, Wa-Era* 13 (197); *Tanḥ. B, Wa-Era* 14 (2, 29); *Exod. R.* 9,12; *Deut. R.* 7,9.
[21]= Onq.
[22]*Exod. R.* 10,3 takes HT to mean that the frogs sexually mutilated the people.

Notes, Chapter 8

[1]Omitted in Lond. and *ed. pr.*
[2]= Onq.; also in vv. 2, 12, 13; 7:5, 19; 9:22, 23; 10:12, 13, etc.
[3]See 7:19, and n. 14 to that verse.
[4]Ps.-J. explains why it was Aaron rather than Moses who stretched forth his hand. Cf. *Tanḥ. A, Wa-Era* 14 (198); *Exod. R.* 9,10; 10,4. See also Ps.-J.'s version of v. 12, where HT also says explicitly that Aaron was to strike the dust.
[5]= Onq. The same Heb. verb (*'tr*) is also translated by *ṣly,* "pray," in vv. 5, 24, 25, 26; 9:28; 10:17, 18. See also Gen 25:21.

and from your people. Only those that are in the river shall remain." 8. Then Moses and Aaron went out from Pharaoh, and Moses *prayed before* the Lord concerning the frogs which he had inflicted upon Pharaoh. 9. And the Lord did as Moses said; the frogs died out of the houses, out of the courtyards, and out of the fields. 10. And they gathered them in heaps,[6] and the land stank. 11. But when Pharaoh saw that there was relief *from his anguish*, his heart became obdurate,[7] and he did not listen to them, as the Lord had spoken. 12. And the Lord said to Moses, "Say to Aaron, '*Raise* your rod and strike the dust of the earth that it may become vermin in all the land of Egypt.' *But it is not possible that the earth be struck by you, for through it you found deliverance when you killed the Egyptian and it received him.*"[8] 13. And they did so. Aaron *raised* his hand with the rod and struck the dust of the earth, and there was *a plague of* vermin on *the flesh of* man and beast; all the dust of the earth *was turned* into vermin in all the land of Egypt. 14. The magicians (who practiced) *sorcery* did the same with their spells to bring forth vermin, but they could not. And *the plague of* vermin was *in control of* man and beast. 15. And the magicians *of* Pharaoh said, "*This is not*[9] *from the power of the strength*[10] *of Moses and Aaron, but* it is *a plague sent from before the Lord.*"[11] But *the inclination of* Pharaoh's heart was hardened, and he did not listen to them as the Lord had spoken. 16. And the Lord said to Moses, "Rise early in the morning and station yourself before Pharaoh. Behold, he is coming out *to observe omens on* the water *like a magus.*[12] You shall say to him, 'Thus says the Lord: Let my people go that they may worship *before* me. 17. For if you do not let my people go, I will *let loose*[13] *a mixture*[14] *of wild beasts* against you, against your servants, and against your people. And the houses of the Egyptians, and even the ground on which they stand, will be filled with *a mixture of wild beasts.* 18. On that day *I will perform miracles*[15] in the land of Goshen where my people dwell, so that no mixture of wild beasts may be seen there, that you may know that I am the Lord *ruling in the midst of the land.* 19. And I will grant redemption to my people, but *upon*

Notes, Chapter 8

[6]Lit.: "heaps and heaps"; = HT. Ps.-J. uses the word *k(y)rwwn,* which is also the word in Nf, P, and V. Onq. uses the word *dgwryn.*

[7]Lit.: "made his heart heavy"; cf. also vv. 11 and 28; 9:34; 10:1.

[8]See above, n. 4 to v. 2, and the texts from *Tanḥ.* and *Exod. R.* mentioned in that note.

[9]Reading *l',* "not," with *ed. pr.,* rather than *wl',* "and not," of Lond.

[10]Or: "from the mighty strength." On the idiom (*kḥ gbwrt'*) used here by Ps.-J., see Ps.-J. Gen 44:13, and n. 7 to that verse (Maher, 1992, 145). In our present verse the word *gbwrt* is abbreviated to *gbwr* in Lond.

[11]Onq.: "It is a plague from before the Lord." The Targums clarify the meaning of the anthropomorphic words of HT: "This is the finger of God." See also *Exod. R.* 10,7. See further Grossfeld, 1988B, 21, n. 6.

[12]See above, Ps.-J. 7:15.

[13]The play on HT *šlḥ,* "let go; send," is lost in Ps.-J. (and in Nf). When *šlḥ* refers to God's sending punishment, the Targums often render it by *gry,* "let loose, incite," as do Ps.-J. and Nf in our present verse; see, e.g., Nf, Onq., Ps.-J. Lev 26:22, 25; Num 21:6 (also in Frg. Tgs.); Deut 7:20.

[14]*'yrbwb.* Ps.-J. (twice in our present verse) links HT *'rb,* "swarms" (RSV, v. 21), with *'rbb,* "mix up, confuse." See also Nf, V. See also vv. 18, 20 (twice), 25, 27. See *Exod. R.* 11,2: "beasts and birds combined."

[15]Ps.-J. and Nf link HT *plḥ* (Hif.), "set apart," with *pl'* (Hif.), "do something in a marvelous way." See also 9:4 (Ps.-J.). But compare 11:7.

your people *I will bring a plague.* [16] *During* tomorrow this sign shall come to pass.'"
20. And the Lord did so. *He brought a* mighty *mixture of wild beasts* to Pharaoh's
house and to the houses of his servants in all the land of Egypt. And *the inhabitants
of* the land of Egypt were destroyed because of *the mixture of wild beasts.*
21. Pharaoh summoned Moses and Aaron and said, "Go, *worship (with) festive offerings before the Lord* your God in this land." 22. But Moses said, "It would not
be right to do so, for *we would take lambs* [17] that are idols of the Egyptians and offer
(them) *before* the Lord our God. Behold, if we offer *the idols of* the Egyptians before them, *behold,* [18] *it would be right* (for them) to stone us *with stones.* 23. Let us
go a three days' journey in the wilderness and sacrifice *festive offerings before* the
Lord [19] our God, as he may say to us." 24. Pharaoh said, "I will let you go to sacrifice *before* the Lord your God in the wilderness; but do not go very far. *Pray* for
me." 25. And Moses said, "Behold, I am going out from you, and I *will pray before*
the Lord, and tomorrow the *mixture of wild beasts* will depart from Pharaoh, from
his servants and from his people; but let Pharaoh not continue to deal falsely by
not letting the people go to sacrifice *festive offerings before* the Lord." 26. And
Moses went out from Pharaoh and *prayed before* the Lord. 27. The Lord did according to *the request of* Moses, and he removed *the mixture of wild beasts* from
Pharaoh, from his servants, and from his people. Not one remained. 28. But this
time also Pharaoh made *the inclination of* his heart obdurate, and he did not let the
people go.

CHAPTER 9

1. The Lord said to Moses, "Go in to Pharaoh and speak with him: 'Thus says
the Lord, the God of the *Jews*: Let my people go that they may worship *before* me.
2. For if you refuse to let (them) go, and hold them any longer, 3. behold, *the blow
of* the hand of the Lord [1] is *now about to be let loose, as it never has been, also*
against your cattle that are in the field, against the horses, the asses, the camels, the
oxen and the sheep, a very great *death.* [2] 4. But the Lord will *perform miracles* [3]

Notes, Chapter 8

[16] = Onq. See Grossfeld, 1988B, 21, n. 8.
[17] Onq.: "cattle." See Ps.-J. Gen 43:32, and n. 15 to that verse.
[18] Reading *h',* rather than *hw'* of Lond. and *ed. pr.*
[19] "The Lord" is omitted in *ed. pr.*

Notes, Chapter 9

[1] Or: "the plague of. . ." Onq.: "a plague (or a blow) from before the Lord." Ps.-J. does not avoid the anthropomorphic
word "hand." See above Ps.-J. 7:4 and n. 5 to that verse.
[2] = Onq., LXX. See above Ps.-J. 5:3, with n. 5 to that verse.
[3] See above Ps.-J. 8:18 and n. 15 to that verse.

among the livestock of Israel and the livestock of the Egyptians, and nothing shall die of all that belongs to the children of Israel. 5. The Lord has fixed the time, saying, Tomorrow the Lord will do this thing in the land.'" 6. The Lord did this thing the next *day*; all the cattle of the Egyptians died, but of the cattle of the children of Israel not one died. 7. And Pharaoh sent *scouts*[4] *to see*, and behold, not even one of the cattle of *the children of* Israel[5] had died. But *the inclination of* Pharaoh's heart was obdurate, and he did not let the people go. 8. And the Lord said to Moses and Aaron, "Take handfuls of *fine* ashes from the furnace, and let Moses scatter it towards the heavens in the *sight of* Pharaoh. 9. It shall become dust over all the land of Egypt, and it shall become, on man and beast, an inflammation *developing*[6] (into) blisters in all the land of Egypt." 10. So they took the ashes of the furnace and stood before Pharaoh. Moses scattered it towards heaven, and it became an inflammation *developing* (into) blisters on man and beast. 11. The magicians were not able to stand before Moses because of the inflammation, for the *plague of* inflammation was upon the magicians and upon all the Egyptians. 12. But the Lord hardened *the inclination of* Pharaoh's heart, and he would not listen to them, as the Lord had said to Moses. 13. And the Lord said to Moses, "Rise early in the morning, and station yourself before Pharaoh and say to him. 'Thus says the Lord, the God of the *Jews*: Let my people go that they may worship *before* me. 14. For this time I will send *you a plague from heaven, and it will bring back to your heart*[7] all the plagues *with which I smote you*, against your servants and your people, *because they were sent from before me, and not by the sorcery of human beings,*[8] that you may know that there is *none who is like* me in all the earth. 15. If I had sent the *blow of my strength,*[9] *it would have been just* that I should smite you and your people with a plague, and that you should be wiped out from the earth. 16. But, *in truth*, I did *not* keep you alive *that I might do good*[10] to you but to show you my power, and that you might tell of my holy name in all the earth. 17. You[11] are still exalting yourself over my people and will not let them go. 18. Behold, *this*[12] time tomorrow I will *bring down from the storehouses of the heavens*[13] a very great hail such as has not been in Egypt from the day that *its foundations were completed* until now. 19. And now, have your livestock and everything you have in the

---

Notes, Chapter 9

[4]See also v. 27; 10:16; Num 16:12; 22:10; Deut 20:10, where Ps.-J. adds the same word in similar contexts.

[5]LXX: "of the sons of Israel"; Pesh.: "of the house of Israel."

[6]Or: "producing"; = Onq. See also v. 10.

[7]Ps.-J.'s rendering takes into account the different prepositions of HT: "*toward* (*'l*) your heart," and "*against* (*b-*) your servants."

[8]Cf. Ps.-J. 8:15. Ps.-J. seems to admit implicitly that sorcerers might have brought on the plagues. On Ps.-J.'s attitude to magic, see Maher, 1992, 6.

[9]= Onq.; HT: "my hand." See above, v. 3 (Ps.-J.), and n. 1.

[10]Lit.: "that we might do good."

[11]"You" is omitted in Lond.

[12]= Onq. Cf. *Exod. R.* 12,2.

[13]See Job 38:22, which mentions "the storehouses of the hail"; *b. Hag.* 12b. Compare also Ps.-J. Exod 16:4, which says that the manna had been reserved in heaven.

field *gathered*;[14] the hail shall come down upon every man and beast that is found in the field and has not been gathered indoors, and they shall die.'" 20. *Job*,[15] who among the servants of Pharaoh feared the word of the Lord, gathered his servants and his herds indoors. 21. But *Balaam*,[16] who did not heed the word of the Lord, left his servants and his herds in the field. 22. And the Lord said to Moses, "*Raise* your hand towards heaven, and there will be hail in all the land of Egypt, upon man and beast, and upon all the plants of the field in the land of Egypt." 23. So Moses *raised* his rod *towards* heaven, and the Lord sent thunder and hail, and fire *flashed* upon the earth, and the Lord *sent down* hail upon the land of Egypt. 24. And there was hail and fire *leaping* in the midst of the hail; (it was) very severe, so that there had not been the likes of it in all the land of Egypt since it became a nation *and a kingdom*. 25. In all the land of Egypt the hail struck everything that was in the fields, both man and beast; and the hail struck every plant of the field, and it broke *and uprooted* all the trees of the field. 26. Only in the land of Goshen, where the children of Israel were, there was no hail. 27. And Pharaoh sent *scouts* to call Moses and Aaron, and he said to them, "I am guilty this time. *I know that* the Lord *is a* just God. *But* I and my people are *guilty of each and every plague*.[17] 28. *Pray before* the Lord that he may bring to an end[18] the thunder *of malediction*[19] *from before the Lord*, and the hail, and I will let you go. Do not delay any longer." 29. Moses said to him, "When I go out, *close to*[20] the city, I will stretch out my *hands in prayer*[21] before the Lord; the thunders will cease, and there will be no more hail, so that you may know that the earth *is* the Lord's. 30. But as for you and your servants, I know that before *you let the people go*, you shall fear from before the Lord God." 31. The flax and the barley were smitten, because the barley was ripening and the flax *had produced* buds. 32. But the wheat and the spelt were not smitten, for they are late (crops). 33. Moses[22] went out from Pharaoh, *close to* the city,[23] and stretched out his *hands in prayer before* the Lord. And the thunder *of*

Notes, Chapter 9

[14]Lit.: "send, gather your livestock"; = Onq.

[15]*Exod. R.* 12,2; *j. Sotah* 5, 20c. See also *Exod. R.* 1,9; *b. Sotah* 11a. On Ps.-J.'s tendency to name people who are anonymous in the Bible (cf. also the mention of Balaam in v. 21), see n. 10 to Ps.-J. Gen 6:4 (Maher, 1992, 38).

[16]There is no source for this identification; cf. Schmerler, 1933, 41. But see, e.g., *Exod. R.* 1,9; *b. Sotah* 11a, which say that Balaam was one of Pharaoh's counselors.

[17]The meaning seems to be that Pharaoh and his people became more and more guilty as they refused to repent on the occasion of each plague. Compare *Exod. R.* 11,2: "(Pharaoh) hardened his heart in the face of the first three plagues."

[18]Lit.: "that there may be much before him."

[19]= Onq. See also Ps.-J. (but not Onq.) vv. 33, 34. Compare "the cup of malediction" in Ps.-J. Deut 32:33; Nahum 1:1; see Cathcart-Gordon, *The Aramaic Bible*, vol. 14, p. 131, n. 1.

[20]Cf. *Mek. RI* Exod 12:1 (1,3-4). See also below, n. 23 to v. 33.

[21]= Onq. See also v. 33. The same idiom, "stretch out (*prs*) one's hands in prayer," occurs again in Ps.-J. and Onq. Exod 17:12, and in Ps.-J. Deut 32:31.

[22]*Ed. pr.* adds "and Aaron."

[23]*Exod. R.* 12,7 (149): "Though he was still in the city's boundary." The construction *'t h'yr,* "(went out) of the city," in HT is unusual. The midrash takes *'t* to indicate closeness to the city.

malediction and the hail ceased, and the rain *that was coming down*[24] did not *reach*[24] the earth. 34. But when Pharaoh saw that the rain ceased and that the hail and the thunder *of malediction had stopped*, he sinned yet again, and he made *the inclination of* his heart obdurate, he and his servants. 35. And *the inclination of* Pharaoh's heart was hardened, and he did not let the children of Israel go, as the Lord had said through Moses.

CHAPTER 10

1. And the Lord said to Moses, "Go in to Pharaoh. For I have made *the inclination of* his heart and *the inclination of* the hearts of his servants obdurate, in order that I might display[1] these my signs among them, 2. and that you may tell in the hearing of your son and of your son's son *the miracles I performed*[2] in Egypt, and the signs I displayed among them, and that you may know that I *am* the Lord." 3. So Moses and Aaron went in to Pharaoh and said[3] to him, "Thus says the Lord the God *of Israel*,[4] 'How long will you refuse to humble yourself before me? Let my people go that they may worship *before* me. 4. For if you refuse to let my people go, behold, tomorrow I will bring locusts on your territory. 5. They will cover the *view*[5] of the earth, so that no one will be able to see the land. They will *wipe out* the remnant of what was saved, what was left to you after the hail, and they will *wipe out* every tree of yours that grows in the field. 6. Your houses shall *be* filled (with them), and the houses of all your servants, and the houses of all the Egyptians, something that neither your father nor your fathers' fathers saw from the day they came[6] on the earth to this day.'" Then he turned and went out from Pharaoh.

Notes, Chapter 9

[24] = Onq. According to *Tanḥ. A, Wa-Era* 16 (202); *Tanḥ. B, Wa-Era* 22, (2,37) and *Exod. R.* 12,7, the rain remained suspended in mid-air. See also *b. Ber.* 54b; see also Pesh.: "the rain did not reach (*smk*) the earth."

Notes, Chapter 10

[1] Lit.: "place, put, set"; = Onq., HT. See also v. 2.
[2] = Onq. See Grossfeld, 1988B, 26, n. 2.
[3] The verb is in the singular in Lond.
[4] Onq.: "The God of the Jews." HT.: "the God of the Hebrews."
[5] HT (literally): "the eye." Onq.: "the view (lit.: the eye) of the sun." See also v. 15 and Num 22:5, 11, where the different Targums render the same Heb. idiom as they do in our present verse. See further Grossfeld, 1988B, 27, n. 5. G. A. Rendsburg (1990, 15–17) recalls that the Egyptian phrase "eye of Ra" designated the sun, and he goes on to claim that Onq. realized that the Hebrew phrase "the eye of the (whole) earth" in the biblical texts just mentioned refers to the sun. Onq. makes this clear by adding the word "sun" to his translation of this phrase. I find Rendsburg's argument rather forced.
[6] Lit.: "were"; = HT.

7. Pharaoh's servants said to him,[7] "How long will this *man* be a snare to us? Let the men go that they may worship *before* the Lord their God! Are you not yet aware that *the land of* Egypt is *destined to* be destroyed *by him*?"[8] 8. So *the order was given* that Moses and Aaron be brought back to Pharaoh. And he said to them, "Go and worship *before* the Lord your God. Who are *these that are* to go?" 9. Moses[9] said, "We will go with our young and our old; *we will go* with our sons and daughters; we will go with our flocks and herds; for it is for us a feast *before* the Lord." 10. And he said to them, "May *the Memra of* the Lord be *at your assistance*, just as[10] I will let you and your little ones go! See that there is *an* evil *snare for you* before you *on the way in which you are going until you reach the place where you are to encamp.*[11] 11. It shall not be as *you think*! *But* let the men go and worship *before* the Lord, for that[12] is what you are requesting." And they were driven out from Pharaoh's presence. 12. And the Lord said to Moses, "*Raise* your hand over the land of Egypt *for* the locusts, that they may come upon the land of Egypt and *wipe out* every plant of the land, everything that the hail has left." 13. So Moses *raised* his staff over the land of Egypt, and the Lord drove an east wind over the land of Egypt all that day and all night. In the morning the east wind had brought the locusts. 14. The locusts came up over all the land of Egypt and settled in all the territory of Egypt, a very dense (swarm). Never before had locusts been so dense, and there will never be so many[13] again. 15. They covered the *view*[14] of all the land *until* the land was darkened, and they *wiped out* all the plants of the land and all the fruit of the trees which the hail had left, so that nothing green was left, on tree or plant, in all the land of Egypt. 16. Then Pharaoh hurried and *sent scouts* to call Moses and Aaron, and he said, "I have incurred guilt *before* the Lord your God and against you. 17. And now, forgive, I pray, my sin, just this time, and *pray before* the Lord <your God>[15] that he may but remove this death from me." 18. So he went out from Pharaoh and *prayed before* the Lord. 19. And the Lord caused a change to a very strong wind *from the west*,[16] and it lifted the locusts and threw them into the Sea of Reeds. Not one locust was left in all the territory of Egypt. *Even what they*

Notes, Chapter 10

[7]"To him" is omitted in *ed. pr.*

[8]HT (literally): "Do you not know that Egypt is destroyed?" Onq. translates literally. Ps.-J. interprets the text to refer to the future, referring implicitly to the interpretation of Pharaoh's dream (Ps.-J. 1:15). On Ps.-J.'s tendency to take up the same haggadic tradition on several occasions, see Maher, 1992, 5.

[9]Omitted in Lond.

[10]Ps.-J.'s translation gives one possible meaning of HT; Onq. ("when") gives another possible meaning of HT.

[11]Ps.-J.'s interpretation of HT seems to be like that of Rashi, who, borrowing from the midrash (Yalkut), said that Pharaoh saw by astrological means that evil would befall the Israelites on their journey through the wilderness. See Schmerler, 1933, 44; Ginzberg, *Legends* 2, 358; 5, 431, n. 196; Komlosh, 1973, 193–94.

[12]Lond., using the feminine suffix (*yth*), translates HT directly. *Ed. pr.* has the masculine suffix, i.e., it takes "Lord" to be the object of the verb. See Durham, *Exodus,* 133, n. 11b; Speier, 1967, 115.

[13]Lit.: "such."

[14]See above, v. 5 and n. 5 to that verse.

[15]Omitted in Lond. and *ed. pr.*

[16]= Onq. Ps.-J. and Onq. correctly interpret the idiom "sea wind" of HT as "west wind." See also *Exod. R.* 13,7.

had salted in vessels for their food requirements the west wind took, and they went away.[17] 20. But the Lord hardened *the inclination of* Pharaoh's heart, and he did not let the children of Israel go. 21. And the Lord said to Moses, "*Raise* your hand *towards* heaven, that there may be darkness over the land of Egypt *at dawn; but let* the darkness *of night first depart.*"[18] 22. So Moses *raised* his hand *towards* heaven, and there was thick darkness in all the land of Egypt for three days. 23. People could not see one another, and no one rose from *his place*[19] for three days. But all the children of Israel had light[20] *so that they could bury the wicked among them who had died,*[21] *and so that the just could be occupied with the commandments*[22] in their dwellings. 24. *At the end of three days*[23] Pharaoh called Moses and said, "Go, worship *before* the Lord. Only let your flocks and herds stay *with me.* Even your little ones may go with you." 25. But Moses[24] said, "You yourself must also provide us[25] with sacrifices of *holy things*[26] and burnt offerings, so that we may sacrifice *before* the Lord our God. 26. Our livestock also shall go with us. Not *one* hoof *from them* shall remain; we must take of them to worship *before* the Lord our God. *And if we leave them behind,*[27] we will not know with what we are to worship *before* the Lord until we arrive there." 27. But the Lord hardened *the inclination of* Pharaoh's heart, and he did not wish to let them go. 28. And Pharaoh said to him, "Go away from me! Take care that you do not see my countenance again *to speak before me another terrible word such as these.* For on the day that you see my countenance *my anger* will *be enkindled against you, and I will deliver you into the hands of those*

Notes, Chapter 10

[17]*Tanḥ. A, Wa-Era* 14 (200); *Exod. R.* 13,7; *Sefer Ha-Yashar* 80 (240).

[18]Onq.: "after the darkness of the night has departed." Onq. and Ps.-J. derive HT *wymš*, not from *mšš*, "feel, touch," but from *mwš*, "depart, be removed"; cf., e.g., Petermann, 1829, 48; Bacher, 1874, 61; Komlosh, 1973, 129. In saying that the darkness was to come after the darkness of the night had departed, Onq. and Ps.-J. are indicating that there would be no doubt about the miraculous nature of the darkness.

[19]= Pesh. LXX: "from his bed." HT (literally): "from under it"; = Onq.

[20]Lit.: "there was light in all (*bkl;* read *lkl*, 'for all,' with Onq. and Nf) the children of Israel."

[21]*Mek. RI* Exod 12:27 (1,95) says that many Israelites died during the three days of darkness, and that their fellow Israelites buried them lest the Egyptians should rejoice over the deaths. *Tanḥ. A, Wa-Era* 14 (200) and *Exod. R.* 14,3 take up this tradition and specify that those Israelites died because they were unwilling to leave Egypt. Ps.-J. simply alludes to this tradition in our present verse. On Ps.-J.'s tendency to allude to well-known haggadic traditions, see Maher, 1992, 6.

[22]Le Déaut (1981, 527) thinks the reference is to the study of the Law. The mention in HT of "light," which is often associated with the Law, would have prompted this reference. Schmerler, 1933, 45, believes that the reference is to the observance of the *mitzwoth,* e.g., the burial of the dead.

[23]Ps.-J. fixes the time. Ps.-J. often specifies times that are vague in HT. See Ps.-J. Gen 4:3 and n. 6 to that verse. See Maher, 1992, 31.

[24]Omitted in Lond.

[25]Lit.: "must put in our hand"; = HT.

[26]= Onq.; Nf, Nfmg: "sacrifices"; = HT. See also 18:12, where Onq., Ps.-J., and Nf translate HT "sacrifices" as "sacrifices of holy things." This latter formula is normally used in the Targums to translate HT *(zbḥ) šlmym,* "peace offering"; cf., e.g., 20:21(24); 24:5; 29:28; Lev 3:1, 3, 6, 9; 4:10, 26, 31, 35, and the Targums of Lev 7 *passim.* On the distinction between "most holy sacrifices," to which category the peace offering belonged, and "lesser holy sacrifices," see, e.g., *m. Zeb.* 1,2; 5,1.4.7.

[27]Lit.: "one of the hard words such as these."

men who were seeking your life[28] *to take it.*" 29. Moses said: "You have spoken *fittingly. While I was still dwelling in Midian, it was said to me in a word from before the Lord that the men who sought to kill me had become impoverished and were accounted as dead.*[29] *It is not because*[30] *mercy was shown you*[31] *that I prayed and the plague ceased from you.* But *now* I shall not see your face again."

CHAPTER 11

1. And the Lord said to Moses, "I will bring upon Pharaoh and upon the Egyptians one more affliction, *which will be the most severe of all for them.* After that he will let you go from here. When he lets (you) go *he will experience total destruction*[1] (and) he will drive you out from here. 2. Speak, then, in the hearing of the people, and let them borrow, each man from his *Egyptian friend,*[2] and each woman from her *Egyptian friend,*[2] objects of silver and objects of gold." 3. The Lord granted to the people (that they would find) *mercy before* the Egyptians. Moreover, the man Moses was very great in the land of Egypt *before* Pharaoh's servants and *before* the people. 4. Moses said *to Pharaoh,*[3] "Thus says the Lord, *Tomorrow* night, *at this hour,*[4] *I will reveal myself* in the midst of the Egyptians, 5. and every first-born in

Notes, Chapter 10

[28]Lit.: "your soul." The corresponding Hebrew phrase is used in the same context in Exod 4:19. See also, e.g., 1 Sam 20:1; 22:23 (twice); 23:15. With the formula "I will deliver you into the hands of these men (lit. 'these sons of man')," compare Mk 9:31.

[29]See above, Ps.-J. 4:19.

[30]Lit.: "from the end that"; = Nf, Nfmg, V.

[31]Lit.: "was upon you." P and V (see also Nf) go on to threaten Pharaoh with the tenth plague, thus giving a clearer text than Ps.-J.

Notes, Chapter 11

[1]HT (literally): "as (for) his sending, it is complete (*kšlḥw klh*)." On these difficult Hebrew words, see Durham, *Exodus,* 144–45. The word *klh* can also mean "destruction," and Ps.-J. understands it in that sense in our present verse, as do Onq. and Nfmg. See also Ps.-J. Gen 18:21 and n. 34 to that verse (Maher, 1992, 68).

[2]Ps.-J. translates HT *r',* "fellow, friend, neighbor," by *rḥm',* "friend, lover," while Onq. and Nf use *ḥbr',* "fellow, associate, friend," which is a more faithful rendering of the Hebrew word.

[3]Since it has not been said that Moses left Pharaoh's presence (see Exod 10:28-29), Ps.-J. concludes that Moses now addresses the Pharaoh.

[4]According to *b. Ber.* 4a, R. Ashi specified that the plague would come "tomorrow" (see also Ps.-J.) and that it would come "at midnight," lit., "like the midnight." This interpretation takes *k* in *kḥṣt,* "about midnight," to mean "like," i.e., "exactly at" rather than "about." Compare *kš't'* of Ps.-J., which we have translated as "at this hour." Another view expressed in the text from *Berakhoth* just mentioned, states that Moses deliberately said "about midnight" rather than "at midnight." One could also take Ps.-J.'s phrase to mean "at about this hour."

the land of Egypt shall die, from the first-born *son* of Pharaoh who *was destined to*[5] sit upon his *royal*[5] throne to the first-born of the *least* maidservant *in Egypt*, (*the child*) *who was born to her when she was grinding* behind the millstones, and all the first-born of the cattle. 6. And there will be a great cry in all the land of Egypt, because there never was such *a night* in which there was *a plague like this*; and never again will there be such *a night* (in which there will be) *a plague like this.* 7. But no dog, *by barking* with its tongue,[6] shall *harm* any of the children of Israel either man or beast, that you may know that the Lord makes a distinction between the Egyptians and Israel. 8. Then all these your servants will come down to me, and they will *ask a favor of* me,[7] saying, 'Go out, you and all the people who are *with* you.'[8] After that I will go out." And he went out from Pharaoh in hot anger. 9. And the Lord said to Moses, "Pharaoh will not listen to you in order that I may multiply my wonders in the land of Egypt." 10. Moses and Aaron performed all these wonders before Pharaoh. But the Lord hardened *the inclination of* Pharaoh's heart, and he did not let the children of Israel go from his land.

CHAPTER 12

1. The Lord said to Moses and Aaron in the land of Egypt, saying, 2. "This month[1] you *shall fix*[2] as the beginning of the months. *From it you shall begin to count the feasts, the (liturgical) times and the seasons.*[3] It shall be the first (month) for you *for numbering* the months of the year. 3. Speak to all the congregation of[4]

Notes, Chapter 11

[5]= Onq.
[6]HT: "not a dog shall move (or: whet) its tongue." The Targums explain this to mean barking. Ps.-J.'s version agrees with that of Onq. See further Grossfeld, 1988B, 31, n. 6.
[7]Onq.: "they will beg of me." See further Grossfeld, 1988B, 31, n. 7.
[8]= Onq. HT (literally): "at your feet." The Targums explain the Hebrew idiom. See also the rendering of the same idiom in Ps.-J. and Onq. Deut 11:6.

Notes, Chapter 12

[1]One might expect Ps.-J., who often specifies times that are vague in the Bible (see above, Ps.-J. 10:24 and n. 23 to that verse) to identify the month as Nisan, just as P does. See also *Mek. RI* Exod 12:2 (1,16). In Lev 23:5, Ps.-J. names Nisan as the month in which Passover is celebrated.
[2]Lit.: "(shall be) to you to fix it."
[3]*Mek. RI* Exod 12:2 (1,17–18); *Mek. RSbY* Exod 12:1 (9); cf. also *b. Rosh Hash.* 2a-b; *j. Rosh Hash.* 1, 1a.
[4]*Ed. pr.* adds "the children of"; = Nf, Pesh., LXX.

Israel, saying, 'On the tenth of this month—*its time is fixed on this occasion but not for (future) generations*[5]—let <each man>[6] take a lamb to a family.[7] *But if the number is too great,*[8] *let them take* a lamb for a house.[9] 4. But if *the members of*[10] the household are fewer than *the number ten,*[11] *that is enough to eat* the lamb, then he and his neighbor who is closest to his house shall take according to the *total* (number) of persons.[12] You shall *slaughter*[13] the lamb according to *the amount* each person can eat. 5. You shall have a perfect lamb, a male, a year old; you may take it from the lambs or from the *kid*[14] goats. 6. You shall have it *tied and* kept until the fourteenth day of this month, *so that you may know that you need not fear the Egyptians who see it.*[15] And all the assembly of the congregation of Israel shall slaughter it at twilight *according to the regulations.*[16] 7. They shall take some of the blood and put (it) on the two doorposts and on the *upper*[17] lintel, *on the outside*[18] of the houses (in which) they are to eat it *and in which they sleep.*[19] 8. They shall eat the flesh that night *of the fifteenth of Nisan until midnight;*[20] roasted by fire, with unleavened bread, with *chervil and endives*[21] they shall eat it. 9. Do not eat any of it *while it is* raw[22] or when it is boiled *in wine or oil or (other) liquids,*[23] or boiled in water, but roasted by fire, *with* its head, its legs and its entrails. 10. You

Notes, Chapter 12

[5]*m. Pesah.* 9,5; *Mek. RI* Exod 12:3 (1,25); *Mek. RSbY* Exod 12:3 (9); *b. Pesah.* 96a.

[6]Omitted in Lond. and *ed. pr.*

[7]Lit.: "to a family house." Compare *Mek. RI* Exod 12:3 (1,26): "'father's houses' merely means families."

[8]Lit.: "if they are greater than the number."

[9]*Mek. RI* Exod 12:3 (1,26); *Mek. RSbY* Exod 12:3 (9).

[10]Or: "the men of." See above, Ps.-J. 1:1 and n. 1 to that verse.

[11]No rabbinic source says that the group who eat the Passover cannot be less than ten; cf. Schmerler, 1933, 49. Describing a census that took place under Agrippa, *b. Pesah.* 64b says that at the Passover "there was not a single paschal lamb for which more than ten people had not registered." But this does not mean that less than ten could not have shared a lamb. Cf. Gronemann, 1879, 39.

[12]Onq.: "according to the number of persons"; = LXX.

[13]*Mek. RI* Exod 12:4 (1,28); *b. Pesah.* 61a.

[14]= Onq.

[15]*Mek. RI* Exod 12:6 (1,39); *Exod. R.* 16,3.

[16]Lit.: "the *halakah*." See also v. 11.

[17]Rashi, in his commentary on this verse, also states that the reference is to the *upper* post. See also below, v. 22 (Ps.-J.).

[18]See the debate in *Mek. RI* Exod 12:7 (1,44) about whether the blood should be on the inside or the outside. *Mek. RSbY* Exod 12:13 (16) says that the blood should be put where passers-by could see it, i.e., on the outside. Rashi, on the same verse, holds that the blood should be on the inside. See also below, v. 22 (Ps.-J.).

[19]*Mek. RI* Exod 12:7 (1,45); cf. *ibid.* to 12:13 (1,56). See *Mek. RSbY* Exod 12:13 (16) and *t. Pesah.* 8, 17 (Zuckermandel, 169), which distinguish between the Passover in Egypt and later Passovers.

[20]*Mek. RI* Exod 12:7 (1,45-46); *m. Zeb.* 5,8 (the paschal lamb had to be eaten . . . only until midnight); *t. Pesah.* 5,13 (Zuckermandel, 164); *b. Ber.* 9a; *Pesah.* 120b.

[21]Ps.-J. interprets HT *mrrym,* "bitter herbs," using the names of two herbs that are mentioned among others in *m. Pesah.* 2, 6 as suitable for fulfilling the Passover. Tg. Song of Songs 2:9, using the same two words (*tmk'* and *'wlsyn*) that Ps.-J. uses in our present verse, also states that chervil and endives were eaten with unleavened bread at the Passover meal. Nf, CTg HH, and Onq. use neither of these words in our present verse. Heb. *mrrym,* "bitter herbs," occurs also in Num 9:11, and in that verse Ps.-J. renders it by its Aramaic cognate, as do Nf and Onq.

[22]*kd hy;* = Onq. *Mek. RI* Exod 12:9 (1,48).

[23]According to *Mek. RI* Exod 12:9 (1,49), the words "or boiled in water" of HT include all liquids. See also *m. Pesah.* 2, 8; *b. Pesah.* 41a; *j. Pesah.* 2, 29c.

shall not leave any of it over until morning; and any of it left over until morning *you shall put aside, and on the evening of the sixteenth* you shall burn (it) with fire, *because what is left over from the holy sacrifices cannot be burned on the festival day.*[24] 11. *According to these regulations*[25] you shall eat it *on this occasion, but not throughout (future) generations:*[26] *let* your loins *be* girded, your shoes on your feet, and your staffs in your hands. And you shall eat it in the *haste*[27] *of the Shekinah of the Lord of the world, because* it is *a mercy*[28] *from before* the Lord *for you.* 12. On that night I will *be revealed* in the land of Egypt *in the Shekinah of my Glory, and with me there will be ninety thousand myriads of destroying angels.*[29] I will slay every first-born in the land of Egypt, both man and beast, and I will execute *four* judgments on all the *idols* of Egypt: *the molten idols will be melted, the idols of stone will be smashed, the idols of clay will be reduced to sherds, and the idols of wood will be reduced to ashes,*[30] *that the Egyptians may know that* I am the Lord. 13. The blood *of the Passover sacrifice and (that) of the cut of circumcision will be mixed*[31] by you *so as to make of it* a sign on the houses in which you *dwell.* When I see *the merit of* the blood, *I will spare*[32] you, and *the Angel of Death,*[33] *to whom authority to destroy has been given,* will *have no power* over you when I slay in the land of Egypt. 14. This day shall be for you a memorial day, and you shall celebrate it as a feast *before* the Lord; throughout your generations you shall celebrate it as a perpetual ordinance. 15. Seven days you shall eat unleavened bread; but *from the middle of* the day *before the feast*[34] you shall remove leaven from your houses. For any-

Notes, Chapter 12

[24]*Mek. RI* Exod 12:10 (1,50-51); *Mek. RSbY* Exod 12:10 (14); *j. Shabb.* 2, 4c; *b. Shabb.* 24b. These texts say that the burning may not take place until the *morning* of the sixteenth. None of them put it back to the *evening* of that day as does Ps.-J. The word *'wrt'*, which we translate as "evening," can mean "light," and might therefore refer to the morning. But it usually refers to the evening light; cf. Jastrow, 35; Levy 1, 16. Notice that Ps.-J. not only specifies the time for the burning (on Ps.-J.'s interest in precise times, see above Ps.-J. 10:24 and n. 23 to that verse), but also the reason for the choice of that time.

[25]Lit.: "this halakah." See above, Ps.-J. v. 6.

[26]*m. Pesah.* 9, 5; *b. Pesah.* 96a. See above v. 3 (Ps.-J.) and n. 5 to that verse.

[27]According to one opinion expressed in *Mek. RI* Exod 12:11 (1,52), the haste referred to in HT is that of the Shekinah.

[28]HT: *psh*, "passover, pass over," is here translated by Ps.-J. as *hyys'*, "mercy, protection." See also v. 27ab (Onq., Ps.-J.), and v. 13 (Onq., Ps.-J.). The word *hws* is often used in connection with the word *psh*. See, e.g., *Mek. RI* Exod 12:13 (1,56) and to Exod 12:23 (1, 87): "Passing over *(psyh')* merely means protection *(hyys)*." See further R. Weiss, "*PSH = HML, HWS,* (in Hebrew)," *Leshonenu* 27–28 (1964), 127–30; Brock, 1982A, 27–34; idem, 1982B, 222–33, especially 224–25.

[29]*j. Sanh.* 2, 20a says that when God came to deliver Israel, he was accompanied by his entire staff of angels. On the destroying angels, see above 4:25 (Ps.-J.) and n. 24 to that verse.

[30]*Mek. RI* Exod 12:12 (1,55); *Mek. RSbY* Exod 12:12 (15). See also Ps.-J. Num 33:4.

[31]*PRE* 29 (210): "The Israelites took the blood of the covenant of circumcision, and they put (it) upon the lintel of their houses, and when the Holy One . . . saw the blood . . . of circumcision . . . and the blood of the paschal lamb, he was filled with compassion." Cf. *Exod. R.* 19,5. On the redemptive power of the two bloods (of circumcision and of the Passover lamb), see, e.g., *Mek. RI* Exod 12:6 (1,33-34); *PRK* 7,4; *Exod. R.* 15,12; 17,3; Tg. Ezek 16:6. On the value of circumcision, see above Ps.-J. 4:24-26. See further Le Déaut, 1963, 209–12.

[32]= Onq. See above, v. 11 and n. 28 to that verse.

[33]On destructive angels, see above, 4:25 and n. 24 to that verse.

[34]The time for putting leaven away is debated in *m. Pesah.* 1, 4; *Mek. RI* Exod 15:11 (1,63-64); *j. Pesah.* 1, 27c; *b. Pesah.* 4b.

one who eats what is leavened from the first day *of the feast* until the seventh day, that *man* will be wiped out from Israel. 16. On the first day you shall hold a holy convocation, and on the seventh day a holy convocation; no work shall be done on them; only what *must be done so that* everyone may eat, that alone may be prepared by you. 17. You shall observe *the kneading of*[35] the Unleavened Bread, for on this very day I brought out your hosts *redeemed* from the land of Egypt; you shall observe this day throughout your generations (as) a perpetual ordinance. 18. In Nisan,[36] on the fourteenth day of the month, *you shall slaughter the Passover (victim),* and on the evening *of the fifteenth* you shall eat unleavened bread until the twenty-first day of the month; on the evening *of the twenty-second*[37] *you may eat what is leavened.* 19. For seven days no leaven shall be found in your houses. For whoever eats of what is leavened, that *person* will be wiped out from the congregation of Israel, whether he is a sojourner or a native of the land. 20. You shall not eat any *mixture*[38] that is leavened. In every *place* where you dwell you shall eat unleavened bread.'" 21. Then Moses called all the elders of Israel and said to them, "*Withdraw your hands from the idols*[39] *of the Egyptians,* and take *of the young*[40] of the flock for your families and slaughter the Passover *lamb.* 22. And take a bunch of hyssop and dip it in the blood that is in the *earthen* vessel,[41] and *sprinkle* the *upper* lintel *on the outside* and the two doorposts with the blood that is in the *earthen* vessel.[41] And none of you shall go outside the door of his house until morning. 23. *The Glory of* the Lord will *be revealed* to smite the Egyptians, and he will see the blood *that is* on the lintel and on the two doorposts, and *the Memra of* the Lord will *protect*[42] the door and will not allow the Destroying *Angel* to enter and smite your houses. 24. You shall observe this rite[43] as an ordinance for you and for your *male*[44] children forever. 25. And when you enter the land which the Lord is going to give you, as he promised, you shall observe this rite *from the time that you reach it.*[45] 26. And when your children say to you at that time, 'What do you mean by this rite?' 27. you shall say, 'It is a sacrifice *of mercy*[46] *before* the Lord, who *in*

Notes, Chapter 12

[35]I.e., watch the dough lest it become leavened; cf. *Mek. RI* Exod 12:17 (1,73).

[36]= Onq. See Grossfeld, 1988B, 33, n. 10.

[37]Ps.-J. counts the evening of the twenty-first, i.e., the evening when the feast day ends, as belonging to the next day, the twenty-second. See Schmerler, 1933, 56.

[38]*m. Pesah.* 3,1; *Mek. RI* Exod 12:20 (1,79); *b. Pesah.* 43a.

[39]*Mek. RI* Exod 12:21 (1,82); *Mek. RSbY* Exod 12:21 (25). See Ps.-J. 6:9, which says that the Israelites in Egypt engaged in idolatry.

[40]= Onq.

[41]*Mek. RI* Exod 12:7 (1,44) and to 12:22 (1, 84) explain that *sp* of HT means "vessel"; cf. *Mek. RSbY* Exod 12:22 (25). We know of no source for Ps.-J.'s specification that it was an *earthen* vessel. Cf. Schmerler, 1933, 56–57.

[42]= Nf; Nf also uses *psh,* "pass over." On the root *gnn* (Af.) used here by Ps.-J. and Nf to translate HT *psh,* see Brock, 1982A, 27–34; idem, 1982B, 224–25. See also above, v. 11, and n. 28 to that verse.

[43]Lit.: "word," or "thing."

[44]*Mek. RI* Exod 12:24 (1,89).

[45]*Mek. RI* Exod 12:25 (1,89).

[46]= Onq. See above, v. 11, and n. 28.

his Memra spared[46] the houses of the children of Israel in Egypt when he *destroyed the Egyptians but saved our houses.'" When the house of Israel heard this word from the mouth of Moses,* they bowed down and worshiped. 28. And the children of Israel went and did so; as the Lord commanded Moses and Aaron, so did they *hasten to do.* 29. In the middle of the night *of the fifteenth (of Nisan) the Memra of* the Lord *slew* all the first-born in the land of Egypt, from the first-born *son* of Pharaoh who *was to* sit upon his *royal* throne to the first-born *sons of the kings who were taken captives and who were hostages in the dungeon in the hand of Pharaoh. But because they rejoiced in the slavery of Israel, they too were smitten.*[47] And all the first-born of the cattle *which the Egyptians worship died.*[48] 30. Pharaoh rose that night, he and all *the rest of* his servants and all *the rest of* the Egyptians, and there was a great cry <in Egypt>,[49] for *there was* not a house *of the Egyptians* where there was not *a first-born* dead. 31. *Now the territory of the land of Egypt extended for a distance of four hundred parasangs,*[50] *and the land of Goshen, where Moses and the children of Israel were, was in the middle of the land of Egypt, and Pharaoh's royal palace was at the beginning of the land of Egypt.*[51] *But when* he summoned Moses and Aaron on the night *of Passover, his voice was heard as far as the land of Goshen.*[52] *Pharaoh was supplicating in an anguished voice,*[53] and he said *thus*: "Arise, go forth from among my people, both you and the children of Israel. Go, worship *before* the Lord as you said. 32. Take also your flocks and your herds, *and some of what is mine,*[54] as you said, and go. *And I ask nothing of you, except that you pray for me*[55] *that I may not die."* 33. *When Moses and Aaron and the children of Israel heard Pharaoh's mournful voice, they paid no attention until he and all his servants*[56] *and all* the Egyptians *went and* urged the people[57] *of the house of Israel* to hurry, in order to let them go out of the land, for they said, "*If these tarry here one hour,* behold, we shall all be dead." 34. So the people took their dough *upon their heads* before it was leavened, *and whatever unleavened bread and bitter herbs they had left over*[58] *they carried* wrapped in their clothes upon their shoulders.

Notes, Chapter 12

[47]*Mek. RI* Exod 12:29 (1,98). There is no source for Ps.-J.'s view that the captives were sons of kings.

[48]*Mek. RI* Exod 12:29 (1,99); *Tanḥ. A, Bo* 7 (208); *PRK* 7,9.

[49]Omitted in Lond. and *ed. pr.* By adding "the remainder" (twice) Ps.-J. takes into account the fact that many Egyptians had died; see v. 29. See also Ps.-J. 32:12 and n. 27 to that verse.

[50]*b. Pesah.* 94a; *Ta'an.* 10a; *Tanḥ. A, Wa-Era* 14 (199).

[51]We know of no source for this addition ("and the land of Goshen . . . the land of Egypt").

[52]Cf. *j. Pesah.* 5, 32c: the voice of *Moses* was heard in all the land of Egypt. See also *Tanḥ. A, Bo* 9 (210).

[53]The idiom "in an anguished voice" occurs in Dan 6:21. See also Ps.-J. Exod 32:5. There is no source for Ps.-J.'s application of this phrase to Pharaoh. See Schmerler, 1933, 59.

[54]*Mek. RSbY* Exod 12:32 (29); *Mek. RI* Exod 12:32 (1,102).

[55]Onq.: "pray for me." *Mek. RI* Exod 12:32 (1,102): "Pray for me that this visitation may cease from me."

[56]We know of no source for this "pre-translation haggadah." The phrase we translate as "Pharaoh's mournful voice" reads literally: "the sound of Pharaoh's weeping."

[57]*Ed. pr.* has "all the people," reading *lkl* instead of *'l.*

[58]Onq.: "that which was still left in their kneading trough." Cf. *Mek. RI* Exod 12:34 (1,104); *Tanḥ. A, Bo* 8 (209).

35. The children of Israel did according to the word of Moses, and they borrowed from the Egyptians vessels of silver and vessels of gold, and <clothing>.[49] 36. And the Lord granted to the people (that they would find) favor *and grace before* the Egyptians, so that they lent them (to them). And they emptied out[59] the Egyptians *of their possessions.* 37. The children of Israel set out from *Pelusium*[60] to Succoth, *a hundred and thirty mils.*[61] *There they were covered by the seven clouds of glory, four on their four sides, and one above them, so that rain or hail would not fall on them, and so that they would not be burned by the burning heat of the sun; and one beneath them so that thorns and serpents and scorpions would not harm them; and one went before them to level the valleys and to lower the mountains, to prepare a dwelling place for them.*[62] *They were* about six hundred thousand *men, and they went* on foot, *and not riding on horses,*[63] except for the little ones, *five for each man.* 38. Moreover, *foreigners*[64] (who were) *more* numerous *than they—two hundred and forty myriads*[65]—went up with them, and flocks and herds, *and* very many livestock. 39. *And they cut off some of* the dough they had brought out from Egypt *and placed (it) on their heads,*[66] and it was baked into unleavened cakes for them *by the heat of the sun,* for it was not leavened, because they had been driven out from Egypt and they could not tarry. *They had enough to eat until the fifteenth day of the month of Iyar.*[67] *In fact,*[68] they had prepared no provisions for themselves. 40. *The days* that the children of Israel dwelt in Egypt (were) *thirty weeks of years,*[69] *that is two hundred and ten years. But the number was* four hundred and thirty years *since the Lord had spoken to Abraham, from the time he had spoken to him on the fifteenth of Nisan between the pieces*[70] *until the day they went forth from*

Notes, Chapter 12

[59]See above, Ps.-J. 3:22 and n. 32 to that verse.

[60]HT: Rameses. See Ps.-J. Gen 47:11 and n. 9 to that verse (Maher, 1992, 152).

[61]Cf. *Mek. RI* Exod 12:37 (1,107); see the different figures (120, 130, 160) given in the variant readings in the H. S. Horowitz-I. A. Rabin edition of the *Mekilta de Rabbi Ishmael,* Jerusalem, 1960, p. 47.

[62]*Mek. RI* Exod 13:21 (1,183); *Sifre Num.* 83 (Horovitz, 79); *Tanḥ. A, Be-Shallah* 3 (219); Tg. Song of Songs 2:6. See also *Mek. RI* Exod 12:37 (1,108). Ps.-J. takes up this tradition again in Exod 13:20; Num 14:14; 33:5; Deut 1:31; 32:5. Cf. also Ps.-J. Exod 14:19. See Luzarraga, 1973, 104, 127, 138. There is a certain contradiction between our present verse, which says that a cloud protected the people from the burning sun, and v. 39, which says that the sun baked their cakes.

[63]We know of no source for this addition. On Ps.-J.'s addition, "five for each man," see below, Ps.-J. 13:18.

[64]= Onq.

[65]*Mek. RI* Exod 12:38 (1,109).

[66]See also v. 34 (Ps.-J.).

[67]According to *Mek. RI* Exod 12:39 (1,110), they ate those cakes until the manna came down. Cf. *b. Qidd.* 38a. See also Ps.-J. Exod 16:2.

[68]Lit.: "because, since."

[69]Or: "thirty septennial periods"; cf. Jastrow, 1595. In vv. 40–41 Ps.-J. solves the problem raised by the contradictory data of Gen 15:13 (400 years) and Exod 12:40 (430 years). See *Mek. RI* Exod 12:40 (1,111); *PRE* 48 (375–76); cf. *Gen. R.* 92,2; *Exod. R.* 18,11.

[70]That is, the pieces of the victims in the ritual described in Gen 15. Ps.-J. Gen 15 does not associate this ritual with Nisan. But see *Mek. RI* Exod 12:41 (1,112). On events which Ps.-J. associates with Passover, see Ps.-J. Gen 14:13 and n. 30 to that verse (Maher, 1992, 57).

Egypt. 41. Thirty years passed *from the time that this covenant was made until Isaac was born*, and four hundred <years> *from (the time) that Isaac was born*[71] *until they went out redeemed from Egypt*, and on that very day all the hosts of the Lord went out *redeemed* from the land of Egypt. 42. *Four nights*[72] *are inscribed in the Book of Memorials before the Master of the world. The first night, when he was revealed to create the world; the second, when he was revealed to Abraham; the third, when he was revealed in Egypt, and his hand slew all the first-born of Egypt, and his right hand delivered the first-born of Israel; the fourth, when he will be revealed to redeem the people of the house of Israel from among the peoples. And he called all of them "nights of watching."*[73] *Therefore, Moses says clearly:* "It is a night reserved for redemption *from before* the Lord, to bring out *the people of the children of Israel* from the land of Egypt. That is the night that was protected *from the Destroying Angel* for all the children of Israel *who were in Egypt, and (it is) also (reserved) for their deliverance from their exiles* throughout their generations." 43. And the Lord said to Moses and Aaron, "This is the ordinance of the Passover: no gentile, *and no Israelite who has apostatized*[74] *and has not repented*, shall eat of it. 44. Every *foreigner who has been sold as* a slave *to an Israelite man*, (who has been) bought for money, you shall circumcise him *and bathe him*;[75] then he may eat it. 45. A resident *stranger* and a *foreign* hireling[76] may not eat of it. 46. It shall be eaten in one *company*; you shall not take any of the flesh out of the house, outside *the company*,[77] *not even to send gifts from one to another.*[78] And you shall not break a bone of it, *to eat what is within it.*[79] 47. All (the members of) the congregation of Israel *shall mix with one another, one family with another family*,[80] to celebrate it. 48. If a *proselyte is converted*[81] among you and would celebrate the Passover *before* the Lord, let him circumcise all his males; then he *shall be fit* to celebrate it; he shall be as a native of the land. But no uncircumcised *Israelite*[82] shall eat it.

Notes, Chapter 12

[71]The word "years" is omitted in Lond. and *ed. pr.*, and the words "from (the time) that Isaac was born" are omitted through homoioteleuton in *ed. pr.*

[72]Since the haggadah of the Four Nights occurs at much greater length in Nf's version of v. 42, we refer the reader to the notes on that verse.

[73]"Nights of watching, (or: vigil, *nṭyr*)"; = Onq.; compare HT: "a night of watching (*šmwrym*)."

[74]= Onq. Nf: "no gentile." Ps.-J. combines the reading of Onq. and Nf. Ps.-J. agrees with *Mek. RI* Exod 12:43 (1,118); *Mek. RSbY* Exod 12:43 (35). See also *b. Pesah.* 96a; *Yeb.* 71a.

[75]*Mek. RI* Exod 12:48 (1,127); *Mek. RSbY* Exod 12:48 (37); *b. Yeb.* 46a. On the question of a ritual bath for proselytes, cf. Ohana, 1974, 322, n. 3, with bibliography.

[76]*Mek. RI* Exod 12:45 (1,121); *Tanḥ. A, Bo* 10 (211).

[77]*Mek. RI* Exod 12:46 (1,122–23); *b. Pesah.* 86a-b.

[78]We know of no source for this addition; cf. Schmerler, 1933, 67.

[79]*Mek. RI* Exod 12:46 (1,124).

[80]*Mek. RI* Exod 12:47 (1,125).

[81]= Onq. *Mek. RI* Exod 12:48 (1,125). On the Targums' (Nf, Onq., Ps.-J.) rendering of this verse, see Ohana, 1973, 392–93; see further, idem, 1974, 317–32.

[82]*Mek. RI* Exod 12:48 (1,127–28).

49. *With regard to all the commandments,*[83] there shall be one law for the native and for the *proselyte* who will *be converted* among you."[84] 50. All the children of Israel did (so); as the Lord commanded Moses and Aaron so they did. 51. That very day the Lord brought the children of Israel out of the land of Egypt by their hosts.

CHAPTER 13

1. The Lord spoke to Moses, saying, 2. "Consecrate *before* me every *male*[1] first-born; whatever opens the womb among the children of Israel, both of man and of beast, is mine." 3. And Moses said to the people, "Remember this day, on which you came out *redeemed* from Egypt, from the *bondage of* slaves;[2] for by the *strength of* a mighty hand the Lord brought you out from here. No leavened bread may be eaten. 4. This day you are to go forth *redeemed, on the fifteenth of Nisan, that is* the month of Abib. 5. And when the Lord *your God* brings you into the land of the Canaanites, the Hittites, the Amorites, the Hivites, and the Jebusites, which he swore *by his Memra* to your fathers to give you, a land *that produces*[3] milk and honey, you shall perform this rite in this month: 6. Seven days you shall eat unleavened bread, and on the seventh day there shall be a feast *before* the Lord. 7. For seven days unleavened bread shall be eaten. No leavened bread shall be seen with you, and no leaven shall be seen with you in all your territory. 8. And you shall tell your son on that day, saying 'Because of this *precept*[4] *the Memra of* the Lord performed *miracles and wonders* for me when I came out of Egypt.' 9. You shall have *this miracle clearly inscribed on the phylactery of* the hand, *at the upper part of the left (hand),* and as a memorial *clearly inscribed on the phylactery of the head, fixed before* your eyes, *at the upper part of your head,*[5] so that the Law of the Lord may be in your mouth, because the Lord brought you out from Egypt with *the strength*

Notes, Chapter 12

[83]*Mek. RI* Exod 12:49 (1,128); *Mek. RSbY* Exod 12:49 (37).
[84]Lond.: "among the."

Notes, Chapter 13

[1]*Mek. RI* Exod 13:2 (1,128–29).
[2]Lit.: "from the house of slavery of the slaves." This idiom occurs in Ps.-J., v. 14; 20:2 (also P, CTg F); Deut 5:6 (also Nf); 6:12 (also Nf); 7:8 (also Nf); etc., etc.
[3]= Onq. See above, 3:8 (Ps.-J.) and n. 16 to that verse.
[4]HT reads (literally): "because of this." The *meturgeman* took "this" to refer to the unleavened bread (*mṣwt*). Then, by playing on the word *mṣwt*, he gets the translation *mṣwh*, "precept." Compare *Mek. RI* Exod 12:17 (1,74).
[5]*Mek. RI* Exod 13:9 (1,151); *Mek. RSbY* Exod 13:9 (40); *b. Men.* 36b, 37b. These texts specify that the phylacteries were to be on the upper part of the left hand and on the upper part of the head. See also Ps.-J. Deut 6:8. According to Ps.-J., the miracles of the Exodus are the sign for Israel (cf. Rashi to Exod 13:9), and they are to be written on the phylacteries. For the texts usually written on the phylacteries, see *EJ* 15, 898–904.

of a mighty hand. 10. You shall observe this statute *of the phylacteries* at the *appropriate* time,[6] *on workdays but not on sabbaths or festivals, by* day, *but not by night.*[7] 11. And when the Lord has brought you into the land of the Canaanites, as he swore to you and to your fathers, and has given it to you, 12. you shall *set apart*[8] *before* the Lord everything that opens the womb; everything that opens *the womb* of the cattle that you have, *that its mother has dropped,*[9] (all the) males you shall *consecrate before*[10] the Lord. 13. But everything that opens *the womb* of an ass you shall redeem with a lamb; if you do not redeem (it), you shall strike it mortally. You shall redeem *with money*[11] every first-born of man, (that is), of *your* son, *but not of your servant.*[12] 14. And when, in time to come, your son asks you, saying, 'What is this *precept of the first-born?*' you shall say to him, 'With *the strength of* a mighty hand the Lord brought us out *redeemed* from Egypt, from the *bondage of* slaves.[2] 15. It happened, *when the Memra of the Lord* hardened[13] Pharaoh's *heart* against letting us go, the Lord slew all the first-born in the land of Egypt, both the first-born of man and of beast. Therefore I sacrifice *before* the Lord every male that opens the womb, but every first-born among my sons I redeem *with money.'* 16. It shall be as a sign *clearly engraved* upon your *left*[14] hand, and as *phylacteries*[15] between your eye-*lids*;[16] for with *the strength of* a mighty hand the Lord brought us out from Egypt." 17. Now when Pharaoh let the people go, *the Lord* did not lead them by the way of the land of the Philistines, although it was nearer; for *the Lord* said, "Perhaps the people will change their minds when they see *their brothers who died in the war, two hundred thousand men, men of valor from the tribe of Ephraim." Seizing shields and spears and (other) weapons, they went down to Gath to plunder the livestock of the Philistines. And because they transgressed the decree of the Memra of the Lord and went forth from Egypt thirty years before the appointed time, they were delivered into the hands of the Philistines, who slew them. These were the dry bones which the Memra of the Lord brought to life through the mediation of Ezekiel the prophet in the valley of Dura. If (the departing Israelites) had seen that, they would have taken fright*[17] and returned to Egypt. 18. So *the Lord* brought the

Notes, Chapter 13

[6]Onq.: "from season to season." Cf. Grossfeld, 1988B, 35; Díez Macho, *Neophyti 1*, IV, 32*.

[7]*Mek. RI* Exod 13:10 (1,155–57); *b. Men.* 36b.

[8]*Mek. RI* Exod 13:12 (1,159); *Tanḥ. A, Bo.* 12 (213).

[9]*Mek. RI* Exod 13:12 (1,160); *m. Bek.* 3,1.

[10]"Consecrate before" = Onq. LXX, Vulg.: "consecrate to."

[11]Cf. Num 18:16. See also below v. 14 (Ps.-J.); *b. Qidd.* 8a.

[12]According to Levine (1971, 44–45), the early Karaites held that the first-born of slaves had to be redeemed. Ps.-J. rejects such a view.

[13]*Mek. RI* Exod 13:15 (1,167).

[14]See above v. 9 (Ps.-J.), with n. 5 to that verse.

[15]= Onq. *Mek. RI* Exod 13:9 (1,150); *ibid.,* 13:16 (1,168); *b. Men.* 36b. See further Grossfeld, 1988B, 36, n. 7.

[16]Onq.: "between your eyes; = HT. Compare Ps.-J. v. 9 above; Deut 11:18.

[17]*Mek. RI* Exod 13:17 (1,172–73); *b. Sanh.* 92b; *Exod. R.* 20,11; *PRE* 48 (377); *Machsor Vitry* (Hurwitz, 305); Ps.-J. Gen 50:25, with notes to that verse (Maher, 1992, 166). Tg. 1 Chr 7:21; Tg. Ezek 37: 1-16; Tg. Song of Songs 2:7. See M. J. Mulder, 1975, 141–66; Heinemann, 1974A, 131–41; idem, 1975, 1–15.

people around by the way of the wilderness of the Sea of Reeds, and the children of Israel, *each one with five little ones*,[18] went up from the land of Egypt. 19. Moses *raised up*[19] *out of the Nile the ark in which* Joseph's bones *were contained and* took (them) with him, for he had made the children of Israel swear solemnly, saying, "*The Lord* will surely *remember* you; then you shall bring up my bones with you from here." 20. They set out from Succoth, *a place where they had been covered by the clouds of glory*,[20] and encamped at Etham, *which is* at the edge of the desert. 21. *The Glory of the Shekinah of* the Lord was *leading* before them by day in a pillar of cloud, to guide them on the way; at night *the pillar of cloud went back behind them to create darkness for those who pursued them*,[21] *and* (they had) the pillar of fire to give light before them, that they might travel by day and by night. 22. The pillar of cloud by day and the pillar of fire by night did not cease *to lead* before the people.

CHAPTER 14

1. The Lord spoke to Moses, saying, 2. "Speak to the children of Israel, and let them turn *backwards*[1] and encamp before the 'Mouths-*of-the-Prostrate-Licentious-Things*'[2] *that were created like human beings, male and female, with their eyes open. That is the region of Tanis*[3] *that is* between Migdol and the sea, before the *idol* Zephon *that remained of all the idols of Egypt, so that the Egyptians would say, 'Baal Zephon is more glorious than all the idols, because it has survived and has not been struck down.'*[4] *They will go and worship it, and they will find that you are*

Notes, Chapter 13

[18]LXX: "in the fifth generation"; Theodotion: "doing (this) on the fifth day." These texts and Ps.-J. link HT *ḥmšyn*, "equipped for battle," (RSV) with *ḥmš*, "five." See also above, 12:37 (Ps.-J.). For different rabbinic interpretations of *ḥmšyn*, see *Mek. RI* Exod 13:18 (1,174); *PRK* 11,11. See further Le Déaut, 1981, 525–33.

[19]*w'syq* = Onq. For the legend about the raising of the coffin of Joseph, see, e.g., *Mek. RI* Exod 13:19 (1,176–77); *b. Sotah* 13a; *Tanḥ. A, Be-Shallah* 2 (218). See Gen 50:26 (Ps.-J.), and n. 30 to that verse (Maher, 1992, 166).

[20]*Mek. RI* Exod 13:20 (1,182). Cf. *b. Sukk.* 11b. See above 12:37 (Ps.-J.), and n. 62 to that verse.

[21]There is a certain contradiction between Ps.-J.'s version of our present verse (the pillar of cloud brought darkness on the Egyptians) and Ps.-J. 14:20 (the pillar of cloud was part light, part darkness, bringing darkness on the Egyptians, and giving light to Israel at night).

Notes, Chapter 14

[1]*Mek. RI* Exod 14:2 (1,189).

[2]We take Aramaic *mrby't* to be derived from *rb'*, "lie." See further P. Grelot's review of *Biblia Polyglotta Matritensia*, vol. 2, *Exodus*, in *RB* 89 (1982) 596. See also Ps.-J. Num 33:7. For different interpretations of Heb. *ḥyrt* in the Hebrew place-name Pi-Hahiroth, see *Mek. RI* Exod 14:2 (1,188); *Num. R.* 20,23.

[3]*Mek. RI* Exod 14:2 (1,188): "In the past it had been called Pithom." HT "Pithom" is rendered as Tanis in the Pal. Tgs. of Exod 1:11. See above n. 21 to that verse (Ps.-J.).

[4]*Mek. RI* Exod 14:2 (1,190).

encamping opposite it, by the *shore of* the sea. 3. And Pharaoh will say to *Dathan and Abiram*, Israelites *who had remained in Egypt,*[5] *'The people of the house of Israel* are wandering around[6] in the land. *The idol Zephon has closed the passes of*[7] the wilderness on them.' 4. I will harden *the inclination of* Pharaoh's heart and he will pursue them, and I will gain glory through Pharaoh and all his soldiers, and the Egyptians will know that *it is* I who am the Lord." And they did so. 5. *The guards who had gone with Israel*[8] told <the king of Egypt> that the people had fled, and the heart of Pharaoh and his servants was changed *to malice* against the people. And they said, "What is this that we have done, letting Israel go from our service?" 6. He[9] *himself, in person,*[10] harnessed his chariot, and *with persuasive words*[11] he brought his people with him. 7. He took six hundred picked chariots and the chariots of the Egyptians, *his servants who had feared the word of the Lord and who had not died of the plague or in the hail;*[12] and to each *chariot he added a third mule to pull (it) and to pursue (them) in haste.*[13] 8. And the Lord hardened *the inclination of* the heart of Pharaoh, king of Egypt, and he pursued the children of Israel; and the children of Israel were going out with uplifted hand, *prevailing over the Egyptians.*[14] 9. The Egyptians pursued them, and they overtook them while they were encamped at the sea *gathering pearls and precious stones which the Pishon had taken from the garden of Eden into the Gihon, and which the Gihon had taken to the Sea of Reeds, and which the Sea of Reeds had cast up on its shore.*[15] All the chariot horses of Pharaoh, his horsemen, and his soldiers were at the "Mouths-*of-the Rocks*," which is opposite the idol Zephon. 10. Pharaoh *saw that the idol Zephon had been saved, and he offered offerings before it.*[16] The children of Israel raised their eyes, and behold, the Egyptians were on the move after them; and they feared greatly. And the children of Israel *prayed before*[17] the Lord. 11. *And the wicked of*

Notes, Chapter 14

[5]We know of no source for this tradition: cf. Schmerler, 1933, 75.

[6]Lit.: "are being knocked (or tossed) about." See Nf and Nfmg Num 12:12, where the same verb (*ṭrp*) is used with reference to the wandering of Israel or of Miriam in the desert.

[7]Reading *ngdwy* with Nf, which Levy (2,89) renders as "plains" ("Steppen"), and which Jastrow (872) translates as "narrows." Lond.: *nghwy*; ed. pr.: *nghwy*. See *Mek. RSbY* Exod 14:3 (48).

[8]*Mek. RI* Exod 14:5 (1,194).

[9]V. 6 is omitted in Lond. However, Lond. does have the *lemma* for that verse.

[10]*Mek. RI* Exod 14:6 (1,198).

[11]*Mek. RI* Exod 14:6 (1,200) records Pharaoh's words.

[12]See Exod 9:6, 20. The Targum solves the problem raised by 9:6 ("all the cattle of the Egyptians died") and 14:7 (Pharaoh still had beasts to draw chariots). Cf. *Mek. RI* Exod 14:7 (1,201); *Tanḥ. A, Be-Shallah* 8 (220).

[13]Ps.-J. takes HT *šlšm*, "officers" (RSV), to be derived from *šlš*, "three." Cf. *Mek. RI* Exod 14:7 (1,202); *j. Kilayim* 8, 31c.

[14]*Mek. RI* Exod 14:8 (1,204).

[15]There is no known source for this tradition. Cf. Schmerler, 1933, 77. See also Ps.-J. Exod 35:27; *Exod. R.* 33,8.

[16]*Mek. RI* Exod 14:10 (1,205); *Tanḥ. A, Be-Shallah* 8 (221). The verb *hqryb*, "drew near," can also mean "offer," and it is taken in that sense by the midrash. On the survival of the idol Zephon, see above, v. 2 (Ps.-J.).

[17]Cf. *Mek. RI* Exod 14:10 (1,206); *Tanḥ. A, Be-Shallah* 9 (221). HT *ṣʿq*, "cried out," is often taken to mean "pray"; see, e.g., Exod 8:8 (Onq., Nf, Ps.-J.) 14:15 and 15:25 (Onq., Nf, Ps.-J., P, V, N).

(that) generation[18] said to Moses, "Is it because there was no grave *for us* in Egypt that you brought us to die in the wilderness? What have you done to us, taking us out of Egypt? 12. *Is* not this what we said to you in Egypt—*May the Lord be revealed to you and judge*[19]—saying: 'Leave us alone and let us serve the Egyptians, for it is better for us to serve the Egyptians than to die in the wilderness'?" 13. *The children of Israel were formed into four groups*[20] *at the shore of the Sea of Reeds. One said: "Let us go down into the sea!" Another said, "Let us return to Egypt!" Another said, "Let us arrange battle lines against them!" Another said, "Let us shout at them and confuse them!" To the group that said, "Let us go down into the sea,"* Moses said: "Do not be afraid! Stand by, and see the redemption of the Lord which he will perform for you today." *To the group that said: "Let us return to Egypt,"* Moses said: "Do not return, for as you have seen the Egyptians today, you shall not see them again forever." 14. *To the group that said, "Let us arrange battle lines against them," Moses said: "Do not fight, for it is from before* the Lord *that your victorious battles will be conducted." To the group that said, "Let us shout at them,"* Moses said: "Be silent, *and give glory and praise and exaltation to your God.*" 15. The Lord said to Moses, "Why *are you standing (there), praying*[21] *before* me? *Behold the prayer of my people has preceded yours.*[22] Speak to the children of Israel, and let them go forward. 16. And you, lift up your rod, and incline your hand *with it* over the sea and split it, and let the children of Israel go into the sea on dry ground. 17. As for me, behold I will harden *the inclination of* the hearts of the Egyptians, and they will go in after them, and I will gain glory through Pharaoh and all his soldiers, through his chariots and his horsemen. 18. And the Egyptians will know that *it is* I who am the Lord when I gain glory through Pharaoh, through his chariots and his horsemen." 19. And the angel of *the Lord* who was leading before the camp of Israel moved and came behind them; and the pillar of cloud moved from before them and settled behind them *because of the Egyptians who were throwing arrows and stones against Israel, and the cloud intercepted them.*[23] 20. It came between the camp of Israel and the camp of the Egyptians, and it was *part light and part* darkness; *on one side it cast darkness over the Egyptians, and on the*

Notes, Chapter 14

[18]Only the wicked complained. Those who "prayed before the Lord" (Ps.-J. v. 10) would not have complained. Ps.-J. protects the honor of the ancestors by limiting the complaint to the wicked. See also Ps.-J. 32:19 and n. 37 to that verse, and Num 11:8, 33.

[19]*Mek. RI* Exod 14:12 (1,209). This *Mekilta* text and Ps.-J. record the words from Exod 5:21 which the people addressed to Moses and Aaron in Egypt. In quoting the words from 5:21 in our present verse, Ps.-J. translates them not as he had done in 5:21, but according to Nf's version of that verse.

[20]This haggadah about the four groups, which is found in P and in *Machsor Vitry* (Hurwitz, 307) at Exod 15:3, occurs in *Mek. RI* Exod 14:13 (1,214–15); *j. Ta'an.* 2, 65d; *LAB* 10, 3; *Sefer Ha-Yashar* 81 (243). See further Speier, 1950, 58–61; Heinemann, 1974A, 92–93; Towner, 1973, 113–17. The haggadah seems to be based on Judg 5:15-16 or Ps 68.

[21]*Mek. RI* Exod 14:15 (1,216); *b. Sotah* 37a. See above, v. 10 (Ps.-J.) and n. 17 to that verse.

[22]*Exod. R.* 21,1.

[23]*Mek. RI* Exod 14:20 (1,227).

other side it gave light *over Israel*[24] *all* the night. And through the whole night *one camp* did not approach *against* the other[25] *to engage in battle.* 21. And Moses inclined his hand over the sea, *holding the great and glorious rod that had been created in the beginning, and on which the great and glorious Name was clearly inscribed, as well as the ten signs with which he had smitten the Egyptians,*[26] *the three fathers of the world, the six matriarchs, and the twelve tribes of Jacob.*[27] And immediately the Lord drove back the sea with a strong east wind all the night, and he turned the sea into dry land. And the waters were split *into twelve divisions, corresponding to the twelve tribes of Jacob.*[28] 22. The children of Israel went into the midst of the sea on dry ground, and the water *became solid like* walls,[29] *three hundred mils* high,[30] to their right and to their left. 23. The Egyptians pursued, and went in after them into the sea, all Pharaoh's horses, his chariots and his horsemen. 24. At the morning watch, *at the time when the hosts from on high come to praise,*[31] the Lord looked *with anger*[32] on the camps of the Egyptians from[33] the pillar of fire *to throw burning coals on them,* and from[33] *the pillar of* cloud *to throw hail on them,*[34] and he threw the camp of the Egyptians into confusion. 25. He

Notes, Chapter 14

[24]Onq.: "and the cloud became darkness for the Egyptians but illumination for the Israelites." *Mek. RI* Exod 14:20 (1,226). See above 13:21 (Ps.-J.) and n. 21 to that verse. Note that at the beginning of our present verse Ps.-J. inverts the order of Egypt-Israel.

[25]*Mek. RI* Exod 14:20 (1,227).

[26]See above, 2:21 (Ps.-J.), with nn. 27-28 to that verse, and 4:20 (Ps.-J.), with n. 20 to that verse.

[27]We know of no source for this addition ("the three fathers . . ."); cf. Schmerler, 1933, 81.

[28]*PRE* 42 (330): "the waters were made into twelve valleys, corresponding to the twelve tribes . . ." See also *Mek. RI* Exod 14:16 (1,223); Lauterbach's edition says that the sea was divided into "two parts." Other editions read "twelve parts"; cf., e.g., the edition of M. Friedmann (Vienna, 1870), reprinted in Israel, 1968, p. 30a); *ARN* A 33 (134); *Deut. R.* 11,10; *Sefer Ha-Yashar* 81 (244). See Deut 1:1 (Ps.-J., Nf); CTg PP Exod 14:29-31 [Klein, 1986, 1, 230–231]). This tradition is illustrated in Kraeling, 1956, 84–85 and 352. In his Homily V on Exodus, Origen writes: "I have heard a tradition from the ancients that in that parting of the sea individual divisions of the waters were made for each individual tribe of the sons of Israel and a special way was opened in the sea for each tribe . . ." See *Origen, Homilies on Genesis and Exodus.* (*The Fathers of the Church. A New Translation,* vol. 71. Translated by R.E. Heine [Washington, D.C.: Catholic University of America Press, 1982]) 282–83. Cf. also Eusebius, *In Psalm.* 77:13 (*PG* 23, 913); Theodoret, *Quaest. 25 in Exod.* (*PG* 80, 256B,C).

[29]*Mek. RI* Exod 14:16 (1,224): "The sea congealed on both sides . . ."; *PRE* 42 (330): "(the waters) were made into walls of water. . . ."

[30]Reading *rmyn* with Lond.: ed. pr.: *dmym.* We know of no source for the view that the walls of water were three hundred *mils* high; cf. Schmerler, 1933, 82.

[31]Ps.-J. may here be alluding to the tradition about the angels who wanted to chant their hymns when the Egyptians were being drowned in the sea, which is recorded in *b. Meg.* 10b. On Ps.-J.'s tendency to make allusions to well-known traditions, see Maher, 1992, 6. For other references in Ps.-J. to the praise of the angels, cf. Ps.-J. Gen 27:1 and n. 2 to that verse (Maher, 1992, 94).

[32]HT: *wyšqp,* "and (the Lord) looked down." *Tanḥ. A, Ki Tissa* 14 (311): "Wherever the word *šqp* is used, the reference is to trouble (or grief; *ṣ'r*)." The *Tanḥuma* includes our present verse (14:24) in its list of examples.

[33]Lit.: "in."

[34]*Mek. RI* Exod 14:27 (1,245): "The ministering angels then began hurling at them arrows, great hailstones, fire and brimstone . . ."

sawed the wheels of the armed chariots *of Pharaoh* so that *they* drove *them* with difficulty, *and they were gradually leaving (them) behind.* The Egyptians said *one to another*, "Let us flee before *the people of the children of* Israel,[35] because *it is the Memra of* the Lord *who* engages in battle for them against the Egyptians." 26. Then the Lord said to Moses, "Incline your hand over the sea, and let the waters come back over the Egyptians, over their chariots and horsemen." 27. So Moses inclined his hand over the sea, and at morning time the sea returned to its normal state. The Egyptians were fleeing in front of its *waves*, and the Lord *strengthened* the Egyptians in the middle of the sea *so that they would not die in the middle of it but would receive the (full) punishment that was sent to them.*[36] 28. The *waves of the sea* returned and covered the chariots, the horsemen, and all the camp of Pharaoh that had gone in after them into the sea; not even one of them remained. 29. But the children of Israel went through the sea on dry ground, and the waters were *like* walls for them on their right and on their left. 30. On that day the Lord *redeemed*[37] *and* saved Israel from the hands of the Egyptians, and Israel saw the Egyptians dying *but not (yet) dead*,[38] *thrown*[39] upon the seashore. 31. And when Israel saw *the strength*[40] of the mighty hand *with* which the Lord had performed *miracles* against Egypt, the people feared *from before* the Lord, and they believed *in the name of the Memra of* the Lord, and in *the prophecy of*[41] his servant Moses.

CHAPTER 15

1. *Behold*, then Moses and the children of Israel sang this song *of praise*[1] *before* the Lord and said thus: *"Let us give thanks and praise before* the Lord, *the eminent one* who is exalted *above the exalted*[2] *and elevated above the elevated. Through his*

Notes, Chapter 14

[35] *Ed. pr.*: "of the house of Israel."

[36] *Mek. RI* Exod 14:27 (1,246).

[37] This verb (*prq*) is also added by Nf, so that Ps.-J. and Nf give a double translation of HT *wywš'*, "and (the Lord) saved." Onq. and P translate the Hebrew verb by *prq*.

[38] *Mek. RI* Exod 14:30 (1,250). Ps.-J.'s phrase (*mytyn wl' mytyn*) is the Aramaic rendering of the idiom used in the *Mekilta.*

[39] Cf. *b. Pesah.* 118b: "The Holy One . . . ordered . . . 'spew them forth' on dry land."

[40] = Onq.

[41] = Onq. See Grossfeld, 1988B, 40, n. 13.

Notes, Chapter 15

[1] Lit.: "the praise of this song" (*šbḥ šyrt' ḥd'*); = P, V, N, *Machsor Vitry* (Hurwitz, 307).

[2] *Mek. RI* Exod 15:1 (2,13); *b. Ḥag.* 13b.

Memra he takes revenge on anyone who exalts himself before him. Because the wicked Pharaoh plotted before the Lord, was elevated in his heart, and pursued the people of the children of Israel, horses and riders he cast (them) *and drowned them in the Sea of Reeds.*[3] 2. Our[4] strength and *the (object of) our many*[5] *praises, feared by all the ages,* the Lord. *He declared through his Memra and he was for me a redeeming God." From their mother's breasts*[6] *the sucklings*[7] *would indicate with their fingers to their fathers and would say:* "This *is our* God *who had us suck honey from the rock*[8] *and oil from the flint stone at the time when our mothers went out into the open country and gave birth to us and abandoned us there. He would send an angel who would bathe us and swaddle us. And now let us praise him,* the God of *our* fathers, *and let us* extol him." 3. *The children of Israel said,* "The Lord is a *hero who wages our* wars *in every generation.*[9] *He makes his strength known to his people,*[10] the house of Israel. The Lord is his name; *like his name is his strength. May his name be blessed forever and ever!* 4. The chariots of Pharaoh and his armies he has thrown into the sea. *The best of his brave young men,*[11] *he cast (them) and* drowned *them* in the Sea of Reeds. 5. The deeps covered them over. They went down *and sank* in the depths *of the sea; they were* like stones. 6. Your right hand, O Lord, *how* praiseworthy *it is* in (its) strength! Your right hand, O Lord, exterminates the enemies *of your people who rise up against them to harm them.*[12] 7. In your great exaltation[13] you demolish *the walls of the enemies of your people.*[14] You *let loose against them* your *mighty* anger, *you destroy them as burning fire takes control* in straw.[15] 8. *With a word from before you* the waters *were formed into* many heaps; they stood up *firmly* like *water-skins*[16] *of* flowing *water.* The deeps became solid over them in *the depths*[17] of the *Great* Sea. 9. *For*[18] *the wicked Pharaoh,* the hater[18]

Notes, Chapter 15

[3]Cf. *Mek. RI* Exod 15:1 (2,13). See also *Tanḥ. B, Be-Shallah* 14 (2,61); *Exod. R.* 23,13.

[4]*Machsor Vitry* (Hurwitz, 307); Targumic Tosefta to Exod 15:2 (Klein, 1975, 62).

[5]Reading *rb* of Lond. as *rwb* (= Nf, P, V, N, and Targumic Tosefta [see preceding note]). *Ed. pr.* reads *rab,* "Lord of."

[6]For the haggadic tradition that follows, see *b. Sotah* 11b; *Exod. R.* 1,12; 23,8; *PRE* 42, (332); Tg. Ezek 16:4. See further Grelot, 1961, 49–60.

[7]Read *ynqy'* with V, N. Lond. and *ed. pr.*: *'qy'*; Rieder is wrong in claiming that Lond. reads *ynqy'.*

[8]See Deut 32:13.

[9]*Mek. RI* Exod 15:3 (2,31).

[10]Compare Ps 28:8.

[11]Lit.: "the best of the young men of his warriors"; = P.

[12]Compare *Mek. RI* Exod 15:6 (2,42): "It does not say 'hast dashed,' but 'wilt dash,' that is, in the future. . . ."

[13]Onq.: "In your great power." See Grossfeld, 1988B, 42, n. 12.

[14]Onq.: "You shattered those who rose up against your people." See Grossfeld, 1988B, 42, n. 14. For Ps.-J.'s idiom ("demolish the walls of the enemy"), see also Ps.-J., Nf (cf. also Onq.) Gen 49:6.

[15]See *Mek. RI* Exod 15:7 (2,48).

[16]Lit.: "bound together (*ṣryryn*) like waterskins." Cf. *Mek. RI* Exod 15:8 (2,51): "Just as a skin bottle, when it is tied up (*ṣrwr*), stands still. . . ." The midrashic interpretation is based on a play on HT *nd (nêd),* "heap," and *nwd,* "water-skin." See Tg. Pss 33:7; 78:13; cf. also Tg. Josh 3:13. See Schmerler, 1933, 88.

[17]*pylgws*; = Gr. *pelagos.*

[18]= Onq.

and enemy, said, 'I will pursue *the people of the children of Israel, and we*[19] *will* come upon *them (when they are) camping on the seashore, and we will draw up battle lines against them, and we will perform a great and mighty slaughtering among them; we will plunder great spoils from them, and we will take many captives from them.* I will divide *their* spoils *among my people who conduct my war. And when* my soul has had its fill of *the blood of their slain, after that* I will draw my sword, and *I* will wipe them out *with* my *right* hand.' 10. You blew with a wind *from before you,*[20] *O Lord; the waves of* the sea covered them over; *they went down and* they sank like lead <in>[21] the majestic waters. 11. Who is like you among the gods *on high,* O Lord? Who is like you,[22] glorious in holiness, revered through praises, working miracles *and wonders for his people the house of Israel?*" 12. *The sea*[23] and *the earth were arguing together, one with the other. The sea said to the earth, "Receive your children!" And the earth said to the sea, "Receive your slain!" The sea did not want to sink them, and the earth did not want to swallow them. The earth was afraid to receive them, lest they would be demanded of her on the day of great judgment in the world to come, just as the blood of Abel will be demanded of her. Immediately, O Lord,* you inclined your right hand *over the earth with an oath that they would not be demanded of her in the world to come.* The earth then *opened its mouth and* swallowed them. 13. "In your steadfast love you led this people whom you redeemed. You *gave them possession*[24] *of the mountain of your Sanctuary,*[25] the dwelling place of your holy *Shekinah.* 14. The nations heard, they were agitated.[26] Fear seized *them, all the pillars*[27] of the inhabitants of *the land of* the Philistines. 15. *Behold,* then the chiefs of the Edomites were dismayed; trembling seized the mighty ones of the Moabites. All *the pillars*[27] *of* the inhabitants of *the land of* the

Notes, Chapter 15

[19]The verbs in the plural in this verse, "we will come upon," "we will draw up," etc., may be examples of the use of the first person plural form with the meaning of the first person singular. Cf. Le Déaut, 1978, 95, n. 13. *Mek. RI* Exod 15:9 (2,55) states clearly that "the enemy" mentioned in HT is Pharaoh in person.

[20]Onq.: *"You spoke through your Memra."*

[21]Omitted in Lond. and *ed. pr.*

[22]Onq.: "there is no one besides you; you are God, O Lord, there is no God but you." By turning the question of HT— which might be taken to presuppose the existence of other gods—Onq. avoids any possible misunderstanding. See also Deut 3:24b, where Onq. avoids a similar question. See Klein, 1976, 534. Compare *Mek. RI* Exod 15:11 (2,61): "Who is like unto thee among those who serve before thee in heaven. . . ?"

[23]*Mek. RI* Exod 15:12 (2,67–68); *Lam. R.* 1,9.37; *PRE* 42 (334–35); *Midrash Psalms* 22:17 (Braude, 1958-59, 1, 312; cf. *b. Pesah.* 118b. The midrash explains the connection between HT "thou didst stretch out thy right hand," which is usually understood by the Targums to refer to an oath; see above Ps.-J. 6:8 and n. 6 to that verse—and "the earth swallowed them." It also explains why the Egyptians were not swallowed up by the sea but were cast up on the seashore (cf. Exod 14:30). See further Rodríguez Carmona, 1978, 114–26.

[24]HT *nhlt,* "thou hast guided," seems to anticipate events. Ancient translators tried to avoid the difficulty in different ways. Onq. reads: "you *led it forth*"; LXX: "you have called them." Ps.-J. translates as if HT read *nhlt,* "you have given as a possession." This is also the reading in the Samaritan Pentateuch. See Geiger, 1928, 465.

[25]*Mek. RI* Exod 15:13 (2,70); cf. *Sifra, Be Hukkotai* 5,2 (ed. Weiss, 111d).

[26]Or: "became angry." Onq.: "trembled." Ps.-J. reads *ytrgzwn;* better *'trgzwn* (cf. Nf, P).

[27]See Ps.-J. Gen 46:28, with n. 28 to that verse (Maher, 1992, 151).

Canaanites, *their heart* melted *within them*. 16. *Cause* a *deadly* terror[28] and dread *to fall* upon them. Through the might of your *strong* arm may they become as silent as stones, until your people, O Lord, cross *the torrents of the Arnon*,[29] until this people whom you acquired crosses *the ford of the Jabbok*. 17. You will bring them in and plant them on the mountain of your *Sanctuary*.[30] You have established, O Lord, *a place that corresponds to the throne of your Glory*,[31] *made ready opposite the dwelling place*[32] *of your holy Shekinah. Your* Sanctuary, *O Lord*, your own *two*[33] hands completed it." 18. *When the people, the house of*[34] *Israel saw the miracles and wonders which the Holy One, may his name be praised, performed for them at the Sea of Reeds, and the strength of his hand between*[35] *the waves, they spoke up and said one to another: "Come, let us place a crown of greatness on the head of our Redeemer, who makes (things) pass away but does not pass away, who causes (things) to change but does not change; for the crown of kingship is his, and he is king of kings in this world, and his is the kingship for the world to come;*[36] *it is his, and let it be* (so) *for ever and ever!"* 19. For the horses of Pharaoh, with his chariots and horsemen, went into the sea; and the Lord turned the waters of the sea back on them; but the children of Israel went on dry ground in the midst of the sea. *There sweet springs sprang up,*[37] *as well as fruit trees, green plants, and choice fruit*[38] *at the bottom of the sea.* 20. Then Miriam the prophetess, Aaron's sister, took the timbrel in her hand; and all the women went out after her; *they were dancing* to the sound of timbrels and *playing the hingas.*[39] 21. And Miriam *sang* to them, "*Let us give thanks and praise before* the Lord *because might and eminence are his; he is exalted above the exalted, and he is elevated above the high. Because the wicked Pharaoh plotted and pursued the people of the children of Israel, his* horses and his *chariots,* he threw (them) *and sank them* in the *Sea of Reeds.*" 22. Then Moses caused Israel

Notes, Chapter 15

[28]*'ymt' dmwt'*; V,N: *'ymtyh dmwt'*, which Klein (1980, 2, 130) translates as "the dread of death." See the Hebrew idiom *'ymwt mwt*, "the terrors of death," in Ps 55:5(4).

[29]*Mek. RI* Exod 15:16 (2,75). Cf. Deut 2:24. In our present verse HT twice uses the verb "cross" without a direct object. The Targums (Ps.-J., Nf, P, V, N, CTg W, Onq.) specify the rivers which the Israelites would cross.

[30]*Mek. RI* Exod 15:17 (2,77). See also above, v. 13 (Ps.-J.), and n. 25 to that verse; Deut 33:19 (Onq., Nf, V, N, L, Ps.-J.).

[31]*Mek. RI* Exod 15:17 (2,78). See Ps.-J. Gen 28:17 and n. 27 to that verse (Maher, 1992, 100).

[32]Lit.: "the house."

[33]*Mek. RI* Exod 15:17 (2,79); *ARN* A 1 (16). Notice the gross anthropomorphism in the reference to God's two hands (Nf, Frg. Tgs., Ps.-J.).

[34]Lond.: "the children of."

[35]Reading *byny* rather than *bny* of Lond. and *ed. pr.*

[36]Ps.-J. takes the seemingly redundant idiom "for ever and ever" of HT to refer to this world and to the world to come. There is no rabbinic parallel to the long addition which Ps.-J. (see also Nf, V, N) makes to this verse. Shinan (2, 1979, 333–34) draws attention to the similarity between this addition and the final part of the blessing *Emeth we-Emunah*, which is recited in conjunction with the evening *Shema* and which is explicitly linked with Exod 15:11.

[37]*Mek. RI* Exod 15:8 (2,51); *Tanh. A, Be-Shallah* 10 (222); *Tanh. B, Be-Shallah* 18 (2,64).

[38]*Exod. R.* 21,10: "they would . . . pluck an apple or a pomegranate from the sea."

[39]These musical instruments (*hyngyy'*), which cannot be identified (cf. Jastrow, 458; Levy, 1, 269), are referred to again in Ps.-J. Exod 32:19.

to set out from the Sea of Reeds, and they went to the wilderness of *Haluzah.*[40] They traveled three days in the wilderness, *neglecting the commandments,*[41] and they found no water. 23. They came to Marah, but they could not drink the water of Marah, because it was bitter. That is why it was named Marah. 24. And the people murmured against Moses, saying, "What shall we drink?" 25. So *he prayed before* the Lord, and the Lord showed him a *bitter oleander*[42] tree. *He wrote the great and glorious Name on it*[43] and threw (it) into the water, and the water became sweet. There *the Memra of the Lord* enjoined on him the decree *of the sabbath, the statute to honor (one's) father and mother,* the judgments *for wounds and blows, the penalties to be imposed on the guilty,*[44] and there he tested him *with the tenth temptation.*[45] 26. And he said, "If you listen carefully to *the Memra of* the Lord your God, doing what is fitting *before* him, obeying his commandments and observing all his statutes, I will not inflict on you any of the *evil* diseases that I inflicted on the Egyptians. *But if you transgress the words of the Law, they shall be sent upon you. If you repent, I will remove them from you,*[46] for I *am* the Lord, your healer." 27. And they came to Elim, and *in Elim* there were twelve springs of water, *a well for each tribe,* and seventy palm trees, *corresponding to the seventy elders of Israel.*[47] And they encamped there beside the water.

CHAPTER 16

1. They[1] set out from Elim, and the whole congregation of Israel[2] came to the wilderness of Sin, which is between Elim and Sinai, on the fifteenth day of the

Notes, Chapter 15

[40]Cf. Ps.-J. Gen 16:7 and n. 10 to that verse (Maher, 1992, 63).

[41]*Mek. RI* Exod 15:22 (2,89–90); 15:27 (2,98); *b. B. Qam.* 82a; *Tanh. A, Be-Shallah* 19 (233). Since the Torah was compared with water (see, e.g., the text from *Mek. RI* Exod 15:22 just mentioned), Ps.-J. associates lack of water with neglect of Torah, not only in our present text but also in Exod 17:1; Num 21:20; 33:14.

[42]*Mek. RI* Exod 15:25 (2,92). Ps.-J. employs the word *'rdpny.* The *Mekilta* text uses the corresponding Hebrew word, which Lauterbach translates as "ivy." See also *Tanh. A, Be-Shallah* 24 (236); *Tanh. B, Be-Shallah* 18 (2,65); *LAB* 11,15.

[43]Cf. Nfmg 2. Compare Ps.-J. Exod 2:21, and see n. 28 to that verse. We know of no source for the statement in Ps.-J. and Nfmg 2 to the effect that Moses wrote the Holy Name on the tree at Marah.

[44]*Mek. RI* Exod 15:25 (2,94); *b. Shabb.* 56b.

[45]*PRE* 44 (345).

[46]*Mek. RI* Exod 15:26 (2,96); *b. Sanh.* 101a. On the importance of observing the Law, see Ps.-J. Gen 3:24 and n. 60 to that verse (Maher, 1992, 31).

[47]*Mek. RI* Exod 15:27 (2,98). See also Num 33:9 and the Targums (Ps.-J., Nf, Nfmg, V, N) of that verse.

Notes, Chapter 16

[1]For a study of the Targums of this chapter, see Malina, 1968, 42–63.

[2]HT: "the whole congregation of the children of Israel."

month *of Iyar, that is,* the second *month*[3] after they had gone out from the land of Egypt. 2. *On that day the dough which they had brought out from Egypt came to an end,*[4] and all the children of Israel murmured against Moses and Aaron in the wilderness. 3. And the children of Israel said to them, "*Would that* we had died by *the Memra of* the Lord in the land of Egypt when we sat by the fleshpots, *when* we were eating bread *and* had our fill. For you have brought us out into this wilderness to kill all this assembly with hunger." 4. And the Lord said to Moses, "Behold, I will *bring down*[5] for you bread from heaven, *which has been reserved for you from the beginning.*[6] And the people will go out and gather a day's portion every day, in order to test them, (to see) whether they *observe the precepts of* my Law or not. 5. But on the sixth day they shall prepare what they brought in *before them to eat on the sabbath day and they shall prepare an erub*[7] *in the houses, and they shall form a shittuf*[8] *in their courtyards*[9] *so that they may take (an object) from one to another.* And *they shall take* twice the amount they gather each day." 6. So Moses and Aaron said to all the children of Israel, "By evening you shall know that the Lord brought you out *redeemed* from the land of Egypt; 7. and in the morning the Glory of *the Shekinah of* the Lord *will be revealed to you,* when your murmurings *before* the Lord have been heard *before him.* As for us, what are we that you should murmur against us?" 8. And Moses said, "*By this you shall know that* the murmuring you are uttering against him has been heard *before* the Lord, when the Lord *prepares* flesh for you to eat in the evening, and bread to the full in the morning. As for us, *of* what *importance* are we? Your murmuring is not against us but against *the Memra of* the Lord." 9. Moses said to Aaron, "Say to the whole congregation of the children of Israel: 'Draw near before the Lord, because your murmurings *have been heard before him.*'" 10. As Aaron spoke to the whole congregation of the children of Israel, they turned towards the wilderness, and behold, the Glory of *the Shekinah of* the Lord appeared in the cloud *of glory.*[10] 11. And the Lord spoke to

Notes, Chapter 16

[3]*Mek. RI* Exod 16:1 (2,99); *b. Shabb.* 87b. If Nisan is the first month (see above Ps.-J. 12:1 and n. 1 to that verse), *Iyar* is the second. Ps.-J. follows a different reckoning in Gen 7:11 (see n. 12 to that verse; Maher, 1992, 41) and 8:4, 5, 13, 14 (see nn. 2, 4, 13 and 14 to these verses; Maher, 1992, 42–43).

[4]*Mek. RI* Exod 16:1 (2,99–100). *Exod. R.* 3,4 and 25, 4; Josephus, *Ant.* III.i.3. Ps.-J.'s "pre-translation haggadah" takes up a theme which Ps.-J. had recorded in 12:39; see above, n. 67 to that verse. On Ps.-J.'s tendency to repeat traditions, see Maher, 1992, 6.

[5]= Onq. HT: "I will rain." See Malina, 1968, 53–54.

[6]See also below, v. 15. The manna was among the ten things which, according to rabbinic tradition, were created on the eve of the first sabbath; cf. Ps.-J. Num 22:28. See Ps.-J. Gen 2:2 and n. 4 to that verse (Maher, 1992, 21).

[7]The reference is to an *erub ḥaṣeroth,* "an *erub* of the courts." Where houses were built around a court, it was forbidden to carry anything from one house to another, or from a house into the yard, on the sabbath, unless one prepared an *erub* beforehand. This was done when the dwellers of the houses contributed their share to a quantity of food which was then placed in one of the houses. The dwellers of the houses were then considered to form one community or association. Cf. *b. Erub.* 71a–71b. See further *EJ* 6 (Jerusalem, 1972), 849–50.

[8]*Shittuf,* "partnership, association," was the name given to the association formed by those who prepared an *erub ḥaṣeroth;* see preceding note.

[9]*Mek. RI* Exod 16:5 (2,104).

[10]See Ps.-J. Gen 2:6 and n. 11 to that verse (Maher, 1992, 22).

Moses, saying: 12. "The murmuring of the children of Israel *has been heard before me.*[11] Speak to them, saying, 'At twilight you shall eat flesh, and in the morning you shall *eat* bread, and you shall know that I *am* the Lord your God.'" 13. And in the evening *pheasants*[12] came up and covered the camp; and in the morning there was *a fall*[13] *of congealed*[14] dew, *prepared like tables,*[15] round about the camp. 14. *The clouds* went up *and brought down the manna on the fall*[13] *of* dew.[16] And *it was* a fine layer[17] on the surface of the wilderness, as fine as hoarfrost on[18] the ground. 15. When the children of Israel saw (it), *they were amazed,* and they said to one another, "What is it?"[19] For they did not know what it was. And Moses said to them, "It is the bread *that was reserved for you from the beginning in the heavens on high;*[20] *and now* the Lord is giving it to you to eat. 16. This is what the Lord has commanded: 'Let each one gather as much of it as he can eat, an omer a head, according to the number of persons. Each one shall take according to *the total of the men* of his tent.'" 17. The children of Israel did so, and they gathered *the manna,* some much, some little. 18. They measured by the omer, <and>[21] there was nothing left *of the measure of* him who *gathered* much, and there was nothing lacking *from the measure of* him who *gathered* little; each gathered according to what he could eat. 19. And Moses said to them, "Let no one leave any of it over until morning." 20. But they did not listen to Moses; *Dathan and Abiram, sinful* men,[22] left some of it until morning. It was *crawling*[23] with worms, and it became foul. And Moses was angry with them. 21. So they gathered it *from* morning *time until the fourth hour of the day,*[24] each according to what he could eat. *But from the fourth hour onwards* the sun grew hot *over it* and it would melt, *becoming wells of water flowing to the Great Sea. And clean beasts and animals came and drank from*

Notes, Chapter 16

[11]*Ed. pr.*: "before him"; = Nfmg.

[12]*pysyywnyn* = Nfmg; = Gr.: *phasianos*. Cf. *b. Yoma* 75b: "There are four kinds of quails: thrush, partridge, pheasant (*psywny*), and quail proper."

[13]= Onq. *Mek. RI* Exod 16:14 (2,111). See also Grossfeld, 1988B, 47, n. 7.

[14]Reading *mtqrs'* rather than *mtqds'* of Lond. and *ed. pr.* See Ps.-J. Num 11:7.

[15]*Mek. RI* Exod 16:14 (2,111); *Midrash Psalms* 78:4 (2,24).

[16]According to *Sifre Num.* 89 (ed. Horovitz, 90), the hoarfrost formed a kind of tray on which the manna fell.

[17]Lit.: "a fine lined (substance)."

[18]= *Ed. pr.,* HT, Nf, Onq.; Lond.: "which is on."

[19]Ps.-J. (*m'n hw'*) preserves the play on words which occurs in HT (*mn hw'*; RSV: "What is it?"). On the translation of HT *mn hw'* in the Targums, in the LXX, and in Josephus, see Malina, 1968, 55–56.

[20]See above v. 4 (Ps.-J.) and n. 6.

[21]Omitted in Lond. and *ed. pr.*

[22]*Tanh. A, Shemot* 10 (167-68); *Exod. R.* 1,29; 25,10; *Tanna debe Eliyyahu* 18 (Braude-Kapstein, 273–74). Since in our present verse (Exod 16:20) the word *'nšym,* (lit. "men"; RSV: "some"), is used, and in Num 16:25-26 the term *'nšym rš'ym* is applied to Dathan and Abiram, the midrash concludes that the *'nšym* of Exod 16:20 are also Dathan and Abiram. See above, Exod 2:13 (Ps.-J.) and n. 20 to that verse.

[23]= Onq.

[24]*Mek. RI* Exod 16:21 (2,117); *j. Ber.* 4, 7b; *b. Ber.* 27a.

it, and the children of Israel[25] *were hunting them and eating them.*[26] 22. On the sixth day they gathered double the amount of food, two omers for each *man.* And all the chieftains of the congregation came and told Moses. 23. And *Moses* said to them, "*You have done* what the Lord said. Tomorrow is a day of rest, a holy sabbath *before* the Lord. Bake *today* what *you would need to* bake tomorrow, and cook *today* what *you would need to* cook tomorrow. And whatever is left over *from what you eat today,* put it aside, *and let it be kept* until morning." 24. So they put it aside until morning as Moses had commanded; it did not become foul, and there were no maggots in it. 25. And Moses said: "Eat it today, for today is a sabbath *before* the Lord. You will not find it today in the field. 26. Six days you shall gather it; but on the seventh day, *which is* the sabbath, *the manna* will not *come down.*" 27. But on the seventh day some *wicked persons*[27] of the people went out to gather *manna,* but they did not find (any). 28. And the Lord said to Moses, "How long will you refuse to keep my commandments and my Law? 29. See that the Lord has given you the sabbath. Therefore he gives you bread for two days on the sixth day. Let everyone remain *in his place. Do not move anything more than four cubits from domain to domain,* and let no one leave his place *to walk more than two thousand cubits*[28] on the seventh day." 30. So the people rested on the seventh day. 31. The house of Israel called its name manna. It was like coriander seed, white, and its taste was like cakes made with honey. 32. And Moses said, "This is what the Lord has commanded: '*Put aside* a full omer of it to keep (it) throughout your generations, so that *the rebellious generations*[29] may see the bread that I gave you to eat in the wilderness when I brought you out of the land of Egypt.'" 33. And Moses said to Aaron, "Take an *earthen*[30] flask, and put a full omer of manna in it, and put it aside before the Lord to keep it throughout your generations." 34. As the Lord had commanded Moses, Aaron put it aside before the Testimony to keep (it). 35. The children of Israel ate the manna for forty years, *during the life of Moses,* until they came to inhabited land. They ate the manna *for forty days after his death*[31] until *they crossed the Jordan and* came to the border of the land of Canaan. 36. Now the omer is a tenth of *three seahs.*[32]

Notes, Chapter 16

[25]Schmerler (101–102), and Rieder in his edition of Ps.-J., suggest that we should follow the *Mekilta* and the *Tanḥuma* (see next note) and read "children of the nations."

[26]*Mek. RI* Exod 16:21 (2,117); *Tanḥ. B, Be-Shallah* 21 (2,66).

[27]= Nfmg. *Mek. RI* Exod 16:27 (2,120): "those of little faith." *Mek. RI* Exod 16:20 (2,116) had used the same idiom. Compare Ps.-J.'s version of 16:20, where the term "sinful" is used.

[28]*Mek. RI* Exod 16:29 (2,122); *Mek. RSbY* Exod 16:29 (114); *b. Erub.* 48a; 51a; *Jub.* 2,30; 50,8.

[29]See *Mek. RI* Exod 16:33 (2,125–26), which says that the prophet Jeremiah showed the bottle containing the manna to his contemporaries who did not busy themselves with the Torah.

[30]*Mek. RI* Exod 16:33 (2,125).

[31]*Mek. RI* Exod 16:35 (2,126); *t. Sotah* 11,2 (Zuckermandel, 314); *b. Qidd.* 38a. Ps.-J. Deut 34:8 records a different tradition. See further Malina, 1968, 62.

[32]= Onq. HT: "an ephah." *b. Men.* 77a explains that an ephah is three *seahs.*

CHAPTER 17

1. All the congregation of the children of Israel set out by stages from the wilderness of Sin according to *the word of* the Lord. They encamped at Rephidim, *a place where their hands neglected the commandments of the Law, so that their wells dried up,* [1] and there was no water for the people to drink. 2. And the *wicked ones of* the people quarreled with Moses and said, "Give us water to drink." Moses said to them, "Why do you quarrel with me? And why do you test *before* the Lord?" 3. But the people thirsted there for water; and the people murmured against Moses and said, "Why did you bring us up from Egypt to kill us and our children and livestock with thirst?" 4. So Moses *prayed* [2] *before* the Lord, saying, "What shall I do with this people? In a *little* while they will be stoning me!" 5. Then the Lord said to Moses, "Pass before the people, taking with you some of the elders of Israel; and take in your hand the rod with which you struck the river, and go, *because of their murmuring.* [3] 6. Behold, I will be standing there before you, *at the place where you will see the track of a foot* [4] on the rock [5] at Horeb. Strike *it with the rock* [6] *of your rod*, and *drinking* water will come out of it, and the people will drink." And Moses did so *before* the elders of Israel. 7. And he called the name of *that* place "Testing" and "Quarreling," because the children of Israel quarreled *with Moses*, and because they tested *before* the Lord, saying, "Is *the Glory of the Shekinah of the Lord in truth dwelling* among us or not?" 8. Amalek came *from the land of the South. That night he leapt one thousand six hundred mils,* [7] *and because of the enmity that existed between Esau and Jacob* [8] *he came* and waged war with Israel at Rephidim. *And he took and slew men of the house of Dan, because the cloud was not receiving them on account of the idolatry they practiced.* [9] 9. Moses said to Joshua, "Pick out for us men *(who are) strong and mighty (in the observance) of the commandments* [10]

Notes, Chapter 17

[1] *Mek. RI* Exod 17:1 (2,129); 17:8 (2,135); *b. Sanh.* 106a; *Bek.* 5b; *Tanḥ. A, Be-Shallah* 25 (238). The Midrash read the place-name Rephidim as "they slackened (their) hands (*rpw ydym*)." The texts referred to say that when the Israelites slackened their hands from the Torah, i.e., neglected the Torah, the enemy (Amalek) came upon them. They do not mention the drying up of the wells as does Ps.-J. See above 15:22 (Ps.-J.) and n. 41 to that verse.

[2] = Onq. See above 14:10 (Ps.-J.) and n. 17 to that verse.

[3] *Mek. RI* Exod 17:5 (2,131); *Tanḥ. A, Be-Shallah* 21 (234).

[4] *Mek. RI* Exod 17:6 (2,133); *Tanḥ. A, Be-Shallah* 22 (235). The midrash is playing on the Hebrew word ṣwr, which means both "rock" and "draw, design."

[5] "On the rock" is omitted in *ed. pr.*

[6] According to Ps.-J. Exod 4:20, the rod was made of sapphire. Cf. *Mek. RI* Exod 17:6 (2,133).

[7] *Mek. RI* Exod 17:8 (2,137); *Tanḥ. A, Be-Shallah* 25 (237); *PRK* 3,8.

[8] *PRE* 44 (346); *PRK* 3,11; Tg. Song of Songs 2:15.

[9] Lit.: "that was in their hands" (Lond.); *ed. pr.*: "that was among them." The Danites were well known as idolators; see *Tanḥ. A, Ki Teze* 10 (666); *b. Sanh.* 103b; *PRK* 3,12. Tg. Song of Songs 2:15; Ps.-J. Num 11:1; 22:41; Deut 25:18. See further Le Déaut, 1979, 142, n. 7.

[10] *Mekilta, Tanḥuma, Exod. R,* (see next note): "heroes . . . fearers of sin." LXX, Pesh.: "mighty men." Ps.-J., like the midrashim, interprets HT "choose for us men" (RSV) in spiritual rather than physical terms.

and victorious in battle. Go out *from beneath the clouds of glory*[11] and draw up *battle lines* against *the camps of* Amalek. Tomorrow I will stand, *fasting*[12] *(and) relying on the merits of the patriarchs,* the heads of *the people, and on the merits of the matriarchs, who are comparable to* the hills,[13] with the rod, *by which miracles were performed from before the Lord,*[14] in my hand." 10. Joshua did as Moses told him and waged war with Amalek, while Moses *and* Aaron and Hur went up to the top of the hill. 11. Whenever Moses held up his hands *in prayer,*[15] *those of the house of* Israel prevailed; but whenever he lowered his hands *and ceased praying, those of the house of* Amalek prevailed. 12. But Moses' hands grew heavy, *because he delayed the battle until the following day*[16] *and was not zealous on that day for the liberation of Israel. So he was not able to hold them up in prayer. But because he wished to afflict himself,*[17] they took a stone and put it under him and he sat on it. Aaron and Hur, one on each side, supported his hands; so his hands remained *stretched out in faith, in prayer, and (in) fasting*[18] until the setting of the sun. 13. And Joshua *smashed* Amalek, *for he cut off the heads of the heroes*[19] *of* his people according to *the word of the Lord,*[20] *slaying (them)* by the sword. 14. Then the Lord said to Moses: "Write this as a memorial in the Book *of the Ancients of Old*[21] and declare[22] *these words* in the *hearing* of Joshua, that I will utterly blot out the memory of Amalek from under heaven." 15. And Moses built an altar and named it *"The Memra of* the Lord is my miracle,"[23] *because (Moses said), "the miracle which the Place performed was for my sake."*[24] 16. And he said, "Because *the Memra of the Lord swore by* the throne *of his Glory that he, through his Memra, would wage* war against *those of the house of* Amalek,[25] *he will wipe them out for the three generations,* from the generation *of this world,* from the generation *of the Messiah, and from the generation of the world to come."*[26]

Notes, Chapter 17

[11]*Mek. RI* Exod 17:9 (2,141); *Tanḥ. A, Be-Shallah* 26 (238); *Exod. R.* 26,3; Tg. Song of Songs 2:16.

[12]*Mek. RI* Exod 17:9 (2,142).

[13]*Mek. RI* Exod 17:9 (2,142). *Tanḥ. A, Be-Shallah* 26 (238). HT: "the top of the hill" is taken to refer to the patriarchs ("the top") and the matriarchs ("the hill"). See also Ps.-J. Num 23:9; Deut 33:15; Tg. Song of Songs 2:8.

[14]= Onq. See above, 4:20 (Ps.-J.), where the same formula is used.

[15]*Mek. RI* Exod 17:11 (2,143); *PRE* 44 (347).

[16]*Mek. RI* Exod 17:12 (2,145).

[17]*Mek. RI* Exod 17:12 (2,145); *b. Ta'anit* 11a; *Tanḥ. A, Be-Shallah* 27 (239).

[18]Onq.: "in prayer." Cf. *Mek. RI* Exod 17:12 (2,145); cf. Maneschg, 1981, 236–38.

[19]*Mek. RI* Exod 17:13 (2,146); *Tanḥ. A, Be-Shallah* 28 (239–40).

[20]*Mek. RI* Exod 17:13 (2,147).

[21]This addition probably comes from a faulty reading of *Mek. RI* Exod 17:14 (2,148), which quotes the words of Scripture, "Write this as a memorial in a book," and then goes on to say, "The former sages say, . . ." Cf. Ginsburger's edition of Ps.-J., 130, n. 6.

[22]Lit.: "place, set"; = HT.

[23]Or possibly: "and *the Memra of* the Lord named it, 'This Miracle is Mine.'" Cf. Le Déaut, 1979, 145, and n. 14, ibid.

[24]*Mek. RI* Exod 17:15 (2,159). Ps.-J.'s use of the title "the Place" for God, a usage otherwise unknown in the Targums, is due to the fact that this title is used in the *Mekilta* text just mentioned.

[25]*Mek. RI* Exod 17:16 (2,160); *PRE* 44 (347).

[26]*Mek. RI* Exod 17:16 (2,161). See further Levey, 1974, 14; Rodríguez Carmona, 1978, 37.

CHAPTER 18

1. Jethro, the *ruler*[1] of Midian, Moses' father-in-law, heard all that *the Lord* had done for Moses and for Israel his people, how the Lord had brought Israel out of Egypt. 2. And Jethro, Moses' father-in-law, took Zipporah, Moses' wife, after he had sent her away *from him when he was going to Egypt,*[2] 3. as well as her two sons—one of whom was named Gershom, for he said, "I have been a resident in a foreign land *that was not mine*";[3] 4. and the other was named Eliezer, for *he said,* "The God of my father *was* at my assistance, and he delivered me from the sword of Pharaoh." 5. Jethro, Moses' father-in-law, came with *Moses'*[4] sons and his wife to Moses in the wilderness, where he was encamped *close to* the mountain *on which the Glory of the Lord was revealed to Moses at the beginning.*[5] 6. He said to Moses, "I, your father-in-law Jethro, am coming to you *to become a proselyte.*[6] *And if you do not wish to receive me for my own sake, receive me for the sake of*[7] your wife and her two sons *who are* with her." 7. Moses went out *from beneath the clouds of glory*[8] to meet his father-in-law; he bowed down and kissed him, *and made a proselyte of him.*[9] Each asked about the other's welfare, and they came to the tent *of the academy.*[10] 8. Moses then told his father-in-law all that the Lord had done to Pharaoh and the Egyptians for the sake of Israel, all the hardship that had befallen them on the way, *at the Sea of Reeds, at Marah and at Rephidim, and how Amalek had attacked them,*[11] and (how) the Lord had delivered them. 9. And Jethro rejoiced over all the good that the Lord had done to Israel, *in that he gave them the manna and the well,*[12] *and* in that he delivered them from the hand of the Egyptians. 10. Jethro said, "Blessed be *the name of* the Lord who delivered you from the hand of the Egyptians and from the hand of Pharaoh, and who delivered the people from under the *domination*[13] of the Egyptians. 11. Now I know that the Lord *is* powerful *over* all the gods. For the scheme *which the Egyptians had wickedly devised—to judge Is-*

Notes, Chapter 18

[1] *Mek. RI* Exod 18:1 (2,166). See above, 2:16 (Ps.-J.), and n. 22 to that verse.

[2] *Mek. RI* Exod 18:2 (2,167).

[3] *Mek. RI* Exod 18:3 (2,168). See above 2:22 (Ps.-J.), where the same idiom ("a resident in a foreign land that is not mine") occurs.

[4] *Mek. RI* Exod 18:5 (2,172).

[5] See above, 3:1 (Ps.-J.) and n. 3 to that verse.

[6] *Mek. RI* Exod 18:6 (2,173); *Exod. R.* 27,2.

[7] *Mek. RI* Exod 18:6 (2,172); *Tanḥ. A, Yitro* 6 (245).

[8] Since HT says that Moses "went out" rather than "went," as one would expect, Ps.-J. concludes that Moses went out from beneath the clouds of glory. The same tradition occurs in the late (12th century) work *Midrash Aggadah* (Buber's edition, Vienna, 1894), p. 150.

[9] *b. Sanh.* 94a; *Zeb.* 116a; *Tanḥ. A, Yitro* 7 (245).

[10] Lit.: "the tent of the house of instruction." Cf. *Mek. RI* Exod 18:7 (2,174). On the Targumic interpretation of "tent" as "schoolhouse," see n. 23 to Ps.-J. Gen 9:27 (Maher, 1992, 46).

[11] *Mek. RI* Exod 18:8 (2,174). Ps.-J. is the only Targum to specify the hardships that had befallen Israel on the way. See also v. 8, where Ps.-J. specifies the good which God had done for Israel.

[12] *Mek. RI* Exod 18:9 (2,174).

[13] = Onq.

rael by water—he turned (this) judgment against them *so that they were judged by water.*[14] 12. And Jethro, <Moses' father-in-law>,[15] took burnt offerings and sacrifices *of holy things before the Lord*;[13] and Aaron came with all the elders of Israel to eat bread before *the Lord* with Moses' father-in-law. *And Moses was standing and serving before them.*[16] 13. On the day after *the Day of Expiation*,[17] Moses sat to judge the people, and the people stood *before* Moses from morning until evening. 14. Moses' father-in-law saw all *the trouble he took and* what he did for *his* people, and he said, "What is this that you are doing for the people? Why are you sitting alone *to judge*, with all the people standing *before* you from morning until evening?" 15. Moses said to his father-in-law, "It is because the people come to me to seek *instruction from before the Lord*.[18] 16. When they have a *case for judgment*,[19] *they* come to me, and I judge between a man and his neighbor, and I make known *to them* the statutes of *the Lord* and his Law." 17. And Moses' father-in-law said to him, "The thing you are doing is not right. 18. You will become utterly weary, both you and *Aaron and his sons and the elders*[20] who are with you; for the task[21] is too heavy; you cannot do it by yourself. 19. Now listen to *me*. I will give you advice, and may *the Memra of the Lord be at your assistance!*[22] Let you be for the people *the one who seeks instruction from before the Lord*, and bring *their* problems *before the Lord*. 20. You shall explain to them the statutes and the Law. You shall make known to them *the prayer they should pray in their synagogue*, the way *to visit*[23] *the sick*, and (the way) to go *about burying the dead and performing (deeds of) kindness*, as well as the demands *of the line of strict justice*, and how they are to deal, *within the line (of justice), with the wicked.*[24] 21. And you shall choose from all the people men of valor who fear *the Lord*, trustworthy men who hate *to accept money through dishonesty*,[25] and *appoint* (them) over them as chiefs of thousands, chiefs of hundreds, chiefs of fifties, chiefs[26] of tens. 22. They shall judge the people at all time; every major problem they shall bring to you, and every minor problem they shall

Notes, Chapter 18

[14]*Mek. RI* Exod 18:11 (2,176-77); *b. Sot.* 11a; *Tanḥ. A, Yitro* 7 (245).

[15]Omitted in Lond. and *ed. pr.*

[16]*Mek. RI* Exod 18:12 (2,177). See also Ps.-J. Gen 18:8 and n. 13 to that verse (Maher, 1992, 66–67).

[17]*Mek. RI* Exod 18:13 (2,179).

[18]= Onq. HT: "to inquire (*drš*) of God." See Gen 25:22 (Ps.-J.) and n. 28 to that verse (Maher, 1992, 89–90).

[19]= Onq. See Grossfeld, 1988B, 51, n. 8.

[20]*Mek. RI* Exod 18:18 (2,181).

[21]Lit.: "the thing"; = HT.

[22]= Onq. See Ps.-J. Gen 26:3 and n. 2 to that verse (Maher, 1992, 91).

[23]Reading *ybqrwn* with *ed. pr.* rather than *ypqdwn* of Lond.

[24]*Mek. RI* Exod 18:18 (2,182); *b. B. Qam.* 99b-100a; *B. Mez.* 30b. Compare Ps.-J. Deut 34:6. On the duty of mourning the dead, see Ps.-J. Gen 35:9 and n. 13 to that verse (Maher, 1992, 120). The phrase "within the line (of justice)" must, in accordance with the texts from the *Mekilta, b. B. Qam.* and *B. Mez.* just mentioned, be taken to mean that the wicked are to be judged leniently; cf. Levy, 2, 464; Schechter, 1961, 215–16.

[25]Onq.: "who hate *to accept* money." See *Mek. RI* Exod 18:21 (2,183): "who when sitting in judgment hate to accept money."

[26]= Lond., *ed. pr.*; HT: "and leaders." See also Ps.-J. v. 25.

judge themselves. Thus they will lighten *the burden that* is upon you, and they will bear (it) with you. 23. If you do this, *namely, that you become free from (the task of) judging*, then *the Lord* will reveal *his commandments* to you,[27] and you will be able to stand *to hear them. Aaron*, too, *as well as his sons and all the elders of*[28] this people, will be able to come in peace to the place *of their courthouse.*" 24. Moses listened to *the word of* his father-in-law and did everything he had said. 25. Moses chose men of valor out of all Israel, and he appointed them heads over the people—chiefs of thousands: *six hundred*; chiefs of hundreds: *six thousand*; chiefs of fifties: *twelve thousand*; and chiefs of tens: *six myriads.*[29] 26. They judged the people at all time, bringing the difficult matters to Moses and judging the minor matters themselves. 27. Then Moses bade farewell to[30] his father-in-law, who went off *to make proselytes of all his fellow countrymen.*[31]

CHAPTER 19

1. In[1] the third month after the departure of the children of Israel from the land of Egypt, that very day, *on the first of the month*,[2] they came to the wilderness of Sinai. 2. They set out from Rephidim, and coming to the wilderness of Sinai, they encamped in the wilderness. Israel encamped there, *united in heart*,[3] in front of the mountain. 3. *On the second day*[4] Moses went up *to the top of the mountain*,[5] and

Notes, Chapter 18

[27]Lit.: "and the Lord will command you commandments." Our understanding of this text is that of Schmerler, 1933, 116.

[28]*Mek. RI* Exod 18:23 (2,185).

[29]*Mek. RI* Exod 18:21 (2,183); *b. Sanh.* 18a.

[30]Lit.: "let go, sent away"; = HT.

[31]Lit.: "all the sons of his land"; = *ed. pr.*; Lond.: ". . . of the land." *Mek. RI* Exod 18:27 (2,186): "I (Jethro) shall . . . convert all the people of my country."

Notes, Chapter 19

[1]For a synoptic presentation of the Targums of Exodus 19–20, see Díez-Macho, *Neophyti* 1, I, 115*–27*. For a study of the traditions of the Sinai covenant in chapters 19–20, see Potin, 1971. M. Serra (1971), followed by B. Olsson (1974), claims that Ps.-J.'s version of Exodus 19–24 clarifies the structure of Jn 1:19–2:12. B. Lindars (1976, 65) does not find this thesis convincing.

[2]*Mek. RI* Exod 19:1 (2,195); *b. Shabb.* 86b. Ps.-J. gives a precise time sequence to the Sinai events; see vv. 3, 7, 9, 10, 16. Cf. Ps.-J. 24:1.

[3]*Mek. RI* Exod 19:2 (2,200); *PRE* 41 (321); *Lev. R.* 9,9. The fact that in HT the verb "encamp" occurs first in the plural and then in the singular gave rise to the midrashic exegesis. The *Mekilta* text uses the idiom *lb 'ḥd,* which Lauterbach translates as "of one mind." Compare similar idioms in Acts 1:14; 2:46; 4:32; 5:12.

[4]*Mek. RI* Exod 19:3 (2,201); *b. Shabb.* 88a.

[5]HT: "to God." LXX: "to the mountain of God"; cf. Exod 3:1. See Geiger, 1928, 465–66.

the Lord called to him from the mountain, saying, "Thus shall you say to *the women of*[6] the house of Jacob, and declare to *the house* of Israel: 4. 'You have seen what I did to the Egyptians, and (how) I bore you *on clouds as on* eagles' wings[7] *from Pelusium, and carried you* to *the site of the Sanctuary to celebrate the Passover there*, bringing you back to Pelusium *that same night; and from there I brought you close to the instruction of my Law.*[8] 5. And now, if you really *listen* to my *Memra*[9] and keep my covenant, you shall be *more beloved before me*[10] than all the peoples *who are upon the face of*[11] the earth. 6. And you will be *before* me *kings adorned*[12] *with the crown, ministering* priests,[13] and a holy people. These are the words you shall speak to the children of Israel.'" 7. *That same day*[14] Moses came and summoned the elders of the people and put before them all these words which the Lord had commanded him. 8. All the people replied as one, saying, "All that the Lord has spoken we will do." And Moses brought back the people's words *before* the Lord. 9. *On the third day*[15] the Lord said to Moses, "Behold, I will *reveal* myself to you in the thickness of the cloud *of glory,*[16] so that the people may hear when I speak with you, and also that they may trust you forever." Then Moses related the words of the people *before* the Lord. 10. *On the fourth day*[17] the Lord said to Moses, "Go to the people and *prepare*[18] them today and tomorrow, and let them wash their garments. 11. Let them be ready for the third day; for on the third day the Lord will *reveal himself*[19] in the sight of all the people, on Mount Sinai. 12. You shall set bounds for the people *so that they will stand* round about *the mountain*, saying, 'Be careful that you do not go up the mountain or *approach* the border of it; whoever *approaches* the mountain[20] shall surely *be killed.* 13. No hand

Notes, Chapter 19

[6]*Mek. RI* Exod 19:3 (2,201); *Exod. R.* 28,2; *Tanḥ. A, Mezora* 9 (425); *PRE* 41 (321).

[7]See above 12:37 (Ps.-J.), where it is said that there was a cloud beneath the Israelites as they traveled. All the Targums, including Onq. ("*as* on eagles' wings"), as well as Pesh. and LXX, had difficulty with the image of the Israelites being carried "on eagles' wings." See further Potin, 1971, 1, 51; Luzarraga, 1973, 131.

[8]*Mek. RI* Exod 19:4 (2,202): "*And how I brought you on eagles' wings:* . . . This refers to the day of Rameses . . . *And I brought you unto myself.* To the Temple." (Rameses = Pelusium; see above Ps.-J. 1:11.) However, this *Mekilta* text does not offer a parallel to the haggadah which we find in Ps.-J., and in Ps.-J. alone. Cf. Shinan, 2, 1979, 247, n. 17; idem, 1983A, 2, 420, n. 6. On Ps.-J.'s tendency to record miraculous events, see Maher, 1992, 6.

[9]= Onq.

[10]= Onq. Cf. *Mek. RI* Exod 19:5 (2, 204). See further Grossfeld, 1988B, 53, n. 5.

[11]See Deut 7:6, which is a parallel to our present verse (Exod 19:5).

[12]Lit.: "tied."

[13]Cf. *Mek. RI* Exod 19:6 (2,205), which explains that the Israelites are not kings who go around making conquests, and that they are true functioning priests. See further McNamara, 1966, 227–30; idem, 1972, 148–59; Potin, 1971, 1, 218–30.

[14]See above, v. 3. Cf. *b. Shabb.* 88a: "On the second day Moses ascended and descended."

[15]*b. Shabb.* 88a; *Sifra, Shemini, Mekhilta de Milluim,* 1,1 (ed. Weiss, 43c).

[16]See above, 16:10 (Ps.-J.) and n. 10 to that verse.

[17]*Mek. RI* Exod 19:10 (2,210).

[18]= Onq.; cf. v. 14 (Ps.-J., Onq.); Num 11:18 (Ps.-J., Onq.). Grossfeld, 1988B, 53, n. 8.

[19]= Onq. HT: "will come down." See also vv. 18, 20. See above, 3:8 (Ps.-J.) and n. 13 to that verse.

[20]*Ed. pr.* uses the Heb. *hr.*

shall touch him; for he must be stoned *with hailstones*, or *arrows of fire*[21] will be thrown *at him*; whether beast or man he shall not live.' *But* at the prolonged *sound* of the horn they will *be authorized*[22] to go up on the mountain." 14. *That same day*[23] Moses came down <from the mountain>[24] to the people; he *prepared* the people, and they washed their garments. 15. And he said to the people, "Be prepared for the third day, and do not *engage in sexual intercourse.*"[25] 16. On the third day, *on the sixth of the month,*[26] in the morning *time*, there were claps *of thunder*, and lightning, and a thick cloud *enveloping*[27] the mountain, and a very loud blast of the horn, and all the people who were in the camp trembled. 17. And Moses brought all the people out of the camp to meet *the Shekinah of the Lord*, and *immediately the Lord of the world uprooted the mountain and lifted it up in the air and it was transparent like glass,*[28] and they stationed themselves *under* the mountain.[29] 18. Mount Sinai was all in smoke because the Lord[30] *had inclined the heavens to it*[31] *and revealed himself* upon it in *glowing* fire; and the smoke of it went up like the smoke of a furnace, and the whole mountain trembled violently. 19. The sound of the horn grew louder and louder. Moses spoke, and he received an answer *from before the Lord* in a *sweet*[32] *and majestic* voice, *and sweet (was) the tone.*[33] 20. The Lord *was revealed* on Mount Sinai, on the top of the mountain, and the Lord called Moses to the top of the mountain and Moses went up. 21. The Lord said to Moses, "Go down, warn the people not to *direct (themselves) towards*[34]

Notes, Chapter 19

[21]Compare Isa 30:30, where fire and hailstones are mentioned as divine punishments. See also Ps.-J. Num 1:51; 3:10, 38. Unlike HT and the other Targums (see also *Mek. RI* Exod 19:13 [2,214]; *b. Sanh.* 45a), Ps.-J. implies that the punishment is to come directly from God. We know of no source for this interpretation.

[22]= Onq. *Mek. RI* Exod 19:13 (2,214).

[23]*b. Shabb.* 88a: "on the fourth day (cf. Ps.-J. v. 10) he descended and ascended no more."

[24]Omitted in Lond. and *ed. pr.*

[25]Lit.: "do not approach the use of the bed." Cf. *Mek. RI* Exod 19:15 (2,216-217); *PRE* 41 (323). The Targums make it clear that only sexual intercourse is excluded. See Schmerler, 1933, 122. On the translation of Onq. (lit.: "do not come beside a woman"), see Levy, 2, 320.

[26]*Mek. RI* Exod 19;11 (2,212). "The sixth of the month" fits in with Ps.-J.'s sequence of events; cf. vv. 1, 3, 9, 10, 11.

[27]*qtyr 'l*; Ps.-J. uses the same verb (*qtr*) in a similar context in Gen 22:4, in an addition that is special to this Targum.

[28]*'spqlry'*; = Latin *specularis (lapis)*, "a kind of transparent stone, mica." Ps.-J. uses this word again in Exod 38:8; Deut 33:19. See also Tg. Job 28:17.

[29]*Mek. RI* Exod 19:17 (2,219); *b. Shabb.* 88a; *Abod. Zar.* 2b. The midrash that God suspended the mountain over the Israelites is based on HT, which says (literally) that the people stood *beneath* the mountain. The sources just mentioned do not say that the mountain was transparent. We know of no source for this addition by Ps.-J. Cf. Ps.-J. Num 21:14 (= Nf, Nfmg, P, V, N, v. 15), which says that the mountains moved to crush the enemies of Israel.

[30]Omitted in *ed. pr.*

[31]*Mek. RI* Exod 19:20 (2,224). See Ps 18:9. Compare v. 11 (Ps.-J.) in our present chapter, and see n. 19 to that verse.

[32]*n'ym.* The same word (*n'ymh*; rendered as "tone" in Lauterbach) is used in the *Mekilta*; see next note.

[33]Reading *ḥlyy'* with Lond. *Ed. pr.* has: "*and* pleasant (were) the words (*mly'*)." In either case, the meaning seems to be that the words which Moses spoke to the people were pleasant. Cf. *Mek. RI* Exod 19:19 (2,223); *Sifre Num.* 116 (ed. Horovitz, 132).

[34]Lit.: "*direct themselves before.*" Ps.-J. is the only Targum of this verse to use the verb *kwn*, "direct, aim." See also v. 24.

the Lord to gaze, lest (even) *a chief who is among them*[35] should fall. 22. The priests also, who approach *to minister before*[36] the Lord, must sanctify themselves, lest the Lord *slay* (some) of them."[37] 23. Moses said *before* the Lord, "The people cannot come up to Mount Sinai, for you have warned us, saying, 'Set bounds about the mountain and sanctify it.'" 24. So the Lord said to him, "Go, descend; and come up together with Aaron; but let not the priests or the people *attempt*[38] to go up *to gaze before*[39] the Lord, lest he *slay* them." 25. So Moses went down *from the mountain* to the people and said to them, "*Come near! Receive the Law with the ten words.*"[40]

CHAPTER 20

1. *The*[1] *Lord* spoke all these words, saying: 2. *The first word, when it came forth from the mouth of the Holy One, may his name be blessed, was like shooting stars, like lightning, and like flames of fire; a fiery torch on its right, and a fiery torch on its left, flying and floating in the air*[2] *of the heavens; it returned and was seen over*

Notes, Chapter 19

[35]We follow the translations of Le Déaut (1979, 159), and Rieder (1984; vol. 1, Hebrew section, 134), both of whom quote the *Mekilta* version (Horovitz-Rabin, 217) which reads '*pylw rb 'ḥd mhm šypwl*, "if even one chief among them should fall."

[36]"Before" is omitted in Lond.

[37]Lit.: "slay (some) among them"; = Onq.

[38]Lit.: "direct (themselves)"; see v. 21 and n. 34.

[39]*"To gaze before"* may have been added under the influence of v. 21. Cf. Ginsburger, 1903, 134.

[40]The ten commandments were known at an early date as the "ten words." Cf., e.g., Josephus, *Ant.* III.v.4. See also Ps.-J. Exod 34:28; Num 7:86; Deut 32:10 (P, V, Nf). See further Bacher, 1965, 1, 19–20; 2,36.

Notes, Chapter 20

[1]For Targumic versions, other than Onq., Nf, Frg. Tgs., CTg. and Ps.-J. of Exod 20, see Hurwitz, *Machsor Vitry*, 337–44. The Strasbourg MS published by Landauer, (1908, 19–26); = CTg S. Díez Macho, 1956; = CTg Q. The Parma MS published by Díez Macho, 1981B, 239–41 (Aramaic text), 250–57 (commentary). R. Kasher, 1989, 1–17. For a synoptic view of the Targums of chapter 20, see Díez Macho, *Neophyti 1,* I,115*–27*; Potin, 1971, 2, 37–79. Potin's text contains a considerable number of errors.

For special studies of the Targums of chapter 20, see Kuiper, 1971; idem, 1972, 69–90; Komlosh, 1963, 289–95; essentially the same material is published in Komlosh, 1973, 259–67; Díez Merino, 1975, 23–48; S. A. Kaufman and Y. Maori, "The Targumim to Exodus 20: Reconstructing the Palestinian Targum," *Textus* 16 (1991) 33–78. Since the haggadic additions in Ps.-J.'s version of this chapter are essentially the same as those in Nf, we refer the reader to the comments on Nf, and we limit ourselves to occasional notes on the text of Ps.-J.

[2]'*wyr*, = Nf, P, CTg S; = Gr. *aêr*. See also, e.g., Ps.-J. Gen 1:20, 26; 7:23; Exod 19:17; 20:2, 3; 32:19.

the camps of Israel; it circled round and was engraved on the tables of the covenant that had been given into the palm of Moses' hands, and it was changing from one side to another on them. [3] Then he cried out and said, "My people, children of Israel, I *am* the Lord your God who *redeemed* you and brought (you) out *redeemed* from the land of the Egyptians, from the bondage of slaves."[4] 3. *The second word, when it came forth from the mouth of the Holy One, may his name be blessed, was like shooting stars, like lightning, and like flames of fire; a fiery torch on its right, and a fiery torch on its left, flying and floating in the air*[2] *of the heavens; it circled round and was seen over the camps of Israel; it returned and was engraved on the tables of the covenant, and it was changing from one side to another on them.*[3] *Then he cried out and said, "My people, house of Israel,* <you shall have no other God *besides me*>.[5] 4. You shall not make for yourselves an image *or a figure* or any likeness of what is in the heavens above, or of what is on the earth below, or of what is in the waters below the earth. 5. You shall not bow down to them or worship *before* them. For I am the Lord your God, a jealous *and an avenging God who takes revenge with jealousy, remembering*[6] the sins of the *wicked* fathers against the *rebellious* sons, against the third and the fourth *generation* of those who hate me,[7] 6. but *reserving* kindness *and goodness* for thousands of *generations*, for *the righteous* who love me, and for those who keep my commandments *and my Law.*[8] 7. *My people, children of Israel, let none of you swear* in vain by the name of *the Memra of* the Lord your God, for *on the day of great judgment*[9] the Lord will not acquit *anyone* who *swears* in vain by his name. 8. *My people, children of Israel,* remember the sabbath, to sanctify it. 9. Six days you shall labor and do all your works, 10. but the seventh day is a sabbath *and rest*[10] *before* the Lord your God; you shall not do any work, you, your sons, your daughters, your menservants, your maidservants,[11] nor the strangers[12] who are in your *cities.* 11. For in six days the Lord *created* heaven and earth, *and* the sea, and everything that is in them, and he rested on the seventh day.

Notes, Chapter 20

[3]Cf. Exod 32:15: "written on both sides" (RSV). One can conclude from *b. Shabb.* 104a that the engraving went through the tables from side to side. See also v. 3.

[4]See 13:3 (Ps.-J.) and n. 2 to that verse. Notice the plural forms "your," "you." See also the plurals "you shall not make," "yourselves" (v. 4), etc.

[5]Omitted in Lond. and *ed. pr.,* because of the fact that the phrase that is omitted begins with *l',* as does v. 4.

[6]= CTg F, S, *Machsor Vitry* (Hurwitz, 338); Onq., P, HT: "visiting." See 3:16 and n. 24 to that verse.

[7]Onq. adds: "when the children follow their fathers in sinning." Like the other Targums, Onq. had added "rebellious" in the body of the verse. By adding "rebellious" the Targums protect the righteousness of God, who could not punish the innocent descendants of wicked fathers. See also, e.g., Exod 34:7 (Ps.-J., Nf, V, N, Onq.); Lev 26:39 (Ps.-J., Onq.); Num 14:18 (Ps.-J., Nf, V, N, Onq.); Deut 5:9 (Ps.-J., Nf, Onq.); Tg. Jer 2:9; 32:18. See Potin, 1971, 1, 90; Shinan, 1979, 2, 312–13; Grossfeld, 1988B, 55, n. 2.

[8]Cf. Nfmg, P, CTg F, S; Deut 5:10 (Ps.-J., Nf).

[9]= Nf, Nfmg, CTg, F, S. These texts specify when God will punish the guilty. See also Tg. Deut 5:11 (Ps.-J., Nf). On "the day of great judgment," see Ps.-J. Gen 3:19 and n. 41 to that verse (Maher, 1992, 29).

[10]"A sabbath and rest" = Nf, CTg F, S. The same idiom is used, e.g., in Lev 23:3a, 32 (Ps.-J.), 23:3b (Nf, CTg F). See also Ps.-J. Exod 35:2.

[11]Lond. and *ed. pr.* (and also the Samaritan Targum) omit "or your cattle."

[12]Or possibly "proselytes." See note to Nf.

Therefore God blessed the sabbath day and hallowed it. 12. *My people, children of Israel, let everyone be careful about the honor of his* father and *the honor of his* mother, so that your days may *increase* in the land which the Lord your God is giving you. 13. *My people, children of Israel, you shall not be murderers, nor friends nor partners of murderers; and let murderous people not be seen in the congregations of Israel lest your children rise up after you, and they too learn to be a murderous people, because for the sins of murderers the sword comes forth upon the world.* 13/14. *My people, children of Israel, you shall not be adulterers,*[13] *nor friends nor partners of adulterers; and let adulterous people not be seen in the congregation of Israel, lest your children rise up after you and they too learn to be an adulterous people, because for the sins of the adulterer death goes forth upon the world.* 13/15. *My people, children of Israel, you shall not be thieves, nor friends nor partners of thieves; and let thieving people not be seen in the congregation of Israel, lest your children rise up after you and they too learn to be a thieving people, because for the sins of thieves famine goes forth upon the world.*[14] 13/16. *My people, children of Israel,* do not bear false witness against your fellows; *do not (be) friends or partners of bearers of false witness; and let people who bear false witness not be seen in the congregation of Israel, lest your children rise up after you and they too learn to be people who bear false witness, because for the sins of false witnesses the clouds go up and the rain does not fall, and drought comes upon the world.* 14/17. *My people, children of Israel, do not be covetous, nor friends nor partners of the covetous; and let covetous people not be seen in the congregation of Israel, lest your children rise up after you and they too learn to be covetous people.* And let none *of you* covet <*his* fellow's house, and let none *of you* covet>[15] *his* fellow's wife or his manservant or his maidservant or his ox or his donkey or anything that belongs to *his* fellow, *because for the sins of the covetous the kingdom attacks*[16] *people's possessions to take them,*[17] *and those who are rich in possessions become poor,*[18] *and exile comes upon the world.*" 15/18. All the people were watching the thunder, *how it was changed in the hearing of each one of them,*[19] and *how it came out from the midst of* the torches, and the sound of the horn, *how it revived the dead,*[20] and the mountain

Notes, Chapter 20

[13]*gyywryn*. The Pal. Tgs. use the word *gy(y)wr'*, "adulterer," and the feminine form *gywrth* in our present verse, in the corresponding text in Deut 5:18 and in Lev 20:10. In this latter verse a verbal form is also used. We do not have this usage in Onq. See Ohana, 1974, 326, n. 3.

[14]Cf. *b. Shabb.* 32b: "For the crime of robbery locusts make invasion, famine is prevalent. . . ."

[15]Omitted in *ed. pr.* through homoioteleuton. Or the omission may be due to the fact that the author took "house" to be synonymous with "wife," as is sometimes the case in rabbinic literature; cf. Díez Macho, 1981B, 257.

[16]Or: "are incited against."

[17]Lit.: "and to take them." Ps.-J. is the only Targum to refer to people's possessions in our present verse. But see Ps.-J. and Nf Deut 5:21.

[18]The words "and those who . . . become poor" are not in Ps.-J. Deut 5:21.

[19]*Mek. RI* Exod 20:18 (2,267): "They (the thunderings) were heard by each man according to his capacity." Cf. *ibid.* Exod 19:16 (2,218); *PRK* 12,25; *Exod. R.* 5,9; 28,6; Philo, *De Decalogo* IX §33; XI §46.

[20]*Mek. RI* Exod 20:18 (2,270); *b. Shabb.* 88b; *PRE* 41 (325). Cf. 1 Cor 15:52; 1 Thess 4:16. See further Rodríguez Carmona, 1978, 61–73; see also Cathcart-Gordon, 1989, 223, n. 7.

smoking. When *all*[21] the people saw it they trembled, and they stood at a distance *of twelve mils.*[22] 16/19. And they said to Moses, "You speak to us, and we will listen; but let us not be addressed[23] *again from before the Lord*, lest we die." 17/20. Moses said to the people, "Do not be afraid; for *the Glory of the Lord has been revealed to you* in order to test you, and in order that the fear of him should ever be before your eyes[24] so that you do not sin."[25] 18/21. So the people stood at a distance *of twelve mils,*[22] and Moses approached towards[26] the dense cloud where *the Glory of the Shekinah of the Lord* was. 19/22. The Lord said to Moses: "Thus shall you say to the children of Israel: 'You have seen that I have spoken to you from heaven. 20/23. *My people, children of Israel*, you shall not make, *for the purpose of bowing down (to it), any likeness of the sun, the moon, the stars, or the planets, or of the angels who minister before* me;[27] you shall not make for yourselves *deities* of silver or *deities* of gold. 21/24. You shall make an altar of earth to *my name*, and sacrifice on it your burnt offerings and your *sacrifices of holy things*[28] *from* your sheep and *from* your oxen; in every place where I will *cause* my *Shekinah to dwell*[29] *and where you will worship before me, I will send my blessing upon* you[29] and I will bless you. 22/25. And if you make an altar of stones to *my name*, do not build it of hewn stones; for if over *the stone* you *raise iron*[30] *from which the* sword *is made*, you have profaned it. 23/26. *As for you priests, who stand to minister before me*, do not ascend my altar by steps *but by a (sloping) plank,*[31] so that your nakedness may not *be seen* upon it.'

Notes, Chapter 20

[21]Cf. LXX and Samaritan Pentateuch.

[22]*Mek. RI* Exod 20:18 (2,269); *ibid.* Exod 20:21 (2,273); *t. Arakh.* 1,10 (Zuckermandel, 543); *b. Shabb.* 88b.

[23]Lit.: "Let it not be spoken with us"; = Onq., Nf.

[24]Lit.: "upon your faces"; = Onq.

[25]Or: "become guilty"; = Onq.

[26]= some MSS of Onq.; see Sperber, 1959, 123; Sperber's own reading is "to the side of"; see also Grossfeld, 1988B, 57 and Apparatus *f.*

[27]*Mek. RI* Exod 20:23 (2,276); *ibid.* Exod 20:4 (2,242–43); *b. Abod. Zar.* 42b; *Rosh Hash.* 24b. *Ed. pr.* here reads "before him" for "before me" of Lond.

[28]HT: "peace offerings." See 10:25 (Ps.-J.) and n. 26 to that verse.

[29]= Onq.

[30]Pesh. replaces HT "sword" with "iron." See note to Nf.

[31]*Mek. RI* Exod 20:26 (2,290).

CHAPTER 21

1. "These are the ordinances that you are to *arrange*[1] before them:[2] 2. When you buy *an Israelite*[3] as a slave *because of a theft he has committed*,[4] he shall serve six years, and *at the beginning of*[5] the seventh he shall go out as a free man, without payment. 3. If he comes in alone, he shall go out alone; *and* if he is the husband of *an Israelite woman*,[6] his wife shall go out with him. 4. If his master gave him *a servant*[7] as wife and she has borne him sons or daughters, the wife and her children shall belong to his master, and he shall go out alone. 5. If the slave *declares and* says,[8] 'I love my master, my wife, and my children, I do not wish to go out as a free man,' 6. his master shall bring him *before the judges*[9] *to receive authorization from them*, and he shall bring him to the door *that is on*[10] the doorpost; and his master shall perforate his *right*[11] ear with a needle, and he shall be his slave, *serving (him) until the Jubilee.*[12] 7. If a man, *an Israelite*, sells his daughter, *a minor*,[13] into *servitude*, she shall not go out as *Canaanite* slaves, *who are freed with a tooth or an eye*, go out.[14] *But (she shall go out) in the sabbatical years, when the signs (of puberty) appear, in the Jubilee, at the death of her master, and (by) redemption with money.*[15] 8. If she *does not find favor before*[16] her master who designated her[17] (for himself), *her father*[18] will redeem her; he will not have the right to sell

Notes, Chapter 21

[1] = Onq. *Mek. RI* Exod 21:1 (3,1): "arrange them in proper order." See Grossfeld, 1988B, 59, n. 1. The Aramaic idiom (*sydry dyny'*, literally "the orders of judgments"; compare Nf, Onq.: *dyny'*; HT: *mšpṭym*) which we translate as "ordinances," occurs frequently in the Pal. Tgs.; see, e.g., Lev 18:4, 5, 26.

[2] Maori (1983, 245) noted the great similarity that exists between Ps.-J. Exod 21:2-11 and the *Mekilta de R. Ishmael* to the same verses. He remarks that Ps.-J. must have known a version of the *Mekilta* that is very similar to that which has come down to us. On Ps.-J.'s halakic additions to Exod 21-23, see Itzchaky, 1982, 40ff.

[3] = Onq. See *Mek. RI* Exod 21:2 (3,3-4); *b. B. Mez.* 71a.

[4] *Mek. RI* Exod 21:2 (3,3). See also *b. Qidd.* 14b; Ps.-J. Exod 22:2.

[5] *Mek. RSbY* Exod 21:2 (160): "at the beginning, and not at the end." See also Ps.-J. Deut 15:12.

[6] *Mek. RI* Exod 21:3 (3,9).

[7] *Mek. RI* Exod 21:4 (3,10); *Mek. RSbY* Exod 21:4 (162).

[8] *Mek. RI* Exod 21:5 (3,13): "unless he says it once and repeats it." See also *Mek. RSbY* Exod 21:5 (162); *b. Qidd.* 21b.

[9] = Onq. *Mek. RI* Exod 21:6 (3,14). See Grossfeld, 1988B, 59, n. 4. HT: "to God." See also the Targums of 22:7, 8, 27, where "God" is also rendered as "judges." See also Gen 6:2 (Nf); Deut 10:17 (Onq., Ps.-J.).

[10] See Onq.; cf. Grossfeld, 1988B, 58, with *Apparatus f.*

[11] *Mek. RI* Exod 21:6 (3,15); *Mek. RSbY* Exod 21:6 (163); *b. Qidd.* 15a. In Deut 15:17 Ps.-J. does not specify that it is the *right* ear that is to be pierced.

[12] *Mek. RI* Exod 21:6 (3,17); *Mek. RSbY* Exod 21:6 (164); Ps.-J. Deut 15:17. Cf. *m. Qidd.* 1,2.

[13] *Mek. RI* Exod 21:7 (3,18). On the Targums of vv. 7-11, see Díez Macho, 1972, 81-84.

[14] *Mek. RI* Exod 21:7 (3,23); cf. ibid. 21:3 (3,9); R. Akiba's view in *Mek. RSbY* Exod 21:7 (165); *b. Qidd.* 16a.

[15] *m. Qidd.* 1,2; *Mek. RI* Exod 21:7 (3,23-24); *b. Qidd.* 16a.

[16] *Mek. RI* Exod 21:8 (3,24).

[17] Reading *yth* (with Nf) rather than *ytyh* of Lond. and *ed. pr.* See also Onq. and LXX. See Berliner, *Targum Onkelos*, 2,232; Díez Macho, 1972, 82.

[18] *Mek. RI* Exod 21:8 (3,24).

her to *another man*,[19] since *her master has exercised his right* over her.[20] 9. If he designates her for his son,[21] he shall treat her as is the custom with the daughters *of Israel*.[22] 10. If he takes for himself another *daughter of Israel as well as her*, he shall not withhold *from her* her food, her *ornaments*,[23] or her conjugal rights.[24] 11. If he does not do these three things for her, *(namely), to designate her for himself or for his son, to have her redeemed*[25] *by her father*,[26] she shall go out without money; *nevertheless he shall give her a bill of divorce*.[27] 12. Whoever strikes *a son of Israel or a daughter of Israel*[28] and *kills him*[29] *shall surely be killed by the sword*.[30] 13. But if he did not *attack him*,[31] but *his misfortune came about from before the Lord*, I will assign you a place to which he can flee. 14. If a man acts wickedly against his fellow to kill him treacherously, *even if he is a priest and serving upon my altar*, you shall take him *from there and kill him*[32] *with the sword*. 15. He who *does violence to*[33] his father or his mother shall surely be *killed by strangulation*[34] *with a scarf*.[35] 16. He who kidnaps *a person from among the children of Israel*,[36] whether that person has been sold or is still *in his power*,[37] shall surely *be killed by strangulation*[38] *with a scarf*. 17. He who curses his father or his mother *by the explicit Name*[39] shall surely *be killed by stoning*.[40] 18. If men quarrel and one strikes the other with a stone or with a fist, and he does not die but falls *sick*,[41] 19. if he gets up *from his sickness* and walks in the street upon his staff,[42] he who struck

---

Notes, Chapter 21

[19]= Onq. Cf. Grossfeld, 1988B, 59, n. 7.

[20]*Mek. RI* Exod 21:8 (3,26); *b. Qidd.* 18b.

[21]Lit.: "(to be) beside his son."

[22]= Onq. *Mek. RI* Exod 21:9 (3,27).

[23]= PVN, Nfmg. Cf. Díez Macho, 1972, 83–84.

[24]Lit.: "his going in unto her."

[25]*Mek. RI* Exod 21:11 (3,29-30); *Mek. RSbY* Exod 21:11 (168).

[26]See v. 8.

[27]*Mek. RI* Exod 21:11 (3,30).

[28]*Mek. RI* Exod 21:12 (3,32).

[29]= Onq. *Mek. RI* Exod 21:12 (3,32).

[30]*Mek. RI* Exod 21:12 (3,34); *Mek. RSbY* Exod 21:12 (169).

[31]Lit.: "and he who did not join himself to him." Ps.-J. interprets HT *ṣdh*, "lie in wait," as if it were derived from *ṣd*, "side," and so gets the meaning "come beside," "join oneself to." Cf. Levy, 1, 213; Schmerler, 1933, 136.

[32]*Mek. RI* Exod 21:14 (3,37); *Mek. RSbY* Exod 21:14 (171).

[33]*Mek. RI* Exod 21:15 (3,42); *b. Sanh.* 84b.

[34]*Mek. RI* Exod 21:15 (3,43); *m. Sanh.* 11,1; *b. Sanh.* 84b.

[35]The method of strangulation (by a scarf) is described e.g., in *m. Sanh.* 7, 3; *Mek. RI* Exod 21:15 (3,43–44). Strangulation by a scarf is mentioned again in Ps.-J. v. 16; Lev 20:10; Deut 22:22; 24:7.

[36]= Onq. See Grossfeld, 1988B, 61, n. 13.

[37]*Mek. RI* Exod 21:16 (3,45). HT: "in his hand." See Ps.-J. Exod 22:3 and n. 7 to that verse.

[38]*Mek. RI* Exod 21:16 (3,46); *m. Sanh.* 11,1.

[39]*Mek. RI* Exod 21:17 (3,48); *m. Sanh.* 7,8; *m. Shebu.* 4,13; Ps.-J. (*šm' mprš'*) follows the *Mekilta* (*šm hmpwrš*) in using the term "the explicit Name." The Mishnah text has simply "the Name." The explicit Name is, of course, God's proper name *Yhwh*. See also Exod 33:6 (Nf, P; cf. Ps.-J.); Lev 20:9 (Ps.-J.). See further Le Déaut, 1979, 176, n. 13; M. Reisel, 1957, 77–88.

[40]*Mek. RI* Exod 21:17 (3,49); *m. Sanh.* 7,4.

[41]= Pesh. Onq.: "fell into idleness."

[42]Onq.: "upon his (own) strength (lit.: health)"; = *Mek. RI* Exod 21:19 (3,53).

(him) shall be acquitted *of the death penalty*;[43] he must only compensate (him) for his *loss of work, for his pain, for his injuries, and for his shame*; and *he shall pay the doctor's fees until*[44] he is cured. 20. If a man strikes his *Canaanite*[45] manservant or his *Canaanite* maidservant with a staff and he dies *that same day* under his hand, he shall *be punished by the sentence of death by the sword.*[46] 21. However, if he survives *one* day, *from (a certain) time to (a certain) time*, or two *incomplete* days,[47] he shall not be *punished*, because *he had bought* him with money. 22. If men struggle and strike a pregnant woman and she *aborts* her child, but it does not result *in death to her*, he (who struck her) shall be fined *for the child*,[48] according to what the woman's husband imposes on him, and he shall give according *to the word of the judges.*[49] 23. But if it did result in *death*[50] *for her*, you shall *condemn* the life *of the murderer* for the life *of the woman*, 24. *the value*[51] *of* an eye for an eye, *the value of* a tooth for a tooth, *the value of* a hand for a hand, *the value of* a foot for a foot, 25. *the value of the pain*[52] *of* a burn for a burn, *the value of* a wound for a wound, *the value of* an ulcer for an ulcer. 26. If a man strikes the eye of his *Canaanite*[53] manservant or the eye of his *Canaanite* maidservant and *blinds* it,[53] he shall let the slave go free on account of the eye. 27. If he knocks out the tooth of his *Canaanite* manservant or the tooth of his *Canaanite* maidservant, he shall let the slave go free on account of the tooth. 28. If an ox gores a man or a woman to death, the ox shall surely be stoned, and *it shall not be slaughtered*[54] so that its flesh may be eaten; but the owner of the ox shall be acquitted *of the death penalty, and also of (paying) the value of the manservant or the maidservant.*[55] 29. But if the ox has been a gorer for some time, and testimony has been borne (to this) *three times in the presence of* its owner,[56] and he did not guard it, and *afterward*s it killed a man or a woman, the ox shall be stoned, and the owner too shall *be put to death with the death that shall be sent to him from heaven.*[57] 30. If *however*, a *monetary*[58] fine is imposed on him, he shall give (it) as a ransom for his life, according to whatever the *Sanhedrin of*

Notes, Chapter 21

[43]*Mek. RI* Exod 21:19 (3,54).

[44]*Mek. RI* Exod 21:19 (3,54); *m. B. Qam.* 8, 1.

[45]*Mek. RI* Exod 21:20 (3,56–58).

[46]*Mek. RI* Exod 21:20 (3,60–61); *b. Sanh.* 52b.

[47]A period of 48 hours, but regarded only as 24 hours when the night hours are not counted. Cf. *Mek. RI* Exod 21:21 (3,61). The midrash explains HT "a day or two."

[48]*Mek. RI* Exod 21:22 (3,65): "for the children."

[49]= Onq.; *Mek. RI* Exod 21:22 (3,66); *PRE* 47 (370).

[50]= Onq.; *Mek. RI* Exod 21:23 (3,66).

[51]*Mek. RI* Exod 21:24 (3,67); *b. B. Qam.* 84a; *Ketub.* 32b. See also Ps.-J. Lev 24:20; Deut 19:21.

[52]*Mek. RI* Exod 21:25 (3,69); *b. B. Qam.* 84a.

[53]*Mek. RI* Exod 21:26 (3,70).

[54]*Mek. RI* Exod 21:28 (3,78); *b. B. Qam.* 41a.

[55]*Mek. RI* Exod 21:28 (3,81); *b. B. Qam.* 42b. Cf. Gronemann, 1879, 138.

[56]*Mek. RI* Exod 21:29 (3,83); *m. B. Qam.* 2,4; *b. B. Qam.* 24a.

[57]*Mek. RI* Exod 21:29 (3,85). The punishment must come from God. The judges may not condemn a man to death if his ox kills a man; cf. *b. Sanh.* 15b.

[58]Onq., Pesh.: "(a fine of) money"; *b. B. Qam.* 40a.

Israel[59] shall impose on him. 31. *If the ox* gores a son *of Israel*[60] (or) a daughter *of Israel,*[60] he shall be dealt with according to this same rule. 32. If, *however,* the ox gores a *Canaanite*[61] manservant or a *Canaanite* maidservant, he shall give thirty *selas* of silver to the master *of the manservant or the maidservant,* and the ox shall be stoned. 33. If a man opens a pit, or if a man digs a pit *in the street*[62] and does not cover it, and an ox or an ass falls into it, 34. the owner of the pit shall pay compensation; he shall give back money to its owner, *the price of his ox or ass,* and *the carcass* shall be his.[63] 35. If a man's ox wounds his fellow's ox and it dies, they shall sell the live ox and divide its *price*; they shall also divide *the price of*[64] the dead animal. 36. If it was known that the ox had been a gorer for some time and its owner had not guarded it, he shall surely repay ox for ox; but *the carcass and the skin*[65] shall be his. 37. If a man steals an ox or a sheep and slaughters it or sells it, he shall pay five oxen for *one* ox, *because he has prevented him from ploughing,* and four sheep for *one* sheep, *because he carried it when stealing it, and (because) it cannot work.*[66]

CHAPTER 22

1. "If the thief is found (in the act of) breaking in *through a wall* and he is struck and dies, (he who struck him) is not *guilty of the shedding of innocent* blood. 2. If *the matter is as clear as*[1] the sun, *that he did not go in to kill someone and (the owner) kills him, the guilt of shedding innocent* blood is upon him.[2] *If (the thief) es-*

Notes, Chapter 21

[59]*Mek. RSbY* Exod 21:30 (181): "the court (*byt dyn*)."
[60]= Onq. Cf. Grossfeld, 1988B, 62, n. 23.
[61]*Mek. RI* Exod 21:32 (3,89). *Mek. RSbY* Exod 21:32 (183). See also vv. 20, 26, 27.
[62]*b. B. Qam.* 49b: "In the case of a pit on a public ground . . . there should be liability." See the debate *ibid.* 50a, and *m. B. Qam.* 5, 5.
[63]Ps.-J. seems to say that the dead animal will belong to the man who dug the pit. See the discussion in *Mek. RI* Exod 21:34 (3,93–94). Cf. also *b. B. Qam.* 10b, where there is a similar discussion with regard to v. 36. See, however, Schmerler, 1933, 142.
[64]Or: "the value of" = Onq. See Grossfeld, 1988B, 62, n. 25.
[65]We know of no source for Ps.-J.'s mention of the skin. There is, in fact, no need of such a mention, since the skin is part of the carcass. See Schmerler, 1933, 143.
[66]*Mek. RI* Exod 21:37 (3,99); *t. B. Qam.* 7,10 (Zuckermandel, 359); *b. B. Qam.* 79b. Ps.-J. combines the views of R. Meir and R. Johanan that are expressed in the *Mekilta.*

Notes, Chapter 22

[1]*b. Sanh.* 72a. Onq.: "If the eye of witnesses falls upon him"; see Grossfeld, 1988B, 63, n. 1.
[2]Cf. *b. Sanh.* 72a: "But if it is as clear to thee as the sun that his intentions are peaceable, do not slay him." See also *Mek. RI* Exod 22:2 (3,102).

capes from his hands,[3] he must make restitution. If he does not have anything *with which to make restitution,* he shall be sold for *the value of*[4] his theft *and until the sabbatical year.*[5] 3. If, *before witnesses,*[6] what was stolen is found in his *possession,*[7] whether ox or ass or sheep, *while they are still* alive, he shall pay two *for one.*[8] 4. If a man *breaks into*[9] a field or a vineyard and lets his cattle loose and they *graze*[10] in the field of another *man,* he shall pay compensation (from) the best of his field and the best of his vineyard. 5. If a fire breaks out and catches on in thorns, and destroys stacked corn, or *anything*[11] that is standing, or the crop,[12] he who kindled the fire shall make full restitution. 6. If a man gives to his fellow money or goods to keep, *without reward for the keeping,*[13] and they are stolen from the man's house, if the thief is found, *he* shall pay two *for one.* 7. If the thief is not found, the owner of the house shall be brought *before the judges,*[14] *and he shall swear*[15] that he has not put forth his hand to his fellow's goods. 8. Concerning everything that is *lost through willful negligence,* concerning an ox, an ass, a sheep, clothing, or any (other) lost thing, *he shall swear,* when (someone) says, 'This is it.' *And when what was lost is later found in the possession of the thief, the case* of both parties, *the case of the owner of the house and the case of the thief,* shall come *before the judges,*[16] and he *whom the judges* find guilty, *the thief,* shall pay two *for one* to his fellow. 9. If a man gives to his fellow an ass, an ox, a sheep, or any (other) animal to keep, *without reward for the keeping,*[17] and it dies, or is torn *by a wild beast,*[18] or is carried off, with no *witness*[19] who sees *and who (can) bear witness,* 10. let there be an oath of the Lord between the two of them; *he shall swear* that he

Notes, Chapter 22

[3]The logic of Ps.-J.'s rendering requires this addition, since the first part of the verse regards the thief as dead, and the second part speaks of his making restitution. Cf. Maori, 1983, 236.

[4]Or: "in compensation for"; = Lond.: *bdmy; ed. pr.: br mn,* "outside."

[5]Ps.-J.'s mention of the sabbatical year contradicts the halakah; cf. *Mek. RI* Exod 22:2 (3,103); *b. Nid.* 48a. See Exod 21:2.

[6]*Mek. RI* Exod 22:3 (3,104); *b. B. Qam.* 64b.

[7]*Mek. RI* Exod 22:3 (3,104). HT: "in his hand." See Ps.-J. 21:16, and n. 37 to that verse.

[8]= Onq. See Grossfeld, 1988B, 63, n. 3.

[9]Ps.-J. and Nfmg use the verb *pqr,* which Jastrow (1212) renders as "break into, trespass," and to which Levy (2, 285) gives the meaning "make free (to all), turn over to common use." Cf. CTg A, which uses the verb *bqr,* "clear, declare free"; cf. Jastrow, 187. See Ps.-J. Exod 23:11 and n. 18 to that verse. See note to our present verse in Nf.

[10]Lit.: "eat"; = Onq. On the translation of this verse in Onq., see Grossfeld, 1988B, 63, and n. 4. Cazelles, 1986, 329–36.

[11]*Mek. RI* Exod 22:5 (3,111) includes trees. Cf. *b. B. Qam.* 60a.

[12]Lit.: "field"; = HT.

[13]*Mek. RI* Exod 22:6 (3,113); cf. also *b. B. Qam.* 64b.

[14]= Onq.; *Mek. RI* Exod 22:7 (3,116). See above, 21:6 (Ps.-J.) and n. 9 to that verse.

[15]*Mek. RI* Exod 22:7 (3,116); LXX: "and shall swear."

[16]*Mek. RI* Exod 22:8 (3,119).

[17]*Mek. RI* Exod 22:9 (3,121). *b. B. Mez.* 94b says that vv. 9-12 deal with one who is paid to mind something. Therefore Ginsburger (1903, 139) omits the negative particle in v. 9 and reads *b'gr,* "for a reward," rather than *bl' 'gr,* "without a reward"; cf. v. 11.

[18]*Mek. RI* Exod 22:9 (3,121).

[19]*Mek. RI* Exod 22:9 (3,122); *Mek. RSbY* Exod 22:9 (205).

did not put forth his hand to his fellow's goods, and his master shall accept *his oath*[20] and he shall not make restitution. 11. But if it was stolen from him *who had (received) a reward for keeping (it)*,[21] he shall make restitution to its owners. 12. If it was torn *by a wild beast*, he shall bring him *witnesses*,[22] *or he shall take him to the body of* (the animal) that was torn;[23] he shall not make restitution. 13. If a man borrows *something* from his fellow, and *the vessel* is broken[24] or *the animal* dies, its owner not being with it, he shall surely make restitution. 14. If its owner was with it, he shall not make restitution; but if it was hired, *its loss* is added to the hiring fee.[25] 15. If a man seduces a virgin who is not betrothed and lies with her, he shall take her as wife by paying the bride price. 16. If *she is not fit for him*,[26] *or if* her father *does not wish* to give her to him,[27] *he shall be fined fifty selas of* silver,[28] in accordance with the bride price of virgins. 17. *My people, children of Israel*, you shall not let *anyone who practices sorcery* live;[29] *they shall be killed by stoning.* 18. . . . [30] 19. *Whoever* sacrifices to the *idols of the nations* shall be *put to death by the sword*,[31] *and his possessions* shall be destroyed;[32] *therefore you shall offer worship* only to *the name of*[33] the Lord. 20. You shall not annoy a stranger *with words*,[34] and do not distress him *by taking his possessions.*[34] *My people, children of Israel*, remember that you were sojourners in the land of Egypt. 21. You shall not afflict any widow or orphan. 22. If you do afflict him, *beware*; for if he *rises up and* cries out *against you in prayer before* me, I will hear *the voice of his prayer and I will avenge him.*[35] 23. My anger will be enkindled,[36] and I will put you to death by the sword

Notes, Chapter 22

[20] = Onq.; *Mek. RI* Exod 22:10 (3,124); *b. B. Qam.* 106a; *b. Shebu.* 45a.

[21] *Mek. RI* Exod 22:11 (3,124); see also the text from *b. B. Mez.* referred to in n. 17.

[22] = Onq.; *Mek. RI* Exod 22:12 (3,125); *b. B. Qam.* 11a.

[23] *Mek. RI* Exod 22:12 (3,125). Cf. *b. B. Qam.* 11a. Ps.-J. has a conflate reading, combining the views of both R. Ahai and R. Jonathan as recorded in the *Mekilta.*

[24] See *b. B. Mez.* 94b: "Or again (refer it) to the borrowing of utensils." Ps.-J. refers HT *nšbr* (RSV: "is hurt"; lit.: "is broken") not to an animal, but to a vessel. See Geiger, 1928, 466.

[25] Lit.: "Its loss comes into." The meaning seems to be that the person who hired something must make good its loss by paying the difference between the hiring fee and the value of the thing hired. *Mek. RI* Exod 22:14 (3,129): "the hirer should . . . pay for theft and loss." One might also translate Ps.-J.'s phrase as "the hire covers its loss." See Levy, 2, 276.

[26] Cf. *Mek. RI* Exod 22:15 (3,131): "where the girl is fit to be his wife."

[27] The repetition in HT (*m'n ym'n*) gives Ps.-J. occasion to refer to two cases ("is not fit," "does not wish"). Cf. Gronemann, 1879, 60.

[28] *Mek. RI* Exod 22:16 (3,133); *b. Ketub.* 38a. Cf. Deut 22:29.

[29] *Mek. RI* Exod 22:17 (3,133): "whether it be a man or a woman"; cf. *b. Sanh.* 67a.

[30] Verse 18 is omitted through homoioteleuton ("by stoning") in both Lond. and *ed. pr.* The Mekilta (3,133–34) gives stoning as the penalty in both verses 17 and 18. Lond. leaves a blank space for v. 18.

[31] Ps.-J. (see also Ps.-J. Exod 32:27) is against the teaching that idolatry is punished by stoning; cf. Deut 17:5; *m. Sanh.* 7,4.6; cf. *b. Yoma* 66b. But see *m. Sanh.* 10,4, which refers to a case in which many idolators are involved. See further Gronemann, 1879, 68–69; Schmerler, 1933, 149.

[32] Compare *m. Sanh.* 10,4, which distinguishes between single idolators and many idolators.

[33] = Onq. See Grossfeld, 1988B, 65, n. 12.

[34] *Mek. RI* Exod 22:20 (3,137); *m. B. Mez.* 4,10. See Ps.-J. Lev 25:17.

[35] *Mek. RI* Exod 22:22 (3,144).

[36] "My anger will be enkindled" = Onq. Compare Nf, CTg A. See Klein, 1976, 535–36.

of death; your wives shall become widows, and your children orphans. 24. If you lend money to my people, to the poor person *who is*[37] with you, do not treat him like a creditor; do not *oblige him to have witnesses and guarantors*; do not (lend to him) at interest or *at usurious rates.*[38] 25. If you take your fellow's garment in pledge, you shall return it to him before the sun sets, 26. for it is the only cloak *with which he can cover himself*, it is *the undershirt*[39] *that touches* his skin, *and if you take the mattress of his bed,*[39] on what shall he sleep? If he cries out *before* me, I will accept *his prayer*, for I am *a* compassionate *God*. 27. *My people, children of Israel*, do not slight *your judges,*[40] and do not curse the leaders *who have been appointed* rulers of your people. 28. You shall not delay *to offer the first of your fruit*[41] and *the first wine of your winepress*[42] *at the appropriate time*[43] in the (dwelling) *place of my Shekinah.*[44] *You shall set* the first-born of your sons *apart*[45] *before* me. 29. You shall do likewise with *the first-born of*[46] your cattle and your flocks; seven days it shall *suck*[47] its mother, and on the eighth day you shall *set it apart before* me. 30. You shall be holy men *before* me, *eating*[48] *ordinary food in (a state of) purity;*[49] *but* you shall not eat flesh torn *from a living animal;*[50] you shall throw[51] it to the dog *as his reward.*[52]

Notes, Chapter 22

[37]= Lond.: *d'ymk*; = Nf; *ed. pr.*: "of the people (*d'm'*)."

[38]*Mek. RI* Exod 22:24 (3,149); *m. B. Mez.* 5, 11; *b. B. Mez.* 75b. Cf. Gronemann, 1879, 68.

[39]*Mek. RI* Exod 22:26 (3,151). Cf. *b. B. Mez.* 113b, which says that a couch and matting must be left to a poor man.

[40]Onq.: "a judge." *Mek. RI* Exod 22:27 (3,151); *b. Sanh.* 66a. See above, 21:6 (Ps.-J.) and n. 9 to that verse.

[41]Onq.: "your first fruits." *Mek. RI* Exod 22:28 (3,153).

[42]LXX, Pesh.: "(the first fruits of) your wine press." Cf. Geiger, 1928, 466–67.

[43]See *Mek. RI* Exod 22:28 (3,153), which discusses the order in which the offerings should be made.

[44]The same idiom ("the place of my Shekinah") occurs in Ps.-J. 23:20.

[45]= Onq. See also v. 29. Cf. Grossfeld, 1988B, 65, n. 15.

[46]*Mek. RI* Exod 22:29 (3,154).

[47]*Mek. RI* Exod 22:29 (3,155–56).

[48]Lit.: "tasting." The same verb is used in Ps.-J. Lev 11:1, where the same idea is expressed.

[49]*Tanna debe Eliyyahu* 15/16 (Braude-Kapstein, 202–3).

[50]= Onq.; *b. Ḥul.* 102b. See Silverstone, 1931, 139.

[51]*trmwn* = Onq. See above 4:3 (Ps.-J.) and n. 2 to that verse.

[52]According to *Mek. RI* Exod 22:30 (3,159) and *Exod. R.* 31,9, this reward was given because the dogs did not bark against the Israelites on the night they left Egypt. Cf. Gronemann, 1879, 99. On the word *swṭr'*, which we translate as "reward" in our present verse, see above, n. 15 to 2:9 (Ps.-J.).

CHAPTER 23

1. *"My people, children of Israel,* do not accept the lying *words of a man who informs on*[1] *his fellow before you.*[2] Do not join hands with the wicked man *who is* a false[3] witness. 2. *My people, children of Israel,* do not follow the multitude to do evil, *but to do good;*[4] *let none of you be prevented from proclaiming the innocence of his fellow* in a lawsuit, *saying, 'Behold,* the *legal decision* follows the majority.'*[5] 3. You shall not *show favor*[6] in his lawsuit to a poor man *who is guilty, pitying him;*[7] *for one cannot show favor in judgment.* 4. If you come upon the ox of your enemy *whom you hate for a sin of his which you alone know,*[8] or upon (his) ass that strayed *from the way,* you must take it back to him. 5. If you see, lying under its burden, the ass of your enemy *whom you hate for a sin of his which you alone know,*[8] and you would refrain *from approaching* it, *at that very moment you must forget the hatred against him that is in your heart,* and you must *unload and re-load (it)*[9] with him. 6. *My people, children of Israel,* you shall not pervert the justice due to the poor man in his lawsuit. 7. Keep far from a false charge;[10] and do not put to death *one who goes forth* acquitted *from your courthouse*[11] *and whose guilt is (later) discovered, or one who goes forth convicted and whose* innocence *is (later) discovered;*[12] for I do not declare him innocent *if he is* guilty. 8. You shall not accept a bribe, for a bribe blinds *the eyes of those who take it,*[13] *drives the sages from their seats,*[14] corrupts the *upright* words *that are written in the Law,*[15] and *confuses the words* of the innocent *in their mouths at the hour of judgment.*[16] 9. You shall not oppress a stranger; you know the stranger's *anguish of* soul, for you were sojourners in the land of Egypt. 10. For six years you shall sow your land and gather in its produce; 11. but in the seventh you shall let it rest, *by not working it,*[17] *and*

Notes, Chapter 23

[1] Or: "who slanders"; lit.: "who eats pieces." The same Aramaic idiom is used by Ps.-J. in Gen 49:23; Lev 19:16 (= Onq.). We find it also, e.g., in Dan 3:8; 6:25; Tg. Pss 15:3; 120:3. See further Levy, 2, 390.

[2] *Mek. RI* Exod 23:1 (3,160); *b. Pesah.* 118a.

[3] = Onq. Cf. *Mek. RI* Exod 23:1 (3,160); *Mek. RSbY* Exod 23:1 (214).

[4] *Mek. RI* Exod 23:2 (3,161); *m. Sanh.* 1,6.

[5] On the translation of v. 2 in the Pal. Tgs., see R. Kasher, 1986, 11–12. On the translation of the second part of the verse in Onq., see Grossfeld, 1988B, 66–67, and nn. 5-6.

[6] See Lev 19:15.

[7] See Onq.

[8] *b. Pesah.* 113b. See Gronemann, 1879, 99–100.

[9] *Mek. RI* Exod 23:5 (3,167); *m. B. Mez.* 2,10; *b. B. Mez.* 31a. Cf. Tg. Deut 22:4 (Nf, P, V, N, L). See Klein, 1982, 135*–36*.

[10] Lit.: "from a word of lying"; = HT.

[11] Cf. Onq. See Grossfeld, 1988B, 66–67, and n. 10.

[12] *Mek. RI* Exod 23:7 (3,171); *Mek. RSbY* Exod 23:7 (216). See also *b. Sanh.* 33b.

[13] LXX: "the eyes of the seeing." Onq.: "the eyes of the wise." Pesh.: "the eyes of the wise in judgment." Cf. Deut 16:19; *Mek. RI* Exod 23:8 (3,172): "(the eyes) of those learned in the law." Cf. *m. Pesah.* 8,9.

[14] Compare *Mek. RI* Exod 23:8 (3,173): "his mind will become confused with respect to the knowledge of the Torah."

[15] *Mek. RI* Exod 23:8 (3,173).

[16] Cf. the Pal. Tgs. (including Ps.-J.) of Deut 16:19.

[17] Lit.: "from work." *Mek. RI* Exod 23:11 (3,175).

you shall declare its fruit[18] *free.*[19] Let the poor of your people eat (of it), and what they leave let the beasts of the field eat. You shall do the same with your vineyard and your olive tree. 12. For six days you shall do your work, but on the seventh day you shall rest, so that your ox and your ass may rest, and that the *uncircumcised*[20] son of your maidservant, as well as the stranger, may take their rest. 13. Give heed to all *the commandments*[21] that I have spoken to you. Do not bring to mind the name of the *idols of the nations,*[22] and let it not be heard from your mouth. 14. Three *times*[23] a year you shall celebrate a feast *before* me. 15. You shall observe the Feast of Unleavened Bread; seven days you shall eat unleavened bread, as I have commanded you, at the appointed time in the month of Abib, for in it you went forth from Egypt. None shall appear before me empty-handed. 16. And (you shall observe) the Feast of Harvest, of the first fruits of your work, of what you sow in the field; and the Feast of Ingathering at the end of[24] the year, when you gather in (the results of) your work from the field. 17. Three times a year all your males shall appear before the Master *of the world,*[25] the Lord. 18. *My people, children of Israel,*[26] you shall not offer the blood of my *Passover* sacrifice *while there is* leavened bread *in your houses;*[27] and the fat of my *Passover sacrifice* shall not remain overnight, until morning, *away from the altar,*[28] *nor*[29] *(any) of the meat you eat in the evening.* 19. The best of the first fruits *of the fruits* of your land you shall bring to the *Sanctuary*[30] of the Lord your God. *My people, house*[31] *of Israel, you are not permitted* either to boil *or to eat meat and* milk *mixed together,*[32] *lest my anger be enkindled and I boil your grain, wheat and straw, the two of them together.*[33] 20. Behold, I am *dispatching* an angel before you to guard you on the way and to bring you into the (dwelling) place *of my Shekinah*[34] which I have prepared.

Notes, Chapter 23

[18]*Mek. RI* Exod 23:11 (3,175).
[19]Ps.-J. uses the verb *pqr*. P uses the verb *bqr* (= Nf as corrected by Díez-Macho [*Neophyti 1,* II, 151]). A marginal gloss in P notes that *bqr* has the same meaning as *pqr*. See above 22:4 (Ps.-J.) and n. 9 to that verse.
[20]*Mek. RI* Exod 23:12 (3,178); *b. Yeb.* 48b.
[21]*Mek. RI* Exod 23:13 (3,179).
[22]= Onq. See also 22:19 (Ps.-J., Onq.).
[23]= Onq., Pesh., LXX.
[24]Lit.: "at the going out of"; = Nf, Onq., HT. Cf. also 34:22 (Ps.-J., Nf, Onq.).
[25]= Onq. See Gen 18:31 (Ps.-J.) with n. 42 to that verse (Maher, 1992, 69).
[26]= Nfmg.
[27]= Onq. *Mek. RI* Exod 23:18 (3,185); *m. Pesah.* 5,4; *b. Pesah.* 5a; *j. Pesah.* 5, 32b. Cf. Tg. Exod. 34:25 (Onq., Ps.-J., V, N.).
[28]= Onq.; *Mek. RI* Exod 23:18 (3,185–86); Ps.-J. Exod 34:25; Deut 16:4.
[29]Lond.: *wl'*; *ed. pr.*: *l'*.
[30]Or: "Temple"; = Onq.; cf. Grossfeld, 1988B, 68, n. 17.
[31]= P.
[32]Onq.: "Do not consume meat with milk." *Mek. RI* Exod 23:19 (3,190); *b. Ḥul.* 115b. Tg. Exod. 34:26 (Onq., Ps.-J., Nf, V, N); Deut 14:21 (Onq., Ps.-J., Nf, Nfmg). Cf. Grossfeld, 1988B, 69, n. 18.
[33]This motivation ("lest my anger, etc."), which is also added (with variations) in Nf and P in our present verse, in 34:26 (Ps.-J., Nf) and in Deut 14:21 (Nf), has no parallel in Talmudic literature. Cf. Bamberger, 1975, 29; Gronemann, 1879, 92. But see *Tanḥ. A, Re'eh* 17 (645) and *PRK* 10,9, where the prohibition against boiling a kid in its mother's milk is linked with the command to pay tithes. See Schmerler, 1933, 163.
[34]See above 22:28 (Ps.-J.) and n. 44 to that verse.

21. Pay heed to him and obey his *Memra*. Do not rebel against his *words*, for *I* will not forgive your sins, because *his Memra* is in my name.[35] 22. But if you obey his *Memra* and do all that I say *through him*, I will hate *him* who hates you, and I will oppress those who oppress you. 23. For my angel will go before you and bring you in to the Amorites, the <Hittites>,[36] the Perizzites, the Canaanites, the Hivites, and the Jebusites, and I will wipe them out. 24. You shall not bow down to their *idols* nor worship them, nor do according to their *evil* deeds, but you shall utterly abolish *their places of worship*[37] and smash their pillars *and their images* to bits. 25. You shall worship *before* the Lord your God, and he will bless *the food that you eat*[38] and your *drink*.[39] And I will remove the *plague of jaundice*[40] from your midst. 26. No woman will miscarry or be barren in your land. I will complete the number of the days *of your life from day to day*.[41] 27. I will send my terror before you, and I will throw into confusion all the peoples against whom you come, *drawing up battle lines*,[42] and I will make all your enemies *turn* their back[43] before you. 28. I will send hornets before you, and they will drive out before you the Hivites, the Canaanites, and the Hittites. 29. I will not drive them out before you in a single year, lest the land become desolate, and the wild beasts outnumber you—*when they come to eat their corpses—and do you harm*. 30. I will drive them out before you little by little, until you have increased and possess the land. 31. I will set your borders from the Sea of Reeds to the sea of the Philistines, and from the desert to the *Euphrates*;[44] for I will deliver *all* the inhabitants of the land into your hand, and *you*, you shall drive them out before you. 32. You shall make no covenant with them or with their *idols*. 33. *You shall not make dwellings for them*[45] in your land, lest *they cause you to err and* cause you to sin[46] *before*[47] me; for you would worship their *idols*, since *they* would be a snare to you."

Notes, Chapter 23

[35] = Onq. See Maybaum, 21; Grossfeld, 1988B, 69, n. 22.

[36] Omitted in Lond. and *ed. pr.*

[37] Lit.: "their place of bowing down." Ps.-J. uses the same idiom in Num 31:10 and 33:52.

[38] Lit.: "the foods of your eating (*mzwny myklk*)," which seems to be a conflate reading. Onq.: *myklk*. From the words "and he will bless your bread" the rabbis concluded that one must pronounce a blessing before meals; cf. *Mek. RI* Exod 13:3 (1,137); *b. B. Qam.* 92b.

[39] = Onq.

[40] Lit.: "of the gall, bile." HT: *mḥlh*. Cf. *b. B. Qam.* 92b: "*Maḥalah* means gall." Cf. *b. B. Mez.* : 107b.

[41] *b. Sotah* 13b; *Rosh Hash.* 11a. Ps.-J.'s idiom (*mywm' lywm'*) corresponds to that used in these texts, *mywm lywm*.

[42] Onq.: "against whom you will come to fight."

[43] Lit.: "those who turn their back"; = Onq.

[44] Nfmg: "the river of the Euphrates." HT: "the river." See also Ps.-J. Gen 36:37 and Num 22:5, where "the river" is also rendered as "the Euphrates."

[45] See *b. Abod. Zar.* 20a, where the words of Deut 7:2, "show no mercy to them (the Girgashites, the Amorites, etc.)," are taken to mean "(you shall not) allow them to settle on the soil."

[46] Ps.-J. has a conflate reading; Onq.: "lest they cause you to sin."

[47] = *Ed. pr.*; = Onq., Nf; Lond.: "before him," using the third person instead of the first; cf. Díez-Macho, 1981A, 61–89.

CHAPTER 24

1. *Michael, the prince of wisdom,*[1] said to Moses *on the seventh day of the month*:[2] "Come up *before* the Lord, you and Aaron, Nadab and Abihu, and seventy of the elders of Israel, and bow down from afar. 2. Moses alone shall approach *before* the Lord. They shall not approach, and the people shall not come up with him." 3. Moses came and related to the people all the words of the Lord and all the ordinances. And all the people answered with one voice and said, "All[3] that the Lord has said we will do!" 4. Moses wrote <all>[4] the words of the Lord. And he rose early in the morning and built an altar at the foot of the mountain, with twelve pillars for the twelve tribes of Israel. 5. He sent *the first-born*[5] of the sons of Israel—*for until that time the worship was in (the hands of) the first-born, because the tent of meeting had not yet been made, and the priesthood had not yet been given to Aaron*[6]—and they offered up burnt offerings, and they <slaughtered>[4] bulls as sacrifices of *holy things before*[7] the Lord. 6. Moses took half of the blood *of the sacrifice* and put (it) in the dashing-basins,[8] and the (other) half of the blood *of the sacrifice* he dashed against the altar. 7. Then he took the book of the covenant *of the Law* and read (it) *before* the people. And they said, "All *the words* that the Lord has spoken we will do and we will obey."[9] 8. Then Moses took *the half of* the blood *that was in the dashing-basins* and dashed (it) *against the altar to make atonement for* the people;[10] and he said, "Behold, *this is* the blood of the covenant which the Lord has made with you in accordance with all these words." 9. Then Moses and Aaron, Nadab and Abihu, and seventy of the elders of Israel went up. 10. *Nadab and Abihu*[11] *lifted up their eyes and* saw *the glory of* the God of Israel; under the

Notes, Chapter 24

[1]According to *b. Sanh.* 38b, it was Metatron who spoke to Moses. Michael, whom Ps.-J. calls "the prince of wisdom" in our present verse, is called "prince of Israel" in Tg. Song of Songs 8:9. Cf. Dan 12:1. Michael is mentioned several times in Ps.-J.; see Ps.-J. Gen 32:25 and n. 18 to that verse (Maher, 1992, 114). Metatron is mentioned by Ps.-J. in Gen 5:24 (see n. 10 to that verse; Maher, ibid., 37) and Deut 34:6.

[2]Here Ps.-J. takes up the chronology which he had followed up to 19:16. See above, n. 2 to 19:1 (Ps.-J.). Ps.-J.'s mention of the seventh day contradicts *Mek. RI* Exod 19:10 (2, 210) and *b. Shabb.* 88a, which give us to understand that the events described in Exod 24 took place on the fifth day.

[3]Lond. and *ed. pr.*, probably under the influence of v. 7, omit "the words."

[4]Omitted in Lond. and *ed. pr.*

[5]= Onq., Nfmg; *Mek. RSbY* Exod 24:5 (220). See Grossfeld, 1988B, 71, n. 2.

[6]*m. Zeb.* 14,4; *b. Zeb.* 115b; *Gen. R.* 63,13.

[7]"Holy sacrifices before" = Onq. See above, 10:25 (Ps.-J.) and n. 26 to that verse.

[8]*mzyrqy'* = Onq. HT: *'gnt,* "basins." Ps.-J. adds this word in v. 8. See 27:3 (Ps.-J., Nf, V, N, Onq.) and 38:3 (Ps.-J., Nf, Nfmg, Onq.), where the Targums use this word to translate the corresponding Hebrew word *mzrq.*

[9]Lit.: "will accept"; = Onq.

[10]This addition ("against the altar, etc."), which we also find in Onq., may have been made to counteract the Christian doctrine of the atoning power of the blood of Christ. See Ginzberg, *Legends,* 6, 34, n. 195; Berliner, *Targum Onkelos* 2, 164. See also Grossfeld, 1988B, 71, n. 5.

[11]Ps.-J. is the only Targum of this verse to specify that Nadab and Abihu (but not Moses) saw the Glory of God; see *Exod. R.* 3,1; *Lev. R.* 20,10; *PRK* 26,9; *Tanḥ. A, Aḥare Mot* 6 (432). See also Ps.-J.'s version of v. 11.

footstool[12] *of his feet that was placed*[13] *under his throne* (there was) the likeness [14] of a work of sapphire *stone,* [15] *recalling the slavery with which the Egyptians had en-slaved the children of Israel with clay and* bricks.[16] *As the women treaded the clay with their men, there was a delicately reared maiden there who was pregnant. She lost the embryo, and it was tread on with the clay. Gabriel*[17] *came down and made a brick out of it, and bringing it up to the heavens on high, he placed it as a platform under the footstool of the Lord*[18] *of the world.*[19] *Its splendor was like (that of) a work in precious stone* and like *the glorious beauty*[20] *of the heavens when they are clear*[21] *of clouds.* 11. But, *at that time,* he did not send his *plague* against *the handsome young men Nadab and Abihu.* But *it was reserved for them until the eighth day of or-dination, when it would afflict them.*[22] And they saw *the Glory of the Shekinah of the Lord,* and *they rejoiced in their offerings that had been accepted with favor, as if* they ate and drank.[23] 12. And the Lord said to Moses, "Come up *before* me to the mountain and remain there, and I will give you the tables of stone *where the rest of the words of* the Law *and the six hundred and thirteen*[24] commandments, which I wrote for their instruction, *are intimated.*" 13. So Moses and his attendant Joshua rose, and Moses went up the mountain *on which the Glory of the Shekinah of the Lord was revealed.*[25] 14. And he said to the *sages,*[26] "Wait here for us until we re-turn to you. Behold, Aaron and Hur are with you. Let anyone *who has a legal case*[27] approach *you.*"[28] 15. Then Moses went up the mountain, and the *cloud of glory* covered the mountain. 16. The Glory of *the Shekinah of* the Lord dwelt on the mountain of Sinai, and the cloud *of glory* covered (it) for six days. On the sev-enth day he called to Moses from the midst of the cloud. 17. Now the appearance of *the splendor of* the Glory of the Lord was like a *burning* fire *and (like) sparks of inextinguishable fire*[29] <on top of the mountain>.[30] *And the children of Israel saw*

Notes, Chapter 24

[12]*'pypwryn* = P. (Ps.-J. uses this word in the same form later in the verse.). Nf: *'pypwdn*; Gr.: *hypopodion.*
[13]Lit.: "spread." Jastrow (589) says the reference is to a folding stool.
[14]Lit.: "like."
[15]Or: "a pavement (lit.: a stone work) of sapphire."
[16]According to *j. Sukk.* 4, 54c and *Lev. R.* 23,8, the pavement, which was a reminder of the harsh slavery of Egypt, dis-appeared when Israel was redeemed.
[17]*PRE* (see next note) identifies the angel as Michael. Gabriel is mentioned by Ps.-J. in Gen 37:15; Deut 32:9; 34:6.
[18]*PRE* 48 (385–86). See also *3 Baruch* 3,5.
[19]On the title "Lord of the world," see Ps.-J. Gen 14:13 and n. 28 to that verse; Maher, 1992, 57.
[20]Lit.: "like the might of the beauty."
[21]*bryryn*; Nf, Nfmg, P, V, N: *nqyyn*; = *j. Sukk.* 4, 54c.
[22]*Tanḥ. A, Be-Ha'alothka* 16 (530). See v. 10 and n. 11.
[23]= Onq. Cf. *b. Ber.* 17a. See Grossfeld, 1988B, 73, n. 12.
[24]The 613 commandments are referred to, e.g., in *b. Makk.* 23b; *Shabb.* 87a; *Num. R.* 13, 15 and 18. See further, Urbach, *The Sages,* 342–43.
[25]See above, 3:1 and n. 3 to that verse.
[26]Onq.: "elders." See above, 3:16 and n. 23 to that verse.
[27]*'sq dyn'*; = Nf; Onq.: *dyn',* "a case."
[28]= Lond.; *ed. pr.*: "to them"; = HT.
[29]Lit.: "fire devouring fire"; = Nf. Ps.-J. uses the same idiom in Gen 38:25; Deut 4:24.
[30]Omitted in Lond. and *ed. pr.*

(it), and they were amazed. 18. Then Moses went into the midst of the cloud and went up the mountain. And Moses was on the mountain forty days and forty nights *learning the words of the Law from the mouth of the Holy One*[31]—*may his name be praised.*[32]

CHAPTER 25

1. The Lord spoke to Moses, saying, 2. "Speak to the children of Israel, and let them bring an *offering of separation*[1] *before* me; you shall accept an *offering of separation* for me from everyone[2] who offers willingly,[3] *and not under duress.* 3. And this is the *offering of separation* you shall accept from them: gold, silver, and bronze; 4. blue, purple, and crimson material, linen and goats' hair; 5. tanned[4] rams' skins, sasgona[5] skins, and acacia wood; 6. *and*[6] olive oil for lighting, *and* spices for *the preparation of* the anointing oil and for *the preparation of* aromatic incense; 7. *gems of beryl, they are gems* for setting, *to be inlaid and inserted in* the ephod and *in* the breastpiece. 8. Let them make a sanctuary to *my name,*[7] and I will *make my Shekinah* dwell among them. 9. According to all that I show you, the pattern of the tabernacle and the pattern of its utensils, so shall you make it. 10. Let them make an ark of acacia wood, two and a half cubits long, a cubit and a half wide, and a cubit and a half high. 11. You shall overlay it with pure gold; inside and outside you shall overlay it, and you shall make upon it a gold molding round about. 12. You shall cast four gold rings for it, and you shall put them on its

Notes, Chapter 24

[31]*j. Hor.* 3, 48b; *Tanḥ. A, Ki Tissa* 36 (330); *Exod. R.* 41,6; *PRE* 46 (359–60).
[32]Ps.-J. also uses this formula in Exod 15:18.

Notes, Chapter 25

[1]Lit.: "what is set apart." Cf. Jastrow, 109; Levy 1,57. See also, e.g., the Targums of Exod 29:27; 30:13, 14; 35:5. On the meaning of the underlying Heb. word (*trwmh*), see Driver, *Exodus,* 263.
[2]Lond., *ed. pr.: kl.* The word *gbr* should probably be added as in Onq. and Nf; cf. HT. See 35:21.
[3]Lit.: "whose heart delights (or: chooses) to offer"; = Onq. Our translation is influenced by the continuation of the verse in Ps.-J., where the addition "and not under duress" explains the phrase "who offers willingly." See also the late (eleventh century) midrash *Leq. Tob,* which explains that the Heb. idiom *ydbnw lbw,* "whose hearts prompt them" (RSV), in our present verse means "who is not forced" (*wl' 'nws*); see *Leq. Tob,* ed. S. Buber (2 vols.; Berlin, 1900), vol. 1, p. 176. Cf. also *m. Arakh.* 5,6.
[4]Lit.: "reddened"; = Nf, Onq.
[5]The underlying Heb. word (*tḥšym,* "sea cows"? "dolphins"? "porpoises"?) is obscure. The word *sasgona* used by Nf, Ps.-J., and Onq. may be the name of an animal, or it may refer to a color (scarlet); cf. Jastrow, 1009; Levy, 2, 176–77. See *b. Shabb.* 28a: "we translate it (*taḥash*) *sasgawna* (meaning) that it rejoices in many colors."
[6]The conjunction is also found in the Heb. *lemma.* See also Pesh. and LXX.
[7]= Nf; Onq.: "before me"; HT: "to me."

four feet,[8] two rings on one of its sides, and two rings on its other side. 13. You shall make poles of acacia wood and overlay them with gold. 14. Then you shall insert the poles into the rings on the sides of the ark, to carry the ark by them. 15. The poles shall *be placed* in the rings of the ark; they shall not be removed from it. 16. You shall place within the ark *the tables*[9] of the testimony which I will give you. 17. You shall make a propitiatory of pure gold, two and a half cubits long, a cubit and a half wide; *and its thickness shall be a handbreadth.*[10] 18. You shall make[11] two cherubim of *pure* gold; you shall make them of hammered work, at the two sides of the propitiatory. 19. You shall make one cherub on one side, and the other cherub on the other side. You shall make the cherubim of one piece with the propitiatory[12] on its two sides. 20. The cherubim shall have their wings spread upwards, *in front of their heads,*[13] covering the propitiatory with their wings; one will be turned towards the other,[14] (and) the faces of the cherubim will be (turned) towards the propitiatory. 21. You shall place the propitiatory on top of the ark, and within the ark you shall place *the tables of* the testimony which I will give you. 22. I will appoint *my Memra* to meet you[15] there, and I will tell you, from above the propitiatory, from between the two cherubim that are upon the ark of the testimony, all that I will command you concerning the children of Israel. 23. You shall make a table of acacia wood, two cubits long, a cubit wide, and a cubit and a half high. 24. You shall overlay it with pure gold, and you shall make a gold molding for it round about. 25. You shall make for it a rim a handbreadth *high*[16] round about, and you shall make a gold molding for its rim round about. 26. You shall make four gold rings for it, and you shall put the rings on the four corners at its four legs. 27. The rings shall be against the rim as *holders*[17] for the poles to carry the table. 28. You shall make the poles of acacia wood and overlay them with gold; and they shall carry the table with them. 29. You shall make its bowls,[18] its dishes, its flagons,[19] and its jugs which *will be used* to pour libations; you shall make them of pure gold. 30. You shall *arrange* on the table the *interior* bread,[20] (to be) before me

Notes, Chapter 25

[8]On *'yztwwr* used here and (with a slight variation in spelling) in 37:3 by Ps.-J., and only by Ps.-J., see E. M. Cook, 1986, 250.

[9]Only in Lond.; not in *ed. pr.* See v. 21.

[10]*b. Sukk.* 5a; *Shabb.* 92a.

[11]The verb is in the singular in Ps.-J., as is also the case in the LXX. Nf and Onq., like HT, have the plural.

[12]Lit.: "from the propitiatory." "From" in this context is taken to mean "part of, made from."

[13]Ps.-J.'s source, *b. Sukk.* 5b, discusses whether the wings of the cherubim were above their heads or on a level with them.

[14]Lit.: "and their faces (shall be) one opposite the other."

[15]Lit.: "to you"; = Onq., Nf.

[16]= Onq. Cf. also 37:12. (Ps.-J., Onq.). See Grossfeld, 1988B, 75, n. 7.

[17]Lit.: "a place"; = Onq.; HT: "houses." Cf. Grossfeld, *ibid.,* n. 8. See also, e.g., Exod 26:29; 30:4; 36:34.

[18]*pyyltwy*; Gr.: *phialê.* Ps.-J. uses this word also in Gen 40:12; Exod 37:16; Num 4:7 and fourteen times in Num 7.

[19]*qsww'*; this word, used also by Nf and Onq., refers to a kind of dish or bowl, especially a bowl for libation. See also Ps.-J., Nf, Onq. 37:16; Num 4:7. See Jastrow, 1395; Levy 2, 374.

[20]In translating HT *lḥm hpnym,* "the bread of the Presence" (RSV), Ps.-J. usually takes *pnym* in its second meaning of "inside, interior" (cf. Jastrow, 1190). In 35:13 and 39:36, Ps.-J., like Onq. and Nf, takes *pnym* to mean "presence." See also Num 4:7, where Ps.-J., Nf, and Onq. add "bread" to that text.

always. 31. You shall make the lampstand of pure gold; the base[21] and the shaft of the lampstand shall be made[22] of hammered work; <its cups>,[23] its calyxes and its flowers shall be of one piece with it. 32. Six branches shall extend from its sides, three branches of the lampstand from one side, and three branches of the lampstand from the other side. 33. There shall be three cups *engraved with their figures* on one branch, (each with) calyx and flower; three cups *engraved with their figures* on another branch, (each with) calyx and flower; so for the six branches that extend from the lampstand. 34. And on the lampstand there shall be four cups *engraved with their figures*, each with its calyxes and its flowers: 35. a calyx of one piece with it under a pair of branches; and a calyx of one piece with it under (the second) pair of branches; and a calyx of one piece with it under (the third) pair of branches; (so) for the six branches that extend from the lampstand. 36. Their calyxes and their branches shall be of one piece with it, the whole of it one hammered piece of pure gold. 37. You shall make its seven lamps, *and the priest*[24] *who is appointed shall light*[25] its lamps, and *they* will give light in front of it. 38. Its snuffers[26] and its trays shall be of pure gold. 39. It shall be made, with all these *its* accessories, out of a *centenarius* of pure gold. 40. See that you make (them) according to the patterns for them that you are being shown on the mountain.

CHAPTER 26

1. You shall make the tabernacle with ten curtains of fine twisted linen, of blue, purple, and crimson material; <you shall make them>[1] *embroidered with*[2] cherubim, <the work of an artisan>.[1] 2. The length of a curtain shall be twenty-eight cubits; <and the width>[3] of a curtain <four cubits>.[3] All the curtains shall have the same measurement. 3. Five curtains shall be joined to one another, and the five *other* curtains shall be joined to one another. 4. You shall make loops of blue on the hem[4] of one curtain, on the side, at the point of the joining; and you shall do

Notes, Chapter 25

[21] *bsys*, = Nfmg, and cf. Nf; = Gr. *basis*. HT reads, literally, "thigh." See also 37:17, where Ps.-J. and Nf again use *bsys* to translate the same Heb. word.

[22] = Lond.; *ed. pr.*: "you shall make," which is also the reading in Pesh., LXX.

[23] Omitted in Lond. and *ed. pr.*

[24] See Exod 30:8; Num 8:2. See further Schmerler, 1933, 176.

[25] = Onq.; HT: "elevate." Cf. also 27:20; 30:8; 40:4, 25; Lev 24:2.

[26] Or: "(wick) removers"; *mlqt'* (= Nf) from *lqt*, "pick up"; see Jastrow, 718 and 793. Compare Heb. *mlqh*, from *lqh*, "take, seize."

Notes, Chapter 26

[1] Omitted in Lond.; but there is a blank space in the MS.

[2] Lit.: "(with) embroidery." Onq.: "(with) a design."

[3] Omitted in Lond. and *ed. pr.*

[4] The word *'ymr'* used by Ps.-J. in this verse (twice) and in v. 10 is a Hebraism. Cf. E. M. Cook, 1986, 230.

likewise on the hem of the curtain at the second point of the joining. 5. You shall make fifty loops on one curtain, and you shall make fifty loops at the end of the curtain, at the other point of the joining, the loops directed[5] towards one another. 6. You shall make fifty golden hooks and join the curtains to one another with the hooks, so that the tabernacle will be *fastened to* become one whole. 7. And you shall make curtains of goats' hair *to spread*[6] over the tabernacle; you shall make eleven such curtains. 8. The length of each curtain shall be thirty cubits, and the width of each curtain shall be four cubits; the eleven curtains shall have the same measurement. 9. You shall join five curtains by themselves, *corresponding to the five books of the Law,* and six curtains by themselves, *corresponding to the six orders of the Mishnah.*[7] And you shall fold the sixth curtain over[8] the front of the tent. 10. You shall make fifty loops on the seam of one curtain, at the side, at the point of joining, and fifty loops on the hem of the curtain at the second point of joining. 11. You shall make fifty bronze hooks, and insert the hooks into the loops, and join the tent so that it becomes one whole. 12. The remaining part that hangs from the curtains of the tabernacle, the half of the curtain that remains, shall hang over the rear of the tabernacle. 13. The cubit on either side in the remaining (part of the) length of the curtain of the tabernacle shall hang over the sides of the tabernacle, on either side, to cover it. 14. And you shall make for the tabernacle a covering of tanned rams' skins, and a covering of sasgona skins above. 15. You shall make the planks for the tabernacle of acacia wood, upright, *the way they are planted.*[9] 16. The length of each plank shall be ten cubits, and the width of each plank a cubit and a half. 17. Each plank shall have two tenons, *the end of* one fitting[10] into the other; thus you shall do with all the planks of the tabernacle. 18. You shall make the planks for the tabernacle, twenty planks for the side facing south.[11] 19. You shall make forty sockets of silver under the twenty planks, two sockets under one plank for its two tenons, and two sockets under another plank for its two tenons; 20. and for the second side of the tabernacle, on the north side, twenty planks, 21. with their forty sockets of silver, two sockets under one plank, and two sockets under another plank. 22. And for the rear[12] of the tabernacle, to the west, you shall make six planks; 23. and you shall make two planks for the corners of the tabernacle, at the rear.[13] 24. They shall be joined at the bottom, and they shall be joined, as a unit, at the top, in one ring; thus shall it be for the two of them; they

Notes, Chapter 26

[5]I.e., facing one another; opposite one another; = Onq.

[6]= Onq. See also 36:14.

[7]We know of no source for Ps.-J.'s reference to the Torah and the Mishnah. The idea is taken up in *Midrash Ha-Gadol* to this verse (edition Margulies, Mosad Harav Kook, Jerusalem, 1966, p. 590). See also Exod 36:16 (Ps.-J., Nfmg).

[8]Lit.: "opposite."

[9]Ps.-J.'s sources, b. *Sukk.* 45b and *Yoma* 72a, use the phrase "the way they grow (*drk gdyltn*)." The meaning seems to be that the (pointed) top will be on top. See b. *Shabb.* 98b: "the boards . . . tapered to a fingerbreadth at the top." In his commentary on Exod 26:15, Rashi says that "standing, upright" of HT means that the boards are to be placed in a perpendicular position. See also Ps.-J. 36:20.

[10]Lit.: "*the side of* one directed."

[11]Lit.: "for the side of the south side"; = Onq. HT reads, literally, "to the south side, southward."

[12]Lit.: "the end"; = Onq.

[13]Lit.: "at their ends"; = Onq. See also v. 27.

shall form the two corners. 25. Thus there will be eight planks with their sockets of silver: sixteen sockets, two sockets[14] under one plank, and two sockets under another plank. 26. You shall make bars of acacia wood: five for the planks of one side of the tabernacle, 27. five bars for the planks of the second side of the tabernacle, and five bars for the planks of the side of the tabernacle at the rear, to the west. 28. The middle bar, halfway up the planks, crossing from end to end, *(shall be made) of the tree that Abraham planted in Beer-sheba.*[15] *When Israel crossed the sea, the angels cut the tree and threw it into the sea. It floated on the surface of the waters, and an angel called out and said, "This is the tree that Abraham planted in Beer-sheba when he prayed there in the name of the Memra of the Lord." The children of Israel took it, and from it they made the middle bar, which was seventy cubits*[16] *long. Wonders were worked in it, for when they erected the tabernacle, it twisted itself*[17] *round about like a serpent in the middle of the planks of the tabernacle; and when they took it apart, it straightened out like a rod.*[18] 29. You shall overlay the planks with gold, and you shall make their rings of gold, *holders*[19] for the bars; and you shall overlay the bars with gold. 30. Thus you shall erect the tabernacle according to the plan[20] that you were shown on the mountain. 31. You shall make a veil[21] of blue, purple, and crimson material, and fine twisted linen; it shall be made[22] *embroidered with* cherubim, the work of an artisan. 32. You shall *arrange* it upon four pillars of acacia overlaid with gold, with their clasps of gold, and (set) in four sockets of silver. 33. You shall place the veil beneath the hooks and bring the ark of the testimony in there, behind the veil, so that the veil will separate the Holy Place from the Holy of Holies for you. 34. You shall place the propitiatory, *with the cherubim that are of hammered work and of one piece with it,*[23] <upon the ark of the testimony>[24] in the Holy of Holies. 35. You shall place the table outside the veil, with the lampstand opposite the table, on the south side of the tabernacle. And you shall *arrange* the table on the north side. 36. You shall make a screen for the entrance of the tent, of blue, purple, and crimson material, and fine twisted linen, done in embroidery *with the needle.*[25] 37. You shall make five pillars of acacia for the screen and overlay them with gold; their clasps shall be of gold, and you shall cast five sockets of copper for them.

Notes, Chapter 26

[14] = *Ed. pr.* Lond.: "planks." Rieder, in his edition of Ps.-J., has "sockets," without noting that he has corrected the text.

[15] Cf. Gen 21:33.

[16] *Gen. R.* 94,4 and *Song of Songs R.* 1,12.1 tell us that the middle bar of the tabernacle was made from the tree which Abraham planted and which had been stored by the Israelites. See further Ginzberg, *Legends* 3, 164, and 6, 66, n. 344. We know of no source for Ps.-J.'s account of the intervention of the angels; cf. Shinan, 1979, 2, 263.

[17] *m(y)sglgl* = Lond., *ed. pr.* Read *m(y)tglgl*. In his edition of Ps.-J., Rieder suggests that the use of *s* for *t* indicates that the scribe was Ashkenazi.

[18] *b. Shabb.* 98b: "It lay there by a miracle."

[19] See 25:27 (Ps.-J.) and n. 17 to that verse.

[20] Lit.: "its rule, law"; = Onq. Cf. HT: *kmšpṭw*, "according to the plan for it" (RSV).

[21] *prgwd'*; Nf, Onq.: *pr(w)kt'*. Ps.-J. generally uses the form *prgwd'*, while Nf and Onq. use *pr(w)kt'*. See 26:33 (three times), 35; 27:21; 30:6; 35:12; 36:35, etc. In 40:3, however, Ps.-J., like Nf and Onq., uses *prwkt'*.

[22] Lit.: "he shall make it"; = Nf, Onq., HT. LXX, Pesh.: "you shall make."

[23] See 25:18-19. In our present verse Ps.-J. reads, literally, "that go out hammered from it."

[24] Omitted in Lond. and *ed. pr.*

[25] Cf. *b. Yoma* 72b: "The embroiderer's (work) is needlework."

CHAPTER 27

1. You shall make the altar of acacia wood, five cubits long and five cubits wide: the altar is to be square, and three cubits high. 2. Make its horns on its four corners: its horns are to be of one piece with it, *erected upwards*;[1] you shall overlay it with bronze. 3. You shall make pots to remove[2] its ashes, as well as its shovels, sprinkling basins, forks, and fire-pans; you shall make all its utensils of bronze. 4. And you shall make for it a grating[3] of network in bronze; and on the net make four bronze rings on its four corners.[4] 5. You shall place it under the ledge[5] of the altar, downwards, so that the net extends to[6] the middle of the altar. *If a bone or a burning coal falls from the altar, it will fall upon the grating and will not reach the ground.*[7] *And the priests will take it off the grating and put it back on the altar.* 6. You shall make poles <for the altar, poles>[8] of acacia wood, and you shall overlay them with bronze. 7. The poles shall be inserted into the rings, so that the poles will be on the two sides of the altar when *the altar* is being carried. 8. You shall make it hollow, of boards, *filled with earth.*[9] As *I have shown*[10] you on the mountain, so shall they do. 9 You shall make the courtyard of the tabernacle: for the side facing south,[11] there shall be hangings of fine twisted linen for the courtyard, a hundred cubits long for (that) one side; 10. its pillars shall be twenty, with their twenty sockets of bronze; the clasps of the pillars and their bands will be of silver. 11. So also for the north side, in its length, there shall be hangings a hundred (cubits)[12] long, with their twenty pillars, and their twenty sockets of bronze; the clasps of the pillars and their bands shall be of silver. 12. (For) the width of <the courtyard>[8] on the west side, hangings of fifty cubits, with their ten pillars and their ten sockets. 13. The width of the courtyard on the east side, to the orient, will be fifty cubits. 14. There will be fifteen cubits of hangings on one side, with their three pillars and their three sockets. 15. ...[13] 16. And for the gate of the courtyard, a screen of twenty cubits, of blue, purple, and crimson material, and of fine

Notes, Chapter 27

[1]According to *m. Middoth* 3,1, the horns were cubes, measuring a cubit at each edge. See also Ps.-J. Exod 30:2; 37:25; 38:2.

[2]Read *lm(y)drd'* with *ed. pr.* rather than *lmrdd'* of Lond. Ps.-J. uses the verb *drd* again in Num 4:13.

[3]*qnql* = Nf, V, N; = Gr. *kigklis*; Latin: *cancelli*; HT: *mkbr*. In v. 5 P uses *qnql* to translate HT *krkb*, "ledge" (RSV).

[4]Lit.: "sides"; = Onq.

[5]Or: "gallery"; = Onq. Cf. Grossfeld, 1988B, 78, n. 1.

[6]Lond. and *ed. pr.* read "upon" (*'l*) instead of "to" (*'d*).

[7]Cf. Ps.-J. 38:4. We know of no source for Ps.-J.'s explanation of the purpose of the grating mentioned in vv. 4-5. According to *b. Zeb.* 53a, it served as "a barrier to distinguish between the upper and the lower bloods"; cf. *m. Middoth* 3,1. See further, Schmerler, 1933, 182.

[8]Omitted in Lond. and *ed. pr.*

[9]*Mek. RI* Exod 20:21 (2,284): "Issi b. Akiba says: An altar of copper filled in with earth." See also *b. Zeb.* 54a. See also Ps.-J. Exod 38:7.

[10]= Onq. See Grossfeld, 1988B, 78, n. 2.

[11]See 26:18 and n. 11 to that verse.

[12]"Cubits," which we add for clarity, is also added in LXX.

[13]v. 15 is omitted in Lond. and *ed. pr.*

twisted linen, done in embroidery *with the needle*;[14] their pillars will be four, with their four sockets. 17. All the pillars round about the courtyard shall be banded with silver; their clasps will be of silver and their sockets of bronze. 18. The length of the courtyard shall be a hundred cubits, and its width fifty *to the west*[15] *and* fifty *to the east*,[15] and its height five cubits, (with hangings) of fine twisted linen and sockets of bronze. 19. All the utensils of the tabernacle, for all its service, and all its pegs, and all the pegs of the courtyard *round about*,[16] shall be of bronze. 20. You shall command the children of Israel to bring you pure oil of crushed olives for lighting, for *lighting*[17] lamps regularly.[18] 21. In the tent of meeting, outside the veil that is over the testimony, Aaron and his sons shall set it in order from evening to morning before the Lord. (This shall be) a perpetual ordinance for the children of Israel throughout their generations.

CHAPTER 28

1. You shall bring near to you, from the midst of the children of Israel, Aaron your brother, and his sons to *minister before* me:[1] Aaron, Nadab, Abihu, Eleazar, and Ithamar, the sons of Aaron. 2. You shall make sacred vestments for Aaron your brother, for glory and honor.[2] 3. You shall speak to all who are wise of heart,[3] whom I have filled with the spirit of wisdom, and they shall make Aaron's vestments, to consecrate him to *minister before* me. 4. These are the vestments they are to make: a breastpiece, an ephod, a robe, checkered tunics, turbans, and sashes.[4] They shall make the sacred vestments for Aaron your brother and for his sons, so that *they may minister before* me.[5] 5. And they shall receive *of their wealth*,[6] gold, blue, purple, and crimson material and fine linen. 6. They shall make the ephod

Notes, Chapter 27

[14]See 26:36 and n. 25 to that verse.
[15]For the additions "to the west" and "to the east" see vv. 12-13. See also *b. Erub.* 23b.
[16]See 38:20, 31.
[17]= Onq. See 25:37 and n. 25 to that verse.
[18]In the context the meaning is "regularly," i.e., each night (cf. v. 21) rather than "continually." See also Ps.-J. 30:8 and n. 6 to that verse.

Notes, Chapter 28

[1]Or: "to serve before me"; = Onq. HT has a curious idiom, literally, "to minister him as priest to me." Ps.-J. agrees with Onq. in its rendering of this phrase; cf., e.g., 28:3, 4, 41. See the comment on our present verse in Nf.
[2]Lit.: "praise"; = Onq. See also v. 40.
[3]The Aramaic idiom which we translate as "all who are wise of heart" corresponds to the idiom in HT which is rendered as "all who have ability" (RSV) or "all who are skillful" (JPS).
[4]Or: "belts" (*qmwryn*). Nf and Onq. use the word *hmyyn*, "belt, girdle." See also, e.g., 28:39-40; 29:9; 39:29. In 28:42 Ps.-J. uses the word *qmwr* with *'sr* (= Nf), "band, fastening."
[5]Lond.: "before him"; = Nf. But in vv. 1 and 3, Ps.-J. has "before me." See Díez-Macho, 1981A, 76.
[6]The reference seems to be to the offerings made by the people (cf. 25:2-7). See Schmerler, 1933, 183.

<of gold>,[7] blue, purple, and crimson material, and of fine twisted linen, the work of an artisan. 7. *And*[8] it shall have two shoulder-pieces attached to its two ends, and (so) it will be attached.[9] 8. The belt that is on it for fastening it shall be made like it, of one piece with it: of gold, blue, purple, and crimson material, and of fine twisted linen. 9. You shall take two *gems* of *beryl* and inscribe on them the names of the sons of Israel, 10. *part of* their names,[10] six, on one *gem*, and the names of the six that remain on the second *gem, arranged* according to their birth. 11. The *gems*[11] *shall be* the work of an artisan, inscribed and (*clearly*) engraved; *as one inscribes* a signet ring you shall inscribe the two *gems* with the names of the sons of Israel; you shall have them[12] mounted artistically, in settings of gold. 12. You shall *arrange* the two *gems* on the shoulder-pieces of the ephod, as *gems* that remind the children of Israel of *the merit* (of the Fathers).[13] And Aaron shall carry the names *of the sons of Israel*[14] on his two shoulders, as a memorial. 13. You shall make settings of gold, 14. and two chains of pure gold. You shall make them like cords, plaited work, and place the plaited chains on the settings. 15. You shall make a breastpiece of judgment—*through which*[15] *is made known the judgment of Israel that is hidden from the judges, as well as the order of their victorious wars,*[16] *(and which serves) to make atonement for the judges*[17]—the work of an artisan. After the manner[18] of the ephod you shall make it; you shall make it of gold, blue, purple, and crimson material, and of fine twisted linen. 16. It shall be square, doubled, a span in length and a span in width. 17. You shall set in it a setting of *precious gems*, four rows of *precious gems*[19] *corresponding to the four corners of the world.*[20] The *first* row: a cornelian, a topaz, and a smaragd, one row. *On them shall be clearly engraved the names of the tribes Reuben, Simeon, and Levi.*[21] 18. *The names*[22] of the second row: a turquoise, a sapphire, and a chalcedony. *On them shall be clearly engraved the names of the three tribes Judah, Dan, and Naphtali.*

Notes, Chapter 28

[7]Omitted in Lond. and *ed. pr.*

[8]Both the Aramaic version and the Hebrew lemma add "and."

[9]The meaning seems to be that the two "sides" of the Ephod (its front and back) will be joined by the shoulder-pieces.

[10]Ps.-J. translates HT *mšmtm*, "of their names" as *mn qṣt šmhthwn*, "of *part of* their names." Compare *j. Sotah* 7, 21d. See Schmerler, 1933, 184–85.

[11]Onq.: "precious stone."

[12]Lit.: "you shall make them."

[13]Ps.-J. takes the word "remembrance" of HT to refer to a remembrance of the merits of the ancestors. For references to the merits of the fathers in Ps.-J. see, e.g., Gen 15:11; 22:18; 28:14; Exod 40:4, 8; Num 22:30; 23:9.

[14]Cf. LXX.

[15]Through the Urim and Thummim that were in the breastpiece; cf. v. 30.

[16]*m. Yoma* 7,5: "and they did not inquire of them (the Urim and Thummim) except for a king or for the court. . . ." Cf. Num 27:21.

[17]*b. Arakh.* 16a: "The breastpiece procures atonement [for errors] in legal decisions." Cf. also *b. Zeb.* 88b; *j. Yoma* 7, 44b.

[18]Lit.: "like the work of."

[19]Cf. Bacher, 1894, 79–90. See further Le Déaut, 1979, 223, n. 8.

[20]We know of no source for Ps.-J.'s reference to the four corners of the world. See also 39:10 (Ps.-J.).

[21]For the stones, with their corresponding names, that are listed in vv. 17-20, see *Exod. R.* 38,9; *Num. R.* 2,7. Cf. Ps.-J. Num 2:3, 10, 18, 25. See also Nf Exod 28:17-20 and the notes to those verses.

[22]Lit.: "the name." See also vv. 19-20.

19. *The names of* the third row: a jacinth, an agate, and an amethyst.[23] *On them shall be clearly engraved the names of the three tribes Gad, Asher, and Issachar.* 20. *The names of* the fourth row: a beryl *of the Great Sea,* a chrysoberyl, and a jasper. *On them shall be clearly engraved the names of the three tribes Zebulun, Joseph, and Benjamin.* They shall be inserted in gold in their settings. 21. *The gems* shall be *taken* according to the names of the sons of Israel; *they* shall be twelve, according to their names. They shall be inscribed, *clearly engraved as one inscribes* a signet ring. They shall represent the twelve tribes, each with *its gem* corresponding to its name. 22. On the breastpiece you shall make corded chains, plaited work, in pure gold. 23. On the breastpiece you shall make two rings of *pure* gold, and put the two rings at the two sides of the breastpiece. 24. You shall put the two plaits of gold in the two rings at the ends of the breastpiece. 25. The two plaits *that are at* its two ends you shall put on the two settings, and you shall put (them) on the shoulder-pieces of the ephod, at its front. 26. You shall make two rings of gold and put them at the two ends of the breastpiece, on its inner edge, against[24] the ephod. 27. You shall make two rings of gold and put them on the two shoulder-pieces of the ephod, low down on its front, at the point of joining above the belt of the ephod. 28. They shall bind the breastpiece with a *twisted* cord[25] of blue from its rings to the rings of the ephod, so that it is *fastened* to the belt of the ephod, and so that the breastpiece does not come loose from the ephod. 29. Aaron shall carry the names of the sons of Israel on the breastpiece of judgment upon his heart, when he enters the holy place,[26] as a *good* remembrance before the Lord continually. 30. You shall put into the ephod of judgment the Urim—*the words of which are enlightening*[27] *and make public the hidden things of the house of Israel*—and the Thummim—*which fulfills*[27] *the oracles of the high priest, who, through them, seeks instruction from before the Lord. On them is clearly inscribed the great and holy Name*[28] *through which the three hundred and ten worlds were created,*[29] *and which was clearly inscribed on the foundation stone with which the Lord of the world sealed the mouth of the great deep from the beginning.*[30] *And everyone who brings this holy*

Notes, Chapter 28

[23]Lit.: "calf's eye"; HT: *'ḥlmh.* Nf, V, and N use this term in v. 18 to translate HT *yhlm.*

[24]Lit.: "to the side of."

[25]Lit.: "a twisted thread (*šzyr,* = Nf) of cord (*ḥwṭ';* = Onq.)." See also v. 37; 39:31. Cf. also 28:31, where Ps.-J. uses this idiom.

[26]Lit.: "the holy"; = HT. See also v. 43; 29:30; 31:11; 35:19; 36:1, 6; 39:1.

[27]The midrash is based on a popular etymology of the words *Urim* (taken to be derived from *'wr,* "light") and *Thummim* (taken to be derived from *tm,* "to be complete," or, in this context, "fulfilled"). See *b.* Yoma 73b; *j.* Yoma 7, 44c. The phrase which we translate as *"which fulfills the oracles of the high priest"* reads literally: *"which fulfills by their deeds (b'wbdyhwn)* [compare *b.* Yoma 73b: *dbryhn] for the high priest."*

[28]We know of no source for the statement that the holy Name was written on the Urim and Thummim; cf. Ginzberg, *Legends,* 6, 69, n. 358; Shinan, 1979, 2, 281.

[29]*b. Sanh.* 100a. Cf. *m. Uktsin* 3,12, which, however, seems to be a late addition to the Mishnah. Compare Exod 20:7 (P): "for through my great Name the world was created." See further Ginzberg, *Legends,* 5, 12, n. 30.

[30]Tg. Qoh 3:11; Tg. Song of Songs 4:12. The "foundation stone" referred to is the stone that remained in the Temple after the ark was taken away; cf. *m.* Yoma 5,2; *PRE* 35 (266). See further Ginzberg, *Legends,* 5, 14-15, n. 39; Heinemann, 1974, 191–92; Shinan, 1979, 2, 281, n. 188.

Name to mind in the hour of affliction is saved, and hidden things are revealed[31] *to him.*[32] They shall be upon Aaron's heart when he comes in before the Lord. And Aaron shall carry the judgment of the children of Israel upon his heart before the Lord continually. 31. You shall make the robe[33] of the ephod of *twisted thread* of blue. 32. The opening for the head shall be in the middle. There will be a band *on its border*, the work of a weaver, surrounding the opening round about. It will be like the opening of a coat of mail, (so that)[34] it is not torn. 33. On its hem you shall make pomegranates of blue, purple, and crimson material, round about on the hem, with bells of gold between them round about: 34. a golden bell and a pomegranate *of blue and crimson*, a golden bell and a pomegranate *of blue and crimson*, round about on the lower hem of the robe.[35] *Their total: seventy-one.*[36] 35. It shall be *wrapped* on Aaron when he ministers,[37] and the sound of it will be heard when he comes into the sanctuary before the Lord and when he goes out, so that he may not die *in the glowing fire*. 36. And you shall make a plate of pure gold, and you shall inscribe on it, *clearly* engraved:[38] "Holy to the Lord." 37. You shall *arrange* it on a *twisted* cord[39] of blue, *to make atonement for the insolent*;[40] it shall be on the turban, *above the phylactery for the head*;[41] it shall be on the front of the turban. 38. It shall be on the forehead of Aaron's *face, reaching from temple to temple*;[42] and Aaron shall carry the guilt[43] associated with the holy things that the children of Israel shall consecrate as[44] their sacred donations *in which they have defrauded*. It shall be on his forehead continually to win favor for them before the Lord. 39. You shall weave the tunic of fine linen in checkers, to make *atonement for the shedding of innocent blood*;[45] you shall make the turban of fine linen to make atonement *for the haughty*;[46] and you shall make a sash, done in embroidery. 40. For Aaron's

Notes, Chapter 28

[31]We know of no source for this latter addition by Ps.-J. But cf. *b. Qidd.* 71a: "He who knows it (the divine Name) . . . is beloved above and popular below, feared by man, and inherits two worlds. . . ." On Ps.-J.'s interest in the divine Name and in its power, see Maher, 1992, 7.

[32]"To him" is omitted in *ed. pr.*

[33]Ps.-J. has the conflate reading "the tunic (*mnṭr*), the robe (*m'yl'* = Nf, Onq.)." See also v. 34; 29:5; 39:22, 23, 24, 25, 26; Lev 8:7.

[34]See 39:23, where Ps.-J. adds "so that."

[35]See v. 31 and n. 33.

[36]In 39:26 Ps.-J. reads "seventy." Rieder, in his edition of Ps.-J., reads "seventy-two" in both texts. He follows *b. Zeb.* 88b and *Lev. R.* 21,7.

[37]Lit.: "to minister"; = HT.

[38]Onq.: "in clear script."

[39]See above, v. 28 and n. 25.

[40]Lit.: "the insolent (*ḥṣypy*) of face." See *b. Arakh.* 16a, literally, "for the deeds of the insolent (*'zy pnym*)." Cf. also *b. Zeb.* 88b; *j. Yoma* 7, 44c.

[41]Compare *b. Zeb.* 19a-b. See also Ps.-J. 39:31.

[42]*b. Sukk.* 5a: "stretching from ear to ear."

[43]= Onq.; Nf: "sins."

[44]Lit.: "for all"; = HT.

[45]*b. Arakh.* 16a.

[46]Or: "the presumptuous"; literally: "those who make their minds bold (*mgysy r'ywnyhwn*)." See the corresponding Hebrew phrase in Ps.-J.'s source, *b. Arakh.* 16a: *gsy hrwḥ*, literally: "the bold of spirit."

sons also you shall make tunics, and make sashes for them, and make headdresses for them for glory and honor. 41. You shall put them on your brother Aaron and on his sons with him; you shall *purify*[47] them, and *offer their offering*,[48] and consecrate them that they may *minister before* me. 42. You shall also make linen breeches[49] for them to cover the flesh of (their) nudity; they shall extend from the *fastening of the sash*[50] *of* their loins to their thighs. 43. They will be on Aaron and on his sons when they enter the tent of meeting or when they approach the altar to minister in the holy place,[51] so that they do not incur guilt <and die>[52] *in glowing fire.*[53] (It shall be) a perpetual ordinance for him and for *his sons* after him.

CHAPTER 29

1. This is what you shall do to them to consecrate them to *minister before him*: take a bull *that is not a hybrid*,[1] and two perfect rams, 2. unleavened bread, unleavened cakes kneaded with *olive*[2] oil, and wafers[3] of unleavened *bread* smeared with *olive*[2] oil. You shall make them of fine wheat flour.[4] 3. You shall put them in one basket and bring them near in the basket; the bull and the two rams *will be carried*

Notes, Chapter 28

[47] = Lond.: *tdkyh*; Rieder and Clarke, in their editions of Ps.-J., read *trbyh*; *ed. pr.*: *trby*. See also 29:29, 36.

[48] = Onq. Nf: "you shall complete the offering of their hands"; HT: "fill their hands." The idiom "fill the hand," meaning "ordain to priestly office," is translated by Onq. and Ps.-J. as "offer the offering." Cf., e.g., 29:9, 29, 33, 35; Lev 8:33; 16:32; 21:10; Num 3:3. Cf. also Exod 32:29. See further the note on our present verse in Nf, and cf. Grossfeld, 1988B, 81, n. 6.

[49] *'wwrqsyn*; Nfmg: *'brqsyn*; cf. V, N. Latin: *braccae*. Cf. Levy, 1, 7. See also 39:28 (Ps.-J.); Lev 6:3 (Ps.-J., Nfmg, P, V, N); 16:4 (Ps.-J., Nfmg).

[50] Ps.-J. has a conflate reading *'sr qmwr*. See v. 4 and n. 4.

[51] See v. 29 and n. 26.

[52] Omitted in Lond. and *ed. pr.*

[53] The idiom "(to die) in glowing fire" is used frequently in Ps.-J.; see also v. 35; 30:20, 21, 29; Lev 16:1, 13; 22:9; Num 1:51; 3:4, etc. Cf. Rodríguez Carmona, 1983, 111.

Notes, Chapter 29

[1] See *b. Nid.* 41a: "'a bullock' excludes *kil'ayim*, (that is, a hybrid)," and *b. Ḥul.* 78b: "wherever *'sheep'* is stated the hybrid (*kl'ym*) is excluded." See also Ps.-J. Lev 16:3, 5; 23:18, 19; Num 15:24, 27; 28:11; Deut 14:4; 21:3.

[2] See also, e.g., Gen 35:14; Exod 35:28; Lev 2:15; 6:14; 7:12 (three times); 9:4, where Ps.-J. also adds "olive."

[3] Read *'rykyn* (=Nf) rather than *'yrwbyn*, which is the reading in Lond. and *ed. pr.* The mistake is due to the influence of v. 1, where the word *'yrwbyn* occurs.

[4] *smyd'*; = Gr. *semidalis*. Nf, Onq.: *slt*. Ps.-J. usually employs *smyd'* when Onq. and Nf use *slt*; cf. v. 40; Lev 2:1, 4, 5, 7; 5:11; 6:8, etc.

on a pole.[5] 4. You shall bring Aaron and his sons near to the entrance of the tent of meeting, and bathe them in *forty seahs of running* water.[6] 5. You shall take the vestments, and clothe Aaron with the tunic, the robe[7] of the ephod, the ephod, and the breastpiece, and you shall gird him with the belt of the ephod. 6. You shall put the turban on his head, and on the turban you shall put the crown on which the holy *name is inscribed.*[8] 7. You shall take the anointing oil and pour (it) on his head and anoint him. 8. Then you shall bring his sons near, and clothe them with tunics, 9. and gird them with sashes, Aaron and his sons, and bind headdresses on them. And the priesthood will be theirs by perpetual ordinance. *You shall offer the offering* of Aaron and *the offering*[9] of his sons. 10. Then you shall bring the bull before the tent of meeting, and let Aaron and his sons lay their hands on the head of the bull. 11. You shall slaughter the bull before the Lord at the entrance of the tent of meeting. 12. You shall take some of the bull's blood and put (it) on the horns of the altar with your finger; then pour out all (the remaining)[10] blood at the base of the altar. 13. You shall take all the fat that covers the entrails, the appendage on *the lobe of* the liver,[11] and the two kidneys with the fat on them, and *arrange*[12] *(them) on* the altar. 14. The flesh of the bull, its hide and its dung, you shall burn by fire outside the camp; it is a sin offering. 15. Then take one of the rams, and let Aaron and his sons lay their hands on the head of the ram. 16. You shall slaughter the ram, and take its blood, and dash (it) against the altar, round about. 17. You shall cut the ram into pieces, rinse its entrails and legs, and *arrange* (them) on its *limbs* and on its head. 18. You shall offer[13] up the whole ram on the altar; it is a burnt offering *before* the Lord *to be accepted with favor*; it is *an offering before* the Lord. 19. Then you shall take the second ram, and let Aaron and his sons lay their hands

Notes, Chapter 29

[5] *'sl'*; Gr. *asilla.* See also Ps.-J. Lev 16:27; Num 4:10; 13:23. This word, although used in Hebrew, is not used in Aramaic contexts except in Ps.-J. Cf. E. M. Cook, 1986, 231. In our present verse Ps.-J. makes it clear that the bull and the rams were not in the basket, as one might try to argue from HT.

[6] *m. Men.* 12,4; *Mikvaoth* 1,7; *b. Erub.* 4b; *Pesah.* 109b. These texts specify that a ritual bath must contain 40 *seahs* of water. The verb which we translate as "bathe" in this verse is *tbl,* "immerse, bathe for purification." The verb in HT is *rhs,* "bathe, wash," and it is translated in Onq. as *shy,* which has the same meaning. Nf renders it by *qds,* "sanctify." Cf. Lev 8:6, where Onq. and Ps.-J. translate *rhs* by *shy,* while Nf again uses *qds.* See below, Ps.-J. 30:18 and n. 15 to that verse.

[7] See 28:31 and n. 33 to that verse.

[8] Cf. 28:36.

[9] = Onq. See 28:41 and n. 48 to that verse.

[10] LXX adds "the remaining."

[11] Lit.: "that which is left on the lobe of the liver." Ps.-J., Nf, Nfi, Onq., Pesh., and LXX all take HT *ytrt* (RSV "appendage") to mean "lobe." In our present verse and in v. 22, Ps.-J. and Nf translate HT *ytrt* twice, first deriving it from the Hebrew root *ytr,* "to remain over," and then rendering it as "lobe." Nf usually has this double translation of *ytrt,* whereas Ps.-J. usually agrees with Onq. and translates that word simply as "lobe." See the Targums of Lev 3:4, 10, 15; 4:9; 7:4, etc.

[12] = Nf. Onq.: "offer"; literally, "cause to go up." HT (literally): "cause to go up in smoke." The Pal. Tgs., apart from Ps.-J., usually translate this verb (*qtr,* Hif.) as "arrange, set in order." Ps.-J. usually agrees with Onq., using "cause to go up" as in v. 18; 30:20; Lev 1:9, 13, 15, 17, etc., or using the Aramaic cognate of the Hebrew verb (Exod 30:7 [twice], 8). In 29:25 Ps.-J. agrees with Nf. In Lev 6:15 Ps.-J. combines the readings of Nf and Onq. In Exod 30:1 and 40:27 the three Targums use different words.

[13] Lit.: "cause to go up"; = Onq. Nf: "arrange." See preceding note.

on the head of the ram. 20. You shall slaughter the ram and take some of its blood, and put (it) on the lobe[14] of Aaron's *right*[15] ear, and on the lobes of his sons' right ears, on the thumbs of their right hands, and on the big toes of their right feet; and you shall dash *the rest of* the blood on the altar, round about. 21. Then you shall take some of the blood that is on the altar and some of the anointing oil and sprinkle upon Aaron and his vestments, and upon his sons and his sons' vestments with him <...>[16] 22. You shall take from the ram the fat and the fat tail, the fat that covers the entrails, the appendage on *the lobe of* the liver,[17] the two kidneys with the fat that is on them, and the right thigh—for it is a ram of *the offerings*[18]— 23. and one round loaf of bread, one cake of bread *kneaded in* oil, and one wafer, from the basket of unleavened bread that is before the Lord. 24. You shall place all these on the *hands* of Aaron and on the *hands*[19] of his sons, and *raise* them as an *offering of elevation*[20] before the Lord. 25. Take them from their hands and *arrange*[21] (them) on the altar in addition to the burnt offering, *to be accepted with favor* before the Lord; it is *an offering before* the Lord. 26. You shall take the breast of the ram of Aaron's *offerings*, and *raise* it as an *offering of elevation* before the Lord; it shall be your portion. 27. You shall consecrate the breast of the *offering of elevation* and the thigh of the *offering of separation*, that which was *raised up* and that which was *separated*, from the ram of the *offerings*, from that of Aaron and from that of his sons. 28. And it shall be[22] for Aaron and his sons a perpetual due[23] from the children of Israel <because it is an *offering of separation*; it will be an *offering of separation* by the children of Israel>[24] from their sacrifices of *holy things*, their offering that has been set apart *before* the Lord. 29. Aaron's sacred vestments shall belong to his sons after him, to be anointed[25] in them, and to *offer* their *offerings*[9] in them. 30. The priest from among his sons—*but not from among the Levites—who will come after* him,[26] shall wear them for seven days when *they* enter the tent of meeting to minister in the sanctuary.[27] 31. You shall take the ram

Notes, Chapter 29

[14]*ḥsḥws*. Ps.-J. uses this word to translate HT *tnwk*, "lobe, tip," in our present verse (twice), and in Lev 8:23; 14:17. Nf and Onq. regularly translate this word by *rwm*. See Lev 8:24; 14:14, 25, 28, where Ps.-J. renders it as "the middle protuberance." Rashi on Lev 14:14 explains *tnwk* as "the inner wall of the ear."

[15]Added also in Pesh. and LXX, probably because "right" is mentioned three times in this verse with reference to Aaron's sons.

[16]The end of the verse is omitted through homoioteleuton.

[17]See v. 13 and n. 11.

[18]= Onq. See 28:41 and n. 48 to that verse.

[19]Omitted in Lond. Here, and earlier in the verse, HT has "palms."

[20]Lit.: "as an elevation (*'rm'*)"; = Onq.; Nf: "as a wave offering (*'npw*)." See also vv. 26, 27; 35:22, 24; 38:24, 29, where Ps.-J. agrees with Onq., against Nf.

[21]= Nf; Onq.: "offer." See v. 13 and n. 12.

[22]Nfmg: "they shall be." This makes it clear that the offerings mentioned in the preceding verse are being referred to.

[23]Lit.: "an everlasting ordinance."

[24]Omitted in Lond. and *ed. pr.* through homoioteleuton.

[25]= Lond.: *lrb'ḥ*; *ed. pr.*: *ldk'ḥ*, "to be purified." Onq., Nf, HT: "to be anointed." See 28:41 (Ps.-J.).

[26]On the demands made by the Levites in 64 C.E. to wear the white linen vestment of the priest, see J. Jeremias, 1975, 212–13.

[27]See 28:29 (Ps.-J.) and n. 26 to that verse.

of the *offerings* and boil its flesh in a holy place. 32. Aaron and his sons shall eat the flesh of the ram, and the bread that is in the basket, at the entrance of the tent of meeting. 33. They shall eat those things[28] with which atonement was made, at the *offering* of the *offering*[29] for their consecration *to minister before me*. No layman may eat (them), for they are holy. 34. If any of the flesh of the *offerings*[29] or any of the bread is left till morning, you shall burn what is left by fire; it shall not be eaten, for it is holy. 35. Thus you shall do to Aaron and his sons, according to all I have commanded you. For seven days you shall *offer* their *offering*.[29] 36. Each day you shall offer a bull as a sin offering,[30] for atonement; you shall *purify*[31] the altar when you make atonement on it, and you shall anoint it[32] to consecrate it. 37. For seven days you shall make atonement for the altar, and (thus) you shall consecrate it, and the altar will become most holy. Whoever[33] *from among the sons of Aaron* approaches the altar will be consecrated. *But it is not possible for the rest of the people to approach, lest they be burned in glowing fire that would come forth from the holy things.* 38. This is *the offering* you are to make on the altar: two year-old lambs each day, continually. 39. You shall offer[34] one lamb in the morning, and you shall offer the second lamb at twilight. 40. (You shall offer) a tenth (of a measure) of fine flour kneaded with a quarter of a *hin* of oil of *crushed* olives and a libation of a quarter of a *hin* <of wine>,[35] for one lamb. 41. You shall offer the second lamb at twilight; you shall offer with it a cereal offering and its libation as in the morning, *to be accepted with favor* as *an offering before* the Lord. 42. (It shall be) a continual burnt offering, throughout your generations, at the entrance of the tent of meeting before the Lord, where I will have *my Memra* meet you, to speak with you there. 43. There I will have *my Memra* meet the children of Israel, and *I shall be sanctified in your*[36] *princes*[37] *for the sake of* my glory. 44. I will consecrate the tent of meeting and the altar; and I will consecrate Aaron and his sons to *serve before* me.[38] 45. And I will *make my Shekinah* dwell in the midst of the children of Israel, and I will be their God. 46. And *the children of Israel* will know that I am the Lord their God who brought them forth *redeemed* from the land of Egypt to *make my*[39] *Shekinah* dwell among them; I am the Lord their God.

Notes, Chapter 29

[28]Lit.: "them"; = HT.

[29]= Onq. See 28:41 (Ps.-J.) and n. 48 to that verse.

[30]Lit.: "you shall make a bull of sin offering"; = Onq., HT. Compare Nf.

[31]= Lond.: *tdky*; *ed. pr.*: *trby*, "you shall anoint." Nf also reads *trby*. Klein (1974, 226) proposes that this should read *tdky*. See also Díez-Macho's edition of Neofiti in *Biblia Polyglotta Matritensia*, vol. 2, *Exodus*, 232. See above v. 29 and n. 25.

[32]*Ed. pr.*: "on it."

[33]HT is ambiguous and can mean "anything" or "anyone." We know of no source for Ps.-J.'s application of this text to the sons of Aaron.

[34]Lit.: "make"; = Onq., HT. Compare Nf. See also v. 36 and n. 30, and v. 41.

[35]Omitted in Lond. and *ed. pr.*

[36]*Ed. pr.*: "their."

[37]Cf. *b. Zeb.* 115b: "in your honored ones," which in the context refers to the priests. See Ps.-J. Lev 10:3.

[38]= *Ed. pr.*, Nf, Onq.; Lond., Nfmg: "before him."

[39]= *Ed. pr.*; Lond.: "his."

CHAPTER 30

1. You shall make an altar *to* offer up *aromatic* incense[1] *on it*; you shall make it of acacia wood. 2. It shall be a cubit long and a cubit wide. It shall be square, and two cubits high. Its horns shall be *erect*,[2] of one piece with it. 3. You shall overlay it with pure gold, its top, its sides round about, and its horns; and make a gold molding for it round about. 4. You shall make two gold rings for it; you shall make them under its molding, at its two corners, on its two sides; they will be *holders*[3] for the poles with which to carry it. 5. You shall make the poles of acacia wood, and you shall overlay them with gold. 6. You shall place it in front of the veil that is over the ark of the testimony, in front of the propitiatory which is over the testimony, where I will have *my Memra* meet with you.[4] 7. Aaron shall burn[5] aromatic incense on it; morning by morning, when he prepares the lamps, he shall burn[5] it. 8. And when Aaron *lights* the lamps at twilight, he shall offer[5] it, a regular[6] *aromatic* incense before the Lord throughout your generations. 9. You shall not offer on it *aromatic* incense of foreign *nations*,[7] or a burnt offering, or a cereal offering, nor shall you pour out libations on it. 10. Aaron shall make atonement on its horns once a year. With the blood of the sin offering for atonement he shall make atonement on it once a year, on the *Day of Atonement*, throughout your generations. It shall be most holy *before* the Lord." 11. The Lord spoke to Moses, saying: 12. "When you take a census[8] of the children of Israel according to their number,[9] each shall give a ransom for himself *before* the Lord, when you count them, lest they suffer any *mortal damage*[10] when you count them." 13. This *standard had been shown to Moses on the mountain as a dinar of fire, and thus he*[11] *said to him*:[12] "*Thus shall* everyone who passes through the counting give: a half-shekel according to the shekel *of the coin* of the sanctuary—twenty *meahs*[13] to the shekel—a half-

Notes, Chapter 30

[1]Ps.-J. uses basically the same idiom as Onq. Ps.-J. employs the verb *nsq* (Af.), "cause to go up, offer," while Onq. uses *qtr*, "cause to smoke, offer (incense)." See 29:13 (Ps.-J.) and n. 12 to that verse.

[2]Cf. Ps.-J. 27:2 and the note to that verse.

[3]Lit.: "the place"; see Ps.-J. 25:27 and n. 17 to that verse.

[4]Lit.: "to you."

[5]Lit.: "cause to smoke"; = Onq. See 29:13 (Ps.-J.) and n. 12 to that verse.

[6]"Regular" is a more appropriate rendering than "continual," since the reference is to incense that was offered each morning and evening. See also 27:20 (Ps.-J.) and n. 18 to that verse.

[7]Ps.-J. explains that HT "strange incense" (RSV: "unholy incense") means the incense of foreign nations. But this explanation is inadequate, since any incense other than that described in vv. 34-38, even if made in Israel, is not permitted. See Schmerler, 1933, 206-7.

[8]Lit.: "the number (*ḥwšbn*)"; = Onq.

[9]Or: "count (*mnyyn*)"; = Onq.

[10]Lit.: "so that there will be no mortal damage in them." The last part of the verse ("lest they . . . count them") is omitted in Rieder's edition.

[11]The context and the parallel texts (see next note) show that God is the subject.

[12]*j. Shek.* 1, 46b; *PRK* 2,9; *Tanḥ. B, Ki Tissa* 6 (2,108). The superfluous word "this" at the beginning of the verse (HT) gave rise to the midrash, which also occurs in Nfmg.

[13]= Lond. (*m'yn*); *ed. pr.*: *mnyn*, "manehs."

shekel as an *offering of separation before* the Lord. 14. Everyone who passes through the counting, from the age of twenty years upwards, shall give the *offering of separation before* the Lord. 15. One who is rich shall give no more, and one who is poor shall give no less than half a shekel when giving the *offering of separation before* the Lord to make atonement for yourselves. 16. You shall take the money of the atonement from the children of Israel and give it for the service of the tent of meeting, that it may be a *good* memorial for the children of Israel before the Lord, to make atonement for yourselves." 17. And the Lord[14] spoke to Moses, saying, 18. "You shall make a laver of bronze with its base of bronze, for *sanctification*;[15] you shall *arrange* it between the tent of meeting and the altar, and you shall put water into it. 19. *Let some of it be taken with the ladle*[16] *that is in it*,[17] and Aaron and his sons shall *sanctify* their hands and their feet *in its water*. 20. *At the time* when they enter the tent of meeting they shall *sanctify* themselves in the water, lest they die *in glowing fire*;[18] or[19]*at the time* when they approach the altar to minister, to offer up[20] *the offering before* the Lord, 21. *they shall take water from the laver with the ladle that is in it*,[21] and they shall *sanctify* their hands and their feet lest they die *in glowing fire*.[18] It shall be for them a perpetual ordinance, for him and for his *sons*, throughout their generations." 22. And the Lord spoke to Moses, saying, 23. "You yourself shall take the best spices: *choice*[22] myrrh *weighing* five hundred *manehs*, half that *weight of* aromatic cinnamon, two hundred and fifty *manehs*, and aromatic cane *weighing* two hundred and fifty *manehs*; 24. cassia *weighing* five hundred *manehs, selas* according to the *sela* of the sanctuary, and olive oil, *a full kista*,[23] *amounting to twelve logs*,[24] *a log for each tribe, for the twelve tribes*.[25] 25. You shall make of these[26] a holy anointing oil, an aromatic blend, the work of a mixer[27] *of blended perfume*.[28] It shall be a holy anointing oil. 26. With it you shall anoint the tent of meeting, the ark of the testimony, 27. the table and all its utensils, the lampstand and its accessories, and the altar of *aromatic* incense, 28. the altar of burnt offering and all its utensils, the laver and its base. 29. You shall consecrate them, and they will be most holy; any one *among the priests* who

Notes, Chapter 30

[14]Omitted in Lond.

[15]= Onq. Nf. See also vv. 19, 20, 21; 40:30, 31, 32. See also Nf 29:4. Cf. Grossfeld, 1988B, 85, n. 6.

[16]The Rabbis take "from it" (JPS) of HT to mean that the water must be taken out of the laver; cf. *b. Zeb.* 21a; 22a.

[17]Reading *dbyh* with Lond.; so also in v. 21. Clarke, in his edition of Ps.-J., reads *dkyh* both in v. 19 and in v. 21. *Ed. pr.* reads *dkyh*, "pure," in v. 19. Part of v. 21 is omitted in *ed. pr.* See Ps.-J. 40:31 and Num 5:17, which do not use the word "pure."

[18]See 28:43 and n. 53 to that verse.

[19]The section from "glowing fire" in this verse to "It shall be" in v. 21 is omitted in *ed. pr.* through homoioteleuton.

[20]Lit.: "cause to go up"; = Onq. See 29:13 and n. 12 to that verse.

[21]This section may have been added from v. 19 by mistake.

[22]Nf, V, N; Onq.: "pure."

[23]*qsṭ'*; Gr. *xestes*. The word used in the plural in Ps.-J. Lev 19:36; Deut 25:15.

[24]*b. Men.* 89a; *Hor.* 11b; *Kerithoth* 5b.

[25]See *j. Shek.* 1, 46a, with reference to Exod 30:13.

[26]Lit.: "you shall make it."

[27]*mmzyg* with *ed. pr.*; Lond.: *mmzyt*.

[28]Reading *mtbśm* with *ed. pr.*; Levy (1, 102) suggests that we read *mbśm* for *mtbśm*. This word is omitted in Lond.

approaches them shall be consecrated, *but (anyone) from the rest of the tribes shall be burned in glowing fire before the Lord.*[29] 30. You shall anoint Aaron and his sons, and you shall consecrate them to *minister before* me.[30] 31. And you shall speak to the children of Israel, saying, 'This shall be a holy anointing oil *before* me throughout your generations. 32. It shall not be *rubbed* on the flesh of any person, and you shall not make anything like it, in the same proportions.[31] It is holy; it shall be holy for you. 33. Whoever mixes any like it, or puts any of it on a layman, *(on one) who is not of the sons of Aaron,*[32] shall be blotted out from his people.'" 34. The Lord said to Moses, "Take spices: balm, costus,[33] and galbanum, *choice* spices and pure frankincense; they shall be of equal *weight.*[34] 35. Make them[35] into *aromatic* incense, a perfume, the work of a perfumer, *mixed,*[36] pure, holy. 36. You shall crush some of it, *and* grind it into powder, and place some of it before the testimony in the tent of meeting where I will have *my Memra* meet you. It shall be most holy to you. 37. The *aromatic* incense that you are to make, you shall not make any in the same proportions[37] for yourselves; it shall be holy for you *before* the Lord. 38. Whoever makes any like it, to smell it, shall be blotted out from his people."

CHAPTER 31

1. The Lord spoke to Moses, saying, 2. "Behold, *Moses,* I have called Bezalel, son of Uri, son of Hur, of the tribe of Judah, by *a good* name. 3. I have filled him with a spirit *of holiness*[1] *from before the Lord,* with wisdom and intelligence, and with knowledge in every craft, 4. to plan *in his* mind[2] *how* to work in gold, silver, and bronze, 5. in cutting *gems* for setting, in carving wood, to practice every (kind

Notes, Chapter 30

[29]See 29:37 (Ps.-J.).

[30]= *Ed. pr.*; Lond., Nfmg: "him."

[31]"In the same proportions"; lit.: "like it."

[32]Having translated HT *zr,* "layman," as *ḥylwnyy,* "layman" (= Onq., Nf), Ps.-J. goes on (unnecessarily) to explain what that means.

[33]*kšṭ*; Gr. *kostos.*

[34]= Onq., Nf. Cf. Grossfeld, 1988B, 87, n. 13.

[35]Lit.: "it"; = HT.

[36]*m'rb*; = Onq. It is probable that salt was mixed with the ingredients. Cf. HT: "seasoned with salt" (RSV).

[37]Lit.: "like it." See v. 32.

Notes, Chapter 31

[1]See 35:31, where Ps.-J. uses the phrase "a spirit of prophecy" in the same context. On the terms "a spirit of holiness" and "a spirit of prophecy," see Schäfer, 1970, 304–14; idem, 1972, 21–26. See also "a spirit of wisdom" in v. 6 below.

[2]Lit.: "in their thought." Perhaps the plural suffix in Ps.-J. is due to the mention of wisdom, intelligence, and knowledge in the preceding verse.

of) craft. 6. And behold, I have *appointed* Oholiab son of Ahisamach, of the tribe of Dan, (to be) with him. And I have *added a spirit of* wisdom in the heart of all who are skilled,[3] and they will make everything that I have commanded you: 7. the tent of meeting, the ark of the testimony, the propitiatory that is upon it, and all the furnishings of the tent; 8. the table and *all* its utensils, the pure lampstand and all its accessories, and the altar of *aromatic* incense; 9. the altar of burnt offering and all its utensils, and the laver and its base; 10. the vestments for ministering,[4] the sacred vestments of Aaron the priest and the vestments of his sons, for *ministering*; 11. the anointing oil and the aromatic incense for the sanctuary.[5] According to all that I have commanded you, they shall do." 12. And the Lord said to Moses, saying, 13. "You shall speak to the children of Israel saying, 'Be sure[6] that you keep my sabbath *days*,[7] for this is a sign between *my Memra* and you <throughout your generations>,[8] that you may know that *it is* I, the Lord, who sanctifies you. 14. You shall keep the sabbath, for it is holy for you. *Anyone* who desecrates it shall surely be killed; for whoever does work on it, that *man*[9] will be blotted out from his people. 15. Six days shall work be done, but on the seventh day (there shall be) a sabbath of solemn rest, holy *before* the Lord. Whoever does work on the sabbath day *shall* surely be killed *by stoning*.[10] 16. The children of Israel shall keep the sabbath, preparing *the delicacies*[11] *of* the sabbath throughout your generations (as) a perpetual ordinance. 17. It shall be a sign for ever between *my Memra* and the children of Israel. For in six days the Lord *created and completed*[12] the heavens and the earth, and on the seventh day he rested and reposed.'" 18. When he finished speaking with him on Mount Sinai, he gave Moses the two tables of the testimony, tables of *sapphire*[13] stone *from the throne of Glory,*[14] *which weighed forty seahs*, written with the finger of *the Lord*.

Notes, Chapter 31

[3]Lit.: "wise of heart"; = Nf, Onq. HT has the corresponding idiom in the singular.

[4]Lit.: "of ministry, service"; = Onq., Nf, Pesh.; cf. LXX. HT: "finely worked" (RSV).

[5]Lit.: "the holy"; see 28:29 and n. 26 to that verse.

[6]Lit.: "surely, (*brm*)"; = Onq.; Nf: *lḥwd,* "only."

[7]= Onq.

[8]Omitted in Lond. and *ed. pr.*

[9]*br nš'*; Onq., Nfi: *'nš'*.

[10]*m. Sanh.* 7,4; *Mek. RSbY* Exod 31:15 (222). This latter text quotes Num 15:35, which states that a man who broke the sabbath was stoned to death. See also Ps.-J. Exod 35:2.

[11]*b. Shabb.* 118b; 119a; Tg. Isa 58:13. This latter text uses the same word for "delicacies" (*tpnwqyn*) as Ps.-J. uses in our present verse.

[12]*šklyl.* Ps.-J. uses this verb with reference to the completion of the world in Gen 7:11; 22:13; Exod 31:17 (our present verse); Num 22:28.

[13]*Sifre Num* 101 (Horovitz, 99–100); *Lev. R.* 32,2; *PRE* 46 (361). *j. Shek.* 5, 49a mentions precious stones and gems rather than sapphire.

[14]Ps.-J. Deut 34:12; cf. 4:13; Tg. Song of Songs 1:11. Compare Ps.-J. Exod 4:20, which describes the rod of Moses.

CHAPTER 32

1. The [1] people saw that Moses delayed in coming down from the mountain, and the people gathered around Aaron *when they saw that the time he had fixed for them had passed. And Satan went and led them astray,* [2] *and their hearts became proud.* And they said [3] to him: "Arise! Make us *deities* [4] that will go before us, because this Moses, the man who brought us up from the land of Egypt, *was burned on the mountain in glowing fire from before the Lord.* [5] We do not know what became of him *in the end.*" [6] 2. Aaron said to them, "Take off the gold rings [7] that are on the ears of your wives, your sons, and your daughters and bring (them) to me." 3. *But the women refused to give their ornaments to their husbands.* [8] *And immediately* all the people took off the rings of gold that were on their ears and brought (them) to Aaron. 4. He took (them) from their hands, *wrapped them* [9] *in a cloak,* [10] *and* threw them [9] into *a mold,* [11] and made them [9] into a molten calf. And they said, "These are your *deities,* [4] O Israel, who brought you out from the land of Egypt." 5. Aaron saw *Hur slain before him; and he was afraid;* [12] and he built an altar before it. And Aaron cried out *in an anguished voice* [13] and said, "Tomorrow (shall be) a festival *before* the Lord *for the slaughtering to death of his enemies, those who denied their Lord* [14] *and exchanged the Glory of his Shekinah for this calf."* [15] 6. They rose early the next day and offered burnt offerings and brought *sacrifices.* [16] And

Notes, Chapter 32

[1] For studies on certain aspects of the Targums of this chapter, see the first note to Nf chap. 32. Ps.-J. ignored the rabbinic injunction against the translation of certain sections of this chapter. Cf. Klein, 1988, 88–89.

[2] *b. Shabb.* 89a; *Tanh. B, Ki Tissa* 13 (2, 112–13); *Tanh. A, Ki Tissa* 19 (317); *Exod. R.* 41,7. Ps.-J. is the only Targum to mention Satan in this context. See also vv. 19, 24.

[3] Lond. and *ed. pr.:* "he said."

[4] = Onq. See Ps.-J. Gen 31:30 and n. 24 to that verse (Maher, 1992, 110).

[5] We know of no source for this addition, which, in fact, contradicts the continuation of the verse. For if the people knew that Moses was burned, they knew his end. See also v. 23 (Ps.-J.).

[6] Cf. Nf. Also v. 23 (Ps.-J., Nf). See Ps.-J. Gen 42:13 and n. 14 to that verse (Maher, 1992, 140).

[7] On the word for ring (*qdš'*) used here and in v. 3, see Ps.-J. Gen 24:47 and n. 27 to that verse (Maher, 1992, 86). See also Ps.-J. Gen 35:4; Num 31:50.

[8] *PRE* 45 (354); *Tanh. A, Ki Tissa* 19 (317). These texts state that when the women refused to give their ornaments, thus making the construction of an idol impossible, the men, who at that time wore earrings, took off their ornaments and gave them to Aaron. See the view of Ephraem referred to by Le Déaut, 1979, 250, n. 3.

[9] Lit.: "them."

[10] Ps.-J. takes HT *wyṣr,* "and fashioned" (RSV), to be derived from *ṣrr,* "wrap," or *ṣwr* (1), "bind." He interprets *ḥrṭ,* "graving tool" (RSV), as "cloak." (On the interpretation of the two Hebrew words just mentioned, see Durham, 1987, 415 and 416). Ps.-J.'s first interpretation corresponds to that of Onq., which can be translated as "he rolled it up in a cloth"; cf. Levy, 1, 220. Ps.-J. then adds a second interpretation ("and threw them into a mold"; = Nf, Pesh.) of HT.

[11] Reading *bṭwps'* (= Nf) rather than *ṭwpr'* of Lond. and *ed. pr.*

[12] *b. Sanh.* 7a; *Lev. R.* 10,3; *PRE* 45 (353); *Exod. R.* 51,8. See note to Nf (v. 5.).

[13] See Ps.-J. 12:31 and n. 53 to that verse.

[14] The idea seems to be that Aaron hoped that Moses would return, and that the worshipers of the calf would be slaughtered. Compare Exod 33:5. See Schmerler, 1933, 217.

[15] Ps.-J. paraphrases Ps 106:20. See also *Sifra, Shemini, Mekilta de Milluim* 4 (ed. Weiss, 43c).

[16] = Onq.

the people sat down [17] to eat and drink, and then rose to *sport in idolatry.* [18] 7. The Lord spoke to Moses, "Go! Go down *from the greatness of your glory, for I have not given you greatness except for the sake of Israel.* [19] *And now,* your people, whom you brought up from the land of Egypt, have performed base *deeds.* [20] 8. They have quickly gone away from the way which I commanded them *at Sinai: 'You shall not make for yourselves an image, or a figure, or any likeness.'* [21] *And now* they have made for themselves [22] a molten calf and bowed down to it; and they have sacrificed to it, and *they have proclaimed before it*: 'These are your *deities,* [4] O Israel, who brought you out of the land of Egypt.'" 9. And the Lord said to Moses, "*The haughtiness of* this people is *manifest before me,* [23] and behold it is a stiff-necked people. 10. And now, abandon *your prayer* [24] and *do not entreat on their behalf before* me; [25] I will arouse a mighty burning anger against them, and I will *wipe* them *out,* and make of you a great nation." 11. Moses *trembled with fear and began to pray before* [26] the Lord his God, and he said, "Why, O Lord, is your anger kindled against your people, whom you brought out from the land of Egypt with great power, and with a mighty hand? 12. Why *then* should the Egyptians *who remain* [27] say, 'With evil (intent) he brought them out, to slay them *between* the mountains, *Tabor and Hermon, Sirion and Sinai,* [28] and to wipe them off the face of the earth'? Turn from your blazing anger, and let there be regret *before* you concerning the evil *which you threatened* [29] *to bring upon* your people. 13. Remember Abraham, Isaac, and Israel your servants, to whom you swore by *your Memra,* and to whom you said, 'I will multiply your *children* like the stars of the heavens, and all this land of which I spoke I will give to you and to your *children,* and they will take possession of (it) forever.'" 14. And there was regret *from before* the Lord concerning the evil

Notes, Chapter 32

[17] On the verb *shr,* which Ps.-J. and Onq. use here, see Ps.-J. Gen 27:19 and n. 12 to that verse (Maher, 1992, 95).

[18] Onq. translates HT *ṣhq* literally as "to indulge in revelry." The Pal. Tgs., including Ps.-J., take it to refer to idolatrous worship. See *Tanḥ. B, Ki-Tissa* 13 (2,113); *Exod. R.* 1,1. See also Ps.-J. Gen 21:9 and n. 7 to that verse (Maher, 1992, 75).

[19] *b. Ber.* 32a. Ps.-J.'s wording is very similar to this text. See also *PRE* 45 (355); *Exod. R.* 42,3.

[20] Lit.: "they have corrupted their deeds." Nfmg: "they have corrupted their good deeds." See Deut 32:5, where Ps.-J. uses the idiom "corrupt their good deeds" against "corrupt their deeds" of P, V, N, L; Nf reads "they have acted corruptly (lit.: 'corrupted') before him." See also Deut 4:16, 25 (Ps.-J., Nf); 31:29 (Ps.-J.), where the idiom "corrupt one's deeds" occurs. In all these texts, as in our present verse, HT uses the verb *šḥt.*

[21] Exod 22:4 (Ps.-J.; cf. Nf). See below v. 19 (Ps.-J.). See also Num 17:5 and Deut 9:12, where Ps.-J. also quotes a passage from a different section of Scripture in his translation of a particular verse.

[22] = *Ed. pr.*; Lond.: "for you."

[23] = *Ed. pr.*; Lond.: "before him."

[24] Or: "let go of your prayer; leave your prayer"; = Onq. The same idiom occurs in Deut 9:14 (Ps.-J., Onq.). *b. Ber.* 32a, quoting Exod 32:10 (our present verse) and Deut 9:14, goes on to say that Moses prayed urgently when he heard God's threatening words. See Grossfeld, 1988B, 89, n. 6.

[25] Cf. Jer 7:16; 11:14; 14:11.

[26] Ps.-J. interprets HT *wyḥl,* "But (Moses) besought," in three different ways: from *ḥyl,* "writhe, tremble"; from *ḥll* (1), "begin"; and from *tplh,* "prayer." Onq.: "Then Moses prayed before." See Grossfeld, 1988B, 89, n. 7; Maher, 1990, 231.

[27] This addition takes into account the fact that many Egyptians had died at the time of the Exodus (cf. Exod 12:29-30) and at the Reed Sea (14:26-29). See also Ps.-J. 12:30 and n. 49 to that verse.

[28] We know of no source for this addition. Ps 89:12 (13) mentions Tabor and Hermon together. For Sirion see Deut 3:9; Ps 29:6.

[29] Lit.: "spoke"; = Onq.

which he *planned*[30] to do to his people. 15. And Moses turned and came down from the mountain, with the two tables of the testimony in his hand, tables with writing[31] on both sides; they had writing[32] on the one side and on the other. 16. The tables were the work of *the Lord*, and the writing was the writing of *the Lord, clearly* inscribed on the tables. 17. Joshua heard the sound of the people *shouting*[33] *with joy before the calf,* and he said to Moses, "(There is) the noise of battle[34] in the camp." 18. But he said, "It is not the sound of *warriors who are victorious in battle*[34] nor the sound of the weak *who are conquered in battle*[34] *by their enemies*; it is the sound of *those who practice idolatry*[35] *and sport before it* that I hear." 19. When *Moses* came near the camp, he saw the calf, and the musical instruments[36] *in the hands of the wicked*[37] people who played and bowed down before it. Satan was in the middle of it,[38] *leaping and jumping before the people. And immediately the heat of* Moses' anger blazed forth, and he threw the tables from his hands and broke them at the foot of the mountain. *But the sacred writing that was on them flew and floated in the air of the heavens.*[39] *And he cried out and said, "Woe to the people that heard on Sinai from the mouth of the Holy One: 'You shall not make for yourselves an image, or a figure, or any likeness,'*[40] *but (who), after forty days, made a molten calf which in reality is nothing."*[41] 20. He took the calf that they had made and burned (it) in the fire; he ground (it) until it was powder, scattered (it) on the surface of the water *of the brook,*[42] and made the children of Israel drink (it). *Whoever had given an object of gold there, a mark came out on his face.*[43] 21. And Moses said to Aaron, "What did this people do to you that you brought a great sin upon them?" 22. And Aaron said, "Let not the anger of my master be enkindled. You know that the people *are children of righteous men. But it is the evil inclination that led them astray.*[44] 23. And they said to me, 'Make us *deities* that will go before us, because this Moses, the man who brought us up from the land of

Notes, Chapter 32

[30]Onq.: "spoke."

[31]Lit.: "written."

[32]Lit.: "they had writing."

[33]= Onq. The basic meaning of the verb *ybb* used by Ps.-J. and Onq. is "sound the alarm."

[34]Lit.: "battle lines."

[35]Cf. *j. Ta'an.* 4, 68c. Onq.: "those who indulge in revelry." Ps.-J.'s interpretation of this verse is essentially that of Onq. See Grossfeld, 1988B, 90–91, and n. 11; see also the note to this verse in Nf.

[36]See Ps.-J. 15:20 and n. 39 to that verse.

[37]Ps.-J. limits the blame to the wicked among the people. See also v. 22, with n. 44; 33:8. See Ps.-J. 14:11 and n. 18 to that verse.

[38]*PRE* 45 (355) says that Sammael (or Satan) entered into the calf. See also v. 24 below. But perhaps Ps.-J. in our present verse means that Satan was in the middle of the camp. Ps.-J. is the only Targum to mention Satan in this context. See above v. 1 and n. 2.

[39]*b. Pesah.* 87b; *ARN* A 2 (20); *PRE* 45 (355); Ps.-J. Deut 9:17.

[40]See v. 8 and n. 21. We know of no source for Ps.-J.'s final addition ("and he cried out . . . is nothing") to this verse.

[41]Lit.: "in which there is no reality, substance."

[42]Added from Deut 9:21.

[43]*PRE* 45 (356–57); *b. Abod. Zar.* 44a; *LAB* 12,7. See Ps.-J. v. 28.

[44]Ps.-J. avoids saying that the people are "set on evil." See also v. 19 and n. 37. See v. 1, where Satan is blamed for the people's lapse.

Egypt, *was burned on the mountain in glowing fire from before the Lord*. We do not know what became of him *in the end*.'[45] 24. So I said to them, 'Those who have gold, take (it) off.' So they gave (it) to me, and I threw it into the fire, and *Satan entered it*,[46] and *the likeness of* this calf came out *of it*." 25. Moses saw that the people were stripped[47]—for, *because of* Aaron *they* had stripped off *the holy crown that had been on their heads, (and) on which the great and glorious name was clearly inscribed*[48]—*and that their bad reputation had spread abroad*[49] *among the nations of the earth, and they acquired a bad name for themselves for their generations.*[50] 26. Moses stood up at the entrance to *the Sanhedrin*[51] of the camp and said, "Let those *who fear* the Lord *come* to me!" And all the sons of Levi gathered to him. 27. He said to them, "Thus says the Lord, the God of Israel: '*Whoever has sacrificed to the idols of the nations shall be slain by* the sword.[52] *And now*, go back and forth throughout the camp, from the entrance *of the Sanhedrin*[53] to the entrance *of the courthouse; beseech*[54] *from before the Lord that this sin be forgiven you, and take revenge on the wicked, those who practiced idolatry, and* kill, each one *even* his brother, each one his companion, and each one his neighbor.'" 28. The sons of Levi did according to the word of Moses, and that day, of the people *who had the mark on their faces*,[55] there fell, *slain by the sword*, about *the number of* three thousand men. 29. And Moses said, "*Offer your offering*[56] <today> *for the blood that* your hands *have shed*,[57] *to make expiation for yourselves*[58] *before* the Lord—for each one

Notes, Chapter 32

[45]See v. 1 and nn. 5–6.

[46]= Nfmg. *PRE* 45 (355). On the reference to Satan see v. 1 and n. 2. In our present verse Ps.-J. and Nfmg shift some of the blame from Aaron by mentioning Satan.

[47]Like the other Pal. Tgs., Ps.-J. uses the same verb as HT (*pr'*, "break loose"), but they use it in the sense of "strip." Cf. Vulg.: *nudatus.*

[48]*b. Shabb.* 88a; *Tanḥ. A, Tezavveh* 11 (295); *PRK* 16,3; *Exod. R.* 45,2 and 3; 51,8; *Song of Songs R.* 4,12.2; 8, 5; *PRE* 47 (367); Tg. Song of Songs 2:17. See Ps.-J. Exod 33:4, 6.

[49]Lit.: "had gone forth." See Ps.-J. Gen 34:30 and n. 10 to that verse (Maher, 1992, 118).

[50]Cf. Nf, P, Onq., and see Grossfeld, 1988B, 90–91, and n. 14.

[51]Since the elders sat at the city gate to judge (cf., e.g., Deut 21:19; 25:7) Ps.-J. takes HT "gate" to refer to the Sanhedrin. Cf. *b. Sotah* 48a. See also v. 27.

[52]Cf. *b. Sanh.* 66b. See Ps.-J. 22:19.

[53]*Tanḥ. A, Ki Tissa* 26 (321). According to HT, Moses gave a command to have the rebels killed. In Ps.-J. that command becomes a condemnation to death that is issued by a court. See also n. 51 above.

[54]We know of no source for this reference to prayer for forgiveness. The idea of prayer may have been suggested by the fact that the verb '*br*, "cross, pass," employed here in HT, was used by the Sages to refer to the person who led the congregation in the recital of the Tefillah. Cf. Schmerler, 1933, 223; Maher, 1990, 235.

[55]Ps.-J. takes up and completes the tradition he has recorded in v. 20. See n. 43 to that verse. On Ps.-J.'s tendency to introduce particular haggadic traditions into different verses, see Maher, 1992, 5.

[56]Onq.: "let your hands offer an offering"; Nf: "complete the offering of your hands." HT: "fill your hands." On the translation of the biblical idiom "fill the hand," which usually means "ordain to the priestly service," see Ps.-J. 28:41 and n. 48 to that verse. The Hebrew idiom "fill the hand" is difficult in our present verse, but it seems to mean that the Levites, by their loyalty, merited a special ordination to the service of Yahweh. Nf translates the idiom in this verse as it does on other occasions, while Onq. and Ps.-J. each modify their usual rendering of the phrase. Both Lond. and *ed. pr.* omit "today" of HT.

[57]Lit.: "for the shedding of blood that is in your hands." According to Ps.-J., the sons of Levi must make atonement for the killing they carried out at the command of God and of Moses (cf. vv. 26–27).

[58]Lit.: "and let expiation be made for you." Our translation is required by the end of the sentence.

of you *has smitten* his son and his brother—and to bring the blessing upon you today." 30. The next day Moses said to the people, "You have sinned a great sin. And now I will go up *and pray before* the Lord. *O that* I may make atonement for your sins!" 31. Moses returned *and prayed before* the Lord, and said, "*If you please,*[59] *Lord of all the worlds! The darkness as well as the light is manifest before you.*[60] *And now*, this people has sinned a great sin, and they have made for themselves *deities* of gold. 32. And now, if you will forgive their sins, *forgive*;[61] but if not, blot me out, I pray, from the book of *the righteous*[62] *in which* you have written *my name!*" 33. But the Lord said to Moses, "*It is not fitting that I should blot out your name, but* he who has sinned *before* me, him will I blot out from my book. 34. And now, go, lead the people to *the place*[63] of which I have spoken to you. Behold, my angel will go before you. But on the day of my visitation I will visit[64] their sins upon them." 35. Thus *the Memra of* the Lord destroyed the people because *they bowed down to* the calf that Aaron made.

CHAPTER 33

1. The Lord spoke to Moses, "Go, ascend from here, *lest the heat of my anger blaze forth against the people and I wipe them out.*[1] *Therefore, set out*, you and the people that you brought up from the land of Egypt, to the land which I swore to Abraham, Isaac and Jacob, saying, 'To your *children* I will give it.' 2. I will *appoint*[2] an angel before you, and *through him* I will drive out the Canaanites, the Amorites, the Hittites, the Perizzites, the Hivites, and Jebusites. 3. (Go up)[3] to a land *producing*[4] milk and honey; for *it is not possible that* I would remove *the Shekinah of my Glory from* among you.[5] *But my Glory will not dwell where you re-*

Notes, Chapter 32

[59]*bmṭw mynk.* See Ps.-J. Gen 43:20 and n. 9 to that verse (Maher, 1992, 143).
[60]Cf. Ps 139:12.
[61]= Samaritan Targum, LXX.
[62]*b. Rosh Hash.* 16b.
[63]= Onq., LXX. See Ps.-J. Exod 15:17.
[64]In this verse Onq. and Ps.-J. twice translate the root *pqd* by *s'r*. Nf and Nfmg use *dkr* on both occasions. Cf. also 34:7; Lev 18:25; Num 14:18. See Ps.-J. 3:16 and n. 24 to that verse.

Notes, Chapter 33

[1]Compare Ps.-J. 32:10, 12.
[2]*w'yzmn.* HT: *wšlḥty.* See also Gen 24:7, 40, where Ps.-J. also uses *zmn* with reference to God's sending (HT: *šlḥ*) an angel. But see Num 20:16, where Ps.-J. uses *śdr* in the same context (HT: *šlḥ*; = Onq., Nf). In Exod 15:2, in a Targumic addition, Ps.-J. uses *śdr*, again with reference to God's sending an angel.
[3]HT has no verb. LXX: "and I will lead you in." Vulg.: *et intres.*
[4]= Onq. See Ps.-J. 3:8 and n. 16 to that verse.
[5]Onq.: "I will not remove my Shekinah from among you." See also Nf, Nfmg. Ps.-J., Onq., and Nf state the opposite of what we find in HT. See Klein, 1976, 530; Grossfeld, 1988B, 92, n. 3.

side in your camps—for you are a stiff-necked people—lest I wipe you out on the way." 4. When the people heard this harsh[6] word they went into mourning, and no one put on the *armament*[7] *that had been given to them on Sinai (and) on which the great and holy Name was clearly engraved.*[8] 5. The Lord said to Moses, "Say to the children of Israel, 'You are a stiff-necked people. Were I to remove *the Glory of my Shekinah* for one *short* moment from among you, I would wipe you out. And now, take off your *armament,*[7] *for* what I should do to you *has been revealed before me.*'"[9] 6. So the children of Israel were stripped[10] of their *armament*[7] *on which the great Name was clearly*[11] *written (and) which had been given to them as a gift* from Mount Horeb. 7. Moses *took them*[12] *and hid them in his tent for instruction in the Law. But* he took the tent *from there* and pitched it outside the camp, and removed *it* some distance from the camp *of the people who had moved* a distance of two thousand cubits.[13] He called it the tent *of the house of instruction.*[14] And anyone who *repented*[15] *before* the Lord[16] *with a perfect heart* went out to the tent *of the house of instruction* which was outside the camp. *He confessed his sins and prayed about his sins, and praying, he was forgiven.* 8. Whenever Moses went out *of the camp and went* to the tent, all *the wicked ones*[17] *of* the people would stand up and station themselves, each at the entrance of his tent, and watch Moses *with an evil eye*[18] until *the time* he entered the tent. 9. And when Moses entered the tent, the *glorious* pillar of cloud would descend and stand at the entrance of the tent, and *the Memra of the Lord would converse* with Moses. 10. All the people saw the pillar of cloud standing at the entrance of the tent, and *immediately* all the people arose and bowed low *towards the tent*[19] *while* each *stood* at the entrance of his tent. 11. The Lord *would converse* with Moses *in direct <speech*[20]—*he would hear the voice of the Dibbura, but he would not see the splendor of the face*—*as a man speaks>*[21] to his

Notes, Chapter 33

[6]Lit.: "evil"; = Onq., Nf, HT.

[7]Lit.: "the adornment of his armament"; = Onq.

[8]See Ps.-J. Exod 32:25 and n. 48 to that verse.

[9]Cf. Onq.; HT ("that I may know"; RSV) might be taken to mean that God did not yet know what he would do.

[10]Lit.: "were emptied." Cf. P: "stripped off"; lit.: "emptied."

[11]*mprš.* See 21:17 (Ps.-J.) and n. 39 to that verse.

[12]That is, the elements of the armament mentioned in vv. 4-6. See *b. Shabb.* 88a.

[13]*Tanḥ. A, Ki Tissa* 27 (322); *Exod. R.* 45,3.

[14]= Onq. Cf. Grossfeld, 1988B, 92–93, and n. 6. See also the note to Nf v. 11.

[15]Lit.: "returned in repentance." See the same idiom in Ps.-J. Gen 25:17; Exod 40:7.

[16]Onq., Nf, Nfmg: "anyone who sought instruction from before the Lord." These Targums take HT "sought" to refer to the seeking of instruction from God. Ps.-J. takes it to refer to repentance. We know of no source for this interpretation or for Ps.-J.'s further addition ("He confessed . . . he was forgiven") to this verse; cf. Schmerler, 1933, 227. The *tannaim* formulate the view that God was ready to forgive Israel when they would make atonement for the sin of the golden calf; cf., e.g., *Sifra, Shemini, Mikilta de Milluim* 1,3 (ed. Weiss, 43c). See Mandelbaum, 1990, 207–23.

[17]See Ps.-J. 32:19 and n. 37 to that verse.

[18]*b. Qidd.* 33b; *j. Shek.* 5, 49a; *Exod. R.* 51,6.

[19]According to *Tanḥ. B, Ki Tissa* 15 (2, 115), the people knew that the Shekinah was revealed to Moses.

[20]Lit.: "speech opposite speech." For rabbinic interpretations of the anthropomorphic idiom "face to face" of HT, see, e.g., *b. Ber.* 63b; *Exod. R.* 45,2; *Deut. R.* 3,15. See also the Targums of Deut 5:4; 34:10, and cf. the Targums of Num 12:8. On the word *Dibbura* used later in our present verse by Ps.-J., see McNamara, 1992, 38.

[21]Omitted in Lond.

fellow man. *And when the voice of the Dibbura had gone up*, (Moses) would return to the camp *and relate the words to the congregation of Israel. But* his attendant, Joshua, son of Nun, *was* a boy, (and) would not move from within the tent. 12. Moses said *before* the Lord, "See *what* you say to me, 'Bring up this people!' But you have not let me know whom you are sending with me. You have said *in your Memra*, 'I have *designated* you by a *good* name, and you have also found *mercy before* me.' 13. And now, I pray, if I have found *mercy before* you, let me, I pray, know the way *of your goodness*,²² that I may know *your mercy, how you deal with human beings—to the just it happens as to sinners, and to sinners as (to) the just;²³ and, on the other hand, it happens to the just according to their merits, and (to) sinners it happens according to their sins*—so that I may find *mercy before* you. And *it is manifest before you* that this people is your people." 14. And he said, "*Wait until* (my) countenance *of anger*²⁴ has passed, *and after that* I will give you rest." 15. And he said to him, "If (your) Presence²⁵ does not go *among us*,²⁶ do not bring us up from here *with a countenance of anger*. 16. For how will it be known that I have found *mercy before* you, <I and your people>,²⁷ unless *your Shekinah* speaks with us and *wonders are performed for us*²⁸ *when you remove the spirit of prophecy*²⁹ *from the nations*³⁰ *and speak in the Holy Spirit to* me and *to* your people, *so that we become different*³¹ from all the peoples that are on the face of the earth?" 17. And the Lord said to Moses, "I will also do this thing that you have asked,³² for you have found *mercy before*³¹ me, and I have *designated* you by a *good* name." 18. And he said, "Let me, I pray, see your Glory." 19. And he said, "*Behold*, I will make the whole *measure of* my goodness³³ pass before you, and I will proclaim the name of *the Memra of* the Lord before you, and I will show favor to him *who is worthy of* favor,³⁴ and I will show mercy to him *who is worthy of* mercy. 20. But," he said, "it is not possible for you to see my countenance, for man may not see me and *survive*."³¹ 21. And the Lord said, "Behold, (there is) a place *prepared before* me, and you are to station yourself on the rock. 22. And when the

Notes, Chapter 33

²²= Onq. See Grossfeld, 1988B, 94, n. 10.

²³*b. Ber.* 7a; Tg. Qoh 8:14. Compare the dispute recorded in Tg. Gen. 4:8 (Ps.-J., Pal. Tgs.). Ps.-J. is the only Targum to introduce this topic into our present verse.

²⁴The Hebrew idiom in Ps.-J.'s source (*b. Ber.* 7a) corresponds exactly to that used by Ps.-J. See also v. 15.

²⁵Lit.: "(your) face"; Onq.: "your Shekinah"; HT: "your face."

²⁶We correct Lond. and *ed. pr.* ("among us") according to Nf and Onq.

²⁷Omitted in Lond. and *ed. pr.*

²⁸Cf. Onq. and Nf. See note to this verse in Nf, and Grossfeld, 1988B, 94–95, and n. 15. See also Ps.-J. 8:18 and n. 15 to that verse.

²⁹Cf. Schäfer, 1972, 75. See Ps.-J. Exod 31:3 and n. 1 to that verse.

³⁰*b. Ber.* 7a; *B. Bat.* 15b.

³¹= Onq.

³²Lit.: "spoken"; = HT.

³³= Nf. *Tanḥ. A, Ki Tissa* 27 (323): "the measure of goodness and the measure of punishment." See the note to this verse in Nf. On vv. 18-23 in general, see the note to these verses in Nf.

³⁴Compare *b. Ber.* 7a: "(And I will show mercy . . .) although he may not deserve it."

Glory *of my Shekinah* passes by, I will put you in a cleft [35] of the rock, and I will *protect* you *with my Memra* until *the moment* I pass by. 23. *And I will make the bands of angels that stand and minister before me pass by,* [36] and you will see *the knot of the phylacteries* [37] *of the Glory of my Shekinah*; but *it is* not *possible for you to* see the face *of the Glory of my Shekinah.*

CHAPTER 34

1. The Lord said to Moses, "Cut for yourself two tables of stone like the first ones, and I will write on the tables the words that were on the first tables, which you broke. 2. Be prepared by morning, and in the morning go up to Mount Sinai, and station yourself *before* me there on the top of the mountain. 3. No one shall go up with you, and no one shall be seen anywhere on the mountain; neither shall the flock or the herd graze in front of this mountain." 4. So Moses cut two tables of stone like the first ones. And Moses rose early in the morning and went up on Mount Sinai as the Lord had commanded him, and he took the two stone tables in his hand. 5. The Lord *revealed himself* [1] in the clouds *of the Glory of his Shekinah.* And *Moses* stationed himself there with him, and *Moses* proclaimed the name of *the Memra of* the Lord. 6. The Lord caused *his Shekinah* to pass before him and called out, "The Lord! The Lord! A God merciful and gracious, patient and *bringing mercy near,* [2] and bounteous *in doing* [3] kindness and truth, 7. keeping kindness *and goodness* [4] for thousands *of generations*, remitting *and forgiving* sins, *passing over* the rebellious, and *making atonement* for sins, *pardoning those who return to the Law,* [5] but not acquitting, *on the day of the great judgment, those who do not*

Notes, Chapter 33

[35] *'splyd'*; cf. Gr. *spêladion* (diminutive of *spêlaion*), "grotto, cave."
[36] *PRE* 46 (365).
[37] Ps.-J. is obscure. Our translation, which is that of Le Déaut (1979, 267) and which agrees with *b. Ber.* (see further), leaves the word *dbyr'* (= *ed. pr.*; Lond.: *dbyd'*) untranslated. This word (*dbyr'*, with variations in spelling) occurs in the other Pal. Tgs., and Ps.-J.'s rendering may be a conflate reading. Chester (1986, 361) reads *dbyd'* with Lond. and translates Ps.-J.'s phrase as "the knot on the hand of the tephillin." See *b. Ber.* 7a: "The Holy One . . . showed Moses the knot of the tefillin."

Notes, Chapter 34

[1] See above, 3:8 (Ps.-J.) and n. 13 to that verse.
[2] = V, N.
[3] = Onq.
[4] Onq., V, N: "keeping *goodness.*" Ps.-J. and Nf have a conflate rendering of HT *ḥsd*, "steadfast love."
[5] "Pardoning . . . the Law." This addition is also in Onq.

repent, [6] visiting the sins of the fathers on *rebellious* [7] children, upon the third and fourth *generations.*" 8. Moses hastened to bend down to the ground and to worship. 9. And he said, "If, I pray, I have found *mercy before* you, *O Lord*, let *the Shekinah of your Glory, O Lord*, go between us, although this is a stiff-necked people; forgive our guilt and our sin, and give us possession *of the land that you promised to our fathers,* [8] *so that you do not exchange us for another people.*" [9] 10. So he said, "Behold, I am making a covenant *that I will not exchange this people for another.* [9] *But from you shall multitudes* [10] *of righteous people go forth.* [11] Before all your people I shall work wonders *for them when they go into exile by the rivers of Babylon. And I will bring them up from there, and I will have them dwell on the banks of the river Sambatyon.* [12] *Such wonders* have not been performed among any *of the inhabitants of* the earth or in any nation. And all the people among whom *you dwell* will see the deed of the Lord *on that day,* for what I am going to do with you is awesome. 11. Observe what I command you this day. Behold, I will drive out before you the Amorites, the Canaanites, the Hittites, the Perizzites, the Hivites, and the Jebusites. 12. Take care that you do not make a covenant with the inhabitants [13] of the land into which you are entering, lest they become a snare in your midst. 13. Rather, you shall shatter their altars, smash their pillars, and cut down their Asherim. 14. For *you are* not *permitted to* bow down to another god, for the Lord, whose name is 'Jealous *and Avenger,*' is a jealous *and an avenging* God. 15. You shall not make [14] a covenant with the inhabitants [13] of the land, for when they go astray after their *idols* and sacrifice to their *idols,* and invite you, you may eat of what has been sacrificed to *their idols,* 16. and take their daughters for your sons, so that *when* their daughters go astray after their *idols,* they will *also* lead your sons astray after their *idols.* 17. You shall not make molten *deities* for yourselves. 18. You shall observe the Feast of Unleavened Bread; seven days you shall eat unleavened bread, as I have commanded you, at the appointed time in the month of Abib, for in the month of Abib you went out *redeemed* from Egypt. 19. Everything that opens the womb *is* mine, and (of) all your animals *you shall consecrate the males,* both cattle and sheep. 20. But the first-born of an ass you shall redeem with

Notes, Chapter 34

[6]Ps.-J. interprets the difficult Heb. *wnqh l' ynqh,* "who will by no means clear the guilty" (RSV), in essentially the same way as Onq. See Grossfeld, 1988B, 96-97, and n. 8. On "the day of great judgment," which is added by Ps.-J. (cf. Nf, V, N), see Ps.-J. Gen 3:19 and n. 41 to that verse (Maher, 1992, 29).

[7]Cf. Onq., Nf, V, N. The Targums protect the justice of God by limiting his punishment to rebellious sons. See also Exod 20:5 (Ps.-J.) and n. 7 to that verse.

[8]Lit.: "that you swore to our fathers." Cf., e.g., Gen 24:7; Exod 13:5; 33:1.

[9]In the light of Ps.-J. 33:16, this addition seems to be a request that God will not remove his spirit from Israel and give it to another people. See also next verse.

[10]*'wklwsyn;* = Gr. *ochlos.* Ps.-J. uses this word again in Num 21:6, 34; 24:24. See McNamara, 1992, 20.

[11]Cf. *b. Ber.* 7a: More than sixty myriads came forth from Israel. See also *Num. R.* 16,25.

[12]*Gen. R.* 73,6; *j. Sanh.* 10, 29c; *Lam. R.* 2,5.9; *Num. R.* 16,25. The river Sambatyon was a mythical river that was said to cease flowing on the sabbath. It is mentioned by Josephus and by Pliny. Cf. Ginzberg, *Legends,* 6, 407–8, n. 56.

[13]Lit.: "inhabitant"; = Onq., HT.

[14]Lit.: "lest you make."

a lamb; and if you do not redeem (it), you shall strike it *with a hatchet.*[15] You shall redeem every first-born of your sons.[16] None shall appear before me empty-handed. 21. Six days you shall work, but on the seventh day you shall rest; (even) at ploughing (time) and harvest (time) you shall rest. 22. You shall celebrate[17] the Feast of Weeks *at the time of* the first fruits of the wheat harvest, and the Feast of Ingathering at the end of[18] the year. 23. Three times a year all your males shall appear before the Master *of the worlds,*[19] the Lord, the God of Israel. 24. For I will drive out peoples before you, and I will extend your borders; no one will covet your land when you go up to appear *before* the Lord your God three times a year. 25. You shall not offer[20] my *Passover* sacrifice[21] before *you have removed* leavened bread, and *the fat of* the Passover sacrifice shall not remain overnight, until morning, *away from the altar.*[22] 26. The best of the first fruits *of the fruits* of [23] your land you shall bring to the sanctuary of the Lord your God. *You are not permitted either to* boil *or to eat meat* and milk *both mixed together, lest my anger be enkindled against you*[24] *and I destroy*[25] *the fruit of your trees, with the unripe fruit, with their blossoms and leaves together."*[26] 27. And the Lord said to Moses, "Write these words, for in accordance with *the decree of* these words I have made a covenant with you and with Israel." 28. And he was there *before* the Lord forty days and forty nights; he ate no bread and drank no water. And he wrote on the *second*[27] tables the terms[28] of the covenant, the Ten Words[29] *that were written on the first tables.* 29. *At the time that* Moses came down from Mount Sinai,[30] with the two tables of the testimony in Moses' hand as he came down from the mountain, Moses did not know that *the splendor of the features*[31] *of his face shone because of*[32] the *splendor of the Glory of the Shekinah of the Lord* at *the time* that he spoke with him.

Notes, Chapter 34

[15]*m. Bek.* 1,7. The word we translate as "hatchet" (*qwpyṣ*) is the same as that used in the Mishnah. See Exod 13:13, where Ps.-J. does not mention the hatchet.

[16]Lit.: "your son," to be understood in the plural. HT: "your sons."

[17]Lit.: "you shall make for yourself"; = HT. LXX: "you shall make to me."

[18]Lit.: "at the going out of"; = Nf, Onq.; HT: "at the turn of the year." See 23:16 and n. 24 to that verse.

[19]Perhaps we should read "of the world" with Onq.; cf. 23:18 (Ps.-J., Onq.). With *kl,* "all," the idiom is usually "of all the worlds." See Ps.-J. Gen 18:31 with n. 42 to that verse (Maher, 1992, 69).

[20]Lit.: "slaughter"; cf. 23:18.

[21]*b. Pesah.* 64a.

[22]See 23:18 (Ps.-J.).

[23]*pyry.* Compare V,N: *'lltkwn.*

[24]See 23:19 (Ps.-J.) and n. 32 to that verse.

[25]Jastrow (1501) and Levy (2, 439) mention no other text apart from our present verse (Ps.-J.) where the verb *ršn,* which is used here, occurs. Levy takes it to mean "destroy, spoil," while Jastrow suggests that we read *'ybšyl* as in 23:19.

[26]Compare 23:19 and see n. 33 to that verse.

[27]Lit.: "the other."

[28]Lit.: "the words"; = HT.

[29]See 19:25 (Ps.-J.) and n. 40 to that verse.

[30]"Sinai" is omitted in Lond.

[31]*'yqwnyn.* See Gen 4:5 (Ps.-J.) and n. 12 to that verse (Maher, 1992, 32).

[32]Lit.: "which he had from." The view that the splendor of Moses' face derived from the Shekinah is expressed in several rabbinic texts; see Grossfeld, 1988B, 99, n. 20.

30. Aaron and all the children of Israel saw Moses, and behold, *the features*[31] *of* his face shone; and they were afraid to go near him. 31. But Moses called to them, and Aaron and all the princes *who had been appointed leaders* in the congregation returned to him, and Moses spoke with them. 32. After that all the children of Israel came near, and he enjoined on them all that the Lord had spoken to him on Mount Sinai. 33. When Moses ceased speaking with them, he put a veil[33] on *the features*[31] *of* his face. 34. Whenever Moses went in before the Lord to speak with him, he would remove the veil *that was on the features*[31] *of his face* until he came out. And he would come out and tell the children of Israel what he had been commanded. 35. The children of Israel would see Moses' *features,*[31] that *the splendor of the features*[31] *of* Moses' face *shone.* Then Moses would put the veil[33] back on his face until he went in[34] to speak with him.

CHAPTER 35

1. Then Moses gathered all the congregation of the children of Israel and said to them: "These are the things Yahweh has ordered to be done:[1] 2. Six days shall work be done, but the seventh day shall be holy for you, a sabbath *(and) rest*[2] *before* the Lord. Whoever does any work *on the sabbath day* shall surely be killed *by stoning.*[3] 3. *My people, children of Israel,* you shall not kindle a fire on the sabbath day in any *place* where you dwell."[4] 4. And Moses said to all the congregation of the children of Israel, saying, "This is what the Lord has commanded, saying: 5. Take from among you an *offering of separation before* the Lord; let everyone who is willing[5] bring *the offering of separation* of the Lord, gold, silver, and bronze; 6. blue, purple, and crimson material, linen and goats' hair; 7. tanned rams' skins, sasgona skins, and acacia wood; 8. oil for lighting, spices for the anointing oil and for the aromatic incense,[6] 9. *gems (that) are*[7] of beryl, and gems for setting, *to be*

Notes, Chapter 34

[33]*swdr';* = Nf; Gr. *soudarion*; also vv. 34 and 35.
[34]Lit.: "until *the time of* his going in."

Notes, Chapter 35

[1]Lit.: "to do them."
[2]For the idiom "a sabbath and rest," see 20:10 (Ps.-J.) and n. 10 to that verse.
[3]See 31:15 (Ps.-J.) and n. 10 to that verse.
[4]HT: "in all your habitations" (RSV). The word "place" is added also in Nf, V, and N. So also in the translation of the same phrase in 12:20 (Ps.-J., Nf); Lev 23:3, 31 (Ps.-J., Nf).
[5]Lit.: "everyone whose heart delights, chooses"; = Onq. See vv. 21, 22, 26, 29 and 25:2 (Ps.-J.).
[6]Compare 25:6, where Ps.-J. makes several additions to HT.
[7]See also 25:7 (Ps.-J.).

inserted[8] into the ephod and into the breastpiece. 10. Let all the skilled persons[9] *who are* among you come and make all that the Lord has commanded: 11. the tabernacle, *its screen* and its covering, its hooks, its planks, its bars, its pillars, its sockets; 12. the ark and its poles, the propitiatory, and the veil for the screen; 13. the table, its poles, and all its utensils, and the bread of the Presence; 14. the lampstand for lighting, its accessories and its lamps, and the oil <for lighting; 15. the altar of *aromatic* incense and its poles, the oil>[10] for anointing and the aromatic incense, and the entrance screen for the entrance of the tabernacle; 16. the altar of burnt offerings, its bronze grating, its poles and <all>[11] its utensils, the laver and its base; 17. the hangings of the courtyard, its pillars and its sockets, and the screen for the gate of the courtyard; 18. *and* the pegs of the tabernacle and the pegs of the courtyard, and their cords; 19. the vestments of service for ministering in the sanctuary,[12] the sacred vestments of Aaron the priest, and the vestments of his sons for *ministering.*" 20. So the whole congregation of the children of Israel went out from the presence of Moses. 21. And they came, every man who was willing,[13] and everyone whose spirit *was filled with the prophecy* which he had,[14] (and) brought the *offering of separation before* the Lord for the making of the tent of meeting, for all its worship, and for the sacred vestments. 22. The men as well as the women came, everyone who was willing;[13] they brought chains,[15] earrings, rings, pendants,[16] and all (sorts of) golden *ornaments*, everyone who would raise an *offering of elevation* of gold *before* the Lord. 23. And everyone who had in his possession blue, purple, and crimson material, linen and goats' hair, tanned rams' skins, sasgona skins, brought (them). 24. Everyone who would raise an *offering of elevation* of silver or bronze brought the *offering of separation before* the Lord; and everyone who had in his possession acacia wood for any work of the worship brought (it). 25. And every skilled woman[17] spun with her own hands, and when[18] they had spun they brought blue, purple, and crimson material, and linen. 26. And all the women who were willing[19] spun goats' hair *on their bodies*[20] with skill, *and carded (it) while they were alive.* 27. *The clouds of heaven went to Pishon, drew from it the stones of chrysoberyl* and the stones for setting *to be inserted* in the ephod and

Notes, Chapter 35

[8]= Onq., Nf. See 25:7 (Ps.-J., Nf, Onq.).

[9]Lit.: "all the wise of heart"; = Onq.

[10]Omitted in Lond. through homoioteleuton.

[11]Omitted in Lond. and *ed. pr.*

[12]Lit.: "the holy." See 28:29 (Ps.-J.) and n. 26 to that verse.

[13]Lit.: "whose heart delighted, chose"; = Onq. See v. 5 and n. 5.

[14]Lit.: "that was with him." Ps.-J. translated HT *'tw*, "him," as "with him." See also v. 26 and n. 19.

[15]*šyryn*; = Onq., Nfmg; Jastrow (1568): "chain, necklace, bracelet."

[16]*mḥwkyn*; = Onq.; cf. Nfmg; Jastrow (758): "gold hooks over the female bosom."

[17]Lit.: "every woman (who was) wise of heart"; = HT.

[18]Reading *kd* (= Onq.) rather than *kl*, "all," of Lond. and *ed. pr.*

[19]Lit.: "whose heart delighted (chose) with them." Ps.-J. translates *'tnh*, "them," as "with them." See also v. 21, with n. 14, and v. 29 with n. 24.

[20]That is, while the hair was on the goats' bodies; cf. *b. Shabb.* 74b; 99a; Tg. 1 Chr 2:18. See Schmerler, 1933, 244; Ginzberg, *Legends* 6, 70, n. 363.

in the breastpiece, *and they let them down on the surface of the desert.*[21] And the princes *of Israel went and* brought *them for the requirements of the work.* 28. *Then the clouds of heaven returned and went to the garden of Eden, and took from there choice* spices,[22] *olive*[23] oil for lighting and *pure balsamum* for the anointing oil and for the aromatic incense. 29. Thus the children of Israel, every *Israelite* man and every *Israelite* woman who was willing[24] to bring (something) for all the work that the Lord, through Moses, had commanded to be done, brought a freewill offering *before* the Lord. 30. And Moses said to the children of Israel, "See *that* the Lord has *designated* by a *good* name Bezalel, son of Uri, son of Hur, of the tribe of Judah, 31. and filled him with a spirit of *prophecy*[25] *from before* the Lord, with wisdom, with intelligence, with knowledge, and with every craft, 32. to *teach the skills* of working in gold, in silver, and in bronze, 33. to cut *precious gems* to be set in the things that are *to be made,*[26] to carve wood, and to practice every (kind of) artistic work. 34. And he has put *knowledge* into his heart, (into) him and Oholiab, son of Ahisamach of the tribe of Dan, to teach *craftsmanship to the rest of the artisans.* 35. He filled them with skill to do all the work of a carpenter, and of an artisan, and of an embroiderer in blue, purple, and crimson material, and linen, and of a weaver, workers in all crafts, and *teachers of crafts.*

CHAPTER 36

1. Bezalel and Oholiab and every skilled person to whom the Lord has given wisdom and intelligence to know (how) to do all the work for the service of the sanctuary shall do according to all that the Lord has commanded." 2. So Moses called Bezalel and Oholiab, and every skilled person in whose heart the Lord had put skill, everyone who was willing,[1] to take on[2] the work (and) to carry it out. 3. They

Notes, Chapter 35

[21] According to *b. Yoma* 75a and *Exod. R.* 33,8, precious stones came down with the manna. This explains how precious stones were available in the wilderness for the making of the tabernacle. There is no parallel for Ps.-J.'s mention of Pishon in this context. Cf. Schmerler, 1933, 243. See Ps.-J. Exod 14:9, which records that precious stones had been brought from Pishon to the Sea of Reeds. See also Ps.-J. Gen 6:16, where there is reference to a gem from Pishon (Maher, 1992, 38).

[22] See *b. Yoma* 75a: ". . . there came down to Israel with the manna the cosmetics for women." We know of no source for Ps.-J.'s mention of the garden of Eden in this context.

[23] See 29:2 (Ps.-J.) and n. 2 to that verse.

[24] Lit.: "whose heart delighted (chose) with them." Ps.-J. translates HT *'tm,* "them," as "with them." See v. 26 and n. 19.

[25] See 31:3 (Ps.-J.) and n. 1 to that verse.

[26] Lit.: "for setting *the work* with them."

Notes, Chapter 36

[1] Lit.: " everyone whose heart delighted, chose."

[2] Lit.: "to approach"; = HT.

took from Moses all the *offerings of separation* that the children of Israel had brought for carrying out the work connected with the service of the sanctuary.[3] And they still brought freewill offerings every morning out *of their wealth.* 4. And all the skilled men who were doing all the work for the sanctuary came, each man from the work he was doing, 5. and said to Moses, "The people are bringing more than is required for doing the work that the Lord has commanded to be done." 6. So Moses gave a command, and they had a public crier[4] pass throughout the camp, saying, "Let no man or woman do any more work for the *offering of separation* for the sanctuary." And the people stopped bringing. 7. What they had brought[5] was sufficient for all the work; and when they had done it, there was *even* some left over. 8. All the skilled <among those who were doing the work>[6] made the tabernacle of ten curtains of fine twisted linen, of blue, purple, and crimson material; he[7] made them with *designs of* cherubim, the work of an artisan. 9. The length of each curtain was twenty-eight cubits, and its width four cubits: the *total* (measurement) of each curtain. All the curtains had the same measurement. 10. He joined five curtains to one another, and he joined (the other) five curtains to one another. 11. He made loops of blue on the border of the curtain, at the side, at the point of joining; he did the same on the border of the (second) curtain,[8] at the second point of joining. 12. He made fifty loops for one curtain, and he made fifty loops at the end of the curtain, at the second point of joining, the loops directed towards[9] one another. 13. He made fifty hooks of gold and joined the curtains to one another with the hooks, so that the tabernacle was one whole. 14. He made curtains of goats' hair *to spread*[10] over the tabernacle; he made eleven curtains. 15. The length of each curtain was thirty cubits, and the breadth of each curtain was four cubits; the eleven curtains had the same measurement. 16. He joined five curtains by themselves—*corresponding to the five books of the Law*—and six curtains by themselves—*corresponding to the six orders of the Mishnah.*[11] 17. He made fifty loops on the border of the curtain, at the side, at the point of joining, and he made fifty loops on the border of the curtain, at the second point of joining. 18. He made fifty hooks of copper to join the tent, so that it became one whole. 19. He made for the tabernacle a covering of tanned rams' skins, and (a covering of) sasgona skins above, *to cover (it).*[12] 20. He made the planks of the tabernacle of

Notes, Chapter 36

[3]This part of the verse ("They took . . . of the sanctuary") is repeated in Lond. because of homoioteleuton (see the end of v. 2 and the end of the section that is repeated).

[4]See note to this verse in Nf.

[5]Lit.: "the work."

[6]Omitted in Lond. and *ed. pr.*

[7]The "he" referred to here and in the rest of the chapter is Bezalel; see 37:1.

[8]Perhaps we should add "at the side" (as in the first part of the verse), as proposed by Rieder in his edition of Ps.-J. See Onq. and Nf.

[9]See 26:5 (Ps.-J.) and n. 5 to that verse.

[10]See 26:7, where Ps.-J. also uses the verb "to spread."

[11]See 26:9 (Ps.-J.).

[12]See 26:14 (Ps.-J.), where we do not find this addition.

acacia wood, upright, *the way they are planted.*[13] 21. The length of a plank was ten cubits, and the width of each plank was a cubit and a half. 22. Each plank had two tenons, *the end*[14] of one fitting into *the end* of the other; thus he did with all the planks of the tabernacle. 23. He made the planks for the tabernacle, twenty planks for the side facing south.[15] 24. He made forty sockets of silver under the twenty planks, two sockets under one plank for its two tenons, and two sockets under the next[16] plank for its two tenons. 25. For the second side of the tabernacle, the north side, he made twenty planks, 26. with their forty sockets of silver, two sockets under one plank, and two sockets under the next[16] plank. 27. And for the rear of the tabernacle, to the west, he made six planks. 28. He made two planks for the corners of the tabernacle at their rear. 29. They were joined at the bottom, and they were joined as one at the top by one ring; thus he did with both of them at the two corners. 30. There were eight planks with their sockets of silver, sixteen sockets, two sockets under each plank. 31. He made bars of acacia wood, five for the planks of one side of the tabernacle, 32. and five bars for the planks of the second side of the tabernacle, and five bars for the planks of *the side of* the tabernacle at the rear, to the west. 33. The middle bar (that was) to cross halfway up the planks, from end to end, he made *from the tree that our father Abraham had planted in Beer-sheba where he prayed in the name of the Memra of the Lord, the God of the world.*[17] 34. He overlaid the planks with gold, and he made their rings of gold, as holders[18] for the bars; and he overlaid the bars with gold. 35. He made the veil of blue, purple, and crimson material, and fine twisted linen; he made it *embroidered with*[19] cherubim, the work of an artisan. 36. He made four pillars of acacia *wood* for it and overlaid them with gold, with their clasps of gold. And he cast four sockets of silver for them. 37. He made hangings *spread*[20] at the entrance of the tent, of blue, purple, and crimson material, and fine twisted linen, done in embroidery, 38. and five pillars with their *five* clasps. He overlaid their tops and their bands with gold, and their five sockets were of bronze.

Notes, Chapter 36

[13]See 26:15 (Ps.-J.) and n. 9 to that verse.

[14]See 26:17 (Ps.-J.). In that verse Ps.-J. adds "the end" only once, whereas this addition is made twice in our present verse.

[15]See 26:18 and n. 11 to that verse.

[16]Lit.: "one."

[17]See 26:28 (Ps.-J.).

[18]= Onq. See 25:27 (Ps.-J.) and n. 19 to that verse.

[19]See 26:31 (Ps.-J.).

[20]*wwylwn prys.* Compare Onq., Nf: *prs,* "a screen"; Nfmg: *ḥpyy.* "a covering." Ps.-J. has a conflate reading, combining a word of his own with the reading of Onq. and Nf.

CHAPTER 37

1. Bezalel made the ark of acacia wood, two and a half cubits long, a cubit and a half wide, and a cubit and a half high. 2. He overlaid it with pure gold, inside and outside, and he made a gold molding for it round about. 3. He cast four gold rings for it, for its four feet:[1] two rings on one side and two rings on the other side. 4. He made poles of acacia wood, overlaid them with gold, 5. and inserted the poles into the rings on the sides[2] of the ark for carrying the ark. 6. He made the propitiatory of pure gold, two and a half cubits long and a cubit and a half wide; *but its thickness was a handbreadth.*[3] 7. He made two cherubim of *pure*[4] gold; he made them of hammered work, at the two sides of the propitiatory, 8. one cherub on one side, and another cherub on the other side, *of hammered work; the cherubim were looking at each other*[5] *and were not separated*[6] from the propitiatory; *for with the wisdom of the spirit of prophecy*[7] he made the two cherubim on its two sides. 9. The cherubim stretched their wings, *as well as*[8] *their heads,* upwards, covering the propitiatory with their wings, with their faces (turned) towards one another; the faces of the cherubim were (turned) towards the propitiatory. 10. He made the table of acacia wood, two cubits long, one cubit wide, and a cubit and a half high. 11. He overlaid it with pure gold, and made a gold molding for it round about. 12. He made a rim for it a handbreadth *high*[9] round about, and he made a gold molding for it round about. 13. He cast four gold rings for it, and put the rings on the four corners at its four legs. 14. The rings were against the rim, as *holders*[10] for the poles to carry the table. 15. He made the poles of acacia wood for carrying the table, and he overlaid them with pure gold. 16. The utensils that (go) on the table—its bowls, its dishes, its jugs, its flagons *with which they covered (the bread)*[11]—he made of pure gold. 17. He made the lampstand of pure gold. He made the base and the shaft of the lampstand of hammered work; its cups, its calyxes, and its flowers were of one piece with it. 18. Six branches extended from its sides, three branches of the lampstand from one side, and three branches of the lampstand from the other side. 19. There were three cups *engraved with their figures* on one branch, (each with) calyx and flowers; and three cups *engraved with their figures* on

Notes, Chapter 37

[1] See 25:12 (Ps.-J.) and n. 8 to that verse.
[2] Lond. and *ed. pr.*: "side."
[3] Cf. 25:17 (Ps.-J.).
[4] Cf. 25:18 (Ps.-J.).
[5] Cf. 25:20.
[6] I.e., it will be of one piece with the propitiatory; cf. 25:19.
[7] See 35:31 (Ps.-J.) and n. 25 to that verse.
[8] Lit.: "with, in the presence of." Cf. 25:20 (Ps.-J.).
[9] = Onq. See 25:25 (Ps.-J., Onq.).
[10] = Onq. See 25:27 (Ps.-J.) and n. 17 to that verse.
[11] Ps.-J. derives HT *ysk,* "to pour" (RSV), from *skk* in the sense of "cover." Cf. Schmerler, 1933, 248. Compare 25:29, where Ps.-J. correctly understands HT *ysk* to be derived from *nsk,* "pour, offer a libation." In our present verse Ps.-J. seems to be referring to covering the bread of the Presence; cf. 25:29-30.

another branch, (each with) calyx and flowers; so for the six branches extending from the lampstand. 20. On the lampstand there were four cups *engraved with their figures*, [12] (each with) its calyx and flowers: 21. a calyx of one piece with it under a pair of branches; a calyx of one piece with it under (the second) pair of branches; and a calyx of one piece with it under (the third) pair of branches; (so) for the six branches extending from it. 22. Their calyxes and their branches were of one piece with it, the whole of it one hammered piece of pure gold. 23. He made its seven lamps, its snuffers [13] and its trays, of pure gold. 24. He made it, with all its accessories, out of a *centenarius* of pure gold. 25. He made the altar of *aromatic* incense *of* acacia wood, a cubit long and a cubit wide, square, and two cubits high; its horns were *erect*, [14] of one piece with it. 26. He overlaid it with pure gold, its top, its sides round about and its horns; and he made a gold molding for it round about. 27. He made two gold rings for it under its molding, at its two corners, on its two sides, as *holders* [10] for the poles with which to carry it. 28. He made the poles of acacia wood and overlaid them with gold. 29. He made the holy anointing oil and the pure aromatic incense, the product of the art of making perfumes.

CHAPTER 38

1. He made the altar of burnt offerings of acacia wood, five cubits long and five cubits wide; (it was) square, and three cubits high. 2. He made its horns on its four corners; its horns were of one piece with it, *erect*; [1] and he overlaid it with bronze. 3. He made all the utensils of the altar, the pots, the shovels, the sprinkling basins, the forks, and the fire-pans; he made all its utensils of bronze. 4. He made for the altar a grating of network in bronze, under its rim, downwards, to its middle, *to receive coals or bones that might fall from the altar*. [2] 5. He cast four rings at the four corners of the bronze grating as *holders* [3] for the poles. 6. He made the poles of acacia wood and covered them with bronze. 7. And he inserted the poles into the rings on the side of the altar, to carry it with them. He made it hollow, of boards, *filled*

Notes, Chapter 37

[12]See 25:34 (Ps.-J.).
[13]See 25:38 (Ps.-J.) and n. 26 to that verse.
[14]See 27:2 (Ps.-J.) and n. 1. to that verse.

Notes, Chapter 38

[1]See 27:2 (Ps.-J.) and n. 1 to that verse.
[2]See 27:5 (Ps.-J.) and n. 7 to that verse.
[3]See 25:27 (Ps.-J.) and n. 17 to that verse.

with earth.[4] 8. He made the laver of bronze and its base of bronze from the mirrors[5] *of bronze* of the *chaste*[6] women,[7] *(who), when they came to pray*[8] at the entrance of the tent of meeting, *stood beside their offering of elevation, praising (God) and giving thanks. Then, when they were purified from the uncleanness of their blood, they returned to their husbands and bore righteous children.*[9] 9. He made the courtyard: on the side facing south[10] the hangings of the courtyard were of fine twisted linen, a hundred cubits. 10. Their pillars were twenty <and their sockets twenty>,[11] of bronze. The clasps of the pillars and their bands were of silver. 11. On the north side, a hundred cubits; their pillars were twenty and their sockets twenty, of bronze. The clasps of the pillars and their bands were of silver. 12. On the west side, fifty cubits of hangings; their pillars were ten and their sockets ten. The clasps of the pillars and their bands were of silver. 13. On[12] the east side, to the orient, fifty cubits. 14. Fifteen cubits of hangings were on one side; their pillars were three and their sockets three. 15. On the other side, on either side of the gate of the courtyard, fifteen cubits of hangings; their pillars were three and sockets three. 16. All the hangings round about the courtyard were of fine twisted linen. 17. The sockets for the pillars were of bronze; the clasps of the pillars and their bands were of silver; the overlay of their tops was of silver, and they were banded with silver. All the pillars of the courtyard *were made in this way.* 18. The screen for the gate of the courtyard was done in embroidery *with the needle*, in blue, purple, and crimson material, and fine twisted linen. It was twenty cubits long; its height, like its width, was five cubits, corresponding to the hangings of the courtyard. 19. Their pillars were four, and their sockets were four, of bronze; their clasps were of silver; the overlay of their tops and their bands were of silver. 20. All the pegs for the tabernacle and for the courtyard round about were of bronze. 21. These are the amounts[13] *of the weights and the totals* (of the materials) for the tabernacle of the testimony[14] that were counted according to *the word*[15] of Moses; *but* the work of the Levites *was (done)* under the direction of Ithamar, son of Aaron the priest. 22. Bezalel, son of Uri, son of Hur, of the tribe of Judah, made all that the Lord had commanded Moses, 23. and with him was Oholiab, son of

Notes, Chapter 38

[4]See 27:8 (Ps.-J.) and n. 9 to that verse.

[5]*'spqlyry*; Latin: *specularis*. See also Ps.-J. Exod 19:17 and n. 28 to that verse; Deut 33:19.

[6]Or: "modest."

[7]Cf. *Mek. RI* Exod 13:4 (1,140); see also the note to Nf to our present verse.

[8]= Onq.; Cf. Nf, Pesh.; HT: *ṣb'w*, "(who) ministered," is obscure. Ps.-J. and the versions just listed take it to refer to prayer. Compare Nfmg, P, V, N. See Vulg.: *quae excubabant*. See Komlosh, 1973, 197; Grossfeld, 1988B, 105, n. 2.

[9]I have found no source for this addition which praises the virtue of the Israelite women.

[10]The same idiom is used in Ps.-J. 26:18; 27:9.

[11]Omitted in Lond. through homoioteleuton.

[12]In Lond. v. 15 is placed before v. 13.

[13]Or: "the numbers." Ps.-J. employs the word used by Onq. (*mnyn*, "amount, number") and the word used by Nf (*skwm*, "total, sum").

[14]HT, Nf, Onq.: "the tabernacle, the tabernacle of the testimony."

[15]*'l pm mymr'*; Onq. *'l mymr'*.

Ahisamach, of the tribe of Dan, a carpenter, an artisan, an embroiderer in blue, purple, and crimson material, and in fine linen. 24. All the gold that was used for the work, in all the work of the sanctuary—*the total of* the gold of the *offering of elevation*—was 29 *centenarii* and 730 *selas* according to the *selas* of the sanctuary. *This was the gold of the offering of elevation which the children of Israel had raised, everyone who was willing to make an offering of separation.* 25. The silver of those of *the children of Israel*, who were numbered, *which they gave, each as a redemption for himself, when Moses made a census of them,*[16] (came to) 100 *centenarii* and 1,775 *selas*, according to the *selas* of the sanctuary. 26. A *daric*[17] a head, half a *sela* according to the *selas* of the sanctuary, for everyone who passed through the counting, from the age of twenty years upwards, 603,550 (men). 27. The 100 *centenarii* of silver were for casting the sockets of the sanctuary and the sockets of the veil, 100 sockets for a 100[18] *centenarii*, a *centenarius* for a socket. 28. And with the 1,775 *selas* he made the clasps for the pillars, overlaid their tops, and banded them. 29. The bronze from *the offering of elevation* (came to) 70 *centenarii* and 2,400 *selas*. 30. With it he made the sockets for the entrance of the tent of meeting, the altar of bronze and its bronze grating, and all the utensils of the altar, 31. the sockets of the courtyard round about,[19] the sockets of the gate of the courtyard, all the pegs of the tabernacle, and all the pegs of the courtyard round about.

CHAPTER 39

1. From the blue, purple, and crimson material they made the vestments of service for ministering in the sanctuary, and they made the sacred vestments for Aaron *the priest*,[1] as the Lord had commanded Moses. 2. He made the ephod of gold, blue, purple, and crimson material, and fine twisted linen. 3. They hammered out the sheets[2] of gold and cut them into threads to be worked into[3] the blue and the purple, and into the crimson, and into the fine linen, the work of an artisan.

Notes, Chapter 38

[16]See 30:11-15.
[17]See Gen 24:22 (Ps.-J.) and n. 12 to that verse (Maher, 1992, 84).
[18]"a hundred" is omitted in *ed. pr.*
[19]From here on Lond. is confused and reads: "and all the pegs of the gate of the courtyard, and all the sockets of the courtyard round about."

Notes, Chapter 39

[1]Also added in some printed editions of Onq. See Sperber, 1959, 160, *Apparatus.* See also Exod 31:10.
[2]*ṭsy*; = Onq., Nf; Gr. *tasis* (cf. Levy, 1, 311).
[3]Lit.: "to work into the midst of"; = Nf, Onq., HT.

4. They made for it attached shoulder-pieces; it was attached[4] at its two ends.
5. The belt that was on it for fastening it was one piece with it; it was made like it,
of gold, blue, purple, and crimson material, and of fine twisted linen, as the Lord
had commanded Moses. 6. They made the *gems* of *chrysoberyl*, inserted and set
<in gold>,[5] inscribed, in *clearly* engraved *writing*, with the names of the children
of Israel. 7. He placed them on the shoulder-pieces of the ephod as stones of remembrance for the children of Israel, as the Lord had commanded Moses. 8. He
made the breastpiece, the work of an artisan, in the same way as the ephod: of gold,
blue, purple, and crimson material, and fine twisted linen. 9. It was square. They
made the breastpiece doubled, a span in length and a span in width, doubled.
10. They set in it four rows of *precious gems corresponding to the four corners of the
world*. The first row: a cornelian, a topaz, and a smaragd, one row. *On them were
clearly engraved the names of three tribes, Reuben, Simeon, and Levi. 11. The
names of* the second row: a turquoise, a sapphire, and a chalcedony. *On them were
clearly engraved the names of three tribes, Judah, Dan, and Naphtali. 12. The
names of* the third row: a jacinth, an agate, and an amethyst. *On them were clearly
engraved the names of three tribes, Gad, Asher, and Issachar. 13. The names of* the
fourth row: a beryl *of the Great Sea*, a chrysoberyl, and a jaspar. *On them were
clearly engraved the names of three tribes, Zebulun, Joseph, and Benjamin.* They
were inserted (and) set in gold, in their settings. 14. The *gems* corresponding to the
names of the children of Israel <were>[5] twelve, like their names. They were inscribed *with writing, clearly engraved, like the inscription of*[6] a signet ring, each with
its gem according to its name, for the twelve tribes. 15. On the breastpiece they
made corded chains, plaited work, in pure gold. 16. They made two settings of gold
and two rings of gold, and they put the two rings at the two ends of the breastpiece.
17. They put the two plaits of gold into the two rings at the ends of the breastpiece.
18. The two plaits *that were arranged at* its two ends they put on the two settings
and put them on the shoulder-pieces of the ephod, at its front. 19. They made two
rings of gold and put them at the two ends of the breastpiece, on its inner edge,
against the ephod. 20. They made two rings of gold and *arranged* them on the two
shoulder-pieces of the ephod, low down on its front at the point of joining, above
the belt of the ephod. 21. They bound the breastpiece with a cord of blue from its
rings to the rings of the ephod, so that it was *fastened* to the belt of the ephod, and
so that the breastpiece did not come loose from the ephod, as the Lord had commanded Moses. 22. He made the robe,[7] the work of a weaver, *of twisted (thread)* of
blue. 23. The opening of the robe *was double*, in the middle of it, like the opening
of a coat of mail; there was a band *on its border surrounding* its opening round
about, *so that* it would not be torn. 24. On the hem of the robe they made pomegranates of blue, purple, and crimson material, twisted. 25. They made bells of

Notes, Chapter 39

[4]Lond.: "it will be attached." This is the form used in 28:7 (Ps.-J., Onq.). See n. 9 to that verse.
[5]Omitted in Lond. and *ed. pr.*
[6]= Onq.
[7]See 28:31 (Ps.-J.) and n. 33 to that verse. In our present verse *mnṭr* is written in the margin of Lond.

gold and put the bells among the pomegranates, on the hem of the robe round about, among the pomegranates, 26. a bell and a pomegranate, a bell and a pomegranate, *in all seventy*,[8] round about on the hem of the robe for serving, as the Lord had commanded Moses. 27. They made the tunics of fine linen, the work of a weaver, for Aaron and his sons; 28. and the turban of fine linen, and the decoration of the headdresses of fine linen, and the linen breeches[9] of fine twisted linen; 29. and sashes of fine twisted linen, of blue, purple, and crimson material, done in embroidery, as the Lord had commanded Moses. 30. They made the plate of the holy crown of pure gold, and they wrote on it, inscribed, *clearly* engraved; "Holy to the Lord." 31. They *arranged* on it a *twisted* cord[10] of blue to fix (it) on the turban, above *the phylactery for the head*,[11] as the Lord had commanded Moses. 32. Thus was completed all the work of the tabernacle, of the tent of meeting. The children of Israel did (so); as[12] the Lord had commanded Moses, so they did. 33. Then they brought the tabernacle to Moses *to his schoolhouse*,[13] *where Moses and Aaron and his sons were sitting. And he determined*[14] *the order of the priesthood for them.*[15] *There also sat the ancients of Israel. And they showed him*[16] the tent and all its utensils, its hooks, its planks, its bars, its pillars, its sockets. 34. The covering of tanned rams' skins, the covering of sasgona skins, and the veil for the screen; 35. the ark of the testimony and its poles, the propitiatory *and the cherubim of hammered work, of one piece with it, one on one side, and one on the other side*;[17] 36. the table and all its utensils, and the bread of the Presence; 37. *and* the <pure>[18] lampstand *and* its lamps, lamps set in order,[19] *that are arranged to correspond to the seven planets*[20] *that move in their orbits in the firmament day and night*; <all its utensils>,[18] and the oil for lighting; 38. the altar of gold, the anointing oil, the aromatic incense, and the screen *that is at* the entrance of the tent; 39. the altar of bronze with its grating of bronze, its poles and all its utensils, the laver and its base; 40. the hangings of the courtyard, *and* its pillars and its sockets, the screen for the door of the courtyard, its cords and its pegs, and all the utensils for the service of the tabernacle, for the tent of meeting; 41. the vestments of service for ministering in the sanctuary, *and*[21] the sacred vestments for Aaron the priest, and the vest-

Notes, Chapter 39

[8]Compare 28:34 (Ps.-J.), and see n. 36 to that verse.

[9]Cf. Nfmg. See 28:42 (Ps.-J.) and n. 49 to that verse.

[10]See 28:28 (Ps.-J.) and n. 25 to that verse.

[11]See 28:37 (Ps.-J.) and n. 41 to that verse.

[12]Nfint and the Samaritan Pentateuch are essentially the same as Ps.-J. HT, Onq.: "according to all that."

[13]Ps.-J. takes *'hl*, "tent," of HT to refer to the schoolhouse. See also, e.g., Ps.-J. Gen 9:27; 25:27 (Maher, 1992, 46, 90).

[14]Lit.: "straightened out," i.e., settled the difficulties (relating to the functioning of the priests).

[15]We know of no source for this addition.

[16]According to *Tanḥ. A, Pekude* 11 (354), neither the skillful people, nor Bezalel and Oholiab, were able to erect the tabernacle. So the people showed it to Moses, who then erected it. See also *Tanḥ. B, Pekude* 8 (2, 133).

[17]See 25:18 and 26:34.

[18]Omitted in Lond. and *ed. pr.*

[19]Lit.: "lamps of the order, arrangement"; = HT.

[20]Cf. *Num. R.* 15,7; *Tanḥ. A, Be-Ha'alothka* 5 (520). See also Ps.-J. Exod 40:4.

[21]Lond.; cf. Samaritan Pentateuch and Pesh.

ments of his sons for *ministering*. 42. According to all that the Lord had commanded Moses, so had the children of Israel done all the work. 43. Moses saw all
the work, and behold, they had done it just as the Lord had commanded; so they
had done. And Moses blessed them *and said: "May the Shekinah of the Lord dwell
in the works of your hands."* [22]

CHAPTER 40

1. And the Lord spoke to Moses, saying, 2. "In the first month,[1] *that is the
month of Nisan,*[2] on the first of the month, you shall erect the tabernacle, the tent
of meeting. 3. Place there the ark of the testimony, and cover the ark with the veil.
4. You shall bring the table into[3] *the north side, for it is from there that wealth is
given,*[4] *and from there the drops of the late rains pour upon the plants,*[5] *so that the
inhabitants of the world may be sustained by them. You shall set its rows in order,
two rows of interior bread,*[6] *six loaves in a row, corresponding to the tribes of Jacob.*[7]
You shall bring the lampstand into *the south side,*[8] *for it is from there that the
paths*[9] *of the sun and the moon (come), and from there (come) the ways of the luminaries; and there (are) the treasuries of wisdom*[10] *that are likened to the luminaries.*[11]
You shall *light its seven lamps, corresponding to the seven planets*[12] *that are likened
to the righteous*[13] *who by their merit give light to the world.*[14] 5. You shall put the

Notes, Chapter 39

[22]*t. Men.* 7, 8 (Zuckermandel, 522); *Tanḥ. A, Pekude* 11 (355). See the comment on this verse in Nf, and Le Déaut,
1964B, 85–90, especially 86–87.

Notes, Chapter 40

[1]Lit.: "On the day of the first month."
[2]*Tanḥ. A, Pekude* 11 (355); *Num. R.* 13,2; Cf. *Tanḥ. B, Pekude* 6 (2,131); *Exod. R.* 52,2. See Ps.-J. Lev 9:1.
[3]Lit.: "in." For the location of the table in the north side, see 26:35; 40:22. On Ps.-J.'s rendering of our present verse,
see Böhl, 1987, 141–44.
[4]*b. B. Bat.* 25b: " . . . the north wind which makes gold flow"; cf. Philo, *De vita Mosis* II.xxii §104.
[5]Compare *b. B. Bat.* 25b: ". . . the south wind which brings up showers and causes the grass to grow." See also ibid.,
147a. Cf. Schmerler, 1933, 254.
[6]= *ed. pr.* (*gw'h*); Lond.: *m'h.* For "interior bread" see 25:30 (Ps.-J.) and n. 20 to that verse.
[7]This idea occurs in the late 10th-century work *Midrash Tadshe* 10; cf. Schmerler, 1933, 254.
[8]See 26:35; 40:24.
[9]*ysrtwwn*; = Latin *strata.* See also Ps.-J. Num 20:19; 22:22, 23 (twice), 31; Deut 1:1; 22:6.
[10]*b. B. Bat.* 25b: "He who desires to become wise should turn to the south. . . ."
[11]*b. Ta'an.* 7b: "'light' surely means Torah."
[12]See 39:37 and n. 20 to that verse.
[13]*j. Ned.* 3, 38a.
[14]Cf. Dan 12:3.

altar of gold for the *aromatic*[15] incense before the ark of the testimony, *for the sake of the Sages who occupy themselves with the Law, and whose odor spreads like aromatic incense.*[16] You shall place the screen for the entrance of the tabernacle, *for the sake of the righteous, who with their merits protect the people of the house of Israel.* 6. You shall place the altar of burnt offerings before the entrance of the tent of meeting, *for the sake of the rich who set the table before their doors to provide for the poor, and whose sins are forgiven them as if they had offered a burnt offering on the altar.*[17] 7. You shall place the laver between the tent of meeting and the altar, and put water in it *for the sake of the sinners*[18] *who repent*[19] *and who shed their perversity like water.*[20] 8. You shall set up the courtyard round about *for the sake of the merits of the fathers of the world who surround the people of the house of Israel round about.* You shall put in place the screen for the door of the courtyard *for the sake of the merits of the mothers of the world, who (are like a screen) spread at the entrance of Gehenna so that the souls of the young children of the people of Israel do not enter there.*[21] 9. You shall take the anointing oil and anoint the tabernacle and all that is in it; you shall consecrate it[22] *for the sake of the royal crown*[23] *of the house of Judah, and of the King Messiah who is destined to redeem Israel at the end of days.*[24] 10. You shall anoint the altar of burnt offerings and all its utensils, and consecrate the altar, and the altar will be most holy *for the sake of the crown of the priesthood of Aaron and his sons, and of Elijah the high priest who is to be sent at the end of the exiles.*[25] 11. You shall anoint the laver and its base, and consecrate it *for the sake of Joshua, your attendant, the head of the Sanhedrin of his people, by whom the land of Israel is to be divided, and (for the sake of) the Messiah, the son of Ephraim,*[26] *who will be descended from him, and through whom the house of Israel is to be victorious over Gog and his associates at the end of days.*[27] 12. You shall

Notes, Chapter 40

[15] = Onq. See also 30:1, 8 (Ps.-J., Onq.); 37:25 (Ps.-J., Onq.).

[16] *b. Ber.* 43b: "The young men of Israel are destined to emit a sweet fragrance. . . ." See also Tg. Song of Songs 4:6.

[17] Cf. *b. Ber.* 55a. Ps.-J.'s addition to this verse reflects a spiritualizing attitude toward sacrifices. Cf. Gordon, 1974, 288, n. 20.

[18] = Lond.: *ḥyby'*; Rieder and Clarke, in their editions of Ps.-J., read *ḥwby'*, "sins," which is the reading of *ed. pr.*

[19] Lit.: "who return in repentance." See 33:7 (Ps.-J.) and n. 15 to that verse.

[20] See the same expression ("shed . . . like water") in Tg. Lam 2:19. There is no source for Ps.-J.'s addition to this verse. See Ginsburger, *Pseudo-Jonathan* XXI.

[21] We know of no source for Ps.-J.'s addition to this verse; cf. Schmerler, 1933, 255. On the merits of the patriarchs and the matriarchs, see also Ps.-J. Exod 17:9; Num 23:9; cf. Deut 33:15.

[22] Lond. and *ed. pr.* omit "and all its utensils, and it will be holy."

[23] The reference to the three crowns (kingship, the Messiah, the priesthood) in vv. 9-10 may have been prompted by the triple "you shall anoint" in vv. 9-11. We know of no source for Ps.-J.'s additions to these three verses. Cf. Schmerler, 1933, 255–56.

[24] Cf. Gen 49:10 (Nf, P, V, N, Ps.-J., Onq.).

[25] See Ps.-J. 4:13; 6:18, and the notes to these verses.

[26] *b. Sukk.* 52a; *Tanḥ. B, Wa-Yiggash* 3 (1,205); *Num. R.* 14,1; *Midrash Psalms* 60,9 (Braude, 1958–59, 1,516); 87, 4 (Braude, 1958–59, 2,77). Tg. Song of Songs 4:5; 7:4. See Heinemann, 1974A, 131–41; = idem, 1975, 1–15; D. Berger, "Three Typological Themes in Early Jewish Messianism: Messiah Son of Joseph, Rabbinical Calculations, and the Figure of Armilus," *Journal of the Association for Jewish Studies* 9 (1984) 141–64.

[27] Cf., e.g., *b. Sanh.* 97b; *Abod. Zar.* 3b; *Gen. R.* 88,5; Num 11:26 (Nf, P, V, N, L, Ps.-J.); 24:17 (Ps.-J.); Tg. Song of Songs 8:4.

bring Aaron and his sons near to the entrance of the tent of meeting and bathe them in water.[28] 13. You shall clothe Aaron with the sacred vestments; anoint him and consecrate him, that he may *minister before* me.[29] 14. You shall bring his sons near, and clothe them with tunics, 15. and anoint them as <you will have anointed>[30] their father, that they may *minister before* me.[29] Their anointing will confer an everlasting priesthood on them throughout their generations." 16. And Moses did (so); according to all that the Lord had commanded, so he did. 17. In the first month, *that is the month of Nisan*,[31] in the second year, on the first of the month, the tabernacle was erected. 18. Moses erected the tabernacle, put (down) its sockets, placed its planks, put (in) its poles, and erected its pillars. 19. He spread the *screen*[32] over the tabernacle and placed the covering of the tent on top of it, as the Lord had commanded Moses. 20. He took *the two tables of stone, the tables of the covenant that had been given to him at Horeb and that had been erected on a standard*[33] *in the house of instruction—these were the tables* of the testimony *and the fragments of the tables (that were placed)* in the ark.[34] He placed the poles on the ark and put the propitiatory, *with the cherubim that are of hammered work and of one piece with it*,[35] on top of the ark. 21. He brought the ark into the tabernacle, placed the veil of the screen, and covered the ark of the testimony, as the Lord had commanded Moses. 22. He placed the table in the tent of meeting, on the north side of the tabernacle, outside the veil. 23. On it he arranged the rows of bread before the Lord, as the Lord had commanded Moses. 24. He placed the lampstand in the tent of meeting opposite the table, on the south side of the tabernacle. 25. And he *lit* the lamps before the Lord, as the Lord had commanded Moses. 26. He placed the altar of gold in the tent of meeting, before the veil. 27. On it he offered up aromatic incense, as the Lord had commanded Moses. 28. He put in place the screen for the entrance of the tabernacle. 29. He placed the altar of burnt offerings at the entrance of the tabernacle <of the tent of meeting>,[36] and on it he offered the burnt offering and the cereal offering, as the Lord had commanded Moses. 30. He placed the laver *on its base* between the tent of meeting and the altar, and, he put in it, for *sanctification*,[37] *running*[38] water *that would never cease or become foul.*[39] 31. Moses and Aaron and his sons[40] *took some of it with the ladle*[41] and

Notes, Chapter 40

[28]Compare Ps.-J. 29:4.
[29]= Onq.
[30]Omitted in Lond.
[31]See v. 2 (Ps.-J.).
[32]Cf. Nf and note.
[33]Compare Num 21:8-9 (Onq.).
[34]Deut 10:2; *b. Men.* 99a; *B. Bat.* 14b; Tg. 2 Chr 5:19; 32:31.
[35]See Ps.-J. 26:34; 39:35.
[36]Omitted in Lond. and *ed. pr.*
[37]= Onq. See 30:18 (Ps.-J.) and n. 15 to that verse.
[38]*b. Zeb.* 22b. See above 29:4 (Ps.-J.).
[39]Cf. *m. Yoma* 3,10.
[40]"And his sons" is omitted in Lond.
[41]See 30:19 (Ps.-J.).

sanctified[37] their hands and their feet with it. 32. *At the time* when they entered the tent of meeting, and when they approached the altar, they *sanctified*[37] themselves, as the Lord had commanded Moses. 33. He set up the courtyard round about the tabernacle and the altar, and put in place the screen *that is* at the door of the <courtyard>.[42] Thus Moses completed the work. 34. The cloud *of glory* covered the tent of meeting, and the Glory of *the Shekinah of* the Lord filled the tabernacle. 35. And *it was* not *possible for* Moses to enter the tent of meeting, because the cloud *of glory* had settled upon it, and the Glory of *the Shekinah of* the Lord filled the tabernacle. 36. *At the moment* when the cloud *of glory* rose from upon the tabernacle, the children of Israel set out on all their journeys. 37. But if the cloud *of glory* did not rise, they did not set out until the day when it did rise. 38. For the cloud *of the Glory* of the Lord *would overshadow*[43] the tent by day, and *the pillar of* fire *would shine*[44] by night. *And* all the *children* of Israel *saw* (that) in all their journeys.

Notes, Chapter 40

[42]Lond. and *ed. pr.* read "the tabernacle."
[43]See Ps.-J. Num 9:15.
[44]HT "in it" is omitted in Lond. and *ed. pr.*

BIBLIOGRAPHY

Alexander, P.: 1972, "The Targumim and Early Exegesis of 'Sons of God' in Genesis 6," *JJS* 23, 60–71.

idem: 1976, "The Rabbinic Lists of Forbidden Targumim," *JJS* 27, 177–191.

Aptowitzer, V.: 1927, *Parteipolitik der Hasmonäerzeit im rabbinischen und pseudoepi-graphischen Schriftum.* Vienna: Kohut Foundation.

Azita, C.: 1987, "L'Utilisation polemique du recit de l'Exode chez les ecrivains alexandrins (IVème siècle av. J.-C.–Ier siècle ap. J.-C.)," *Aufstieg und Niedergang der römischen Welt,* Teil II. Principat. Band 20, ed. H. Temporini and W. Haase. Berlin-New York: Gruyter, 41–65.

Baars, W.: 1961, "A Targum on Exod. XV 7-21 from the Cairo Geniza," *VT* 11, 340–342. This text is now published by M. Klein, 1986 (see below), 1, 244–247.

Bacher, W.: 1874, "Das gegenseitige Verhältniss der pentateuchischen Targumim," *ZDMG* 28, 59–72.

idem: 1894, "Une ancienne liste des noms grecs des pierres précieuses relatées dans Exode XXVIII, 17-20," *RÉJ* 29, 79–90.

idem: 1899, 1965, *Die exegetische Terminologie der jüdischen Traditionsliteratur,* two parts. Leipzig; 2 parts in one, reprint Darmstadt: Wissenschaftliche Buch-gesellschaft, 1965.

Bamberger, B. J.: 1975, "Halakic elements in the Neofiti Targum: A Preliminary State-ment," *JQR* 66, 27–38.

Baskin, J. R.: 1983, *Pharaoh's Counsellors: Job, Jethro and Balaam in Rabbinic and Patristic Tradition.* Chico, Calif.: Scholars Press.

Beer, B.: 1883, *Leben Moses nach Auffassung der jüdischen Sage.* Leipzig: Leiner.

Berliner, A.: 1884, *Targum Onkelos.* Herausgegeben und erläutert von A. Berliner. Berlin: Gorzelanczyk.

Bienaimé, J.: 1984, *Moïse et le don de l'eau dans la tradition juive ancienne: Targum et Midrash.* Rome: Biblical Institute Press.

Bloch, R.: 1955, "Quelques aspects de la figure de Moïse dans la tradition rabbinique," in *Moïse. L'homme de l'Alliance.* See below, Botte, B., 93–167.

Bogaert, P.-M.: 1976, *Pseudo-Philon. Les Antiquités Bibliques.* 2 vols. Paris: Cerf. See also under Pseudo-Philo.

Böhl, F.: 1987, "Die Metaphorisierung (Metila) in den Targumim zum Pentateuch," *Frankfurter Judaistische Beiträge* 15, 111–149.

Botte, B., Bloch R., and Vermes, G.: 1955, *Moïse l'homme de l'Alliance.* Cahiers Sioniens 2–4. Paris: Desclée.

Braude, W. G.: 1958–59, *The Midrash on Psalms.* Translated from the Hebrew and Aramaic by W. G. Braude. 2 vols. Yale Judaica Series XIII. New Haven: Yale University Press.

idem: 1968, *Pesikta Rabbati.* 2 vols. Translated by W. G. Braude. Yale Judaica Series XVIII. New Haven: Yale University Press.

Braude, W. G., and Kapstein, I. J.: 1975; 2nd impression 1978, *Pesikta de-Rab Kahana.* Translated from the Hebrew and Aramaic. Philadelphia: Jewish Publication Society.

idem: 1981, *Tanna debe Eliyyahu. The Lore of the School of Elijah.* Translated from the Hebrew. Philadelphia: Jewish Publication Society.

Brock, S. P.: 1982A, "An Early Interpretation of *pāsaḥ*: '*aggēn* in the Palestinian Targum," in *Interpreting the Hebrew Bible. Essays in Honour of E. I. J. Rosenthal,* ed. J. A. Emerton and S. C. Reif. Cambridge: Cambridge University Press, 27–34.

idem: 1982B, "Passover, Annunciation, and Epiclesis: Some Remarks on the Term *aggen* in the Syrian Versions of Lk. 1:35," *NT* 24, 222–233.

idem: 1985, "A Dispute of the Months and Some Related Syriac Texts," *JSS* 30, 181–211.

Burchard, C.: 1966, "Das Lamm in der Waagschale," *ZNTW* 57, 219–228.

Cathcart, K. J. (and Gordon, R. P.): 1989, *The Targum of the Minor Prophets.* The Aramaic Bible 14. Wilmington, Del.: Michael Glazier.

Cazelles, H.: 1986, "D'Ex 22,4 à Is 6,13 par les Targums," in *Salvación en la Palabra. Targum. Derash. Berith.* En memoria del profesor Alexandro Díez Macho. Madrid: Ediciones Cristiandad, 329–36.

Charlesworth, J. H.: 1976, 1981, *The Pseudepigrapha and Modern Research,* 1976; reprint with a supplement. Chico, Calif.: Scholars Press, 1981.

idem (ed.): 1983, 1985, *The Old Testament Pseudepigrapha.* 2 vols. London: Darton, Longman and Todd.

Chester, A. N., 1986, *Divine Revelation and Divine Titles in the Pentateuchal Targumim.* Tübingen: Mohr.

Chilton, B. D.: 1983, *The Glory of Israel.* Sheffield: University of Sheffield Press.

idem: 1978: see under Davies, P. R.

Chronicles of Moses. See below, Gaster, M.

Clarke, E. G., with Aufrecht, W. E.; Hurd, J. C.: Spitzer, F.: 1984, *Targum Pseudo-Jonathan of the Pentateuch: Text and Concordance.* Hoboken, N.J.: Ktav.

Cook, E. M.: 1986, *Rewriting the Bible: The Text and Language of the Pseudo-Jonathan Targum.* Unpublished Ph.D. dissertation. Los Angeles: University of California.

Daube, D.: 1956, *The New Testament and Rabbinic Judaism.* London: Athlone Press.

Davies, P. R.: 1979: "Passover and the Dating of the Aqedah," *JJS* 30, 59–67.

Davies, P. R., and Chilton, B. D.: 1978, "The Aqedah: A Revised Tradition History," *CBQ* 40, 514–546.

Denis, A. M.: 1970, *Introduction aux Pseudépigraphes Grecs d'Ancien Testament.* Studia in Veteris Testamenti Pseudepigrapha I. Leiden: Brill, 146–149.

Díez Macho, A.: 1956, "Nuevos Fragmentos de Tosefta Targumica," *Sefarad* 16, 313–324.

idem: 1958, "Un segundo fragmento del Targum palestinense a los Profetas," *Biblica* 39, 198–205.

idem: *Neophyti 1.* Targum Palestinense. MS de la Biblioteca Vaticana. Madrid-Barcelona: Consejo Superior de Investigaciones Científicas.
1 *Génesis,* 1968; 2 *Éxodo,* 1971; 3 *Levitico,* 1971; 4 *Numeros,* 1974; 5 *Deuteronomio,* 1978.

idem: 1972, *El Targum. Introducción a las Traducciones Aramaicas de la Biblia.* Barcelona: Consejo Superior de Investigaciones Científicas.

idem: 1977–89, *Biblia Polyglotta Matritensia.* Series IV. *Targum Palaestinense in Pentateuchum.* Additur Targum Pseudojonatan ejusque hispanica versio. Editio critica curante A. Díez Macho, adjuvantibus L. Díez Merino, E. Martínez Borobio, T. Martínez Saiz. Pseudojonathan hispanica versio: T. Martínez Saiz. Targum Palaestinensis testimonia ex variis fontibus: R. Griño. Madrid: Consejo Superior de Investigaciones Científicas. L. 1, *Genesis,* 1989; L. 2, *Exodus,* 1980; L. 3, *Leviticus,* 1980; L. 4, *Numeri,* 1977; L. 5, *Deuteronomium,* 1980.

idem: 1981A, "L'Usage de la troisième personne au lieu de la première dans le Targum," in *Mélanges Dominique Barthélemy.* Études Bibliques offertes à l'occasion de son 60ᵉ Anniversaire. Ed. P. Casetti, O. Kiel, and A. Schenker. Orbis Biblicus et Orientalis 38. Fribourg: Éditions Universitaires; Göttingen: Vandenhoeck und Ruprecht, 61–89.

idem: 1981B, "Nueva Fuente para el Targum Palestino del Dia Septimo de Pascua y Primero de Pentecostes," in *Escritos de Biblia y Oriente.* Miscelánea conmemorativa del 25ᵒ aniversario del Instituto Español Biblico y Arqueológico (Casa de Santiago) de Jerusalén. Bibliotheca Salmanticensis, Estudios 38; ed. R. Aguirre, F. García López. Salamanca-Jerusalem: Universidad Pontificia, 233–257.

Díez Merino, L.: 1975, "El decálogo en el Targum Palestinense. Origen, estilo y motivaciones," *Est. Bíb.* 34, 23–48.

idem: 1984, "Maria, hermana de Moises, en la tradición targumica," *Scripta de Maria* 7, 56–57.

Driver, S. R.: 1911, *The Book of Exodus*. Cambridge Bible for Schools and Colleges. Cambridge: University Press.

Durham, J. I.: 1987, *Exodus*. Word Biblical Commentary. Waco, Tex.: Word Books.

Elbogen, I.: 1931, *Der jüdische Gottesdienst in seiner geschichtlichen Entwicklung*, 3rd ed. Frankfurt.

Epstein, J. N., and Melamed, E. Z.: n.d., *Mekilta de-Rabbi Shimon bar Yohai*, ed. J. N. Epstein and E. Z. Melamed. Jerusalem: Hillel Press.

Esh, S.: 1957, *Der Heilige Er sei gepreisen*. Leiden: Brill.

Etheridge, J. W.: *The Targums of Onkelos and Jonathan ben Uzziel on the Pentateuch: With the Fragments of the Jerusalem Targum: From the Chaldee*. 2 vols. London: Longman, Green, Longman, and Roberts, 1862, 1865; reprint in one vol., New York: Ktav, 1968.

Ezekiel the Tragedian, *Exagôgê*. English trans. with introduction and notes by R. G. Robertson in *The Old Testament Pseudepigrapha*, ed. J. H. Charlesworth. London: Darton, Longman and Todd, 1985, 803–819.

Field, F.: 1875, *Origenis Hexapla quae supersunt*. 2 vols. Oxford: Clarendon Press.

Fraade, S. D.: 1984, *Enosh and his Generation*. Chico, Calif.: Scholars Press.

Friedlander, G.: 1981 (4th ed.), *Pirke de Rabbi Eliezer. The Chapters of Rabbi Eliezer the Great*. Translated and annotated by G. Friedlander. New York: Sepher-Hermon. (In the notes to Ps.-J., page references to this translation are given in brackets.)

Gager, J. G.: 1972, *Moses in the Greco-Roman World*. Nashville and New York: Abingdon.

Gaster, M.: 1899 (1971), *The Chronicles of Jerahmeel: or, The Hebrew Bible Historiale*. London, 1899. Republished with a Prolegomenon by H. Schwarzbaum. New York: Ktav, 1971. (This work is referred to as "The Chronicles of Moses," with a reference to Gaster's pagination.)

Geiger, A.: 1928, *Urschrift und Übersetzungen der Bibel*. 2nd ed. Frankfurt am Main: Madda.

Ginsburger, M.: 1891, "Die Anthropomorphismen in den Thargumim," *JFPT* 17, 262–280, 430–458.

idem: 1900, "Verbotene Thargumim," *MGWJ* 44, 1–7.

idem: 1903, *Pseudo-Jonathan*. Thargum-Jonathan ben Usiël zum Pentateuch. Nach der Londoner Handschrift (Brit. Mus. Add. 27031). Berlin: Calvary.

Ginzberg, L.: 1909–46, *The Legends of the Jews*. 7 vols. Philadelphia: Jewish Publication Society. Referred to as *Legends*.

Gordon, R. P.: 1974, "Targumic Parallels to Acts XIII 18 and Didache XIV 3," *NT* 16, 285–289.

idem: 1989. See above, Cathcart, K. J., and Gordon, R. P.

Grabbe, L. L.: 1979, "The Jannes/Jambres Tradition in Targum Pseudo-Jonathan and its Date," *JBL* 98, 393–401.

Grelot, P.: 1961, "Sagesse 10,21 et le Targum de l'Exode," *Biblica* 42, 49–60.

Gronemann, S.: 1879, *Die Jonathan'sche Pentateuch-Uebersetzung in ihrem Verhältnisse zur Halacha.* Leipzig: Friese.

Grossfeld, B.: 1984, "The Translation of Biblical Hebrew *pqd* in the Targum, Peshitta, Vulgate and Septuagint," *ZAW* 96, 83–101.

idem: 1988A, *The Targum Onqelos to Genesis.* The Aramaic Bible 6. Wilmington, Del.: Michael Glazier.

idem: 1988B, *The Targum Onqelos to Exodus.* The Aramaic Bible 7. Wilmington, Del.: Michael Glazier.

Guillamont, A.: 1977, "Un Midrash d'Exode 4:24-26 chez Aphraate et Ephrem de Nisibe," in *A Tribute to Arthur Vööbus,* ed. R. E. Fischer. Chicago: Lutheran School of Theology, 89–95.

Hamp, V.: 1938, *Der Begriff 'Wort' in den aramäischen Bibelübersetzungen.* Munich: Neuer Filser.

Harrington, D.: 1985, "Pseudo Philo. A New Translation and Introduction," in *The Old Testament Pseudepigrapha,* ed. J. H. Charlesworth. London: Darton, Longman & Todd, vol. 2, 297–377.

Hayward, R.: 1978, "Phinehas—the same is Elijah: The Origins of a Rabbinic Tradition," *JJS* 29, 22–34.

idem: 1981A, *Divine Name and Presence: The Memra.* Totowa, N.J.: Allenheld, Osmun.

idem: 1981B, "The Present State of Research into the Targumic Account of the Sacrifice of Isaac," *JJS* 32, 127–150.

idem: 1987: *The Targum of Jeremiah.* The Aramaic Bible 12. Wilmington, Del.: Michael Glazier.

Heinemann, J.: 1969, "Targum of Exodus 22:4 and Early Halakhah" (in Hebrew), *Tarbiz* 38, 294–296.

idem: 1973, "Remains of Piyyut-type Compositions of the Ancient Targumists" (in Hebrew), *Ha-Sifrut* 4, 362–365.

idem: 1974A, *Aggadah and Its Development.* Jerusalem: Keter.

idem: 1974B, "Early Halakhah in the Palestinian Targumim," *JJS* 25, 114–122. The same article appeared in *Studies in Jewish Legal History in Honour of David Daube,* ed. B. S. Jackson. London: Jewish Chronicle Publications, 1974, 114–

122. It was published, with slight modifications, in Hebrew, in *Aggadah and Its Development* (see preceding entry), 143–150.

idem: 1975, "The Messiah of Ephraim and the Premature Exodus of the Tribe of Ephraim," *HTR* 8, 1–15. Essentially the same article had been published in Hebrew in *Tarbiz* 40 (1970–71) 450–461.

Herr, M. D.: 1971, "The Mekhilta of R. Simeon ben Yohai," *EJ,* vol. 6 (Jerusalem), cols. 1269–1270.

Horovitz, H. S., and Rabin, I.: *Mekilta de-Rabbi Ishmael.* Frankfurt: Kauffmann, 1931; reprint Jerusalem: Bamberger and Wahrmann, 1960.

Hurwitz, S., *Machsor Vitry,* nach der Handschrift im British Museum (Cod. Add. No. 27200 u. 27201). Leipzig, 1899; 2nd ed. Nürnberg: Bulka, 1923; reprint Jerusalem: Aleph, 1963, 305–344.

Isenberg, S. R.: 1968, *Studies in the Jewish Aramaic Translations of the Pentateuch.* Unpublished Ph.D. dissertation. Cambridge, Mass.: Harvard University.

Itzchaky, E.: 1982, *The Halakah in Targum Jerushalmi I.* Pseudo-Jonathan b. Uzziel and Its Exegetic Methods (in Hebrew). Unpublished Ph.D. dissertation. Ramat-Gan: Bar-Ilan University.

Jackson, B. S.: 1973, "The Problem of Exodus XXI 22–25 (Ius Talionis)," *VT* 23, 273–304.

idem: 1974, "The Fence-Breaker and the *actio de pastu pecoris* in Early Jewish Law," *JJS* 25, 127–129.

James, M. R.: 1917, *The Biblical Antiquities of Philo,* (London). Reprint with Prolegomenon by L. H. Feldman. New York: Ktav, 1971.

Jastrow, M.: 1950 (etc.; reprints; preface 1903), *A Dictionary of the Targumim, the Talmud Babli and Yerushalmi, and the Midrashic Literature.* 2 vols. New York: Pardes.

Jellinek, A.: 1853–77, *Bet ha-Midrasch. Sammlung kleiner Midraschim und vermischter Abhandlungen aus der ältern jüdischen Literatur,* 6 vols. Leipzig; republished Jerusalem: Wahrmann, 1967.

Jeremias, J.: 1967, "Moses," in *Theological Dictionary of the New Testament* 4. Grand Rapids: Eerdmans, 852–873.

idem: 1975, *Jerusalem in the Time of Jesus.* Philadelphia: Fortress.

Jerome, *Hebraicae quaestiones in libro Geneseos,* ed. P. de Lagarde, in CCL 72, 1–56. Turnhout: Brepols, 1959.

idem: *Epistolae* (Epistle 73, Ad Evagrium (Evangelum), ed. J.-P. Migne. *Patrologia Latina* 22. Paris, 1864), cols. 676–681.

Josephus (Flavius), *The Antiquities of the Jews* (ed. with Eng. trans. by H. St. J. Thackeray and Ralph Marcus in the Loeb Classical Library).

idem: *Contra Apionem* (ed. with Eng. trans. by H. St. J. Thackeray and Ralph Marcus in the Loeb Classical Library).

Kadushin, M.: 1965, *The Rabbinic Mind.* New York: Jewish Theological Seminary of America.

Kahle, P.: 1927, *Masoreten des Westens.* Vol. 1. Stuttgart: Kohlhammer.

idem: 1959: *The Cairo Geniza.* 2nd ed. Oxford: Blackwell.

Kapstein, I. J. See above, Braude, W. G., and Kapstein, I. J.

Kasher, M.: 1954, *Torah Shelemah.* Vol. 6: Exodus. New York: American Biblical Encyclopaedia Society.

idem: 1974, *Torah Shelemah.* Vol. 24. *Targumey ha-Torah. Aramaic Versions of the Bible. A Comprehensive Study of Onkelos, Jonathan, Jerusalem Targums and the Full Jerusalem Targum of the Vatican Manuscript Neofiti 1.* Jerusalem.

Kasher, R.: 1976-77, "A Targumic Tosephta to Gen 2:1-3" (in Hebrew), *Sinay* 78, 9–17.

idem: 1986, "Targumic Conflations in the MS Neofiti I" (in Hebrew), *HUCA* 57, Hebrew section 1–19.

idem: 1989, "A New Targum to the Ten Commandments According to a Geniza Manuscript," (in Hebrew), *HUCA* 60, Hebrew section 1–17.

Kaufman, S.: 1991, see below, Maori, Y.

Klein, M. L.: 1974, "Notes on the Printed Edition of MS Neofiti I," *JSS* 19, 216–230.

idem: 1975, "The Targumic Tosefta to Exodus 15:2," *JJS* 26, 61–67.

idem: 1976, "Converse Translation: A Targumic Technique," *Biblica* 57, 515–537.

idem: 1980, *The Fragment-Targums of the Pentateuch According to Their Extant Sources.* 2 vols. Rome: Biblical Institute Press.

idem: 1982, "Associative and Complementary Translation in the Targumim," *Eretz-Israel* 16 (H. M. Orlinsky volume), 134*–140*.

idem: 1986, *Genizah Manuscripts of Palestinian Targum to the Pentateuch.* 2 vols. Cincinnati: Hebrew Union College Press.

idem: 1988: "'Not to be translated in Public—*l' mtrgm bsybwr,*'" *JJS* 39, 80–91.

Koch, K.: 1966, "Das Lamm, das Ägypten vernichtet," *ZNW* 57, 79–93.

Komlosh, Y.: 1959, "The Targum Version of the Crossing of the Red Sea" (in Hebrew), *Sinay,* 45, 223–228.

idem: 1962, "A Fragment of the Palestinian Targum of the Song of Moses" (in Hebrew), in *Sefer Seidel.* ed. H.M.L. Gevaryahu et al. Jerusalem, 7–11.

idem: 1963, "The Ten Commandments in the Palestinian Targums" (in Hebrew), *Sinay,* 52, 289–295.

idem: 1977, "Characteristics of Targum Neophyti of Exodus" (in Hebrew), in *Proceedings of the Sixth World Congress of Jewish Studies.* Jerusalem: Academic Press, 183–189.

idem : 1973, *The Bible in the Light of the Aramaic Translations* (in Hebrew). Tel-Aviv: Bar Ilan University-Dvir.

Kraeling, C.: 1956, *The Synagogue. The Excavations at Dura-Europos.* New Haven: Yale.

Kuiper, G. J.: 1971, "Targum Pseudo-Jonathan in Relation to the Remaining Targumin at Exodus 20:1-18, 25-26," *Augustinianum* 11, 105–154.

Landauer, S.: 1908, "Ein interessantes Fragment des Pseudo-Jonathan," in *Festschrift zu Ehren des Dr. A. Harkavy*; ed. D. v. Günzburg and I. Markon. St. Petersburg, 19–26. The same text has recently been republished: M. L. Klein, *Genizah Manuscripts* (see above under "Klein"), 1, 273–274.

Lauterbach, J. Z.: *Mekilta de-Rabbi Ishmael.* 3 vols. Edited and translated by J. Z. Lauterbach. Philadelphia: Jewish Publication Society, 1933–1935; reprint 1949.

Le Déaut, R.: 1963, *La Nuit Pascale.* Rome: Biblical Institute Press.

idem: 1964A, "Miryam, soeur de Moïse, et Marie, mère du Messie," *Biblica* 45, 198–219.

idem: 1964B, "Actes 7,48 et Matthieu 17,4 (par.) à la lumière du Targum Palestinien," *Recherches de Science Religieuse,* 52, 85–90.

idem: 1966, *Introduction à la Littérature targumique.* Rome: Biblical Institute Press.

idem: 1978, 1979, *Targum du Pentateuque.* Vol. 1: *Genèse,* 1978; vol. 2: *Exode et Lévitique,* 1979. Paris: Cerf.

idem: 1981, "A Propos du Targum d'Exode 13,18: La Tôrah, arme secrète d'Israël," in *De la Tôrah au Messie.* Mélanges Henri Cazelles. Ed. J. Doré, P. Grelot, and M. Carrez. Paris: Desclée, 525–533.

Levey, S. H.: 1974, *The Messiah: An Aramaic Interpretation.* The Messianic Exegesis of the Targum. Monograph of the Hebrew Union College 2. Cincinnati/New York: Hebrew Union College-Jewish Institute of Religion.

Levine, E.: 1971, "A Study of Targum Pseudo-Jonathan to Exodus," *Sefarad* 31, 27–48.

idem: 1973, "*Neofiti* I. A Study of Exodus 15," *Biblica* 54, 301–330.

Levy, J.: 1881, 1966, *Chaldäisches Wörterbuch über die Targumim und einen grossen Theil des rabbinischen Schriftthums.* Leipzig; reprint Köln: Melzer, 1966. Referred to as "Levy."

idem: 1924, *Wörterbuch über die Talmudim und Midraschim.* 4 vols. Reprint of 2nd ed. Berlin-Vienna; Darmstadt: Wissenschaftliche Buchgesellschaft, 1963.

Lindars, B.: 1977, "The Place of the Old Testament in the Formation of New Testament Theology. Prolegomena," *NTS* 23, 59–66.

Luzarraga, J.: 1973, *Las tradiciones de la nube en la Biblia y en el Judaismo primitivo.* Rome: Biblical Institute Press.

Lyonnet, S.: 1962, "Tu ne convoiteras pas," *Neo-Testamentica et Patristica.* Leiden: Brill, 157–165.

McNamara, M.: 1966, *The New Testament and the Palestinian Targum to the Pentateuch.* Rome: Biblical Institute Press.

idem: 1967, "*Logos* of the Fourth Gospel and *Memra* of the Palestinian Targum (Ex. 12, 42)," *Expository Times* 79, 115–117.

idem: 1972, *Targum and Testament.* Shannon: Irish University Press.

idem: 1992, *Targum Neofiti 1: Genesis.* The Aramaic Bible 1A. Collegeville, Minn.: Liturgical Press.

Maher, M.: 1988, *Targum Pseudo-Jonathan of Exodus 1–4.* Unpublished Ph.D. dissertation. Dublin: National University of Ireland (University College Dublin).

idem: 1990, "The Meturgemanim and Prayer," *JJS* 41, 226–246.

idem: 1992, *Targum Pseudo-Jonathan: Genesis.* The Aramaic Bible 1B. Collegeville, Minn.: Liturgical Press.

Malina, B.: 1968, *The Palestinian Manna Tradition.* Leiden: Brill.

Mandelbaum, I. J.: 1990, "Tannaitic Exegesis of the Golden Calf Episode," in *A Tribute to Geza Vermes,* ed. P. R. Davies and R. T. White. Sheffield: Sheffield Academic Press, 207–223.

Maneschg, H.: 1981, *Die Erzählung von der ehernen Schlange (Num 21, 4-9) in der Auslegung der frühen jüdischen Literatur. Eine traditionsgeschichtliche Studie.* Frankfurt am Main/Bern: Lang.

Maori, Y.: 1975, *The Peshitta Version of the Pentateuch in Its Relation to the Sources of Jewish Exegesis* (in Hebrew). Unpublished Ph.D. dissertation. Jerusalem: Hebrew University.

idem: 1983, "The Relationship of Targum Pseudo-Jonathan to Halakhic Sources" (in Hebrew), *Te'uda* 3, 235–250.

Maori, Y. and Kaufman, S.: 1991, "The Targumim to Exodus 20: Reconstructing the Palestinian Targum," *Textus.* Studies of the Hebrew Bible Project 16, 33–78.

Marmorstein, A.: 1927, *The Old Rabbinic Doctrine of God. I: Names and Attributes of God.* London: Jewish College Publications.

Maybaum, S.: 1870, *Die Anthropomorphien und Anthropopathien bei Onkelos.* Breslau: Schletter.

Mulder, M. J.: 1975, "1 Chronik 7:21B-23 und die rabbinische Tradition," *JSJ* 6, 141–166.

Muñoz León, D.: 1974, *Dios-Palabra. Memra en los Targumim del Pentateuco.* Granada: Institución San Jeronimo.

286   *Bibliography*

idem: 1977, *Gloria de la Shekina en los Targumim del Pentateuco*. Madrid: Instituto Francesco Suárez.

Noah, M. M.: 1840, *Sefer ha-Yashar or The Book of Jasher. Referred to in Joshua and Second Samuel*. Translated by M. M. Noah. New York: Noah and Gould. (In the notes to Ps.-J., page references to this translation are given in brackets.)

Odeberg, H.: 1965, "'Iannês, 'Iambrês," *TDNT* 3, 192–193.

idem: 1973, *3 Enoch,* reprinted with Prolegomenon by J. C. Greenfield. New York: Ktav.

Ohana, M.: 1973, "Agneau Pascal et circoncision," *VT* 13, 385–399.

idem: 1974, "Prosélytisme et Targum Palestinien: Données nouvelles pour la datation de Néofiti I," *Biblica* 55, 317–332.

idem: 1975, "La polémique judéo islamique et l'image d'Ismaël dans Targum Pseudo-Jonathan et dans Pirke de Rabbi Eliezer," *Augustinianum* 15, 367–387.

Okamoto, A.O.H.: 1976, "A Geonic Phrase in Ms. Targum Yerushalmi, Codex Neofiti I," *JQR* 66, 160–167.

Olsson, B.: 1974, *Structure and Meaning in the Fourth Gospel*. Coniectanea Biblica, New Testament Series 6. Lund: Gleerup.

Pérez Fernández, M.: 1984, *Los capitulos de Rabbi Eliezer*. Valencia: Institución S. Jeronimo.

Petermann, I. H.: 1829, *De duabus Pentateuchi paraphrasibus chaldaicis*. Part I. *De indole paraphraseos, quae Ionathanis esse dicitur*. Berlin: Academic Press.

Philo, *De agricultura* (in *Philo with an English Translation,* vol. III), The Loeb Classical Library.

idem: *De confusione linguarum* (in *Philo with an English Translation,* vol. IV), The Loeb Classical Library.

idem: *De congressu quaerendae eruditionis gratia* (in *Philo with an English Translation,* vol. IV), The Loeb Classical Library.

idem: *De Decalogo* (in *Philo with an English Translation*, vol. VII), The Loeb Classical Library.

idem: *De migratione Abrahami* (in *Philo with an English Translation,* vol. IV), The Loeb Classical Library.

idem: *De mutatione nominum* (in *Philo with an English Translation,* vol. V), The Loeb Classical Library.

idem: *De vita Mosis* (in *Philo with an English Translation,* vol. VI), The Loeb Classical Library.

idem: *De sobrietate* (in *Philo with an English Translation,* vol. III), The Loeb Classical Library.

idem: *De somniis* (in *Philo with an English Translation,* vol. V), The Loeb Classical Library.

idem: *De specialibus legibus* (in *Philo with an English Translation,* vols. VII and VIII), The Loeb Classical Library.

idem: *Quaestiones et solutiones in Exodum* (in *Philo with an English Translation,* Supplement vol. II), The Loeb Classical Library.

idem: *Legum Allegoriae* (in *Philo with an English Translation,* vol. I), The Loeb Classical Library.

Pietersma, A., and Lutz, R.: 1985, *Jannes and Jambres,* in *Old Testament Pseudepigrapha.* Vol. 2. Ed. J. H. Charlesworth. London: Darton, Longman and Todd, 427–442.

Potin, J.: 1971, *Le Fête juive de la Pentecôte.* 2 vols. Paris: Cerf.

Pseudo-Philo, *Liber Antiquitatum biblicarum.* See under Bogaert, P.-M., Harrington, D. and James, M. R.

Rahmer, M.: 1861, *Die hebräischen Traditionen in den Werken des Hieronymus.* Breslau: H. Skutsch.

Rashi, *Pentateuch with Targum Onkelos, Haphtaroth and Rashi's Commentary.* Hebrew text with trans. by M. Rosenbaum and A. M. Silbermann with A. Blashki and L. Joseph. 5 vols. Jerusalem: Silbermann Family, 1973.

Reisel, M.: 1957, *The Mysterious Name of Y.H.W.H. The Tetragrammaton in connection with the names of Ehyeh-ašer-Ehyeh-hūhā and Šem Hammephoraš.* Assen: Van Gorcum.

Rendsburg, G. A.: 1990, "Targum Onqelos to Exod 10:5, 10:15, Numb 22:5, 22:11," *Henoch* 12, 15–17.

Rieder, D.: 1965, "Comments and Clarifications on Targum Jonathan ben Uzziel" (in Hebrew), *Sinay* 56, 116–119.

idem: 1974, 1984–85, *Pseudo-Jonathan*: Targum Jonathan ben Uziel on the Pentateuch copied from the London MS. (British Museum add. 27031). Jerusalem: Salomon's, 1974. Reprinted with Hebrew translation and notes. 2 vols. Jerusalem, 1984–85.

idem: 1975, "Notes on the Aggadoth in Targum Jonathan ben Uzziel" (in Hebrew), *Beth Miqra,* 62, 428–431.

Robertson, R. G.: see under Ezekiel the Tragedian.

Rodríguez Carmona, A.: 1978, *Targum y Resurrección. Estudio de los textos del Targum Palestinense sobre la resurrección.* Granada.

idem: 1983, "Concepto de 'muerte' en el Targum Palestinense del Pentateuco," *Est. Bíb.* 41, 107–136.

Schäfer, J. P.: 1970, "Die Termini 'Heiliger Geist' und 'Geist der Prophetie' in den Targumim und das Verhältnis der Targumim zueinander," *VT* 20, 304–314.

idem: 1972, *Die Vorstellung vom Heiligen Geist in der rabbinischen Literatur.* Munich: Kösel.

Schäfer, P.: 1972, *Die Vorstellung vom Heiligen Geist in der rabbinischen Literatur.* Munich: Kösel.

Schechter, S.: 1909, 1961, *Aspects of Rabbinic Theology. Major Concepts of the Talmud.* New York: Macmillan, 1909; Schocken, 1961.

Schelberg, G.: 1958: "Exodus XXI 4 im palästinischen Targum," *VT* 8, 253–263.

Schmerler, B.: 1933, *Sefer Ahavat Yehonathan* (in Hebrew). *Exodus.* Bilgary.

Schoeps. H. J.: 1949, *Theologie und Geschichte des Judenchristentums.* Tübingen.

Schürer, E.: 1973, 1979, 1987, *The History of the Jewish People in the Age of Jesus Christ (175 B.C.–A.D. 135).* A new English version revised and edited by G. Vermes, F. Millar, M. Black. Literary editor P. Vermes. 3 vols. Edinburgh: Clarke.

Séd, N.: 1964, "R. Le Déaut. La Nuit Pascale. Essai sur la signification de la Pâque juive à partir du Targum d'Exode xii, 42," *RÉJ* 123, 529–533.

Sefer-Ha-Yashar. See above, Noah, M. M.

Serra, A. M.: 1971, "Le tradizioni della teofania sinaitica nel Targum dello pseudo-Jonathan Es. 19.24 e in Giov. 1,19–2,12," *Marianum* 23 (1971) 1–39.

Shinan, A.: 1977, *Dibre ha-Yamim Shel Mosheh Rabbenu* = "The Chronicles of Moses" (in Hebrew), *Ha-Sifrut* 24 (1977) 100–116. This Midrash had been published by A. Jellinek, *Bet ha-Midrasch* (see under Jellinek), Zweiter Theil, 1–11.

idem: 1979, *The Aggadah in the Aramaic Targums to the Pentateuch* (in Hebrew). 2 vols. Jerusalem: Makor.

idem: 1983A, "Miracles, Wonders and Magic in the Aramaic Targums of the Penta-teuch" (in Hebrew), in *Essays on the Bible and the Ancient Near East.* Festschrift I. L. Seeligman. 2 vols. Ed. A. Rofé and Y. Zakovitch. Jerusalem, 2, 419–426.

idem: 1983B, "The Angelology of the 'Palestinian' Targums on the Pentateuch," *Sefarad* 43, 181–198.

idem: 1984, *Midrash Shemot Rabbah. Chapters I–XIV.* A Critical Edition Based on a Jerusalem Manuscript with Variants, Commentary and Introduction (in He-brew). Jerusalem: Dvir.

Silverstone, A. E.: 1931, *Aquila and Onkelos.* Manchester: University Press.

Smolar, L. and Aberbach, M.: 1968, "The Golden Calf in Postbiblical Literature," *HUCA* 39, 91–116.

Speier, S.: 1950, "Beiträge zu den Targumim," *Schweizerische theologische Umschau* 20, 52–61. This volume of the journal is entitled *Festschrift für Ludwig Köhler zu dessen 70. Geburtstag.*

idem: 1967, "Pseudojonathan Exodus 10,11," *Biblica* 48, 115.

Sperber, A.: 1959, *The Bible in Aramaic.* Vol. 1: *The Pentateuch According to Targum Onkelos.* Leiden: Brill.

Stemberger, G.: 1982, *Einleitung in Talmud und Midrasch* by H. L. Strack. Fully revised edition. Munich. English translation by M. Bockmuehl, *Introduction to the Talmud and Midrash.* Edinburgh: Clark, 1991.

Strack, H. L.: 1982. See Stemberger.

Strack, H. L. and Billerbeck, P.: 1922–69, *Kommentar zum Neuen Testament aus Talmud und Midrasch.* 4 vols. Munich: Beck.

Syrén, R.: 1986, *Aspects of Rabbinic Theology.* Abo: Abo Akademie.

Teicher, J. L.: 1951, "A Sixth Century Fragment of the Palestinian Targum?" *VT* 1, 125–129.

Towner, W. S.: 1973, "Form-Criticism of Rabbinic Literature," *JJS* 24, 101–118.

Urbach, E. E.: 1969, 1979, *The Sages. Their Concepts and Beliefs.* Jerusalem: Magnes (Hebrew); English translation (with same title), 2 vols. Jerusalem: Magnes, 1979.

Vermes, G.: 1961, 1973, *Scripture and Tradition in Judaism.* Studia Post-Biblica 4. Leiden: Brill, 2nd rev. ed. 1973.

idem: 1969, "He Is the Bread," in *Neotestamentica et Semitica: Studies in Honour of M. Black.* Ed. E. E. Ellis and W. Wilcox. Edinburgh: Clark.

idem: 1973–87. See Schürer, E.

idem: 1973A, "Circumcision and Exodus IV 24–26," in *Scripture and Tradition in Judaism.* 2nd ed. (see above), 178–192.

idem: 1973B, "Redemption and Genesis xxii," in *Scripture and Tradition* (see above), 193–227.

Vermes, P.: 1973, "Buber's Understanding of the Divine Name related to the Bible, Targum, and Midrash," *JJS* 24, 147–166.

York, A. D.: 1974, "The Dating of Targumic Literature," *JSJ* 5, 49–62.

idem: 1979, "The Targum in the Synagogue and in the School," *JSJ* 10, 74–86.

Zuckermandel, M. S.: 1880, 1983, *Tosephtha, Based on the Erfurt and Vienna Codices with parallels and variants.* Pasewalk, 1880; Jerusalem: Wahrmann, 1983.

INDEXES TO TARGUM NEOFITI 1:
EXODUS

BIBLICAL

TARGUMIM

Targum Onqelos

Pseudo-Jonathan

Neofiti 1

Neofiti Margin

Fragment Targum P

Fragment Targum V

Cairo Genizah Palestinian Targum Fragments

(ed. M. Klein 1, 1986)

Samaritan Targum

Targum Nebi'im

Targum Ketubim

RABBINIC
I. Tosefta, Mishnah, Talmud

II. Midrash

POST-BIBLICAL

ANCIENT VERSIONS

COMMENTARIES

ANCIENT AUTHORS

MODERN AUTHORS

INDEXES TO TARGUM PSEUDO-JONATHAN: EXODUS

HEBREW BIBLE

NEW TESTAMENT

SAMARITAN PENTATEUCH

APOCRYPHAL/DEUTEROCANONICAL BOOKS

APOCRYPHA AND PSEUDEPIGRAPHA

TARGUMIM
Targum Pseudo-Jonathan

Targum Neofiti and Neofiti Glosses

Fragment Targums

Palestinian Targums

Cairo Genizah Targums

Targum Tosefta

Machsor Vitry

Targum Onqelos

ANCIENT VERSIONS
Septuagint

Theodotion

Peshitta

Vulgate

JEWISH WRITERS

Pseudo-Philo

CHRISTIAN WRITERS

RABBINIC

I. Tosefta, Mishnah, Talmud

II. Midrash

INDEX OF SUBJECTS

(Page numbers followed by *n.* refer to
footnotes; page numbers alone refer to the text of Ps.-J.)

INDEX OF AUTHORS